JEWELS OF THE MIDDLE WAY

Studies in Indian and Tibetan Buddhism

This series was conceived to provide a forum for publishing outstanding new contributions to scholarship on Indian and Tibetan Buddhism and also to make accessible seminal research not widely known outside a narrow specialist audience, including translations of appropriate monographs and collections of articles from other languages. The series strives to shed light on the Indic Buddhist traditions by exposing them to historical-critical inquiry, illuminating through contextualization and analysis these traditions' unique heritage and the significance of their contribution to the world's religious and philosophical achievements.

STUDIES IN INDIAN AND TIBETAN BUDDHISM

JEWELS OF THE MIDDLE WAY

The Madhyamaka Legacy of Atiśa and His Early Tibetan Followers

James B. Apple

Wisdom

Wisdom Publications
199 Elm Street
Somerville, MA 02144 USA
wisdompubs.org

Library of Congress Cataloging-in-Publication Data
Names: Apple, James B., author.
Title: Jewels of the middle way: the Madhyamaka legacy of Atīśa and his early Tibetan followers / James B. Apple.
Description: Somerville, MA: Wisdom Publications, 2018. | Series: Studies in Indian and Tibetan Buddhism | Includes bibliographical references and index. | Description based on print version record and CIP data provided by publisher; resource not viewed.
Identifiers: LCCN 2018009216 (print) | LCCN 2018036556 (ebook) | ISBN 9781614295013 (ebook) | ISBN 9781614294764 (pbk.: alk. paper)
Subjects: LCSH: Atīśa, 982–1054 | Buddhism—Tibet Region—Doctrines. | Mādhyamika (Buddhism)
Classification: LCC BQ7950.A877 (ebook) | LCC BQ7950.A877 A67 2018 (print) | DDC 294.3/92092—dc23
LC record available at https://lccn.loc.gov/2018009216

ISBN 978-1-61429-476-4 ebook ISBN 978-1-61429-501-3

22 21 20 19 18
5 4 3 2 1

Cover and interior design by Gopa & Ted2, Inc. Set in Diacritical Garamond Premier Pro 10.5/13. Cover image: "Portrait of the Indian monk Atisha." Courtesy of the Metropolitan Museum of Art. Gift of Steven Kossak, The Kronos Collections, 1993.

Wisdom Publications' books are printed on acid-free paper and meet the guidelines for permanence and durability of the Production Guidelines for Book Longevity of the Council on Library Resources.

This book was produced with environmental mindfulness.
For more information, please visit wisdompubs.org/wisdom-environment.

Printed in the United States of America.

This book is dedicated to the memory of my spiritual teacher Geshé Lhundup Sopa (1923–2014), my mentor Leslie Kawamura (1935–2011), and my devoted colleague Jim Blumenthal (1967–2014) —jewel-like teachers of the Middle Way.

Contents

Preface

Geshé Lhundup Sopa (1923–2014) enthusiastically introduced me to a biography of Atiśa in the early summer of 1992 while on retreat at Deer Park Buddhist Center outside of Oregon, Wisconsin. In the spring of 1996, Geshé Sopa led my graduate school classmates and I through Atiśa's biography in a second-year classical Tibetan class at the University of Wisconsin-Madison. The following academic year we read Atiśa's *Open Basket of Jewels*.

Over the summers from 1998 to 2002 at Deer Park Monastery in Oregon, Wisconsin, Geshé Sopa also introduced me to the Madhyamaka thought of Tsongkhapa (1357–1419) in seminars on the major works—the *Great Treatise on the Stages of the Path*, the *Essence of Eloquence*, *Elucidation of the Thought*, and *Ocean of Reasoning*. I was intensely interested in Tsongkhapa, but could not help noticing that Atiśa was always only mentioned in passing in these works. In the back of my mind was the question, "Did Atiśa have any sustained teachings or writing on Madhyamaka other than the *Open Basket of Jewels*?" That question was left unanswered for a number of years as I tried to gain stable employment as an academic scholar.

When I landed a tenure-track position at the University of Calgary in 2008, and having published a book related to Tsongkhapa (*Stairway to Nirvāṇa*), I noticed that a scholar in Japan, Izumi Miyazaki, had published a Tibetan critical edition of Atiśa's *Open Basket of Jewels*, the "Annotated Tibetan Text and Japanese Translation of the *Ratnakaraṇḍodghāṭamadhyamakopadeśa* of Atiśa" (2007). I immediately found my class notes from Geshé Sopa's class, revised the English translation and annotation of Miyazaki's paper, and published this in 2010 as "Atiśa's Open Basket of Jewels: A Middle Way Vision in Late Phase Indian Vajrayāna." At the same time that I arrived at the University of Calgary, the availability of the the *Collected Works of the Kadampas*, unknown to Tibetan scholars after the seventeenth century and published in fascimiles only recently, had been announced.

Noticing that a number of the works were no longer extant elsewhere, I secured grant funds to acquire the *Collected Works of the Kadampas* in 2008.

I can remember the day that the boxes arrived and my late, lamented mentor-colleague Leslie Kawamura (1935–2011) and I unpacked and shelved the first ninety volumes in my office. I was excited to see what these texts would say, particularly with regard to the *Abhisamayālaṃkāra*, on which the collection contained a number of commentaries. As a number of the works were written in hard-to-read cursive (*dbu med*) Tibetan script, I began to write down all the ligatures that I could not read.

Thanks to my training, I could read a majority of the texts, and over time and through comparison I was able to discern a number of abbreviations (*sdus yig*) and other scribal features of the texts that I wished to investigate. I began to notice several volumes on Madhyamaka whose authorship was considered anonymous. I analyzed, transcribed, and translated a number of them wherever and whenever I could find the time. In the spring of 2012, Shōryū Katsura arranged for me to present a lecture on "An Early Tibetan Commentary on Atiśa's *Satyadvayāvatāra*" at the Ryukoku University Research Institute for Buddhist Cultures in Asia (BARC) in June 2012. In Kyoto preparing for the lecture, I realized that the volume *A Collection of Special Instructions on the Middle Way* in the Kadampa collection, the text that was the basis for the lecture, contained elements of Madhyamaka thought and practice I had not read before. I later revised and published this lecture in 2013, which became the basis for chapters 2 and 3 of this book. Upon returning to Canada, and interspersed among other research projects and publications from 2014 to 2016, I gradually edited and published the texts that would eventually become chapters 4–7.

I had every incentive to rework these articles into a book on the Madhyamaka thought and practice of Atiśa and his followers. Not only are the introductory essays and translations based on recently recovered Tibetan texts never before studied, but I was also motivated to counter the misperception of some modern scholars that Atiśa was not an important figure either in Indian or Tibetan Buddhist history. As the book demonstrates, this is decidedly not the case. I have also been motivated by a recent generation of scholars, particularly those who do not read Tibetan, who, with a disregard for sociohistorical context and philological precision, have tried to turn the profound spirituality of Indian and Tibetan Buddhist Madhyamaka into some type of analytical philosophy.

Organization and Structure of the Book

The book is organized in three parts based on the chronology of Atiśa's teaching of Madhyamaka in India and Tibet. Each part focuses on a specific text, or set of texts, specifically related to Atiśa's Middle Way. The authorship and date of composition for each work is discussed along with an outline of the work's textual sources followed by an analysis of the content. Part 1 introduces and is a translation of Atiśa's *Open Basket of Jewels*, an extensive teaching that he composed in India and that was translated by his Tibetan disciples while in India. This text provides an early record of Atiśa's extensive instructions on the Middle Way in which he elaborates his lineage of teachers, the importance of the "mind of awakening" (*bodhicitta*), and the scriptural sources that influence his understanding of Madhyamaka.

Part 2 introduces and provides translations of Atiśa's understanding of the two realities (*satyadvaya*), the basis for his exegesis of the Middle Way. Chapter 2 is a text that Atiśa wrote on the two realities, *Entry to the Two Realities* (*Satyadvayāvatāra*). I have included this brief work of twenty-eight verses as a reference text for the Kadampa commentary *Collection on the Two Realities* in chapter 3, the earliest known commentary on Atiśa's *Entry to the Two Realities.* I introduce the *Collection on the Two Realities* with a discusion on Atiśa's understanding of conventional reality (*saṃvṛtisatya*) and ultimate reality (*paramārthasatya*), and the role of valid cognition (*pramāṇa*) and reasoning (*yukti*) in Atiśa's thought. Chapter 4 is an extended work attributed to Atiśa entitled *A General Explanation of, and Framework for Understanding, the Two Realities.* I introduce the work with a discussion of the evidence for its attribution to Atiśa, provide a topical outline, and furnish a summary and analysis of the content.

Part 3, "How Mādhyamikas Meditate," concentrates on Atiśa's *Special Instructions on the Middle Way* (*Madhyamakopadeśa*) along with two commentaries to the work, one by the Indian scholar Prajñāmukti, who was among the entourage accompanying Atiśa while he traveled in Tibet, and the other by an anonymous Tibetan Kadampa author affiliated with the monastic center of Radreng. Chapter 5 introduces and translates the base text of Atiśa's *Special Instructions on the Middle Way.* Chapter 6 consists of Prajñāmukti's *Commentary on the Special Instructions on the Middle Way* (*Madhyamakopadeśavṛtti*), which furnishes evidence of how Madhyamaka was understood by a contemporary Indian student of Atiśa. Chapter 7 provides a Tibetan commentary to Atiśa's base text *Collection of Special Instructions on the Middle Way* that demonstrates the faith-based contemplative nature of the Middle Way among Atiśa's early followers. Altogether, these chapters bring together the primary sources of Atiśa's Madhyamaka thought and its understanding among his early Kadampa followers.

Manuscripts and Sources

The works of Atiśa and his early Kadampa followers included in this book are based on recently published manuscripts of the *Collected Works of the Kadampas* (*Bka' gdams pa gsung 'bum*).[1] This collection consists of a number of lost Tibetan manuscripts that were recovered from temples within Drepung and Sera monasteries outside of Lhasa in 2003, as well as works gathered from private collections of individual Tibetan scholars. Currently consisting of 120 volumes, the collection contains facsimiles of manuscripts related to Buddhist scholastic topics such as Madhyamaka (*dbu ma*), Pramāṇa (*tshad ma*), and Abhidharma (*chos mngon pa*) by Tibetan authors from the late tenth century up to the early fifteenth century.

The original manuscripts were found loosely piled in muddled, dusty, and moldy stacks of folios in the storerooms of Drepung and Sera monasteries. Under the direction of Alak Zenkar Rinpoche Tupten Nyima (Thub bstan nyi ma, b. 1943), these stacks of manuscripts were cleaned, put in order, organized into distinct books, and shelved. Over the course of several years, facsimiles of the manuscripts were made available for purchase in four sets of thirty volumes each. Volumes 1–30, published in 2006, contain works of scholars such as Rinchen Sangpo (958–1055), Ngok Loden Sherap (1059–1109), Patsap Nyimadrak (b. 1055), and Chapa Chökyi Sengé (1109–69). Volumes 31–60 (2009) include works by figures like Gyamar Jangchup Drak (eleventh century) and Chim Namkha Drak (1210–85). Volumes 61–90 (2009) have texts by authors such as Mapja Jangchup Tsöndrü (d. 1185), Chomden Rikpai Raldri (1227–1305), and Gyalsé Thokmé Sangpo (1295–1369). Among volumes 91–120 (2015) are works of Atiśa, Rinchen Sangpo, and Potowa Rinchen Sal (1027–1105). Each of these four sets contains works by numerous other authors; some works are anonymous or have authors yet to be identified. The facsimiles of the manuscripts are unedited. Some manuscript folios are out of order, some manuscripts are in block print, and the majority are written in different varieties of cursive Tibetan script.

The authors of these works are generally considered to belong to the Kadampa tradition of Tibetan Buddhism. The volumes of handwritten manuscripts were purportedly a part of the library of the fourth Tsang king, Karma Tenkyong Wangpo (r. 1622–42), a patron of Kagyüpa groups, and were confiscated by the Fifth Dalai Lama, Ngawang Losang Gyatso (1617–82). Although the banning of books owing to doctrinal content is well known in Tibetan history,[2] the confiscation of these manuscripts is most likely not due to their content. As suggested by Gareth Sparham (cited in Hopkins 2007, 10–12), the seventeenth-century political situation in Tibet involving the Gelukpa, their Mongolian patrons, and rival kings in Tsang province may not reflect the banning of individual works based on philosophical or doctrinal content but rather political conflict over maintenance of patronage. Nevertheless, the fact that these texts were deposited away in the mid-seventeenth century indicates that prominent Tibetan scholars, particularly Gelukpa exegetes such as Changkya Rölpai Dorjé (1717–86) and Thuken Chökyi Nyima (1737–1802), or even a Kadampa literature specialist like Yeshé Döndrup (1792–1855),[3] did not have access to texts such as *A General Explanation of the Two Realities* after the seventeenth century. It gives pause for thought that these texts are available to scholars today through the sheer contingency of historical factors that enabled their recovery.

Most studies of Indian Buddhism and Madhyamaka are based on extant manuscripts, xylographs, or blockprints centuries away from the authors of these works. These texts are preserved in Tibetan Tengyurs and, once translated into Tibetan, have been systematically and anonymously edited over the centuries. The manuscripts I have selected for this book bring us closer to the eleventh-century figure of Atiśa, as they appear to be the earliest and most relevant to Atiśa's Madhyamaka in the currently available *Collected Works of the Kadampas. Open Basket of Jewels*; *Entry to the Two Realities* and its Kadampa commentary, *Collection on the Two Realities*; *A General Explanation of the Two Realities*; and the Kadampa commentary *Collection of Special Instructions on the Middle Way* are all translated from manuscripts of the *Collected Works of the Kadampa*s and are texts attributed to Atiśa or his early Kadampa followers. Although physically copied in the mid-seventeenth century, the textual readings they contain are earlier than the block print editions of the Tengyur, most of which were created and anonymously edited in the early part of the eighteenth century (1730s).[4]

I have also utilized other early commentaries preserved from the *Collected Works of the Kadampa*s for insight into Atiśa's Madhyamaka teachings in Tibet. These include the *Explanation of [Atiśa's] Special Instructions of the Middle Way*; *The System of Potowa and His Spiritual Son* (*Dbu ma'i man ngag gi bshad pa, Pu to yab sras kyi lugs*) [abbr. *Potowa's Middle Way*][5] by an anonymous Kadampa author; as well as an early Kadampa commentary on the *Satyadvayāvatāra*, *Sherab Dorjé's Explanation of Atiśa's "Entry to the Two Realities,"* attributed to Naljorpa Sherap Dorjé (ca. 1125), who was a direct disciple of Sharawa Yönten Drak (1070–1141).[6]

My translations and analyses are supplemented with anecdotes from the early biographies of Atiśa and his numerous works and translations that are preserved in Tibetan. The stories of Atiśa's life are preserved only in Tibetan sources. Based on the extensive studies of Helmut Eimer (1977, 1979, 1982,

2003), over forty Tibetan sources are known that provide biographical information about Atiśa. Among these sources, *The Extensive Biography* (*Rnam thar rgyas pa*), attributed to Ja Dülzin Tsöndrü Bar (1091–1166 or 1100–1174), and *The Universally Known Biography* (*Rnam thar yongs grags*), attributed to Chim Namkha Drak (1210–85), furnish almost all material known about the life of Atiśa (Eimer 1982). Excerpts from these biographies have been studied and translated (Decleer 1996, 1997a, 1997b; Jinpa 2006), although complete translations have yet to be published. In addition, recently recovered manuscripts published in facsimile by the Paltsek Institute for Ancient Tibetan Manuscripts has complicated, yet also enhanced, the available sources for Atiśa's life and its transmission history. In addition to known sources on Atiśa's life that have not been translated, the Paltsek Institute's recent publication of the *Collected Works of Tibetan Histories and Biographies* (*Bod kyi lo rgyus rnam thar phyogs bsgrigs* 2010) contains six biographies of Atiśa based on texts previously unknown or presumed lost. These older versions of Atiśa's life story have recently been published in Tibetan as the *Collected Biographies of the Glorious Lord Atiśa*.[7] Although material found in these biographies overlaps with material found in *The Extensive Biography* and *The Universally Known Biography*, there are also strands of information in the older biographies that were previously unknown. A good example is a biographical episode translated by Thupten Jinpa (2006, 27–58) entitled "How Atiśa Relinquished His Kingdom and Sought Liberation," attributed to Atiśa's disciple Dromtönpa. This is one of four biographical works on Atiśa found in *The Book of Kadam*. Two of the biographies in the *Collected Biographies of the Glorious Lord Atiśa*, both attributed to Dromtönpa, also contain this episode, but these older biographies provide an additional twenty pages of narrative not found in *The Book of Kadam*. In sum, the biographical and historical information for Atiśa's instruction on Madhyamaka that is available in these sources has not been preserved for other Indian Buddhist scholars and teachers. The accounts of the journeys of Tibetan translator-monks to bring Atiśa to western Tibet, along with accounts of Atiśa's life and his own writings, supplemented with recently discovered Kadampa manuscripts, provide new evidence for the practice of Madhyamaka in eleventh-century India and Tibet.

The old Tibetan manuscripts published by the Paltsek Institute, hidden away in the basement storerooms of Drepung Monastery, Sera Monastery, and the Potala Palace for over four hundred years, bring to light an understanding and exegesis of Atiśa's Madhyamaka thought and practice that, in many respects, is totally opposite from the views of post-sixteenth-century Gelukpa thinkers. These texts illustrate how unique the Gelukpa presentation of Madhyamaka is from the standpoint of Atiśa and the majority of early

Kadampa thinkers. They implicitly demonstrate just how reliant a number of modern interpreters of Madhyamaka are on Gelukpa understandings of Madhyamaka and its related practices, and just how different modern interpreters are in their soteriological understanding of Madhyamaka in the context of Buddhist thought.[8]

These available historical resources provide evidence for a general chronology of when and where Atiśa taught and translated his teachings on the Middle Way. Based on them, the introductory essays to the translations discuss the Indian Buddhists that Atiśa studied under, as well as the texts that he studied and taught, to gain a clear picture of the influences that shaped his understanding of Madhyamaka in India.

Acknowledgments

At Wisdom Publications, I especially thank David Kittelstrom, whose editorial insights significantly improved the book. I thank Mary Petrusewicz, whose meticulous line editing notably improved the quality of the book.

I would like to thank my parents, Jeanne Bedwell and James Apple, for their support and advice. Finally, but certainly not least, I would like to thank my wife, Shinobu, who step by step has supported me throughout the writing of this book.

Chapters of this book were originally published as journal articles. Chapter 1: "Atiśa's Open Basket of Jewels: A Middle Way Vision in Late Phase Indian Vajrayāna," *Indian International Journal of Buddhist Studies* 11 (2010): 117–98. Chapters 2 and 3: "An Early Tibetan Commentary on Atiśa's *Satyadvayāvatāra*," *Journal of Indian Philosophy* 41.3 (2013): 263–329, and "An Early Tibetan Commentary on Atiśa's Satyadvayāvatāra: Diplomatic Edition with Introduction and Notes," *Journal of Indian Philosophy* 41.5 (2013): 501–33. Chapter 4: "An Early Bka'-gdams-pa Madhyamaka Work Attributed to Atiśa Dīpaṃkaraśrījñāna," *Journal of Indian Philosophy* 44.4 (2016): 619–725. Chapters 5–7: "A Study and Translation of Atiśa's *Madhyamakopadeśa* with Indian and Tibetan Commentaries," *Acta Tibetica et Buddhica* 7 (2014): 1–82.

Calgary, Alberta
August 7, 2017

Introduction: Atiśa's Middle Way in India and Tibet

Dīpaṃkaraśrījñāna (982–1054), also known under the title Atiśa,[9] is famous for his journey to Tibet and his teachings there over the course of thirteen years. His lucid expositions on Mahāyāna and Vajrayāna Buddhist thought and practice came to influence all subsequent traditions of Buddhism in Tibet. However, Atiśa's teachings on Madhyamaka (Middle Way religious thought and practice)[10] are not extensively discussed nor commented on in the works of known and extant indigenous Tibetan scholars. In modern scholarly overviews or sourcebooks on Indian Buddhist thought and practice, Atiśa's Madhyamaka teachings, if even discussed, are minimally acknowledged. The essays and translations in this book reveal Atiśa's pure Madhyamaka lineage from Nāgārjuna that was significantly influenced by the works of Candrakīrti. This Madhyamaka lineage was contemplative in nature and based on faith, compassion, and resolutions to attain a miraculous form of buddhahood rather than on formal logical proof, linguistic semantics, or metaphysical speculation. Moreover, it was actively taught and followed for at least fifty years after Atiśa came to Tibet. The works that follow open a window into a lineage of Madhyamaka that pre-dates the infusion of epistemology that developed at the famous monastery of Sangphu Neuthok in the twelfth century and its later systemization in the Geluk tradition after the fifteenth century. These introductory essays and translations therefore fill an important gap in the historical knowledge of Madhyamaka teachings in eleventh-century India and Tibet.[11] They constitute new knowledge and understanding concerning Madhyamaka and its practice according to Atiśa and his early followers, known as Kadampas (*bka' gdams pa*).[12] Although there have been previous studies on Atiśa (e.g., Chattopadhyaya 1967; Sherburne 1983; Sherburne 2000), the materials in this book are based on recently recovered texts of the *Collected Works of the Kadampas* (*Bka' gdams gsung 'bum*) published by the Paltsek Institute for Ancient Tibetan Manuscripts (*dpal brtsegs bod yig dpe rnying zhib 'jug khang*). Unknown to even indigenous Tibetan scholars after the seventeenth century and collected and published in facsimile form only in the early twenty-first century, these materials shed new light on Atiśa's teachings in Tibet and bring to the forefront a forgotten legacy of Madhyamaka thought that disappeared from Tibetan Buddhist communities after the thirteenth century.

Atiśa's Study of the Middle Way

Atiśa traveled far and wide both as a student and as a scholar to learn and teach Madhyamaka thought and practice. The biographies mention him traveling throughout central India, South India, Kashmir, Bengal, and Sumatra to learn the Dharma of the Buddha.[13] Based on the lineage lists that record his early education, Atiśa received extensive teachings on Mahāyāna Buddhism in both the way of the perfections (*pāramitā*) and the way of mantras (*mantra*). Atiśa's lineages within the way of perfections are classified as either the lineage of the view (*lta ba*) or the lineages of extensive practices (*spyod pa*). Atiśa will later be renowned in Tibetan forms of Buddhism for unifying the vision and practices found within these two lineages.

In the works translated in this book, Atiśa identifies himself as a follower of the Middle Way (*dbu ma pa*) from the lineage and teachings of the Ārya Nāgārjuna. Nāgārjuna, in Atiśa's eyes, is a Mahāyāna Buddhist figure equivalent to the Buddha, one who is placed at the beginning of numerous lineage lists encompassing the way of the perfections, the way of mantras, and the lineage of view within the Tibetan biographical tradition of categorizing Atiśa's received teachings. The basis of Atiśa's understanding of Mahāyāna Buddhist thought and practice descends from Nāgārjuna and encompasses all of Atiśa works included in this book.

The early biographies on Atiśa's life begin with his training under numerous Indian masters. Five masters that are prominent in his early education include the *brāhmaṇa* Jitāri, the scholar-monk Bodhibhadra, the contemplative-monk Vidyākokila, and the tantric yogis Avadhūtipa and Rāhulagupta. Atiśa would study under these masters from around the age of ten up to the age of twenty-one. Biographies expand the number of Atiśa's teachers from seven, then twelve, and up to fifty-two (Vetturini 2013, 80).

The narratives depict him learning about Madhyamaka from scholarly monks in Indian Buddhist monasteries and from contemplative monks and tantric yogis in remote forest retreats. Atiśa lived during the the Pāla dynastic period (eighth century to 1200) in eastern India, where great educational and monastic centers of Buddhism flourished. Institutions such as Vikramaśīla, Nālandā, Somapurī, Trikaṭuka, Uddaṇḍapura, and Jagaddala received royal funding and state support from the Pāla emperors for infrastructure costs and teaching appointments.[14] As the young prince *Candragarbha (*zla ba'i snying* *po*), Atiśa seeks out his teachers in monastic institutions, forest retreats, or cave dwellings. The idealized portraits of Atiśa's life perserved in the Potala Palace depict meetings with teachers in forest retreats.[15] Among Atiśa's teachers related to Madhyamaka or meditation, Bodhibhadra is mainly connected with a monastery, Nālandā, but his primary teacher of Madhyamaka, Avadhūtipa, is a yogi who resides in the forest. Among Atiśa's early teachers, Jitāri, Bodhibhadra, Vidyākokila, and Avadhūtipa are the most formative for Atiśa's understanding of Madhyamaka.

Although Jitāri is not listed among Atiśa's lineage of Madhyamaka teachers, early biographies portray him as the first major teacher in Atiśa's life and one who encourages the young Atiśa to seek out and study under Bodhibhadra. Jitāri[16] was a lay (*upāsaka*) Buddhist scholar and master of tantra who was educated at home because his parents had a mixed-caste marriage (Franco 2015). Jitāri taught at Vikramaśīla Monastery and was considered an excellent teacher, both in epistemology (*pramāṇa*) and tantra, based on his known works and his having received the honor of paṇḍita during the reign of Mahāpāla (Tucci 1956, 250–52). Biographical sources mention that Atiśa was a young boy around the age of ten (ca. 992) when he studied under Jitāri. The Tibetan biographical narratives depict Jitāri instructing the young Atiśa to travel away from Vikramaśīla Monastery, which was closer to his home, and to the more distant monastery of Nālandā in Magadha in order to study under Bodhibhadra.

The young prince *Candragarbha met Bodhibhadra upon arrival at Nālandā in 994 and received novice vows from the scholar-monk. The Tibetan Tengyur preserves five major works attributed to Bodhibhadra. These include the *Bodhisattvasaṃvaravidhi* (Toh 3967 and 4491), the *Bodhisattvasaṃvaraviṃśakapañjikā* (Toh 4083), *Jñānasārasamuccayanibandhana* (Toh 3852), *Samādhisambhāraparivarta* (Toh 3924), and *Yogalakṣaṇasatya* (Toh 2458 and 4536). Atiśa often cites these works of Bodhibhadra in his own corpus of writings.[17] Bodhibhadra is an authoritative figure for Atiśa in bodhisattva conduct, the practice of tranquility (*śamatha*), and his understanding of Madhyamaka. In the section on tranquility in Atiśa's *Bodhipathapradīpa*, the *Samādhisambhāraparivarta* is cited multiple times and Atiśa supports his classifications and branches of tranquility based on this work. Along these lines, Atiśa provides a brief exegesis on Madhyamaka in his *Bodhimārgapradīpapañjikā* (see Appendix) influenced by the thought of Bodhibhadra. In relation to Atiśa's lineage of Madhyamaka, as represented in the *Bodhipathapradīpa* and its autocommentary, Bodhibhadra is a major figure. Atiśa considers this tradition of Madhyamaka as being passed from Nāgārjuna through Āryadeva, Candrakīrti, Bhāviveka, and Śāntideva down to Bodhibhadra. Atiśa praises Bodhibhadra in the *Bodhimārgapradīpapañjikā* as follows:

> Bodhibhadra attained accomplishment by means of the special instructions of Ārya Nāgārjuna and acquired the approval of Ārya Mañjughoṣa. He obtained supersensory knowledge and perceived reality, manifesting in his mind the intention of all the tantras, all the sūtras, and the tradition of vinaya at the same time. Therefore, since the spiritual teacher of the successively transmitted lineage is the glorious Bodhibhadra, one should follow him.[18]

In the works translated in this book, however, Bodhibhadra is not significantly cited in Atiśa's articulation of Madhyamaka. Atiśa mainly cites the works of Nāgārjuna in his own works composed in India and Tibet. Atiśa does cite Bodhibhadra as an authoritative figure in his *Bodhipathapradīpa*, and this may have been due to Bodhibhadra's status as a celibate monk when the *Bodhipathapradīpa* was commissioned by King Jangchup Ö in the west Tibet region of Shangshung.

Bodhibhadra gives the young prince *Candragarbha instruction on generating the resolve for the awakening mind (*cittotpāda*, *sems bskyed*) (Dromtönpa Gyalwai Jungné 2014a, 4–6; Jinpa 2006, 41). Bodhibhadra also gives the prince instruction on death and impermanence, encouraging him to renounce his kingdom and become a fully ordained monk. He then directs the prince to receive instruction on Dharma from *Vidyākokila, a monk living north of Nālandā in solitary retreat. Atiśa left Bodhibhadra and sought instruction from Vidyākokila.

Vidyākokila is often noted in Tibetan biographies and histories as a master who comes after Nāgārjuna and Candrakīrti in the accounts of Atiśa's lineages of received teachings. *The Dromtön Itinerary*, attributed to Atiśa's foremost disciple, Dromtönpa Gyalwai Jungné ('Brom ston pa rgyal ba'i 'byung gnas, 1004–64), provides a third-person account of Naktso Lotsāwa Tsultrim Gyalwa seeing Vidyākokila at a noontime gathering of monks at Vikramaśīla Monastery and mistaking him for Atiśa. In Naktso Lotsāwa's account, Vidyākokila is described as "a great accomplished master who directly trained under the great Ācārya Candrakīrti."[19] The Kadampa *Collection on the Two Realities* and *General Explanation* mention that Vidyākokila, along with Nāgārjuna and Candrakīrti, were long-lived figures who perceived reality. Ruegg (2010, 9–10n10) has noted that the Tibetan translator Patsap Nyimadrak's Indian mentors, Kanakavarman and Hasumati, were disciples of Vidyākokila.

After studying under Vidyākokila, Atiśa, according to early Kadampa biographies, went to study with Avadhūtipa. Historical information for Avadhūtipa is elusive in that there are at least four individuals with this name in works preserved in the Tibetan Tengyur. Tibetan historians writing after the fourteenth century also provide varied accounts of his life and his relationship to Atiśa.[20] I therefore limit the references about Avadhūtipa and his teachings to works written by Atiśa, the early Kadampa biographies of Atiśa, and the early Kadampa commentaries on Atiśa's Middle Way. A traditional biography of Atiśa attributed to Dromtönpa Gyalwai Jungné (2012b, 45–46) states that Atiśa first received Madhyamaka teachings under the tantric yogi Avadhūtipa, with whom he studied for seven years from the age of twelve to eighteen. The biography mentions that Atiśa learned the Madhyamaka principles of subtle cause and effect under Avadhūtipa, a point specifically mentioned in the *Collection on the Two Realities* (folio 7b). Atiśa's study of Madhyamaka under Avadhūtipa is also supported by the colophon to the *Sūtrasamuccayasañcayārtha*, which mentions that he received the special instruction (*upadeśa*) of *apratiṣṭhita* [*madhyamaka*] *darśana* under Avadhūtipa. This work was translated by Atiśa and a Tibetan student while in India.[21] In another work translated while in India, Atiśa's *Open Basket of Jewels* directly cites Avadhūtipa three times. The first citation emphasizes the nondifference between gnosis and the *dharmadhātu*, the second citation advocates practicing the vehicle of secret mantra and attaining Mahāmudrā, and the third citation prescribes not judging others while continuously meditating on emptiness. As we shall see, the nondifference between gnosis and the *dharmadhātu* (the realm of reality) will be a major source of controversy between Atiśa and his students trained in Tibet. *A General Explanation* lists Avadhūtipa in the lineage of Atiśa's Madhyamaka teachers and describes him as a bodhisattva who obtained the fourth level (*bhūmi*). The Kadampa *Collection on the Two Realities* mentions that Atiśa gained the Middle Way vision (*dbu ma'i lta ba*) from Avadhūtipa, but later states that Avadhūtipa is not recorded in lists of Atiśa's Madhyamaka teachers. The *Collection of Special Instructions on the Middle Way*[22] states that Avadhūtipa bestowed on Atiśa the special instructions on nonarising.

The chronology of Atiśa's life after his study with Avadhūtipa is not fully clear. The biographical sources tell of Atiśa receiving consecration and oral teachings from the tantric master Rāhulagupta into the cult of Hevajra and then traveling in central and northwest India practicing asceticism and studying various classes of tantra. In the course of his ascetic practices during this time, Atiśa is inspired to become a monk. At the age of twenty-eight or twenty-nine, Atiśa is ordained at Uddaṇḍapura by Śīlarakṣita, who belonged to the

Lokottaravāda branch of the Mahāsāṃghika school. The biographies mention that Atísa acquires full mastery of the great commentary of the Mahāvibhāṣā and three piṭakas at the age of thirty-one.

During Atiśa's time at Uddaṇḍapura, he learns of the great Buddhist teacher Dharmakīrti of Suvarṇadvīpa, known in Tibetan as Serlingpa, "the man from Sumatra Island." The biographies portray Atiśa's inspiration to study with this teacher through either prophecies from his teachers, visions from his meditational deities, or by word of mouth while on pilgrimage in Bodhgayā. Atiśa is inspired to undertake the arduous journey to Sumatra to study under Serlingpa because of this teacher's prestigious knowledge of Mahāyāna path systems, especially his teaching on how to properly cultivate the resolution to attain full buddhahood for the benefit of all beings. Atiśa embarked on the dangerous voyage around the year 1012 (Chattopadhyaya 1967, 85). According to the traditional sources, he stayed for twelve years.

Atiśa was considered one of Serlingpa's four great disciples, along with Ratnākaraśānti, Jñānaśrīmitra, and Ratnakīrti. Serlingpa was the author of the *Durbodhālokā*, a well-known subcommentary on Haribhadra's *Abhisamayālaṃkāravivṛti*. Indeed, Atiśa's biographies mention that he directly heard lectures on the *Abhisamayālaṃkāra* in fifteen sessions from Serlingpa. Serlingpa's mastery of the *Abhisamayālaṃkāra* enabled him to teach Atiśa topics such as mind training, the exchange of self and others, and bodhicitta, which Atiśa would later disseminate to his Kadampa followers. Serlingpa was also credited with works related to Śāntideva's *Śikṣāsamuccaya* and *Bodhicaryāvatāra*.

Atiśa studied under Serlingpa and returned to India in 1025 around the age of forty-four. *The Universally Known Biography* states that Serlingpa instructed Atiśa to study with Ratnākaraśānti at Vikramalaśīla upon returning to India. *The Extensive Biography* describes Atiśa carrying out religious work in the Vajrāsana area before going on to Vikramaśīla Monastery.[23] Atiśa may have arrived at Vikramaśīla after being appointed as *Upādhyāya* (preceptor) at Vikramaśīla with responsibility also for Uddaṇḍapura under King Bheyapāla, who reigned according to Tāranātha as the predecessor of Neyāpāla (r. ca. 1027–43). Atiśa's teachers and colleagues at Vikramaśīla included such figures as Tathāgatarakṣita, Kamalarakṣita, Jñānaśrīmitra, Ratnakīrti, and Ratnākaraśānti. Atiśa most likely studied under Ratnākaraśānti during the initial period of settling into life at Vikramaśīla.

Ratnākaraśānti (ca. 1000), also known as Śāntipa in Tibetan sources, was a formidable figure at Vikramaśīla, renowned for his enormous breadth of learning and prolific scholarship. He is said to have held the position of eastern gatekeeper[24] at Vikramaśīla and to have been a teacher of the Tibetan translator Drokmi Śākya Yeshé (993–1077) in addition to being Atiśa's teacher. He composed at least thirty works in a variety of subjects such as valid cognition (*pramāṇa*), the *Perfection of Wisdom* (*prajñāpāramitā*), Yogācāra, tantra, as well as Buddhist verse metrics (*cansaḥśāstra*) and riddles (Isaacson 2013). Many of them are preserved only in Tibetan, but a fair number of his compositions also survive in Sanskrit. His works on valid cognition include the *Antarvyāptisamarthana*, a digest wherein he formulated the position of "intrinsic entailment" (*antarvyāpti*) (Kajiyama 1999). His compositions on the *prajñāpāramitā* include the *Sārottamā*, a commentary on the eight-thousand-line discourse, and the *Śuddhamati*, a commentary to the twenty-five-thousand-line text. Ratnākaraśānti's compositions on tantric philosophy and practice were significant for explaining the "method of mantras" (*mantranaya*) in terms of Buddhist scholasticism. His tantric works included commentaries and instruction manuals (*sādhana*) on the *Hevajratantra* and the *Guhyasamājatantra*. Ratnākaraśānti also composed works in which he systematized the thought of Maitreya, Asaṅga, and Vasubandhu with the thought of Nāgārjuna to establish his version of the Middle Way (*madhyamā pratipat*) along the lines of yogācāra thought. The Middle Way for Ratnākaraśānti consisted of a Yogācāra position in which mental images, or aspects, in cognition are false (**alīkākāravāda*). Ratnākaraśānti articulated his position in several of his independent writings, such as the *Madhyamakālaṃkāropadeśa* (MAU), the *Madhyamakālaṃkāravṛtti-madhyamapratipatsiddhi* (MAV), the *Vijñaptimātratāsiddhi* (VMS), the *Sūtrasamuccayabhāṣya* and *Prajnāpāramitopadeśa* (PPU). As discussed below, Atiśa and Ratnākaraśānti did not share the same view and practice of the Middle Way.

Atiśa presumably taught courses and served as a supervisor for students at Vikramaśīla and Somapurī. Although the narratives of this phase of Atiśa's life in the Tibetan biographies emphasize and are framed in terms of prophetic expectations for Atiśa to come to Tibet, the sources also indicate that Atiśa was willing to accept Tibetans as students. The two Tibetan figures who come to study with Atiśa and translate texts under him are Gya Tsöndrü Sengé (aka Gya Lotsāwa), who arrived first, and Naktso Lotsāwa Tsultrim Gyalwa, who followed. Both these monastic student-translators were sent to India by Jangchup Ö (984–1078) to bring Atiśa back to west Tibet to revitalize the Buddha's discipline and teaching there. The Tibetan biographical accounts record that Atiśa initially rejected invitations to Tibet, and that although the two translators eventually succeed in their mission to recruit Atiśa, they stayed at Vikramaśīla for several years waiting for Atiśa's decision.

Gya Tsöndrü Sengé and Naktso studied under Atiśa during this time and together translated works by Atiśa and his disciples. Atiśa's *Entry to the Two*

Realities and its commentary were translated into Tibetan at Vikramaśīla, as was *Open Basket of Jewels*. Colophons of works preserved in Tibet and biographical anecdotes mention that Atiśa utilized the *Madhyamakaratnapradīpa* (MRP) and the *Tarkajvālā* at Somapurī while teaching courses on Madhyamaka around the year 1034. The MRP was translated in India by Gya Lotsāwa and Naktso while at Somapurī, after Atiśa himself had requested a personal copy of the text from a Ceylonese monk. This anecdote not only records that Atiśa's Tibetan students accompanied him on teaching tours to other monasteries but also that Atiśa kept a personal copy of the MRP for the study and teaching of Madhyamaka.

The MRP is the base text for Atiśa's understanding of Madhyamaka. A number of Atiśa's standpoints on Madhyamaka thought, as well as the Buddhist scriptural sources to substantiate them, are found in the MRP. Atiśa also taught Madhyamaka at Somapurī utilizing the *Tarkajvālā*. However, the *Tarkajvālā* was translated into Tibetan by Atiśa and Naktso only years later when Atiśa presented his special instructions on the Madhyamaka in Lhasa. What is notable is that Atiśa taught the MRP and the *Tarkajvālā*, both works that he attributed to Bhāviveka, as sources for introducing Madhyamaka thought. The *Tarkajvālā* is cited in the commentaries throughout the following chapters.

Atiśa accepted the invitation to teach in Tibet at some point between 1037 and 1040. The biographies depict Atiśa's decision to leave Vikramaśīla for Tibet as one based on his consultation with teachers, colleagues, and tutelary deities, who ostensively advocate that Atiśa will benefit a great number of beings by teaching in Tibet. The sources also indicate that Atiśa realized that his life might be shortened by traveling to Tibet. At the same time, the Tibetans had to negotiate with Vikramaśīla's senior monks to gain permission for Atiśa to leave, indicating that elder monks at the monastery had greater authority and power than did Atiśa in the adminstration of affairs at Vikramaśīla. The sources tell only the Tibetan side of the story and we do not know what the state of affairs were at Vikramaśīla that provoked Atiśa, at nearly sixty years of age, to leave on a multiyear journey to Tibet by horseback. If we understand philosophical views and practices to be affiliated with power and prestige, then Atiśa may well have felt outnumbered in the environment of Vikramaśīla, where a number of his supervisors and colleagues were affliated with Yogācāra views and were experts in the utilization of valid cognition for apologetics. The invitation to be an honored guest in a foreign land may have attracted Atiśa for a number of reasons, including the opportunity to lead eager Buddhist students who had an enthusiasm for Madhyamaka and the practice of Vajrayāna.

Whatever the reasons for his decision to journey to Tibet, Atiśa and his Tibetan translators, accompanied by an Indian entourage, left Vikramaśīla in 1040. On their journey through Nepal, Gya Lotsāwa unexpectedly died and Atiśa almost decided to turn back. Eventually, after two years of travel, they arrived in west Tibet, where Atiśa took up residency at Tholing Monastery. Atiśa met with the great Tibetan translator Rinchen Sangpo at this time and also began translating tantric texts. Atiśa's first years in Tibet were under royal patronage. He translated numerous works as well as composed his most important public work, the *Bodhipathapradīpa*, while residing in west Tibet.

TABLE 1. ATIŚA'S PRINCIPAL TEACHERS

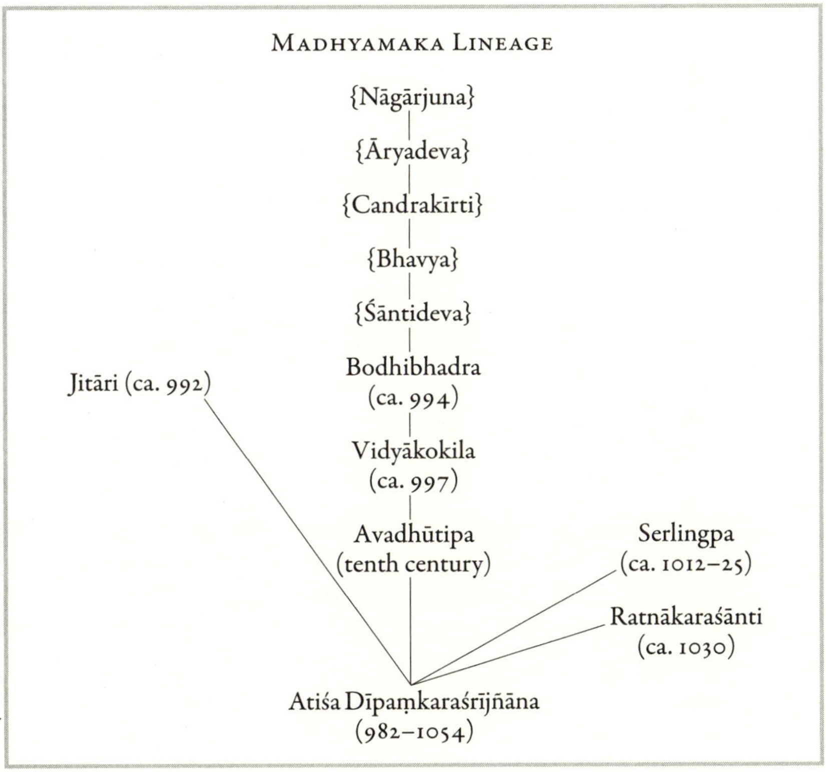

Individuals listed in brackets represent lineage figures not met by Atiśa in person.

Atiśa's Years in Tibet

After his first three years in Ngari, Atiśa resided in Tibet for ten more years, meeting important disciples, translating texts, and giving teachings in public and in private. The primary historical sources outline Atiśa's remaining time in Tibet as an itinerant teacher who journeyed to central Tibet with his entourage, residing for four years in the regions of Ü and Tsang and for six years in the Nyethang region.[25] Atiśa had initially planned to return to India according to the three-year leave-of-absence agreement made with his monastic superiors at Vikramaśīla. However, as several accounts emphasize, the road through Nepal was blocked owing to regional conflicts, impeding his return. At this time Atiśa met Dromtönpa Gyalwai Jungné, a layperson trained in eastern Tibet who would become Atiśa's foremost Tibetan disciple. The Kadampa biographical accounts depict Atiśa as anticipating meeting a lay disciple according to predictions he received in visions from his tutelary deity Tārā. The accounts portray Dromtönpa as an educated layman with high ambitions, gathering patronage and support for a future monastery on his journey to west-central Tibet to meet a newly arrived Indian master.

Atiśa met Dromtönpa at a temple in Purang and the Indian master gave him a tantric consecration and teaching after they met.[26] Dromtönpa gained Atiśa's confidence as a loyal disciple while Atiśa and his entourage determined their next course of action to return to India. *The Blue Annals* (Roerich 1976, 253) describes Atiśa and his entourage as spending a year (1045) in Kyirong, a district of Mangyul, while the roads were closed. During this time Dromtönpa suggested that Atiśa go to central Tibet. He emphasized to Atiśa, at least as represented in several accounts, that travel to central Tibet would benefit the many good monks who resided there and that Atiśa would also be able to visit the Tibetan Buddhist temples and see the Sanskrit manuscripts preserved at Samyé Monastery. Atiśa agreed to go to central Tibet if he received an invitation from the Buddhist community (*dge 'dun*). Dromtönpa then sent a letter through Shang Wangchuk Gön for delivery to Geshé Kawa Shākya Wangchuk. The letter consisted of nineteen verses and addressed the Buddhist dignitaries of central Tibet to invite the Indian master to the region.[27]

Influenced by Dromtönpa, Atiśa and his entourage then initiated a journey east across to central Tibet rather than south to Nepal. Dromtönpa had enticed Atiśa to central Tibet with descriptions of monks of pure conduct, wondrous Buddhist temples, and treasures of Sanskrit manuscripts. Yet Atiśa and his entourage were on the cusp of encountering a number of unanticipated sociopolitical challenges in the Buddhist culture of eleventh-century Tibet. Competing local clan-based rule would challenge not only Atiśa's authority as a monastic official but also the form and content of what Buddhist doctrines that he could teach publicly. As recent scholarship has demonstrated, eleventh-century Buddhist central Tibet lacked a strong central authority and the foundational stability of the Imperial Era. In place of unifying power, monastic communities consisting of master and disciple lineages in succession, supported by local clan-based factions, represented political agency in the competitive sociopolitical environment of central Tibet.[28] The network of monastic communities bound by lineage ordination directly interacted with local clan-based factions who controlled the lands where monastics settled for patronage, allegiance, and social cohesion.[29]

These monastic communities in competition consisted of four main groups (*sde ba bzhi*) derived from the Lower Vinaya tradition of eastern Tibet and they were all ordination descendants of Lachen Gongpa Rabsel (832–915). The four groups and their local supporters were from Lumé, Ba, Rak, and Dring and upheld the Mūlasarvāstivāda ordination lineage.[30] The fact that Atiśa and his entourage were upholders of the Lokottaravāda ordination lineage of the Mahāsāṃghika Vinaya had a number of problematic consequences for his travels and teaching in a dominant Mūlasarvāstivāda environment. As Davidson (2005, 110–11) has aptly described, because of these conditions Atiśa rarely established temples or institutions and he had no choice in the curriculum of the teaching agenda he was requested to follow. Moreover, as indicated below, all of Atiśa's early primary Tibetan disciples were educated in the Lower Vinaya curriculum of Buddhist subject matter, such as the Abhidharma, *Perfection of Wisdom*, and Madhyamaka.[31] Thus not only were the temples where Atiśa taught as a guest lecturer controlled by the Eastern Vinaya tradition but the structure and content of his teachings were also often translated according to the framework of this conservative Tibetan tradition.

As mentioned, the layman Dromtönpa became Atiśa's primary disciple. The fact that one of the main disciples of Atiśa, as well as the de facto founder of the Kadampa tradition, was a layperson (*dge bsnyen*) who upheld the precepts of the Mūlasarvāstivāda Vinaya may indicate a tension between the dominant Tibetan monastic community, who upheld the same ordination lineage, and Atiśa, who upheld the Mahāsāṃghika Vinaya. Along these lines, the Kadampa historical accounts of the life of Dromtönpa place great emphasis on the fact that he took his lay precepts from Shang Chenpo of Gyal, also known as Shang Nanam Dorjé Wangchuk (976–1060), one of the "four pillar" disciples of Lumé Sherap Tsultrim of the Eastern Vinaya tradition.[32] The biographical tradition also emphasized that Dromtönpa studied at monastic institutes in Denma, eastern Tibet, for a number of years under the masters Setsun Wangchuk Shönu and Smṛtijñānakīrti.[33] In brief, Kadampa authorial communities stressed the relations of ordination and education that Dromtönpa shared with members of the Eastern Vinaya tradition and portrayed him as part of the conservative monastic establishment.

Early in Atiśa's journey east across to central Tibet, he met Khutön Tsöndrü

Yungdrung (1011–75). Khutön was a powerful dignitary from Yarlung who, like the other primary early disciples of Atiśa, had studied in Khams under Setsun and was ordained in the Lower Eastern Vinaya tradition from Lumé. He was considered a master of Abhidharma and, as indicated below, received a number of teachings from Atiśa.[34] Atiśa also met around this time Ngok Lekpai Sherap (eleventh century), a monk in the Eastern Vinaya tradition who had been ordained by Dring Yeshé Yönten and who had also received his monastic education in eastern Tibet under Setsun Wangchuk Shönu. Ngok Lekpai Sherap had followed Khutön to central Tibet a year after Dromtönpa went to meet Atiśa.[35]

Atiśa then traveled to central Tibet into the Ü and Tsang regions. The histories mention that by the time Atiśa arrived in Ü, he had three primary Tibetan disciples, including Khutön of Yarlung, Ngok Lekpai Sherap, and Dromtönpa, collectively known as Khu-Ngok-Drom-Sum (*khu rngog 'brom gsum*). In central Tibet, Atiśa met Geshé Naljorpa and Gönpawa. The *Universally Known Biography* mentions that Atiśa met Geshé Naljorpa (1015–78), also known as Amé Jangchup Rinchen, at Nyantso in Tsang.[36] Geshé Naljorpa, born in Domé Tsongkha in the year of the female wood rabbit (*shing mo yos lo*), became one of Atiśa's foremost students on the subject of the two realities (*bden pa gnyis*).[37] As mentioned below, Geshé Naljorpa became an important figure in the monastic community of Radreng after Atiśa passed away. Gönpawa Wangchuk Gyaltsen (1016–82), born in Dokham in the year of the male fire dragon, also met Atiśa in Nyantso. He became an important figure in the monastic community of Radreng and was known for his meditative abilities and insight.

The biographies mention that Atiśa met these Tibetan disciples during his initial travels in west-central Tibet but do not provide details regarding the teachings he might have given them. Be that as it may, several accounts mention that an individual named Setön Drachan Dzin, after following Atiśa for seven months, requested and received instructions in the Madhyamaka view.[38] *The Blue Annals* (Roerich 1976, 857) refers to Setön Drachan Dzin as a pupil of Drok Jhośe Dorjé Bar, a translator who later invites the Indian teacher Vajrapāṇi (Phyag Na) to central Tibet from Nepal. Although the available sources do not provide further details concerning Atiśa's teachings to this individual, they do indicate that Atiśa was quite hesitant to teach Madhyamaka and would do so only after persistent requests. As a number of histories mention Atiśa teaching Madhyamaka to Setön Drachan Dzin, this individual must have been known to earlier Tibetan audiences. In the next section we shall see that Atiśa had been questioned about emptiness in Ngari by scholars from central Tibet, which illustrates that Atiśa's understanding of

Madhyamaka was based on textual sources not yet available to Tibetans, and at this juncture he may have provided only a general overview on Madhyamaka to Setön Drachan Dzin.

When Atiśa arrived in central Tibet he received invitations and requests from a local king named Lhatsün Bodhirāja, who was said to be a descendent of the early emperor Songtsen Gampo. Lhatsün Bodhirāja provided resources to Atiśa and his entourage and requested empowerment for tantric practices related to the *Buddhakapālatantra* and then the *Nīlāṃbaradharavajrapāṇisādhana*. At this time Atiśa and his Tibetan disciple-translator Naktso translated several texts, including Candrakīrti's *Pañcaskandhaprakaraṇa*, the *Sūtrasamuccayopadeśa*, the *Bodhisattvamaṇyāvali*, and the *Bodhisattvacaryā sūtīkṛtāvavāda*.[39] While at Chimphu, slightly northeast of Samyé, Devarāja, Nāgarāja, Gargewa, and Lotsāwa requested that Atiśa give teachings on "the special instructions of the Great Brahmin [Saraha]" (*bram ze chen po'i gdams pa*),[40] but Dromtönpa prevented Atiśa from giving these teachings. On the same occasion, Atiśa gave numerous instructions in esoteric Buddhist ritual and practice to Dromtönpa. This account illustrates the difference in content between Atiśa's public teaching and the instructions he gave to close disciples in private.[41]

At the Kachu temple near Samyé, a location controlled by the Eastern Vinaya tradition, Khutön and Ngok Lekpai Sherap requested Atiśa to give lectures on the *Six Collections of Middle Way Reasonings* (*Dbu ma rigs tshogs drug*).[42] This grouping of six texts related to the Middle Way teachings of Nāgārjuna, and affiliated with reasoning (*yukti* ≈ *rigs*), was a Tibetan genre classification based on the curriculum inherited from the Eastern Vinaya tradition. This can be inferred from the fact that all the earliest biographies, reflecting early oral Kadampa traditions, explicitly utilize this classification in describing how these two disciples, trained in the curriculum of the Eastern Vinaya, requested these teachings from Atiśa. More important, though, is the fact that Atiśa did not group the texts of Nāgārjuna in this fashion either in *Open Basket of Jewels* or *Lamp for the Path to Awakening* (Sherburne 2000, 237–41). *Open Basket of Jewels*, as pointed out by Brunnhölzl (2007, 30–31), provides the most comprehensive Indian layout of Nāgārjuna's compositions, listing over forty-five works. Nāgārjuna's works on Middle Way reasoning are neither listed nor classified as "six works on reasoning."[43]

This request from Atiśa's early prominent disciples that he give lectures on the Middle Way reasonings of Nāgārjuna therefore indicates that Atiśa was obligated to publicly teach Madhyamaka thought within the classifications and literary structures presumed by his Tibetan students and that there was a conceptual presumption that Nāgārjuna's works on reasoning were necessarily separate from his other works, such as the *Dharmadhātustava* (Hymn to the Realm of Reality), a devotional praise that Atiśa considered essential for understanding Nāgārjuna's thought. Unfortunately, although we can definitely state that Khutön, Ngok Lekpai Sherap, and Dromtönpa studied Madhyamaka in eastern Tibet before meeting Atiśa, what exact texts comprised the Eastern Vinaya tradition's Middle Way curriculum is currently unknown.[44] Be that as it may, his circle of early students must have been trained in the Madhyamaka tradition of Śāntarakṣita and Kamalaśīla, along with the texts of Nāgārjuna and related commentaries translated during the early imperial period. Indeed, based on the colophons of Tibetan translations, Nāgārjuna's works that are explicitly affiliated with reasoning, such as the *Mūlamadhyamakakārikā* (Toh 3824) and *Vigrahavyāvartanī* (Toh 3828), were translated during the early imperial period. Other Nāgārjuna texts affiliated with reasoning, such as the *Śūnyatāsaptati* (Toh 3831) and *Yuktiṣaṣṭikā*, were also translated in the imperial period, although the basic texts were embedded within commentaries (e.g., *Yuktiṣaṣṭikāvṛtti*, Toh 3864). These translations would be revised by Tibetan translators, but only after Atiśa's lifetime. On the other hand, the works of Nāgārjuna that Atiśa regarded as essential to understanding Madhyamaka, texts such as the *Bodhicittavivaraṇa* (Toh 1801), *Bhāvanākrama* (Toh 3908), and *Acintyastava* (Toh 1128), were either translated into Tibetan by Atiśa himself, by his disciples, or decades after Atiśa's lifetime.

While in central Tibet, Atiśa continued to teach topics in accord with the Eastern Vinaya tradition's curriculum. This is clearly demonstrated when he accepted an invitation by Khutön to Sölnak Tangboché, an Eastern Vinaya monastery southwest of Lhasa near the Yarlung Valley. At Khutön's monastery, Atiśa was offered one hundred srang to teach Haribhadra's *Abhisamayālaṃkārālokā* as well as texts affiliated with Maitreya, the *Uttaratantra* and *Dharmadharmatāvibhāga*.[45] Atiśa and his retinue stayed at Sölnak Tangboché for one month, but had a serious falling out with Khutön and left the area against the wishes of Khutön.[46] After several stops in various locations, Atiśa and his retinue journeyed on to the monastic complex at Samyé.

Atiśa and his entourage arrived at Samyé Monastery in 1047. Atiśa examined the treasury of Sanskrit manuscripts held in the monastery's temple. According to the biographies, the temple contained many manuscripts that did not exist in India at the time. *The Extensive Biography* mentions that the lack of Sanskrit manuscripts in India was due to three different fires that razed the libraries.[47] The biographies mention in particular the Sanskrit manuscripts of the *Madhyamakāloka* (*Dbu ma snang ba*) and *Avataṃsakasūtra* (*Phal po che*). As discussed by Keira (2004, 8–9), Kamalaśīla composed the *Madhyamakāloka* in Tibet at the behest of the Tibetan king rather than writing it in

India. This work was therefore not known among most, if any, Indian Buddhist thinkers. Atiśa may have been surprised, if not perplexed, at the content of the *Madhyamakāloka*, which utilizes Dharmakīrti's theory of valid cognition to realize ultimate reality in the context of Madhyamaka thought. Atiśa is said to have requested that copies of the *Madhyamakāloka* be made and sent back to India.

Atiśa and his retinue decided to leave Samyé after hearing of a prominent noble woman's protest against his presence in the area. Dromtönpa sent a message out to Bangtön Jangchup Gyaltsen, a religious companion (*mched grogs*) who had previously studied under Setsun and Dromtönpa. Bangtön later arrived with two hundred horsemen and the entourage moved on to Lhasa.[48] The group stopped for two weeks at the religious settlement of Gyaphip of Sri, a dependency aligned with the Dring community.[49] Ngok Lekpai Sherap, a lineage successor (*mkhan bu*) of the Dring community, invited Atiśa to Lhasa.

Atiśa and his entourage then journeyed to Lhasa. Atiśa taught Madhyamaka and also translated a number of texts while residing there. The extant historical records, colophons to the Tibetan translations, and early Kadampa commentaries indicate that Atiśa taught Bhāviveka's *Tarkajvālā* commentary and gave special instructions on Madhyamaka (*madhyamakopadeśa*) at the invitation and request of his disciple Ngok Lekpai Sherap. This disciple, also known as Sangphuwa, later founded the early Kadampa monastery of Sangphu Neuthok around 1073.[50] *The Extensive Biography,* one of the earliest accounts, records the episode in the following manner:

> Ngok Lekpai Sherap, having negotiated with the authorities, requested teachings of Madhyamaka, and [Lord Atiśa] taught the *Madhyamakatarkajvālā*. The Master himself composed the greater and lesser *Special Instructions* for Madhyamaka, offering that as realization for Geshé Naljorpa, stating, "I have confidentially written about how to be guided [in the Middle Way] teaching, a little bit about the celebrated profound." Having translated this with the translator [Naktso], at the bottom of [the translation] the Lord [Atiśa] stated, "This document has been composed in the Manifested Temple (*'Phrul snang gtsug lag khang*) of Lhasa (lit. *ra sa*), having been requested by the Śākya monk, the honorable Ngok, Lekshé.[51]

This early account provides several important details. Notable is that Ngok Lekpai Sherap had to negotiate with temple authorities for Atiśa to teach there. Atiśa and his translator-disciple Naktso Lotsāwa Tsultrim Gyalwa then translated Bhāviveka's *Tarkajvālā* (*Rtog ge 'bar ba*) commentary to his *Madhyamakahṛdayakārikās* at Lhasa's main temple, the Trulnang Tsuglakhang. The request to teach and translate Bhāviveka's *Tarkajvālā* commentary was most likely sanctioned for public instruction, since it furnished an important set of additional teachings to the Eastern Vinaya tradition's curriculum.[52] These teachings on Bhāviveka built on the precedent Tibetan translations of Bhāviveka's *Prajñāpradīpa* commentary to Nāgārjuna's *Mūlamadhyamakakārikā* and the accompanying *Prajñāpradīpaṭīkā* subcommentary of Avalokitavrata carried out during the Imperial Era. This style of Madhyamaka teaching not only fulfilled the expectations of the central Tibetan audience of Eastern Vinaya affiliated monks but also complemented Atiśa's pedagogical approach, as documented above in his teaching at Somapurī of introducing Madhyamaka thought through the works of Bhāviveka.

In contrast to these public teachings, Atiśa's *Madhyamakopadeśa* instructions were initially offered in private to his disciple Geshé Naljorpa. The accounts state that Atiśa composed the greater and lesser *Special Instructions on the Middle Way* (*Dbu ma'i man ngag che chung*) at this time in Lhasa. The "greater" special instruction is a reference to *Open Basket of Jewels*,[53] while the "lesser" is Atiśa's *Special Instructions on the Middle Way*.[54] However, according to the colophon of the canonical version of *Open Basket of Jewels*, this work was written in the great temple of Vikramaśīla, under the patronage of King Devapāla. The colophon to the so-called short *Special Instructions on the Middle Way* does mention that it was composed in the main temple of Lhasa and that Atiśa and Tsultrim Gyalwa translated and edited the text together. Therefore *Open Basket of Jewels* was composed first, in India, and then *Special Instructions on the Middle Way* was composed years later in Tibet. As *Special Instructions on the Middle Way* has similar content to some sections of *Open Basket of Jewels*, Atiśa may have composed it as a brief instruction based on extracts from the latter work. Atiśa may have used both texts to give lectures in private on Madhyamaka to his close disciples during his time in Lhasa. Along these lines, the biographical literature also records occasions where Atiśa gave teachings on Madhyamaka that are no longer extant. Notable in this regard are teachings that Atiśa gave on the view of his Indian teacher Vidyākokila while residing at Nyethang. Although these specific teachings are not preserved, related teachings on Madhyamaka in the lineage of Vidyākokila and Candrakīrti are preserved in *A General Explanation*.

Atiśa traveled for several years in central Ü translating texts and giving teachings on a variety of different topics, including the Vinaya and perfections (*pāramitā*). He complained to Dromtönpa that he was not allowed to establish his Mahāsāṃghika ordination lineage nor teach on tantric songs (*dohā*). While traveling in central Tibet to Yerpa, he received an invitation from Bangtön to go to Nyethang.[55] Atiśa and his entourage traveled to Nyethang, where Atiśa would reside during the final years of his life. The biographies relate that once Atiśa settled in Nyethang, he attracted Buddhist scholars and dignitaries throughout Tibet to hear his teachings on Dharma.[56] One such dignitary was Khutön, who, despite previous disagreements with Atiśa's entourage, arrived at Nyethang and requested teachings on the *Perfection of Wisdom*. Atiśa gave public lectures on the *Aṣṭasāhasrikāprajñāpāramitā*, which were written down by Geshé Chakdar. These teachings were called the Khams System of the Perfections (*Pha rol tu phyin pa khams lugs*). During the time that Atiśa gave public teachings on the perfections, topics familiar to an Eastern Vinaya educated audience, his close disciple Dromtönpa endeavored to master the thought of the Indian Madhyamaka master Candrakīrti. An early biography of Atiśa records the occasion in the following words:

> When Geshé Tönpa offered the noble lord his realization of Candrakīrti's system, the Lord [Atiśa] pressed his palms together in salutation and said, "Nowadays in Eastern India, this is the only view upheld."[57]

This episode demonstrates, once again, that while Atiśa publicly taught topics related to the curriculum of the Eastern Vinaya tradition, in private he guided his close disciples in esoteric practices, meditative cultivation, and his lineage of Madhyamaka, a lineage passing through Candrakīrti to Vidyākokila. Along these lines, the public Tibetan audience for Atiśa's teaching at this time did not have the familiarity with Candrakīrti's works, such as his *Madhyamakāvatāra* and its *Bhāṣya*, that would have been needed to record either orally or in writing an account of these teachings. Without Tibetan translations of the basic Madhyamaka works of Candrakīrti, a tradition of study and practice related to this lineage of Madhyamaka was difficult to initiate and preserve. The Kadampa commentaries translated in chapters 3, 4, and 7 of this book provide evidence that Atiśa and Naktso were preparing a Tibetan translation of Candrakīrti's *Madhyamakāvatāra*, but Naktso would not complete an initial Tibetan translation of the *Madhyamakāvatāra* until after Atiśa had passed away.[58]

Be that as it may, Atiśa taught his early disciples the system of Candrakīrti through his own *Entry to the Two Realities* and *Special Instructions on the Middle Way*. As indicated below, it is not clear if Atiśa's first tier of Tibetan disciples, such as Dromtönpa, Khutön, and Ngok Lekpai Sherap, who were trained in the older tradition of the Eastern Vinaya curriculum, fully understood or accepted Candrakīrti's Madhyamaka system. An issue that appeared problematic to those trained in eastern Tibet was whether buddhas see appearances or whether buddhas have a continuum of wisdom. A citation from Dromtönpa in the *Collection of Special Instructions on the Middle Way* indicates that he himself was ambivalent about whether a buddha has a continuum of wisdom. As will be discussed, Atiśa did not accept a buddha having a continuum of wisdom. In addition to these factors, several sections in the biographies describe Dromtönpa as not understanding the translation during a teaching on the *Entry to the Two Realities*;[59] as not accepting Atiśa's offer to teach Serlingpa's system of the *Śikṣāsamucccaya* and *Bodhicaryāvatāra*, since Dromtönpa had already studied these texts under Setsun;[60] and as questioning his own intellectual ability at times.[61] The above passage demonstrates that Dromtönpa made efforts to understand Candrakīrti's system despite his background education and the lack of polished Tibetan translations. As discussed below, the evidence indicates that Atiśa's early disciples who were not educated at monastic institutes in Denma, eastern Tibet—disciples such as Amé Naljorpa Jangchup Rinchen and Gönpawa Wangchuk Gyaltsen—were more receptive to Atiśa's Madhyamaka teachings on the two realities and lectured on Atiśa's Madhyamaka teachings while at Radreng.

The biographical sources do not indicate that Atiśa gave additional Madhyamaka teachings in his remaining years at Nyethang. At the end of his life, Atiśa is depicted as residing at Nyethang and having visions of Maitreya, Mañjuśrī, and numerous esoteric deities while reciting tantric songs and being surrounded by *ḍākinī*s (*mkha' 'gro ma*). At the age of seventy-two, Atiśa passed away in Nyethang in the year of the male wood horse (1054) and took rebirth, according to tradition, as the bodhisattva Stainless Space (*nam mkha' dri ma med pa*) in Tuṣita Heaven.[62]

The Early Contemplative Community of Radreng

After the passing of Atiśa, four of Atiśa's lead disciples established monastic centers that received support from among the four clan-based groups of Lumé, Ba, Rak, and Dring. Khutön, with support from the Lumé group, established the Lhading or Sedur monastic center of Dren in Yarlung. Bangtön established the monastic center of Nyethang Ö with the support of the Ba and Rak groups. Ngoktön, supported by the Dring group, established the monastic center of Sangphu, including the seat of Gyaphip. Dromtönpa and Naljorpa Chenpo Jangchup Rinchen built the monastic center of Radreng and the Khyung Gochen or "Garuḍa-headed" temple.[63] Among these early communities of Atiśa's followers, I briefly focus on Radreng Monastery, as it was considered the spiritual base of Atiśa's teaching and "a small satellite of Vikramaśīla."[64] Moreover, the only Kadampa community mentioned among the manuscripts translated in the following chapters is Radreng Monastery.[65]

Radreng Monastery was founded in the year of the male fire monkey (1056) under the impetus of Dromtönpa and Gönpawa Wangchuk Gyaltsen. According to Chim Namkha Drak's (1210–85) *Spiritual Biography of Geshé Tönpa*, after Atiśa passed away, Dromtönpa resided in Nyethang for a year and intended to build a small reliquary monument for Atiśa's ashes. However, Bangtön spoke with Dromtönpa and Naljorpa about constructing a more extensive place for Atiśa's ashes, along with a temple. They first considered building a temple in the desert valley of Nam. Geshé Gönpawa and some others went to the location and found it was not suitable for spiritual practice. After an initial failure and a second invitation from Dromtönpa's Shang patron, Drangkha Berchung, Dromtönpa arrived from the Phenyul region of the Uru Jang district north of Lhasa. After Dromtönpa's favorable visit to the area and some discussion with colleagues, Radreng was chosen as a suitable location.[66] The *Spiritual Biography of Geshé Tönpa* states:

> After that, Geshé Tönpa, Naljorpa, Gönpawa, Sherap Dorjé, Jampai Lodrö, Trichok, Tongten Nago, Chakdar Tönpa, Yogdzong, and Nyené Yönten Bar fulfilled the intention of Lord [Atiśa], and all of the above went to Radreng in the year of the male fire monkey. Further, first, since it is the land of Danma, in the language of Danma, it was called Radreng. In the Tibetan language it is called "water is not far away" (*chu mi ring mo*).[67]

The nine individuals mentioned in this excerpt who came to Radreng with Dromtönpa are classified as "yogis" (*rnal 'byor pa*), or practitioners of meditation, in the historical sources. Amé Naljorpa Jangchup Rinchen, referred to as Naljorpa in this passage, along with Gönpawa, Sherap Dorjé, and Chakdar Tönpa, are collectively referred to as the "four brothers of Kham."[68] Jampai Lodrö is often included as a fifth brother of Kham. These individuals, along with Trichok, were disciples of Atiśa who followed Dromtönpa to Radreng. Tongten Nago, Yokzong (also known as Yongzok Naljorpa), and Nyené Yönten were disciples of Dromtönpa. Amé Naljorpa Jangchup Rinchen, Gönpawa, Sherap Dorjé, Jampai Lodrö, and Trichok resided in residences that were constructed at Radreng, each residence supported with an individual sponsor (*yon bdag*).[69] The fact that the majority of the founding members of

Radreng Monastery had the title "yogi" illustrates how Radreng was, from its beginnings, a contemplative community.

The *Spiritual Biography of Geshé Tönpa* also describes the early curriculum at Radreng:

> The Dharma initially taught at Radreng was the perfections consisting of both the *Aṣṭasāhasrikā* and its commentary, along with the twenty-thousand-verse *Perfection of Wisdom*, and the small commentary *Abhisamayālaṃkāra*, along with its *pañjikā*, the *Śikṣāsamuccaya*. The *Bodhicaryāvatāra*, *Bodhipathapradīpa*, *Bhāvanākrama*, and so forth were taught many times. A little bit of the Mind Only (*sems tsam*) texts of the *Abhidharmasamuccaya* and *Mahāyānasaṃgraha* were taught many times. The three Madhyamaka texts of the Easterners appears to have been taught many times, it is said.[70]

This account is significant for several reasons. First, every text mentioned in the early Radreng curriculum, except for Atiśa's *Bodhipathapradīpa*, was translated during the early imperial period. Thus the curriculum that Dromtönpa adapted, and which a number of the monks at this time at Radreng taught, was more than likely based on the educational program of the Eastern Vinaya tradition. These texts represented an early curriculum that emphasized Mahāyāna Buddhist teachings on cultivating the perfections. A number of these texts had been publicly taught by Atiśa while in Tibet and had already been translated into Tibetan. These texts represented a public curriculum that did not emphasize esoteric Buddhist teachings. *The Blue Annals* mentions that although Dromtönpa was knowledgeable in both tantras and sūtras, he was secretive about esoteric teachings and did not widely teach them. Rather, Dromtönpa taught and refined the translations of the *Aṣṭasāhasrikāprajñāpāramitā*, the *Abhisamayālaṃkārālokā* (*Brgyad stong 'grel chen*), the *Vivṛti*, and Āryavimuktisena's *Commentary on the 25,000 Stanza Perfection of Wisdom*.[71] All these texts fit a curriculum for teaching the perfections practiced on the bodhisattva path. Notable as well is that the early Radreng curriculum focused on the "three Madhyamaka texts of the Easterners" (*dbu ma shar ba gsum ka*). These three texts consisted of Śāntarakṣita's *Madhyamakālaṃkāra* (MAK), Kamalaśīla's *Madhyamakāloka* (MĀ), and Jñānagarbha's *Satyadvayavibhaṅga* (SDV). Again, these texts had been translated and studied since the Imperial Era and were suitable for introducing Madhyamaka teachings in a public setting. However, they do not represent Atiśa's Middle Way thought.

Atiśa's explicit teachings on Madhyamaka, in particular his *Entry to the Two Realities* and *Special Instructions on the Middle Way*, had initially circulated among select disciples at Radreng and only later became more widely disseminated. This scenario matches the evidence from the manuscripts and the earliest historical sources. The above episode on Atiśa's teaching on the *Special Instructions on the Middle Way* translated from *The Extensive Biography* mentions that Atiśa gave these teachings privately to Geshé Naljorpa. Along these lines, an early commentary on these teachings, *Potowa's Middle Way*, mentions that Geshé Gönpawa also gave teachings on Madhyamaka instructions in private.[72] Although not emphasized in the traditional biographies, Dromtönpa likewise gave instructions on Madhyamaka to his closest disciples. *The Blue Annals* records Dromtönpa's Madhyamaka position as one in which nothing ultimately exists and where objects are nonimplicatively negated.[73] This accords with statements attributed to Dromtönpa in the Kadampa *Collection on the Two Realities,* where he clarified that ultimate reality "is [in] reality not established as anything" because form, nonform, cause, effect, knowledge, object of knowledge, and so forth do not exist in ultimate reality. Citations of Dromtönpa in the *Collection of Special Instructions on the Middle Way* indicate that he considered that ultimate reality, the unproduced, to be discernable only by buddhas and tenth-stage bodhisattvas but not by scholars or *ācāryas*. Dromtönpa taught that conventional realities are illusory dependent-arisings, but differentiated between correct and incorrect conventional realities following Atiśa's teaching in the *Entry to the Two Realities*. In the Kadampa *Collection on the Two Realities*, Dromtönpa is quoted for his position that purified states of awareness that occur after one has reached the path of vision (*mthong lam*) are called "correct conventional reality." As mentioned above, Dromtönpa is ambivalent concerning appearances at the level of buddhahood, stating that, even though they do not exist, such appearances occur for the purpose of sentient beings. The following translations indicate that Dromtönpa's Madhyamaka position was based on Atiśa's *Entry to the Two Realities* and *Special Instructions on the Middle Way*, as well as on Candrakīrti's *Madhyamakāvatāra*. Atiśa's Madhyamaka teachings became more widely disseminated and were eventually written down among the generation of scholars that came after Dromtönpa.

Dromtönpa resided at Radreng for nine years up until his passing in 1064. He maintained a spiritual community consisting of eighty members while at the monastic center. Among these students, he had three primary disciples: Potowa Rinchen Sal (1027/31–1105), Chengawa Tsultrim Bar (1038–1103), and Phuchungwa Shönu Gyaltsen (1031–1106). Each of these disciples had met Atiśa in their youth and had been ordained as monks before they arrived at Radreng. These three became known as the *ku-ché-sum* (*sku mched gsum*), the "three [spiritual] brothers." Although they shared the same teacher, the traditional sources indicate that Geshé Tönpa emphasized specific teachings for each of them. Dromtönpa taught Phuchungwa the doctrine on the nobles' four realities.[74] Dromtönpa taught Chengawa to focus on emptiness and also gave him instruction on Atiśa's esoteric teachings.[75] Potowa learned the instructions for spiritual accomplishment from Dromtönpa and understood as soon as he heard them.[76] After the passing of Geshé Tönpa, these three Dharma brothers focused on their spiritual practice and maintained respect for Amé Naljorpa Jangchup Rinchen, who became the second abbot of Radreng. During this time, the yogis and the three brothers became known as the "spiritual guides of Radreng."[77]

Amé Naljorpa Jangchup Rinchen became known as the Great Yogi (*rnal 'byor pa chen po*) for residing in solitude while at Radreng.[78] He had learned many teachings from Atiśa and was considered the foremost of Atiśa's disciples in the teachings on the two realities, that is, ultimate reality and conventional reality. The sources describe him as more knowledgeable about the two realities than Dromtönpa. Amé Jangchup Rinchen also mastered the subtle threads of karmic action.[79] The Kadampa teachings translated in parts 2 and 3 of this book mention him in several places, and he must have lectured on the two realities during the thirteen or fourteen years that he served as abbot of Radreng.[80] His most prominent student was Tölungpa Rinchen Nyingpo (1032–1116). After the passing of Amé Jangchup Rinchen in 1078, Gönpawa Wangchuk Gyaltsen became the third abbot of Radreng for five or seven years, roughly from 1078 to 1082.[81] As Gönpawa was the immediate successor of Naljorpa, it is conceivable that he received the oral transmission for the teachings on Atiśa's *Entry to the Two Realities* as well as *Special Instructions on the Middle Way*. The anonymous Kadampa author of the *Collection on the Two Realities* commentary explicitly mentions that he witnessed Gönpawa giving teachings on the two realities at Radreng. Based on this account, Atiśa's works on Madhyamaka became part of the public curriculum while Radreng was under the leadership of Naljorpa and Gönpawa.

Potowa became the fourth abbot of Radreng in the early 1080s when he was around fifty years of age. At this time the three spiritual brothers became more prominent and the term "Kadampa" became popularized as a referent for those who follow the precepts and practices given by Atiśa and Dromtönpa. Potowa popularized the use of six texts (*gzhung*) in his pedagogy, including the *Jātaka* (*Skyes rabs*), *Udānavarga* (*Ched du brjod pa'i tshoms*), *Bodhisattvabhūmi* (*Byang sa*), *Mahāyānasūtrālaṃkāra* (*Mdo sde rgyan*), *Bodhicaryāvatāra* (*Spyod 'jug*), and *Śikṣāsamuccaya* (*Bslab btus*). Additional texts utilized by Potowa included Atiśa's *Entry to the Two Realities* and *A Lamp for the Path to Awakening*.

After leaving Radreng, Potowa wandered in nearby valleys for several years. He soon established himself as a popular teacher of doctrines from the Kadampa tradition. At the age of sixty-one he established Poto Monastery in Tré in the Phenyul region and had up to two thousand monk-disciples residing in this monastery.[82] He came to prominence by his style of teaching through analogies and parables that utilized a mixture of regional Tibetan folklore and similes drawn from Buddhist canonical sources. These teachings would be recorded by his disciples in a collection known as *Teachings Exemplified* (*Dpe chos*). Potowa's most important disciples were Langri Thangpa Dorjé Sengé (1054–1123) and Sharawa Yönten Drak. Langri Thangpa compiled a stages of the path (*lam rim*) text and is most well-known for his teachings on mind training (*blo sbyong*). Sharawa, who belonged to the Patsab clan, had first been a disciple of Geshé Phuchungwa and Chengawa. Sharawa composed several texts including a long and short *lam rim* that are extant. In addition to these works, a recovered manuscript found in *The Collected Works of the Kadampas* entitled *Explanation of [Atiśa's] Special Instructions on the Middle Way, the System of Potowa and His Spiritual Son* (*Dbu ma'i man ngag gi bshad pa, Pu to yab sras kyi lugs*; *Potowa's Middle Way*) documents the Madhyamaka thought of Potowa Rinchen Sal and his spiritual son Sharawa Yönten Drak.

Potowa's Middle Way, preserved in a brief and partly illegible manuscript, is a short commentary (*tig chung*) on Atiśa's *Special Instructions on the Middle Way*. The contents clearly indicate that Potowa and Sharawa closely followed the Madhyamaka thought of Atiśa and Dromtönpa based on the teachings of Nāgārjuna, Āryadeva, Candrakīrti, and Avadhūtipa. A great amount of its structure and content is shared with the Kadampa *Collection of Special Instructions*. *Potowa's Middle Way* outlines the Middle Way of Nāgārjuna (321.1–2), the proper observance of cause and effect (321.2–6), the distinction between conventional and ultimate reality (321.6–322.2), the four great reasonings among Madhyamakas and its application in meditation (322.3–329.4), the nature of mind and the use of reasoning (329.5–330.4), the faults of sinking and agitation in meditation (330.1–331.1), the vajra-like concentration (*vajropamasamādhi*) (332.4–332.5), Avadhūtipa and Candrakīrti's system of buddhahood (332.5–6), and the ambivalent position of Dromtönpa regarding the relation of appearances and buddhahood (333.5–334.1). An interlinear note in the text states that "Ācārya Asaṅga accepts a wisdom of postmeditative and a continuum of wisdom. Atiśa does not accept a wisdom of postmeditative attainment, as [a buddha's] continuum of wisdom is always in meditative equipoise."

Among Dromtönpa's other major disciples, Chengawa studied under Dromtönpa for eight years and is a highly regarded lineage figure in the Kadampa tradition. In *The Blue Annals* Dromtönpa gives Chengawa instruction on emptiness based on Atiśa's *Entry to the Two Realities*. Specifically, Dromtönpa paraphrased verses 16 and 17 of the *Entry to the Two Realities* to instruct Chengawa that, although there are numerous Buddhist teachings, meditation on emptiness is like a panacea that cures all disease.[83] After the passing of Dromtönpa, Chengawa received teachings on the two realities from Naljorpa, teachings on meditation from Gönpawa, and teachings on tenets from Naljorpa Sherap Dorjé.[84] Chengawa is later acclaimed in the Kadampa sources as the founder of the "lineage of instructions" (*gdams ngag*). He would go on to found the monastery of Lo, and his notable students included Tölungpa Rinchen Nyingpo, Nyukrumpa (1042–1109), Tsöndrü Gyaltsen (1042–1109), and Jayülwa Shönu Ö (1075–1138). As the historical sources and manuscript evidence suggest, the instructions that Chengawa received on Madhyamaka and emptiness were based on Atiśa's *Entry to the Two Realities, Special Instructions on the Middle Way,* and the oral traditions of commentarial exegesis affiliated with these texts. Chengawa Tsultrim Bar was considered to be the origin of the explanatory transmission (*bshad rgyun*) of Atiśa's *Entry to the Two Realities* for some Tibetan authors.[85] Be that as it may, there are no extant individual writings by Chengawa and he is only mentioned in passing among the translations in the following chapters.

As mentioned above, Potowa became the fourth abbot of Radreng and served for around three years. He departed Radreng, however, after disagreements with patrons and several pupils. When Potowa departed, Radreng Monastery was unable to replace the abbatial position for a great number of years, a period referred to as a "Dharma famine" (*chos kyi mu ge*, ca. 1085–1115).[86] The lack of leadership and administration at Radreng contributed to the spread of other Kadampa-affiliated communities in the region of Phenyul. Over time, the center for Kadampa-based monastic training and education would shift from Radreng to Sangphu Neutok, a monastery founded in 1073 by Ngok Lekpai Sherap.[87] All of the Kadampa texts translated in parts 2 and 3 of this book are related to a tradition of Madhyamaka that was preserved at Radreng[88] from its founding by Dromtönpa Gyalwai Jungné in 1056/57 up until the end of the thirty-year "Dharma famine," circa 1115.

The Development of Atiśa's Midde Way Thought in India

Atiśa's Indian teachers in both the monastery and the forest retreat shaped his understanding of Madhyamaka thought and practice. The textual evi-

TABLE 2. ATIŚA'S EARLY TIBETAN PRINCIPAL DISCIPLES

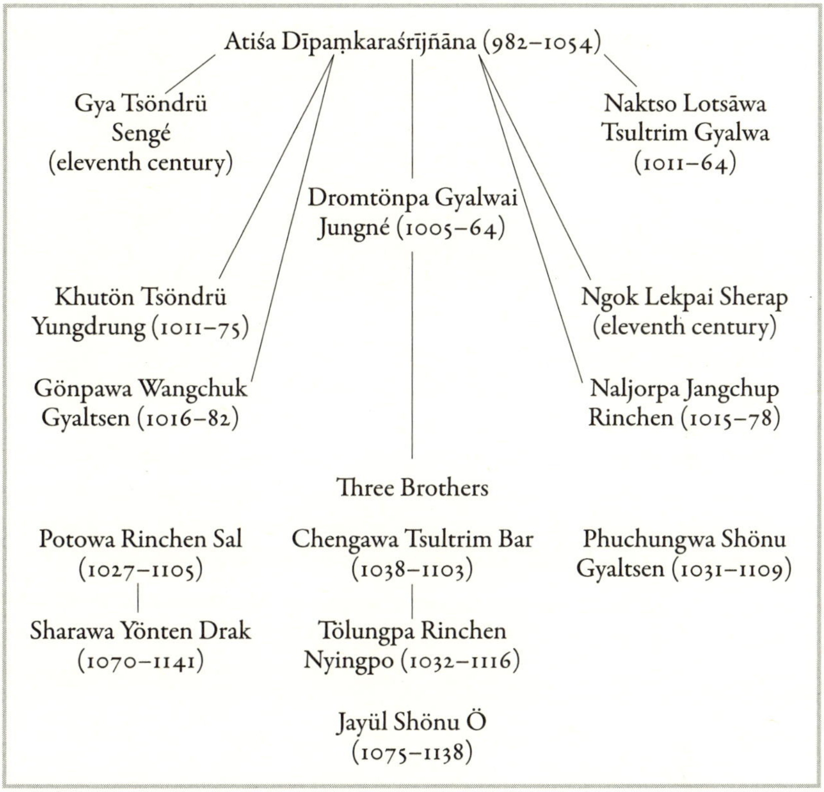

dence found in his teachers' extant works as well as early historical accounts of discussions with his teachers furnish clues for how Atiśa's understanding of Madhyamaka developed while he was in India. As mentioned earlier, the well-regarded layman Jitāri instructed the young Atiśa at Vikramaśīla. Jitāri wrote around one hundred short works on valid cognition and tantra during his lifetime.[89] Among the works that influenced Atiśa's Madhyamaka was Jitāri's base text with a commentary entitled *Sugatamatravibhaṅgakārikā*.[90] This text contains eight verses that are identical to the *Jñānasārasamuccaya* (vv. 21–28) of the second Āryadeva (eighth century) (Mimaki 2000, 233–35). It discusses four main schools of Buddhist thought (Vaibhāṣika, Sautrāntika, Yogācāra, and Madhyamaka), the Mādhyamika arguing for the nonsubstantiality of even consciousness through the reasoning that things have neither a single nor a plural nature. Jitāri utilized the Yogācāra standpoint as a step toward reaching the ultimate reality of the Mādhyamika. Jitāri emphasizes, as well, that the "Mādhyamika knows reality, which is free from the four extremes." In this respect, Jitāri's understanding of valid cognition closely followed that of Śāntarakṣita and Kamalaśīla.[91] Jitāri also considered Dharmakīrti's thought to be in agreement with Nāgārjuna. Among other notable works, Jitāri wrote the *Bodhicittotpādasamādānavidhi*,[92] which provides instruction on cultivating the resolution for awakening. Atiśa most likely learned basic principles of Buddhist thought from Jitāri, including hierarchical categorization of Buddhist doxography, modes of Madhyamaka reasoning, and the importance of cultivating the resolution for awakening.

Although not directly cited in this book, Bodhibhadra certainly influenced Atiśa. Bodhibhadra's *Jñānasārasamuccayanibandhana* provides textual evidence for several important themes that are influential in Atiśa's Madhyamaka. His *Nibandhana* discusses the importance of the spiritual teacher (*bla ma* ≈ *guru*), describes the appearance of Nāgārjuna in this world in terms of predictions (*vyākaraṇa*) (D, folio 29a–b), and mentions that Nāgārjuna composed his works within the framework of the five fields of knowledge (D, 29b). Bodhibhadra provides an exegesis on the natural luminosity of the mind (D, 33a), a theme found in Atiśa's *Open Basket of Jewels* and *General Explanation*. Bodhibhadra also articulates how ultimate reality for the Mādhyamika is free from the four extreme positions of existence, nonexistence, neither, and both that is structured by dichotomizing conceptualization (*vikalpa*) (D, 44a3).[93] He posits the two realities as indivisible, and that the bodhisattva directly cognizes ultimate reality in space-like equipoise and then views, in the postmeditative state, conventional realities to be like illusions (D, 45a3–4), based on the *Avikalpapraveśadhāraṇī*. Atiśa follows this structure for the meditative cultivation of the Madhyamaka vision in his works as well.

Writing in the same milieu as Jitāri, Bodhibhadra composed compendia in which four great Buddhist schools were outlined—the Vaibhāṣika as the lowest to the Madhyamaka as the highest (Kajiyama 1987, 76). In Bodhibhadra's *Nibandhana*, the Yogācāra are considered lower than the Madhyamaka. Bodhibhadra differentiates Bhāviveka and Śāntarakṣita based on how they posit conventional realities, but he does not classify them into different "schools" of Madhyamaka.[94] Rather, individuals within Indian Madhyamaka during this time period were differentiated according to their particular commentarial standpoints, but nevertheless were still considered followers of an undifferentiated Madhyamaka tradition. Atiśa utilized a basic outline of four Buddhist schools of thought in his works, but in Atiśa's own works there is no evidence of divisions among Madhyamakas. Bodhibhadra and Jitāri's way of categorizing Buddhist thought greatly influenced later Tibetan Buddhist thinkers in their doxographical literature (*grub mtha'*, *siddhānta*), and as demonstrated below, Atiśa's early Tibetan followers had several different classifications for Atiśa's Madhyamaka.

Atiśa's teacher Vidyākokila is mentioned, but not directly cited, in a number of chapters in this book. The difficulty in identifying Vidyākokila and his thought is that he is not known to have composed any treatises. An early version of Atiśa's biography attributed to Dromtönpa records a dialogue of key instructions on Madhyamaka that Atiśa learned from Vidyākokila. In the biography, after Atiśa's offering and request, Vidyākokila pledges to confer Atiśa with blessings of nonduality (*gnyis su med pa'i byin rlabs*) and truthful words of reality's unchanging nature (*chos nyid 'gyur ba med pa'i bden tshig*), comprised within the instruction of the resolution for awakening.[95] Vidyākokila instructs Atiśa, and the biographies provide the following verses of that teaching based on Nāgārjunagarbha (*klu sgrub snying po*), an alternative name for Nāgārjuna.

Vidyākokila states:

> The nature of all, dreamlike, illusionlike, is devoid of elaborations.
> The mind itself is uncontrived and abides in the innate nature.
> He who fails to contemplate these two in his thoughts
> will remain entrapped in the mires of cyclic existence.
>
> O prince, abide in meditative equipoise on the spacelike ultimate.
> In the illusionlike subsequent periods, reflect on karma and its fruits.
> When the teacher revealed this profound teaching, [the prince]
> attained the path of preparation and realized the "heroic" meditative absorption.[96]

Atiśa then recounts his realization from Vidyākokila's instruction with the following verses:

> When I remain in equipoise, one-pointed in meditative absorption,
> like the sky that is totally free of clouds,
> everything is clear, translucent, and devoid of obscurations.
> O teacher, is this reality's true mode of being?
>
> Then as I rise from this meditative absorption,
> without clinging to appearances, thoughts of sentient beings arise;
> though [appearances are] false, I find respect for the minute facets of karma.
> O teacher, are these experiences of mine deluded?[97]

Vidyākokila responds by telling Atiśa that, indeed, his system of the two realities consists of purifying the mind in spacelike meditative equipoise followed by leading sentient beings with compassion in the postconcentrative periods. This episode indicates that Atiśa received instruction in a Madhyamaka tradition on the two realities that was contemplative in nature and consisted of a focus on emptiness in meditation while having compassion for sentient beings and being conscientious about the repercussions of one's actions when one is not meditating. Atiśa prescribes similar instructions in his *Open Basket of Jewels* when he states that one cultivates the nonconceptual spacelike realm of reality in meditative stabilization and then views things as illusions in the postmeditative state. Although Vidyākokila's teachings to Atiśa represented in this account cannot be textually related to the works of Nāgārjuna and Candrakīrti, it is feasible that Vidyākokila's lineage transmitted to Atiśa represented a contemplative tradition of Madhyamaka that empasized the realization of nonduality, the cultivation of compassion, and the resolution for awakening based on teachings attributed to Nāgārjuna and Candrakīrti.

Avadhūtipa taught the works of Nāgārjuna and Madhyamaka to the young Atiśa, and several works quote this tantric yogi. The few works that cite Avadhūtipa's teachings to Atiśa are informative. *A General Explanation* directly quotes Atiśa as stating the following about this teacher:

> I was associated with Avadhūtipa for seven years. I studied under Avadhūtipa. I was pleased with his knowledge. He was in agreement with the texts of the Ācārya Nāgārjuna. The prediction of Lady Tārā said that he has the unmistaken accepted position of Ārya [Nāgārjuna].[98]

A General Explanation later cites Avadhūtipa as instructing Atiśa:

> For as long as self-grasping is not exhausted, the most subtle of subtle karmic actions should be understood to yield a result.[99]

A final oral teaching is recorded in chapter 14 of *The Jewel Garland of Dialogues* where Avadhūtipa instructs Atiśa on how unfindability leads to realizing the *dharmadhātu*, or the realm of reality:

> The nature of conceptualization is the realm of reality. When [conceptualizations] arise, it is joyful, for they are an excellent impetus. Of what use are they, since they cannot be found? They are but the effulgence of the ultimate mode of being.[100]

These three citations attributed to Avadhūtipa indicate that Atiśa studied with him for seven years and that Avadhūtipa taught him the Middle Way of Nāgārjuna, emphasizing attaining unity with the realm of reality, presumably while meditating on ultimate reality. Avadhūtipa also emphasized vigilance to the young Atiśa with regard to observing one's actions. The Kadampa commentaries record that Atiśa also emphasized this point in his own oral teachings. In fact, when Atiśa first arrived in west Tibet, he was known as the "teacher of cause and effect," due to his placing great attention in his initial teachings there on the importance of karma.[101]

Atiśa studied with Dharmakīrti of Suvarṇadvīpa primarily to learn Mahāyāna path systems and not for the thought and practice of Madhyamaka. The Tibetan biographies of Atiśa depict Serlingpa as affiliated with the Yogācāra tradition that posited aspects, or images, as real (*sems tsam rnam bden* ≈ *sākāravijñānavāda*). In his *Bodhimārgapradīpapañjikā*, Atiśa stated that the Yogācāra, or Mind Only, understanding of the *Prajñāpāramitā* was elucidated by Asaṅga, and that his teachers Serlingpa and Ratnākaraśanti followed that interpretation (Sherburne 2000). Based on these sources, the doctrinal affiliation of Serlingpa was some type of Yogācāra.

Yogācāra (lit. "practice of yoga") was one of the two major Mahāyāna Buddhist traditions of thought and practice in India, developed since at least the sixth century.[102] Yogācāra-based traditions were well known for the doctrines of "mere cognitive representation" (*vijñaptimātra*) and "mind only" (*cittamātra*), in which external objects do not exist but are posited to be of a mental nature. Atiśa listed in *Open Basket of Jewels* figures such as Asaṅga, Vasubandhu, Sthiramati, Prajñākaragupta, and Devendrabuddhi as belonging to this tradition.[103] The arguments throughout the early Kadampa commentaries of Atiśa's works are directed against those who hold Yogācāra tenets. The problem with Yogācāra tenets, at least according to how they are represented by Atiśa and his followers, was that they ultimately held reality to be substantially existent as consciousness (*vijñāna*). For Atiśa and his followers, who uphold the Middle Way free from the extremes of existence and nonexistence, adhering to this tenet falsely imputes an extreme of existence and is therefore outside of the Middle Way.

A succinct presentation of Yogācāra tenets according to Atiśa's early followers is found in the Kadampa *Collection on the Two Realities* (chapter 3, fols. 3b4–4a4), where the doctrine of three characterstics, or three natures (*trisvabhāva*), is described. The three characteristics presented in the Kadampa commentaries to Atiśa's works are the imagined (*parikalpita*), the dependent (*paratantra*), and the perfected (*pariniṣpanna*). These terms are discussed in detail in Yogācāra texts but may be briefly described in the following manner:

The three characteristics, or natures, are often considered to be three qualities that all things are endowed with. The imagined nature for Yogācāra adherents is considered false, as it consists of appearances that are construed as different from the perceiving consciousness. However, for Yogācāra traditions, objects do not exist apart from a perceiving subject, as they arise in dependence on consciousness. Consciousness arises from latent seeds of representation that have been stored in the subconscious since the beginningless past. All objects and subjects are dependent on other conditions and causes for their existence, and this quality of dependency is called the dependent characteristic. The absence of the imagined characteristic in the dependent is said to be the perfected nature. That is, the perfected nature is ultimate reality constituted by pure consciousness without the duality of the apprehended object and apprehending subject.[104]

According to Atiśa's teacher Bodhibhadra, there were two kinds of Yogācārins who differed regarding the nature of images in cognition (*ākāra*). The Sākāravādins (*rnam pa dang bcas pa*) maintained that cognition was always endowed with images (*sākāra*) and the Nirākāravādins (*rnam pa med pa smra ba*) maintained that cognition in its ultimate state was without images (*nirākāra*).[105] Bodhibhadra claimed that Dignāga and his followers were Sākāravādins, as they taught that the images of cognition belonged to dependent natures. On the other hand, Asaṅga and his followers were considered Nirākāravādins, as they maintained that the images of cognition belonged to imagined natures and were false and unreal. In the narratives of Atiśa's life, Serlingpa is considered a Sākāravādin.

Although Atiśa and some of his biographers represent Serlingpa as a Yogācāra follower, the content of his works descibed earlier points toward a Madhyamaka orientation influenced by Yogācāra concepts. The early Kadampa commentaries on Atiśa's *Entry to the Two Realities* mention that Atiśa composed this brief work in order to convert Serlingpa from a Yogācāra to a Madhyamaka view. In relation to this account, an interesting anecdote is preserved in a version of one of the early Kadampa biographies attributed to Dromtönpa that is not found among other biographies.[106] In this vignette recounted by Dromtönpa, one day while praying in front of Tārā, Serlingpa becomes troubled over the view that Atiśa upholds and immediately requests his monk-attendant Devamati to deliver a handwritten letter to Atiśa at Vikramaśīla expressing his concerns.[107] Upon receiving this letter, Atiśa immediately traveled to Sumatra to meet with Serlingpa. When Atiśa arrived in Sumatra, Serlingpa inquired about his view.

Atiśa responded with the following example:

During an unreal dream while sleeping,
a magician conjures two elephants.
When one elephant kills the other,
does the slaying, death, or the illusion itself exist?[108]

Serlingpa replied:

Whatever a magician conjures in a false dream,
whatever slaying or death of the elephant conjured by him,
Dīpaṃkara, is this an example of dream awareness?
Or an example of the awareness of the two elephants?[109]

Atiśa replied:

Awareness while dreaming is apprehended as real.
Little attachment appears to the awareness that is awake.
The part of the analogy of mistaken awareness while dreaming
illustrates only the vividness for [sensory] objects.

Awareness while awake is an analogy for correct awareness.
The apprehended object and apprehending subject of the elephant is a metaphor for an ultimate object.
However, what appears as the apprehended object and apprehending subject is a conventional mere name, but is not the ultimate.[110]

Atiśa then tells Serlingpa that all of the Buddha's teachings are based on the two realities, which consist of conventional reality in relation to the worldly and ultimate reality realized by holy ones. Atiśa then continues:

The analogy of mistaken awareness corresponds to those who cling to things as truly real.
The conventional of mere appearance is pleasing to ordinary individuals.
The conventional of mere name is acceptable for the supreme individual.
The ever-present reality of things is the supreme ultimate.

The two elephants, which are objects seen in a dream, if they are consciousness, will they no longer exist or will they become three [things]?

Otherwise, what is there for the proponent of Mind Only?
If at the time of waking up a nonexistent object is known, is that consciousness yesterday evening's awareness or is it a momentary appearance not previously seen?
If it is the very same [thing] as the previous awareness, the following morning [awareness] is contradicted and diminishes what is previously the case.
If it is the very same momentary-like appearance, in that case, even the two elephants are not apparent for that long.
Therefore the elephant as a sense object or subjective perception does not exist, and the mind and the object that is construed as an elephant are neither the same nor different.
The perceiver and the object are fundamentally unreal; that is to speak of the final ultimate reality.[111]

Serlingpa then asks Atiśa that if this is the case, how does one understand dependent-arising as emptiness? How is dependent-arising ceaseless, peaceful from the beginning (*rten 'brel bar med bzod nas zhi*)? Atiśa responds by explaining his understanding of dependent-arising:

When a sprout arises in dependence on a stalk of rice at first, all understand that the sprout does not exist.
When merely dependent on a seed, at that time the sprout does not exist.
At the time of the sprout, the seed ceases because, although the supported exists, the supporter does not.
This nonexistence [of the supported and supporter] at the same time is emptiness.
Powerless in itself, reliant on another, devoid of being internally established, this is the nature of reality abiding from the beginning.[112]

Atiśa concludes by stating:

Without knowing the reality of things, even the wise remain in the superficial.
In this manner, completely realizing this true nature of things and at the same time permeating its expanse is the supreme dependent-arising.[113]

After Atiśa proclaims these words, the episode concludes with Serlingpa praising this teaching as a pure view that, even though imperceptable, leads to the realization of nonduality. Whether or not the episode actually occurred, this dialogue between Atiśa and Serlingpa represents, for the Kadampa authorial community, a contrast between the views of Yogācāra and the Madhyamaka of Atiśa. As mentioned, Yogācārins posit that the world is nothing but our cognition and that external reality does not exist at all. For a number of Yogācārins, images of cognition are appearances of our mind and the implication is that "a cognition is always endowed with an image (*sākāra*) that is represented by our mind" (Kajiyama 1965, 426). Every cognition is endowed with an image, and so the conceptual thought of an ordinary individual, according to some Yogācārins, dichotomizes the subjective and objective aspects of cognition. One who realizes the absence of a real nature for the subjective and objective aspects (*grāhyagrāhakākāra*) of the mind is liberated, according to Yogācāra. Thus in this story Atiśa uses the analogy of a dream, a favorite example utilized by Yogācārins, to represent a Yogācāra position that understands the cognitions, or consciousness, to really exist. Atiśa understands these images as dependent designations that do not really exist. Atiśa elucidates a brief mereological analysis of the objects in the dream to illustrate that conciousness, or cognitive images, cannot be existent or nonexistent. Rather, as Atiśa illustrates with the example of the seed and sprout, things are dependent-arisings that lack any intrinsic essence.[114] The enhancement of this realization of things lacking any essence to all things is the meaning of great dependent-arising for Atiśa. As this episode in his life illustrates, Atiśa, as a Mādhyamika, follows the principles of the Middle Way based on the teaching of dependent-arising through the framework of conventional and ultimate reality.

A number of scholars at Vikramaśīla followed various forms of Yogācāra thought and worked within the textual and philosophical traditions of epistemology founded by the seventh-century Buddhist thinker Dharmakīrti. Atiśa's biographies mention that a number of these scholar-monks held the Yogācāra view of either *Sākāravāda* or *Nirākāravāda*. Atiśa's colleague Jñānaśrīmitra was an exponent of the Sākāra tradition, while Ratnākaraśānti, a senior scholar to Atiśa, is said to have held the rival position of Nirākāra.

The philosophical position of Ratnākaraśānti was quite complex and does not easily fit into the traditional categories of Buddhist thought represented in the Tibetan doxographical literature (*grub mtha'*). In brief, Ratnākaraśānti articulated a Middle Way based on Yogācāra principles that incorporated the theory of the three characteristics with an emphasis on self-awareness (*svasaṃvedana*) as equivalent to luminosity (*prakāśa, gsal ba*). For Ratnākaraśānti, self-awareness as luminosity constituted the intrinsic nature of all dharmas and was the highest form of valid cognition.

The early biographies of Atiśa mention that he learned the perfections and Yogācāra-Madhyamaka while studying the eight-thousand-line *Perfection of Wisdom* under Ratnākaraśānti.[115] An early biography also states that Atiśa, at first, upheld the *Nirākāravāda* view of Śāntipa, and later discarded it for the view of Ācārya Nāgārjuna. This discord on view may have been a source of dispute between Ratnākaraśānti and Atiśa.[116] Atiśa himself is reported to have said:

> When my guru Śāntipa was teaching the eight-thousand-verse [*Perfection of Wisdom*], for all the explanations of Madhyamaka, he refuted each and every one of them, and my Madhyamaka view itself became refreshed. The Yogācāra-Madhyamaka [system] became extremely clear, I had great faith in the system of Candrakīrti.[117]

Based on the biographical material, we can surmise that the Madhyamaka teachings that Atiśa received in his youth were in conflict with the views of Ratnākaraśānti that Atiśa learned while studying under him at Vikramaśīla. A brief comparison of the works of Ratnākaraśānti with Atiśa's affiliated works translated in this book indicates that they differed on a number of points of thought and exegesis. Although both Atiśa and Ratnākaraśānti claimed to follow the Middle Way of Nāgārjuna, Atiśa's thought was also influenced by Candrakīrti, whereas Ratnākaraśānti expounded his system based on Yogācāra sources. Ratnākaraśānti also differentiated two groups of Mādhyamikas in his *Triyānavyavasthāna* based on their application of the tetralemma in negating either the binaries of existence/nonexistence or permanence/impermanence.[118] Atiśa, on the other hand, does not differentiate Madhyamaka based on this distinction. Moreover, in his *Bodhimārgapradīpapañjikā* (BMPP), Atiśa incorporates both sets of binaries in his application of the tetralemma. That is, in this work Atiśa applies the tetralemma twice, once to the fourfold negation of existence/nonexistence and permanence/impermanence. Even though Atiśa and Ratnākaraśānti both accepted the luminous nature of the mind, awareness for Atiśa dependently arises and lacks any essence, whereas for Ratnākaraśānti, awareness, at least on the level of nonduality, is ultimately real. Atiśa and Ratnākaraśānti differed as to the interpretation of the same Buddhist scriptural sources as well. A good example was the interpretation of Nāgārjuna's *Yuktiṣaṣṭikā* (verse 34), where Atiśa posited mental qualities as mere appearances that dependently arise, whereas Ratnākaraśānti framed the ultimate nature of mental qualities as their "mere shining forth of nonduality" (*advayaprakāśamātra*). Ratnākaraśānti criticized positions that advocated "mere appearance" and Atiśa clearly articulated an interpretation of Madhyamaka emphasizing mere appearances in his *General Explanation*.[119]

Atiśa and Ratnākaraśānti also differed as to the role of negation in realizing what they considered as the ultimate; Atiśa emphasized only nonimplicative negations (*prasajyapratiṣedha*) in his *General Explanation* and Ratnākaraśānti described in his *Prajnāpāramitopadeśa* the perfected nature as a implicative negation (*paryudāsapratiṣedha*).[120] Ratnākaraśānti criticized the Madhyamaka position that conventional reality exists "without analysis," a position that is explicitly stated in Atiśa's *Satyadvayāvatāra* (verse 3).[121] Ratnākaraśānti also refuted Candrakīrti's "what is renowned in the world position" for conventional reality and advocated the means of valid cognition for realizing ultimate reality.[122] As discussed in part 2, Atiśa strongly opposed the means of valid cognition for realizing ultimate reality. Lastly, Ratnākaraśānti severely criticized the position that buddhahood was "inconceivable" and exhausted of all mind and mental functions. Instead, Ratnākaraśānti advocated that a buddha's realization has mental qualities (Yiannopoulos 2012, 194). The understanding of buddhahood as without conceptuality and as inconceivable is found in Candrakīrti and is strongly advocated throughout the works of Atiśa and his Kadampa followers.

In addition to these points, the Kadampa works also mention that Atiśa and Ratnākaraśānti had discordant philosophical views. An early history records that Atiśa's system of following Nāgārjuna displeased Ratnākaraśānti; for Śāntipa, the student and teacher should share the same view.[123] A Kadampa manuscript also mentions that Ratnākaraśānti broke up a class session when he overheard Atiśa teaching emptiness to several students. The philosophical differences between Atiśa and Ratnākaraśānti may have been a contributing factor for Atiśa to leave for Tibet.

Atiśa's Middle Way in Tibet

The Questioning of Atiśa in Western Tibet

An important event occurred after Atiśa's initial arrival in western Tibet that illustrates his understanding of Madhyamaka in relation to his Buddhist thought and practice. The event was the Tibetan king Jangchup Ö's invitation to a number of Tibetan scholars from central Tibet to visit and have a dialogue with Atiśa. This episode in Atiśa's life is recorded in a diverse number of early biographies of Atiśa, Kadampa works, and later Tibetan histories.[124] The story represents an early collective memory of how Atiśa's followers differentiated themselves from other practices and doctrines among Tibetan

Buddhists around that time. A significant portion of the dialogue concerns the Tibetans' inquiries into Atiśa's understanding of Madhyamaka. The dialogue not only provides evidence for how early Kadampas understood Atiśa's Madhyamaka but also demonstrates how early followers of Atiśa represented Tibetan forms of Madhyamaka that differed from Atiśa's. One may infer that the Madhyamaka presumptions of the Tibetan scholars at this time were still based on the earlier imperial-period teachings of Śāntarakṣita (ca. 725–88), Kamalaśīla (ca. 740–95), Jñānagarbha (eighth century), and of Śrīgupta and Haribhadra, among others, that had continued since the collapse of the Tibetan empire in 842.

As mentioned, the teachings of Śāntarakṣita, Kamalaśīla, and Jñānagarbha are known in early Kadampa sources as the "as the teachings of the Easterners" (*shar ba dag*) because these three authors were from Bengal. The texts included within this early classification of Madhyamaka were Śāntarakṣita's *Madhyamakālaṃkāra* (MAK), Kamalaśīla's *Madhyamakāloka* (MĀ), and Jñānagarbha's *Satyadvayavibhaṅga* (SDV).[125] The Tibetan scholars at this time must also have known of Śāntarakṣita's *Madhyamakālaṃkāravṛtti* (MAV) and *Tattvasaṃgraha* (TS) and Kamalaśīla's *Madhyamakālaṃkārapañjikā* (MAP) and *Tattvasaṃgrahapañjikā* (TSP). Although there is evidence for monastic colleges and for a tradition of studying Madhyamaka and Pramāṇa from the time of Śāntarakṣita, we do not currently know the extent of the Tibetans' study of such texts in the imperial period or in the postimperial period before Atiśa's arrival in western Tibet.[126] Be that as it may, what is clear from the following dialogue is that the Tibetan understanding of Madhyamaka at this time was based on the texts of the Easterners and comprised a type of Madhyamaka that utilized the integration of valid cognition and Mind Only thought with the Middle Way of Nāgārjuna as found in the works of Śāntarakṣita and Kamalaśīla. In fact, the dialogue begins with the Tibetan interlocutors asking Atiśa about his view of Madhyamaka and Cittamātra, an inquiry that illustrates the presumptions of the Tibetan questioners, who assumed that Atiśa had views similar to those of Śāntarakṣita.

This assumption may have been related to beliefs based on geographical affiliations rather than on textual or doctrinal statements. The Kadampa narratives of Atiśa's life depicted Atiśa as being from the same royal lineage as Śāntarakṣita in Bengal, and the ceremonies to welcome Atiśa into Tibet were similar to those for Śāntarakṣita's arrival, an understanding that the Tibetan interlocutors in west Tibet must have shared as well.[127] However, Śāntarakṣita and Atiśa upheld different lineages of Vinaya and had dissimilar individuals of influence in their lineage of Madhyamaka. Śāntarakṣita upheld the Mūlasarvāstivāda Vinaya, which became the official ordination lineage in all of Tibet during the imperiod period, and his lineage of Madhyamaka teachers included Śrīgupta and Jñānagarbha.[128] Atiśa, as has been discussed, was ordained within the Mahāsāṃghika Vinaya, and his Madhyamaka was significantly influenced by Candrakīrti, by the Madhyamaka found in the *Madhyamakaratnapradīpa* attributed to Bhāviveka, and by his teachers Vidyākokila and Avadhūtipa. More important, Śāntarakṣita and Kamalaśīla's Madhyamaka accommodated the means of valid cognition of Dignāga and Dharmakīrti for realizing emptiness, whereas Atiśa upheld valid cognition as useful only for debating non-Buddhists.

The differences between the Tibetan questioners' and Atiśa's understanding of Madhyamaka was due not only to their background knowledge of Buddhist thought but also to the ironic contingencies of history. This is because what also underlies the dialogue is the Tibetans' understanding of Madhyamaka based on Kamalaśīla's *Madhyamakāloka*, where Dharmakīrti's theory of inference was utilized for realizing ultimate reality. However, neither Atiśa nor any other Indian Buddhist scholar before him had read Kamalaśīla's *Madhyamakāloka*. This text had been written in Tibet for the Tibetan king in the late eighth century and, at least according to Atiśa, had not been available to Indian Buddhist scholars.[129] At the same time, Atiśa was fully versed in the thought of Candrakīrti, whose works had yet to be fully translated in Tibet. These differences of textual knowledge and tradition based on varied Indian and Tibetan Buddhist historical conditions infuse the dialogue. The translation is presented here with explanatory comments in between segments to further clarify Atiśa's Madhyamaka thought and its reception upon arrival in Tibet.

The dialogue concerning Atiśa's view begins with the Tibetan interlocutors asking Atiśa about his understanding of Madhyamaka, Cittamātra, and other schools of thought.

> [The Tibetans asked,] "What do you accept?" and "Do you accept Madhyamaka, Cittamātra, and so forth according to the ancient ways?" [Atiśa replied,] "I posit things according to scripture and logic." Everyone said, "This is excellent." When asked by a single-minded one from among the three areas of Ngari, a Ngaripa named Losal, "How can this appear in common to all, as you do not teach according to assertions?" [Atiśa replied,] "Since I am a monk who trains in accordance with the Buddha, what I say is in accord with the thoughts of those to be trained." Again, one known as Metsun Yönten Sherap asked, "Well then, what do you assert?" [Atiśa replied,] "I do not assert anything." [They then asked,] "Since [you]

> do not have any assertions ultimately, what do you accept conventionally?" Atiśa stated, "All these [conventionals] are seen like hairs in the vision of one with eye disease. That is how they abide. Precisely, if someone asks how, [they] do not exist." Thinking that this was a unique view that was in disagreement with everyone, again, someone asked the Lord whether one clears away or does not clear away appearances. [Atiśa said,] "It is the same as getting rid of hairs in cooked rice for one with eye disease, but you must experience it yourself."[130]

In this segment Atiśa clarified that he teaches the Buddha's Dharma according to the needs of his disciples but that he does not make propositional assertions. This relates to Atiśa's understanding that a Mādhyamika is not engaged in the establishment of philosophical assertions. Rather, as indicated in his *General Explanation*, reasonings are utilized to refute erroneous assertions while one's own nonacceptance is not invalidated. For Atiśa, no proof of a philosophical position is ever posited by a Mādhyamika.

Along these lines, the Tibetan interlocutor named Losal asked Atiśa, "How can this appear in common to all?" (*kun la mthun par 'gyur snang pa ji ltar lags*) if he does not make assertions. The interlocutor's question presumes, as well as invokes, in an eleventh-century Tibetan context, the principle of common establishment (*ubhayasiddhatva*), which became in later Tibetan scholarship the contentious issue of "commonly appearing subjects" (*chos can mthun snang ba*).[131] The principle of common establishment, traceable to statements made by Dignāga (fifth–sixth century), was that the reason and subject must be established for both parties in a debate. The idea is that for both parties in a debate there is something that similarly appears (*mthun snang ba*) in order for logical debate and discussion to take place. Some Mādhyamikas in India accepted this principle, while others did not. It was accepted, at least on the conventional level, by Indian Madhyamaka thinkers like Śāntarakṣita, Kamalaśīla, and Jñānagarbha.[132] On the other hand, Candrakīrti appears to be one of the few scholars among Indian Madhyamaka traditions not to have followed the rule of common establishment.[133] As recent scholarship has demonstrated, Candrakīrti presented Madhyamaka teachings based on reasonings-for-others in the form of either consequences (*prasaṅgas*) or other-acknowledged inferences (*paraprasiddhānumāna*). In this type of inference, the subject, as well as the reason, are established only for an opponent and not the Mādhyamika. This kind of reasoning enabled a Mādhyamika such as Candrakīrti or Atiśa to debate without following a Dignāga-based rule of common establishment or contravening their understanding of emptiness and nonsubstantiality. This tradition of Madhyamaka was not yet known in Tibet, so Atiśa responded to the inquiry by stating that he, in the pragmatic tradition of the Buddha, answers "in accord with the thoughts of those to be trained."

Based on statements in the Kadampa *Collection on the Two Realities* and *A General Explanation*, Atiśa followed a lineage of Madhyamaka that advocated the use of consequences that exposed contradictions and employed other-acknowledged inferences.[134] In the context of this dialogue in west Tibet, the Tibetan interlocutor does not seem to be familiar with a tradition of Madhyamaka that did not concede to the principle of common establishment. Atiśa did not further explore this issue, according to the narrative, but merely provided a polite and nonconfrontational response. Nevertheless, the question and its response points toward a difference of understanding between Atiśa and his Tibetan interlocutors on this issue in Madhyamaka thought in 1042. The early Kadampa commentaries provide evidence that Atiśa's early followers accepted his position on Madhyamaka reasoning of not adhering to the principle of common establishment. The later evidence from the works of Shangthak Sakpa (first half of the twelfth century) and Chapa Chökyi Sengé demonstrate that the issue of common establishment became a contentious and passionately debated point from at least the twelfth century onward in the history of Tibetan Buddhist thought.[135]

This segment also demonstrates Atiśa's understanding of conventional reality being a false projection of ignorance, like a person who sees hairs while suffering from eye disease. This metaphor—of the eye disease of ignorance constituting conventional reality—will occur again at the end of this dialogue and is fully explained in *A General Explanation.* As discussed in chapter 4, Atiśa's emphasis on conventional reality being a false projection is, in his interpretation, congruent with the teachings of Nāgārjuna and Candrakīrti. However, this point troubled the Tibetans and they asked Atiśa if appearances (*snang ba*, *pratibhāsa*) are cleared away or not. The Tibetan questioner may have been thinking along the lines of Śāntarakṣita's statement that, "as for us, we do not eliminate entities insofar as they are appearances to the eye and other sense consciousnesses."[136] As will be demonstrated below, and throughout this book, appearances for Atiśa are due to ignorance and are falsities that do not withstand analysis. As Tillemans has made clear, Śāntarakṣita and Kamalaśīla accepted appearances at the conventional level as existing in a similar manner to the way in which Yogācāra-based epistemologists posited particulars (*svalakṣaṇa*). Śāntarakṣita stated in his *Madhyamakālaṃkāra* that cause and effect is consciousness only and that "whatever exists in its own right is consciousness."[137] For Śāntarakṣita and Kamalaśīla an object that is perceived by ordinary people is an appearance of consciousness that is conventionally established. In their view, accepting appearances on the conventional level was necessary for engaging in debate without falling into the pitfalls of the subject being unestablished (*āśrayāsiddha*), for the basis of inference, and to explain cognition in meditation. In brief, for Śāntarakṣita and Kamalaśīla, something remains at the level of conventional reality that is more than the mere nominal appearance of conventional reality that Atiśa dependently designates. As discussed in *A General Explanation*, appearances for Atiśa are "mere appearances" (*snang ba tsam*) in which both the object and the cognition are dependently designated and are therefore mere imputations (*prajñāptimatra*). This interpretation of Madhyamaka, as characterized by Tillemans, would "duly horrify" a thinker like Kamalaśīla, for whom conventional realities at a certain level must be established by valid cognition. If things are accepted just by what is acknowledged in the world without "epistemic instruments" being conventionally established, then, for Kamalaśīla, "it would follow absurdly that everything whatsoever would be established by everything."[138] Atiśa, following his intepretation of Nāgārjuna and Candrakīrti, posited appearances based on dependent designation without epistemic warrants being conventionally established.[139]

Related to this question regarding appearances, the dialogue continues with a question concerning the nature of discerning awareness and its relations to the subject under investigation.

> Furthermore, Lord [Atiśa] was asked whether or not a subject (*chos can*) appears to a discerning awareness (*rig pa'i shes rab*).[140] [Atiśa replied,] "In regard to discerning awareness, the subject does not appear, as it does not exist, nor does the object appear, as it does not exist, in the context of the purview of that awareness; since the subject does not exist, there is nonappearance (*mi snang ba*)."
>
> Lord [Atiśa] asked, "Do you assert appearances or do you assert nonappearances?" In replying that they accept appearances, the Tibetans stated that a subject withstands [analysis] by asserting that it appears.[141]

This question by the Tibetan interlocutor relates to the fundamental question of the role of reasoned analytical knowledge (*rigs pa'i shes pa*) and its relation to the property-possessor (*chos can, dharmin*), or subject, that is examined in the context of debate or, by extension, is examined by a reasoning procedure in the context of meditation. The Tibetan interlocutors on this point may be thinking about Śāntarakṣita's well-known statement in the *Madhyamakālaṃ-*

kāra that "I do not refute the entity that appears," and Kamalaśīla's follow-up comment in *Madhyamakālaṃkārapañjikā* that "we have established the refutation of the superimposition of an ultimate nature on the appearing subject but we do not refute the nature (*rang gi ngo = svarūpa, svabhāva*) of the subject."[142] As recent scholarship has noted, most all Mādhyamikas refute the "superimpositions" (*samāropa*) of intrinsic nature (*svabhāva*) that are projected on conventional realities perceived in the world. Even so, what constituted conventional reality was a point of contention and dispute among Indian (and Tibetan) Madhyamaka thinkers. Some Madhyamakas granted a certain level of existence to conventional realities that, when bereft of superimpositions, can still function as means of valid cognition and are nondeceptive as long as they are not analyzed. On the other hand, some Madhyamakas, such as Atiśa, held that all conventional realities are false appearances that are unreal at any level as objects and, as such, are either deceptive appearances that perpetuate *saṃsāra* or mere appearances that are false but are conducive to awakening (*bodhi*).

As mentioned, Śāntarakṣita and Kamalaśīla were Madhyamaka thinkers who argued that entities are established on the conventional level,[143] and perhaps surprisingly from Atiśa's perspective, Kamalaśīla argued in the *Madhyamakāloka* that inference could be employed to realize ultimate reality.[144] Atiśa, based on his interpretation of Nāgārjuna and Candrakīrti, considered conventional realities to be deceptive and false appearances that appear owing to ignorance, and he fully rejected the claim that ultimate reality, or emptiness, can be realized by either direct perception (*pratyakṣa*) or inference (*anumāna*) (SDA, vv. 12–14). For Atiśa, nothing withstands analysis and this unfindability is the ultimate (SDA, v. 21). Atiśa stated in his *Satyadvayāvatāra* (v. 5) that "there is neither a subject nor its property [for inferential reasoning] in the ultimate." The Kadampa commentary on Atiśa's text clarifies that there is no conceptual diversity (*spros pa*) in relation to the ultimate. For Atiśa and his followers, the ultimate is understood in a nonconceptual manner that is conventionally designated as "seeing" that is a "nonseeing" (SDA, vv. 7ab). Moreover, for Atiśa and his followers, reasoning is a conventional process that dissolves itself at the end of a procedure that seeks to establish the existence of an object. Once reasoning consumes the fuel of conceptual thought, as metaphorically described by Atiśa, the fire of reasoning itself dissipates and one comes to rest in nonappearance. In Atiśa's outline of Madhyamaka meditation in his *Madhyamakopadeśa*, analytical reasoning dissolves itself and this leads to a nonconceptual meditative state of nonduality in which there are no longer any appearances of ignorance. On this point Atiśa is following a tradition of exegesis found in the *Madhyamakaratnapradīpa* (MRP), where analytical reason dissipates after dissolving conceptual thought. In the dialogue Atiśa therefore responded that "there is nonappearance" in the purview of a discerning awareness or reasoned analytical knowledge.

The dialogue continues with the Tibetan scholars inquiring about the existence of a continuum of wisdom at the level of buddhahood.

> [Atiśa] was asked whether or not there is a continuum of wisdom at the level of a Buddha. [Atiśa replied,] "A Buddha does not have at all [a continuum of wisdom]. He is incomparable."
>
> Then the Lord said, "It is like a magician deceiving a minister, but you should experience for yourself; positing [a buddha] to not have a continuum of wisdom is like striking victory everywhere." The Lord said, "You Tibetans will not even be receptive (*mi bzod*) to the teaching of Mind Only through my Madhyamaka view."[145]

Similar to the previous questions, the issue of whether or not a continuum of wisdom, or gnosis (*jñāna, ye shes*), exists at the level of buddhahood was a contentious issue in both eleventh-century India and in Tibet. In her meticuluous study on the controversies concerning the existence of gnosis in relation to the understanding of buddhahood, Almogi (2009, 139–48) has pointed out that the variety of positions that accepted the existence of gnosis at the level of a buddha were primarily affiliated with Yogācāra traditions and their subschools. The degree to which later Mādhyamika thinkers such as Śrīgupta, Jñānagarbha, Śāntarakṣita, Kamalaśīla, and Haribhadra, among others, were willing to accommodate Yogācāra as well as epistemological structures into their arguments and understanding of Buddhist doctrines provoked a number of controversies and passionate debates. Śrīgupta, for instance, a teacher of Jñānagarbha, clearly posited the existence of nonconceptual gnosis and pure mundane gnosis at the level of a buddha. Dharmamitra (ca. 800), a commentator to Haribhadra's *Abhisamayālaṃkāravivṛti*, while rejecting pure mundane gnosis, accepted the existence of nonconceptual gnosis for a buddha. On the other hand, Śāntarakṣita and Kamalaśīla's standpoint on this issue is not fully clear.[146]

In addition to whether or not an individual Indian Mādhyamika author accepted some type of gnosis for a buddha, the subtleties of the fine points debated within an Indian Buddhist context were not always clearly discernible in the early Tibetan translations of Indian Buddhist digests. In texts such as Śāntarakṣita's *Madhyamakālaṃkāravṛtti* or Śāntideva's *Bodhicaryāvatāra*, whether a debated point of contention was from a Yogācāra or Mādhyamika standpoint was not always clear. Moreover, Tibetan exegetes, from the time of the imperial period until Atiśa's arrival, could interpret texts such as Śāntideva's *Bodhicaryāvatāra* from a Yogācāra-Madhyamaka standpoint rather than a strictly Mādhyamika interpretation.[147] Factors such as this may have influenced the Tibetan interlocutors to question Atiśa on whether wisdom exists at the level of buddhahood or not.

In agreement with his reply, Atiśa emphatically advocated in his works that buddhas are completely fused with ultimate reality in a nondualistic fashion whereby all conceptual thought has been eliminated and not even nonconceptual wisdom exists. Throughout his writings, Atiśa references Mahāyāna sūtras, tantras, the works of Nāgārjuna, Āryadeva, Candrakīrti, and Śāntideva as proof texts for this standpoint. Atiśa, in his *Open Basket of Jewels* (section 3.2), provides an extended discussion, based on the works of Nāgārjuna, on the point that buddhahood does not have any mind or mental factors. Related to Atiśa's understanding of buddhahood as bereft of any mental qualities is his position that a buddha does not have a continuum of wisdom. This issue is specifically related to the interpretation of part of a stanza in Śāntideva's *Bodhicaryāvatāra* that states, "upon conditions having their continuum cut, [an illusion] does not arise even conventionally."[148] The point of contention in the interpretations of this verse is what exactly has its continuum cut and what exactly does not arise. Atiśa directly repeats this portion of Śāntideva's stanza in his *Satyadvayāvatāra* (vv. 23cd). The Kadampa commentary, likely following an oral tradition of Atiśa's teachings, explains that appearances occur due to various causes and conditions, and if the continuance of the conditions for such appearances are interrupted, then appearances will no longer arise even conventionally. For Atiśa and his Kadampa followers, all appearances are due to ignorance and are comprised of ignorance. Therefore when the conditions for any type of appearance are exhausted, including wisdom or gnosis (*jñāna*), then such appearances will no long occur.

In addition to the *Satyadvayāvatāra*, Atiśa directly addressed the status of gnosis at the level of a buddha in the *Bodhisattvacāryāvatārabhāṣya*, a summary on Śāntideva's *Bodhicaryāvatāra*.[149] Several sections of the text are composed in the form of a dialogue with the bodhisattva Mañjuśrī to address difficult points of exegesis. Atiśa discusses the gnosis at the level of a buddha in a section describing the vision of liberating gnosis (*rnam par grol ba'i ye shes mthong ba ≈ vimuktijñānadarśana*) at the level of a buddha (see Appendix for a translation of the passage). Atiśa's discussion in this work clearly demonstrates that he did not accept a buddha having a continuum of wisdom based on Śāntideva's *Bodhicaryāvatāra*. Atiśa's understanding on this point is congruent with a strict Madhyamaka understanding of the nature of buddhahood found in the works of Nāgārjuna, Candrakīrti, and Śāntideva. The understanding that a buddha does not have any mind or mental functions, including even wisdom, was a position that was vehemently refuted by Atiśa's Indian Yogācāra contemporaries such as Jñānaśrīmitra and Ratnākaraśānti.[150] Furthermore, this point was not even fully understood by some of Atiśa's own disciples and became a debated point of contention among Tibetan Madhyamaka scholars in the decades following Atiśa's lifetime.[151]

In this segment of the dialogue, Atiśa also mentions that the Tibetan scholars would not be receptive to his teaching of "mind only" according to his vision of Madhyamaka (*dbu ma'i lta ba*). Atiśa's teaching of "mind only" through his vision of the Middle Way is found in his *General Explanation*. As modern scholars have previously noted, both Madhyamaka- and Yogācāra-affiliated authors had interpretations of what Mahāyāna scriptures mean when they state that things are "mind only."[152] Mādhyamikas, like Yogācārins, posit that things are imputed by the mind and are mind-dependent, as it is the mind that produces designations (*prajñapti*). However, "the difference between the Mādhyamika . . . and the Yogācāra is that the latter considers the mind to be more consistent and real than the imagined external objects. The Yogācāra accepts an ontological hierarchy of mind over objects," for although "both Yogācāra and Madhyamaka maintain that objects are reducible to mind," the Yogācāra accepts that the mind is more real than the object (Tillemans 1990, 65). For Atiśa's Yogācāra contemporaries like Jñānaśrīmitra, this means that nondual cognitive images purified of conceptions ultimately exist in the form of reflexive awareness (*svasaṃvedana*), whereas for Ratnākaraśānti cognitive images are false and what ultimately exists is the luminosity of reflexive awareness. Mādhyamikas like Śāntarakṣita and Kamalaśīla accommodated a form of Yogācāra at the level of conventional reality that posited the mind as more real than objects but rejected the reality of both mind and objects in terms of ultimate reality. As discussed in chapter 4, Atiśa's understanding of Madhyamaka mentalism, based on sources he attributed to Nāgārjuna, is complex and nuanced as a response to his contemporaries who adhered to Satyākāravāda, *Alīkākāravāda, or Māyopamādvayavāda positions. In brief, Atiśa did not make a hierarchical distinction between the ontological status of mind and objects in terms of either conventional or ultimate realities. Rather, as discussed in chapter 4, objects and cognitions for Atiśa were considered imputations of mere appearance that are unestablished and dependently arisen.

In relation to these differences between Mādhyamika and Yogācāra ways of positing "mind only" realities, the dialogue continues with Atiśa questioning the Tibetan scholars on how to posit the example of an illusion. This inquiry brings out further differences of understanding between Atiśa's Madhyamaka and the Tibetans' Madhyamaka that, unconsciously or not, accommodates Yogācāra and/or other Buddhist systems at the conventional level.

> Furthermore, Lord [Atiśa] asked, "How do you posit an example of an illusion for a Mādhyamika?" The Tibetan teachers replied, "It is like pebbles and sticks that appear as horses and elephants when a spell is cast on the eyes." The Lord said with a slight frown, "Tibetans, there is a negative consequence for the systems of Mind Only and below."[153]

The example of an illusion of horses or elephants conjured by a spell on sticks or pebbles is referred to in Mahāyāna Buddhist scriptural sources such as the *Saṃdhinirmocanasūtra*, and is taken up by several Yogācāra authors. In later Tibetan scholasticism the example of the magician's illusion is referred to as the example in which "pebbles and sticks of a magical display do not exist as horses and elephants" (*sgyu ma'i rde'u shing rta glang du med*). This example is utilized by later Gelukpa exegetes to articulate the Madhyamaka philosophical view of Śāntarakṣita and Kamalaśīla. However, the Gelukpa representation of the magician's illusion is different from what occurs in this dialogue (see Lopez 1987). An example of the magician's illusion in Śāntarakṣita and Kamalaśīla's works is, as far as I can currently identify, in Śāntarakṣita's *Madhyamakālaṃkāravṛtti* while commenting on his *Madhyamakālaṃkāra* (v. 52). On this point Śāntarakṣita states:

> Consciousness is ultimately like a pure crystal and is not composed of distinctive cognitive images like blue and so forth. Again with respect to this, cognitive images appear owing to erroneous latencies from beginningless time, just as horses, elephants, and so forth appear on a lump of clay to eyes that have been disturbed by a mantra and so forth.[154]

Although this example is mentioned by Śāntarakṣita in the *Madhyamakālaṃkāra*, verse 52 and its commentary represent Śāntarakṣita's depiction of the Alīkākāravāda-Yogācāra position that Śāntarakṣita refutes in the verses that follow (55–60).[155] The form of Yogāracāra that Śāntarakṣita and Kamalaśīla accept at the conventional level, whether of Satyākāravāda, *Alīkākāravāda, or something different from these two, is a complex issue that cannot be further explored here.[156] The Tibetan interlocutors may have understood the magician's illusion in this section of Śāntarakṣita's *Madhyamakālaṃkāravṛtti* as an example of how a Mādhyamika posits a magician's illusion. Alternatively, the Tibetans' understanding may have come from another unknown source translated during the imperial period. Be that as it may, what is at stake in the Tibetans' positing of illusion from Atiśa's Madhyamaka perspective is that the illusion is presumed to have a real basis of pebbles and sticks. A position like this resembles the manner in which Yogācāra-based thinkers posited a dependent nature that serves as a real basis for conceptual designations to take place (*prajñaptyadhiṣṭhāna*). Indeed, the Yogācāra understanding of a real entity for conceptual designation is found in Asaṅga's *Bodhisattvabhūmi*, where it is stated that "if the real entity for conceptual designation does not exist, being without substratum, conceptual designation would also not exist (*tatra prajñapter vastu nāstīti niradhiṣṭhāṇa prajñaptirapi nāsti*)." For the Yogācāra adherent, the real entity that serves as a basis is constituted by mental qualities. In brief, the Yogācāra posits an ontology where a dependent nature, constituted by a succession of dependently arisen mental qualities, exists as a basis for designations.[157] The Madhyamaka thinker who accommodates Yogācāra at the level of conventional reality would accept projected mental objects to conventionally exist as bases for designation. The Tibetans' manner of positing the magician's illusion presumes such a conventionally real basis (*vastu*) of pebbles and sticks from which the superimposed horses and elephants are imputed, or imagined, due to the spell of erroneous subconscious latencies. Atiśa classifies this manner of positing an illusion as applicable to followers of "Mind Only (*cittamātra*) and below," due to the presumption of an underlying basis, mental or otherwise, that is real at least on the conventional level. Atiśa, as a pure Mādhyamika, posited illusions in a slightly different manner with different presumptions, as indicated in his reply:

> "In that case, how to do you posit for a Mādhyamika," they asked. [Atiśa said,] "Through merely casting a spell upon the eyes, various horses, elephants, and so forth appear in empty space. In this way, this appearance has a delusive basis in which things variously appear. Things like this are not even accepted as a mere conventionality."[158]

Atiśa's *General Explanation* repeatedly states that all appearances are mere designations that are not existent, real, or substantially existent. Conventional realities, whether correct or mistaken, are mere nominal designations. For Atiśa, the basis of designation and the agent that designates both lack substantial existence and are dependent designations that arise totally due to ignorance, whether from the coarse ignorance of ordinary individuals or from the subtle latencies of ignorance in the mindstream of an advanced bodhisattva. In brief, Atiśa does not posit things as having a real basis; rather, things do not have a basis (*avastuka*) and are without foundation. Atiśa clarifies in his *General Explanation*, based on Candrakīrti's *Yuktiṣaṣṭikavṛtti* (vv. 26–27), that the universe appears like an illusion that is without basis or foundation. Atiśa also states in his *Satyadvayāvatāra* (v. 8) that reality is without support and without basis. In this way, Atiśa accords with the "cardinal tenet of Mādhyamikas" that things are only nominal designations (*prajñapti*) that are dependently designated (*upādāya prajñapti*).[159]

This part of the dialogue also indicates that Atiśa follows Candrakīrti in understanding that things such as elephants and horses that appear based on spells cast upon the eyes do not even exist as "mere conventions" (*kun rdzob tsam*). The classification "mere convention" (*saṃvṛtimātra*) is found in Candrakīrti's *Madhyamakāvatārabhāṣya* and *Madhyamakāvatāra* 6.28 where he makes a distinction between the perspective of conventional reality according to ordinary beings and the perspective of those, the *āryas*, who have understood emptiness, who perceive things as "mere conventions." For the *āryas*, conditioned things are false, artificial, and are like reflections of a magician's illusion, while an ordinary individual perceives things as true and real. Atiśa specifies that the elephants and horses that appear based on a spell are not even a "mere convention," insofar as they are dependent-arisings that appear false even to those who have ignorance.[160] Note that, following Candrakīrti, Atiśa in his *General Explanation* clarifies that things appear as inherently existent to ordinary individuals due to afflicted ignorance, that things appear like reflections or a magician's illusion due to the latencies of unafflicted ignorance, and that conventional reality no longer appears to buddhas who have totally removed all vestiges of misknowledge and no longer have any mind or mental factors.

At this point in the narrative of the dialogue, the Tibetan biographer stresses that even though Tibetans thought they were Mādhyamikas before Atiśa's arrival, their understanding, at least as Atiśa's early Kadampa biographers see it, does not even qualify as Madhyamaka. The biography states at this point:

> At the time before Lord [Atiśa] arrived, all Tibetans accepted a Madhyamaka view. After Atisa arrived, all appeared to be in error about being a Madhyamaka.[161]

The questioning of Atiśa in regard to his understanding of Madhyamaka comes to a conclusion with a request for Atiśa to provide an example that demonstrates how beings are afflicted with the eye disease of ignorance. Atiśa responds with the example of an old woman, suffering from eye disease, who sees hair in a bowl of rice offered by her daughter-in-law while her son is away on business. The example is explained in Atiśa's *General Explantion* and referenced in the Kadampa commentary on Atiśa's *Satyadvayāvatāra*. In the dialogue narrated in the biographies, Atiśa responded to his Tibetan questioner as follows:

> At that time, one named Manang Gomchen (Ma snang sgom chen) then asked [Atiśa] to provide an example that illustrates how one is afflicted with eye disease. [Atiśa replied,] "In India, there was an old woman who had a son who showed great kindness and care for her. As he was traveling for business, he worried about leaving his mother behind, so he asked his wife to serve and venerate his mother until his return. Having instructed her, he departed. At that time, the daughter-in-law made rice cakes for the old woman, but her eyes were diminished. As the old woman was confused and the interior [of her eyes] swollen, the food was perceived to have hair in it. The daughter-in-law became saddened, and when the son returned the old woman made an accusation. The son asked his wife how this could be, and the wife replied that she was respectful but that the old woman suffered from visual confusion. She added that the son himself had provided the food. The son saw the well-prepared food that he had provided. The old woman spoke, asking if the son would prepare [tainted] food like that. The son replied that he would not, and that since she was mistaken, and disturbed about this food, a skillful doctor was summoned who nourished her eyes by applying external and internal medicine to them. Then, through the natural healing of her eye disease, she understood that the food did not have hairs in it. Likewise, the Dharma teachings of the Three Baskets (*sde snod gsum*) remove external superimpositions. The special instructions of the excellent spiritual teacher remove internal superimpositions." As all the Tibetan teachers were speechless and filled with wonder, they said, "We must invite the Indian bearded one for his Dharma teaching," and all of their doubts were removed.[162]

In this segment of the biographical narrative, Atiśa provided a conservative response for healing the disease of ignorance. He merely replied that the "Dharma teachings of the Three Baskets remove external superimpositions while the spiritual teacher removes internal superimpositions." The example of the old woman's eye disease is specifically related to teachings found in Candrakīrti's *Madhyamakāvatārabhāṣya* and the teachings of Nāgārjuna (see discussion in chapters 3 and 4). In brief, Atiśa recognized that the Tibetan scholars questioning him in west Tibet were not familiar with his understanding of Madhyamaka based on Candrakīrti and skillfully avoided the reference to teachings they would not have known at this time.

Atiśa's Middle Way in the Bodhimārgapradīpapañjikā *and* Stages of the Path to Awakening

After the questioning of Atiśa about emptiness, he took up residency at Tholing Monastery and began teaching, writing, and translating works into Tibetan. During his residency, Atiśa's Tibetan translator-disciple Naktso reminded the Tibetan king Jangchup Ö that he had promised the abbott of Vikramaśīla that Atiśa would return to India after three years. Prompted by Atiśa's anticipated return to India, Jangchup Ö then asked Atiśa a number of questions regarding Buddhist thought and practice and requested that he write a text that would detail the teachings from the lineages of Nāgārjuna and Maitreya. The king also requested that Atiśa clarify the relations between teachings found in Buddhist sūtras and tantras and provide instructions for how to train one's mind and cultivate the gradual states of the path to awakening. These instructions represented Jangchup Ö's interest in establishing a structured monastic Buddhism. Atiśa then composed the *Lamp for the Path to Awakening* (*Byang chub lam gyi sgron ma* ≈ *Bodhipathapradīpa*), a work of sixty-eight verses outlining the integration of three forms of discipline, including the vows of the *prātimokṣa*, bodhisattva precepts, and precepts of the way of mantras, within Mahāyāna and Vajrayāna practices and cultivations. Atiśa's *Lamp* became "one of the most influential of Indian texts received by Tibetans" and was "the model for mainstream Tibetan monastic Buddhism for the next nine hundred years."[163]

Atiśa does not explicitly discuss Madhyamaka in the verses of this work, but rather outlines (vv. 41–46) the necessity of insight (*shes rab, prajñā*) joined with means (*thabs, upāya*) for progress toward awakening. He then briefly outlines insight as the vision of the unproduced nature of things that is indicated by analysis that leads to nonconceptual cultivation (vv. 47–54). Atiśa concludes this segment by emphasizing that the world arises from conceptualization and that the total elimination of conceptualization is supreme *nirvāṇa* (vv. 55–56). Atiśa references Nāgārjuna's *Śūnyatāsaptati* and *Mūlamadhyamakakārikā* (v. 51) while outlining the importance of insight in the path, but does not provide a further discussion. Although the verses of the

Lamp do not fully articulate his understanding of the Middle Way, a discussion on Madhyamaka is referenced in Atiśa's autocommentary to the *Lamp*, the *Bodhimārgapradīpapañjikā*.[164]

The *Bodhimārgapradīpapañjikā* describes Atiśa's Madhyamaka as the Great Madhyamaka (*dbu ma chen po*) in its section on insight, a classification that he does not explain but that becomes polemical in later Tibetan scholasticism. Atiśa provides an overview of Madhyamaka but does not provide a clear, detailed description of his thought as he does in the *General Explanation*. Atiśa states at the end of the section on insight: "I did not write out the doctrine in detail" (*grub pa'i mtha' rgyas par ni ma bris te*, D281a4; Miyazaki 2007a, 78). Later in the text, Atiśa clarifies that he did not describe details of the path for "fear of too long a text" (*rnam gzhag ni/ gzhung mang 'jigs pas 'dir ma bris*, D285b). Moreover, the two realities, the basis of Atiśa's Madhyamaka exegesis in his *Satyadvayāvatāra* and *General Explanation*, are not discussed in the *Bodhimārgapradīpapañjikā*. Rather, the *Bodhimārgapradīpapañjikā* outlines Atiśa's Madhyamaka in a concise overview wherein he outlines the four great reasons (*gtan tshigs chen po bzhi*) to prove emptiness (D, 279a–80; Sherburne 2000, 228–35), a lineage of his Madhyamaka teachings and its textual sources (D, 280a–81a; Sherburne 2000, 237–41), a meditation on emptiness (D, 281a–82a; Sherburne 2000, 241–45), and proof statements from scripture (D, 283b–85a; Sherburne 2000, 253–61). Along these lines, Atiśa's Madhyamaka overview in the *Bodhimārgapradīpapañjikā* furnishes a summary of his thought consisting of thirty-three verses based on instructions from his teacher Bodhibhadra (D, 282a–83a; Sherburne 2000, 247–53). In introducing these verses Atiśa states that "[the following] verses are the meaning of all the texts previously cited."[165] These verses, nearly half the length of the *Lamp* itself, are important in that they provide significant information for understanding Atiśa's standpoint on a number of issues in his Madhyamaka thought (see the Appendix for an annotated translation of the verses).

Atiśa indicates in verses 1–10 of the *Bodhimārgapradīpapañjikā* that, upon analysis and by the analogies of eye disease and the sleep of ignorance, all appearances and philosophical tenets are false and mistaken. As mentioned, the ocular analogy is based on Candrakīrti and is explained in *A General Explanation*. Atiśa's standpoint is that all appearances are false, unreal, and constituted by ignorance. Verses 11–12 address Atiśa's standpoint on whether a continuum ceases or not, and Atiśa responds with one of the most famous verses in the history of Mahāyāna Buddhism that has been interpreted by both Madhyamaka and Yogācāra traditions. This verse 13, found in Nāgārjuna's *Pratītyasamutpādahṛdayakārikā*, *Abhisamayālaṃkāra* (vv. 5.21), and *Ratnagotravibhāga* (I.154), among other texts, states that "nothing is to be removed, nothing is to be established, reality should be perceived as it is, and one who sees reality becomes liberated." Mādhyamikas like Bhāviveka, Bodhibhadra, and Atiśa will cite this verse to indicate that nothing is removed from dependent-arising and nothing is added due to emptiness.[166] Yogācāra-based thinkers like Jñānaśrīmitra will argue that nothing is removed nor is anything added to the *tathāgatadhātu*. For Mādhyamikas, as Mathes (2008, 327) has observed, "the objects of all defilements, namely the Self of a person and phenomena, do not need to be removed, since they have been wrongly superimposed by virtue of all the defilements and therefore are nonexistent throughout beginningless time." Verses 14–16 of the *Bodhimārgapradīpapañjikā* emphasize that the Middle Way is beyond the extremes of existence and nonexistence and that it is not realized by means of inference. Inference, for Atiśa, merely serves the purpose of refuting the objections of non-Buddhists.

Atiśa then explains that one should follow the lineage of Nāgārjuna that he describes as the tradition of the Great Middle Way (*dbu ma chen po*) (v. 22), which goes beyond the four points of the fourfold tetralemma related to the binary of existence or nonexistence (v. 20) or of permanence and annihilation (v. 21). Atiśa's Great Middle Way does not involve mental constructs, as one becomes released from knowledge and objects of knowledge. Verses 23–25 clarify that the Great Middle Way is beyond reification (*samāropa*) and deprecation (*apavāda*). Atiśa employs the analogies of gold, sky, and water to indicate the purifying nature of emptiness. These analogies are mentioned in his *Madhyamakopadeśa* as well. They are also found in the *Mahāyanāsūtrālaṃkāra*, a text traditionally adhered to by the Yogācāra tradition. These analogies also occur in the *Ratnagotravibhāga*, a text that may be interpreted from a variety of perspectives. Atiśa interprets the analogies in the BMPP from a Madhyamaka perspective as he relates these verses to the special instruction of the Madhyamaka lineage consisting of figures such as Āryadeva, Candrakīrti, and Śāntideva (v. 26). Verses 28 and 29 connect this Madhyamaka lineage to the tradition of the *Perfection of Wisdom*, where all things have qualities related to the phoneme *A* in the Sanskrit language. The phoneme *A* is the initial letter of a syllabary found in Mahāyāna sūtras, particularly in the *Perfection of Wisdom*. The *Twenty-Five-Thousand-Verse Perfection of Wisdom* employs a syllabary that summarizes different qualities of *Perfect Wisdom* in which all the letters are permeated with the sound of *A*. Atiśa mentions that the first letter *A* is connected with all things being unproduced (*anutpāda*), unceasing (*anirodha*), and naturally in *nirvāṇa*. Verse 29 mentions the ultimate nonexistence of the three spheres of activity (*trimaṇḍala*) found in the *Perfection of Wisdom*, in which the agent, action, and object of an action are interdependent and lack any independent existence (*niḥsvabhāva*).[167] The end of verse 29 through verse 30 relates the tradition of the *Perfection of Wisdom* with the state of buddhahood that resides perpetually in the realm of reality (*dharmadhātu*) without any conceptual thought. As we know, Atiśa follows a tradition of Madhyamaka whereby buddhas, who no longer have any mind or mental qualities, are totally integrated in a nondual mode with the realm of reality. Therefore only advanced bodhisattvas who reside on the stages (*bhūmi*), after having achieved realization on that path of vision, have two phases in their course of practice. Such bodhisattvas directly realize reality while in meditative equipoise and then experience appearances constituted by latencies of ignorance in the postmeditative state. Vidyākokila and Bodhibhadra, as mentioned earlier, taught Atiśa this twofold mode of practicing the Middle Way. This tradition of Madhyamaka, based on the *Avikalpapraveśadhāraṇī*, is explicitly mentioned in these verses and also stated in Atiśa's *Open Basket of Jewels* and *General Explanation*. Atiśa's *Lamp* and its autocommentary, compositions that outlined his integration of mainstream Buddhist, Mahāyāna, and Vajrayāna precepts and path systems, were the most significant public works that he composed while in Tibet.

Atiśa's *Stages of the Path to Awakening* (*Byang chub lam gyi rim pa, *Bodhipathakrama*),[168] a previously unstudied but important work found among the recently published manuscript facsimiles of the *Collected Works of the Kadampas*,[169] briefly mentions the Middle Way. The broader text focuses on the ethics of karmic cause and effect, but in the context of instruction on pointing out a nonconceptual direct vision of the emptiness of one's own mind, Atiśa's *Stages* states:

> All dharmas are the mind, the mind itself is free from all extremes.
> The multiple various causes and effects of virtue and wrongdoing
> is unceasing, definitely free from the extreme of nihilism.
> Since whatever appears of the cause and effect of the round of rebirth and nirvāṇa
> is the nature of one's own mind, which is not at all established,
> it is definitely free from the extreme of permanence.
> Emptiness indivisible with cause and effect is the nature of one's own mind,
> free from the proliferations of extemes, the Great Middle Way.[170]

These two stanzas situate Atiśa's Great Middle Way between the extremes of nihilism and permanence based on the nonduality of emptiness and cause and effect. They occur in the *Stages* instructions on tranquility and insight, and were the type of instruction given to disciples of advanced spiritual capacity. Later Kagyüpa scholars such as Gampopa and Pakmo Drupa will describe them as Mahāmudrā, or Great Seal, teachings.

The Madhyamaka teachings in *Lamp* and its autocommentary provide an overview, and the brief stanzas in *Stages* mention his understanding of the Middle Way, but these works do not furnish details of Atiśa's Madhyamaka system of reasoning and practice. Although *Lamp* and its autocommentary were significant compositions under imperial support and *Stages* was an important work disseminated among close disciples, they were not the only record of Atiśa's teachings on Madhyamaka in Tibet. Atiśa gave numerous teachings on Madhyamaka throughout his remaining years in Tibet, and the record that we have of these teachings, as recorded in translations attributed to Atiśa himself and in commentaries by his Indian and Kadampa followers, furnishes a more complete picture of Madhyamaka in eleventh-century India and Tibet.

Conclusion

As documented in Atiśa's writings, lectures, and the commentaries of his Indian and Tibetan disciples, the specific points Atiśa emphasizes in presenting his understanding of the Middle Way will vary depending on the location—India or Tibet—and the capacities and presumptions of his students. Nevertheless, several general characteristics of his Middle Way thought and practice stand out across the spectrum of these writings and teachings.

Atiśa considered himself first and foremost a follower of Nāgārjuna. For him, Nāgārjuna was a towering figure of Buddhist culture who not only had great insight and realization but also sparked innovations in other areas such as political advice and medicine. Atiśa cites and comments on a number of texts attributed to Nāgārjuna—such as the *Bodhicittavivaraṇa*, *Mahāyānaviṃśikā*, *Pratītyasamutpādahṛdayakārikā*, and *Bhāvanākrama*—that he considered vital to understanding the Middle Way. These texts were not yet fully translated into Tibetan by the eleventh century and are often not included in the exegesis of Madhyamaka by later traditional Tibetan scholars or by modern scholars. Along these lines, Atiśa followed a commentary attributed to Nāgārjuna, the *Akutobhayā*, for his interpretation of verses found in the *Mūlamadhyamakakārikā*. Atiśa understood Nāgārjuna's devotional praises, such as the *Dharmadhātustava*, as complementary to Nāgārjuna's works emphasizing reasoning, such as the *Yuktiṣaṣṭikā*. Nāgārjuna was the principal master of Atiśa's Madhyamaka in this holistic and inclusive way of interpretation. Atiśa also considered Nāgārjuna to have lived for six hundred years and to have written esoteric Buddhist works. Moreover, Atiśa described his teachers' visionary encounters with Nāgārjuna as part of an ongoing revelatory lineage of Madhyamaka. Atiśa's Middle Way lineage descended from Nāgārjuna and Candrakīrti, and was influenced by his immediate teachers Vidyākokila, Avadhūtipa, and Bodhibhadra. Atiśa described Candrakīrti as living for four hundred years in India and as having been a direct disciple of Nāgārjuna.[171]

Atiśa's chronology of Nāgārjuna and Candrakīrti do not fulfill modern historicist expectations. Atiśa was an heir to the Indian Buddhist understanding, present from at least the tenth century onward, of accepting the writers of esoteric Buddhist works as being the same personages who composed much earlier texts of Madhyamaka. For instance, the second-century Nāgārjuna who wrote the analytical *Mūlamadhyamakakārikā* was considered by Atiśa to be the same Nāgārjuna who composed the esoteric *Pañcakrama* commentary to the *Guhyasamājatantra* of the ninth or tenth century (Wedemeyer 2010). Atiśa was obviously not a scribe concerned with documenting a chronological record of events and persons. Rather, as a full-fledged Buddhist scholar-practitioner living in one of the most creative periods of Indian Buddhist culture, Atiśa's understanding of the extraordinary long life spans of his Madhyamaka lineage predecessors fulfilled the cultural expectations of his time. In Indian Buddhist culture, the long life spans of holy persons such as Nāgārjuna fulfilled expectations derived from prophecies attributed to the Buddha, represented the extraordinary compassion of the long-lived holy person to reside in the world for a great amount of time based on the wishes of adherents, and perhaps most important, served as proof for the meditative attainments of the holy person.[172] In this way, Atiśa's emphasis on the long lives of his predecessors conveys the stature that he placed on the contemplative authority embodied in his Madhyamaka lineage.

This lineage represented a contemplative tradition of Madhyamaka that emphasized a cultivation of the resolution for awakening, the development of compassion, and the realization of emptiness leading to the inconceivable state of buddhahood. Although reasoning will have its place in Atiśa's system, he advocated a faith-based Madhyamaka that valued the instructions of the spiritual teacher and held predictions, prayers, and meditative cultivation in high regard. Atiśa's Middle Way synthesized the teachings of Bhāviveka and Candrakīrti, built on the basis of Nāgārjuna's teaching. In both India and Tibet, Atiśa pedagogically utilized the works of Bhāviveka, particularly his *Tarkajvālā* and *Madhyamakaratnapradīpa*, as an introduction to Madhyamaka, and then taught advanced students Candrakīrti's system as exemplified in the *Madhyamakāvatāra*.

Atiśa taught Madhyamaka based on the model of the two realities, that is, ultimate (*paramārtha*) and conventional (*saṃvṛti*) reality. Atiśa did not differentiate ultimate reality. He did not uphold the notion of multiple ultimate realities that the early Kadampa commentaries attribute to Yogācāra positions.[173] Atiśa also accepted that the ultimate is not within the range of the intellect. He did not at all accept a mental factor in the state of buddhahood. This understanding entailed that no continuum of wisdom was present in the awakened state either. Buddhahood, for Atiśa, was a nondual, ever-present state of reality. This understanding of buddhahood as a nondualistic fusion of gnosis and the realm of reality bereft of any mental elements became a major source of controversy between Atiśa, his Tibetan students, and subsequent generations of scholars in Tibet.

Conventional realities for Atiśa are mere nominal designations without real basis in either partless atoms or in a succession of dependently arising mental elements. Things are dependent designations that are based on varying levels of ignorance. In this way, conventionalities are false appearances that are unreal at any level. This understanding will be repeatedly evoked in the works of Atiśa and his followers through the metaphor of a person with eye disease who sees hairs in her line of vision. Conventional reality is a false projection of the eye disease of ignorance. Yet conventional realities are construed as either deceptive appearances that perpetuate *saṃsāra* or mere appearances (*snang ba tsam*) that are necessary falsities that may lead to awakening. Atiśa accepted the distinction between correct and incorrect conventional realities even though he considered conventional realities to be false and unreal. This distinction is structured within a framework of shifting perspectives as one progresses along the path in accord with Candrakīrti's *Madhyamakāvatāra*.

Atiśa did not accept that the Madhyamaka posits a thesis (*dam 'cha' ba* ≈ *pratijñā*), nor that a Madhyamaka concedes to the principle of common establishment. Atiśa advocated a Middle Way that utilized consequences to expose contradictions in the assertions of others. As outlined in chapter 4, Atiśa's understanding of Madhyamaka mentalism, based on sources he attributes to Nāgārjuna, does not make a hierarchical distinction between the ontological status of mind and objects in terms of either conventional or ultimate realities. In brief, objects and cognitions for Atiśa were considered imputations of mere appearance that are unestablished, dependently arisen, and dependently designated.

Atiśa did not emphasize the practice of debate in his contemplative system of Madhyamaka. As emphasized in part 2, valid cognition was considered as *hetuvidyā*, the "science of [justificative] reasons(/evidences)" (Eltschinger 2014, 4). For Atiśa, therefore, the primary purpose of valid cognition was to refute non-Buddhist opponents, but not for the realization of ultimate reality or of emptiness. Atiśa and his followers articulated how emptiness is realized in his *Special Instructions on the Midde Way* (*Madhyamakopadeśa*) and its related commentaries. These texts emphasize that realization of emptiness is based on special instructions from one's spiritual teacher and that realizing the two realities does not come about through "initial hearing and thinking." For Atiśa and his followers, direct realization of emptiness is not possible on levels of training that involve initial rote learning (*śrūta-mayī-prajñā*) and intellectual integration (*cintāmayī-prajñā*) of Buddhist teachings. Rather, the instructions for cultivating the Middle Way are given at the level of meditative cultivation (*bhāvanāmayī-prajñā*).

In Atiśa's meditative cultivation of the Middle Way, reasoning (*yukti*) signifies an internal Buddhist form of critical analysis that is distinct from *hetuvidyā*, the external epistemological devices used to defend Buddhist Dharma and defeat non-Buddhist opponents. For Madhyamaka thinkers like Atiśa, reasoning "designates, in a restrained sense, the fundamental principle or proposition that enounces the law of causality discovered by the Buddha that has issued by inductive reasoning, proceeding to a direct and personal experience."[174] This use of reasoning is part of the mastery of inner discourse and dialogue that leads to transformative judgments.[175] In this way, types of reasoning that were used in debate, such as consequences that expose contradictions, can also be understood as internal dialogue that counters discursive thought in meditation. The works of Atiśa and the Kadampa commentaries will repeatedly stress that appearances from causes and effects are perceived as real at the level of conventional reality until one reaches the path of vision. The *Madhyamakopadeśa* then mentions that, when the conventional as it appears is examined with the great reasons or reasonings, one gains an ascertainment that nothing, even minute things, are established. The great reasons refers to four reasons that Atiśa explains in his *Bodhimārgapradīpapañjikā*[176] and that are discussed in *A General Explanation*. Reasons, for Atiśa, are derived from the reasoning of dependent-arising, and all types of reasoning are accepted as consequences that nonimplicatively negate the intrinsic existence of things but do not negate the mere appearance of causes and effects. The mere appearances that arise from causes and effects are overturned through antidotes cultivated while practicing the path.

Atiśa's *General Explanation* specifies that the object of negation of reasoning is a conceived object (*zhen yul*) based on conceptualization that imputes things as either existent or nonexistent. The object negated by reasoning (*rigs pa'i dgag bya*) consists of conceptual thought that imputes objects as existing with its own-character (*rang gi mtshan nyid*). Atiśa's *General Explanation* offers an early distinction between objects negated by an antidote (*gnyen po'i dgag bya*) while implementing the path, and objects negated by reasoning (*rigs pa'i dgag bya*) when searching out the inherent existence of something. Atiśa also stipulates that the wisdom that arises from reasoning is not established. Atiśa compares the reasoning process to two sticks that, after rubbing together and generating a fire, burn up and become nonexistent. For Atiśa and his followers, reasoning is a conventional process that dissolves itself when seeking to establish the existence of an object. Analytical reasoning that dissolves itself is the meditative process producing the nonconceptual gnosis that comprises pristine awareness (*jñāna*).

Atiśa therefore maintained the use of scripture and reasoning (*yukti*) for realizing reality while rejecting speculative logical reasoning (*tarka*) and valid cognition for this purpose. Atiśa's understanding of scripture and reasoning and its relation to the lineage of spiritual gurus is found in *A General Explanation*, which states that Madhyamaka reasonings consist of nonimplicative negations that are special instructions for meditation directed toward nonverbal realization and are not based on argument or debate. These reasonings consist of consequences that expose contradictions applied with inferences known to others. They are utilized to refute mistaken assertions, even those in one's own thought processes, and lead to nonconceptual realization. According to Atiśa, Madhyamaka reasonings are derived from scriptures such as the *Perfection of Wisdom* and are based on the lineage of the Buddha's teaching of dependent-arising. At the level of discernment arising from meditative cultivation, ultimate reality is cognized introspectively by the meditator through interiorized awareness (*pratyātmavedya*).

Atiśa was an itinerant teacher whose instruction was influenced by historical conditions of time, place, and patronage. Atiśa's teachings on Madhyamaka in Tibet were shaped by the capacities and presumptions of his students in the context of mid-eleventh-century Tibet. The Tibetan Buddhist environment of this time was dominated by an overarching Eastern Vinaya ordination tradition and its curriculum of instruction. Moreover, the Tibetans had almost two centuries of prior affiliation with Madhyamaka teachings that were imported during the earlier Imperial Era in the late eighth century. The presumption of a prior affiliation is indicated in the history of Buddhism's transmission to Tibet and the concomitant development of the Tibetan internal classification of Madhyamaka doctrinal positions (Mimaki 1982).

Along these lines, the late-eighth-century Indian scholars Śāntarakṣita and his disciple Kamalaśīla were the most influential among the exegetes who brought Madhyamaka thought and practice to Tibet. A number of Tibetan histories mention that after the eighth-century great debate at Samyé Monastery, the Tibetan king decreed that Nāgārjuna's theory was henceforth to be accepted and the practice of the perfections, the *pāramitās*, to be observed.[177] Among the consequences of this purported imperial decree was the Tibetan Buddhist cultural norm of representing Madhyamaka as the pinnacle of Buddhist philosophical thought and practice. The earliest-known Tibetan doxographical treatises—the *Lta ba'i rim pa'i man ngag* written by Paltsek at the end of the eighth century and the *Lta ba'i khyad par* written by Yeshé Dé around the year 800—discuss the classifications Sautrāntika-Madhyamaka (*mdo sde pa'i dbu ma*) and Yogācāra-Madhyamaka (*rnal 'byor spyod pa'i dbu ma*). These Tibetan authors made a distinction in the Madhyamaka tradition based on the respective approach to entities on the conventional level of reality. Sautrāntika-Madhyamaka maintained the existence of external objects (*phyi don = bāhyārtha*) and Yogācāra-Madhyamaka maintained that there exist no objects external to the mind (Ruegg 1981, 59). These classifications were coined by Tibetan scholars in their organization and analysis of the reception of Buddhist thought into early Tibetan Buddhism.[178] In sum, the branding of Madhyamaka thought, based on identifiable trends within the exegesis of Indian Buddhist thinkers, not only shaped how Tibetans discussed Madhyamaka thought but also became a mode of creating "a hierarchy of prestige" with its concomintant political ranking of superordinate and subordinate (Smith 2004, 253). As Madhyamaka was considered the top and most prestigious form of Buddhist thought, subclassifications of Madhyamaka quickly developed in Tibetan history to account for what was deemed the most refined, subtle, and ostensively soteriologically efficacious form of Madhyamaka. This Tibetan way of thinking about Madhyamaka was already well in place when Atiśa initially arrived in Tibet in 1042.

As mentioned, Atiśa outlined an undifferentiated Madhyamaka tradition in his works. In *Open Basket of Jewels*, Atiśa emphasized that his teachings focus on the lineage of Nāgārjuna and defended "the Mādhyamika followers of Nāgārjuna" as having no faults. His *Bodhimārgapradīpapañjikā* documents a tradition that passed from Nāgārjuna through Āryadeva, Candrakīrti, Bhāviveka, and Śāntideva down to Bodhibhadra. Atiśa's *Bodhimārgapradīpapañjikā* briefly describes his vision of Madhyamaka as Great Madhyamaka (*dbu ma chen po*) in its section on insight (*shes rab*). Atiśa's *General Explanation* also claims that Great Madhyamaka represents the definitive understanding of Nāgārjuna's thought. In brief, Atiśa's classification of Great Madhyamaka represents his effort to differentiate the meaning of *prajñāpāramitā* as taught by Nāgārjuna as opposed to its meaning taught by the Yogācāra scholar Asaṅga.[179] Atiśa in his own writings, therefore, did not distinguish between the followers of Nāgārjuna, that is, Mādhyamikas. Madhyamaka, for Atiśa, was what Ruegg (1981, 30, 57, 59) has labeled "pure"

Madhyamaka, a designation that signifies a Middle Way tradition that is not differentiated based on features of individual doctrines upheld in the works of Indian Buddhist authors.[180]

In spite of Atiśa's stance, the eleventh century during and after Atiśa's lifetime was a fluid and dynamic era in both India and Tibet for classifications of Madhyamaka. A number of scholars have identified Māyopamādvayavāda and Sarvadharmāpratiṣṭhānavāda as a set of late Indian subclassifications of Madhyamakas employed by eleventh-century Indian and Tibetan authors. The subset Māyopamādvayavāda, translated as "the strand which maintains that [phenomena] are not two, inasmuch as they are like illusions" (*sgyu ma lta bu gnyis su med par smra ba*), is also known as "those who assert things to be like illusions" (*sgyu ma lta bur 'dod pa*) or "those who assert illusions established by reason" (*sgyu ma rigs grub pa*). The subclassification Sarvadharmāpratiṣṭhānavāda, or the "strand which maintains that all phenomena have no substratum whatsoever" (*chos thams cad rab tu mi gnas par 'dod pa*), was known as Apratiṣṭhānavāda (*rab tu mi gnas par smra ba*) for short.[181] These are the only two subdivisions of Madhyamaka found in extant Sanskrit sources, and they are utilized by Atiśa's junior contemporary Maitrīpāda (ca. 1015–86) in his *Tattvaratnāvalī*. The subdivisions are also found in a number of Indian texts preserved in Tibetan translations.[182]

However, the earliest layer of Kadampa commentaries, including the *Collection on the Two Realities*, the *Collection of Special Instructions on the Middle Way*, and *Potowa's Middle Way*, do not mention any divisions or subdivisions within Madhyamaka traditions. Atiśa's Indian disciple Prajñāmukti (Tib. *shes rab thar pa*), commenting on the *Madhyamakopadeśa*, mentions in passing "wisdom that abides like an illusion" (*sgyu ma lta bur gnas pa*, D.121b), as well as the term "nonabiding Madhyamaka" (*rab tu mi gnas pa'i dbu ma*, D. 22a). It is not clear if Prajñāmukti is referring to the classification of a Madhyamaka tradition or is making a descriptive epithet. Along these lines, among the early biographies of Atiśa attributed to his lead disciple Dromtönpa Gyalwai Jungné (2014a), Atiśa is described in verses as having a view that "upholds the Madhyamaka of mere appearance" (*lta ba snang ba tsam gyi dbu ma 'dzin*, 49.22), "conversing in the Madhyamaka of nonabiding" (*mi gnas pa'i dbu ma'i gsungs gleng pas*, 50.1–2), and "drawing out the view of Great Madhyamka" (*lta ba dbu ma chen po drangs gyur kyang*). These verses appear to contain poetic descriptions of the attributes of Atiśa's Madhyamaka by one of his closest disciples that have not yet evolved into doxographic classifications. An early Kadampa commentary that does make doxographic distinctions, *Sherab Dorjé's Explanation of Atiśa's Entry to the Two Realities*, the latest among the early Kadampa commentaries I have examined, posits four types of Madhyamaka:

Madhyamakans who accept external objects, Yogācāra-Madhyamaka, Things Are Like Illusions Madhyamaka, and Mere-Appearance Madhyamaka (*snang tsam dbu ma ba*).[183] This commentary will equate Mere-Appearance Madhyamaka with the Great Madhyamaka (*dbu ma chen po*) of Nāgārjuna, a term, as mentioned above, that is emphasized by Atiśa himself. Notably, none of the works mentioned above utilize the later Tibetan neologisms Consequentialist (*thal 'gyur pa*, **prāsaṅgika*) or Autonomist (*rang rgyud pa*, **svātantrika*).

In sum, the works of Atiśa and his early followers in this volume present the pure Madhyamaka of one of the greatest Indian Buddhist masters to come to Tibet. We see in the early Kadampa commentaries the exegesis of devout Buddhist contemplatives who closely followed in the footsteps of their Indian Madhyamaka master Atiśa. In addition to the primary works of Atiśa translated in chapters 1, 2, and 5, a number of the Kadampa commentaries translated in chapters 3, 4, and 7 more than likely represent oral teachings of Atiśa that were put in writing in the late eleventh century. All of these works clearly demonstrate an active lineage of teaching Candrakīrti that Atiśa brought with him to Tibet. These teachings were disseminated before the rise of the early Kadampa monastery of Sangphu and its debating traditions that, particularly beginning in the twelfth century, placed emphasis on the merger of Madhyamaka and epistemology and that would come to shape all later Tibetan Buddhist scholasticism.[184] The proximity in time and place of these commentaries to Atiśa and his teachings in Tibet represents a rare example in the history of Tibetan Buddhism of a pure Madhyamaka lineage directly transmitted by an Indian Buddhist master to Tibetans. In this way, the following texts and commentaries are like rare jewels that, until now, comprised a forgotten legacy of Indian and Tibetan Buddhist Madhyamaka.

Part 1
Lineage Masters, the Mind of Awakening, and the Middle Way

1. Atiśa's *Open Basket of Jewels*: *Special Instructions on the Middle Way*

ATIŚA'S *Open Basket of Jewels: Special Instructions on the Middle Way* (*Ratnakaraṇḍodghāṭamadhyamakopadeśa*)[185] is one of the primary works among his collected writings and perhaps the most extensive of his extant writings composed in India. The text outlines a number of significant features regarding his theory and practice of Mahāyāna Buddhism in general, as well as his understanding of Madhyamaka in particular. The term *ratnakaraṇḍodghāṭa* refers to an open *karaṇḍa*, a "basket or covered box," made of jewels (*ratna*) or containing jewels.[186] In this instance, the jeweled box or box of jewels is the text itself, containing over 120 citations from sūtras and tantras, as well as śāstras and hymns attributed to seminal Buddhist figures such as Nāgārjuna and Āryadeva. The citations of these sources indicate that Atiśa had access, possibly in a temple or monastic library or depository, to a great number of Indian Buddhist texts when he composed this work.

Date and Place of Authorship

According to the colophon of the canonical version of *Open Basket of Jewels*, the text was written in the great temple of Vikramaśīla, under the patronage of King Devapāla. The colophon explains that Atiśa composed the work at the requests of his Tibetan disciple and translation partner Tsultrim Gyalwa. The colophon also mentions that the translation was redacted by Atiśa, Tsultrim Gyalwa, and the layperson Tsöndrü Sengé. Therefore the text must have been composed before Atiśa left for Tibet circa 1040, as Tsöndrü Sengé passed away in Nepal on the journey to Tibet (Chattopadhyaya 1981, 302). This information also demonstrates the pedagogical relationship Atiśa had with his Tibetan students in India, in that Atiśa composed *Open Basket of Jewels* as an introduction for them to understand his Madhyamaka lineage, its source texts, and its primary practices.

Structure and Content

The text centers on the special instructions (*man ngag* or *gdams ngag*) on the Middle Way (*dbu ma*). As Kapstein (1996, 275) notes, *gdams ngag*, "instruction," is understood in connection with meditational and yogic practice and "refers essentially to the immediate, heartfelt instructions and admonitions of master to disciple concerning directly liberative insight and practice." In this instance, the special instructions provide guidance in developing insight derived from meditative cultivation (*bhāvanā-mayī-prajñā*), the third level of insight that comes after initial rote learning and study (*śrūta-mayī-prajñā*) and intellectual integration (*cintāmayī-prajñā*) of Buddhist teachings. Rather than placing emphasis on Madhyamaka reasoning to realize emptiness (*śūnyatā*), this type of instruction centers on cultivating the mind to rest in the nonconceptual experience of reality.

The Middle Way special instructions that Atiśa imparts are permeated with the values of the Vajrayāna or tantric phase of Buddhism under the socioeconomic influences of the South Asian Pāla dynasty (750–1150). During the Pāla dynasty, Buddhist formations were centered on the scholarly study and practice of Mahāyāna discourses (*sūtra*) and technical digests (*śāstra*), supported and cultivated in tandem with Vajrayāna consecrations, rituals, and blessings. The integration of Mahāyāna discourses with Vajrayāna literature is well illustrated in the text: Atiśa cites over forty-six Mahāyāna sūtras and ten tantras as authoritative for his vision of the Middle Way. As the annotations to the translation illustrate, Atiśa's style is to abbreviate citations from sūtras and tantras. Comparison with the canonical versions of these texts often indicates that Atiśa modifies the meaning of verses to help illustrate the rhetorical points that he wishes to emphasize.

Based on Miyazaki's outline (2007), the text may be divided into six sections: (1) preliminary instructions, (2) instructions on the mind of awakening, (3) the activity of buddhas and bodhisattvas, (4) a listing of previous important Indian Buddhist masters, (5) the teachings of Nāgārjuna and his buddhahood, and (6) a brief discussion regarding the practice of secret mantra.

The initial instructions provide a condensed set of guidelines for meditation on emptiness. These instructions include advice on cultivating an attitude of renunciation and the proper motivation to engage in meditation, which should be based on compassion for beings by remembering their kindness to oneself over the course of previous innumerable lifetimes. The instructions at this point state that

> when the yogi internalizes this cultivation and cultivates the ultimate mind of awakening, then through cultivating the conventional

mind of awakening one will stabilize both minds of awakening, [the two minds each] having the essence of great compassion and emptiness.

The idea is that with the fusion of the conventional mind of awakening to the ultimate mind of awakening—the luminous, unproduced reality of emptiness—one will then stand firm in a state of awareness that has the features conducive to attaining the awakening of buddhahood.

Atiśa then discusses cultivating the conventional mind of awakening in thirteen subsections. The subsections are not discussed in sequential order and include understanding the mind of awakening's (1) cause of arising, (2) condition, (3) nature, (4) aspect, (5) training, (6) apprehension, (7) guarding, (12) increase, (13) benefits, (8) cause of dropping, (9) fault of relinquishing, (10) benefits of causing in others, and the (11) fault of interrupting the mind of awakening in others. Atiśa combines citations of sūtras, tantras, works of Nāgārjuna, Asaṅga's *Bodhisattvabhūmi*, and Śāntideva's *Bodhicaryāvatāra* as proof texts to illustrate how the conventional mind of awakening is properly cultivated. This presentation differs slightly from, yet also complements, the presentation on the mind of awakening found in Atiśa's *Bodhimārgapradīpapañjikā* composed later in western Tibet. In this regard, the importance that Atiśa places on the proper cultivation of the mind of awakening within his instruction on Madhyamaka and in his outline of the Mahāyāna path is indicated by the details of his discussion and the wide range of sources that he cites to justify his guidelines.

The third section of *Open Basket of Jewels* outlines the salvific activity of buddhas and bodhisattvas based on their altruistic compassion for sentient beings. Atiśa provides an interesting excursis on the buddha/bodhisattva Mañjuśrī on this topic, identifying him as a primordial buddha (*ādibuddha*) and connecting him to several different cycles of tantric teachings. Atiśa also mentions the activity of Avalokiteśvara, the activity of his predecessors, and autobiographical statements reflecting personal advice that he received in Somapurī and Bodhgayā to cultivate the mind of awakening based on love and compassion. He also summarizes the structure of the path to buddhahood based on the *Daśabhūmikasūtra* and the *Ratnagotravibhāga*. Following this brief outline of the path, Atiśa then demonstrates through the citation of multiple proof texts that, in his view, buddhahood is a state of realization constituted by a nondual fusion with the realm of reality and does not have any mental element whatsoever, not even the mental element of nonconceptual gnosis. In this regard, Atiśa cites multiple texts by Nāgārjuna to illustrate how the miraculous activities of a buddha are performed effortlessly and without any mental elements in relation to the capacity of beings to be guided. In this section Atiśa responds to those who criticize the Madhyamaka followers of Nāgārjuna and emphasizes that meritorious action and faith in Nāgārjuna's teachings are necessary for progress on the path.

In the fourth section Atiśa lists Buddhist masters of the past that he considers noteworthy. The list of scholars is organized by subject matter in an increasingly hierarchical order that places Madhyamaka scholars at the top. The list is not based on chronology, so there is no need to question Atiśa's scholarly aptitude, as some scholars have recently suggested. Placing scholars of logic—Dignāga and Dharmakīrti—lower than the placement of Vaibhāsika, Sautrāntika, Yogācāra, and Madhyamaka scholars indicates that, for Atiśa, the science of epistemology and logic (*hetuvidyā*) was "a profane secular science that is common to the Buddhist and other Indian non-Buddhist schools such as the Naiyāyikas" (Krasser 2004, 130). Likewise, in Atiśa's *Dharmadhātudarśanagīti*,[187] a text that describes in poetic stanzas the characteristics of Buddhist and non-Buddhist schools of thought, the term *pramāṇa* is only mentioned in relation to Sāṃkhya and Tīrthika doctrines. Notably, Atiśa does not list subclassifications of Madhyamaka nor group Madhyamaka texts according to the so-called six collections of reasoning (*rigs tshogs drug*).

The listing of Buddhist masters culminates in laying out the works of Nāgārjuna in the fifth section. Nāgārjuna is foundational for Atiśa, and he cites Nāgārjuna over sixty-five times in his collected writings (Mochizuki 2015). The list of over forty-five of Nāgārjuna's works in the *Open Basket of Jewels* is significant in that the list provides the "most extensive Indian outline" (Brunnhölzl 2007, 30) known of works attributed to Nāgārjuna. In addition to listing the works of Nāgārjuna composed for various groups such as ministers, kings, and doctors, Atiśa lists the foremost of Nāgārjuna's works, that is, the *Mūlamadhyamakakārikā, Vigrahavyāvartanī*, and *Śūnyatāsaptati*, in the same manner as Candrakīrti's *Yuktiṣaṣṭikāvṛtti.*

The second part of section 5 places emphasis on why Nāgārjuna is actually a buddha, based on extensive scriptural citations that authenticate the Buddha's predictions for Nāgārjuna's buddhahood. Atiśa follows his teacher Bodhibhadra and the *Madhyamakaratnapradīpa* in placing emphasis on authoritative predictions for Nāgārjuna, but Atiśa provides much more extensive citations of the proof texts than do his predecessors. Atiśa then describes Nāgārjuna's maturation body (§5.3) and aspiration body (§5.4), solidifying the authority of Nāgārjuna with oral traditions of Atiśa's lineage masters' visionary encounter with Nāgārjuna.

Open Basket of Jewels concludes with a concise summary on the practice of secret mantra (*gsang sngags*). Atiśa briefly indicates that the practice, for those with sharp faculties, is the quickest way to achieve buddhahood even in one's present lifetime. Atiśa emphasizes, as he does later in the *Bodhimārgapradīpapañjikā*, that receiving a teacher (i.e., *vajrācārya*) empowerment is sufficient to engage in tantric practice and that the empowerments of Tantric consecration involving sexual rituals (i.e., *guhya* and *prajñājñāna*) are off-limits to ordained monastics who uphold vows of celibacy. This abridged treatment on tantric consecration is significant in that it demonstrates Atiśa's position on the monastic practice of Buddhist tantra while in India and before his journey to Tibet. In his abrupt treatment on secret mantra, Atiśa mainly gives importance to gaining a proper consecration, keeping the vows and commitments, and visualizing one's chosen deity along with the recitation of mantras.

The emphasis throughout the *Open Basket of Jewels* is on transmission and authority through the lineage of teaching coming from Nāgārjuna. Atiśa cites Nāgārjuna throughout the text (over twenty times, including the first four citations) and devotes individual sections of the text to Nāgārjuna's teachings (§5), predictions of his buddhahood (§5.2), and his bodies of awakening (§§5.3, 5.4). The emphasis that Atiśa places on Nāgārjuna points toward the visionary inspiration of Nāgārjuna and the continued authority and validity of Nāgārjuna's teaching, as argued by Wedemeyer (2007). The text places emphasis on the oral transmission of these teachings from "mentor's mouth to mentor's mouth" (*guru vaktrād guru vaktraṃ*), unbroken from the time of Śākyamuni Buddha's awakening.

The practices outlined by Atiśa in this text integrate the cultivation of insight (*prajñā*) and compassion (*karuṇā*) through training a bodhisattva to develop the mind of awakening (*bodhicitta*) at both ultimate and conventional levels. The ultimate mind of awakening—the birthless, luminuous, nonconceptual realm of reality equated with emptiness—is cultivated during the meditative state, and the conventional mind of awakening is practiced during the postmeditative state. In this manner the two levels of the awakening mind are integrated and stabilized, having the essence of emptiness and compassion (*śūnyatākaruṇāgarbha*).[188] A snapshot of instructions for this integrated cultivation is found in section 2.5, where Atiśa states:

> Regarding the training, first the mind did not come from anywhere and will not go anywhere at the end. [The mind] does not abide anywhere and is without color and without shape. [The mind] does not arise from the beginning nor does it cease at the end. [The mind is] empty of inherent existence and has the nature of clear light. One should recall this again and again.
>
> On the other hand, one should stabilize through accustoming

> that mind of awakening to love and compassion. One should completely purify [the mind] and stand firm, being continuously mindful of each moment of thought with mindfulness, awareness, thoughtfulness, and conscientiousness.[189]

This integrated mind of awakening is protected (§2.7) and increased (§2.12) while the bodhisattva advances through the ten stages (*bhūmi*), as outlined by the *Daśabhūmikasūtra*. In the course of the training, the bodhisattva alternates between cognizing the nonconceptual spacelike realm of reality in meditative stabilization and viewing things as illusions in the postmeditative state. The alternation ceases at the stage of buddhahood, where for Atiśa, based on numerous citations from the hymns (*stava*) of Nāgārjuna (§3.2), the purified realm of reality directly and constantly fuses with the *dharmakāya* without any mental element or gnosis (*jñāna*) existing at all.

Open Basket of Jewels: Special Instructions on the Middle Way

by Dīpaṃkaraśrījñāna

In the Indian language: *Ratnakaraṇḍodghāṭamadhyamakopadeśa*
In the Tibetan language: *Dbu ma'i man ngag rin po che'i za ma tog kha phye ba*

Homage to the venerable Mañjuvajra.
Homage to the Three Jewels.

1 [Preliminary Instructions]

I will write the special instruction of the lineage of Ācārya Nāgārjuna.[190]

As for this, an individual who remembers the suffering of beginningless saṃsāra, of oneself and [other] beings without exception, should not be attached even to an object [the size] of a mere sesame seed, entirely discarding like a drop of spit all activities and objects of the world. First, one who keeps the pure uncorrupted three vows of morality that have been pledged, who possesses the wisdom of hearing and reflection, who has compassion naturally, who disregards his own life and body for the sake of the holy Dharma, should search for a holy individual having the special instruction of the lineage of Ācārya Ārya-Nāgārjuna, and please [him] for a long time. Since [one] is a beginner, one should reside [where it is] easy to obtain a livelihood, in a great, vast land, or great city, or isolated place at the edge of a mountain [rock], and so forth. Sitting on a soft and smooth seat in front of the images of the Three Jewels, [one should reflect] as follows: "When I survey the five types of sentient beings—[those] born from an egg,[191] [those] born from moisture, [those] born miraculously, [those] possessing form and [those] not possessing form, and those possessing consciousness and those not possessing consciousness—[I see that they] are all my mothers. These mother-like [sentient beings] produce and accumulate polluted actions on account of their own [selfish] purposes, and with the maturation of those [actions], experience much suffering."

Ācārya Nāgārjuna states:

> The intelligent, having seen the sufferings of the three realms [caused] by the faults of conceptual thought and habitual tendencies, should pull out from the abode that is saṃsāra.[192]

Ācārya Nāgārjuna also says:

> As I have brought suffering upon sentient beings living in the prison of existence who are tormented by the fire of the afflictions, since all [of them] previously were dear friends and parents who provided great benefit, now it is suitable to make [them] happy.[193]

By understanding [their] kindness, generate the mind of awakening with the four immeasurables,[194] [thinking, I will] "liberate them [from suffering], set them free, relieve their sufferings, and make them reach nirvāṇa."[195] For this purpose accumulate the two collections [of wisdom and merit].

The immediate sphere of space before one, not separate from the dreamlike mind, is filled with the Three Jewels like a heap of mustard seeds.[196] Remembering the seven mental perceptions and the seven holy [things], utter words of remembrance, and by means of the six antidotes,[197] having made the proper posture of body, prostrate, make offerings, confess transgressions, rejoice, request [the wheel of the teaching] to be turned, make supplication,[198] go for refuge, generate the mind of awakening, offer the body, take the vow, make firm the promise of the vow to remain in the path of the Mahāyāna, and dedicate all of these to great awakening. All of this turns into the realm of reality (*dharmadhātu*), the place of offering, the assembly of offerings—all of these. [Now] first of all, when [one] examines where these come from and where they go, [one realizes that] they do not go anywhere [and] they do not come from anywhere. Since all inner and outer things are exactly like that, all [of them] appear as a false emanation of illusion in one's own mind. These [things] with false appearance belong to the body and also belong to the mind. The mind is without color, without form, by its own-nature clear light, and unarising from the beginning. The wisdom of individual analysis (*so sor rtog pa'i shes rab*) itself turns into clear light. Amidst that, consciousness does not absolutely exist, does not at all abide, is not at all established, is unproduced in any aspect, and is totally pacified of elaborations. One should reside as long as one as is able in the appearanceless *vajrasamādhi*, [like] the sky from which all signs of dust are gone, like the midday sky with a noontime autumn sun. If the mind becomes distracted through the force of not being used to regular practice, stand firm through summoning suchness. In other sessions one should do the same. Many sessions should be done for a short time. At the time of becoming accustomed, when the practice becomes a bit more firm, one should do longer and longer [meditative sessions]. One should pacify with the individual antidotes to the five obstacles [of śamatha],[199] and after that open the eyes, saying, "Eh ma ho! The *dharmadhātu*, without anything existing, appears everywhere. This is amazing. These [things], the nature of one's own mind, an illusory emanation, appear like an unreal apparition and are as false as they appear. Appearances are exemplified by the eight similes of illusion[200] and are not intrinsically real." Then, having offered prayers of aspiration, release slowly [from] the sitting position and take to molding statues and so forth, doing as much virtuous activity as one can. Accordingly,[201] one should make effort to accumulate the two collections in six sessions [of cultivation]. Meditate on *śūnyatā* at the time of sleep and go to sleep in the [sphere] of that. After that, at the last session, think to wake up with the mind of awakening arising from love and compassion. These [above activities] generate the ultimate mind of awakening. Food should be divided into four portions.[202]

Again, Ācārya Nāgārjuna states:

> The mind of ultimate bodhicitta should be produced by the power of cultivation for a bodhisattva who does the activity by way of secret mantra.[203]

In this way, when one strives with devotion for a long time and without stopping, [it will] automatically produce compassion toward sentient beings. Ācārya Nāgārjuna states:

> Accordingly, when yogis cultivate emptiness, the mind no doubt will become joyful for the welfare of others.[204]

Moreover,

> The ultimate, birthless from the beginning, when deeply realized by the mind will effortlessly produce compassion for [those] sinking in the mud of saṃsāra.

Likewise, when the yogi internalizes this cultivation and cultivates the ultimate mind of awakening, then through cultivating the conventional mind of awakening one will stabilize both minds of awakening, [the two minds each] having the essence of great compassion and emptiness.[205] The *Vairocanābhisaṃbodhi* states:

> Awakening, the characteristic [of which is similar to that] of space, is the abandonment of all conceptual thought (*rtog pa*).[206]

The *Prajñāsaṃcayagāthā* says:

> There is not even a mere particle of something to be obtained. One should not apprehend awakening as real. This should be demonstrated to beginners.[207]

The *Śatasāhasrikāprajñāpāramitāsūtra* states:

> I have completely awakened in the essence of awakening without obtaining anything at all.

The *Dharmasaṃgīti* states:

> In this regard, what little desire of a bodhisattva is there? He is one who does not desire even awakening. What is the satisfaction? He is one who does not excessively long for the mind of awakening.

This meaning is indicated in many other precious sūtras as well as tantras of secret mantra. The *Guhyasamājatantra* states:

> Due to the sameness of the essencelessness of things, one's own mind—free of all entities, without aggregates (*skandhas*), elements (*dhātus*), sense spheres (*āyatanas*), and subject and object[208]—[is] unproduced from the beginning, the very nature of emptiness (*śūnyatā*).[209]

The *Aṣṭasāhasrikā* [*prajñāpāramitā*] says:

> Śāripūtra, whatever is thought, that is no thought; thought by its nature is clear light.[210]

As Ārya Nāgārjuna has indicated:

> The mind has not been seen, and will not be seen, by all buddhas. What will one see [of something that has] the nature of having no nature?[211]

The Venerable Āryadeva states:

> When one becomes accustomed to ascertaining the mind with wisdom, then the mind will not be seen.[212]

The *Dharmasaṃgītisūtra* states:

> Devapūtras! Moreover, even the desire to understand the mind of awakening is the activity of Māra.[213] Apprehending the mind as real while seeking out the illusory mind is to be confessed by whomever produces the mind of unsurpassable awakening.

One who has been accustomed to the Great Vehicle for innumerable previous lives, and has a well-purified [mental] continuum and sharp mental faculties, knows the conventional mind of awakening itself as producing the ultimate mind of awakening, and since [that mind] has both great compassion and emptiness, one stands firm in the emptiness endowed with all excellent features (*rnam pa thams cad kyi mchog dang ldan pa'i stong pa nyid*).[214] Intending this meaning, Ācārya Nāgārjuna states:

> The buddhas teach that the awakened mind is not obscured with notions of a "self," "skandhas," and so forth, [but] has the characteristic of being empty [of such notions].[215]

Well then, if someone asks, "How [is the mind of awakening produced)?" [the reply is:] One should produce it conventionally, like a magically created individual or emanated individual arousing the mind of awakening. As is said in the *Sāgaranāgarājaparipṛcchāsūtra*:

> King of Nāgas! Due to one dharma, bodhisattvas will be quickly awakened in unsurpassable fully complete awakening! What, one may ask, is that one dharma? It is the mind of awakening that does not let go of all sentient beings.[216]

This sūtra teaches that it is necessary to generate the [mind of awakening].

2 [The Mind of Awakening]

Regarding that mind [of awakening], one should be knowledgeable about the (1) cause of arising, (2) condition, (3) nature, (4) aspect, (5) training, (6) apprehension, (7) guarding, (12) increasing, (13) benefits of (8) cause of dropping, (9) fault of relinquishing, (10) benefits of causing the arising in another, benefits of rejoicing in the arising in others, and (11) bad fault of causing interruption in the arising of [the mind in] others.

2.1 [The Cause of the Mind of Awakening]

In this regard, the cause is having the sign of the excellent lineage (*gotra*). As the *Sūtra of the Prophecy Spoken Truthfully* (*Bden par smra ba lung bstan pa'i mdo*) states:

> (1) With admiration for the extensive, [one] is without admiration for the inferior. (2) By having great compassion naturally, [one] possesses virtuous qualities. (3) By abandoning polluted friends, [one] is nourished by the spiritual friend. (4) By doing whatever one says, [one] is undeceitful. (5) By pleasing the buddhas wandering in the world, [one] has joy. (6) By being without low activities of body, speech, [and] mind, [one] abandons sin. (7) By [this] faultless superior thought, [one] has trust in the sacred vow. (8) By nonattachment to [one's own] tastes, [one] has the nature of pleasing everyone. (9) One is free from the empowerments of Mārā. (10) By accumulating roots of virtue, [one] performs activities well. (11) Since it is in the sphere of great compassion, one has compassionate love for sentient beings. (12) By freely giving necessary things, one has little attachment to anything.[217]

Ācārya Ārya-Asaṅga states:

> There are four causes: lineage, a spiritual friend, compassion, and enduring the suffering of saṃsāra. [218]

2.2 [The Condition for the Mind of Awakening]

As for the condition [of generating *bodhicitta*], there are two: (1) the condition of application (*prayoga*, *sbyor ba*) and (2) the condition of thought (*āśaya*, *bsam pa*).

[The Condition of Application]

In regard to that, the conditions of application are that one should (1) accumulate the provisions [of merit], (2) purify the [mental] continuum, and (3) perform the superior going for refuge [in the Three Jewels].

[Accumulating Provisions]

(1) To accumulate the provisions, one should perform the seven-limbed *pūjā* three times during the day and three times during the night; memorize, read, and recite the profound sūtra of the Perfection of Wisdom; make extensive offerings to the Three Jewels; make gifts and feast offerings for the saṃgha; give ordinary feasts; give great, extensive charity to the protectorless; and give great extensive sacrificial cakes to spirits.

[Training the Mental Continuum]

(2) Train the mental continuum as before: read, recite, and memorize the profound sūtras, perform the seven-limbed *pūjā*, recite the *Triskandhaka*,[219] and confess transgressions with texts such as the *Karmāvaraṇapratiprasrabdhisūtra* and *Suvarṇaprabhāsasūtra* and so forth.

[Superior Going for Refuge]

(3) The superior going for refuge is distinctively noble (*ārya*, *'phags pa*) in seven excellent aspects: (1) excellence of the individual person,[220] (2) excellence of the Three Jewels as objects of refuge, (3) excellence of time, (4) excellence of thought, (5) excellence of application, (6) excellence of advice, and (7) excellence of benefits.

In this regard—the excellence of the Three Jewels as refuge objects—the object of refuge of the Inferior Vehicle is mentioned in the *Abhidharmakośa*:

> One who goes for refuge in the Three Jewels, goes for refuge in the qualities of the Buddha, the Saṃgha, and the Dharma, and likewise one takes refuge by going for refuge in [the qualities] of nirvāṇa.[221]

Here, the distinction of the Three Jewels is in three aspects: (1) the Three Jewels of ultimate truth, (2) the Three Jewels in front of oneself, and (3) the Three Jewels of realization.[222] One should ask a spiritual teacher for the extensive meaning of this.

Still, I will describe only the excellence of the advice. By means of remembering the excellence of the Three Jewels and their good qualities, one does not relinquish the Three Jewels even for the sake of one's life and body. By means of going for refuge over and over again and remembering [their] great kindness one should, always or from time to time, offer even as much as a full bowl of pure water, as well as offer the first portion of food and so forth. Whatever you do, whatever your purpose, make requests to the Three Jewels but abandon other worldly methods. One should perform activities in this manner for other sentient beings as well. As for advice of the Common Vehicle: since one goes to refuge in the Buddha, one should not make homage and so forth to worldly deities; one should follow this advice for each of the Three Jewels.

[The Conditions Necessary for the Mind of Awakening to Arise]

The *Jñānamūdrasūtra* and the *Karuṇāpuṇḍarīkasūtra* state:

> [Of] (1) the mind generation for the awakening of a buddha, (2) the mind generation at the time of the destruction of the holy Dharma, (3) the mind generation when one has seen the suffering of sentient beings, (4) the mind generation of bodhisattvas, (5) the mind generation when one has made good offerings and worship, (6) the mind generation when one has seen other deities, and (7) the mind generation when one has seen the body of a tathāgata, the first three are the actual mind of awakening.[223]

The *Daśadharmakasūtra* also states:

> [There is] (1) the mind generation when one has been urged by buddhas and bodhisattvas and so forth, (2) the mind generation when one has seen the good qualities of the mind of awakening, (3) the mind generation when one has seen the suffering of sentient beings, (4) the mind generation when one has seen the excellence of the buddhas and bodhisattvas.[224]

[Five Conditions for the Thought of Awakening]

From the *Mahāyānasūtrālaṃkāra*:

> There are five conditions: (1) the power of friend, (2) the power of cause, (3) the power of the root, (4) the power of hearing, and (5) the

> power of being accustomed to virtue. Some of them are firm and some are not firm.[225]

[FOUR CONDITIONS AND FOUR POWERS]

Ācārya Asaṅga speaks of four conditions and four powers.[226] The four conditions are: the mind generation when one has seen the excellence of the tathāgatha, the mind generation when one has seen the benefits, the mind generation at the time of the destruction of the holy Dharma, and the mind generation when one has seen the suffering of sentient beings. The four powers are: the power of cause, the power of activity, one's own power, and the power of others.

In this way, when one thoroughly accumulates the causes and conditions, one will thoroughly generate the mind of awakening.

2.3 [The Nature of Arising]

The nature of arising: the wish (*'dun pa*), the desire (*'dod pa*), and the aspiration (*smon pa*) are synonyms.[227] As Ārya Maitreya states:[228]

> Generation of mind is a desire for perfectly complete awakening for the sake of others.[229]

The essential nature is to perceive the distinctive object of consciousness, which is an intelligence that possesses similarity with compassion and wishing. Like the good foundational earth that produces without exception the crops of [virtuous] white dharma[s], the wish is the mind of awakening that is like earth.

2.4 [The Distinctive Aspect]

The distinction or the particularity of the aspect itself is that it is not even covered by any kind of fault, like deceiving and so forth, and is stainless. For example, like the pure gold that is without the faults of rust, stones, earth, and so forth, that mind itself is a pure thought, like gold. As for the extensive meaning of this, the *Akṣayamatinirdeśasūtra*: states:

> Venerable Śāradvātiputra: Regarding the mind of awakening, what are the aspects of generating the mind like that? [Bhagavan:] Kulaputra, by being unmixed with the Inferior Vehicle, [that mind] arises in the aspect of purity.[230]

Thus it is taught extensively and so forth [in the sūtras].

2.5 [Training the Mind]

Regarding the training, first the mind did not come from anywhere and will not go anywhere at the end. [The mind] does not abide anywhere and is without color and without shape. [The mind] does not arise from the beginning nor does it not cease at the end. [The mind is] empty of inherent existence and is of the nature of clear light. One should recall this again and again.[231]

On the other hand, one should stabilize through accustoming that mind of awakening to love and compassion. One should completely purify [the mind] and stand firm, being continuously mindful of each moment of thought with mindfulness, awareness, thoughtfulness, and conscientiousness.[232]

2.6 [Keeping the Mind of Awakening]

As for keeping the mind of awakening, [this consists of]: (1) the four ways of not letting go of sentient beings, (2) the eight thoughts of a holy individual, (3) the ten masteries of the inner method, (4) the six masteries of the outer method, including the exchange of self and other, as well as equalizing self and others, and (5) dedicating with the *Ten Great Blessings of the Vajra Banner*[233] and the *Bhadracaryā*.

[Not Giving up on Sentient Beings]

In this regard, not giving up on sentient beings entails: (1.1) not letting go of the mind of beings who are beneficial to oneself, (1.2) not letting go of sentient beings who harm oneself, (1.3a) directly suffering, (1.3b) not giving up the cause of suffering and so forth, and (1.4) not giving up on sentient beings in general.

[Not Letting Go Those Who Benefit Oneself]

Regarding that, not letting go those who benefit oneself means to not let go the mind that knows the kindness [of beings] and repays their kindness. As Ācārya Nāgārjuna states:

> Sentient beings—who have resided in the prison of existence suffering with the fire of the defilements since beginningless saṃsāra—were previously my parents. Since they provided great benefit, [I]

> need to make the same repayment. They have been made to suffer by me, now it is suitable to make [them] happy.[234]

One should look at the sūtras for the extensive meaning of this. One needs to understand the benefits that the father, mother, relatives, friends, and so forth of this life have provided and repay [their] kindness. Accordingly, if one will not do so, the downfall of "not to repay a good turn"[235] will occur.

[Not Letting Go Beings Who Do Harm to Oneself]

Not letting go of sentient beings who do harm to oneself means to not mentally relinquish one's control over [one's] actions. As it is said,

> When answered politely, the supreme individual of the Jambudvīpa continent responds politely, and even when receiving a rude response answers in a considerate manner.

The *Aṣṭasāhasrikāprajñāpāramitā* states:

> A bodhisattva, even when faulted by others, does not become disturbed in mind, does not harm them, and does not fight with them. Even in the case of killing, one does not become hostile. One does not have hatred toward any sentient being. Bodhisattvas should firmly produce [this] disposition.

As is further taught:

> Bodhisattvas should perceive all sentient beings as mother, father, sons, and daughters. As one wishes happiness for oneself, [one] should apply happiness to other beings as well. One should liberate from suffering all beings without exception, not giving up on any sentient being. Even if they cut one's body into one hundred pieces, one produces love and compassion and does not have malice toward them.[236]

From the venerable Āryadeva:

> When fierce harm occurs, one should understand that as [one's own] previous karma.

If it is the case that one will not do so, rudimentary downfalls and faults will occur, such as

> "not listening to another's confession," "striking out in anger," "blaming others," "abandoning confession through discussing other's faults,"[237] "disdaining those who are angry," "abusing with abusive replies," and so forth.[238]

[Not Letting Go Beings Who Suffer]

One does not let go of beings who are certainly suffering from heat, cold, hunger, thirst, and so forth, the immediate [suffering of heinous actions],[239] and so forth, and degenerate vows. When seeing them tormented with various sufferings, one does not relinquish the mind of compassion. As the Venerable Āryadeva states:

> I have heard that an iron wheel twelve yojanas long revolves on the head; as soon as the mind of awakening arises, it is dispelled.[240]

Ācārya Aśvaghoṣa says:

> Just as a mother produces anguish for a son tormented by illness, likewise a bodhisattva's love exists especially for those who are inferior.[241]

Ācārya Bhāviveka also states:

> At the time of seeing the sorrowful who are overwhelmed with grief, compassion arises from the bottom of the heart and [one] provides benefit to them.[242]

One should look in the sūtras for the extensive [meaning].

[Not Letting Go Beings Who Have the Cause of Suffering]

Not letting go of sentient beings who have the cause of suffering and so forth means to not let go of the mind that has loving compassion. Undermining precepts, performing heinous actions, cutting life, and committing various transgressions—one should do the opposite from these. The *Smṛtyupasthānasūtra* states:

> Whoever, having received good conduct, does not protect [it] well: that [person's] flesh and bones will certainly burn in the destructive [hell] of Memarmu.

And:

> The *ārya* who obtains and stands firm in desirable qualities, when seeing the breaking of morality, sheds tears, [thinking,] "What rebirth will come of this?"[243]

Also, Ācārya Nāgārjuna says:

> May I always dissuade all at once all beings of any world who intend to engage in negativity, without doing them any harm.[244]

[Not Letting Go of Sentient Beings in General]

Generally, not to let go of sentient beings means not to relinquish the mind of love. The *Pratibhānamatimahāyānasūtra* states:[245]

> Bodhisattvas should view all sentient beings like a son. One should view them like one's own body.[246]

The *Mahāyānasūtralaṃkāra* says:

> Like a pigeon who has supreme love for her young, embracing them closely to herself, a bodhisattva has love like that for sentient beings who suffer.[247]

The *Vidyottamamahātantra* also states:

> Bodhisattvas do not desire their own happiness, are not even bothered by their own sufferings, and suffer because of the sufferings of others. If others are happy, then bodhisattvas are joyful.

The *Śrī-Vajraḍākiṇītantra* and the *Śrī-Paramādibuddha* state:

> For as long as he can, the best wise person bestrides (*gnas*, *adhiṣṭhāna*) existence and for that long he accomplishes unequaled good for sentient beings, without passing beyond suffering.[248]

One should look in the sūtras for the extensive [meaning of this point].

[Eight Special Thoughts of a Holy Individual]

The eight special thoughts of a holy individual: (1) Alas! If possible may I be able to make sentient beings be without the suffering of birth, and likewise (2) without the suffering of aging, (3) the suffering of sickness, and (4) the suffering of death. (5) I will deliver beings who are not delivered and (6) free those who are not free. (7) I will free them from powerful suffering, and (8) I will lead to *nirvāṇa* those who have not yet reached *nirvāṇa*. One should continuously be mindful, moment by moment, thinking these thoughts.

[Mastery of the Inner Method]

Mastery of the inner method: Make others' suffering one's own and clear away the suffering of others with one's own suffering. Exchange (*brje ba*) others' suffering with one's own happiness; always grieve (*gdungs pa*) on account of others' suffering. As the *Vidyottamamahātantra* states:

> Bodhisattvas are not attached to their own happiness; they are not even bothered (*mi mjed kyang*) by their own sufferings. [Their] minds suffer with others' suffering; when others are happy, bodhisattvas are joyful.

One confesses others' transgressions as one's own, rejoices in others' virtue as if it were one's own, rejoices through making one's own virtue the virtue of others, and dedicates having made one's own virtue the virtue of others.

[Mastery of the Outer Method]

The mastery of the outer method includes the four means of gathering disciples,[249] the five objects of knowledge,[250] the ten masteries, the six perfections, the four immeasurables, and so forth. [The following activities] mature all sentient beings without exception: nurturing, terrifying, seducing, conquering, building, and pleasing with presents.

[Dedication with Recitation]

One should avoid relinquishing beings by [reciting] the *The Ten Praises of the Noble Vajra Victory Banner* (*rdo rje rgyal mtshan gyi bsngo ba bcu pa*), *the Bhadracaryāpraṇidhāna*, the *Smon lam nyi shu pa* (*Twenty Aspirational*

Prayers) composed by Ācārya Nāgārjuna, and the eleven verses that occur in the *Salty River Sūtra* (*Ba tshwa chu klung*), and so forth. As the *Kāśyapaparivarta* states:

> Even for the sake of one's life, without speaking lies, one should stand firm with the superior thought that is undeceiving to sentient beings. One should generate the perception that individuals who have the mind of awakening are teachers. One should mature sentient beings who are ready to become established in unsurpassable awakening, but not *śrāvakas* or *pratyekabuddhas*.[251]

Likewise, the *Avalokiteśvaraparipṛcchā* states:

> Kulaputra, bodhisattvas who immediately generate the mind of awakening should train in seven qualities and should not have sexual enjoyment even with mental perception, not to mention joining together the two sexual organs. One should not take up with a nonvirtuous friend even in dreams. With a mind like that of a bird, one should be completely without grasping. With mastery in skill and wisdom, without grasping at pride and the "I," abandon [conceptions of] existence and nonexistence, and firmly cultivate the *samādhi* of emptiness. Pacifying erroneous conceptuality, do not take joy in saṃsāra. In brief, a mind in accordance with mindfulness and introspection will not be separate from conscientiousness.[252]

[And:]

> Befouled by offenses due to the fault of lacking awareness, [conscientiousness] does not stay in the memory of a mind that lacks awareness, like water in a leaky jar.[253]

Again:

> Through mindfulness, awareness, and mental introspection one does not separate from conscientiousness.[254]

This is taught by Ācārya Śāntideva.

Through not forgetting in each moment of thought and by having continual mindfulness, one should apprehend the mind of awakening. In the case where one has not acted appropriately—

> not giving wealth or Dharma, being stingy (*ser sna*) to suffering, protectorless [beings], not offering [Dharma] to those [who] seek Dharma, neglecting to do service [for the] sick, not being a friend in need, doing little for the purpose of sentient beings[255]

—that is how major transgressions and faults will occur.

2.7 [Protecting the Mind of Awakening]

Completely protecting the mind of awakening: One should guard against forgetting, undermining, and giving up [the mind of awakening]. As the *Kāśyapaparivarta* states:

> Causing those without regret to have regret; deceiving the preceptor, teacher, and objects of generosity; not having the superior thought in abundance; deceiving and agitating sentient beings; and insulting individuals who have generated the mind [of awakening].[256]

As the *Sarvapuṇyasamuccayasamādhi* states:

> Son Without Desire! With [these] four qualities [one] will forget the mind of awakening: excessive conceit, not respecting the Dharma, disregarding the spiritual friend, and saying bad words; and four further: making acquaintance with *śrāvaka*s and *pratyekabuddha*s, admiring (*mos*) the Inferior Vehicle, having anger toward and slandering (*sdang zhing skur pa 'debs pa*) bodhisattvas, and pretending not to know the Dharma (*chos la dpe mkhyud byed pa*); and four further: being deceptive [to someone else], deceiving [with one's own faults], being duplicitous to the guru, and having great attachment to profit (*rnyed pa*) and honor (*bkur sti*); and four further: not understanding evil action, [being] obscured with the obscurations of karma, [having] no fortitude for the altruistic attitude, and [being] without skillful means and wisdom. These will cause [one] to forget the mind of awakening.[257]

The Sāgaranāgarājaparipṛcchā states:

> King of Nāgas! That wisdom of all-knowledge is free from the twenty-two bad paths and wrong paths: (1) not being free from the mentality of *śrāvaka*s and not being free from the mentality of *pra-*

> *tyekabuddhas*, (2) [having] pride and excessive conceit, (3) deceiving others and self-deception, (4) conversing with nihilists, (5) [engaging in] erroneous practice, (6) being frightened by birth, (7) being swollen with pride, (8) [engaging in] argument, (9) [having] passionate attachment, (10) [having] hatred, (11) [being] ignorant, (12) [encountering] obstacles of karma, (13) [encountering] obstacles of [powerful] dharmas, (14) praising oneself and demeaning others, (15) not wanting to share the Dharma, (16) being forgetful, (17) [consorting with] sinful friends, (18) [having] a hateful attitude to the spiritual teacher, (19) not being harmonious with the six perfections, (20) [having the extremes] of nihilism and permanency, (21) [performing] the four means of conversion with nonmastery of skillful means, and (22) not separating from all sins. With these [one] will forget the mind of awakening.

Also, the *Gaṇḍavyūha* states:

> Hey! Sons of the Victorious One, [I] do not see a greater karmic retribution than negative thoughts occurring among bodhisattvas.

Likewise, one should look in sūtras that speak extensively on this, such as the *Śraddhābalādhānāvatāramudrā*.

2.8 [The Causes for Downfalls to Occur]

The causes for downfalls to occur: being without a lineage, having little compassion, not being frightened by the misery of saṃsāra, being under the influence of evil friends, thinking that highest awakening is far away, being overpowered by Māra, serving an individual of the Inferior Vehicle, making effort in the texts of the Small Vehicle (*theg pa chung ngu'i gzhung*), abandoning sentient beings, uttering insults and having hostility toward bodhisattvas, and not abandoning a position unharmonious with the mind of awakening. Furthermore, being without awareness, without conscientiousness, without humility, and having many defilements.

2.9 [The Negative Consequence of Letting Go]

The negative consequence (*nyes dmigs*) of letting go: If the sentient beings of the trichiliocosm became arhats and [one] were to kill all of them, and also perform the five heinous actions, the sin of letting go would be even greater.

Moreover, the number of dust particles that pervade the limits of space is known by the Buddha, but the measure of this sin—just this—cannot be known by the Buddha. [One] should look in the sūtras, *Bodhicaryāvatāra*, and so forth for the extensive meaning of this.

2.10 [The Benefit of Causing the Arising in Another of the Generation of the Mind of Awakening]

As for the benefit of rejoicing in the generation of the mind [of awakening] in others, [there is this] from the *Aṣṭasāhasrikāprajñāpāramitā*:

> The measurable number of all the world realms is knowable, but as for the benefit of making others enter into generating [the mind of awakening] . . .

—one should look at Mahāyāna sūtras and the *Bodhicaryāvatāra*.[258]

> Even the buddhas and bodhisattvas of the ten directions are not able to cognize. The measure of merit made by rejoicing in the generation of the mind of awakening in others is unknowable.[259]

One should look in the sūtras for the extensive [meaning].[260]

2.11 [The Negative Consequence of Interrupting Others' Generation of Mind]

As for the negative consequence of interrupting others' generation of mind, the *Kuśalamūlasaṃparigraha* [states]:

> Śāradvatiputra, a person who desires to interrupt the generation of mind or causes interruption . . . will have no opportunity for *nirvāṇa*.

Likewise, the *Aṣṭasāhasrikāprajñāpāramitā* states:

> It is a greater sin than performing the five heinous actions and killing as many arhats as there are sands of the Ganges River [in] three thousand world systems.

Also, the *Bodhicaryāvatāra* states:

> Whoever interrupts and hinders the merit of generating the mind of awakening becomes inadequate for the purposes of sentient beings; limitless are the bad migrations of that [person].[261]

One should look in the sūtras for the extensive meaning.

2.12 [Increasing the Mind of Awakening]

Increasing of the mind of awakening: That mind itself, the mind of awakening, increases in three aspects: the mind of awakening [increases by way of] the discipline of vows *(saṃvara-śila)*, the discipline of collecting virtuous dharmas (*kuśaladharmasaṃgrāhaka-śila*), and the discipline of effecting the aims of sentient beings (*sattvārthakriyā-śila*). For example, like the gradual increase of the waxing moon, this mind will also increase.

> Moreover, since it is superior by [virtue of] its vast and extensive purity, causes great benefit, and is virtuous itself, the pure thought is the superior thought (*adhyāśaya*).[262]

This is taught in the *Mahāyānasūtrālaṃkāra*. The superior thought is like the beginning of the moon (*zla ba tshes*) and is also called the engaging mind of awakening.

[Three Aspects of Conduct]

The *Śīlapaṭalam* [in Asaṅga's *Bodhisattvabhūmi*] states that conduct has three aspects: naturally endowed conduct (*prakṛti-śila*), accustomed conduct (*abhyasta-śila*), and conduct [based on] accepting vows (*samātta-śila*).

[Naturally Endowed Conduct]

Regarding naturally endowed conduct: All sentient beings have a single lineage, possess the essence of the tathāgata (*tathāgatagarbha*), and possess the Mahāyāna lineage. Although one may have the fortune to succeed when practicing, nevertheless, [the lineage] remains covered with four types of faults. As the *Mahāyānasūtrālaṃkāra* states:

> Briefly, the fault of lineage is expressed in four aspects: being accustomed to defilements, having bad friends, being destitute, and being under the power of another.[263]

This said, the individual who possesses the lineage naturally has great compassion and naturally possesses in the mental continuum the virtues of the perfections called "naturally endowed conduct."

[Accustomed Conduct]

Accustomed conduct has three aspects: from a past life up to this life one has great familiarity with the Great Vehicle, has moderate familiarity, or has been accustomed from immeasurable previous lives. For this reason, Maitreya states:

> Venerating the buddhas, producing roots of virtue under them, being protected by the spiritual friend: this is the vessel who hears [the teaching].
>
> Engaging in proper worship and respect of the buddhas, and practicing giving, morality, and so forth: that one is understood by the holy ones as a vessel.[264]

[Discipline]

In this regard, [there is] the discipline based on properly accepting vows: the preceptor (*slob dpon*), having examined well by way of three examinations, should bestow discipline according to the level of the vessel. For the aforementioned individual, the preceptor should give the [vows related to] the four great basic downfalls of the Prātimokṣa, along with the accompanying lesser [restrictions], the four similar downfalls of the Mahāyāna, and the forty-six minor downfalls. For the moderate individual [i.e., an individual with moderate familiarity with Mahāyāna], one should bestow the vows of that moderate individual. On top of that, [one] should bestow [vows related to] the eighteen root downfalls of the *Ākāśagarbha* and so forth, and the fourteen faults mentioned by Ācārya Śāntideva. For the third individual, in addition to these, the four hundred disciplines that are taught in the *Saptaśatikā* and the precepts of the bodhisattva path of accumulation that are taught in the Mahāyāna sūtras should be maintained. As for one on the path of accumulation, the discipline of vows is foremost. For the person on the path of preparation, the discipline that collects virtuous qualities is foremost. For the person who is beyond the worldly path, the discipline that achieves the purpose of sentient beings is foremost. If you calculate (*rtsis na*) in the continuum of a single individual, the individual at the time of the small path of accumulation should make effort in the precepts of the first [type]. The individual at the time of the moderate path of accumulation should make efforts in the precepts of the moderate [individual]. The third individual should make effort in the precepts of the third [type]. Intending the aforementioned accustomed discipline, the *Prasādaprabhāvanā* states:

> The bodhisattva-follower with predispositions for faith in the Mahāyāna follows in this way: whether moving, sitting, sleeping, sick, drunk, or crazy, one will always have faith in the Mahāyāna. The bodhisattva, adhering faithfully to the Great Vehicle in this life as well as future lives, will—even if one has forgotten the mind of awakening in those lives—not be in an inferior situation or have a mind that has inferior fortune. [The bodhisattva] will not even be tempted to identify with *pratyekabuddhas*, *śrāvakas*, and evil friends. How can one be tempted by other *tīrthikas*? When one comes across even a small condition for faith in the Mahāyāna, [one] will swiftly and continuously produce strong faith in the Mahāyāna for that purpose. Therefore, inclinations to faith in the Mahāyāna will increase in later lives, up until unsurpassable fully complete awakening.[265]

2.13 [The Benefits of the Mind of Awakening]

In this regard, the benefits of the mind of awakening have two aspects: (1) the benefits of aspiration (*praṇidhāna*) and (2) the benefit of engaging (*prasthāna*).

[The Benefits of Aspiration]

The benefits of aspiration are limitless. In brief, [the mind of awakening] does not cut off the continuous lineage of the Three Jewels in the world. It is the seed or cause of all virtuous actions, destroying sin, uplifting from downfalls, and rendering nonexistent all interruptions, epidemics (*rims*), devils (*mi ma*), and so forth. The *Kuśalamūlasaṃparigraha* states:

> Śāradvatiputra, firstly, the heap of merit of the mind of awakening is not merely a common or minor matter. Accordingly, one is not able to proclaim [the merit] even in a hundred, a thousand, or a hundred thousand eons. How could one know the measurement of the merit of bodhisattvas' generation of the mind [of awakening]?

The *Aṣṭasāhasrikā* states:

> The merit is greater in someone generating the mind of awakening for one day, half a day, or a finger snap than [in] someone possessed of substantialist views creating for an eon the roots of merit [equal to] the sands of the Ganges River.

Also, the *Bodhicaryāvatāra* states:

> If those who are bound in the prison of saṃsāra generate the mind of awakening for one moment, they will be proclaimed a Son of the Sugata, and will be venerated by gods and men in the world.
>
> Seizing this impure form [the mind of awakening], transform it into the priceless image of the Buddha-gem. Grasp tightly the supreme elixir, the mind of awakening, which must be thoroughly transmuted.[266]

[The Benefit of Engaging]

The benefit of the engaging mind is stated in the *Bodhicaryāvatāra:*

> Although the result of the mind that aspires for awakening is great within the cycle of existence, it is not a source of uninterrupted merit like the mind that engages.[267]

And further,

> From that moment on, an uninterrupted stream of merit, equal to the sky, constantly arises, even when one is asleep or distracted.[268]

Regarding the benefits of both of these, one should look for the extensive meaning in the *Bodhicaryāvatāra*, the *Gaṇḍavyūhasūtra*,[269] and the *Bodhisattvabhūmi* and so forth, as well as in the sūtras.

3 [Buddhas and Bodhisattvas]

3.1 [The Activities of Buddhas and Bodhisattvas]

Buddhas and bodhisattvas do not have any extensive activity other than delivering beings from saṃsāra. Ācārya Nāgārjuna states:

> The excellence of the purpose of others is accepted as the foremost result [of awakening]. Other than buddhahood itself and so forth, these other [benefits] are asserted as the result of this goal [i.e., awakening].[270]

Therefore, the body of a buddha, [the interior body of] of awareness (*jñāna*), qualities, and activities are completed from effecting only that—the aim of others. [It is explained] as follows:

> In other previous inexpressible [numbers of] kalpas, the Bhagavat, the Protector of the Śākyas, was awakened as the tathāgata, the arhat, the fully complete buddha called Crown of Indra (Indraketu), and presently will awaken again (*yang sangs rgyas pa*). Likewise, Ārya-Avalokiteśvara, in other countless kalpas, completely and fully awakened as a fully complete buddha, arhat, tathāgata called Dharma Banner (Dharmadhvaja). Now in Sūkhavati with the Bhagavan Amitābha from the evening till the dawn of nirvāṇa, Avalokiteśvara will become awakened.[271]

And:

> In previous kalpas equal to ninety-two times the [number of] sands of the Ganges River, the venerable Vajrapāṇi became awakened as the Tathāgata Lamp of Wisdom (*ye shes sgron ma*). Now, after the present fortunate kalpa (*bhadrakalpa*) itself, he will awaken as the Tathāgata Diamond Power (*rdo rje rtsal*).[272]

In this regard, [there is] no beginning and no end to saṃsāra, [and] Ārya-Mañjuśrī also has no beginning. He is the primordial buddha (*ādibuddha*).[273] [He is] the gnostic mind of all the buddhas of the three times without exception. All buddhas are grouped into six families. At the heart of the six families, Vajratīkṣṇa (*rdo rje rnon po*, i.e., Mañjuśrī)[274] and so forth dwell as *jñānasattvas*. Samantabhadra Mañjuvajra is the chief deity of the *Guhyasamājatantra*. Mañjuśrī is the foremost deity of the Yamāntaka maṇḍala,[275] in which Śrī-Vajrabhairava [a wrathful form of Mañjuśrī] appears. Heruka [Mañjuśrī] is made chief maṇḍala deity of the *Abhidhana*, explanatory tantra of *Śrī-Cakrasaṃvara*, and [he is known as] Lion Sound, Kumuda, Good Youth, Mañjuśrīkumarabhūta, and so forth. [Mañjuśrī] appears according to the aspiration of the spiritual trainee.[276] Currently, the *Mañjuśrikṣetravyūha-sūtra* teaches that he will be awakened in the eastern direction. Buddhas and bodhisattvas do not relinquish sentient beings until reaching the end of *saṃsāra*; they perform extensive activity of body, speech, and mind, the twenty-seven extensive activities, the thirty-five extensive activities,[277] the three great manifestations and so forth, continuously delivering the sentient beings of *saṃsāra* from *saṃsāra* without exhausting [their number]—because *saṃsāra* is without end. In order to clarify this meaning, Ārya-Avalokiteśvara, from his commitment to draw out sentient beings from *saṃsāra*, has the Bhagavan Amitābha dwelling at the top of his head. [This is] due to the time his head split open when perceiving the realm of sentient beings. All buddhas and bodhisattvas accept immeasurable hardships on their bodies for the purpose of all sentient beings. In this way, even Bhagavan Śākyamuni, [as shown] in the *Jātaka* tales, renounced [the world], practiced great giving, discipline, patience, energetic diligence, and concentration, and accepted immeasurable hardships on his bodies for three countless [kalpas], for the sake of sentient beings. The *Salty River Sūtra* (*Ba tshwa chu klung mdo*) states:

> Wives, son, kingdom, great power, flesh, blood, fat, body, and eyes I have given based on the happiness of others.[278] Anything beneficial to sentient beings is the highest worship for me. If one does harm to sentient beings, one does harm to me.[279]

[This] and other statements were spoken [in] eleven stanzas.

Even recently in this Jampudvīpa [continent], the head of Ācārya Nāgārjuna was given away, Ācārya Āryadeva gave his eye, Ācārya Matṛceta Aśvaghoṣa gave [his] body to a tigress, and my guru, the Brahman Jitāri, died right at the time of giving his broken leg to a tigress.[280] Those [great] beings have trained in the mind of awakening that is moistened with love and compassion. The best bodhisattva produces the mind of awakening very deeply on the path of preparation (*prayogamārga*). In this way, the *Bodhisattvabhūmi* states:

> On the *bhūmi* of conceptual understanding before the path of vision, one who is firm in the roots of virtue produces the mind of awakening.[281]

Therefore, since bodhisattvas need to cherish others, one should train the mind of awakening by exchanging self and others. Previously, when sitting in the forest of Somapurī, I was taught directly by[282] Lokeśvara—"Kulaputra, if desiring the goals of others, to be quickly awakened you must make effort in expanding and training the mind of awakening." Having said [this, he] disappeared. Furthermore, while circumambulating at Vajrāsana (Bodhgayā), the Venerable Tārā and the Venerable Wrathful One said, "Kulaputra,[283] if you desire to be awakened quickly, endeavor in the mind of awakening." Further, when I was staying in Vajrāsana (Bodhgayā), [someone shouted] from a window, "Bhadanta, if you desire to train in the mind of awakening, you should be accustomed to love and compassion." Also, the venerable guru[284] Serlingpa taught: "Āyuṣman, you should train the mind of awakening that arises from love and compassion. If [you] do not train in that, Yogi of Bengal, [you] will not succeed."

The mind of awakening is the root of all qualities of the Great Vehicle: it is the cause, it is the seed. The *Śrī-Vairocanābhisaṃbodhitantra* states:

> The cause of omniscience is the mind of awakening; its root is great[285] compassion.[286]

With mindfulness and mental introspection on each moment of thought, [one] should continuously generate the mind of awakening with love and compassion. As it is said in [the *Vairocanābhisaṃbodhi*] tantra:

> When it has degenerated, there are four qualities that are unsuitable for regaining [this mind of awakening]: giving up the mind of awakening, causing harm to sentient beings, abandoning the holy Dharma,[287] and stinginess.[288]

Regarding this, if the mind of awakening does not degenerate, then it is possible to regain the three [other qualities]. If the [mind of awakening] degenerates, it will not be possible to regain [it] even if the other three [qualities] have not degenerated. Thus one should master the cause of arising and one should be very firm in holding, developing, purifying, and increasing it. For the extensive meaning of this, one should look in the *Maitreyāvatārasūtra*, the *Sāgaranāgarājaparipṛcchā*, the *Sarvapuṇysamuccayasūtra*, the *Ākāśagarbhaparipṛccha*, and so forth.

First, one should protect, as one protects the eyeball, the three trainings of pledged vows. The training of discipline should be protected like the tail of a yak. Having realized cause and effect, one should not waste [time] because death will definitely [come] quickly. Life within Jampudvīpa is without certainty. Now, since it is the degenerate time, there is no ability to remain for a long time.[289] One should recollect death. One [should] meditate [that] since all inner and outer phenomena are caught by the three types of impermanence,[290] [they] quickly and definitely will be nonexistent. One should purify with the four powers[291] all downfalls and obscurations. Moreover, generating the mind of awakening is purifying:

> Entering into the Great Vehicle, even *śrāvaka*s are turned away from harm; by generating love and compassion[292] [one] loves sentient beings like a son. This purifies previously committed transgressions.

Ācārya Nāgārjuna taught this.

Purify by reciting particular *dhāraṇī*s, and confess the downfalls [listed] in the *Karmāvaraṇapratiprasrabdhi*, the *Triskandhakasūtra*, and so forth. A sūtra teaches that it is purifying when one understands that downfalls and obscurations themselves are unproduced. It is imperative to view in a purifying manner when cognizing the equality of all things. Because buddhahood arises from relying on sentient beings, sentient beings should be construed as foremost. The *Madhyamakatarkajvālā* states:

> Those who are bound by the noose of expecting the result will search for and choose the field of giving. Others who, for the purpose of pacifying the suffering of the sick, hungry, and so forth, give while not counting the recipient, will cognize the equality [of] dharma[s]. As is said in the sūtra in another [way]: "By one dharma a bodhisattva will quickly become fully awakened, engaging the equalizing mind to all sentient beings and not discriminating. [If] that bodhisattva [thinks,] 'the Three Jewels are the field of my good qualities but animals and so forth are not,' he will not cognize the equality of *dharmatā* (suchness). With that [view], the Three Jewels and the guru are the good field of giving, but animals and so forth are not. Like a seed planted in a dry, dusty field, that mind will not grow into the quality of a bodhisattva." By teaching thus, the bodhisattva makes firm the superior thought. With the mental continuum moistened by compassion, [bodhisattvas] do not discriminate the field of giving.[293]

The *Tarkajvālā* teaches this.

[This is] also taught in the *Verses That Satisfy Sentient Beings*—drawn from the *Salty River Sūtra*—by Ācārya Nāgārjuna, and taught in other sūtras of the great vehicle. As King Indrabhūti states:

> With equanimity to all beings, one should generate a perfect mind.[294] Anybody who abides without equanimity [in regard to sentient beings] will not generate the wisdom that liberates in the beginning, middle, and end.[295]

One with dull faculties, a fresh beginner—who has not trained the mind, who is not familiar with compassion, and who has little compassion—discriminates the field of giving. As taught extensively in the Dharma commentaries, sūtras, and tantras, a beginner, when not in contemplation, makes sure to attain mental introspection and mindfulness in all activities on the path of preparation (*prayoga-mārga*). For even as long as a finger snap, one should not reside with vulgar individuals. [One should] abandon foolish speech and give sacrificial cakes continually to hungry ghosts. One should read and recite the *prajñāpāramitā* sūtras. Until attaining supernatural knowledge (*abhijña*), one should not teach the Dharma. Not relinquishing sentient beings or abiding in emptiness, one should have those qualities that have been discussed and are blessed by the Sugata. Even at the time of the dream-mind one should not be separate from compassion. One should [perform] all temporal [activities] of the preparatory path as taught in the *Ratnamegha*. Definitely one should satisfy other [beings]. With little desire and sufficient knowledge, one should be disciplined and peaceful. One should suppress the eight worldly dharmas.[296] One should possess and strengthen the ten virtues.[297] One should have little grasping or attachment to any object. One should increase the antidotes for the subsidiary defilements and [root] defilements on account of the equality of all dharmas.[298] When seeing others' suffering, if one is ordained, one should give away nonmonastic necessities. If one is a layperson, one should give without attachment to necessities.

> My body and wealth, and the virtues I have produced in the three times, should be given without attachment for the benefit of all sentient beings.[299]

The venerable guru Avadhūtipa states:

> With sharp eyes, examining one's own faults, be like a blind man when examining the faults of others; frank and without conceit, one should always meditate on emptiness.[300]

The Guru Nāropa taught:

> One should exchange self and others with direct and indirect compassion. For whatever reason, cherish sentient beings [more] than oneself.

Since the bodhisattva needs to cherish others more than himself, he should exchange self and other. The mind of awakening, compassion, and love are also essential for secret mantra [practice]. Among the fourteen root downfalls of the *Mūlāpattisaṃgraha*:

> The Victorious One taught abandoning love for sentient beings as the fourth [downfall]. Abandoning the root of [the] Dharma, the mind of awakening, is the fifth [downfall].[301]

One should go one hundred yojanas to avoid slandering others and making sinful conditions for others:

> The bodhisattva who is ordained should go more than a hundred yojanas from any place where there is a dispute. If she does not go, the bodhisattva degenerates.[302]

One should utilize as much as one can the six perfections. One should recollect the thirteen dharmas of the path of accumulation, the seven noble treasures,[303] the six recollections,[304] the four means of gathering disciples, and the sixteen cognitions of the holy individual. In particular, one should recollect the eight illuminations of the bodhisattva.[305] One should recollect the seven faults of *saṃsāra* as taught by Ārya-Nāgārjuna and the seven[306] faults related to the impermanence of *saṃsāra* taught by Ārya-Asaṅga. One should understand and employ the antidotes for the faults of the five sense desires. Do not do anything that is not Dharma. To effect the purposes of sentient beings, indirectly and directly recollect love and compassion. Think: "Alas! I will take these [beings] out of *saṃsāra*. Alas! What can one do for these [beings]?" One should recollect [this] again and again.

> Those who desire to ascend definitely to this Buddha Vehicle should have an equanimous mind regarding all sentient beings, perceiving [them] as mother and father, and stand firm[307] with a mind of love and beneficial thoughts. Without anger, and frankly, one should speak gentle words.[308]

Thus one should follow accordingly. If one does not quickly dedicate even a tiny virtue, [the situation] will become like the legends of Apalāla (Sog ma med) and Āṭavaka ('Brog gnas).[309] In this manner, for a long time and with humility, the bodhisattva should continuously practice the teachings previously explained, even when not in contemplation, [and] at the time of meditative stabilization, should cultivate the space-like *vajra-samādhi* previously explained. When one has a little clarity toward the ultimate mind of awakening, and does not feel one's own body as existent,[310] one should pacify the defilements a little, and view all worldly activities and verbal conventions, all inner and outer objects, as like misty vapor (*ban bun lang long*) with subtle form. Then a vast, pervasive, smooth, light, joyful, and blissful awareness will occur. Moreover, [it will] also produce the marks taught in the *Saṃcayagāthā*:

> They possess knowledge that is free from perceiving multiplicity;
> they speak suitably.[311]

[One should consider] as well the remaining twenty-four lines taught [in *Saṃcayagāthā*, chapter 17, on the qualities of a bodhisattva].

On account of the four foundations of mindfulness,[312] the four correct exertions, the four miraculous powers,[313] and faith, persistence, mindfulness, absorption, and wisdom, one develops into a person who resides on the path of accumulation (*saṃbhara-mārga*). [Known as] the beginner's ground [or as] residing on the level of faith, this [stage] produces roots of virtue (*kuśalamūla*) that are harmonious with the path of liberation (*mokṣabhāgiya*). After that, the virtuous qualities of the preparatory analytical factors (*nirvedhabhāgiya*) will be produced. As has been indicated, with devotion, with continuous effort for a long time, gradually [one will attain] the five faculties,[314] the five powers,[315] [the stage of] attained illumination (*ālokalabdha*), and [the stage of] expanded illumination (*ālokavṛddhi*). [Then, one will] enter single-pointedly into the meaning of suchness[316] (*tattvārthaikadeśanupraveśa*), attain the uninterrupted concentration (*ānantarya-samādhi*), and, having become cognizant of the ultimate truth, reach the first *bhūmi*, the "very joyous." At that time, the four patiences and the four equanimities also occur. Then, up through the tenth stage,[317] the ten complete perfections, ten powers, eight[fold] brilliance,[318] four ornaments,[319] sixteen compassions,[320] and so forth[321] will be attained; the grounds are established as taught in the *Daśabhūmika Sūtra*. Accordingly, there is meditative stabilization and postmeditative equipoise up through the tenth ground, as the *Avikalpapraveśadhāraṇī* clearly states:

> The bodhisattva in meditative stabilization sees all dharmas as like the middle of the sky and when in the subsequent attainment of that, sees [things] in the manner of the eight similies of illusion.[322]

At whatever time one realizes the highest nonconceptual thought,[323] the vajra-like concentration (*vajropamasamādhi*), one does not have subsequent attainment. Transforming into the realm of reality, one directly realizes the dharmakāya. Because of dwelling in the dharmakāya, apprehending [reality] from that time as long as space endures, one does not possess subsequent attainment.

> Whoever sees me as visible matter, whoever understands me as sound, has entered into a wrong path; that person will not see me. The buddhas are the dharmakāya; the "leaders" see reality (*dharmatā*).[324]

The *Śrī-Vajramālātantra* states:

> All enters into the consciousness aggregate, and even that consciousness is said to be clear light, passing beyond sorrow, totally empty, and the dharmakāya.[325]

The *Dharmasaṃgīti* states:

> The actual buddha is unproduced.

And the *Lokottaraparivarta* states:

> The buddhas are the dharmakāya, completely pure like space.[326]

The teaching of Dignāga states:

> The perfection of wisdom, nondual: that gnosis is the tathāgata.[327]

Also, Ācārya [Nāgārjuna] himself states:

> Immaculate like space, whose nature is unchanging and without elaboration, one who sees you (i.e., *prajñāpāramitā*) sees the tathāgata. Between you who have complete good qualities and the Buddha, the teacher of the world, wise ones see no difference, as with the moon and the light of the moon.[328]

The same Ācārya [Nāgārjuna] also states:

> Not remaining in any phenomena,[329] becoming the reality of the *dharmadhātu*— homage to you, the profound that is the realization of supreme profundity.[330]

Further:

> Therefore there is really no difference between the buddhas and the *dharmadhātu*.[331]

Again:

> Through the nature of nonarising, you do not arise. The Protector does not possess coming and going. Homage to you devoid of an own-being.[332]

Further:

> Buddhas at all times dwell in the *dharmatā* like this.

There are many teachings like this, [but] I will set this aside for the time being. The Venerable Āryadeva states:

> Here, this reality is essenceless, like a lotus born from a sky-forest. [Arising] from both, from self, or from others is also like a rabbit horn. What aspect of liberation [inherently] exists?

Also, the *Vajrajñānasamuccaya* states:

> Even the buddhas—even when they are not affecting the purposes of others—reside pacifying all elaboration while abiding in the limits of purity.[333]

Ācārya Asaṅga states accordingly:

> At the time when all sentient beings have become fully and completely awakened, they will become the *dharmakāya*; all will be buddhas without exception, and having become the purity aspect itself of the *dharmadhātu*, they will remain in suchness.

Thus it is said in the *Viniścayasaṃgrahaṇī*.

This Ācārya does not even accept nondual gnosis in the ultimate [sense], nor does he accept the attainment subsequent to nonconceptual gnosis; because he attained the sovereignty of the third ground, he realized that all things are unproduced.[334] Intending this point, the *Vajramālātantra* states:

> This is ultimate reality, without appearance and without characteristics; it is also called the ultimate truth, the dwelling place of all buddhas.[335]

Ācārya Candrakīrti states:

> The [status of] buddha is proclaimed when the mind resides in the unproduced, the *dharmatā*.[336]

3.2 [Objections against Mādhyamikas]

[Objection:] Because of great attachment to objects from beginningless time, those who do not understand the nature of the two realities say, "If things are as you Mādhyamikas say, then the buddhas, when bodhisattvas, underwent many countless eons of immeasurable hardships and accumulated an immeasurable store of merit for no reason, and the Dharma and the Saṃgha become nothing at all. Since there will not be [any] sentient beings liberated from saṃsāra, one should place this evil view at a great distance. This [Mādhyamika view] is hailstones for crops of virtuous qualities; this [view] is worse than [that of] nihilist outsiders. It is appropriate to abandon and clear away a view such as this."

Mādhyamikas reply: "You whose minds are untrained and foolish, who denigrate the teachings of Ārya-Nāgārjuna—who is prophesized again and again in the *Mahāmegha*, *Laṅkāvatāra*, *Mahābherīhārakaparivarta*, and the *Mahāmañjuśrimūlatantra*—are causing self-defeat. The texts that are accepted by him state that the buddhas become *dharmakāya*, and since even the gnosis of the [buddha], through the abandonment of all conceptual thought, becomes the *dharmadhātu*, the sphere and gnosis are without object and subject, so how can nonconceptual wisdom exist?"

Ācārya Nāgārjuna states:

> If that which has passed does not exist, then the future does not exist, and because the present shifts from place [to] place, where is the presently arisen?[337]

And:

> Whether in meditation or not in meditation, all things lack [true] existence. Being free of things and nonthings is taught by the teacher as [entering into a state of] unity.[338]

According to this teaching, nonconceptual wisdom is not accepted. At the time [of awakening] nonconceptual wisdom does not exist because all elaborations without exception have been pacified. What kind of subsequent attainment wisdom will there be? There is not. The *Laṅkāvatārasūtra* states:

> If error appears, even after all errors have been eliminated, that is the real error, as for one who has not been purified of diseased vision (*rab rib, timira*).[339]

With respect to this, there are three types of diseased vision: (1) the diseased vision of the unskillful, (2) the diseased vision of the skillful, (3) and the completely purified diseased vision of the skillful. Since buddhas are purified [of] diseased vision, diseased vision will not appear again. Well, then, do buddhas have a body, gnosis, virtuous qualities, and extensive activities, or not? On account of one condition and three causes, [these] appear according to the perspective of the disciple; the body variously appears according to the categories of disciples. Furthermore, gnosis is great, self-arisen gnosis (*rang 'byung gi ye shes, svayaṃbhūjñāna*). Guru Avadhūtipa and Guru Tāmradvīpa both teach:

> There is no difference between gnosis and the *dharmadhātu*: the *dharmadhātu* is labeled "self-arisen gnosis," without thought and free from the elaboration of words; that gnosis itself is said to have five aspects from the perspective of those to be trained.[340]

Ācārya Nāgārjuna has taught this as well.

Likewise, the ten powers and so forth, the three miraculous activities, the twenty-five extensive activities, and the thirty-two extensive activities appear to the mind of the trainee. In regard to that, it is as taught by Ācārya [Nāgārjuna]:

> O Protector, you possess neither thought nor mental creation nor movement; [nevertheless,] in this world you fufill a buddha's activity for sentient beings without any effort.[341]

Again:

> You completely fulfill the wishes of all sentient beings like a wish-fulfilling tree unmoved by the fierce winds of conceptual thought.[342]

Again:

> O Protector, your perception of sentient beings does not at all occur, but you send out beneficial compassion for beings tormented by suffering[343]

Again:

> The excellence of the purpose of others is accepted as the foremost result [of awakening]. Other than buddhahood itself and so forth, these other [benefits] are asserted as the result of this goal [awakening].[344]

Furthermore, Ācārya Āryadeva states:

> In many innumerable kalpas [one] always makes effort only for the purpose of others. Finally, when attaining the *dharmakāya*, for the purpose of effecting the goals of others, one does not pass beyond suffering as long as beings abide. For this reason, the bodhisattva does not do [that] which is not [for] the purpose of others. The effort [to fulfill] merely their own aims is carried out by the five types of migrators. When the supreme individual practices for the purposes of others, always being compassionate, they are like joyful parents of migrators.

Establishing the aspects of the three bodies: Ācārya Nāgārjuna established this teaching in other [texts]. Accordingly, from the blessings of the *dharmakāya*, on account of one condition and three causes, the form body [appears] and teaches the profound and vast Dharma. The extensive activity of the *kāya*[*s*] occurs until the end of saṃsāra. Having intended this meaning, a tantra states:

> Just as multiple distinctions occur due to the many aspirations and different inclinations of sentient beings, likewise, a reflection of the moon appears in many vessels of water at one time.[345]

Further, Venerable Āryadeva indicates:

> In an arrangement of vessels of copper, *vaiḍūrya*, precious stones, gems, and coral, the one moon in the middle of the sky becomes transformed to appear different in each one. Likewise the vajra mind of the protector himself abides, variously permeating the mass of beings.[346]

For those with weak faculties and little merit, there is no appearance of the body. As the *Mahāyānasūtrālaṃkāra* states:

> Just as the reflection of the moon does not appear in a broken vessel, likewise the buddha's reflection does not appear to evil beings.[347]

Likewise, the speech [of the Buddha] occurs in relation to the vessel of the trainee:

> The buddhas teach the Dharma in accord with disciples' aspirations. For some, [they] teach the Dharma that turns away from sin. To some, [they] teach the Dharma in which both cause and effect are never wasted. To some, [they] teach the Dharma that classifies [things] into the two realities. To those who are apprehensive about the profound, [they] teach the essence of emptiness and compassion; in this way [they] teach Dharma according to aspiration.[348]

Ācārya Nāgārjuna taught this. Further, [the teachings of buddhas] do not appear to the impure vessel. When requested by Brahmā, [the Buddha said]:

> I have found a Dharma like ambrosia,[349] unconditioned, nectar-like, separated from attachment, profound. No one to whom I show it will comprehend, so [staying] alone by myself, I will meditate in the forest.[350]

Ācārya Nāgārjuna also stated:

> Why does the profound Dharma not appear to beings who are not [proper] vessels? Because only the wise understand that the Buddha is omniscient.[351]

Thus was this meaning taught in the *Tathāgatācintyaguhyanirdeśa*.

Therefore, the Madhyamaka followers of Ārya-Nāgārjuna have no faults whatsoever. Those sentient beings who denigrate these teachings, who abandon the profound and extensive Dharma, will experience the sufferings of hell for a long time.

4 [Previous Buddhist Masters]

Make [an effort to understand] each one of the previous teachers.

4.1 [Logic]

Ācārya Dignāga and Dharmakīrti wrote extensive texts on logic (*tshad ma*).

4.2 [Vaibhāṣika]

Ācārya Dharmatrāta, Ācārya Buddhadeva, Vasumitra, Ghoṣaka, Yid 'ong, and so forth provided the extensive transmission of the *śrāvaka* Vaibhāṣika.

4.3 [Sautrāntika]

Ācārya Śubhagupta, Dharmottara, the earlier Vasubhandu, and so forth wrote extensive texts on the *śrāvaka* Sautrāntika.

4.4 [Yogācāra]

Ācārya Asaṅga, [the later] Vasubandhu, Sthiramati, Prajñākaragupta, Kaliṅga, Devendrabuddhi, Upāsaka Bhadanta Asvabhāva, and so forth wrote extensive texts on the Sākāra (*rnam bcas*) and Nirākāra (*rnam med*) [Yogācāra].

4.5 [Madhyamaka]

Ācārya Bhāviveka, Buddhapālita, Devaśarma, Avalokitavrata, Śāntarakṣita, Kamalaśila, and so forth wrote extensive texts on the Madhyamaka.

4.6 [Mādhyamikas Who Practiced Extensive Deeds]

Ācārya Candragomin, Ācārya Śura, Sāgaramegha, Ācārya Śāntideva, Ācārya Luntaka, and so forth wrote extensive texts for the sake of beginners on the great vast activities of practice, like the four immeasurables, four means of gathering disciples, six[352] perfections, and so forth, starting with the mind of awakening.

4.7 [The Foundations of Madhyamaka]

Ācārya Nāgārjuna, Ācārya Āryadeva, Ācārya Mātṛceṭa, Ācārya Kambala, Ācārya Candrakīrti—the Madhyamaka texts written by these five ācāryas are the foundation of all Madhyamaka texts. Since they are the root of all Madhyamaka texts, they are incomparable.

4.8 [Caryā Tantra and the Yoga Tantra]

Accordingly, for the texts of secret mantra oral precepts, Ācārya Buddhaguhya, Ācārya Śākyamitra, Ācārya Prajñāsiddha, Ācārya Ānandagarbha, and so forth clarified the meaning of the Caryā Tantra and the Yoga Tantra.

4.9 [Tantras]

Ācārya Indrabhūti, Ācārya Buddhajñānapāda, and so forth solely clarified the meaning of the *Guhyasamājatantra*. Ācārya Caryāpāda, Ācārya Vajraghaṇṭā, Ācārya Lūyīpāda, and so forth clarified the meaning of the *Cakrasaṃvaratantra*. Ācārya Ḍombhīheruka, Sararūpa, and so forth clarified the meaning of the *Hevajratantra*. Ācārya Kukuripāda, Dharmapāda, and so forth clarified the meaning of the *Mahāmāyā*.

5 [The Teachings of Nāgārjuna]

5.1 [A Classification of His Teachings]

The teaching of Ācārya [Nāgārjuna] is most kind to all beings.

[Ordinary People]

In order to especially benefit ordinary people, [he] wrote [texts on] calculation and divination.

[Ministers]

In order to benefit ministers, [he] wrote the *Prajñāśataka*, the *Twelve Examinations* (*Brtag pa gnyis pa*), and so forth.

[Kings]

For the [benefit] of kings, he wrote the *Suhṛllekha* and the *Ratnāvalī*.

[The Less Fortunate]

For the [benefit] of the less fortunate, belonging to the retinue of four vowholders (*'khor rnam bzhi*), [he] wrote the great [*Dhūpayogaratnamālā*] and lesser [*Aṣṭāpadikṛtadhūpayoga*] texts on incense preparation (*spos sbyor*).

[Doctors]

For the benefit of doctors, he wrote the *Yogaśataka*, the *Twenty* and *Thirty-Two Practices* (*Sbyor ba sum cu rtsa gnyis pa dang nyis shu pa*), the *Essential Drop of Nectar* (*Bdud rtsi'i snying thigs*), the *Jīvasūtra*, and so forth.

[For Those Entering the Mahāyāna]

For the sake of those entering the Mahāyāna, [he] wrote the *Bodhicittotpāda-vidhi*, *Illuminating the Practice of the Bodhisattva* (*Byang chub sems dpa'i spyod pa gsal ba*), the *Sūtrasamuccaya*, and so forth.

[The Foremost of Texts]

Furthermore, the foremost of those[353] is the *Prajñāmūlamadhyamakakārikā*, and then the *Vigrahavyāvartanī* and the *Śūnyatāsaptati*.

[Ancillary Texts]

The ancillaries to the [foremost texts] are the *Yuktiṣaṣṭikā*, *Mahāyānaviṃśikā*, *Bhavasaṃkrānti*, *Bhāvanākrama*, *Vaidalyaprakaraṇa*, *Akṣaraśataka*, *Bodhicittavivaraṇa*, *Dharmadhātustava*, *Paramārthastava*,[354] *Praise to the Non-Conceptual* (*Rnam par mi rtog par bstod pa*), *Acintyastava*, *Lokātītastava*,[355] *Cittavajrastava*, *Āryaśālistambakamahāyānasūtraṭīkā*, and the *Pratītyasamutpādahṛdayakārikā* along with its *Vyākhyāna*.

[Secret Mantra Texts]

Likewise, for the sharpest of those with sharp faculties, the vessels of the Secret Mantra Great Vehicle, he wrote, [to clarify] the meaning of the *Guhyasamājatantra*, the *Guhyasamājamaṇḍalavidhi*, the *Twenty Rituals* (*Cho ga nyi shu pa*), the *Piṇḍīkṛtasādhana*, the *Guhyasamāja-mahāyogotpattikramasādhanasūtramelāpaka*, the *Pañcakrama*, and the *Vajrāsanacatvumahātantraṭīka*. [He] wrote the *Commentary of the Pure Complete Exhortation* [*Nāmasaṃgīti*], the venerable *Khasarpanasādhana*, the *Six Letters* (*Yi ge drug pa*), the *Arapacana*, the *Vāgīśvara*, and many *sādhanas*, like the *Youthful Verses* (*Tshig sbyin gzhon nu*) and so forth. [He] wrote the *Trisamayavyūha*, the *Siddhaikavīra*, the *Kalyānakāmadhenuvivaraṇa*, the *Thirty Verses of the Sacrificial Cake Ritual* (*Gtor ma sum cu pa*), the *Great Spe-*

cial Instruction on the Completion Stages of Buddhasamāyoga (*Sangs rgyas mnyam sbyor gyi rdzogs pa'i rim pa'i man ngag chen po*), and so forth.

5.2 [Nāgārjuna's Predicted Buddhahood]

Since that supreme individual [Nāgārjuna] is an actual buddha, one should trust the texts written by him. Why is that? From the *Mahāmeghasūtra*:

> Devaputras! Innummerable previous kalpas ago, at the time when the Tathāgata Klu rigs sgron ma (Nāgagotradīpa) appeared in the world, the young Licchavi, Sarvasattvapriyadarśana, was the cakravartin king Holding the Teaching of the Great Effort, his queen was called Upholding Dharma, and his minister was called Upholding the Storehouse of Wonderful Dharma. At that time, the king and minister debated whether relics [of the Buddha] exist or not. The retinue was amazed with the eloquent explanation of the king and they declared to the Bhagavan, "The king understands something profound." Then the Bhagavan extensively explained the qualities of the king.[356]

One should look in the sūtra. [Further:]

> Then the king, along with the retinue, having scattered a handful of jewels, supplicated the Buddha and made vows: "In the future, close to the disappearance of the teaching of Buddha Śākyamuni, at that time I will become ordained. When the Dharma is at its end, I will proclain three times with a great voice, only wearing religious garments, only having shaved hair: 'May I leave the country, may the holy Dharma arise, may I give up my life for the purpose of the holy Dharma.'" Thus [he] prayed. After that, the minister and queen also made a vow.[357] "Devaputras! After many hundred of years have passed since my death, at that time will appear in the southern area a king called Sukhacaryabhadra. At that time, in one hundred years, when even more of the remains of the holy Dharma are disappearing, a disciple of mine will appear, the holy Dharma will be brought out, issue forth, and reappear, and the wheel of the holy Dharma will be turned. The Mahāyāna will be extensively taught to others."[358]

Further:

> Listen to the prophecy of this bhikṣu; he is very pleasing to me. Making my teaching widespread, carrying a great burden, he is a young [member] of my Śākya [clan]. After passing away in the south, in a provincial land called Drang srong byi (Ṛṣyākhu), he will be born in the great northern city called Possessing Merit. [He will be born in] a pure, great lineage, [known as] Bhra go can, that is a lineage of Śākyas. In order to extend my Dharma, the youthful Licchavi, Sarvasattvapriyadarśana, the bodhisattva, this supreme human, will be born in a king's lineage, a great lineage. All his relations will make his name renowned. Then, when he has been ordained, his retinue will protect the teaching by giving up [their] lives for the sake of the holy Dharma.[359]

After that, [the sūtra] later states:

> [A] small [number] will be devoted to his texts, but most will not. Those possessing four qualities will trust and be devoted to his teaching: (1) [They] will be pleased and hear teachings of previous buddhas, (2) [they] will be upheld by the spiritual friend, (3) [they will] stabilize the roots of virtue through relying on the superior thought, and (4) [they will] be devoted to performing extensive deeds publicly with their bodies.[360] All those who do not trust and rejoice in his [teaching] have the ignorance that is blessed by Māra. Those who trust and rejoice in his [teaching] are those who embrace the Buddha's mind.[361]
>
> When venerating him, one is venerating to all the buddhas of the three times. If listening to his spoken word, one is listening to the spoken word of all buddhas of the three times.[362]

Further, after him:

> At the time of his death, my holy Dharma will disappear. Without an individual like that, the [holy Dharma] will become entirely nonexistent.[363]

Also, there will be many teachings after him:

> Those who write extensive texts about him and who uphold his teaching will, when awakened, be the foremost [of the Buddha's]

> retinue. After this good eon, a buddha will not appear for sixty-two aeons. Then, after that, seven buddhas will appear.[364] Subsequent to that, in a world realm called Vivid Clear Light, a tathāgata, arhat, fully awakened buddha called Jñānabhavaprabhā will be fully and completely awakened.[365]

This is taught in many texts. Here I have written just a little bit [of the whole prediction].

Moreover, the *Mañjuśrīmūlatantra* states:

> A bhikṣu called Nāgāhvaya will appear, having the knowledge of suchness that lacks inherent existence; having obtained a spell called peacock, he will live for six hundred years.[366]

Also, from the *Laṅkāvatārasūtra*:

> Oh Mahāmati, you should know . . . In Vedalī, in the south, a bhikṣu most illustrious and distinguished [will be born]; his name is Nāgāhvaya.[367] . . . Having attained the stage of the Joyous, he will go to Sukhāvatī.[368]

There also is a prophecy in the *Mahābherīhārakaparivarta*. There is no verse of prophecy in the *Suvarṇaprabhāsottamasūtra*, but there is a dispute over the relics of the Buddha between the Brahman Kauṇḍinya and this Licchavi Sarvasattvapriyadarśana ("Joyous When Seen by All the World").

Moreover, the honorable Ācārya Candrakīrti states:

> Accordingly, [I] realized the meaning directly from the great Ācārya Ārya-Nāgārjuna himself, who teaches in the world the concentration of Mahāvajradhara that is realized by oneself. [He] has passed beyond the happiness of gods and men, and of the *tīrthikas*, and the happiness of concentration and absorption of *śrāvakas* and *pratyekabuddhas*. He possesses to the utmost all aspects of the body of the tathāgata, which is free of arising and cessation. [One] could never have enough of looking at this body, which has attained the adornment of all qualities of a buddha, the ten powers and the four fearlessnesses and so forth. He went to Sukhavatī and resides [there] possessing the eight qualities of mastery.[369]

This is taught in the *Pradīpodyotana*. Therefore one should learn and understand the texts of Ācārya Nāgārjuna and become one who has the profound instructions of his lineage. The individual who practices [this lineage] will course in the Great Vehicle for immeasurable lifetimes. As long as the Buddha's teaching exists, these oral instructions will not be severed. The Venerable Āryadeva states:

> The Bhagavan Śākyamuni at midnight made manifest the concentration of awakening, and ever since, the Buddha's teaching has existed. Upheld by the Ācārya Ārya-Nāgārjuna, passed from mentor's mouth to mentor's mouth, this oral instruction from the mouth of the Ācārya is a blessing of all the buddhas and bodhisattvas as well as all the *vajraḍākiṇīs*.[370]

The Venerable Ācārya Candrakīrti [states]:

> Yogi, for those desiring to become awakened in this life itself, this difficult-to-obtain special instruction of the profound essential reality for masters from the mouth of the Ācārya [Nāgārjuna] is like treasure, like pouring water of *amṛta* into precious vases. As long as the Dharma of Śākyamunibuddha abides, is transferred and received from mouth to mouth and from ear to ear, for that long this [teaching] will not disappear.

5.3 [Nāgārjuna's Maturation Body]

The maturation body (*rnam par smin pa'i sku, vipakakāya*)[371] of Ācārya Ārya-Nāgārjuna—that very body—dwells on Śrī-Parvata, Glorious Mountain. At one time, the son of King Sukhacaryabhadra went to Glorious Mountain to take the head of the Ācārya. The Ācārya [Nāgārjuna] said, "Prince, cut and take [this body]." Trying five times with a sword, [the Prince] could not cut [him] into pieces. The Ācārya [Nāgārjuna] said, "Take up a blade of Kusha grass." The Prince offered it to him, and having received that, the Ācārya himself wrapped the root around his throat, and [his] head, which dropped to the ground, was offered into the hand of the Prince. [His head] was not carried by the Prince, but went off by itself. Even now the trunk of the body and the head are in a pavilion made of splendid emanated light. They [are] placed on a precious throne, perpetually worshipped day and night by gandharvas, yakṣas, devas, and so forth. There is a long-established oral tradition about this.

5.4 [Nāgārjuna's Aspiration Body]

The aspiration body (*smon lam kyi sku*, *praṇidhānakāya*) dwells in Sukhāvatī. Named Bodhisattva Precious Intelligence (*Byang chub sems dpa' blo gros rin po che*) by the Bhagavan Amitābha, he has two arms, white body color, the right [hand in the gesture] of giving boons and the left [hand] holding a white lotus. From the mouth of the Venerable Guru Avadhūtīpa:

> My lama, the great venerable [one], the lord of yogis, Avadhūtīpa Nāropa,[372] with previously acquired supernatural cognition, had a vision and heard [Nāgārjuna's] teaching, seeing him while dwelling on Śrī-Parvata. A disciple of the Ārya, the Venerable Nāgabodhi, who is renowned as Śrī-Śabaripāda, also always listened to the Dharma.

The Guru Avadhūtīpa taught this.

6 [Regarding the Practice of Secret Mantra]

Casting away their own suffering, tormented by the fire of others' suffering, [those with the] sharpest of sharp faculties aspire not to be frightened of the profound Dharma. Not separating from self-achievement, desiring to be awakened in this life itself, and quickly effecting the purposes of others without difficulty, one should engage in the vehicle of particular skillfulness [i.e., Mantrayāna] with the desire to quickly produce supernatural knowledge. Having requested the *vajrācārya* empowerment from the auspicious guru, one should mainly practice. The secret (*guhya*) and wisdom-gnosis (*prajnajñāna*) empowerments are not authorized for those on the path of liberating pure conduct [i.e., celibacy], and therefore such a student should not take [such empowerments].[373] [These empowerments] terminate pure conduct (*brahmacaryā*), and through causing the disappearance of the Buddha's teaching, undoubtedly cause both disciple and teacher to go to [the realm] of hell beings. If it is secret mantra activity, receive an empowerment and become a follower of any tantra where one has obtained a vase empowerment. Request from the guru the *samādhi* of one's own chosen deity and the mantra to mutter; emphasizing *siddhi*, protecting very purely the twenty vows and commitments (*samaya*), one should succeed. At any time, with the ability to produce [*siddhi*], with [mastery of] the four extensive activities and the eight worldly achievements, [one] will achieve the aims of others without difficulty. With that [in mind] a tantra states:

> Secret mantra [is a] great ocean, a flood of perfection (*siddhi*), erotic (*'khrig pa can*); it cannot be cognized through examples, verbal authority, words, or the insights of inference (*anumāna*).[374]

My guru, Yavadvīpāda, the meritorious Avadhūtīpāda, states:

> Give up the two vehicles [of Hīnayāna and Mahāyāna], enter into this, [and] attain Mahāmudrā. This being the case, what wise person would not practice this vehicle of secret mantra?
>
> Although it has the very same goal [of awakening], the way of secret mantra is superior because it is free from confusion, has multiple methods, is without hardship, and is mastered by those with acute faculties.[375]

In this regard, if one does not gain consecration (*abhiṣeka*, *dbang bskur*), one should not engage in this [vehicle], and one should not cultivate the deity or mutter the mantra. Without one's obtaining the permission blessing (*rjes su gnang ba*), both secret mantra and the perfection [vehicles] become corrupted for attaining liberation. The special instruction (*upadeśa*) of the completion stage that is free from elaboration, the complete mind of vajra-awakening, should not be taught to one who is not a vessel. A fully accomplished *upāsaka* [layperson] who is on the path of desire is without fault in joining the two sexual organs.

> Being content with one's own consort, [one] does not go with the woman of another. Abandoning the aspect of wrongful adultery, that *upāsaka* goes to the abode of the gods.[376]

This is taught in a sūtra.

> One should train [in] the Secret Mantra Vehicle
> for the sake of purifying quickly the two obscurations
> and accumulating quickly the two collections.
> Thus spoke Dīpaṃkaraśrījñāna (Mar me mdzad dpal ye shes),
>
> Sharp-minded bhikṣu of Śākya[muni],
> who possesses the method of love and wisdom.
> [This] was written at the urging of the good disciple
> known as Tshul khrims rgyal ba, Victorious Conduct.

Written by Dīpaṃkaraśrījñāna,
as spoken by the holy gurus,
in the great temple called Vikramaśīla, [supported by]
the solemn oath of [King] Devapāla.

[Dīpaṃkaraśrījñāna did not give these teachings] merely
for the sake of food, wealth, or minor matters.
[This teaching is] not to be given to those unprepared.
One who is not devoted to the teachings of Ārya Nāgārjuna
abandons the profound and goes to hell.

[This] completes the advice by the Mahāpaṇḍita Śrī-Dīpaṃkarajñāna, the so-called Opened Basket of Precious Special Instructions on the Great Vehicle Middle Way. It was translated, requested, and put in order by the Indian master Dīpaṃkarajñāna himself, the great *lotsāwa*[377] *upāsaka* Gya Tsöndrü Sengé, and Bhikṣu Tsultrim Gyalwa.

Part 2
Articulating the Two Realities

2. Atiśa's *Entry to the Two Realities* (*Satyadvayāvatāra*)

ATIŚA, like a number of Indian Madhyamaka forerunners, based his teaching of Madhyamaka thought and practice on the two realities, conventional reality (*saṃvṛtisatya*) and ultimate reality (*paramārthasatya*). *Entry to the Two Realities* succinctly lays out in twenty-eight verses a general exposition on the two realities. The verses not only outline characteristics of the two realities but also present Atiśa's views on valid cognition and reasoning. According to Lindtner (1981, 164), *Entry to the Two Realities* marks the culmination of the Madhyamaka theory on the two realities in India and contains influences from a number of his Indian Madhyamaka predecessors. Such influences include Nāgārjuna's *Mūlamadhyamakakārikā* (*ad* vv. 1, 18cd, 20ab), Bhāviveka's *Madhyamakahṛdaya* (*ad* vv. 20cd), the *Madhyamakaratnapradīpa* (*ad* vv. 2, 3, 14, 21), Candrakīrti's *Madhyamakāvatāra* (*ad* v. 19), and Śāntideva's *Bodhicaryāvatāra* (*ad* v. 23). Traditional Tibetan historians among the Gelukpa regard *Entry to the Two Realities* as among the two foremost textual teachings (*gzhung*) on the view (*lta ba*) within Atiśa's works, the *Special Instructions on the Middle Way* being the other teaching. The Tibetan biographies of Atiśa mention a commentary to *Entry to the Two Realities*, but this commentary is no longer extant.[378]

Atiśa composed *Entry to the Two Realities* between 1012 and 1025 while residing in Sumatra and studying under Serlingpa. As verse 28 indicates, Atiśa was inspired to compose *Entry to the Two Realities* after his guru Serlingpa sent the monk Devamati to deliver a letter to him. Serlingpa inquired about Atiśa's philosophical views (*lta ba*) in the letter and Atiśa composed *Entry to the Two Realities* as a response. This is corroborated, in part, by *Sherab Dorjé's Explanation of Atiśa's Entry to the Two Realities*, which mentions that Atiśa wrote *Entry to the Two Realities* in order to change the philosophical view of Serlingpa from a Yogācāra position, as previously discussed, to that of the Madhyamaka.[379] In this respect, I think that Atiśa's *Entry to the Two Realities* is an introductory text on Madhyamaka that presents his understanding based on the synthesis of a number of previous Madhyamaka thinkers.

Entry to the Two Realities discusses two realities (verse 1), conventional and ultimate. Conventional reality has two aspects (verse 2), mistaken and correct. Mistaken conventional realities also have two aspects, things like optical illusions as well as misconceptions based on faulty doctrines. Correct conventional realities, while unexamined and from the perspective of those of limited vision,[380] arise due to causes and conditions and have causal efficacy (verse 3). Ultimate reality is one (verse 4), undifferentiated (verse 6), and cognized in a nonconceptual (verse 6) and nondual manner (verses 7–9) based on the profound teachings of the Buddha. Buddhists provisionally accept two means of valid cognition (*pramāṇa*) in order to refute opponents, but the ultimate reality of emptiness is not realized by valid cognition (verses 10–13). Rather, ultimate reality is realized through meditation based on the lineage of Nāgārjuna and Candrakīrti (verses 14–17ab). Nevertheless, the cause and effect of conventional realities must be properly observed to serve as the means to reach the goal of realizing ultimate reality (verses 17cf–20). Although the conventional does not intrinsically exist and has the same nature as the ultimate, the appearances of conventional reality occur due to causes and conditions (verses 21–23). Proper observance of the two realities leads to heavenly rebirth (verse 24), and one should therefore follow, in the time available, the authoratative teachings of Nāgārjuna (verses 25–26). The concluding verses discuss the inspiration from Serlingpa to compose the text (verses 27–28).

Entry to the Two Realities (*Satyadvayāvatāra*)

by Atiśa

In the Indian language: *Satyadvayāvatāra*
In the Tibetan language: *Bden pa gnyis la 'jug pa*

Homage to the Great Compassionate One

1. The Dharma taught by Buddhas perfectly relies on two realities: the conventional reality of the world and ultimate reality.

2. The conventional has two aspects: one that is mistaken and one that is correct. The former is twofold: the moon [reflected on] water and the conceptions of bad doctrines.

3. Something that is pleasing only as long as it is not examined, which arises and ceases to exist and which is capable of causal efficiency, is held to be correct convention.

4. The ultimate is one only. Others maintain that it is twofold. How can the nature of reality (*chos nyid*), which cannot be established as anything, be two, three, and so on?

5. [The ultimate] is defined as nonarising, noncessation, and so forth according to the formula [given] by treatises. Because of the way in which different ultimates do not exist, there is neither a subject (*chos can*) nor its property (*chos nyid*) [for inferential reasoning].

6. There is not any differentiation in emptiness. When cognized in a nonconceptual manner, it is conventionally designated that "emptiness is seen."

7. It is said in the very profound sūtras that the state of nonseeing is seeing [ultimate reality]. In that (ultimate reality), there is neither seeing nor seer, but peace without beginning or end.

8. [Reality is] devoid of entity and nonentity, free from conceptions, free from objects, without support, without basis, without coming or going, unexemplified,

9. ineffable, invisible, unchanging, and unconditioned. If a yogi realizes that, the afflictive and cognitive obstructions are eliminated.

10. Direct perception and inference are the two [valid cognitions] accepted by Buddhists. The deluded whose vision is narrow say that emptiness is understood by these two.

11. [If it were,] it would follow that even *tīrthika*s and *śrāvaka*s would understand the nature of reality (*chos nyid*), not to mention the proponents of representation[-only], and the Madhyamakas would be no different [from them].

12ab. This being so, all tenets would also agree because they understand [reality] through valid cognition.

12cd–13. Because all reasonings are not in agreement, would not the nature of reality (*chos nyid*), which is understood through valid cognition, become manifold? Direct perception and inference are useless. In order to refute Tīrthikas, [Buddhist] masters have composed [digests on logic].

14. The master scholar Bhavya stated clearly in scripture that [the ultimate] is not realized by either conceptual or nonconceptual consciousness.

15. Who has understood emptiness? Nāgārjuna, who was predicted by the Tathāgata and saw the truth of the nature of reality, and his disciple Candrakīrti.

16ab. Ultimate reality may be understood by means of the lineage of special instructions from them.

16c–e. The articles of dharma are said to number 84,000. All of them are inclined toward and lead to this [ultimate] reality.

17ab. One is liberated by understanding emptiness. All meditational development is for this purpose.

17c–f. But if one has contempt for the correct conventional reality and meditates on emptiness, the conventional cause and effect, virtue and evil deeds, and so on, will deceive one in the next world.

18. Those who rely on a bit of learning without understanding the meaning of discrimination and do not create merit—such despicable persons are destroyed. Wrongly perceived emptiness will destroy people of little wisdom.

19. The Ācārya Candrakīrti has stated as follows: "Conventional reality functions as a means, and ultimate reality functions as the goal. Those who do not understand the difference between the two have a bad understanding and get a bad rebirth."

20. The ultimate cannot be understood without relying on the conventional. Without the stairway of correct convention a wise man cannot ascend to the top of the palace of reality.

21. When the conventional that appears is analytically examined just as it, nothing whatsoever is found. The unfindable is itself the ultimate and the nature of reality abiding from the beginning.

22ab. The conventional that appears just-as-it-is is established by being produced by causes and conditions.

22cd. If it were impossible to establish it, by whom would the moon in water and the like be produced?

23. Therefore all appearances are established as being produced by various causes and conditions. If the continuance of conditions is interrupted, they do not arise even conventionally.

24. So if one is not deluded with views and one has extremely pure conduct, without following a mistaken path, one will go to the place of Akaniṣṭha.

25. Time is short and things to be known are manifold. But since the span of time is only as long as ignorance, one should select what one prefers, just as a goose extracts milk from water.

26. Although those with narrow vision are not able to ascertain the two realities, this presentation on the two realities of Nāgārjuna's tradition was given relying on the statements of authoritative teachers.

27. If people of today have faith in this demonstration composed under the auspices of the king of Sumatra, it should be accepted after thorough analysis, not just by faith and not just out of reverence.

28. After the King of Suvarṇadvīpa, the Gurupāla, sent the monk Devamati to me, and under his auspices, I composed this "Entry to the Two Realities." It should be examined by present-day scholars.

3. *Collection on the Two Realities*: A Kadampa Commentary

THE FOLLOWING ANNOTATED translation consists of an anonymous Kadampa commentary entitled *Collection on the Two Realities*.[381] The text provides an early Tibetan Madhyamaka exposition on the two realities based on the instruction of Atiśa. We thus have a brief commentary on each of the twenty-eight verses of *Entry to the Two Realities* from a twelfth-century Tibetan perspective. The commentary most likely preserves a tradition of exegesis on Atiśa's work, perhaps based on oral teachings from Atiśa himself, that was brought to Radreng Monastery. It combines the teachings of Candrakīrti and Bhāviveka and exhibits a thorough knowledge of Candrakīrti's *Madhyamakāvatāra*, the major works of Bhāviveka, as well as the work of Jñānagarbha. The commentary does not mention subdivisions within Madhyamaka traditions, indicating that the author of the text and his exegetical lineage did not recognize or know of divisions within Madhyamaka. It does provide clear evidence of an active teaching lineage of Candrakīrti's Madhayamaka that was brought to Tibet with Atiśa. All the arguments in the text are directed against Yogācāra tenets and the use of valid cognition to realize emptiness. The commentary (folio 9a7–10a6) repeatedly emphasizes that valid cognition is used to refute opponents but is not useful for realizing ultimate reality. It (folio 9b3) even cites the *Mahāyānasūtrālaṃkāra* in its claim that logic is not part of Mahāyāna Buddhist teachings. Rather than relying on valid cognition, the commentary emphasizes reliance on the scriptural tradition and the spiritual guru for guidance in realizing emptiness. It surprisingly states that scriptural tradition (*āgama*) is the "supreme of direct perceptions," as it is based on the Buddha's omniscient wisdom. Along these lines, in its exegesis the commentary does not rely on Yogācāra sources to articulate concepts found in the root text. In this manner the commentary explains "causal efficiency" (*don byed nus pa ≈ arthakriyā*) (folio 4a5) or various types of reasoning (folio 14ab) based on Madhyamaka textual sources. In its exegesis the commentary follows what will later become in Tibet the "Prāsaṅgika" interpretation of Candrakīrti and Śāntideva (see Vose 2009, 2010b), as it emphasizes in its interpretation of Atiśa's root text that the ultimate is beyond elaboration (folio 8b), that appearances do not occur at the level of a buddha (folio 6a), and that wisdom has its "continuum cut" (folio 15a), since all awareness is mistaken. I discuss the content of the commentary and the commentary's position on conventional reality, ultimate reality, and valid cognition.

Authorship and Date

The authorship of the *Collection on the Two Realities* is unclear, as the text does not provide a colophon that lists its author. Nevertheless, the text does provide clues in several places for the time of its composition. Early in the text the author acknowledges "Sangphuwa" (1b2), a reference to Ngok Lekpai Sherap. A few lines later he asserts: "Having witnessed Geshé Gönpa, I will state in writing these bestowed special instructions of Atiśa."[382] Other early Kadampa commentaries such as *Potowa's Middle Way* and *Collection of Special Instructions on the Middle Way* also refer to Geshé Gönpa. These references may well be alluding to Geshé Gönpa Wangchuk Gyaltsen, one of the four great spiritual disciples of Atiśa, who was initially from Kham rus dgongs and toward the end of his life served as abbot of Radreng Monastery from 1078 to 1083. Geshé Gönpa's relation to the lineage of transmission of Atiśa's teaching on the two realities may be through Naljorpa Jangchup Rinchen, who was the preceding abbot of Radreng. Thuken Losang Chökyi Nyima (1737–1802) considered Naljorpa to be the principle upholder of Atiśa's lineage of teachings on the two realities (Blo-bzang chos-kyi nyi-ma, Jackson, and Sopa 2009, 107). As Gönpawa was the immediate successor to Naljorpa, it is conceivable that he received the oral transmission for the Madhyamaka special instructions that included the articulation of Atiśa's *Entry to the Two Realities*. Therefore, one piece of evidence for the time of composition is that the author must have been alive toward the end of Geshé Gönpawa's life.

Another clue is found later in the text. While commenting on verse 16 of Atiśa's *Entry to the Two Realities*, the author attempts to draw a parallel between a statement found from the *Prasannapadā* and his current situation in late-eleventh-century Tibet (see translation, folio 11a). The passage refers to "three spiritual sons," a reference to the three famous direct disciples of Atiśa's foremost disciple, Dromtönpa Gyalwai Jungné: Potowa Rinchen Sal, Phuchungwa Shönu Gyaltsen, and Chengawa Tsultrim Bar. For some authors, Chengawa Tsultrim Bar was considered to be the origin of the explanatory transmission (*bshad rgyun*) of Atiśa's *Entry to the Two Realities*.[383] However, our anonymous author does not mention Chengawa but mainly refers to Dromtönpa, Potowa, and Geshé Gönpawa. Based on this information, we can chart the time period of the anonymous author as follows:

Dromtönpa Gyalwai Jungné (active 1057)
|
Three Spiritual Sons (active 1070)
|
Great Disciples (active 1085)
|
Disciples (ca. 1100, anonymous author's time period)

The author of the commentary must have been active around 1100 if not a little earlier. A good candidate, someone who saw Geshé Gönpawa at the end of his life and who is within the time frame of the commentarial statement, would be Neusurpa Yeshé Bar (1042–1118). According to the *Blue Annals* (Roerich 1976, 311), Neusurpa Yeshé Bar was the principle disciple of Geshé Gönpawa and then was a disciple of Potowa. Along these lines, Neusurpa Yeshé Bar was also considered the direct successor of Chengawa Tsultrim Bar in several Kadampa circles of transmission (Sørensen et al. 2007, 466). Another possible candidate would be Sharawa Yönten Drak. Sharawa was a pupil of Potowa and would have been alive at the end of Gönpawa's life. Sharawa was also a leading pupil of the Madhyamaka pioneer Patsap Nyimadrak, and reportedly sent his own students to study with him after reviewing Patsap's early Madhyamaka translations (Roerich 1979, 271; Ruegg 2000, 44–45; Sørensen et al. 2007, 154–55). In any case, a definitive attribution of authorship cannot be made at this time based on the current available evidence. It is most likely that the lineage of Atiśa's teachings represented in this early Kadampa text gradually disappeared after Gönpawa passed away and the following thirty-year period in which Radreng could not fill his abbotship.[384] This gap of abbatial succession coincides with the rise of Sangphu as a center of study and practice and the rise of other Kadampa centers that followed Patsap's interpretations (Vose 2009, 42–61).

Sources and Content of the Early Tibetan Commentary

Collection on the Two Realities is a text on Madhyamaka "spiritual instructions." The author comments on Atiśa's *Entry to the Two Realities* and discusses in a free-flowing style the two realities in terms of how they directly apply to spiritual practice. He directly cites several works of Nāgārjuna, including the *Yuktiṣaṣṭikā, Ratnāvalī, Dharmadhātustava, Prajñādaṇḍa,* and

Pratītyasamutpādahṛdayakārikā. The author also directly cites Jñānagarbha's *Satyadvayavibhaṅgakārikā* and Maitreyanātha's *Mahāyānasūtrālaṃkāra*. He makes paraphrased references to Nāgārjuna's *Vigrahavyāvartanī*, Candrakīrti's *Madhyamakāvatāra*, *Prasannapadā*, and *Pañcaskandhaprakaraṇa*, Bhāviveka's *Prajñāpradīpa* and *Tarkajvālā*, and Avalokitavrata's *Prajñāpradīpaṭīkā*. In addition to these direct and paraphrased citations of Indian *śāstras* the author references early Kadampa teachers, including Geshé Gönpawa, Geshé Tönpa, and Potowa Rinchen Sal.

The commentary does not contain any topical outlines (*sa bcad*) that are found extensively in the works of other early Tibetan scholars such as Ngok Loden Sherap (Kano 2008). The author does provide divisions of the subject matter of *Entry to the Two Realities* and commentary when commenting on verses 7cd–9. At this point in the commentary, the author states that one will remove afflictive and cognitive obstructions if one realizes: the divisions of the two realities (*bden pa gnyis kyi dbye ba*), the divisions of the conventional (*kun rdzob kyi dbye ba*), the nature of each type of conventional (*kun rdzob so so'i rang bzhin*), the indivisible ultimate (*don dam pa dbye ba med pa*), the negation of others' assertions of their existence (*gzhan dag yod par 'dod pa dgag pa*), and the ultimate free from elaborations (*don dam spros bral du bstan pa*). In addition to these divisions, the author uses a double *shad* to mark a new section of the commentary. In the annotated translation, I have placed folio numbers in brackets at the points where the author marks a new section. The folio numbers of these sections, along with my own outline headings that summarize each section's content, are as follows:

1b1 Introduction
2a8 Subject matter of the text [verse 1]
3b4 Yogācāra tenets
4a4 All teachings of a buddha are included within the two realities
4a8 Ultimate reality
4b1 Conventional reality: two aspects [verse 2]
4b7 Bad tenets
4b8 Non-Buddhist bad tenets
5a4 Correct conventional reality [verse 3]
5b3 Objects of knowledge: conditioned or unconditioned
5b6 Conventional reality
6a8 Geshé Tönpa on correct conventional reality
6b3 Two realities and four truths
7a2 Indivisible ultimate reality [verse 4]
7a6 Indicating the ultimate through words [verse 5]
7a8 The ultimate is free from all elaborations

7b2 No differentiation in emptiness [verses 6–7ab]
8b1 Ultimate reality is beyond all elaborations [verses 7cd–9]
9a4 Realizing the ultimate eliminates afflictive and cognitive obstructions
9a7 The means of realizing the ultimate [verses 10–12ab]
9b3 Inference
9b7 Direct perception and inference are useless [verses 12cd–14]]
10a1 The purpose of digests on valid cognition
10a6 How does one realize emptiness? [verses 15–16ab]
11a5 84,000 articles of dharma [verse 16ce]
11b6 The purpose of meditation [verse 17ab]
12b5 Do not have contempt for correct conventional reality [verse 17cf]
13a6 The fault of having contempt for the conventional [verse 18]
13b4 Integrating means and wisdom [verse 19]
13b6 Relying on the convetional [verse 20]
14a1 Meditation on emptiness is necessary
14a4 The two realities are equivalent to the means and the goal
14a6 The two realities are not different entities [verse 21]
14b4 How conventional appearances are established [22ab]
14b6 Appearances are established by causes and conditions [verses 22cd–23]
15a4 The benefit of understanding the integration of the two realities [verse 24]
15b1 Cherish only what achieves integration [verse 25]
16a1 Reason for composing the text [verses 26–28]
16a5 Colophon

The content of the *Collection on the Two Realities* consists of a free-flowing commentary on Atiśa's *Entry to the Two Realities* framed within the context of "Special Instructions on the Middle Way." The text centers on the special instructions (*man ngag* or *gdams ngag*) of Madhyamaka, which provide guidance in developing insight derived from meditative cultivation (*bhāvanā-mayī-prajñā*), the third level of insight that comes after initial rote learning and study (*śrūta-mayī-prajñā*) and intellectual integration (*cintāmayī-prajñā*) of Buddhist teachings. This type of Madhyamaka commentary centers on cultivating a direct, nonconceptual experience of the truth of reality—nonarising (*skye ba med pa*)—based on the special lineage instructions that one has received from an authentic spiritiual teacher. The commentary will repeatedly emphasize that direct realization of ultimate reality comes from nonconceptual meditative cultivation and not through valid cognition, that one must rely on special instructions from a spiritual teacher, and that the teacher should be in the spiritual lineage of Nāgārjuna and Candrakīrti that is upheld by Atiśa.

The Commentary on Conventional Reality, Ultimate Reality, and Valid Cognition

The *Collection on the Two Realities* cites only portions of verses from *Entry to the Two Realities* and then comments on the verses. I have cited verses in bold print apart from the commentary for reference, and I highlight in bold print the verses as they appear in the commentary. In the following pages I examine the opening portions of the commentary and the sections related to conventional reality, ultimate reality, and valid cognition in order to illustrate how early Kadampa thinkers understood the Madhyamaka vision of Atiśa's presentation of the two realities.

The longest portion of the *Collection on the Two Realities* is on the first part of the opening verse (2a8–4b1) of *Entry to the Two Realities*, which covers a number of basic concepts that are well-known to modern scholars. The author understands the opening phrase "The teaching of Dharma by buddhas" to include the four schools of tenets found within the vehicles of the Mahāyāna and Hīnayāna. He then proceeds to discuss the basic tenets of Vaibhāṣika (*bye brag tu smra pa*), Sautrāntika (*mdo sde pa*), Yogācāra (*sems tsam pa*), and Madhyamaka (*dbu ma pa*) in terms of the four points or seals (*bka' rtags kyi phyag rgya*) common to Buddhists: all conditioned things are impermanent, all contaminated things are suffering, all things are selfless, and nirvāṇa is peace. The author notes the different characteristics of these four tenet systems within these four common points. He does not make any distinctions of subschools within the tenet systems of the Vaibhāṣika, Sautrāntika, and, notably, the Madhyamaka. He does, however, briefly mention the Yogācāra subschools of Satyākāravāda (Tib. *rnam bden pa*) and Alīkākāravāda (Tib. *rnam rdzun pa*). The author offers a succinct presentation of Yogācāra tenets (3b4–4a4) primarily based on the teachings of Śāntipa, one of Atiśa's teachers in India.

Conventional Reality

The Kadampa author then proceeds to comment on the second part of the opening verse with a discussion on the two realities. Atiśa and his early Kadampa followers' understanding of conventional reality, based on the *Collection on the Two Realities, A General Explanation*, and other early Kadampa commentaries, is complex and multiform. In general, based on these sources,

Atiśa weaves together an account of conventional reality that brings together the thought of Nāgārjuna, Bhāviveka, Candrakīrti, and Śāntideva to place emphasis on soteriological efficacy in progressing on the path. The overarching structure of his system is based on Candrakīrti's *Madhyamakāvatāra* underlined with the understanding of dependent designation and mutual dependence of Nāgārjuna. Atiśa accepted the distinction between correct and incorrect conventional realities even though conventional realities are false and unreal. It is important to note, based on *A General Explanation*, that conventional realities are classified as mistaken or correct from three different frameworks or perspectives. Conventional realities are dependently designated in relation to the perspectives of (1) the worldly (*lo ka pa*), (2) philosophical tenets (*grub mtha'*), and (3) yogic awareness (*rnal 'byor pa'i blo*). Atiśa's understanding of the dependent-arising of conventional reality in correlation with its states of awareness also accords with what has been called "the relativity theory of the purity and validity of perception" in Madhyamaka works (Wangchuk 2009). In brief, Candrakīrti's *Madhyamakāvatāra* (6.30) and Śāntideva's *Bodhicaryāvatāra* (9.3–4ab) clearly state that the "undefiled cognition of a yogi can invalidate the defiled cognition of a nonyogin and not vice versa" (Wangchuk 2009, 233). Along these lines, the cognitions of advanced yogis successively invalidates the cognitions of lower yogis. For Atiśa and his early Kadampa followers, correct conventional realities are appearances of discerning awareness (*rig pa shes rab*) that occur after the path of vision and are considered pure mundane wisdom (*dag pa lo ka ba'i ye shes*). Correct conventional realities are considered nondeceptive (*mi slu ba*), nonerroneous, and trustworthy (*yid brtan du rung ba*) in that, from the perspective of one after the path of vision, appearances are realized to be unproduced like an illusion and objects are cognized as essenceless entities. Although correct, they are conventional owing to arising through causes and conditions and are considered illusions of pristine awareness (*rig pa ye shes kyi sgyu ma*). Correct conventional realities are nonerroneous illusions (*ma 'khrul ba sgyu ma*) and are imputations conducive to purification, since the causes of purification have nondeceptive individual results. The correct conventional reality that occurs after the path of vision consists of appearances of pure mundane wisdom (*dag pa lo ka ba'i ye shes kyi snang ba* [*dag pa 'ji rten pa'i ye shes ≈ śuddhalaukikajñāna*]) that Atiśa calls the "stairway of correct conventional reality." This system of the relativity of cognitive purity based on progress along the path underlies Atiśa's and his early Kadampa followers' presentation of the two realities.

Accordingly, the *Collection on the Two Realities* comments on the second portion of the first verse by following Candrakīrti's system of Madhyamaka. The Kadampa author's interpretation is based on *Madhyamakāvatāra*

(6.23–28), as he makes a distinction between conventional reality according to an ordinary being's perspective and "mere conventional" according to those who have realization, the *āryas* who have passed beyond ordinary appearances. At this point the Kadampa commentary also mentions that appearances for such *āryas* are "causally efficient and existent," but qualifies this causal efficiency as "merely illusory causal efficiency" (*sgyu ma'i don byed nus pa tsam*). Causal efficiency as a criteria for the conventional is generally found in the work of Madhyamaka scholars such as Śāntarakṣita and Jñānagarbha, but, just as well, the ability to perform actions for dependently designated conventional existents is also described in the works of Nāgārjuna and Candrakīrti.[385] The early Kadampa commentaries emphasize that causally efficient conventional realities lack substantial existence, and on this point move in the direction of illusory causal efficiency and away from an understanding of causal efficiency that may imply substantial existence or underlying real particulars (*svalakṣaṇa*). This point becomes clearer in the exegesis of verse 3.

At first glance, verse 3 seems to be following Śāntarakṣita's *Madhyamakālaṃkāra* (v. 64)[386] and Jñānagarbha's *Satyadvayavibhaṅgakārikā* (v. 12), as alluded to above.[387] However, Atiśa is following the *Madhyamakaratnapradīpa*, *Madhyamakahṛdaya*, and the *Tarkajvālā* attributed to Bhāviveka on this verse in relation to the broader context of Candrakīrti's system. This is because the *Madhyamakaratnapradīpa*, as well as Jñānagarbha's autocommentary to the *Satyadvayavibhaṅgakārikā,* mention that correct conventional reality, qualified by being not examined, produced by causes, and causal efficiency, is from the *perspective of those with narrow vision* (*tshu rol thong ba, arvāgdarśana*), the ordinary worldly person before the path of vision.[388] Correct conventional reality for the yogi, according to Atiśa and his Kadampa followers, occurs only after the path of vision. This accords with appearances of "purified worldly knowledge (*viśuddhalaukikajñāna*) mentioned by Bhāviveka in his *Madhyamakahṛdaya* and *Tarkajvālā*, which he refers to as the stairway of correct conventional reality (*tathyasaṃvṛtisopānam*).[389]

In this way, the *Collection on the Two Realities* provides an extended commentary on verse 3 (folios 5a4–7a2) and follows the *Madhyamakāvatāra* in utilizing the analogy of seeing "hairs with diseased eyes." The author also stresses that conventional reality is not substantially existent even though it is causally efficient. He connects the positing of causal efficiency with substantial existence to the views of Sautrāntika and Yogācāra positions as well as the views in some Madhyamaka texts. Although the author does not name specific Madhyamaka texts, he may be referring to the above works of Bhāviveka and Śāntarakṣita, among others.

The author continues commenting on verse 3 of the *Entry to the Two Reali-*

ties utilizing the *Dharmadhātustava* of Nāgārjuna and relying on a paraphrase of content from chapter 6 of the *Madhyamakāvatārabhāṣya* (La Vallée Poussin 1907–12, 109–10).[390] The commentary's focus in this section on the relativity of conventions based on healthy or degenerated sensory faculties, the notion that convention (*saṃvṛti*) means "concealer," the distinction between "mere convention" and "reality," as well as the discussion of appearances for *ārya* bodhisattvas in the postmeditative state are all found in the sixth chapter of Candrakīrti's autocommentary to the *Madhyamakāvatāra*.

The *Collection on the Two Realities* mentions at this point that appearances both exist and do not exist after the postmeditative state, according to Geshé Tönpa. The commentary is not clear on this point. The question of whether buddhas see appearances will be a point of debate between rival Madhyamaka interpretations among twelfth-century Tibetans.[391] This section of the commentary also discusses Geshé Tönpa's understanding of "correct conventional" reality. The commentary's discussion on Geshé Tönpa matches well a recent excerpt of his thought in the *Instructions on the View* (*lta khrid*) *of the Two Truths* by Prajñāraśmi (1518–84). As recorded in that text, Geshé Tönpa explains "correct conventional" reality as follows:

> In the mind of ordinary beings up to those who reached the Supreme Dharma of the World (*laukikāgradharma, 'jig rten chos mchog*) all appearances only proceed as mistaken conventional [reality], because they are established by mistaken knowledge. Concerning the appearances [perceived by] mistaken knowledge, we do not make the twofold distinction of what is mistaken and what is correct. Both belong to mistaken conventional [reality]. Since they are not suitable as the [correct] path, we do not use the term "correct."
>
> All appearances of the post-meditative period (*pṛṣṭhalabdha, rjes thob*), from the first stage [of bodhisattva] up to the higher ones, are known as correct conventional [reality]. Because they are not interrupted by any appearances, they belong to correct conventional [reality]. These illusory appearances are recognized as illusory by a direct perception (*pratyakṣa, mngon gsum*). Because this is suitable as the [correct] path, we call it correct conventional [reality].[392]

The indication is that the path advocated here is one in which the two realities are "integrated" (*zung du 'jug pa'i lam*): the conventional becomes more and more purified as one collects merit and the ultimate is realized through cognition of selflessness, leading up to the integration of both realities in the final result of buddhahood. The commentary will explain this process through

Candrakīrti's ocular analogy of the "diseased eyes seeing hair" when discussing verses related to ultimate reality.

Ultimate Reality

Atiśa defines ultimate reality in his *Entry to the Two Realities* verse 4 as only one. The *Collection on the Two Realities* relates this definition to the indivisible nature of emptiness that is nondifferentiated (*dbye ba med pa nyid*). The commentary then tersely elaborates on ultimate reality's quality of oneness by connecting it with the single vehicle (*ekayāna*) mentioned in the *Saddharmapuṇḍarīka* and the one moment (*ekakṣana*) of the path of vision advocated in Candrakīrti's *Yuktiṣaṣṭikāvṛtti*. The Kadampa commentary is thoroughly following the understanding of Candrakīrti, as the *Madhyamakāvatārabhāṣya* specifies that since suchness is itself immutable (*rnam par mi 'gyur ba nyid*) the wisdom that takes suchness as its object is also of one nature and undifferentiable from it. Therefore in Candrakīrti's system, followed by Atiśa and his Kadampa adherents, "the equality of all dharmas" (Skt. *sarvadharmasamatā*) in ultimate reality means that there are not multiple vehicles nor multiple moments in the path of vision (see Apple 2015b).

The Mādhyamika stance against the multiplicity and diversity of ultimate reality was not upheld by all Mahāyāna groups, according to Atiśa and his commentators. The remaining commenatry on verse 4 is perhaps the most surprising in terms of philosophical expectations, as the author mentions that "**Others**" in Atiśa's text refers to the Yogācāra. In every modern discussion of *Entry to the Two Realities* verse 4, the referent to the term "**Others**" is considered to refer to Mādhyamikas, who posit multiple types of the ultimate. On this point some scholars see that Atiśa may be referring to Bhāviveka, who states in his *Tarkajvālā*:

> The ultimate is of two kinds: one engages thoroughly effortlessly, passes beyond the world, is undefiled, and lacks proliferation; the second engages with thorough effort, accords with the collection of merit and wisdom, is called "pure worldly wisdom," and possesses proliferations.[393]

Other scholars suggest that Atiśa is pointing toward Indian scholars who posit a concordant ultimate, such as Jñānagarbha, Śāntarakṣita, Kamalaśīla, and Haribhadra (see Nagashima 2004, 74–78). From the late-eleventh to the early twelfth-century perspective of our Tibetan author, the opponents throughout the text are Yogācāras. In the later portion of the commentary (folio 16a1), the author will identify Serlingpa and Śāntipa, teachers of Atiśa known to be Yogācāra thinkers, as qualified scholars (*ācārya*) who, nevertheless, have an inadequate philosophical view.

As mentioned, the commentary explains the process of realizing ultimate reality through an ocular analogy that is found in the works of Candrakīrti. The commentator attributes the basis of his discussion to responses that Atiśa gave to Tibetan scholars on his view of Madhyamaka at Ngari after first arriving in Tibet.[394] This section, which discusses a person with eye disease seeing hair and then becoming purified of seeing hair, is a paraphrase of Candrakīrti's discussion found in chapter 6 (6.29–31) of the *Madhyamakāvatārabhāṣya* (La Vallée Poussin 1907–12, 109–11). The commentarial exegesis makes clear that the *Collection on the Two Realities* follows Atiśa's Madhyamaka tradition of adhering to Candrakīrti.

Atiśa and Early Kadampas on Valid Cognition

In addition to clarifying remarks on conventional and ultimate reality, the *Collection on the Two Realities* provides instructive points on Atiśa's understanding of valid cognition. As modern scholarship and post-thirteenth-century Tibetan scholars have understood, valid cognition was discussed by Indian Buddhist thinkers from the time of Nāgārjuna and utilized by self-proclaimed Mādhyamikas from the time of Bhāviveka onward. The question for a number of Indian Buddhist thinkers was the role that valid cognition had in Buddhist soteriology. Atiśa and his Kadampa commentators have a decisive understanding on this issue.

Contrary to modern and traditional descriptions, Atiśa was not totally averse to valid cognition. According to an early, yet brief, outline of Atiśa's life found in *Sherab Dorjé's Explanation of Atiśa's Entry to the Two Realities*, after taking ordination at Vikramaśīla Monastery, Atiśa studied the science of epistemology and logic (*hetuvidyā*) as a means to refute non-Buddhist opponents. According to Sherab Dorjé, the study of epistemology and logic consisted of digests on valid cognition (*tshad ma'i bstan chos*) that was part of the tenth-century Buddhist university's curriculum necessary to gain omniscience in the five fields of knowledge (*pañcavidyāsthāna*). The study of valid cognition to gain omniscience is found in the *Mahāyānasūtrālaṃkārabhāṣya* as one of five fields of knowledge.[395] The *Mahāyānasūtrālaṃkārabhāṣya* repeatedly mentions that *hetuvidyā* is studied as a means to refute the arguments of those who do not have faith in the Mahāyāna.

According to the colophon, Atiśa also edited and revised an early translation of Dharmakīrti's *Vādanyāyanāmaprakaraṇa*[396] at the request of a king in western Tibet. Van der Kuijp (2013, xii) has recently shown that Atiśa possessed Sanskrit manuscripts of Dignāga's *Pramāṇasamuccya* and of Kamalaśīla's *Tattvasaṃgrahapañjikā*. In brief, Atiśa was fully literate regarding texts on valid cognition. On the other hand, as mentioned in chapter 1, Atiśa lists scholars of epistemology and logic as the lowest of Buddhist groups in *Open Basket of Jewels*. This list of scholars is organized by subject matter in an increasingly hierarchical order that places Madhyamaka scholars at the top. Placing scholars of logic, Dignāga and Dharmakīrti, lower than Vaibhāṣika, Sautrāntika, Yogācāra, and Madhyamaka scholars indicates that for Atiśa the science of epistemology and logic was "a profane secular science that is common to the Buddhist and other Indian non-Buddhist schools such as the Naiyāyikas" (Krasser 2004, 130).

Atiśa's most explicit statement on valid cognition is initially in verse 10 of *Entry to the Two Realities*.[397] We may infer that Atiśa's view of valid cognition in this text represents what he taught in India and not just in Tibet.[398] In this verse Atiśa indicates that Buddhists accept the two valid cognitions of direct perception and inference. He must be referring to Dignāga, Dharmakīrti, and other epistemologists who accept the restriction of the number of valid cognitions to two. Atiśa does not indicate if he himself accepts only these two conventionally. In its comments on this verse, the *Collection on the Two Realities* counts six types of valid cognition upheld by non-Buddhists found in Śāntarakṣita's *Tattvasaṃgraha*, while also noting that Nāgārjuna's *Vigrahavyāvartanī* accepts four types of valid cognition. The commentary merely states without any remarks that there is a distinction between these two sources. The commentary emphasizes (folios 9b7–10a5) that digests on valid cognition are mainly for the purpose of refuting non-Buddhists and protecting the Buddha's teaching.

All the early Kadampa authors state throughout their commentaries that realization of emptiness is based on special instructions from one's spiritual teacher and that realizing the two realities does not come about through "initial hearing and thinking." The authors are alluding to the idea that direct realization of emptiness is not possible on levels of training that involve initial rote learning and study (*śrūta-mayī-prajñā*) and intellectual integration (*cintāmayī-prajñā*) of Buddhist teachings. *Special Instructions on the Middle Way* teachings are given at the level of wisdom cultivated in meditation (*bhāvanāmayī-prajñā*). The *Collection on the Two Realities* commentary considers *āgama*, or scriptural tradition, to be a form of direct perception (*pratyakṣa*), since it is derived from the Buddha's omniscient wisdom. Quite different from Dignāga and Dharmakīrti, who understand *āgama* to be a form of inference (*āgamāśritānumāna*).[399] Rather, this view resembles Candrakīrti's statement that "the word of trustworthy [persons] cognizing supersensible things in a direct [perceptual] manner, this is scripture."[400]

Entry to the Two Realities verses 12cd–14 point out the "inherent epistemological relativism of speculative reasoning" (van der Kuijp and McKeown 2013, xxxvi) with regard to ultimate reality. These verses explicitly reject speculative reasoning (*tarka, rtog ge*) and valid cognition through direct perception and inference to be useless for realizing reality. The verses also substantiate this claim through the justification of scripture (*āgama*). Later verses (*Satyadvayāvatāra*, v. 21) will mention the use of analytical reasoning, *yukti*, for examining the reality of conventional objects. Atiśa therefore maintains the use of scripture and reasoning for realizing reality while rejecting speculative logical reasoning and valid cognition for this purpose.

The early Kadampa understanding of scripture and reasoning and its relation to the lineage of spiritual gurus is explicitly discussed in *A General Explanation*, which states (*ad* 704.14) that Madhyamaka reasonings consist of nonimplicative negations that are special instructions for meditation directed toward nonverbal realization and are not based on argument. These reasonings consist of consequences that expose contradictions that are applied with inferences known to others. They are utilized to refute mistaken assertions and lead to nonconceptual realization (*ad* 706.16–24). They are found in scriptures such as the *Perfection of Wisdom* and *Suvarṇaprabhāsottama*. *A General Explanation* explains that these reasonings based on scriptural authority are constituted by nonimplicative negations and do not involve the valid cognition of those with narrow vision.

A General Explanation and *Entry to the Two Realities* therefore indicate that Atiśa's use of valid cognition is only for conventional reality and not for the ultimate. This appears to be congruent with the position of Dignāga, who, as Krasser (2004) and Kujip and McKeown (2013, xxxii) have recently documented, states that the "teaching of the Tathāgata is not the object of speculative reasoning." Jinendrabuddhi, a commentator on Dignāga, emphasizes that "speculative reasoning" is for "correct knowledge of everyday life" and not the "supermundane religion of the Bhagavan that is the object of personal experience" (Kujip and McKeown 2013, xxxiii).

In this way, Atiśa and his early followers accept the use of logic and epistemology as part of the five fields of knowledge to refute non-Buddhists and Buddhists (Krasser 2004). Valid cognition is utilized at the conventional level only to refute opponents. The application of valid cognition is at the level of intellectual integration (*cintamayī-prajñā*), not during the cultivation of wisdom during meditation (*bhāvanāmayī-prajñā*), the path stage where the realization of the ultimate takes place. For Atiśa and his early Kadampa followers, ultimate reality is cognized introspectively by the yogī through interiorized awareness (*pratyātmavedya*) during meditation.

Atiśa and His Followers on Reasoning

The Kadampa commentaries to Atiśa's *Entry to the Two Realities* as well as the commentaries to Atiśa's *Special Instructions on the Middle Way* differentiate the use of valid cognition and reasoning at the conventional level. Atiśa states in verse 21 of *Entry to the Two Realities* that when conventional realities are analytically examined nothing is found and that "the unfindable" (*ma rnyed pa nyid*) is the ultimate. In his *Special Instructions on the Middle Way*, Atiśa compares the reasoning process to two sticks, which after rubbing together and generating a fire, burn up and become nonexistent. Atiśa states that "wisdom itself, without appearance and luminous, is not established with any nature at all." In *Open Basket of Jewels*, Atiśa states that "the wisdom of individual analysis (*so sor rtog pa'i shes rab*) itself turns into clear light." Prajñāmokṣa in his *Commentary on the Special Instructions on the Middle Way* also clarifies that reasoning negates itself at the culmination of analytical cognition. Such passages indicate that, for Atiśa and his followers, reasoning is a conventional process that dissolves itself when seeking to establish the existence of an object.

On the other hand, Atiśa mentions a different use of analysis toward the end of *Entry to the Two Realities* in verse 27 where he states that followers of his work should accept his teaching after thorough analysis and not just out of faith alone. In commenting on this verse the *Collection on the Two Realities* emphasizes that it is important to examine the sayings of the Buddha and cites the *Mahāyānasūtrālaṃkāra* as a source for examining Dharma with reason.[401] *Sherab Dorjé's Explanation of Atiśa's Entry to the Two Realities* interprets the phrase "after thorough analysis" with the following remarks:

> The text stating "by examining well" is, in practice, not contradictory to perceptible (*pratyakṣa*) objects of valid cognition. It is not contradictory with the inference for imperceptible (*parokṣa*) objects. It is not contradictory with the scriptural authority (*āgama*) for radically inaccessible (*atyantaparokṣa*) objects. On this very topic the Buddhas has taught,
>
> > O monks, just as wise persons accept gold only after cutting, polishing, and comparing it, so too you should accept my words after examining them, and not out of respect for me.

> Well then, does this contradict the explanation given earlier that valid cognition is unnecessary? The explanation given earlier is that "valid cognition does not directly realize final reality." In this case it does not contradict since it is taught in the context of discerning appraisable objects (*gzhal bya*).[402]

Sherab Dorjé's commentary accepts the use of valid cognition for discerning appraisable objects on the level of conventional reality.

These points indicate that early Kadampa authors, in their understanding of Atiśa's *Entry to the Two Realities*, uphold the traditional pre-sixth-century Buddhist separation of *yukti*, an internal Buddhist form of critical analysis, from *hetu-vidyā*, the external epistemological devices used to defend Buddhist Dharma and defeat non-Buddhist opponents (see Eltschinger 2010). Moreover, as the Kadampa author of the *Collection on the Two Realities* never directly cites or references either Dignāga or Dharmakīrti with regard to reasoning, the processes of *yukti* followed by the commentary represent a pure Madhyamaka-lineage tradition of understanding reasoning processes derived from the *Prajñāpāramitā* and the works of Nāgārjuna.

In sum, the commentary indicates that the author understands, like Atiśa, that direct perception and inference are conventionally accepted in order to protect the Buddha's teaching and to debate with non-Buddhists. However, valid cognition is not accepted for realizing ultimate reality, as the realization of ultimate reality relies on nonconceptual gnosis cultivated on the authority of the Buddha's teachings and the spiritual teacher in the lineage of Nāgārjuna and Candrakīrti.

Concluding Remarks

The following annotated translation of the *Collection on the Two Realities* makes a number of points concerning the twelfth-century Kadampa understandings of Atiśa on the two realities. The commentary is primarily concerned with a direct realization of ultimate reality that is integrated with the practices of method based on correct conventional reality. It advocates a faith-based Madhyamaka combined with reasoning that relies on the works of Nāgārjuna and Candrakīrti while maintaining a critique of Yogācāra. Madhyamaka thinkers were not in conflict with one another. The very issues that would polarize later Tibetan thinkers into differentiating Bhāviveka and Candrakīrti's writings on Madhyamaka, and into differentiating the writings of other Madhyamakas such as Jñānagarbha and Kamalaśīla, had yet to develop in Tibet at the time that this commentary was composed. As

Ruegg (2000, 17) notes, "In Dīpaṅkaraśrījñāna's time and circle, Bhavya's and Candrakīrti's schools of Madhyamaka were apparently not clearly differentiated by distinct designations and they were evidently being studied side by side." We may infer that Atiśa and his early Kadampa followers saw Candrakīrti and Bhāviveka as undifferentiated Madhyamakas. Nevertheless, the commentary mentions several factors in Candrakīrti's thought, such as its hostility to Buddhist epistemology and its promoting of scriptural authority, that would become central features of early Prāsaṅgika-Madhyamaka movements in later twelfth- and thirteenth-century Tibet (Vose 2010a, 559).

Collection on the Two Realities

[1a1] ***Collection on the Two Realities*** [emended from *Collection of Special Instructions on the Middle Way*]

[1b1] Homage to the Bhagavan Mañjuśrī

In general, from among the two [types] who engage [in Buddhist practice], that is, the follower of Dharma who possesses wisdom and the follower of faith,[403] it is necessary for us to establish only the one who follows a trustworthy person, one who has faith. In this regard, all these teachings are established as trustworthy or as a place of faith only [for those who] possess great conviction in the meaning of the profound.[404] [This teaching was] requested by Sangphuwa [Lekpai Sherap], who became a great yogi. It was composed by a great paṇḍita who found the status of ācārya in all fields of knowledge (*rig pa'i gnas*) (i.e., Atiśa). It is drawn from the excellent [teaching] translated by the guide who found great intellectual understanding in the Dharma of both India and Tibet. Having witnessed this Geshé Gönpawa, I will comment on these bestowed special instructions of Atiśa, since Atiśa's special instructions are taught as a bestowal that is a completely pure lineage. As it says in the *Satyadvayāvatāra* [15d–16b], "the truth of reality will be realized through the special instructions of the lineage from [Nāgārjuna and his disciple Candrakīrti]." These are held to be the only special instructions. Gönpawa himself, at the time of granting these special instructions of wisdom, conferred uncorrupted words. This Dharma is not only three. Although there are many words given from Lord [Atiśa] that are easy to undersand, this Dharma is unlike an eternalist system and is not an eternalist teaching of paṇḍitas. Since this commentary is freshly written as a bit of intellectual understanding from the teachings of Atiśa, it is a source in which to have confidence. It is unnecessary to lament construing the two realities of Ācārya [Nāgārjuna's] system, as all that is in this *Satyadvayāvatāra* teaching is sufficient. There is not another teaching like this in any Indian or Tibetan language.

[In the Indian language: *Satyadvayāvatāra*
In the Tibetan language: *Bden pa gnyis la 'jug pa*][405]

Based on a discussion among the previous kings, great ministers, and great translators who posited three great necessities, the Indian-language title is written at the top. In this regard, the three necessities are: the necessity to know that it [the *Satyadvayāvatāra*] was created in India and to show gratitude for its creation, the necessity of [showing] its authenticity (*khungs btsun pa*), and the necessity of the Indian-language title's utility to quickly apprehend the words transcribed as an equivalent to the Tibetan language. Regarding that, first, prior to the occurrence of Dharma throughout Tibet there was darkness, [people were] like animals without a distinctive [spiritual] practice. Then appeared a little illumination of wisdom and a little practice for achieving high rebirth and definite goodness. This knowledge is a kindness of the Dharma and [2a] comes about by just that desire for truth. What is called truth in reality when examined by reasoning is the reality of things that has abided from the beginning: the unproduced nature that is ultimate reality. Accordingly, when meditating on the characteristic of the two realities and ultimate reality, it is not realized by the valid cognition of those with narrow vision[406] or by logic, but is realized from the special instructions of the spiritual teacher. In order to achieve liberation through realizing [ultimate reality], if one goes ahead and cultivates the method that relies on conventional reality, then there will be realization, but nonrealizations acquired through listening and reflection will be cut off if [one is] not cultivating an extensive method for [realizing] emptiness. First one should make firm the method by conviction in cause and effect through relying on conventional reality. Then, increasing one's intention to accumulate merit and relying on the spiritual teacher's special instructions, through gradually engaging in meditation that integrates both method and wisdom, one stands firm in a natural state of absorption on reality that interrupts all conventional objects through realizing the object of the ultimate, nonarising. Through the power of that [meditation] one will gradually produce in one's mind a spontaneous and uninterrupted vision of things as they are for other obscured objects, through designation that is said to be both the general meaning of words that appear to the mind and those that are set forth in texts.

[Homage to the Great Compassionate One][407]

The translator's homage is independent, as there is no known decree in India for salutations.[408] The [translator's] purpose is twofold and properly respectful:

to overturn any obstacles and a promise to finish the composition. The present purpose of the translator is that we, as followers of the Mahāyāna who have set about to realize the two realities, offer worship and prayers directly to the Tathāgata and offer prayers to the Tathāgata to attest to the karmic obstructions that impede realizing the two realities. When praying "May we realize the meaning of the two realities just as they are," owing to the blessing of those [prayers], we will realize the two realities, as the two [realities] are not able to be clarified by logic.

[The Dharma taught by buddhas perfectly relies on two realities: the conventional reality of the world and ultimate reality. (v. 1)][409]

The subject matter of the text is "**The Dharma taught by buddhas perfectly relies on two realities** [1ab]," that is, all the pronouncements of a Buddha are grouped together within two realities.[410] [2b] Generally, although the two realities exist for each individual mind, since the Ācārya Nāgārjuna had not yet arrived in the world, there were no established texts for both the Greater and Lesser Vehicles. The Ācārya [Nāgārjuna] established texts of the Great Vehicle. Since Ācārya Asaṅga had not yet appeared, there were no Madhyamaka and Cittamātra [systems]. Asaṅga established the Cittamātra [system]. Since Ācārya Dignāga had not yet appeared in the world, there was no Satyākāravāda (*rnam pa bden*) and Alīkākāravāda (*rnam pa rdzun*) of the Cittamātra [system]. Lord [Atiśa] has said that his (i.e., Dignāga) work is of the Satyākāravāda [system].

Generally, the Buddha's teaching consists of four points: all conditioned things are impermanent, all contaminated things are suffering, all things are selfless, and nirvāṇa is peace.[411] For Buddhists, in general, from among the four great traditions, the eighteen *śrāvaka* schools are grouped by four root schools[412] and uphold the tenets of the Sautrāntikas and the Vaibhāṣikas. As explained from the authoritative root text and commentary of the *Abhidharmakośa*, both are described as positing five bases of knowables.[413] The Lord [Atiśa] has stated that he received the transmission of commitments from the eighteen schools, and there are said to be eighteen dissimilar systems of defining the twelve links of dependent-arising and [dissimilar] systems of asserting all sixteen moments of awareness on the path of vision. Also, each individual school is taught to be devoted to the tenets of the Vaibhāṣikas or to the tenets of the Sautrāntikas. From among the four seals (*bka' rtags kyi phyag rgya bzhi*), [the principle that] all conditioned things are impermanent [refers to] momentary impermanence and the impermanence of a continuum. The impermanence of a continuum (*rgyun gyi mi rtag pa*) is accepted by all Buddhists. Although momentary impermanence is not accepted by some schools, those [schools] are refuted by the *Mahāyānasūtrālaṃkāra.*[414] It is exhausting that they do not accept [momentary impermanence, as they] do not realize their own ignorance in being mistaken on this [point]. In the first place, the reasoning that refutes the extremes of nondisintegrating and nonchanging establishes momentariness. [The principle that] all contaminated things are suffering is accepted by all. As for [the principle that] all things are selfless, there are some schools, such as the Vātsīputrīyas (*gnas ma bu'i sde pa*) and so forth, who say that there is an unspeakable person that exists that is other than the aggregates.[415] This [statement] is established as incorrect only from among all the *śāstra*s that were translated in Tibet. [3a] "Nirvāṇa is peace" is accepted by all, but the Vaibhāṣikas and the Yogācārins accept [*nirvāṇa*] to substantially exist and the Sautrāntikas and Madhyamakas accept [*nirvāṇa*] as merely nominally designated. Also, for these, the first two [points] are grouped together as conventional reality and the later [two] as ultimate reality. The general characteristic of things as being selfless, when construed in terms of reality is the ultimate reality, and when construed in terms of the truth of suffering is conventional reality.

Generally, all objects of knowledge are grouped into five bases of knowables; the Yogācārins specifically assert a base of form that appears. Most schools posit a base of form. A base of the principle mind, a base of mental factors, a base of conditioned forces dissociated from thought, and an immutable unconditioned factor base are not proclaimed as a distinction of appearance. In this regard, the Vaibhāṣikas assert the nature of fifteen dharmas as the base of form. They accept that both color and shape are substantially established. The Sautrāntikas accept fourteen dharmas.[416] They accept that color is substantially established and that shape is nominally designated. It is difficult to find a distinction of substantial and nominal between these two. Both of these schools accept a primary mind and six groups of consciousness, while Cittamātrins have different systems, some of which accept six, some accept eight, and some accept only one.[417] Most Mādhyamikas accept six. Regarding [the different schools'] system [of asserting] production: the Vaibhāṣikas accept production without aspects and the Sautrāntikas accept production with aspects.[418] Further, with regard to assertions up to pervading the ground of a buddha, among those teachings of profound meaning that establish wisdom and so forth, the buddha ground is established as beyond either [type of production]. The Yogācārins accept both production as true and production as false. The Mādhyamikas do not accept production that is substantially established. Mental factors are accepted by some to be nominally existent based on the *Mahāyānasūtrālaṃkāra*. Some accept [mental factors] as substantially established. The conditioned forces dissociated from thought are accepted as substantially existent by the Vaibhāṣikas. The [schools from the] Sautrāntikas on up accept the place of the three later [bases] as nominally existent. There are dissimilar systems for accepting the immutable unconditioned among the four traditions. Mahāyānists, when initially [3b] a monk or novice from the Sautrāntikas, posit all conventional things like the Sautrāntika, and among the Vaibhāṣika, posit conventional things like the Vaibhāṣikas.

In this regard, generally the tenets of schools are easy to establish [as] having relied on the four truths. They are settled by means of the four truths, which are grouped by two, in terms of cause and effect, for defilement and purification. The selflessness of the agent at the time of the cause for defilement is the mere truth of arising of both karma and afflictions. The selflessness of the person at the time of the result is merely suffering. At the time of the cause and effect of purification it is the selflessness of the one who cultivates the path and the one who is liberated. Even for those who accept merely the path and cessation, there is a system to posit a Middle Way whose meaning consists of two realities free from the two extremes. Also, for the Mādhyamikas, the first three truths are grouped as conventional reality, and the truth of cessation is classified as ultimate reality, as stated in the *Yuktiṣaṣṭikāvṛtti*[419] and the *Madhyamakāvatāra*[420] and so forth.

[3b4] The tenets of the Yogācārins are easy to establish by means of three characteristics: they posit as a conventional [characteristic] that which occurs and arises as the basis of form, and the six groups of consciousness that apprehend that are accepted as an imagined [charactereristic] (*kun tu brtag pa, parikalpita*). The base of mind and the base of mental factors [are posited] as the dependent [characteristic] (*gzhan dbang, paratantra*), which is mere cognitive representation, and the base of conditioned forces dissociated from thought is designated within the context of the [dependent]. The base of the immutable unconditioned is accepted as the perfected [characteristic] (*yong su grub pa, pariniṣpanna*). They assert that this system has two realities that [comprise] a middle [way] that has the meaning of being free from the two extremes [of existence and nonexistence]. The imagined [characteristic] is asserted to not conventionally exist at all, or by some [it is accepted] as an erroneous conventional. According to the Satyākāravāda, consciousness is asserted to be produced as the aspects (*rnam pa, ākāra*) of the object, and according to the Alīkākāravāda, consciousness is like a pure crystal undirected by the object. They either assert appearances with various aspects or without various aspects. Moreover, appearances as diverse are cognitions of the appearance itself, and appearance itself has the nature of being erroneous knowledge. In dependence on the former mere cognitive representation, subsequent arisings are the dependent [characteristic] that is conventional reality. In this regard, the perfected [characteristic], which is the immutable base of the unconditioned,

suchness and so forth, is the reality that is empty. The wisdom that is the meditative equipoise on that object and the unmistaken perfected [characteristic] are asserted as ultimate reality. The former is the pure worldly wisdom that is the dependent [characteristic] that functions as an object, and the perfected [characteristic] that is unmistaken is accepted as being ultimate reality. The Ācārya Śāntipa states in his special instructions on the *Perfection of Wisdom* that the nature that is proclaimed as the three characteristics is both conventional reality and ultimate reality.[421] According to the Madhyamaka, through convention, all bases of proclamations are conventional realities, and the imagined [characteristic] is called either a mistaken conventional or a worldly conventional. Also, since the unmistaken perfected [characteristic] is included within the dependent [characteristic], all others have the nature of conventionals. The immutable perfected [characteristic] is asserted to be included within ultimate reality.

[4a4] In this regard, all teachings of a buddha are included within the two realities, and the two realities and their characteristics are taught from multiple sūtras such as the *Daśabhūmika* and so forth. What are these? They are accepted as **"the conventional reality of the world and ultimate reality"** (v. 1cd). As it occurs from the special instruction of the Madhyamaka, all things, which are grouped according to aggregates, elements, and sensory media, are construed based on an ordinary perspective as established according to cause and effect, and what is called reality is that which is merely accepted as reality according to the world.[422] By those who have realized the nature of conventional things and who have passed beyond, things appear as false, but since they are not imputed or presumed to be real, they are called "mere conventional." Trained in language, seeing forms or appearances like a rainbow in the sky, appearances for them are also causally efficacious. They are merely illusory causally efficacious.[423] For the meaning of the two realities, Candrakīrti, with unmistaken intelligence, asserts that what is called conventional reality is merely asserted as reality by the world but is not substantially established.

[4a8] Ultimate reality has the ultimate as its aim. The root of binding sentient beings in saṃsāra is apprehending things as real, and since the antidote that abandons [this false apprehension] is to realize the ultimate meaning, the unproduced, the ultimate is the principle meaning that is to be sought out or to be achieved, as it is the object of the highest wisdom. The true nature of the conventional, from the very beginning, is an unproduced entity.

> **[The conventional has two aspects: one that is mistaken and one that is correct. The former is twofold: the moon [reflected on] water and the conceptions of bad doctrines. (v. 2)]**[424]

[4b1] Regarding this, **the conventional has two aspects: one that is mistaken and one that is correct.** First, mistaken conventionals have **two aspects:** the eight similes of illusion[425] and so forth, like [a moon's] reflection in water. Since it is an actual causally efficacious moon and a mirage in actual water, although [the moon and water are] empty, when they are accepted by the world as mistaken, they are called mistaken. As it is stated:

> Although correct and mistaken conventional [realities] are similar in appearance, they are distinguished by their ability or inability to perform fuctions.[426]

And

> Just as a mirage looks like but is not water . . .[427]

One states as such, but the actual nature of the eight examples is not a mistaken [conventional], since it is known as it is even by pure worldly perception. Therefore, one makes an example for both realities. The various appearances of an illusory cow and so forth that are actually empty is an example of an ultimate, since when one examines by reason the very nature of that appearance, its own-nature is not established. Like those that are actually empty, that which appears from illusory causes and conditions is an example of a conventional, since it appears even though it is not established when examined. Therefore, the Ācārya stated:

> Convinced that impermanent things are like the moon's reflection in water, neither true nor false, one is not carried away by philosophical views.[428]

The **conceptions of bad tenets** are also mistaken conventionals. For all philosophical tenets, including Mere Cognitive Representation (*vijñāptimātra*) on down, are included. Those objects that they impute as real are not existent even conventionally. Those [objects] are said here to be [based on] a mind that conceptualizes. In the wish to abandon tenets, or mistaken views, and be liberated from bonds, holders of philosophical tenets increase mistakes and make bonds out to be supreme, but do not make the correct aim that examines things as they are.

[4b7] As bad tenets [are like] the reflection of [the] moon in water that appears lifeless to monkeys, or [are likened to] beasts that are blindly guided by mirages, they are a cause of being bound in saṃsāra and falling into bad realms

of rebirth, and are especially not the goal. From this point of view, correctness is through having the characteristics of correct conventionals.

[4b8] The bad tenets of Sāṃkhya assert twenty-five *tattvas*[429] and [5a] the Vaiśeṣikas six *padārtha*[430] and the tenets of Vedic knowledge; all this appears as accepting the essence of a single great being—the sun and the moon are its eyes, space is its back, the great earth is its belly, the four directions are the limbs, and the stars are its body hair, as stated by Avalokitavrata. There is little harm for us from them. This tradition of the Bon-po appears from the old manuscripts in the section on the Vaiśeṣika. In the *Tarkajvālā*, all these tenets accept the arising of existence from an egg. The Bon also accept a measure of being like this, [but] that is not established in the texts of the outsiders. There are said to be outside views that occur though one's own bad predispositions, and Potowa has proclaimed that the view that claims cause and effect does not exist as having the greatest harm. A yoga similar to this does not exist in the tradition of the Buddhists. The systems established by our own schools, such as the ones previously indicated, are accepted as being superseded by higher and higher tenets.

> **[Something that is pleasing only as long as it is not examined, which arises and ceases to exist and which is capable of causal efficacy, is held to be correct convention. (v. 3)]**[431]

[5a4] What is correct conventional reality? It is said to be "**not analyzed**" and "**something that arises and ceases that has causal efficacy.**" The Sautrāntika and Yogācāra who accept things as substantially existent also make the distinction that it "**only satisfies when not analyzed.**"[432] In not bearing the burden of reasoning when examined a diminished conventional reality is established. [Some] Madhyamaka texts appear to explain that, since it is mistaken to have the binding and liberation of things that are defiling and purifiying if they are not substantially established, ultimately things are not established and things are conventionally accepted as substantially existent. The nature of things is a false object called the "conventional." Since the cause and effect of defiling and purifying things unmistakenly stands without being substantially existent, it is called "profound."[433] There is not a distinction between the hair that appears to the eye diminished by eye disease and the various appearances in the world that diminish the eye of wisdom by the eye disease of conceptuality. In the sūtras, for example, a magician emananates an illusory person in front of many people, and one may think that in establishing the [path] from the mind of awakening up to unsurpassable awakening [5b], "who is it that generates the mind of awakening?" and accept that there

is not [anyone]. First, just as everything from generating the mind of awakening up to buddhahood occurs due to various dissimilar illusory reasons that arise from aggregations of illusory conditions, even though things are not substantially established, from afar they appear to exist as such due to apprehending things as real, and this does not deny that conventional results arise from conventional causes and conditions. Now, we do not accept to make an ocean of illusion from this. That is said to be eternally unsuitable for this teaching.

[5b3] Generally, objects of knowledge are conditioned and unconditioned. The conditioned is called "conventional." What is called "conditioned" is cause and effect, which dependently arises and is produced dependent on causes and conditions; it is a thing that is destroyed, having been produced, and since it has causal efficacy that is concordant with those causes and conditions, it is **"accepted as correct conventional reality"** [3d]. It is only to fall into an extreme to accept both conventional causal efficacy, while letting go of emptiness, the unproduced, and assert substantial existence. The conventional is not at all substantially established and has the causal efficacy to produce effects that are concordant with each of its [causes]. One does not have to give previous thought to this, as effects arise from merely existent aggregations of causes and conditions such that the effect of rebirth in the lower three realms arises from nonvirtuous causes, and both the maturation and concordant cause when taking rebirth in the upper realms issues forth in a manner such that rebirth in the happy realms arises from contaminated virtue and noble results arise from the uncontaminated path.

[5b6] In this regard, an example that does not exist even as a mere convention is the sky flower or the son of a barren woman. An example that conventionally appears while not ultimately existing is an illusion and so forth. While not substantially established, the effects of defilement and of beneficial qualities arise from defiling or beneficial causes, and, having relied on those, defilements or benefits occur and there is a limited continuity of cause in relation to the cause and a limited continuity of effect in relation to the effect, since it is mere mutual dependence. Therefore, the Ācārya [Nāgārjuna] has expressed that all qualities of production are known as illusory productions [6a]. As stated in his *Praise of the Dharmadhātu* (*Dharmadhātustava*), the example that does not exist conventionally is the rabbit's horn and the example that exists conventionally, while not existing ultimately, is the ox's horn.[434] The worldly who desire sesame oil engage in squeezing sesame, having abandoned sand; for the sake of medicine one seeks a rhinoceros horn or antelope antlers (*rgya ru*), but not a rabbit's horn. One seeks a horn of a wild yak for a bow, but one does not seek the horn of a rabbit. Those of worldly tenets and changeable intelligence accept such things by sight; likewise the world establishes what is

mistaken and correct. That which appears as hair for a sense faculty degenerated by eye disease is accepted as a mistaken conventional, and the color and so forth that appears to a nondegenerated sense faculty is accepted as correct.

Generally, that which obscures is called "convention" or "concealer" for all Madhyamakas. There is afflicted ignorance and unafflicted ignorance that conceals seeing the nature [of things]. Those two are called "conventional" or "concealer," but are not called reality. Mistaken conventionals also are not called "reality." An appearance in the world by the force of afflicted ignorance included among the [twelve] limbs of existence is seized on as real, and from that perspective is called "reality," and an appearance by the force of knowledge obscuration for those *āryas* who perceive appearances are like the former, yet since it is not seized on as true, it is called "mere conventional" but is not called "reality." An *ārya* bodhisattva in meditative stabilization does not see production ultimately, and in the postmeditative state appearances are like mere illusions. These two are suitable from familiarity during the ten [bodhisattva] stages, but with the diminishing of the obscurations of knowledge postmeditative appearances cease, and on the buddha level the establishment of the conventional is not accepted. This is in all the texts. For the level of a buddha, appearances of the postmeditative state are maintained to exist. Although they exist, there is no fault, as a [buddha is a] receptacle of all beneficial qualities and for nourishing all sentient beings. Although appearances do not exist, they spontaneously occur uninterruptedly for the purpose of others, according to Geshé Tönpa.

[6a8] Geshé Tönpa states that purified worldly postmeditative knowledge is called "correct conventional" and that itself is merely the appearance of the essential nature of the conventional. The meaning of the two realities [6b] when one understands them well is known as "an integrated path." For that, it is necessary to have the seed of familiarization previously and to gather the accumulations and be accepted by a spiritual friend. When one realizes both [realities] through these [factors] coming together [then]:

> Those who know the distinction between the two realities are not deluded about the words of the Sage. They, having accumulated the collections in their entirety, accomplish [their own and other's welfare] and go definitely to the perfect other side.[435]

Through this method, all the teachings of the Sage, as previously stated, are grouped within the two realities, and with respect to that, the aim of the deluded is to become nondeluded. Since one is not deluded regarding the conventional, one gathers the accumulations of merit, and by means of not being deluded for the ultimate, one meditates on the two types of selflessness and gathers the accumulations of wisdom, thereby culminating in the completion of the two [accumulations] and reaching the other side of all excellence, arriving at the level of a buddha.

[6b3] Generally, there are multiple teachings for the tenets of schools, the cause and effect of defilement and purification, the grouping together of the four truths. The cause of defilement is virtuous or nonvirtuous contaminated karmic actions, and the motivating condition or root cause is the defilements and the secondary defilements, of which there are many. The result, the truth of suffering, is also grouped into the five types of rebirth of sentient beings whose worldly locations of rebirth are immeasurable. The cause of purification is the three trainings. The antidote for rooting out karma and defilement is superior moral conduct, and the antidote to suppress them is the nature of contemplation, and the antidote for removing them from the root is the three types of wisdom. There are multiple teachings on this. There are multiple factors of abandonment and beneficial qualities among the three types of result or awakening. More than that, the three characteristics are few. More than that, the two realities are few. This is not other than to apprehend the words of the special instructions of Madhyamaka. To elaborate beyond the refutation of others' assertions occurs even in the great texts.[436] The understanding of the ultimate that is known from the Easterners as the "enumerated ultimate" (*rnam grangs kyi don dam*) is based on conventional groups of names, words, and letters that proclaim nonarising and so forth.[437] Both the nature of the expressed and the means of expression are conventional, and the real nature that is indicated through conventional bases is unproduced and is called the "ultimate." Potowa has stated that the two realities are abandoned like connected cultivated fields, or that it is like moving away from [the notion of] day and night being connected when one apprehends [7a] conventional karmic cause and effect to substantially exist. With regard to deprecating the cause and effect of conventionals when focusing on the ultimate object, emptiness, the Ācārya has stated that to wipe away the conventional is just to disappear, and we are said to be sitting as if it were just penetrating to the depths from the very beginning.

> **[The ultimate is one only. Others maintain that it is twofold. How can the nature of reality (*chos nyid*), which cannot be established as anything, be two, three, and so on? (v. 4)]**[438]

Since ultimate reality is real, the nature of emptiness, it is taught as indivisible, **"the ultimate is one only"** (v. 4a). Reality has an indivisible nature only, as it is stated from the *Saddharmapuṇḍarīka*[439] that there are not multiple lineages or multiple vehicles, and the *Yuktiṣaṣṭikāvṛtti*[440] states that since there is only one cause of seeing, the path of vision is only one moment. That is the genuine real nature, and since that state is without degeneration it is an object that is the ultimate to be sought out. It is the one characteristic that is without characteristics. **Others**, as previously indicated, are the Yogācāras, **who maintain as twofold** an ultimate that is the immutable perfected nature (*'gyur ba med pa'i yongs su grub pa'i dang*) and the unmistaken perfected nature (*phyin ci ma log pa'i yongs su grub pa*).[441] Since it is not suitable to divide [the ultimate] by reasoning, during the time of Geshé Tönpa and Khudolbel (Khu-'dol-'bel), it was stated that ultimate reality was not anything at all, that form, nonform, cause, effect, knowledge, object of knowledge, and so forth **"is [in] reality not established as anything,"** and since an entity to be enumerated is not established, **"how can it be specified as two or three, etc."**

> **[[The ultimate] is defined as non-arising, non-cessation and so forth according to the formula [given] by treatises. Because of the way in which different ultimates do not exist, there is neither a subject (*chos can*) nor its property (*chos nyid*) [for inferential reasoning]. (v. 5)]**[442]

[7a6] If it is indivisible, then how can there be multiple statements enumerated, like nonarising, noncessation, emptiness, characterless, wishlessness, suchness, the reality-limit, reality, and so forth? [The root text] states, **"by applying explanatory terms [the ultimate] is characterized by nonarising, noncessation, and so forth."** It is indicated by words that are enumerated, like fingers that point at the moon,[443] through the force of excluding imputations of the dissimilar thoughts of those to be trained, but multiple exclusions for removing imputation construed through the force of the ultimate itself do not exist at all.

[7a8] The ultimate is free from all elaborations, and [7b] as it is characterized in a way that **does not have any differences**, as it does not have an intrinsic nature that is differentiated, it is without either a **subject or property.** Furthermore, conceptual diversity (*spros pa dang bcas pa*) is the activity of both [subject and property] but does not proceed in relation to the ultimate.

> **[There is not any differentiation in emptiness. When cognized in a nonconceptual manner, it is conventionally designated that "emptiness is seen." (v. 6) It is said in the very profound sūtras that the state of nonseeing is seeing [ultimate reality] (vv. 7ab)].**[444]

[7b2] In terms of the subject, its property, or the subject and object, **there does not exist any differentiation in emptiness**. That is the activity of both [subject and object]. If there does not exist the establishment by means of subject, property, object, or object possessor, nor a cultivator and cultivated through the elaborations of whichever subject, and if it is correct to realize the subject and its property in both meditative stabilization and in the postmeditative state, then what will be the unmistaken way of realizing the ultimate if it is not established by means of these? **By means of a nonconceptual manner**, having relied on the ultimate, which is free from elaborations, the scriptural tradition of the Tathāgata, and the special instructions of the spiritual teacher, one gains confidence through hearing. By means of contemplation one obtains certainty, which is called "vision" (*lta ba*). One repeatedly meditates, while not being separated from the factors of method for ascertaining reality, and then at the time of the penultimate meditation, oneself and the realization will become like mixing space with space or like mixing water with water or butter (*mar*) with butter. Through exhausting the imputations that grasp for real objects, the nature of the realm of reality will become evident. Since it is a nonconceptual manner of understanding, it is "**conventionally designated as 'seeing emptiness'**" (v. 6d). Accordingly, it is understood that "**not to see is itself seeing,**" "**as stated in the profound sūtras**" like the *Dharmasaṃgīti*[445] and so forth. The *Laṅkāvatāra* states:

> Whoever sees me as visible matter, whoever understands me as sound, has entered into a wrong path; that person will not see me. The buddhas are the *dharmakāya*; the "leaders" see reality (*dharmatā*).[446]

The *Ārya* [*ratna*]*saṃcaya*[*gāthā*] also states:

> At the time of not objectifying even a mere atom through annihilating wisdom, [whether it be] conditioned, unconditioned, pure, or negative things, the world indirectly understands that as the perfection of wisdom, which is like space and does not stand anywhere.[447]
>
> And
>
> Sentient beings call that "seeing space." Through examining this meaning of how to see space, in this manner, the Tathāgata indicates seeing dharma as [8a] well. [This type of] seeing is not relatable through another example.[448]

In the middle *Perfection of Wisdom* and so forth, it is taught as "gaining conviction for the [perfection of wisdom] but not placing trust in form." For this type of seeing, it is said that "those who see opposite from the worldly do not see conventional reality but see the ultimate, which is the nondual wisdom of buddhas." When Lord [Atiśa] was asked about dispelling or not dispelling appearances,[449] he related the story of the unintelligent person's eye being taken over by eye disease. The story was taught as an example of one's own activity, and although both [a person with eye disease and a person without eye disease] are said to have a sense of "I," the example is intended for just the person [with eye disease]. The beginner is like a person whose eyes are degenerated by eye disease. In all the paths from the great path of accumulation up to the path of preparation, one goes about as if a little bit of darkness has vanished. In generating the path of vision upward, one is like a person who is not purified but recovering from eye disease, and on the third ground of the result, or the Buddha level, it is like one purified [of eye disease]. At the time of recovery from eye disease, not seeing hairs is seeing "emptiness." The *Madhyamakāvatāra*[450] states that a person with cataracts sees a vessel like a rhinoceros horn full of hairs and tries to clear away the hairs by repeatedly overturning the vessel. A person with purified eyes who looks at the object where the eye hairs are said to exist, though searching and focusing visually, will not see eye hairs, and a person who has eye sickness will become cleared of imputed mistakes that think "eye hairs exists." Stating that "eye hairs do not exist" does not deprecate the existence of eye hairs, and the [visual] appearances of a person who has an eye sickness does not harm the appearances of a person with pure eyes. Just as not seeing eye hairs is itself seeing emptiness, likewise conventional appearances, appearances that cover the eye of wisdom by the cataracts of worldly ignorance, that are not seen by the eyes of *āryas*, are called "seeing the ultimate," and that [seeing] is not harmed by [worldly ignorance], and there is no deprecation through negation because of abandoning mistakes. Also, for those whom distant appearances are true, it is said that:

> A form seen from afar is seen clearly by those nearby. If a mirage were really water, why is water not seen by those nearby? The way this world is seen as real by those [positioned] afar is not so seen by those nearby, for whom it is devoid of specific characteristics, as in a mirage.[451]

Likewise, if that which is apprehended by ordinary individuals is true, what need is there for the vision of *āryas*? It is important to train in the view that thinks "if it is not through [an *ārya's*] seeing, then it is false."

> **[In that (ultimate reality), there is neither seeing nor seer, but peace without beginning or end (vv. 7cd). [Reality is] devoid of entity and nonentity, free from conceptions, free from objects, without support, without basis, without coming or going, unexemplified, (v. 8) ineffable, invisible, unchanging, and unconditioned. If a yogi realizes that, the afflictive and cognitive obstructions are eliminated. (v.9)]**[452]

[8b1] Teaching that ultimate reality itself is beyond all elaboration: **in ultimate reality** there is **no thing to see** or **an agent that sees,** and there does not even exist "an agent that sees an object." Just as when a relation is examined, an unsuitable relation that is different is not a suitable relation. Since its nature is not established as conditioned, a **beginning does not occur** in which it is produced, **nor** is there **an end** in which its occurrence is destroyed. Because it is without dependence, since both [beginning and end] do not exist, the nature of the middle is also not established and therefore **it is peaceful.** [As texts state,] "Since what is to be denied does not exist, it is clear that there truly is no negation."[453] "If there is not an object that exists, of what can there be a nonexistent."[454] "Without a thing there is no nonthing; thing and nonthing are not simultaneous."[455] In this way a causally efficient **entity is not established** and is **devoid of a nonentity** in relation to that.

In the *Perfection of Wisdom* sūtras, with regard to any conceptualization, it is stated that "when one goes beyond, from form up to omniscience, on the basis, from form up to omniscience, then there is not any conceptualization whatsoever." Just as it is taught that if one goes beyond these **there is not any conceptualization** with regard to ultimate reality, likewise a nature that is conceptualized for being, nonbeing, form, nonform, and even wisdom is not established because [the ultimate] is **free from any object** to be examined. The wind relies on space, the water relies on that [wind], this great earth relies on [the water], creatures rely on [the great earth], the cause of activity is the action of sentient beings, and so on. That is the thought to this meaning of "to be abiding on space." Similarly, from improper mental activity[456] arise the afflictions of hatred and attachment. Contaminated activity arises from [those afflictions] and the production of the three realms arises from [the contaminated activity]. Since improper mental activity does not have any basis, all things have a base that is baseless and therefore **"[the ultimate] does not have any support or basis."** In terms of conventional causal fact, it is called "the realm of reality," and when meditated on as an object of ultimate reality, nonarising, since it produces all the qualities of the three types of *āryas*, it is said that "all *ārya* [9a] individuals are constituted by the unconditioned."[457]

In the actual reality of the ultimate, the qualities of *āryas*, the wisdom that stands firm, and the final nature of ultimate reality are not at all established as a basis. The noble qualities are **without coming or going** in reality. Likewise, in ultimate reality, the movement from the level of an ordinary individual up to the level of a noble being, and then arriving there, does not exist. Since the nature of the meaning that is to be characterized by examples is not established, it is "**unexemplified.**" Space that is construed as an example is also just an expression. The *Ārya Akṣayamatinirdeśa* states that "since there is no activity of mind, what need is there to even speak of letters?"[458] In this manner, [the ultimate] **is inexpressible** and **invisible** to the mind and the five [kinds of] eyes.[459] The *Perfection of Wisdom* sūtras state that reality is **unchangeable** from the state of an ordinary individual up to the state of a buddha. It is free from the three kinds of changeability of production, cessation, and perdurance that characterize conditioned things. Since it is not fabricated by cause and conditions, it is **unconditioned.**

[9a4] When realized according to the former [nonconceptual manner], the ultimate that is free from elaborations has the benefit of eradicating the two [sets of obstructions] along with their latencies, as the text states "**a yogi**" cultivates according to the former teaching, and at the penultimate state of the path, abandons both the **obstructions of the afflictions**, which are the obstructions of afflictions such as desire-attachment and so forth, and the **cognitive obstructions** that obstruct knowledge. Accordingly, when advancing toward the goal, it is taught that when [a person] **realizes it**—that is, the divisions of the two realities, the divisions of the conventional, the nature of each type of conventional, the indivisible ultimate, the negation of others' assertions of the two realities existence, the ultimate free from elaborations—then she or he will abandon all obstructions.

> **[Direct perception and inference are the two [valid cognitions] accepted by Buddhists. The deluded whose vision is narrow say that emptiness is understood by these two. (v. 10)]**[460]
>
> **[If it were,] it would follow that even *tīrthika*s and *śrāvaka*s would understand the nature of reality (*chos nyid*), not to mention the proponents of representation[-only], and the Madhyamakas would be no different [from them]. (v. 11)**[461]
>
> **[This being so, all tenets would also agree because they understand [reality] through valid cognition. (vv. 12ab)]**[462]

[9a7] What are the means of realizing the ultimate when there exists merely the beneficial vision (*lta phan yon*)? [The ultimate] is not realized by the direct perception and inference of those with narrow vision; rather, it is

taught that realizing [the ultimate] occurs through meditation relying on the special instructions of the spiritual teacher that one places faith in. The text states, "**Direct perception and inference—these two are accepted by Buddhists.**" The *Tattvasaṃgraha* [9b] asserts that outsiders have six types [of valid cognition] including direct perception (*mngon sum, pratyakṣa*), inference (*rjes su dpag pa, anumāna*), verbal testimony (*sgra las 'byung ba, śabda*), examples (*dpe*), analogy (*nye bar 'jal ba, upamāna*), and presumption (*don gyi go ba = arthāpatti*), while the *Vigrahavyāvartanī*[463] accepts four types, including direct perception, inference, analogy, and scriptural tradition. There is a distinction [between these texts]. Scriptural tradition is the supreme of direct perceptions since it is taught from the cognition of the Buddha's omniscient wisdom; therefore, it is included within direct perception. Direct perception has four types, which include the (1) sensory consciousness of the five senses among the faculties and the (2) mental consciousness among mind, and the Yogācāra asserts a (3) self-cognizing consciousness within consciousness and (4) yogic direct perception (*yogipratyakṣa*). All the supersensory knowledges (*abhijñāna*) are yogic direct perception, and the penultimate [yogic direct perception] is omniscient wisdom (*thams cad mkhyen pa'i ye shes*).

[9b3] Inference measures through a logical reason an imperceptible object (*don lkog tu gyur pa = parokṣārtha*) and is a type of knowledge that is generated from the effect (*kārya, 'bras bu*), nature (*svabhāva*), and nonperception (*anupalabdhi*).[464] It is settled by having two relations of identical nature that have arisen from that. There are eleven types of arguments (*prayoga*) for nonperception that are taught in multiple sources,[465] and [as it is said,][466] "logic does not have a base, it has nothing definitive, it lacks extension, it is contingent, it is tired, it is set against the backdrop of childish minds; therefore, the Mahāyāna is not its domain." In this manner, the object of knowledge of inference is not settled as unparalleled. **Those with narrow vision talk in a deluded manner when speaking of realizing emptiness through these two** [, direct perception and inference] [10cd]. Those who view outwardly do not [realize that] the ultimate is to be realized by individually intuited knowledge[467] through nonconceptual gnosis and is a realization that is beyond the object of logic. The latter is not knowledge, and in this way **there would be the consequence** that all the holders of tenets through direct perception and inference, including **even Tīrthika and disciples (*śrāvaka*), would realize reality (*dharmatā*). Not to mention** that there would be **realization even by the Vijñaptivādin. The Madhyamakas would not be incompatible** and would not have any doubt as to whether the Sautrāntika and Yogācāra realize reality or not. **Therefore all tenet systems would become alike because they measure [the ultimate] with valid cognition.** [12ab]

[Because all reasonings are not in agreement, would not the nature of reality (*chos nyid*), which is understood through valid cognition, become manifold? Direct perception and inference are useless. In order to refute Tīrthikas, [Buddhist] masters have composed [digests on logic]. (vv. 12cd–13)[468] The master scholar Bhavya[469] stated clearly in scripture that [the ultimate] is not realized by either conceptual or nonconceptual consciousness. (v. 14)][470]

[9b7] They would not become the same tenet system, since valid cognition differs. **Since all logic differs, even the reality that is measured by valid cognition would become manifold.** (vv. 12cd–13a) Therefore, these two [**direct perception and inference**] **are useless** (v. 13b) as a means to realize reality.

[10a1] Well then, are the digests of valid cognition composed by masters such as Dignāga and so forth useless? **In order to refute Tīrthikas,** to protect the teachings of the Buddha, **[Buddhist] masters have composed [digests on logic]** (v. 13cd).[471] The Lord [Atiśa] has said as such. Philosophers have made the most accurate and most detailed awareness into two, calling them valid cognition and doxography (*grub mtha'*). Generally, since what is construed as the means of valid knowledge is a branch of doxography, everyone from non-Buddhists up through Madhyamakans disprove the positions of others, and all prove their own positions, positing [them] through valid cognition. Lord [Atiśa] has taught that if the realization of the ultimate occurs from these two [i.e., direct perception and inference,] then one is only remaining in their defects, as settling the two realities on initial hearing and thinking[472] is like a finger pointing at the moon when construed from only these two [, direct perception and inference]. Well then, one states "when examined by reasoning." Even this reasoning is not from either [direct perception or inference].[473] Just as if one does not pass beyond the finger, one will not see the moon; likewise, if one does not pass beyond logic, nonconceptual gnosis will not be cultivated and there will not be a realization of ultimate reality. To say that one does not realize [the ultimate] by those two [direct perception and inference] is not careless speech. This has been taught **in the scriptural tradition** of the Buddha, the *Perfection of Wisdom* and so forth. Bhavya, as well, has stated in both the *Prajñāpradīpa* and the *Tarkajvālā* that these two—that is, inference and conceptual realization—are the direct perception of those with narrow vision.[474]

[Who has understood emptiness? Nāgārjuna, who was predicted by the Tathāgata and saw the truth of the nature of real-

ity, and his disciple Candrakīrti. (v. 15) Ultimate reality may be understood by means of the lineage of special instructions from them. (vv. 16ab)][475]

[10a6] How **does one realize emptiness** if it is not realized through direct perception and inference? The **Tathāgata has predicted** in the *Laṅkāvatāra Sūtra*:

> Four hundred years after my nirvāṇa, in Vedalī, in the south, a bhikṣu most illustrious and distinguished [will be born]; his name is Nāgāhvaya.[476] He is the destroyer of the one-sided views based on being and nonbeing. He will declare my vehicle, the unsurpassed Mahāyāna, to the world; having attained the stage of the joyous, he will go to Sukhāvatī.[477]

Also, the *Mahāmeghasūtra* states:

> This Licchavi youth known as *Sarvasattvapriyadarśana* (Joy-When-Seen-by-All-Beings), when four hundred years have elapsed after my parinirvāṇa, will become a monk named Nāga [who will] extensively proclaim my teaching. Finally, in the world realm called Pure Illumination (*Suviśuddhaprabhābhūmi*), he will become [10b] a tathāgata, arhat, samyaksambuddha named Jñānākaraprabha.[478]

Likewise in the *Mahābherīhārakaparivartasūtra*, the *Mañjuśrīmūlatantra*, and the *Suvarṇaprabhāsottamasūtra* the tathāgata predicts [Nāgārjuna].

Also, the cause of that [realization], as the text says, "**the realization of the special instructions of the lineage from Candrakīrti, the disciple of Nāgārjuna who perceived the truth of reality,**" and since one has gathered immeasurable accumulations in previous lifetimes and has a sincere potential for meditating on emptiness [it is said that:]

> Even when they are ordinary beings, when they hear about emptiness, they experience supreme joy again and again inside. The tears from this supreme joy moisten their eyes, and the hairs on their bodies stand on end (6.4). Ones like this have the potential for perfect buddhahood.[479]

And

> Those whose intellect transcends existence and nonexistence, and does not stand [in any extremes], realize the meaning of "condition," which is profound and nonperceived.[480]

Thus those who have qualities such as these rely on a spiritual friend of the Great Vehicle and, as stated in the *Bodhipathapradīpa*, purify their misdeeds and gather the accumulations, firmly meditating on all the factors from understanding karma, cause and effect, up thorough concentration, and having properly received the special instructions from a spiritual friend who has the special instructions of the lineage from Ācārya Candrakīrti, when meditating uninterruptedly for an extended time with devotion to practice that is not devoid of factors of method, one will realize the truth of reality. However, if one becomes familiar with only emptiness while being free from all the protective factors, another illness will emerge, in that, whether realizing or not realizing reality, one will go away as a *śrāvaka*. The special instructions of the lineage from Candrakīrti are the only special instructions of Madhyamaka, and the Madhyamaka *Pañcaskandha*[481] states as such. It is only the definitive meaning, since it is the method of realizing emptiness but is not realized by logic, and even the all[-knowing] Nāropa did not say to train in the means of valid cognition.

From the beginning, the practitioner, having gathered the accumulations and through the blessed words of the spiritual teacher, should realize the concordant process of dependent-arising and realize the nature of reality that is the reverse process of dependent-arising. Dho-bhi-ba,[482] who did not even know the alphabet, through his previous accumulations, having the seed [of knowledge], [11a] and blessings of the spiritual teacher, perceived reality (*bden pa gzigs*). The instruction itself is proclaimed to be the thesis, but this is not generated from instruction that conceives with logic. The *Prasannapadā* states that the Ācārya, his disciple, and the disciples of his disciple have passed on and there are many who cry about the disappearance of their system, but they are not his actual disciples and are holding tenets.[483] It is not definite that those two [Nāgārjuna and Candrakīrti] dwelt here in Jambudvīpa for six hundred and four hundred years. They went, like pouring water from one vessel into another, cultivating for a mere ten years on both the early [portion of Candrakīrti's] and the later part of [Nāgārjuna's] life.[484] Then, at the time of composing the *Prasannapadā*, it did not matter, as all had passed and disappeared. Now, at present, a lifetime passes in lesser or greater of one hundred years, and in my time, the teachings of the three spiritual sons, their great disciples, and the disciples of these disciples are disappearing and various dissimilar teachings are appearing. The Lord [Atiśa] is said to have found the

Middle Way vision[485] from Avadhūtipa. All those ācāryas did not have a lineage from the long-lived Ācārya [Nāgārjuna] and his disciple Candrakirti and *Vidyākokila.[486] When realizing the truth of reality, all obstructions are abandoned, and this method will lead to realization.

> **[The articles of Dharma are said to number 84,000. All of them are inclined toward and lead to this [ultimate] reality. (vv. 16c–e)]**[487]

[11a5] Well then, if one thinks of how the other 84,000 articles of the Buddha's Dharma are considered as teaching, the text states, **"the articles of Dharma are said to number 84,000. All of them are continually inclined toward and directly lead to this [ulimate] reality."** The meaning of "all" is said to be however much is the measure of the article of Abhidharma or however many pronouncements were taught, and this merely indicates that the articles of Dharma are immeasurable.

The system of inclination (*gzhol lugs*): through the teaching of worldly karma, cause and effect, and so forth, [the teaching] entirely proceeds to emptiness. In relation to this, even [if] not [initially] proceeding [to realizing emptiness, the teaching] is inclined to the aim of the three vehicles, the vehicles of the *śrāvaka* and *pratyekabuddha* are inclined toward the Great Vehicle, the four immeasurables of the Great Vehicle are inclined toward the mind of awakening, the mind of awakening inclines one toward the activity of a bodhisattva, the activity-factors of method up through concentration (*dhyāna*) are inclined toward and lead to the realization of reality. [11b] [As it is said,[488]] "the latter arises dependent upon the former," and also for the three things that create merit (i.e., generosity, discipline, and meditation), the former are inclined toward the latter. Likewise for the three trainings [of morality, concentration, and wisdom]. The accumulation of merit is inclined toward the accumulation of wisdom. The [understanding of] the selflessness of the person is inclined [toward understanding] the essencelessness of things.

Among the 84,000 articles of Dharma taught as antidotes to the 84,000 actions, since all actions have as their root the grasping of things as real (*dngos por 'dzin pa*), it is necessary to realize the reality of emptiness in order to abandon actions from the root. In this regard, first, purification practices are necessary to subdue actions, and, even if starting from poor practices of liberation in the beginning, a person will come to the realization of emptiness in the end. As it occurs in the [*Sarvadurgati-pariśodhana*] tantra[489] itself, "do not look down on Tīrthikas, as it creates distance from Vairocana." All the textual systems of the outsiders uplift [the mind] a little with logic or serve as early signs that indicate the teaching of Dharma when the Buddha appears in the world. As [such teachings] appear as a blessing of the Buddha for the purpose of understanding mistaken positions that do not accord with the Buddha's teaching, it is a cause for the lineage that is distant to realizing the reality called "Vairocana." As for our own schools, after overcoming all conceptions contained within the texts by the Vaibhāṣika, the Sautrāntika teaches the fourteen conditioned forces dissociated from thought to not be substantially existent, and the Yogācārins negate apprehended objects and apprehended subjects (*gzung 'dzin, grāhyagrāhaka*), and through the Vijñaptimātra being negated in the Madhyamaka texts, all [these teachings] are **continually inclined toward and directly lead to this [ultimate] reality.**

[One is liberated by understanding emptiness. All meditational development is for this purpose. (vv. 17ab)][490]

[11b6] In this way, although [the teaching is] continually inclined toward and directly leads to [reality], sentient beings are bound by two obscurations that have as their root the grasping of things in *saṃsāra* as real. They will be liberated through eradicating the grasping of things as real when realizing the meaning of nonarising. Well then, if one thinks that other meditations have no purpose, the meaning here is that, as previously indicated, other meditations are necessary to realize reality. The *Madhyamakāvatāra* teaches that without giving, one will need to rely on another for livelihood, without morality one will be reborn in the lower realms, without patience one will be reborn in lower realms, and even if born as a human, because of being ugly, one will not be considered by the spiritual teacher and will not obtain the instructions for meditating on emptiness. Without compassion, even if [12a] meditating on emptiness, one will not become awakened. Without dedicating the roots of virtue for the sake of complete awakening, from lifetime to lifetime sentient beings' meditation on emptiness will be interupted. If they do not respect a bodhisattva, since they will not be able to be taught, as only bodhisattvas [teach] emptiness, they will not encounter a virtuous spiritual friend who teaches emptiness; therefore, all [these meditations] are necessary in order not to deteriorate meditation on emptiness. The *Bodhicaryāvatāra* (9.1) also states that "all these attainments have the purpose of wisdom for oneself and others."[491] The Ācārya [Nāgārjuna] states: "Therefore as long as this Dharma, which destroys egotism, is not thoroughly understood, so long apply yourself with great care to the Dharma of giving, moral conduct, and patience"[492] and "Of the two [virtues], wisdom is the foremost; faith, however, comes first."[493] Thus, just as grammarians are instructed to apprehend

letters and syllables first, likewise in order to realize nonarising it is taught that factors of method are necessary first. The [middle] *Bhāvanākrama* states, "Omniscient wisdom has compassion as its root. It arises from the cause of the mind of awakening. It is the fulfillment of method."[494] Bhāviveka states in the *Tarkajvālā* that "this opportunity to eradicate the eight leisureless states while possessing the lamp of holy Dharma is the lineage that creates the result through the activities of a great person."[495] Thus it is said that the activity of a great individual, who has the religious conduct of the Sage, includes factors of method previous to seeking out reality (*tattvārtha*).

Since "the Sage has said, 'One who is in meditative equipose knows reality as it is,'"[496] concentration (*samādhi*) is necessary for the realization of nonarising through wisdom in meditative equipose. In order to cultivate concentration, it is necessary to have its prerequisites, including pure self-discipline and residing in a solitary place, as well as its conditions, including having few activities and being content and so forth. In the beginning one meditates on the faults of existence, including recollecting death and so forth. After one has obtained aversion through that [meditation], then one needs to understand that the root of all [existence] is grasping things as real. First, meditate on the selflessness of the person. Through that meditation one will become pleasant and free from fear. Having become free from fear, one should not become careless. It is selflessness that presently experiences suffering that arises from [encountering] poison, thorns, and so on, and happiness that arises from [obtaining] food and clothing. [12b] Likewise, one should understand that as long as the view of the self is not cut off, the effects of actions are not wasted and one should have great skill in abandoning transgressions and accomplishing virtue. As a gradual teaching, all that has form and does not have form should be meditated on in a manner in which one would explain that the king's wife is dead. Furthermore, realizations occur when meditating on previous teachings regarding one's support, special instructions, and practices, but the meditation that precisely leaves nothing behind is incomprehensible, as the nonexistent profound from the *Perfection of Wisdom* sūtras is predominately nonperception in the section on the three types of omniscience. From apprehending the support of practice, to not be devoid of both means and wisdom is said to be like increasing cooked food when eating. The Ācārya's assertion is that in not realizing emptiness one does not realize the selflessness of the person. By not realizing [the selflessness of the person], although one obtains the result of *śrāvaka* or *pratyekabuddha*, there is not complete liberation and a *śrāvaka* does not realize the essenceless of things. As there are not all aspects gathered within [a *śrāvaka's*] own support, it is asserted that they do not obtain the final result because they are devoid of factors of method. In this way, when advancing to the goal, both the direct perception and inference of those with narrow vision does not realize reality, and when meditating through relying on the special instructions of the lineage from Nāgārjuna and his disciple Candrakīrti, one will realize that. The complete extent of the Buddha's Dharma is taught as a means for realizing emptiness, and all the other meditations are explained to be necessary for obtaining liberation when realizing [emptiness], as well as for realizing reality.

> **[But if one has contempt for the correct conventional reality and meditates on emptiness, the conventional cause and effect, virtue and evil deeds, and so on, will deceive one in the next world. (vv. 17c–f)]**[497]

[12b5] In this way, those who claim **to meditate on emptiness, having contempt for the correct conventional** from what there is, all that is characterized by cause and effect, who are satisfied by only meditating on emptiness, [thinking that] factors of method are without purpose, who do not refrain from evil deeds, saying there is no harm by anything in emptiness—although they are taught the **conventional**, the nondeceptive **cause and effect** that is similar to being substantially established when grasping things as real from afar, they do not create **virtue**, the benefits of virtue do not occur, and since the faults from [evil deeds] come about because they do not abandon **evil deeds**, they **will be deceived in the next world**. When emptiness is well understood, there is not any reason to do evil deeds. Since doing evil deeds occurs when distinguishing between oneself, one's friends, and one's enemies [13a], and when grasping at one's own body and life as dear, through understanding the selflessness of the evil deeds done for that purpose, there will be no reason to do evil deeds. When examining this whole world in a manner that thinks "there is death for whomever there is," the grasping at one's own body and life as dear will not occur. Therefore by understanding that all things are emptiness, and understanding the selflessness of the self of a person, there is no reason to do evil deeds.

Whether in our system of perfections or in the system of secret mantra, if it is not necessary at all [to distinguish] good and bad views, and to keep one's vows, commitments, and so forth, then at that time one becomes undistinguished from an old layman who has nothing to do or accomplish. It is said that when realizing the nature of things, one will not be obscured even by the [sins of] immediate retribution. What is true here is that, since it is the nature of things to be reborn in Avīci Hell by committing the [sins of] immediate retribution,[498] one is not obscured to make effort in the four opponent powers[499] when realizing the nature of things. The foremost antidote to apply is the meditation on emptiness, and through meditating on that, the encounter with later evil deeds is cut off, as it becomes a prior antidote. If there is no harm later, then [the meditation] will not become a prior antidote. When there is contempt for the conventional, through being obscured by the obscuration of evil deeds, the realization of emptiness will not be produced. Therefore this is the fault of having contempt for the conventional although meditating a bit on emptiness. In accordance with [the statement that[500]] "for whom this emptiness is possible, for them, all things are possible," through emptiness alone all the conventional causes and effects are proper. Since "for whom emptiness is not possible, for them things are not possible," there will be a contradiction when establishing an entity, as its intrinsic nature will be something other, and since there is a contradiction between something with intrinsic nature and something fabricated, a deceptive cause and effect will not be proper.

> **[Those who rely on a bit of learning without understanding the meaning of discrimination and do not create merit—such despicable persons are destroyed. Wrongly perceived emptiness will destroy people of little wisdom. (v. 18)]**[501]

[13a6] The fault of having contempt for the conventional through relying on merely a bit of learning without any meditation on emptiness: **Relying on learning a** mere **bit** of the teaching on emptiness from the sūtras and *śāstras*, **without** the wisdom that is produced from an intellectual **understanding** by contemplating **the meaning of** emptiness with **discrimination**, one is said to be obscured by conceptualizing when trying to create merit. In **not creating any merit**, that **despicable**, foolish **person** who states that one is not harmed in emptiness is reborn in lower realms and unfortunate states and is said to be **destroyed,** since they do not obtain the result of merit. The Ācārya father [Nāgārjuna] and son [Candrakīrti] do not teach only the meaning of the profound, and points like this are given in the *Yuktiṣaṣṭikā*. [13b] The Ārya Mañjuśrī, who did not have any realization other than **the meaning of discrimination**, gathered merit comparable to the [amount of] insatiable water from the great ocean without being satisfied. The bodhisattva of the *Śikṣāsamuccaya*, in the section on remembering the qualities of the saṃgha, states "with canopies of flowers and great mounds of flowers"[502] and so forth, all that is said only for a lord of the tenth stage. With unquenchable eagerness to worship the Three Jewels, first emit light from the palms of one's hands, then emit light from all the pores of one's skin and make offerings emitting light. Presumptuous, clever Buddhists who do not worship this way have only

despicable and foolish actions. Therefore **wrongly perceived emptiness will destroy people of little wisdom.** There are two ways to **wrongly perceive**: (1) if one wrongly perceives emptiness and discards actions and their effects, although one has the seed of liberation, later one will go to lower realms, and (2) when through fear of emptiness, [viewing it like] a precipice, one perceives one who teaches emptiness as an enemy, one will not have the seed of liberation and will go to the lower realms. Here, it is the former.

> **[The Ācārya Candrakīrti has stated as follows: "Conventional reality functions as a means, and ultimate reality functions as the goal. Those who do not understand the difference between the two have a bad understanding and get a bad rebirth."** (v. 19)][503]

[13b4] This being so, it is necessary to integrate means and wisdom though relying on the two realities. The text says "**the Ācārya Candrakīrti has stated,**" and since the two realities are **the means** and **the goal,** it is necessary to integrate both. When **those who do not understand** the characteristics and **divisions of the two** realities and the relation of cause and effect **incorrectly realize** the meaning of the two realities, they **will go to lower realms** or go astray. Candrakīrti himself has stated that one will not achieve liberation if [one's understanding of] the two realities deteriorates when abandoning the system of the Ācārya [Nāgārjuna]. Here, it is not only that.

> **[The ultimate cannot be understood without relying on the conventional. Without the stairway of correct convention a wise man cannot ascend to the top of the palace of reality.** (v. 20)][504]

[13b6] Attentive to scriptural tradition, regarding "**without relying on the conventional,**" the text states: One will not produce an intellectual understanding of ultimate reality if there is not an indication of nonarising, noncessation, and so forth through conventional, transactual meaning. One produces an intellectual understanding through relying on the conventional. Even if meditating on emptiness in an unerring way without relying on factors of method, those meditations will not produce any realizations, as previously explained. From not having contempt for even the slightest evil deed by having great confidence in the causality of cause and effect, up through standing firm in achieving the five perfections that are impelled through the mind of awakening, with necessary complete factors of method one seeks to obtain the king of *samādhi*, which the Buddha [14a] has explained as the equality of all

dharmas. It is said that in this very palace there is no entity that is not offered to the relics of the Tathāgata.

[14a1] In this way, although having methods, if one does not abandon grasping at real things through wisdom, then liberation will not be obtained, and [as it is said,] "if not realizing the ultimate, nirvāṇa will not be obtained."[505] Therefore it is necessary to meditate on emptiness, the ultimate reality. Furthermore, since it is necessary to be accepted by a virtuous spiritual friend who teaches unmistaken instructions regarding emptiness, one should make effort to have a virtuous spiritual friend.

[14a4] The two realities as means and goal are established in other scriptures: "conventional" here means the accumulations of the *ārya* path, as Geshé Tönpa has eloquently said, "the correct conventional." **Without the stairway** of that, the realization of the ultimate being brought to completion will not reach **the top** that is omniscient wisdom, as the wisdom generated in the realization of the path is produced from meditating on ultimate reality. As previously explained, all the factors of method that are known as conventions are necessary for that realization. It is necessary to obtain a happy rebirth for meditation on nonarising and the factors of method are necessary for that. As it is said [in the *Prajñāśataka*], "If one practices well the religion of men, one is not long in arriving at the land of the gods. If one climbs along the ladder of gods and men, liberation is close."[506]

> **[When the conventional that appears is analytically examined just as it is, nothing whatsoever is found. The unfindable is itself the ultimate and the nature of reality abiding from the beginning. (v. 21)]**[507]

[14a6] Teaching that the two realities are not different entities: in accordance with [the statements that] "**the conventional appears just as it is**" [and] "since the nature of ignorance is to veil, it is conventional,"[508] the appearance does not exist due to ignorance. This [appearance] itself is **not found whatsoever when examined** by **reasonings** such as the diamond-splinters[509] and so forth, and since **the unfindable**[510] **is itself the ultimate**, the two realities are not established as different. Since what is held to exist does not [exist] through reasoning, and since it is understood as the nature of things, the text states "**the nature of reality abiding from the beginning.**" This [nature of reality] itself is taught in the sūtras as "the tathāgatagarbha," "lineage," "the mental element," or "the basis-of-all." As for reasoning, the Ācārya [Nāgārjuna] has stated the mere thesis itself as: [14b] "No thing anywhere is ever born from

itself, from something else, from both or without a cause."[511] Generally the intention of the citation is construed as a consequence only in terms of "if it is produced from itself faults will follow here." The reasoning of the lack of being one or many is a reason of nonobservation (*anupalabdhihetu*). The *Perfection of Wisdom* sūtras state that "things themselves, from form up to omniscience, are empty. Why is that? Since their nature is empty," that is said to be a reason of essential nature (*svabhāvahetu*). Everything "existent cannot be produced since it is [already] existent; nonexistent cannot be produced since it is nonexistent"[512] is a perception that is opposed to the presence of itself (*svabhāva-viruddha-upalabdhi*) and so forth. To merely state that "your assertion is not established by direct perception" or "it is contradictory with direct perception" is not an actual reasoning that cognizes ultimate reality.

> [**The conventional that appears just-as-it-is is established by being produced by causes and conditions. (v. 22ab)**][513]

[14b4] Well then, how is the conventional that appears just as it is established? The text states "**by causes and conditions,**" and although it is not ultimately established when examined by reason, **the conventional that appears just-as-it-is is established by being produced by causes and conditions** as a measure of its presence (*snang tshod*). All appearances, including the appearances of hell for the lowest sentient beings through to appearances of the transmigrators among the pure gods, the various appearances of the five types of transmigrators, as well as the extremely pure buddha-fields that appear to *āryas*, are produced by individual causes and conditions. However, all do not appear discordantly due to a single entity but rather are different appearances that are produced from various karmic actions and afflictions.

> **If it were impossible to establish it, by whom would the moon in water and the like be produced? (v. 22cd) Therefore all appearances are established as being produced by various causes and conditions. If the continuance of conditions is interrupted, they do not arise even conventionally. (v. 23)]**[514]

[14b6] If one thinks that there are extensive teachings on dissimilar ways of appearance and dissimilar causes and conditions, and since there is not substantial establishment, then it is unsuitable to establish [things] through causes and conditions: **If it were impossible to establish it** through causes and conditions that are not substantially established, **by whom would the moon in water**, illusions, **and the like be produced?** Even these will become nonap-

pearances in [relation to] causes and conditions, and even though they are not substantially established, it is acceptable for appearances to arise from causes and conditions. Therefore, as previously [explained], **appearances are established as being produced by various causes and conditions,** and **if the continuance of conditions is interrupted,** the result, appearances, **does not arise even conventionally.** Our own texts state that since all these appearances are appearances due to ignorance, they are entirely [composed of] ignorance, and when they are exhausted, any posterior appearances will not occur and [15a] there is only meditative equipoise. Even in the *Bodhicaryāvatāra*, by dwelling only in [meditative equipoise], wisdom is accepted as having its continuum cut.[515] Since there are not causes and conditions that produce sons of barren women and rabbit horns even as mere convention, they are erroneous and do not occur as mere appearances. Rebirth in hell and so forth will not occur if one does not accumulate the causes for rebirth in hell or if one destroys the potentials or interrupts them by the four oppponent powers. As [the practice of not accumulating the causes] does not purify residues, it is called "cessation that is not analytical, since there is not rebirth due to incomplete conditions for conditioned rebirth." Although it is a cessation, it is not liberation from worldly fetters (*'bral ba, visaṃyoga*) as this practice does not purify, and later in dependence on residues, there is another rebirth. In regard to the previous teaching of the *Bodhicaryāvatāra*, since sentient beings are the cause that gives rise to Buddha-gnosis and activity, as long as sentient beings are not extinct, the cause for Buddha-gnosis and activity will not be cut off. The meaning is like this.

> **[So if one is not deluded with views and one has extremely pure conduct, without following a mistaken path, one will go to the place of Akaniṣṭha. (v. 24)]**[516]

[15a4] The benefit of understanding the integration of the two realities: **So if one is not deluded with views** by understanding the ultimate **and if one has extremely pure conduct** through mastery in the cause and effect of the conventional, **without following the mistaken paths** of cyclic existence and the Inferior Vehicle (*Hīnayāna*), **one will go to the place** of the lords of the tenth stage and enjoyment bodies (*saṃbhogakāya*), **Akaniṣṭha.** In order to go into the surroundings of an enjoyment body, one first is not deluded by worldly, correct views and has pure conduct that does not have contempt for even the slightest sin, one does not go astray into places of lower rebirth or unfortunate states, and it is necessary to achieve a happy realm of rebirth as a support for achieving liberation. One proceeds in accordance with the sayings

that "any happiness or suffering should be recognized as karmic actions"[517] or "the aggregates are not from chance, not from time"[518] and so forth. Then, gradually, not straying into lower rebirths and being born in happy realms of rebirth, in accordance with the teaching that "the entire world is cause and effect, in this there is not any being, things that are empty only arise from empty things,"[519] [the entire world is] understood as deceiving and without happiness. One is not deluded with views understanding that merely empty things, such as the person, are results that arise from causes that are merely empty things, such as the self of a person. Through [15b] pure conduct, the three trainings, one does not go astray in the cycle of existence (*saṃsāra*) and achieves liberation, training gradually in the previously mentioned meaning of the two realities.

> **[Time is short and things to be known are manifold. But since the span of time is only as long as ignorance, one should select what oneself prefers, just as a goose extracts milk from water. (v. 25)]**[520]

[15b1] In this way—since it necessary to cherish only what does not go astray by integrating the two realities—"**time is short and things to be known,**" included within the five fields of knowledge, **are manifold,** and due to the shorteness of time it is not possible to completely know all [these fields]. **Since the span of time is only as long as ignorance, one should select what one prefers.** Generally, "if one does not make effort in the five fields of knowledge,[521] then even the most exalted (*'phags mchog*, i.e., *bodhisattvas*) will not become omniscient. For the sake of refuting and supporting others, and for the sake of understanding everything oneself, one makes an effort in these [five fields]."[522] As one is born in a period when time is short, death comes quickly and even an estimate of this short time is not known. In this small quantity of life in the present, there is no time to train in all these [sciences]. As the Ācārya Vasubandhu has said, the completion of a life is not even a mere ninety [years], and one is harmed if one does not even know what is to be abandoned and what is to be practiced over many years. Therefore there is no spare time at all remaining to dwell in practice when deciding here or there to loosely carry out practices with lethargy in the remaining half [of life]. Since one will not be able to do what is to be done when one is old, like a pure goose[523] whose beak can differentiate mixed water and milk that is undifferentiated by others, the wise establish that the outer sciences are like water and that the inner science is like milk. From among them, there are those who willingly carry the burden of the sick and practice to understand the pulse felt with the middle finger (*kan*).[524]

In Tibet, there are not only scriptural systems of the outsiders that subjugate others, but there are also crafts and medical sciences that do not complete others. For the most part, they will become obstacles to oneself, as the former uses one's own erroneous bad intellect, and even the antidotes of the latter position cause unhappiness. Furthermore, one is dependent on the special instruction of the trustworthy spiritual teacher, as one does not know one's own measure. We do not now consider training in the five fields of knowledge as objects to be known. One should subdue the chief enemy of what protects the laity and clergy: the deeds for wealth and so forth of the common are not effective. Excessive [non-Dharma-related] activities of those who engage with the [Buddha's] teaching are only efforts that become weak. Then, as previously indicated, one goes only below [to lower realms] by being deluded with views and actions that cause one to go astray. Earlier, the phrase which states "**selecting what one prefers**" indicates [16a] training in the stages of the three persons.[525] The supports for the root of faith, the four-three-twelve[526] dharmas along with the mind of awakening, are said to be medicines to be applied. In this way, even if the instructions on this from your great spiritual teacher are not necessary, they are instructions for the pure individuals of future generations.

> **[Although those with narrow vision are not able to ascertain the two realities, this presentation on the two realities of Nāgārjuna's tradition was given relying on the statements of authoritative teachers. (v. 26)]**[527]

[16a1] The reason for composing the śāstra is stated as "narrow vision" and so forth. This is stated as such by Candrakīrti, although **the statements of authoritative teachers** such as Avadhūtipa, who later became a yogi [who practices] Yamāntaka, are not recorded as Madhyamaka teachers.

> **[If people of today have faith in this demonstration composed under the auspices of the king of Sumatra, this teaching should be accepted after thorough analysis, not just by faith and not just out of reverence. (v. 27)]**[528]

Although nowadays people have faith in someone other than the spiritual teacher, the text states that "**this teaching should be accepted after thorough analysis, not just by faith and not just out of reverence.**" Thus it is especially important to do likewise for all the sayings of the Buddha as well as this [teaching], in accordance with the statement that "aspiration for the good Dharma after examining with reason can never be interrupted by demons,"[529] [and thus] one will not be deceived by false textual systems. The meaning is that "one may have trust in the text if one examines it well."

> **[After the King of Suvarṇadvīpa, the Gurupāla, sent the monk Devamati to me, and under his auspices, I composed this "Entry to the Two Realities." It should be examined by present-day scholars. (v. 28)]**[530]

The meaning of "guruphala" is good spiritual teacher (*bla ma bzang po*). The views of aged Tibetan teachers are said to be like wandering dogs who do not [practice] through faith alone, but when examining vital points with reasoning reach only their own habitual tendencies (*bag chags ≈ vāsanā*). Serlingpa and Śāntipa are ācāryas, but their views are discordant [from those of Atiśa].

> I have written this memorandum (*brjed byang*)
> for all innumerable sentient beings,
> may they not be deluded with views, and
> with exceedingly pure actions
> may they arrive at the place of Akaniṣṭha
> and not take a wrongful course.
>
> Through the kindness of my spiritual teacher,
> may I make firm [the realizations of] emptiness and compassion
> through exchanging self and others
> to arrive at the "stage of delight."[531]
> The small collection of sayings on reality (*bden chung gi 'bum*)
> is finished.
> It is completed.

4. *A General Explanation of, and Framework for Understanding, the Two Realities*, attributed to Atiśa

A *General Explanation of, and Framework for Understanding, the Two Realities* (*Bden gnyis spyi bshad dang / bden gnyis 'jog tshul*) is a late-eleventh-century Indo-Tibetan Madhyamaka text that records oral teachings attributed to Atiśa on the two realities (*satyadvaya*). The text furnishes an exposition of the Middle Way thought of Nāgārjuna based on an exegesis of conventional reality and ultimate reality within the framework of Mahāyāna path structures found in texts attributed to Maitreyanātha. The commentary preserves an oral tradition of Atiśa's Madhyamaka thought that was disseminated in Ngari, in western Tibet, and Radreng Monastery and transmitted among late-eleventh-century Kadampa scholars of the Phenyul region.

Atiśa's Madhyamaka thought has traditionally been understood based on his *Satyadvayāvatāra*, *Madhyamakopadeśa*, and *Bodhimārgapradīpapañjikā* (D, 3948; Sherburne 2000). Atiśa's Madhyamaka is described as "Great Madhyamaka" in the *Bodhimārgapradīpapañjikā's* section on insight, but the text does not provide a detailed discussion on the topic. The two realities are also not discussed in the *Bodhimārgapradīpapañjikā*. Rather, they are briefly articulated in the condensed twenty-eight verses of the *Satyadvayāvatāra*. *A General Explanation* furnishes previously unknown details to Atiśa's Madhyamaka thought. The text unpacks detailed characteristics of the two realities while contextualizing the nature of these realities within the structures of the bodhisattva path. In the sections that follow, I discuss the sources and content of *A General Explanation*.

Authorship and Date

General Explanation does not have a detailed colophon but merely states at the end of the text, "This is a speech by Atiśa."[532] The Dpal-brtsegs editors of the printed text have added a line to the text, "This is not actually spoken by the Lord [Atiśa],"[533] which is *not* written in the facsimile of the manuscript. As the editors have inferred, the text was not actually written by Atiśa; yet it does quote him directly nineteen times and mentions him over twenty times in the third person. As the written copy of the text attributes the whole discourse to Atiśa, and furnishes previously unknown colloquial statements attributed to Atiśa among its citations, *General Explanation* most likely represents Atiśa's oral teaching on the two realities that were initially given in western Tibet. The strongest philological evidence for its originating in Atiśa's oral teachings is based on the direct correspondence of two citations in the text from the *Bodhicittavivaraṇa* (verses 51 and 73), whose recensions are found only in the works of Atiśa. The citation of verse 73 (746.15) in *General Explanation* directly matches Atiśa's citation in *Open Basket of Jewels*,[534] and the citation of verse 51 matches that found in the *Bodhimārgapradīpapañjikā* (Sherburne 2000, 262). However, the recension of these verses does not match the five other known Tibetan versions of the *Bodhicittavivaraṇa* (on these versions, see van der Kuijp 2014, 129–32). Also, several citations of Indic texts directly match the citations found in the *Madhyamakaratnapradīpa*, a text known to have been utilized by Atiśa for teaching Madhyamaka and translated by his students into Tibetan (see Del Toso 2014). Along these lines, the structure of the text and the many colloquial citations attributed to Atiśa indicate that the work was initially an oral lecture given by Atiśa that was eventually written down.[535] Based on the principle of embarrassment,[536] some statements are not always flattering to the purported author. For instance, the text records Atiśa as stating, "My position is not pleasing, as few accept it and teach it India" (711.22). Likewise, the author tries to employ an Indian cultural example of a monkey in a house to illustrate how he postulates a single mental consciousness (*tshogs gcig*) but, "Alas!, This is not a good example for Tibetans" (713.20). The author then provides the more culturally suitable example for Tibetans of a butter lamp.[537] The text preserves in its numerous citations of Indic works transliterated Sanskrit terms (e.g., *lo ka* for *'jig rten*, *du kha* for *sdug sngal*, *pu nya* for *bsod nams*), instead of Tibetan translations. The intermingled Sanskrit and Tibetan may preserve how an Indian *paṇḍita* who knew Tibetan, a scholar such as Atiśa, recited the citations. After Atiśa's lectures in western Tibet, these teachings were then compiled and progressively modified as they were disseminated among members of its lineage until being written down by a follower of Gya Chakriwa (eleventh century).

General Explanation records in its homage (679.1), and describes within the text (703.6–704.10), one of the earliest known Tibetan Madhyamaka lineage lists. The lineage is described as a "practice lineage" (*grub rgyud*, 707.11; 724.20) that is opposed to unspecified "explanatory lineages" (*bshad rgyud*, 703.7). The exact sequence of figures described in *General Explanation*, although close to the lineage provided in Atiśa's *Bodhipathapradīpapañjikā* (Sherburne 2000, 237–41), is not known in later Tibetan historical works, nor in well-known extant Madhyamaka commentaries or records of received Madhyamaka teachings.[538] The text cites Atiśa's *Satyadvayāvatāra* (vv. 15–16ab) regarding this lineage, indicating that it begins with Nāgārjuna, followed by Candrakīrti and *Vidyākokila (*rig pa'i khu byug*). The lineage discussion then states that these teachings were received by Atiśa from Avadhūtipa, and that Atiśa disseminated them to the famous translator Rinchen Sangpo (958–1055), indicating that they were given in western Tibet sometime during the first three years of Atiśa's residence there.[539] After Rinchen Sangpo, the text's initial homage (697.1) and lineage discussion (703.6–704.10) mention the ambiguous phrase "two gurus" (*bla ma rnam gnyis*). Although the exact individuals that this phrase refers to is not clear, the last lineage figure mentioned in the text provides clues as to who these two gurus might be. The last Madhyamaka lineage figure mentioned in *General Explanation* is Ratna Chakriwa, whom I understand to be Gya Chakri Gongkawa Jangchup Pal, an eleventh-century Kadampa master who was one of several teachers of Gampopa Sönam Rinchen (1079–1153).

In the collected works of Gampopa, which records several dialogues with Chakriwa, Chakriwa's phrase "instruction of the two teachers" (*bla ma rnam gnyis kyi gdams ngag*) (Sherpa 2004, 197–200) describes Chakriwa's instructions from his two teachers, possibly Geshe Gönpawa Wangchuk Gyaltsen and Langri Thangpa Dorjé Sengé. Another story in Gampopa's works records that Geshe Phuchungwa Shönu Gyaltsen did not give instruction to Geshe Langri Thangpa, but later "two yogis" (*rnal 'byor pa rnam gnyis*) received the instructions (Sherpa 2004, 208). The story continues, "It is said that [these two] were the [spiritual] son[s] of the translator Rinchen Sangpo and the great meditator Pūṇya-jñā-bodhi (Bsod nams ye shes byang chub). In Ü, Chakriwa was brought to spiritual maturity." Lechen's Kadampa history, written in 1494, mentions in the section on Rinchen Sangpo that he had two young monk attendants who requested teachings from Atiśa on behalf of Rinchen Sangpo. These monks, after the passing of Rinchen Sangpo, went to central Tibet and met a "Chakriwa (*lcags ri ba*)."[540] A conflation of this account with the sources given above may connect these monks and the phrase "two yogis," in that they refer to Naljorpa Chenpo Jangchup Rinchen and Gönpawa Wangchuk Gyaltsen, who were known to have traveled west to study with Atiśa. Naljorpa and Gönpawa were considered to be two of the four great yogi disciples of Atiśa (Sørensen 2002, 244) and were also counted among ten disciples who served as personal attendants to Atiśa (Vetturini 2013, 101n483). *General Explanation* may conflate the relations that these two gurus had with

Atiśa for Rinchen Sangpo. Be that as it may, these anecdotes indicate that Chakriwa traveled to central Tibet in Ü and received Madhyamaka teachings from two figures who had been associated with Rinchen Sangpo and/or Atiśa in their youth.

A General Explanation, in addition to referring to Naktso Lotsāwa Tsultrim Gyalwa and *lha bstun* Jangchup Ö (eleventh century), directly cites Chakriwa and Naljorpa Chenpo Jangchup Rinchen. A citation from Geshé Phuchungwa is mentioned, but is absent due to a missing folio side. In addition to citing Chakriwa, the text praises him several times as "possessing incomparable knowledge" (704.10) and being "unmistaken" (718). The person who compiled the Madhyamaka lineage teachings of *General Explanation* was a colleague or disciple of Chakriwa. It is conceivable that the person who received these teachings and compiled them was Gampopa Sönam Rinchen. Attributing *General Explanation* to Gampopa early in his career before he met Milarepa (ca. 1028–1111) might be feasible, because it helps to explain why this text was not known among later Kadampa or Kagyüpa communities; the text is like an "orphan" that was not transmitted by either tradition. One can theorize that *General Explanation* was not transmitted by Kadampa communities because Gampopa was scorned for leaving his Kadampa teachers and becoming a student of Milarepa (Vetturini 2013, 139–40), and these teachings were not transmitted by the Kagyüpa because it represents a sūtra level lamrim discourse that does not include any tantric teachings from either Indian or Tibetan masters such as Nāropa or Milarepa. In spite of this hypothesis, the content of the text is not written in Gampopa's style of combining exoteric sūtra discourses with tantra (Davidson 2005), nor does *General Explanation*'s style or content compare with the *Jewel Ornament of Liberation* (*Dam chos yid bzhin nor bu thar pa rin po che'i rgyan*; Guenther 1959). Rather, as the works of Gampopa contain a few idioms of expression and analogies attributed to Chakriwa that are also found in *General Explanation*, we may infer that these points of resemblance derive from discourses that were transmitted and shared among Chakriwa's community of Kadampa scholar-colleagues. In addition to Chakriwa, biographies of Gampopa state that he studied in the Phenyul region under Kadampa masters such as Nyukrumpa Tsöndrü Gyaltsen, Geshe Dreypa, Gya Yöndak, and Jayülwa Shönu Ö.

In relation to the Madhyamaka lineages that Gampopa received, a commentary on Candrakīrti's *Madhyamakāvatāra* by Mikyö Dorjé (1507–54) outlines the main lineages of Madhyamaka (*dbu ma*) in India and Tibet that were transmitted by the later Karma Kagyü tradition. Among three main lines of transmission, including a lineage from Nāropa and Patsap Nyimadrak, a third lineage of transmission from Atiśa Dīpaṃkāraśrījñāna is described as follows:

> "From the preceptors Nāg[ārjuna], Āryadeva, Candrakīrti, and *Vidyākokila this second transmission reached Jo bo Atiśa. From him, it passed on to the *kalyāṇamitra* Tönpa Chenpo [i.e., Dromtönpa Gyalwai Jungné], and then to the latter's disciple Chengawa, and to Jayülwa. From many Kadampa masters, Lord Gampopa then heard it. Alternatively: From Potowa, it passed to the great sage Sharawa, who then handed it down to the glorious Dusum Khyenpa . . ."[541]

General Explanation, however, does not cite or mention either Dromtönpa, Chengawa, or Sharawa. Alternatively, the history of the Kadampa tradition by Lechen Kunga Gyaltsen (b. 1440) describes the dissemination of Atiśa's teachings on the two realities among what came to be known as the lineage of essential instructions (*gdams ngag*) as follows:

> Guidance on the two realities was formulated in order to guide one on the extremely subtle essencelessness of things. The disciple of Lord Atiśa who was extremely skilled in the two realities was Naljorpa Chenpo [Jangchup Rinchen]. His disciples were the masters of yoga Geshe Tölungpa and Chengawa. Chengawa gave oral teachings in secret [on the two realities] to both Tölungpa and Jayülwa. In this way, the one who became skilled in the two realities was the great Tölungpa . . . His disciple Khyung-kham acquired the special instructions of both Tölungpa and Jayülwa . . .[542]

General Explanation cites Naljorpa Chenpo (715.12–15), although Tölungpa is neither cited nor mentioned in the text. A common figure, however, who is mentioned in both of these lineage accounts and who was a teacher of Gampopa and a contemporary of Chakriwa is Jayülwa Shönu Ö. Lechen Kunga Gyaltsen's account states that Atiśa's instructions on the two realities were orally transmitted in secret to the time of Jayülwa. As discussed by Roesler (2015), the eleventh-century Kadampa environment was a transitional phase from oral teachings to textual written works wherein the instructions of significant masters were written down by their disciples. As in the case of Potowa, whose disciples recorded his teachings from memory after his passing in 1105, guidance on the two realities in such texts as *General Explanation* may have been put in writing in the late eleventh century.

As suggested, *General Explanation* may represent an oral teaching of Atiśa that progressively developed during its transmission. The text reflects the development of local autonomous traditions affiliated with Atiśa that emphasized oral tradition and lineage (Vetturini 2013, 22–23). The latest Tibetan figure cited in the text is Geshe Chakriwa. The text represents the Madhyamaka teachings of Atiśa that circulated among communities of eleventh-century Kadampa scholars in the Phenyul region and provides textual evidence for the type of Madhyamaka thought that later figures such as Chapa Chökyi Sengé would vehemently reject (Tauscher 2009; Vose 2009).

General Explanation fills an important gap in the historical knowledge of Madhyamaka teachings in eleventh-century India and Tibet. The text presents a Madhyamaka teaching brought to Tibet by Atiśa and provides previously unknown evidence for the type of pure Madhyamaka teachings that circulated among the communities of early followers of Atiśa. These pure Madhyamaka teachings were disseminated *before* the rise of the early Kadampa monastery of Sangphu Neuthok and its debating traditions that were the basis for most all subsequent forms of Tibetan monastic education that, particularly beginning in the twelfth century, placed emphasis on the merger of Madhyamaka and epistemology. In other words, for Atiśa and his early Kadampa followers the science of epistemology and logic (*hetuvidyā*) was "a profane secular science that is common to the Buddhist and other Indian non-Buddhist schools such as the Naiyāyikas" (Krasser 2004, 130) and not useful for realizing emptiness (see *Satyadvayāvatāra*, vv. 10–14). During the time of Atiśa and his early followers, the use of logic and epistemology were considered part of the five fields of knowledge to refute non-Buddhists and Buddhists. However, valid cognition was *not* part of Atiśa's Madhyamaka and this is demonstrated by the fact that *General Explanation* contains no passages that demonstrate the integration of Madhyamaka and epistemology.

Sources and Content

General Explanation is an exposition on the two realities that integrates the teaching of dependent-arising within the framework of Atiśa's stages of the path (*lamrim*) teachings. The work articulates Nāgārjuna's Madhyamaka of mutual dependence and dependent designation within the system of the five paths (*lam lnga*, **pañcamārga*)[543] found in the technical digests attributed to Maitreyanātha. *General Explanation* outlines the structure of the path integrated with the characteristics of the two realities, providing a framework, or map, for how the soteriological processes based on the works of Nāgārjuna and Maitreyanātha are envisioned. However, it does not provide instructions for how to actually practice or implement its framework. Rather, Atiśa's *Special Instructions on the Middle Way* and its commentaries provide instructions for cultivating the three wisdoms (*prajñā*) of learning, reflection, and meditation within the context of meditative equipoise (*mnyam bzhag, samāhita*) and postmeditative (*rjes las thob, pṛṣṭhalabdhajñāna*) wisdom construed through the purviews of conventional and ultimate realities.

The style of exegesis in *General Explanation* is also found in Atiśa's *Open Basket of Jewels* and *Bodhipathapradīpapañjikā*. As mentioned, *General Explanation* directly quotes Atiśa nineteen times and mentions him over twenty times in the third person. Nāgārjuna is directly cited over forty times in the text from among twelve of his works, including the *Pratītyasamutpādahṛdayakārikā*, the *Mūlamadhyamakakārikā*, the *Yuktiṣaṣṭikā*, and the *Bodhicittavivaraṇa*.[544] Although texts such as the *Dharmadhātustava*, the *Bodhicittavivaraṇa*, and the *Bhāvanākrama* are not attributed by modern scholars to the Nāgārjuna who wrote the *Mūlamadhyamakakārikā*, eleven out of the twelve works cited in *General Explanation* are directly attributed to Nāgārjuna by Atiśa in *Open Basket of Jewels*.[545] *General Explanation* repeatedly connects the thought of Atiśa and Nāgārjuna through comparable citations. The text is explicitly concerned with outlining the path of the Madhyamaka based on the works of Nāgārjuna. It cites the *Mūlamadhyamakakārikā* five times, with four of these verses directly matching the Tibetan translation of the verses preserved in the *Akutobhayā*, a commentary on the *Mūlamadhyamakakārikā* attributed to Nāgārjuna by Atiśa in his *Bodhimārgapradīpapañjikā* and *Ratnakaraṇḍodghāṭa*. Moreover, *General Explanation* (718.2, 740.5) comments on two of these verses (*Mūlamadhyamakakārikā* 13.1, 18.9) with an unacknowledged paraphrase from the *Akutobhayā*. The work also explicitly states that Nāgārjuna and Atiśa agree on certain points, such as the position that appearances are the mind (711.20, 714.4) and that realization of emptiness on the path of vision occurs in a single instant (731.4).

After Nāgārjuna and Atiśa, the most cited textual sources (ten times) are various Mahāyāna sūtras such as the *Suvarṇaprabhāsottama*, the *Laṅkāvatārasūtra*, and the *Vimalakīrtinirdeśa*. Tantric works are not directly cited. *General Explanation* directly cites or mentions other Indian figures such as Maitreyanātha (four times), Āryadeva (twice), Candrakīrti (eight times), and Bhāviveka (three times). The text notes that Nāgārjuna, Candrakīrti, and Atiśa place great importance on utilizing the example of the appearance of hairs for one with eye disease (*rab rib can, taimirika*) in order to illustrate mistaken appearances (743.8).[546] The text also bases its presentation of different frameworks for positing conventional realities on Candrakīrti's

Madhyamakāvatāra (697.10–699.15). It bases its exegesis of the *Yuktiṣaṣṭikā* on the *Vṛtti* of Candrakīrti as well. It advocates the use of consequences that expose contradictions and employing other-acknowledged inferences (706.20), methods supported by Candrakīrti. Yet at the same time, *General Explanation* adapts the metaphor of a stairway (*sopāna*) and the concept of "pure mundane wisdom" (*śuddhalaukikajñāna*) from the works of Bhāviveka. The text integrates the understanding of correct (*tathya, yang dag pa*) and mistaken (*mithyā, log pa*) conventional realities of Bhāviveka with the thought of Candrakīrti while excluding the criteria of causal efficiency for differentiating conventional realities based on the thought of Jñānagarbha.

General Explanation mentions that Atiśa gave three teachings on Madhyamaka in Tibet (703.14–16). The first was the system of Buddhajñāna, which is classified as Yogācāra-Madhyamaka (*rnal 'byor spyod pa'i dbu ma*). The second was the position of Bhavya, which the text classifies as Sautrāntika-Madhyamaka (*mdo sde spyod pa'i dbu ma*). These are classifications of Madhyamaka known in Tibet since the time of Yeshé Dé in the ninth century (Ruegg 1981). The text then explains that Atiśa taught the accepted position of Ācārya Nāgārjuna, which comprises the content of *General Explanation*. The text implies that for Atiśa the thought of Nāgārjuna is considered only Madhyamaka or Great Madhyamaka (697.21, 699.20); the latter classification occurs in Atiśa's *Bodhipathapradīpa* and *Pañjikā* as well as numerous early Kadampa texts.[547] *A General Explanation* also utilizes other classifications for Madhyamaka thought, such as Madhyamakas who hold tenets (*grub pa mtha' 'dzin gyi dbu ma*, 697.20), Madhyamakas who proclaim the nature of dependent-arising (*rten 'brel gshis brjod pa'i dbu ma pa*, 700.7), True Aspectarian Mādhyamikas (*rnam bden dbu ma ba*) and False Aspectarian Mādhyamikas (*rnam rdzun dbu ma ba*, 711.5), and [Proponents] of Illusion-like Nonduality (*sgyu ma gnyis med* ≈ *māyopamādvaya*[*vāda*]). These classifications of Madhyamaka thought were the predominant classifications utilized by Indian and Tibetan authors during the late eleventh century (Almogi 2010), several decades before the well-known classifications "Consequentialist" (*thal 'gyur ba*, **prāsaṅgika*) and "Autonomist" (*rang rgyud pa*, **svātrantika*) were coined in Tibet.[548]

A General Explanation contains topical headings, but they are not always clear or well-organized, providing further evidence that the manuscript may be recorded oral teachings. The Dpal-brtsegs editors have furnished a set of topical outlines (*sa bcad*) in the introductory material to the facsimile of the manuscript, but these outlines do not precisely correspond to the content of the work. I have modified the Dpal-brtsegs editors' topical outlines with headings found in the text. In the annotated translation that follows, I have placed these headings in brackets in order to clarify the content of each section. The topical outline of *A General Explanation* is as follows:

I. Introduction (*klad kyi don bshad pa*)
II. The Main Body of the Work (*gzhung gi don bstan pa*) [697.5–747.10]
A. Explanation of the General Characteristics of the Two Realities (*bden pa gnyis kyi spyi'i mtshan nyid bshad pa*) [697.5–8]
B. Establishing the Framework of the Two Realities (*bden gnyis 'jog tshul so sor bshad pa)* [697.9–698.5]
1. Explanation of Conventional Reality (*kun rdzob bden pa bshad pa*) [698.5–738.6]
a. Explaining the Nature of Conventional Reality (*kun rdzob bden pa'i ngo bo bshad pa*) [698.6–699.15]
b. Explaining the Characteristics of Conventional Reality (*kun rdzob bden pa'i mtshan nyid bshad pa*) [699.15–716.22]
i. Characteristics of Correct Conventional Reality [699.15–714.3]
ii. Characteristics of Mistaken Conventional Realities [714.7–716.22]
c. Objects Indicated by the Words "Correct Obscuration" and "Mistaken Obscuration" (*yang dag pa'i rdzob dang log pa'i rdzob kyi sgra'i don*) [716.22–738.4]
i. Objects Indicated by Conventional Words (*kun rdzob kyi sgra'i don*) [716.23–717.1]
ii. Correct and Mistaken Objects Indicated by Words (*yang dag pa dang log pa'i sgra'i don*) [717.1–723.7]
iii. Objects Indicated by the Words "Reality" or "Truth" and "Obscuration" (*bden pa'i sgra'i don te rdzob kyi sgra'i don*) [723.8–738.4]
1) Objects Indicated by Mistaken Conventional Reality (*log pa'i kun rdzob bden pa'i sgra don*) [723.10–726.10]
2) Objects Indicated by Correct Conventional Reality (*yang dag kun rdzob bden pa'i sgra don*) (726.10–738.4)]
2. Explanation of Ultimate Reality (*don dam bden pa bshad pa*) [738.7–747.10]
III. Three Wondrous Qualities of Practice (*ngo mtshar can gyi spyod pa gsum*) [747.10–751.4]
IV. Conclusion (*mjug gi don bshad pa*) [751.4–5]

A General Explanation does not unfold in a straightforward fashion based on its topical outline, as specific points of exegesis occur throughout the text in a question and answer format. Taking the whole work into account, *General Explanation* frameworks the processes by which one cognizes the ultimate, and thereby progresses to buddhahood, through giving an exegesis on the characteristics and features of conventional reality and ultimate reality according to its theory of the two kinds of reality (*satyadvaya*). The distinction between the two kinds of reality is not made at the pure level of the actual realm of reality, as the Buddha indicates in several Mahāyāna sūtras (738.20) that the conventions of "ultimate" or "conventional" are not applicable in reality. Nevertheless, although actual ultimate reality does not conventionally exist, it may be conventionally indicated through imputations and nonimplicative negations (739.22).

Ultimate reality, which is fully outlined toward the end of the work (738.7–747.10), is beyond references; inexpressible as it is beyond all referents, it is a purified appearance of nonappearance (*snang ba med pa*), like the center of space (739.17), known through individually intuited knowledge (740.5). The "ultimate" is a conventional expression, also embodied by the phrase "realm of reality," consisting of selfless nonappearances that are realized with nonconceptual pristine awareness (*jñāna*) (740.15). The realm of reality is a naturally pure object of realization that is the ever-present real state of things (741.5), which may be cognized in meditative equipoise (721.10) but is not completely actualized until full buddhahood is attained. Ultimate reality does not conventionally exist, as it is devoid of all conventions (700.8). As it does not conventionally exist, ultimate reality does not have characteristics (739.18), nor does it arise due to causes and conditions.[549]

Conventional realities are appearances that arise due to causes and conditions (697.6). All conventional realities are false and deceiving, but they are not nonexistent. Rather, they are mere appearances subject to the principle of cause and effect imputed through dependent-arising. Conventional realities are classified as mistaken or correct from three different frameworks or perspectives (697.9–698.5). The three ways of identifying (*'jogs lugs*) mistaken and correct conventional realities are explained based on Candrakīrti's *Madhyamakāvatāra*. Conventional realities are dependently designated in relation to the perspectives of (1) the worldly (*lo ka pa*), (2) philosophical tenets (*grub mtha'*), and (3) yogic awareness (*rnal 'byor pa'i blo*). The text states that it posits correct and mistaken conventional realities based on the nature of dependent-arising in relation to yogic awareness. A long section of the text (698.5–738.6) focuses on an explanation of conventional reality based on these principles. The exegesis of mistaken and correct conventional realities is based on dependent-arisings rather than causal efficiency advocated by Jñānagarbha (698.1–4). This understanding of the dependent-arising of conventional reality in correlation with its states of awareness accords with what Wangchuk (2010) has called "the relativity theory of the purity and validity of perception" in Madhyamaka works. In the words of *A General Explanation*, "things are not higher or lower; awarenesses are higher or lower" (*chos mtho' dman min / blo mtho' dman yin*, 699.7).

Common appearance is a mere imputation (*btags pa tsam*, 700.18) that is nominally designated (*ming btags*, 708.7). All appearances, including both cognitions and objects, are mere imputations (709.12). All conventional realities are like mistaken illusions (726.15). Mistaken conventional realities are appearances of ignorance that impute impermanent and empty things as either existent or nonexistent. Mistakes (*log pa*) are impermanent and a cause of suffering and they are also deceptive (*slu ba*) and false (*rdzun*). Mistaken appearances are like the hair that is perceived by someone suffering from eye disease (723.10).

Correct conventional realities are appearances of discerning awareness (*rig pa shes rab*) that occur after the path of vision and are considered pure mundane wisdom (*dag pa lo ka ba'i ye shes*, 717.16). Correct conventional realities are considered nondeceptive (*mi slu ba*), nonerroneous, and trustworthy (*yid brtan du rung ba*) in that, from this perspective, appearances are realized to be unproduced like an illusion and objects are cognized as essenceless entities. Although correct, they are conventional due to arising through causes and conditions (733.9) and are considered illusions of pristine awareness (*rig pa ye shes kyi sgyu ma*, 717.7, 735.9). Correct conventional realities are nonerroneous illusions (*ma 'khrul ba sgyu ma*, 717.7) and are imputations (726.5) conducive to purification, since the causes of purification have nondeceptive individual results (733.10).

A General Explanation's presentation of the characteristics of correct conventional reality (699.15–714.3) provides an early account of points of Madhyamaka exegesis that would become polemical points of debate in later decades and centuries in the history of Tibetan Buddhist thought. Topics such as whether Mādhyamikas have a thesis, an inference that is known to others (*gzhan la grags pa'i rjes dpag*), the object that is negated (*dgag bya*), the negation of self-characteristics (*rang gi mtshan nyid* ≈ *svalakṣaṇa*), and the notion that two things are "a single nature but different conceptual isolates" (*ngo gcig ldog pa tha dad*) are discussed, but in a late-eleventh-century Indo-Tibetan Buddhist historical context. The text strongly emphasizes that correct conventional realities are indicated through nonimplicative negations (*med dgag*) and that things are mere appearances that are transactually designated without being established. The work provides an exegesis of how conventional reality is nominally designated based on a technical discussion of verses from

Nāgārjuna's *Dharmadhātustava* (702.1–8) articulating what *A General Explanation* calls the "conventional of mere name" (*ming tsam gyi kun rdzob*) and the "conventional of mere appearance" (*snang ba tsam gyi kun rdzob*). In this way, *A General Explanation* presents a Madhyamaka system of subtle nominalism based on dependent designation in its eludication of five qualities of nonimplicative negation (702.19–22). Objects and cognitions (709.15), as well as emptiness (718.16) and the stages of the path (726.15), are considered nominal designations. Although things are merely imputed, the cause and effect of mere appearance is not refuted (706). Four great Madhyamaka reasons (706.1–706.25) establish all things in *saṃsāra* and *nirvāṇa* as dependent-arisings that lack intrinsic existence. The lack of intrinsic existence is proven by nonimplicative negations based on reasoning employed by the Buddha and found in scripture (707.1–20). Consequences and inferences known to others (706.15–707.1) are utilized to expose the contradictions of those who assert intrinsic existence. A follower of Nāgārjuna does not accept a thesis (739.25–740). Rather, reasonings are utilized to refute erroneous assertions while one's own nonacceptance is not invalidated (706.22). In this way, no proof of a philosophical position is ever posited by a Mādhyamika (697.18). Along these lines, the means of valid cognition (703–703.6), based on statements of Nāgārjuna and Atiśa, are only conventional and are not in the domain of ultimate reality, nor are they able to realize ultimate reality.

A General Explanation specifies that the object of negation of reasoning is a conceived object based on conceptualization that imputes things as either existent or nonexistent. The object negated by reasoning consists of conceptual thought that imputes an object as existing with its own-character (708.20–709.1). However, the text stresses that unestablished mere appearances are not refuted by reasoning. Rather, appearances are overturned through antidotes cultivated while practicing the path, particularly during the path of vision and the path of meditation. *A General Explanation* offers an early distinction between objects negated by an antidote while implementing the path and objects negated by reasoning when searching out the inherent existence of something.

As mentioned, objects and cognitions are considered imputations of mere appearance. *A General Explanation* explains that Atiśa does not accept the existence of external objects (709.20–710.5), as all appearances are imputed by the mind. Atiśa's understanding of mere appearances as mind is based on texts attributed to Nāgārjuna (711.10–20). Atiśa's understanding of Nāgārjuna on this point is similar to suggestions made in previous modern scholarship (Scherrer-Schaub 1991; Lindtner 1997a; Ruegg 2002, 203) on mentalism in Madhyamaka, and what Shulman has recently called "creative ignorance"

(2009, 158–167). That is, Atiśa accepts that owing to conceptualization "the world is created out of ignorance (ibid., 158), that "objects themselves are constructed out of ignorance" (ibid., 159), and that through dependent-arisings "appearances are conditioned by ignorance and caused by conceptualization" (ibid., 162). The appearances created by ignorance are considered by Atiśa (711–711.10) as mistaken conventional realities for all groups, including Madhyamakas who uphold tenets and all those below them. The text mentions that this includes True Aspectarian Madhyamakas, False Aspectarian Madhyamakas, and Māyopamādvayavadins. *A General Explanation* states that its acceptance of mistaken conventional realities, in terms of establishing cognition as mind, is similar to how True Aspectarians (**Satyākāravadins*) posit aspects, or cognitive images (*ākāra*). This process is comparable to Candrakīrti, who, as pointed out by MacDonald (2009, 151), skillfully adapts the Sautrāntika theory of cognition on the conventional level to justify his own views. Atiśa's position on the status of external objects is similar to the presentation of "internal" Madhyamaka (*nang gi dbu ma*) presented in the *Madhyamakaratnapradīpa* (D, 280a3–81a3; Del Toso 2014). However, *A General Explanation* also states, in correlation with Nāgārjuna accepting appearances as mind, that Atiśa asserts, in terms of the mind as *mere* appearance, a perspective equal to correct conventional reality—that all sentient beings are one single continuum (*rgyud gcig*, 712.1–713.5). All sentient beings are considered as one continuum, for even though they have differences of karmic conditions, they share an undifferentiated self-nature (*rang gi ngo bo la tha dad med pa*) that is free from the two extremes of intrinsic essence. Consciousness is also asserted as one group (*tshogs gcig*) by Atiśa (713.5–714.5). In this way, the *General Explanation* presents a mentalist theory of Madhyamaka in which the mind, as mere appearance, is not at all established and is a mere nominal designation free from the extremes of existence and nonexistence.

Appearances from the purview of the relative perspectives of mistaken conventional realities and correct conventional realities are described in a long section entitled "Objects Indicated by the Words 'Correct Obscuration' and 'Mistaken Obscuration'" (*yang dag pa'i rdzob dang log pa'i rdzob kyi sgra'i don*, 716.22–738.4). This section is influenced by Candrakīrti's understanding that all conventional realities are obscured whether they are correct or mistaken, and based on the idea that reality is perceived from different perspectives relative to one's level of awareness. As awareness is transformed and purified, the real condition of mistaken appearance is perceived as mere appearance through gaining cognition of correct conventionals. While from the perspective of correct conventional reality, as one progresses further in purifying awareness, the real condition of correct conventionals is realized as the nonappearance that comprises ultimate reality. Perspectives and awarenesses transform appearances as one progresses on the path to buddhahood. In this way, mistaken obscurations are from the perspective of ordinary individuals who erroneously perceive intrinsic natures in causes and effects, perpetuating the cycle of conditioned existence. Mistaken obscuration is an illusion or appearance of ignorance. Since it is an appearance of ignorance, it is a mistaken illusion (717.5). As mistaken appearances are ignorance, mistaken conventionals are comparable to the state of a person with blurred vision seeing hair in the sky. Such appearances are nonexistent, false, erroneous, and mistaken (723.10). Nevertheless, from the perspective of mere falsity, such appearances are perceived as true/real before reaching the path of vision.

As appearances become purified through implementing the path, the real condition (*gshis*) of mistaken obscurations, that is, mere appearances free from the two extremes of existence and nonexistence, are perceived as correct obscurations after reaching the path of vision. Correct obscuration, as it arises from the conditions of discerning awareness, is an illusion of pristine awareness (*rig pa ye shes kyi sgyu ma*, 717.8) that does not obscure ultimate reality and is suitable as the means to realizing ultimate reality. Based on citations attributed to Nāgārjuna and Candrakīrti, the two realities are explained as cause and effect in that the means, correct conventional reality, serves as the method to realize the goal. *A General Explanation* repeatedly refers to this connection between the dependently arisen means leading to the goal of ultimate reality as "the stairway of correct conventional reality" (*yang dag kun rdzob kyi skas*). A series of citations, some misattributed and one with a significant variant, seeks to unify the thought of Nāgārjuna, Candrakīrti, Bhāviveka, the Buddha, Atiśa, and Chakriwa on this point (720.18–721.4).[550]

The stairway of correct conventional reality that occurs after the path of vision consists of appearances of pure mundane wisdom (*dag pa lo ka ba'i ye shes kyi snang ba* [*dag pa 'ji rten pa'i ye shes* ≈ *śuddhalaukikajñāna*], 717.17). Bhāviveka's *Madhyamakahṛdaya-kārikā* (MHK 3.6c, 3.12c; Iida 1980, 60, 67) employs the metaphor of a stairway and the *Tarkajvālā* (Iida 1980, 62, 69) explains the concept of "pure mundane wisdom" as a synonym of correct conventional wisdom (*yang dag pa'i kun rdzob shes pa, tathyasaṃvṛtijñāna*). Early occurrences of the concept of "pure mundane wisdom" are found in the works of Vasubandhu and Sthiramati, based on their understanding of *nirvikalpajñāna* and the "awareness obtained subsequent to it."[551] The term *śuddhalaukika* also occurs in Kamalaśīla's *Tattvasaṃgrahapañjikā* (Keira 2004, 79–80) as a judgment subsequent to yogic perception. The linking of pure mundane wisdom with correct conventional wisdom is found in the *Madhyamakārthasaṃgraha* attribruted to Bhāviveka, a text that was translated by Atiśa's disciple Tsultrim Gyalwa (Del Toso 2011). Atiśa's understanding of these classifications is influenced by the MRP and is outlined in Atiśa's *Ratnakaraṇḍodghāṭa*, where he articulates his understanding of buddhahood. In the *Madhyamakaratnapradīpa* (D, 282b–83b), the categories "pure mundane wisdom" (*dag pa 'jig rten pa'i ye shes*), "nonconceptual wisdom" (*rnam par mi rtog pa'i ye shes*), "meditative equipoise" (*mnyam par bzhag*), and "post-meditative attainment" (*rjes las thob pa*) are designated based on the inclinations of the disciple to be trained but do not exist in ultimate reality. As outlined in *Open Basket of Jewels*, like the MRP, the distinctions of these categories no longer exist in the state of buddhahood, which is continually, and nondualistically, fused with the realm of reality. In Atiśa's system, the appearances of pure mundane wisdom occur after the path of vision as one traverses the ten stages of a bodhisattva. However, for Atiśa, buddhas never leave meditative equipoise in the realm of reality and therefore do not possess knowledge of illusory conventional phenomena subsequent to meditative equipoise.

In *A General Explanation* the experience of pure mundane wisdom as correct conventional reality is able to realize mere appearance (*snang ba tsam*)—appearances as free from the two extremes of existence and nonexistence. The state of correct conventional reality is also able to recognize experiences of mistaken conventional reality as false, deceptive, and erroneous (726.10–15). Although correct conventional realities are conventional and illusory, they are undeceiving in that the dependent-arising of purification and the path occur compatibly through cause-and-effect relations. *A General Explanation* outlines, in a long and complex discussion (726.25–738.5), the compatibility of purification and the path based on the dependent-arising of correct conventional realities correlated with five effects drawn from the *Madhyāntavibhāga* attributed to Maitreya. Realization of the nonduality of the two realities produces these five effects of correct conventional reality (727.4), enabling one to ascend the stairway of correct conventional reality leading to buddhahood. The five effects—the retributive effect (*vipākaphala*), the predominant effect (*adhipatiphala*), the correlative effect (*niṣyandaphala*), the effect caused by human action (*puruṣakāraphala*), and the separation effect (*visaṃyogaphala*)—are correlated with practices and path structures from a Madhyamaka perspective in that they are dependently designated and lack intrinsic essence. Practices such as the three trainings of morality (*śīla*), concentration (*samādhi*), and insight (*prajñā*), and the three wisdoms arising from study, contemplation, and meditation, are integrated with stages among the five paths and correlated to practices comprising the thirty-seven factors of awakening (*byang chub phyogs kyi chos so bdun*, 727.15–732.15). Atiśa correlates the stages of the path with the thirty-seven factors of awakening in his BMPP

(D, 276b; Sherburne 2000, 213) and *Open Basket of Jewels* (chap. 1, §3.1), but these are brief lists. *A General Explanation* contains a more extended discussion of these factors placed within the context of correct conventional realities (727.15–732.15).

A General Explanation understands the on-going progression of purified states of awareness correlated with effects along the stairway of correct conventional reality within a Mahāyāna-based antidote model that is called "the path that arises eliminates its obscurations" (*skye bar 'gyur ba lam gyis ni / /de'i sgrib pa rab du spong*, 731.5). In this model, the antidote of increasingly refined and purified states of correct conventional reality initially replace and remedy appearances of mistaken conventional realities that have arisen based on the stains of ignorance. After the path of vision, which is equivalent to attaining the first bodhisattva spiritual level, a bodhisattva experiences postmeditative-state appearances due to obstructions to omniscience comprised of unafflicted misknowledge (*nyon mongs pa can ma yin pa'i mi shes pa'i shes bya'i sgrib pa*, 721.7). These obstructions are removed during the path of meditation in conjunction with practices of acquiring great amounts of merit (722.25).

As bodhisattvas become constituted by correct conventional reality after attaining the first spiritual level, they no longer take rebirth due to karma and mental afflictions and function like independent illusions (736.14). *A General Explanation* (733–38) articulates, through a question-and-answer format, the differences between how causation and rebirth function through mistaken appearances for ordinary individuals before reaching the path of vision, and how causation and rebirth function through mere appearances for bodhisattvas after the path of vision is attained. Both mistaken appearances and mere appearances are subject to the principle of cause and effect, as they arise from either mistaken or correct conventional reality according to one's stage on the path to buddhahood.

A General Explanation's discussion of ultimate reality (738.7–747.10), in addition to describing the characteristics mentioned above, furnishes an extended exegesis of the understanding that there is nothing to be removed or established in ultimate reality (740.6–747.10). Ultimate reality, in terms of this exegesis, is the ever-present realm of reality comparable to space, the realization of which is achieved in nonconceptual meditation. As ultimate reality is ever present, yet nonapparent to ignorance, it is immanent. What is removed are the mistaken appearances of ignorance, which are comparable to the hairs perceived by one with eye disease (740.16–741.10). The antidote to the eye disease of the appearance of ignorance is the realization of correct conventional reality, which unloosens the bonds of one's own mind (741.15–742.5).

Realization of ultimate reality, that is, emptiness, liberates one from karma and mental afflictions. However, realization of emptiness must be integrated with the method of correct conventional reality to actualize full awakening (742.10–742.17). The path must be implemented to overturn appearances of ignorance. On this point *A General Explanation* repeatedly asks, "What is the purpose of the path if it does not exist?" (724.8, 726.1, 726.4, 729.25).

A General Explanation then provides a detailed discussion, based on *Yuktiṣaṣṭikā* (vv. 26–27), that all appearances are based on ignorance and that, in reality, they lack intrinsic essence (*svabhāva*). The real nature of things is suchness, whether or not buddhas appear in the world. *A General Explanation*, based on citations from the *Bhāvanākrama* attributed to Nāgārjuna, explains that the true nature of things is nonarising, which is neither existent nor nonexistent (745.7–745.20). The text emphasizes that the actual nature of the mind is suchness (*de bzhin nyid* ≈ *tathatā*) itself, which is comparable to space. As space is unestablished and lacks any position, extreme points, or even a middle, likewise when the mind is bereft of conceptual thought and its latencies, all objects, subjects, emptiness, and even the wisdom that realizes emptiness dissipates (745.21–746.14). In other words, as suggested by MacDonald in her study of Candrakīrti (2009, 145), "the Madhyamaka *nirvāṇa* is the world itself—in its innate and eternal state of peaceful non-arising." When a Mādhyamika yogi no longer apprehends the assertions of others that things exist or do not exist, the object of that wisdom excludes all appearances of ignorance and realizes the ever-present suchness of things (rephrasing Franco 2009, 26).

A General Explanation concludes by emphasizing that the purpose of realizing emptiness is to generate compassion for sentient beings (746.16–747.10) and relates this realization to three wondrous qualities of practice (*ngo mtshar can gyi spyod pa gsum*) (747.10–751.4). Rather than discuss the qualities of buddhahood, the text concludes by stressing practices to be followed by bodhisattvas. These practices are explained based on understanding the indivisibility of the two realities in the context of Atiśa's stairway of correct conventional reality. The exegesis of the three practices and their qualities are derived from verses of the *Bodhicittavivaraṇa*. The three qualities, in brief, are that a bodhisattva (1) closely follows the principles of cause and effect and does not have contempt for karmic effects, (2) has concern only for the welfare of others, and (3) does not turn back from this concern despite sufferings and hardships.

Concluding Remarks

A *General Explanation* is a late-eleventh-century work that thoroughly explains the Madhyamaka thought of Atiśa and his understanding, based on the works of Nāgārjuna, of dependent-arising as mutual dependence and dependent designation. The text outlines Atiśa's understanding of Nāgārjuna within the context of Atiśa's gradual stages of the path and his emphasis on practice. The Madhyamaka advocated in *A General Explanation* is articulated based on the works of Nāgārjuna without any references to Yogācāra doctrinal concepts, such as the storehouse consciousness (*ālayavijñāna*) or the three natures (*trilakṣaṇa*). In fact, the work dismisses the interpretation of Vasubandhu on several points of exegesis (729.20, 735.14). It substantiates a number of its points with citations of Mahāyāna sūtras but does not reference any tantric works. This coincides with the request of Tibetans for Atiśa not to give tantric teachings in Tibet (see Schaeffer 2005, 61–2), as opposed to his *Ratnakaraṇḍodghāṭa*, a text written in India that does contain citations of tantric texts in its teaching of Nāgārjuna. *A General Explanation* does resemble Atiśa's *Open Basket of Jewels* in its emphasis on Nāgārjuna and the works attributed to him. Unlike the BMPP, *A General Explanation* does not reference Bodhibhadra or any of his works. It does not reference Śāntarakṣita or Kamalaśīla either. Rather, like *Open Basket of Jewels*, the text references Avadhūtipa and seeks to support its presentation of Nāgārjuna with citations of Candrakīrti and Bhāviveka. In its discussion of Tibetan figures in its lineage of teachings, the text mentions Rinchen Sangpo, Lhatsun Jangchup Ö, and Naktso Lotsāwa Tsultrim Gyalwa, indicating that these teachings were initially taught in western Tibet by Atiśa. The work does not cite or mention Dromtönpa Gyalwai Jungné, the cofounder of the Kadampa, according to the tradition. Rather, *A General Explanation* mentions and quotes Naljorpa Chenpo Jangchup Rinchen, an early disciple of Atiśa who was considered preeminent among Kadampa communities for his knowledge of the two realities.

A General Explanation is a significant work in that it furnishes an early discussion of exegetical points of Madhyamaka thought that would later become polemical topics for debate in Tibetan Buddhist thought. The work addresses, in an eleventh-century Indo-Tibetan Buddhist historical context, issues such as whether Mādhyamikas have a thesis, how inferences that are renowned to others are applied, specification of the object that is negated, the negation of self-characteristics, and the role of pure mundane wisdom in the ascending path of correct conventional reality. The interpretation of many of these issues would later become conceptual sources for differentiating the Tibetan classifications between "Consequentialist" (*thal 'gyur ba*, **prāsaṅgika*) and "Autonomist" (*rang rgyud pa*, **svātantrika*) types of Madhyamaka. Notably, as exemplified in *A General Explanation*, these concepts are not differentiated for classifying branches of Madhyamaka in the thought of Atiśa and his early Kadampa followers.

A General Explanation fills an important gap in the historical knowledge of Madhyamaka teachings in eleventh-century India and Tibet. The text presents a Madhyamaka teaching brought to Tibet by Atiśa and provides previously unknown evidence for the type of pure Madhyamaka teachings that circulated among the communities of early followers of Atiśa. These teachings were disseminated before the rise of the early Kadampa monastery of Sangphu Neuthok (Gsang phu ne'u thog, founded in 1073) and the development of its debating traditions. The debating curriculum of Sangphu Neuthok, influenced by its renowned abbot Chapa Chökyi Sengé (Tauscher 2009), became the basis for most all subsequent forms of Tibetan monastic education that, beginning in the twelfth century, placed emphasis on the merger of Madhyamaka and epistemology. *A General Explanation* presents evidence for the type of Madhyamaka thought that later figures such as Chapa Chökyi Sengé would forcefully reject and that was lost to subsequent Kagyüpa (*bka' rgyud pa*) and Gelukpa communities.

A General Explanation of, and Framework for Understanding, the Two Realities[552]

[I. Introduction (*klad kyi don bshad pa*)]

[697.1] I pay homage to the holy spiritual teachers. Mañjuśrī, Nāgārjuna, Candrakīrti, Vidyākokila, Mahā-Avadhūtipa, Atiśa, Ratnabhadra (Rinchen Sangpo), the precious two gurus. Homage to the spiritual teacher who is like a lion, free from doubts, indestructible, who has the indivisible intention of the two realities, the lord of yogis, harmonious with the meaning and name.

[II. The Main Body of the Work (*gzhung gi don bstan pa*)]

[A. Explanation of the General Characteristics of the Two Realities (*bden pa gnyis kyi spyi'i mtshan nyid bshad pa*)]

The general characteristics of the two realities and the manner of positing two realities.

First, Atiśa has stated that "a process [697.5] that relies on causes, that is established in dependence on conditions, whose own nature appears like a reflection—that is taught as conventional reality." Conventional reality is that which appears as a reflection from the perspective of an aggregration of causes and conditions. A process that does not rely on causes, is not established in dependence on conditions, whose own-nature does not appear as an object—is said to be ultimate reality. Ultimate reality is not produced by causes and conditions. All things no longer appear. There is no appearance. When cognition loosens its own bonds, that is not conventional [reality].

[B. Establishing the Framework of the Two Realities (*bden gnyis 'jog tshul so sor bshad pa)*]

Conventional reality has two [divisions]: correct conventional reality and mistaken conventional reality. There are three manners of positing [conventional reality]: [it] is put forward in dependence on (1) the worldly, (2) philosophical tenets, and (3) yogic awareness. [697.10]

(1) The manner of positing correct and mistaken conventional reality in dependence on the worldly [is as follows]: All things that do not commonly appear as real to the worldly, from scholar *paṇḍita*s to foolish cowherds, are posited as mistaken [697.15] conventional reality. Regarding this, the Ācārya Candrakīrti has stated:

> That which is apprehended by the six unimpaired sensory faculties and realized by the world—that is reality within the world itself. The remainder is established as mistaken by the world itself.[553]

The proof of this is posited in dependence on the world itself, but there is no proof that is posited in dependence on a Mādhyamika.

(2) The manner of positing correct and mistaken conventional reality in dependence on philosophical tenets [is as follows]: Each individual group, from outsider [non-Buddhists] up through Mādhyamikas who hold tenets, [697.20] have their own manner of positing correct and mistaken conventional reality according to [and in dependence on] their own individual tenets. There is no proof in dependence on the Great Madhyamaka. Regarding this, all these tenets are seen as positions that conceptualize correct dependent-arisings and mistaken conventionals. [698] All positions are not even perceived. For example, a philosophical tenet is like a group of blind men touching a large elephant. The characteristics of correct and mistaken conventionals is in most cases explained by Jñānagarbha, who states that "correct and mistaken conventionals are similar in appearance, but they are distinguished by their ability or inability to be causally efficacious . . ."[554] That teaching should be understood as suitable for his followers.

[1. Explanation of Conventional Reality (*kun rdzob bden pa bshad pa*)]

[a. Explaining the Nature of Conventional Reality (*kun rdzob bden pa'i ngo bo bshad pa*)]

The system of positing correct conventionals and mistaken conventionals that have the nature of dependent-arisings [has three divisions] [698.5]: their nature (*ngo bo*), their characteristics (*mtshan nyid*), and their objects [indicated] by words (*sgra'i don*). The appearance (*snang ba*) of discerning awareness is correct conventional reality. Ignorance that consists of erroneous appearance is mistaken conventional reality. First, an awareness that arises from the condition of wisdom is an appearance due to the cause-and-effect relation of purification enhanced by the three roots of uncontaminated virtue[555] of one's own mind having relied on the advice of a skillful spiritual friend. The characteristic is the knowledge that is after the path of vision. All dharmas within *saṃsāra* and *nirvāṇa* are understood as not distinct from the eight similes [698.10] of illusion.[556] Those are suitable to impute within the path of accumulation. The second, mistaken conventionals, arise from the mistaken condition of ignorance and the cause of karma and mental afflictions. The conditioned cycle of existence—all these appearances in the world: of oneself, of sentient beings, and of the environment—and all that established by the various conceptual thoughts of those who hold tenets, from the lower non-Buddhist forders up through Mādhyamikas who hold tenets, are successively established as mistaken conventional realities. This system of positing correct conventionals and mistaken conventionals [698.15] is posited having relied on the nature of dependent-arising.

(3) To posit based on yogic awareness is [as follows], according to Ācārya Candrakīrti:

> Because delusion obscures intrinsic nature, it is called "all-concealing," and due to this what is fabricated appears to be real. The Sage said this is conventionally real and that an entity that is fabricated is only conventional.[557]

An erroneous appearance of ignorance occurs up to and including the path of preparation (*sbyor lam*). After the path of vision, there are appearances of wisdom, or awareness. Of the appearance of objects within *saṃsāra* and *nirvāṇa*, they are actualized in *saṃsāra* in dependence on the appearance of ignorance. [698.20] The afflicted appearance of ignorance arises as the three poisons. Because of that, through accumulating the two kinds of karmic action,[558] a continuum of aggregates is propelled. *Saṃsāra* is overturned having relied on the appearance of wisdom, or awareness. The appearance of wisdom arises as the three uncontaminated virtuous roots. That is the fifth uncontaminated path. The result of that path appears as the three bodies [of a Buddha]. The actual uncontaminated [path] occurs from the point after the path of vision. In a purely nominal sense it is counted from this point. [698.20] The complete stairway of correct method cannot dependently arise without relying on the condition of the spiritual friend who has skill-in-means. Through meditating on this advice of the gradual stages of the path of three kinds of individuals,[559] [699] the appearance of discerning awareness (*rig pa shes rab*) will occur as antidotes to the three poisons of the afflictions. It is necessary for one's own uncontaminated mind to come forth whether it is nominally designated or substantially existent. If the mind does not emerge as the three uncontaminated virtuous roots, one will not go down the path. It is after the point of the path of vision that one transcends the worldly [view] and extinguishes in particular the worldly proclamations of things.

Now at the time of the beginner, a thing that appears is meditated on as an object that does not exist, and the nonexistence is construed as an object. [699.5] Since a concordant [effect] will erroneously occur, the particular karma will not be extinguished. The root of that [karma], the particular affliction, will not be extinguished. Accordingly, even meditating only [on something] as empty, one will not go down the path. This will not lead to the mind becoming the three uncontaminated virtuous roots. Therefore, things (*chos*) are not higher or lower; awarenesses are higher or lower.[560] When a beginner, who upholds [things as] impermanent, does not cultivate additional Dharma [teachings] and does not refute the familiar, the mind will come forth as the three poisons. Since proceeding on the path will not exist if one does not proceed,[561] it is necessary to meditate on the stages of the path, as method is the stairway of correct conventional reality. Whether this advice of the [699.10] practice lineage (*sgrub brgyud*) exists or not, from the point of view of those with a Dharma-eye, one is joyful and tears stream, as there is no greater kindness than Lord Atiśa. This teaching is not to be refuted as something that leads one astray by those who aspire for the inferior. They will not be able to achieve liberation even if treading the path. One has met with the advice that understands the engagement with, and disengagement from, cyclic existence. Now is the time to accept guidance, if one does not make effort from this time forward, one will necessarily wander [in cyclic existence]. One should take joy in putting forth effort and meditating often.

[b. Explaining the Characteristics of Conventional Reality (*kun rdzob bden pa'i mtshan nyid bshad pa*)]

[i. Characteristics of Correct Conventional Reality]

The characteristics have two [divisions]: the characteristics of the correct conventional and the characteristics of mistaken conventionals. The characteristics of correct conventionals [699.15] has four [divisions]. [The four divisions are] either a nonimplicative negation (*med par bkag pa*) or an implicative negation (*ma yin par dgag pa*), which makes two.[562] [And these two negations are] either substantially (*rdzas*) existent or nominally designated (*btags pa*), which makes two [additional divisions], and this [totals] four. Among the [first] two [divisions], either an implicative or nonimplicative negation, this conventional [reality] is a nonimplicative negation. The conventional is accepted as not established even conventionally. All Mādhyamikas who uphold tenets accept this conventional as conventionally existent. The conventional is by scriptural authority that is established by reason. Since the conventional is asserted by those who establish by reason conventionally, the characteristic of the conventional is accepted as a nonimplicative negation.

[Query:] What about one of the Great Madhyamaka? (*dbu ma chen po ba*) [699.20]

[Reply:] Mistaken conventional [reality] is like an illusion. If that passes as an implicative negation, then the mistaken will become established by reason. A conventional [reality] that is established by reason is not accepted. Since this conventional is not accepted as established by reasoning even conventionally, it is asserted as not being a characteristic of the conventional. This is a system in which the very conventional itself is not established by reasoning. The conventional is accepted to be not established even conventionally.

[Query:] Well then, to whom is the conventional spoken?

[Reply:] The conventional is inquired about by the worldly.

[Query:] Well then, is this appearance for the worldly construed as conventional?

[Reply:] It is not acceptable here to establish this as an implicative negation. Since the conventional [699.25] is accepted as not established even conventionally, it is a nonimplicative negation. Regarding that, the conventional is an understanding that the worldly inquire about. For the common appearance [700] of a pillar, a vase, and a wall, one says to the worldly: "This is a pillar. This is a vase. This is a wall." That appearance is not negated and the Mādhyamika speaks as such. Therefore, from the perspective of common appearance, the conventional is construed in terms of inquiries from the worldly. However, as the worldly impute [things] into the two extremes, a conventional [reality] that is not established even conventionally is not [the case for them]. Therefore, since it is spoken of in terms of appearance but accepted as not established, this conventional is a nonimplicative negation but is not accepted [700.5] as an implicative negation. The Mādhyamika who upholds tenets, having relied on conventional reality, negates an ultimate object, but having relied on the ultimate, it is not acceptable to negate an ultimate object. Having said as such because the ultimate does not exist conventionally, all negations are accepted like this.

[Query:] What about the Mādhyamika who proclaims the nature of dependent-arising?

[Reply:] The ultimate does not conventionally exist, [and] since it is devoid of all conventions, there is nothing to refute or prove. When negating a conventional object, having relied on the conventional, all implicative [700.10] and nonimplicative negations are said to be made conventionally. The characteristic of correct conventional [reality]: as the conventional is free from the two extremes, the conventional is not at all established; since it is not essentially established, there is not a substance that upholds its own-characteristic. Unestablished by reason, it is also not an implicative negation. As it is devoid of the two extremes from the beginning, it is a nonimplicative negation. The example that is free from the two extremes is space. Cause and effect is like space. As it is said, "empty things arise from things that are only empty."[563] In this way, through meditation, [700.15] one should understand that conventionally all things are like space.

[Query:] If this nonimplicative negation is an example like space, what is this common appearance?

[Reply:] This is mere imputation.

[Query:] Well then, if this is established as a mere imputation, then it will occur as an implicative negation.

[Reply:] Since a mere imputation is not accepted as established at all, it will not occur as an implicative negation.

[Query:] Well then, if it is not established as an intrinsically substantial entity, nor established as even a mere imputation, this appearance does not exist at all and is an appearance that is not at all established. Therefore, it is a nonexistent appearance.

[Reply:] [This is] an appearance that is false. An erroneous appearance. A mistaken appearance. For example, [700.20] it is like the person with eye disease who sees hair in the space [before them]. At the time of the appearance of hair in one's vision, the hair in one's vision exists in its own clarity. Even while it exists as an appearance of hair in one's vision in its own clarity, it is an appearance that is not at all established. It is a mere name, a mere word, a mere convention, a mere imputation that is transactually designated, but the establishment of the mere imputation does not at all exist. As it does not exist when established by reason, it is not even an implicative negation. Since it is free of the two extremes and not inherently established, it is not a substantial entity. It is not known to exist from the very beginning. Since conventional [reality] is not at all conventionally established, [700.25] it is a nonimplicative negation. We may take space as an example. In meditation, utilizing the concept of "space," for example, conventionally all things [701] will be understood as being like space. Conventionally, that which is free from the two extremes, is not known to exist from the beginning, is a nonimplicative negation, and is an appearance that is not at all established like space is called a mere imputation. That object is called a convention that is a mere name, a convention that is a mere appearance. The example for the convention of mere name is the rabbit's horn or the sky-flower. [701.4] Atiśa's *Diamond Song* (*rdo rje'i glu*) states: "Existence is the same as a sky-flower." All things within the three realms, the desire realm, form realm, and formless realm—a sky-flower, a yak's horn, and a rabbit's horn—are alike in being mere names. When that which is a name is construed as a mere name, it is not a designated name that arises in speech such as "pillar, vase." It is the aggregate of form. To explain the term "name" as the second aggregate of conditioning factors (*'du byed kyi phung po*), it does not signify the appearance of a generic image in mental consciousness that has conceptuality; it is a nonassociated conditioning factor. It is further explained as a signifier (*brjod byed*, *vācaka*). A generic image (*don spyi*, *arthasāmānya*), is explained as the signified (*brjod bya, vācya*), the conceptual knowledge that has the appearance of a generic image as the signified.

[Query:] If an object is not accepted as expressing its own-characteristic (*rang gi mtshan nyid*), in that case what is a name (*ming*)?

[Reply:] As a sound and concept are a single object, conceptual thought is construed as an object, the measure of which is expressed by sound. It is made an object by being expressed by sound and measured by concept. [701.11] When one expresses [the concept] "rabbit's horn," although a rabbit's horn does not exist for conceptual knowledge, through presumption (*brlom nas*) a faultless horn lucently appears. If that did not exist, the articulation of [the concept] "rabbit's horn" would not occur, and the sound and the concept, as a single object, would not be construed as an object by conceptual thought and would not be able to be expressed by sound. The conceptual mind has a single cognition that apprehends "horn" and the object that appears as horn when lucently appearing as the faultless horn of a rabbit. The object that appears as a horn is a generic image. Through being seized by a cognition [701.15] that apprehends a rabbit's horn, the referent is a term generality (*sgra spyi, śabdasāmānya*) that appears to formulate the thought (*yid byed*) that expresses "rabbit's horn." A person who has apprehended [an object] by expressing the generic image with a term generality may or may not utter the internal expression as speech. The internal expression on the verge of being uttered, approximating its own content, a signifier that expresses the generic image by a term generality that appears, is a name. The term "generality," which is a mental expression (*yid brjod*), the signifier,[564] and the "generic image," that inner mental expression on the verge of descending as speech, the signified, becomes the "expressed."

In this way, the three—the terms "generality," "generic image," and "expression" (*brjod pa*)—are the initial knowledge that is conceptualized by the mind and mental functions. Since the name of the signified (*brjod bya*) is a signifier (*brjod byed*), [701.20] when the term "generality" expresses "rabbit's horn," although the generic image of rabbit's horn is not established, it lucently appears. Naturally grasped, although not established, the mere name "rabbit's horn" appears as a sense object with a subjective perceiver. In a similar manner, a yak's horn, although not established, appears as a horn to deluded perception, and the apprehended horn appears as a sense object with a subjective perceiver. As it is construed particularly by the power of the afflictions of one's own mind, the appearance to one's own mind does not distinguish between *the appearance* (*snang*) of merely the name "yak's horn" and *apprehending* (*'dzin pa*) merely the name "yak's horn." This is, again, similar to the [name] sky-flower. In this way, [701.25] a yak's horn and a rabbit's horn, although not the same, are cognized in the same manner. Likewise, through this illustration, all things within *saṃsāra* [702] and *nirvāṇa* will be understood as not different from the mere name of a rabbit's horn or a sky-flower. This sameness of the yak's horn and rabbit's horn is not independently [established]. As the *Dharmadhātustava* composed by Ārya Ācārya Nāgārjuna states:

> [30] Just as horns on a rabbit's head do not exist and are only imagined, likewise, all things do not exist and are only imagined. [31] As they are not made of solid atoms, the horns of an ox do not exist either. Just as before so it is after, what is to be imagined there? [32] Since arising is a dependent occurrence, and cessation is a dependent occurrence, there is not one single thing that exists—How could the childish think that there is? [33] Through examples like the oxen's and rabbit's horns, the Tathāgata has proven that all things are the Middle Way itself.[565]

[702.8] In this way, the very cognition of a yak's horn and a rabbit's horn appears in the same way as a sensory object; the very cognition is the same in appearing to a subjective perceiver. They are also the same in not being established from the very beginning. The similarity in appearance are examples of mere designation, are similar in not being established from the very beginning, and are examples of nonimplicative negation. This is called "the conventional of mere name" (*ming tsam gyi kun rdzob*). Being posited according to cognition that construes things through mere names it is in agreement with Lord Atiśa, who posits appearances as mind. [702.12] The conventional of mere appearance (*snang ba tsam gyi kun rdzob*): [These are] appearances that are free from the two extremes, appearances that are produced by causes and conditions. The examples of these are the eight similes of illusion. Both a real horse and illusory horse, from the perspective of being an accumulation of causes and conditions, are cognized in a similar manner in being a mere appearance that is free from the two extremes. This is the conventional of mere appearance. In this way, dependent on this understanding, all things within *saṃsāra* and *nirvāṇa* will be understood as mere appearance.

[Opponent:] Others may say: the conventional of mere appearance is established in terms of the object.

[Reply:] Both the subjective perceiver—the appearance of the cognition—and the appearance of the mind—the appearance of the mind that is like an illusion—are established as mere name. The three examples are examples of a nonimplicative negation from the perspective of being free from the two extremes. Appearances, again, are from the perspective of being free from the two extremes; space, a rabbit's horn, and the eight similes of illusion are established as examples of mere imputation. In this way, a nonimplicative negation has five qualities: (1) That which is a nonimplicative negation is free from the two extremes. [702.20] (2) Likewise, a nonimplicative negation is not known to exist from the beginning; the names of a nonimplicative negation are the infinite, the unobservable, and emptiness. (3) The example of a nonimplicative negation is one that is free from the two extremes–space. (4) The examples of mere name are the rabbit's horn or the sky-flower. (5) The examples of mere appearance are the eight, three, or twelve [types of] illusion.

When one applies a nonimplicative negation, the nonimplicative negation is through both scriptural authority and reasoning. Scriptural authority alone is not sufficient. Reasoning alone is not sufficient. Scriptural authority that arises from the doorway of reasoning is a nonimplicative negation. There is not a portion of valid cognition that sees the shore beyond [i.e., supreme] from reasoning. The valid cognition of those with narrow vision, since it comprehends conventions that are mistaken, is not included as a nonimplicative negation. As it is said, [703]

> The Victorious Ones and their sons definitely accept that the ultimate is not an object of speculative logic. All scholars accept valid cognition as only conventional.[566]

The Ārya Nāgārjuna himself refuted the means of valid cognition in his *Vigraha-vyāvartanī*.[567] Since Lord [Atiśa], in his small [text] on the [two] realities, refuted through scriptural authority and reasoning the assertion that suchness is realized by valid cognition, if one thinks "since reasoning does not exist, and since the intention of scriptural authority is inconceivable, we do not understand," the Lord [Atiśa] stated:

> Who has understood emptiness? Nāgārjuna, who was predicted by the Tathāgata and saw the truth of the nature of reality, and his disciple Candrakīrti. (v. 15) Ultimate reality may be understood by means of the lineage of special instructions from them. (v. 16ab)][568] [703.6]

By stating as such, it is unacceptable to apprehend the many thoughts and practices of the explanatory lineage as being on the flooded plain of miserable treatises. The advice of the spiritual teacher is like nectar, as it is apart from the deviate rule-governed way of personal fabrication (*rang bzo*) and selfishness (*gzu lum*). Nonimplicative negations are dependent on the advice of the uninterrupted lineage, who are the followers of Nāgārjuna. Even if we do not have reasoning [703.10] or do not understand the intention of scripture, we have the reasoning by which Ācārya Nāgārjuna perceived reality. He directly perceived the meaning of dependent-arising. He understood the intention of scripture because the Sugata predicted him in the *Laṅkāvatārasūtra*, *Mahāmeghasūtra*, *Mahābherīhārakaparivarta*, and *Mahāmañjuśrīmūlatantra*.[569] If one thinks that we do not understand the intention of the Ācārya Nāgārjuna, the followers of the sole lord, the vajra Lord [Atiśa] has many virtuous qualities. Lord [Atiśa] bestowed three [teachings of] special advice in Tibet. He also taught the nondual, illusory, unproduced system, the system of the Ācārya [703.15] Buddhajñāna, which is characterized as Yogācāra-Madhyamaka. Hereabouts he gave a brief teaching with great blessings on a text he composed, *Special Instructions on the Middle Way* (*dbu ma'i man ngag*). He also taught the Sautrāntika-Madhyamaka, the accepted position of the Ācārya Bhavya. He also taught the accepted position of Ācārya Nāgārjuna. I have the unmistaken advice of the Ācārya Nāgārjuna. The Ācārya Nāgārjuna explained it to the Ācārya Candrakīrti. The Ācārya Candrakīrti explained it to *Vidyākokila (*rig pa'i khu byug*). These three [703.20] perceived reality. The Ācārya *Vidyākokila explained it to the great Avadhūtipa. Avadhūtipa is said to be a bodhisattva who obtained the fourth level. The Lord [Atiśa] said:

> I was associated with Avadhūtipa for seven years. I studied under Avadhūtipa. I was pleased with his knowledge. He was in agreement with the texts of the Ācārya Nāgārjuna. The prediction of Lady Tārā said that he has the unmistaken accepted position of Ārya [Nāgārjuna].

As the Lord [Atiśa] possessed the special advice of the lineage of the Ācārya Nāgārjuna, the followers of Lord Atiśa composed the shorter text on the [Two] Realities and the Diamond-Song (*rdo rje'i glu*). The Lord Atiśa taught the supreme attainment to Rongpa Gargewasel.[570] [703.25] Those of Ngari (*mnga' rigs pa*) and Radreng (*ra sgreng pa*) are predicted by the Yoginī Trathok to attain the supreme in future lifetimes [704], as they are said to reside on the path of preparation. The Lord Atiśa explained it to the Great Translator [Rinchen Sangpo]. The Great Translator is said to have gained the supreme attainment. The Great Translator is an emanation body (*sprul pa'i sku*). The two great gurus [that is, Gönpawa Wangchuk Gyaltsen and Amé Naljorpa Jangchup Rinchen] studied with the Great Translator. Generally, they were associated with him for many years but did well as retreat attendents in the seventh year. Puṇyaratna and Lhatsun Jangchup Ö studied with Naktso [Lotsāwa Tsultrim Gyalwa]. The two aged gurus are said to have studied with Lord [Atiśa] in person. [704.5] The two gurus attained common spiritual realizations. They possessed extensive supersensory powers. Their deeds are said to have gone like water through rocks. The precious guru has stated, "My two gurus will certainly gain the supreme attainment." The incomparable precious spiritual friend studied under the two gurus. By achieving forceful attainment for a long time, his body possessed many virtuous qualities. He mastered extensive supersensory powers and perceived many times the face of the tutelary deity. Ratna Chakriwa,[571] who possesses incomparable distinctive knowledge, [704.10] has attained realization in an unbroken lineage of spiritual teachers. A lineage such as this is an unbroken stream of advice in the practice lineage (*sgrub brgyud*). What other lineage would suffice? There is no doubt in its potency for realization. When meeting a dharma like this, one should make great effort. It is suitable to have great faith and reverence for both the essential meaning and the lineage. Therefore, relying on the advice of this lineage is a nonimplicative negation. When following advice, one should follow advice that cultivates through achieving realization of the path and realization of dependent-arising. It is not a Dharma of verbalization. [704.15] This nonimplicative negation that is above verbal thoughts should be an ascertainment of the three wisdoms. The nonimplicative negation will not occur without the dependent-arising of the means, the stairway of the conventional, the gradual stages of the path of the three individuals, [the meditations on] the difficult-to-find precious human rebirth, karmic causation, the faults of *saṃsāra*, love, compassion, the ordinary conventional mind, the mind of mere appearance, objects like an illusion, up through [cultivating] nonappearance like space. This, through relying on the spiritual friend endowed with skillful means, corresponds with the wisdom arising from study. The wisdom of reflection contemplates [704.20] vividly, producing the distinctive knowledge of certainty that is faith. The opposite of that quality is a turbid mind. Faith, by being free from mental turbidity, produces an ascertaining consciousness for one who reflects on the stages of the path. As it is said,

> Just as a jewel is sufficient to clear turbid water, likewise the jewel of faith purifies the stains of the mind.

The faith that is produced by the wisdoms of hearing and reflection is like a jewel that purifies water, and the turbidity or stains of the mind are purified. Therefore, [704.25] from the condition that purifies the turbidity of the mind with the jewel of faith, one should practice and cultivate in a manner in which all things are like a reflection.

One produces certainty for all things by reflection on the stages of the path. [705] When the mind generates certainty through analysis by establishing reality as the subject, that conviction is due to the perpetuating cause of one's own prior mind and the common condition that is the advice of the guru. The uncommon condition is the predispositions of the ability to realize, having relied on the accumulation of causes, the lack of inherent existence. The accumulation of causes and conditions, although lacking inherent existence, produces an ascertaining consciousness like the eight similes of illusion. That ascertaining consciousness, because it is produced in dependence on an accumulation of causes and conditions, [705.5] stating all things lack inherent existence, is cultivated as a measure of awareness that is a nonappearance, nonexistent like space. Since the condition, although lacking inherent existence, is not negated, an ascertaining consciousness is produced. Empty when merely appearing, appearing as merely empty. That is indivisible. For example, the form in a mirror is empty as a mere appearance. Though not negating the condition, it appears as merely empty. Just as appearance and emptiness are indivisible, the ascertaining consciousness (*nges pa shes*) is also cultivated from the example of the jewel of faith purifying mental turbidity, and one meditates through examining all things as produced in the manner of a reflection. [705.10] That itself is the special advice to meditate on, having established a realization of dependent-arising, a realization of the path. One should cultivate on the stages of the path the twofold aspiration for awakening connected with the verbal commitment. In the time interval of meditating on mind and matter as indivisible, one establishes the five paths along with the results. All purifications, the path, and *nirvāṇa* are given as cause and effect. Therefore, as indicated, all of cyclic existence and the afflictions are understood by anyone as cause and effect. In this way, because all things within *saṃsāra* and *nirvāṇa* are dependent-arisings, they lack inherent existence. [705.15] If they inherently existed it would be contrary to dependent-arising. As the Ācārya Nāgārjuna has stated:

> It is not reasonable for intrinsic nature to arise from causes and conditions. An intrinsic nature that arose from causes and conditions would be something that is made. How is it suitable for there to be "an intrinsic nature which has been made"? An intrinsic nature is not fabricated and is not dependent on anything else.[572]

If a cause was intrinsically established, it would be contrary to being a cause. If it is a cause, it is contrary to being intrinsically established. As a cause is not intrinsically established, and since it is suitable for a cause to have the ability to produce, as well as [actually] produce, a result, a result will be produced by a cause. A result [705.20] that is intrinsically established is contrary to being a result. Since a result is suitable to be produced by a cause, a result is produced by a cause.

Moreover, if causes and effects are intrinsically established, it would not be, rather established as existent nor established as nonexistent. If it was established as existent, an intrinsic nature would not transfer from a transferred intrinsic nature, [and] it is therefore free from the extreme of existence. Since results are produced by causes, it is free from the extreme of annihilation. The *Suvarṇaprabhā sūtra* states:

> Nothing whatsoever is born or ceases to exist by reason of conditions; when conditions are designated [705.25] there is birth and cessation.[573]

The cause and effect that is intrinsically established is refuted. The cause and effect of mere appearance [706] is not refuted.[574] This reasoning of dependent-arising (*rten 'grel gyi rigs pa*) contains four reasonings within it. The mutual relation of cause and effect that lacks intrinsic nature is the very nature of dependent-arising. An effect occurs when causes accumulate is the very nature of dependent-arising. The reasoning of the nature of things (*dharmatāyukti*) and the reasoning of dependence (*apekṣāyukti*) of an effect on a cause [demonstrates that it is] suitable for an effect to arise from a cause. Since it is suitable for reasoning, the reasoning that relates to demonstration of a proof (*upapatti-sādhana-yukti*) is said to establish both cause and effect by the two means of valid cognition. The reasoning of the nature of things [706.5] is like the body, nature, or shape. That [reasoning] contains within it at the same time the four reasonings. All the great reasons (*he tu chen po*)[575] are grouped within the reasoning of dependent-arising. The diamond-splinters (*rdo rje gzegs ma*) is from the point of view of the cause. The negation of existence or nonexistence is through analysis from the perspective of the effect. Free from the one and the many is in terms of intrinsic nature when examining both the cause and effect. Moreover, this is the reasoning of dependence (*apekṣāyukti*). The great reasons (*he tu chen po*) are accepted as consequences. Therefore, this reasoning of dependence is the principal. If all things within *saṃsāra* and *nirvāṇa* were intrinsically established, the activity of the nature [706.10], persisting with a nature that intrinsically exists, by being unfabricated and without change, would be permanent. Since all things within *saṃsāra* and *nirvāṇa* are produced by causes and conditions, they artificially occur. During the time that a cause does not cease, the effect does not exist. At just the point when the cause ceases, the effect is produced. As the effect is produced immediately all at once, the cause in that way ceases, and this implies that it is impermanent.

In this way, when intrinsically established, it is contrary to being a dependent-arising. When it is a dependent-arising, it is contrary to being intrinsically established. All things within *saṃsāra* and *nirvāṇa* [706.15] arise when there is an accumulation of causes and conditions. Since they do arise when [causes and conditions] do not accumulate, it is established as being a dependent-arising. Because it is a dependent-arising, it is empty of intrinsic existence. The text of the Ācārya Nāgārjuna states consequences that expose contradictions (*gal ba brjod pa'i thal 'gyur*); a pseudo-sign similar to what is to be proven; equivalence (*mgo bsgre ba*): "If you accept in this way, because the reason is not different, you must accept this as well." These are bound to the opponent. Inference that is known to others (*gzhan la grags pa'i rjes dpag*) in which one states:[576] "If you yourself accept in this way, your own understanding is contradictory with this [conclusion]." The property of the subject and the entailment are bound [706.20] with the opponent and are established by their acceptance. Even though these [arguments by consequence] are proclaimed through four reasons, they are not different than being included within the reason of dependent-arising.[577] Therefore, [one may state,] "It is suitable to pay homage to you, this nectar that certainly destroys wrong views, dependent-arising." All these reasonings refute erroneous assertions, but one's own nonacceptance is not invalidated. In this way is the special instructions of the lineage of gurus. Through establishing the realization of the path, the realization of dependent-arising, this advice of meditation is a nonimplicative negation. Having designated one's own mind as the subject, the guru's advice that makes nonimplicative [706.25] negations is not contrary to scripture and reasoning.

As this is achieved through the assistance of [707.1] scripture and reasoning, it is necessary to go through the doorway of both scripture and reasoning. Nonimplicative negations are through scripture, the Tathāgata, one who is an authoritative person (*tshad ma'i skyes bur gyur pa*), first negated nonimplicatively. The *Ratnasamuccaya Perfection of Wisdom*, the *Sarvabuddhaviṣayāvatārajñānālokālaṅkāra*, and *The Praise of the Tathāgata by the Bodhisattva Sarvanīvaraṇaviṣkambhin* employ nonimplicative negations. The Protector Maitreya, the second authoritative person, [707.5] employs nonimplicative negations. Reasoning dwells in scripture, one should utilize reasonings that are not contradicted by other [types of] reasons. The special instructions of the guru who possesses both the lineage of meaning and the lineage of words transferred one from another in successive realizations of unbroken attainments of siddhis, this very lineage of meditation that has achieved clear realization of the path, the realization in dependent-arising, dwells in scriptural authority. [Reasoning] dwells in many scriptures, such as the *Perfection of Wisdom*, the *Anavataptanāgarājaparipṛcchasutra*, the *Suvarṇaprabhāsottama*, and so forth. The four reasonings [707.10] are the reasoning of dependence (*apekṣāyukti*), the reasoning of the nature of things (*dharmatāyukti*), the reasoning of function (*kṛtakāraṇayukti*), and the reasoning about valid evidence (*upapattisādhanayuktiḥ*).[578] Through establishing realization of the path, and realization of dependent-arising, this advice of the practice lineage of meditation is connected with scripture. Not invalidated by other reasons, the explication of Ārya Nāgārjuna is unmistaken. The Ācārya Nāgārjuna has stated:

> All the buddhas of the three times are awakened, having relied on this path. Homage to the king of sages who has taught [707.15] dependent-arising, the principle that abandons arising and cessation.

At this point, as this is asserted by a Buddhist, by cultivating this path one is said to be a Buddhist.

> Those whose intellects transcend existence and nonexistence, and do not abide [in any extremes], realize the meaning of "condition," which is profound and nonperceived.[579]

The *Suhṛllekha* states:

> This dependent-arising is the most cherished and profound of the Victor's speech. Whoever sees this correctly, sees the Buddha, the supreme knower of reality.[580]

This reasoning, [707.20] which includes within it the four reasonings, dwells in scripture. It is not invalidated by other reasonings. The essential meaning is taught from the texts composed by the Ācārya Ārya Nāgārjuna that have the means of reliable cognition that perceive the far shore. These special instructions that achieve realization in the path, and realization of dependent-arising, an unbroken lineage from the Ācārya until the present, are nonimplicative negations. The Lord [Atiśa's] *Shorter Text on the Two Realities* states,

> Ultimate reality may be understood by means of the lineage of special instructions from them.[581]

Thus the meaning is that the advice of the lineage of gurus, through both reasoning and scripture, is a nonimplicative negation. In this way, as the conventional is not intrinsically established, since it is conventionally free from the two extremes, [708] it is not substantially established. As the conventional is not itself conventionally established as a substance that upholds its own-characteristic, the conventional is not substantially established. The conventional is merely a nonimplicative negation conventionally, as the conventional is not established by reasoning to be conventionally existent either substantially or imputedly. A conventional that is established by reasoning is not accepted, it is not an implicative negation. In this way, one negates an entity that is not asserted; [708.5] if one were to establish some entity that is asserted, that is interpreted as an implicative negation. That which does not exist as the conventional is not at all established even conventionally, because there is not a entity that is asserted apart from the mere negation of an entity that is not asserted. One only negates without any implications.

[Query:] What is this appearance if it does not exist?

[Reply:] It is merely designated (*btags pa tsam, prajñaptimatrā*). There is not an appearance through being established as existent, real, or substantially existent. It is a mere appearance from the perspective of accumulating conditions. It is merely nominally designated, conventionally designated. Because they are particularly conditioned by one's own mind, since they are merely designated, external objects are not established as anything other than appearances [708.10] in all things within *saṃsāra* and *nirvāṇa*. Therefore, the mind is a mere name, a mere appearance, a mere designation.

[Query:] Through accepting this as a mere designation, wouldn't it become an implicative negation?

[Reply:] Anything that is a "mere designation established by reasoning" is not established.

[Query:] Is this mere appearance that is not at all established a nonimplicative negation?

[Reply:] This is not refuted. [A mere appearance] is not an object negated by reasoning. In this regard, the nearly universal nonimplicative negation of scripture and reasoning [708.15] does not overturn this appearance even though it is fabricated. It is necessary to refute the continuum in refuting an appearance that is an object negated by an antidote (*gnyen po'i dgag bya*), but this appearance is not an object negated by reasoning (*rigs pa'i dgag bya*).[582] Therefore, until the path of vision arises, cause and effect occur from only the sickness of suffering. Since the imputation into two extremes is the object of negation, both reasoning and scripture employ nonimplicative negations. Therefore, one who negates nonimplicatively negates those who speak of things within *saṃsāra* and *nirvāṇa* as existing within the two extremes [of existence and nonexistence] through nonimplicative negations. Furthermore, a conceived object, conceptualized through the two extremes, [708.20] is the imputation that is the object of negation. By refuting the conceived object that seizes on the nonexistent as existent, the Ācārya Nāgārjuna states,

> Since anything negated does not at all exist, I do not deny anything at all. You, therefore, falsely accuse me when you say: "You negate."[583]

Thus a conceived object is refuted.[584] Through refuting the conceived object, clinging is implicitly negated, and since the object that was established as real is [now] established as an unreal subject, the factor of reasoning that apprehends the implicit negation of the factor of clinging is an appearance. It is not an object negated by reasoning. Thus it is conceptual thought [that is negated]. Since it is a conceptual object that is imputed [708.25], the object of negation is imputed. Since the conceived object is an object with its own-characteristic, the object of negation is own-character (*rang gi mtshan nyid*). [709] For one who imputes the object of negation, the Lord [Atiśa] himself has stated in the *Caryāgīti*:

> There is not a distinction between those with blurred vision who see hairs in the sky and those who see the blurred world with concepts. One should meditate on all entities without exception as imputed with conceptuality whose nature is equivalent to the sky.[585]

A mere imputation, the mere appearance which is not at all established, is not an object of negation. Since the mere imputatation itself is construed due to the distinctive conditions of one's own mind [709.5], among the appearances of all things within *saṃsāra* and *nirvāṇa*, external objects are not established and one's own mind is a mere appearance. The Lord [Atiśa] accepts appearances as the mind. All sentient beings are accepted as a single continuum (*rgyud gcig*). All conceptuality is accepted as a single accumulation (*tshogs gcig*). The spiritual friend states there that although there is an object, it does not intrinsically exist. Although there is a mind, it also lacks intrinsic existence. Since if something exists, it exists, and if something does not exist, it equally does not exist, one cannot say an object exists, one cannot say the mind exists. [709.10] One can say it is mere appearance. Just as an animal-headed female deity (*'phra-men-ma*) who slays her own object also slays another's son, one's own view is not established, and the view of another is not refuted, as it is devoid of all kinds of views (*lta bar gyur pa thams cad, sarvadṛṣṭigata*). The Lord [Atiśa] has said: "My vision does not possess a cause for false view. It is mere appearance."

[Objection:] That is wrong. A cognition that understands mere appearance is a distinction of the object that is called mere appearance. A nonobject is also not suitable as an appearance, because when there is not a cognition, an object is not fit as an appearance.

[Reply:] The mere appearance occurs, as both objects and cognitions are mere imputations. [709.15] In this way, when [an appearance] occurs, one cannot say it is an object, one cannot say it is the mind. When one states that an accepted external object exists as a mere appearance, it is accepted as the cause and effect of *saṃsāra* grouped within the twelve limbs of dependent-arising. The Ācārya Ārya [Nāgārjuna] has taught,

> The full Buddha has said, "The world has ignorance as its condition." Therefore, why it is not reasonable for this world to be a conceptual construction? How could it not be clear that once ignorance ceases, what will then cease has been imagined by misknowledge?[586]

[709.20] The twelve limbs of dependent-arising, the cause and effect of *saṃsāra*, are established only from the mental continuum. External objects are not established. If one says, "External objects exist as they are explained by external dependent-arising," to explain further, they do not pass beyond the appearances of the mind. They are counted as distinctions of the mind. The section of the sūtra is of interpretable meaning. The texts of Ārya [Nāgārjuna's] reasonings determine the definitive meaning. Among those [texts], all cause and effect within *saṃsāra* is taught to be grouped as dependent-arisings. As the *Cittavajrastava* composed by Ācārya [Nāgārjuna] states:

> Realization of the mind is awakening; the mind is the five states of transmigration; the characteristics of happiness and suffering do not exist except from the mind [3]. Things seen and heard by all beings and some aspects [710.1] of meditation, they are all in the web of the mind, as it is indicated by the one who speaks of reality.[587]

All things are appearances of the mind is clearly stated in many texts of Ācārya [Nāgārjuna].

[Query:] Regarding this, someone says, "When the Ācārya [Nāgārjuna] teaches that, the meaning is that the mind is primary. The previous mind is the substantial cause. [The mind] does not occur as an appearance from an accumulation of objects and conditions. The principal substantial cause is the appearance of the mind." For example, as smoke arises from a collocation [710.5] of fire and kindling, it is called "fire-smoke" since fire is the principal substantial cause. As all that does not follow from one's own conceptuality, the positions of Ācārya Nāgārjuna are mistakenly twisted.

[Reply:] The Lord [Atiśa] asserts appearance as the mind. External objects that are similar in not intrinsically existing do not appear. The mind is asserted as appearance. The appearance is not an appearance that is construed as an existent or true cause. Since it is an appearance of an accumulation of causes and conditions, the accumulation of causes and conditions as an actual object, the object is suitable as an appearance. Do not pay attention to positing causes and conditions as a real object. The object that is established or unestablished is either an appearance or [710.10] nonappearance. *Saṃsāra* appears as cause and effect as enhanced [30a] by the power of mental afflictions from the mind through the accumulation of causes and conditions in the presence of the mind. *Nirvāṇa* appears as cause and effect through purification as enhanced by the uncontaminated virtuous qualities of one's own mind. All causes and conditions do not pass beyond the mind and are in the presence of the mind.

[Query:] Well then, the understanding of appearance, enhanced by the mind and the object, is appearance, is it not? Is the appearance of a nonobject at all acceptable? If the object exists, the object is necessary to accept as being a mere appearance. [710.15] The understanding of appearance is not said to be enhanced by the mind and object.

[Reply:] [Appearances] are through the power of afflictions from the mind or asserted to appear according to one's own mind, as enhanced by uncontaminated virtuous qualities. For example, a pure crystal will appear with many colors due to conditions. Appearances are like the nature of the crystal. In this way, the understanding of appearances should be that appearances, as an experience of clear presence in all things within *saṃsāra* and *nirvāṇa*, are enhanced by either mental afflictions or uncontaminated virtuous qualities from one's own mind.

[Query:] Well then, is this appearance [710.20] established as the mind?

[Reply:] Even if a fire is not existent, it is suitable for it to have the character of red color, hot, and scorching. Likewise, even if the mind does not exist, as it is a reality that is suitable to experience clarity and knowing, this appearance that is experienced as clarity and knowing is the mind.

There are not logical reasonings, as autonomous [reasonings] are not acceptable. The reasoning of the nature of things is among the four reasonings.[588]

[Query:] Well then, what becomes of the conventional as six lineages [of transmigration]?

[Reply:] Although the mind is established by reasoning, correct conventional will not become [710.25] an implicative negation. Although established as mind, as long as it is not free from the two extremes it is mistaken conventional [reality].

[Query:] What is the difference [711] with a True Aspectarian (*rnam bden pa*, **satyākāravādin*)?

[Reply:] True Aspectarians assert [appearances] as ultimately [real]. This is asserted as a mistaken conventional [reality].

[Query:] What is the difference with the defiled conventional [reality] (*dri ma dang bcas pa'i kun rdzob*) of a False Aspectarian (**alīkākāravādin*)?

[Reply:] The aspect [, or cognitive image,] is accepted as correct conventional [reality] [by False Aspectarians]. Here it is only accepted as mistaken conventional [reality]. This system of establishing cognition as mind is like a True Aspectarian. It is displeasing to posit the factors of defiled conventional [reality] of the False Aspectarians as exactly the same. It is not suitable to accept with the False Aspectarians. Directly here, [711.5] those who speak with great defilement, stating that it is like the system of establishing cognition as mind of True Aspectarian Mādhyamikas and False Aspectarian Mādhyamikas, should be understood as mistaken.[589]

[Query:] The mind, as mere appearance that is free from the two extremes, is accepted as correct conventional [reality]. What is the difference with the ultimate of the [Proponents] of Illusion-like Nonduality (Māyopamādvaya[vāda])?

[Reply:] This is asserted as a nonimplicative negation. [Proponents] of Illusion-like Nonduality assert implicative negations. Therefore the position of Lord Atiśa is that all conventional objects of Mādhyamikas who uphold tenets and [those] below [them] are repudiated as mistaken conventional [reality]. The mind, [711.10] this mere appearance that is free from the two extremes, is taught by Lord Atiśa, based on his understanding of Ācārya

Nāgārjuna, as correct conventional [reality]. The *Yuktiṣaṣṭikā* composed by Ārya [Nāgārjuna] states:

> Things explained, such as the great elements and so forth, are enclosed in consciousness. A result arises when this is understood. Indeed, they are a mistaken construction.[590]

The *Bodhicittavivaraṇa*[591] and the praises of Ācārya [Nāgārjuna] clearly assert [appearances] as the mind. The *Twenty Verses on the Great Vehicle* composed by Ācārya Nāgārjuna states:

> All of these are mere mind. They abide like an illusion. [711.15] Higher and lower rebirths are from virtuous or nonvirtuous actions. When the cycle of the mind ceases, all things will cease. Therefore reality is selfless and reality is pure.[592]

Likewise the *Bhāvanākrama*, composed by Ācārya Nāgārjuna, states:

> External objects are not cognized, as they rely on merely the mind. Standing firm on the object of suchness, one should pass beyond the mere mind. One should recount nonappearance. The yogi who abides in nonappearance sees [711.20] this great vehicle.[593]

As it is explained in many texts of Ācārya Nāgārjuna, the position of Lord [Atiśa] asserting appearance as mind should be understood as the assertion of Ācārya Nāgārjuna.

[Query:] Somone says, the Lord [Atiśa] in meditation and mantra upholds the position of the Yogācāra-Madhyamaka on appearances as mind. This is not compatible with the notion of the mere tiny bit (*en tsam*) as conventional of Ācārya Nāgārjuna.

[Reply:] As Lord [Atiśa] has stated, "My position is not pleasing, as few accept it and teach it India." Therefore [your] comments should be understood as mistaken.

[Query:] Well then, is Lord [Atiśa] a Mādhyamika who upholds tenets?

[Reply:] Lord [Atiśa] addresses what is unfeasible and difficult through reasoning. [711.25] As a Mahāyānist of Nāgārjuna-garbha is unable to be revoked, how could it be possible that Lord [Atiśa] [712] is not compatible with the notion of the mere tiny bit as conventional of Ācārya Nāgārjuna? In this way, it is a system that accepts appearances as mind. Furthermore, Lord [Atiśa] asserts all sentient beings as a single continuum.

[Query:] Well then, as beings would go into lower states of rebirth, all would therefore transmigrate into lower states of rebirth, with the suffering of the lower states of rebirth, and the states of gods and human would not exist. The happiness of gods and humans does not exist in the three lower realms of rebirth. As one can ascertain individual happiness and suffering, are there different continuums?

[Reply:] Ascertaining individual happiness and suffering is not contrary [712.5] to a single continuum. It like the case of a single body, the foot may have the suffering of pain while the head does not. The head may have the suffering of pain while the foot may not.

[Query:] Well then, how is the thought of Lord [Atiśa]?

[Reply:] In ultimate [reality] it is not proper to count single and different continuums. This is posited for conventional [reality]. Conventional reality has two [aspects]. Mistaken conventional reality is like one with blurred vision who sees hairs in space. Since that is nonexistent, false, erroneous, and mistaken, although it is posited as one and the manifold, it does not become a continuum that is manifold and single. The Lord [Atiśa] asserts that correct conventional reality, the perspective of the mind as mere appearance [712.10], is a single continuum.

As the mind is construed as appearance, apprehended object and apprehending subject is rejected. Construed as mere appearance, the particular base that negates the two extremes is the mind as appearance. As it is particularly free from the two extremes, the mind is an appearance that is not at all established. An appearance that is active. Through the perspective of being free from the two extremes, the self-luminous mind that is without subject and object is without different continuums, as all minds are one continuum. Although there are differences of karma and conditions, since self-nature is without differences, all sentient beings are one continuum. The mind arises from the condition of ignorance. As it is enhanced through karma and mental afflictions [712.15], *saṃsāra* appears as cause and effect. Awareness arises from the condition of wisdom. As one's own mind is enhanced through uncontaminated virtuous qualities, purification appears as cause and effect. Although there are different appearances due to different conditions, the self-luminous mind that is free from the two extremes of intrinsic essence is one continuum without differences. It does not become different continuums through different appearances. For example, when spreading out a silk cloth on a white crystal, although the condition of the crystal appears as many colors, the intrinsic nature of the crystal is not different.

[Query:] Well then, what determines each and every happiness and suffering [712.20] for different continuums?

[Reply:] Various causes and conditions of mere appearance from karma and mental afflictions occur as different imputations through various causes and conditions of karma and mental afflictions that are imputed. One imputes intrinsic nature on mere appearances as different due to different conditions. Although held as different, they are not established as different intrinsic natures other than mere appearance. In the very moment when both mere appearance and imputation are different, the self-luminous mind, which is free from the two extremes of intrinsic nature, does not have differences, as it is like a single body. There are different ways of appearing of mere appearance; different imputations are like individually ascertaining the head, feet, [712.25] and limbs. For example, even as many vases occur in multiple spaces, when the many vases are broken apart, the multiple vases are gathered within one great space.[594] A broken vase is an imputation of mistaken conventional [reality].

[Query:] From the perspective of mere appearance, the mind that is free from the two extremes, that is, correct conventional [reality], how is it that you posit a single continuum without differences?

[Reply:] Accordingly, Lord [Atiśa] asserts all sentient beings as a single continuum. Likewise, Lord [Atiśa] asserts consciousness as a single group. Furthermore, ultimately both many groups and single groups do not exist; [713.5] they are counted conventionally. Conventional reality has two [divisions].

Mistaken conventional realities are false, erroneous, and wrong. Although set forth as two groups and many groups, one group and many groups does not suffice at any time. From the perspective of the self-luminous mind that is free from the two extremes, the mind as mere appearance, correct conventional reality, the group of consciousness is asserted as one. In that perspective, if six, eight, or nine groups of consciousness exist, they will not be free from the apprehending subject and apprehended object. Whether they exist or do not exist, it is necessary to gather the path. Correct conventional realities exist, are true, nonerroneous, and [713.10] correct. Since mistaken conventional [realities] are one's own mind, which arises from the condition of ignorance, one will not traverse the path. Correct conventional realities are one's own mind, awarenesses that arise from the condition of wisdom, enhanced by the three roots of uncontaminated virtue. The mind, appearances that are not at all established, the self-luminous awareness that is free from the two extremes, a mind that is dependent-arising without production and cessation, the mind as mere appearance traverses the path. In that perspective, consciousness is not other than one group. Therefore, as Lord [Atiśa] has stated that "it exists or really exists" at [713.15] the time of traversing the path, it is necessary to exist at the time of traversing the path. As there is not other than a single consciousness at the time of traversing the path, the group of consciousness is said to be one.

The group of consciousness appears as different. As different appearances are imputed, it is viewed with clinging. Therefore mistaken conventionals are appearances as various groups of consciousness with various imputations. In this way, although different due to karma and conditions, since it is not different, as it has the same nature, the group of consciousness is taught to be one. Although different by various conditions, consciousness is internally one group, according to the example of the interfering monkey (*spre'u bcug pa*), as [713.20] explained by Lord [Atiśa]. The Lord Atiśa said, "At the time when a monkey exists in an eastern window, he does not exist at the western window. When he exists in the west, he does not exist in the east. Alas, this is not a good Tibetan example!"[595] The Lord [Atiśa] then said, "It is like placing a butter lamp within a water jug. Upon boring many holes in the water jug, externally the many lights are perceived as one. Likewise, when many conditions open the sense doors at one time, many consciousnesses are perceived as one. When the water jug is broken apart, the butter lamp remains as one. The root consciousness is one. When the imputed water jug is broken, [713.25] how is it? As its own-nature is undifferentiated (*tha dad med pa*), consciousness is taught to be one group."[596] In this way, Lord [Atiśa] [714] asserts a system in which consciousness is one group. The assertion of the Ācārya Nāgārjuna is that the mind, which is a mere appearance free from the two extremes, is correct conventional [reality]. In presenting this point, sentient beings emerge as a single continuum and a single group of consciousness, which is the assertion of Lord [Atiśa]. In this way, the Lord [Atiśa] asserts appearances as mind, the assertion of the Ācārya Nāgārjuna.

Accordingly, among the two, nonimplicative negations and implicative negations, [this system] [714.5] is a nonimplicative negation. Among the two, substantially existent and nominally designated, it is a mere nominal designation, the mind is a mere appearance that is not at all established. Correct conventionals are the explanatory position of Lord [Atiśa]. In this way, the nature of mistaken conventionals, the nature of correct conventionals, and the characteristics of correct conventionals are the three [topics] that have been explained.

[ii. Characteristics of Mistaken Conventional Realities]

Now the characteristic of mistaken conventional reality will be taught. Ignorance arises from mistaken conditions, arises from the cause of karma and mental afflictions. The conditioned cycle, this appearance in the worldly environment of oneself and sentient beings, is called a "mistaken obscuration" (*log pa'i rdzob*). Moreover, it is embodied by four characteristics: [714.10] (1) a characterisic that is produced having relied on causes and conditions, (2) a characteristic without beginning and end, (3) a characteristic of a merely nominally designated mind that does not exist, and (4) a characteristic of cyclic existence, the reality of cause and effect, inexpressible to others, that is a principle free from the two extremes. This conditioned cycle, the appearance of the worldly environment, oneself, and sentient beings does not arise from a cause related to a self or what pertains to a self; it arises from a selfless cause. It does not arise from a single permanent cause; it arises from multiple impermanent causes. It does not arise from primary and secondary causes [714.15] issued by a previous mind. It arises from unwavering conditions. It does not arise without a cause or from powerless conditions. As it arises from empowered conditions, it does not arise from incompatible causes and conditions. The six lineages [of transmigration] that occur in mutual dependence on the group of three painful afflictions from the twelve limbs are only a heap of suffering that continuously cycles; like a river, one does not perceive its point of origin. As the beginning point of karma and mental afflictions in cyclic existence is not perceived even by the eyes of the Buddha, it is beginningless. As one does not perceive the object of suchness, not overturning cyclic existence, while mistaken erroneous appearances occur from inexhaustible karma and unceasing mental afflictions [714.20], it is endless. As one wanders while not perceiving the point of its origin, this is the characteristic of the beginningless and the endless.

The six lineages [of transmigration] are in the manner of a three-poled tent (*mdung khyim*), mutually dependent on the group of three painful afflictions from the twelve limbs [of dependent-arising]; they are only a heap of suffering, continuously cycling like a river. The agent of the cycle [is assumed to be] either a self, the principal, the mind, or God. The individuals [714.25] in cyclic existence, the six types of transmigrators, the agent who cycles, the activities of individuals who cycle in cyclic existence, and [715] the actions that are performed in cyclic existence, if one thinks whether the three are substantially established—the activity of cyclic existence, the actions of cyclic existence, and the individual in cyclic existence—these are not substantially established.

The seven mistaken effects (*'bras bu phyin ci log bdun*) that arise from five mistaken causes (*rgyu phyin ci log lnga*)[597] are the world of sentient beings, the harmful external world, and the mere designation "cyclic existence," which are designated as a mere name, a mere word, a mere convention, totally free from intrinsic nature, not at all intrinsically established. A mere [715.5] appearance, which is not at all established, is the characteristic that does not signify sentient beings and [is] a mere designation. As the effects merely arise from five mistaken causes, both cause and effect are not intrinsically transferred. As the cause ceases, the effect is produced; it is free from the extreme of permanance, and because cause and effect cannot be said to be the same, they are not unitary. If the five causes and seven effects were different entities, undistinguished by being other, the consequence would be that everything arises from everything. If one thinks that if all five causes do not exist, the seven causes do arise, and all seven effects arise from only all five causes, as cause and effect would occur as different [entities], [things would arise] without an actual cause. [715.10] As the effect does not arise if there is not a cause, since cause and effect are not different, they cannot be said to be different and they are therefore free from the extremes of annihilation. In this way, as intrinsic nature is not transferred, since existence and so forth does not occur, as it does not exist, as it is free from the extremes of nonexistence, the emptiness that is free from the two extremes of the intrinsic nature of cause and effect is like space. The great Geshé Naljorpa[598] has stated: "Space is accepted as an example of conventional reality, as it is conventionally free from the four extremes. I consider all cause and effect as space." A cause that is like space [715.15] attains the effect.

In this way, those of our and other schools of thought, outsider non-Buddhists and insider Buddhists, impute conventional reality as substantially existent. The very imputation that imputes the ultimate as intrinsically produced distinguishes the basis of designation (*gdags gzhi'*) but does not impute the cause and effect of cyclic existence and the cause and effect of *nirvāṇa* that dependently arises. The cause of conceptuality is an imputation that depends on mistaken scripture and reasoning. In this way, according to the cause of conceptualizing, the object that is the basis of designation, and the consciousness of one who conceptualizes, our own and other schools of thought have an erroneous consciousness that imputes two extremes. Our own [715.20] and other schools of thought, through the imputed basis of designation, the consciousness of one who conceptualizes, and the cause that is conceptualized, assert a cause that is conceptualized to be substantially existent. Since all of that is not known to exist from the very beginning, it is a nonimplicative negation, like space.

Because cause and effect can be neither called the same nor different, the nature of cause and effect is emptiness, which is a nonimplicative negation that is free from the two extremes.

> Empty things arise only from things that are empty, because cause and effect are neither the same nor different.[599]

The nature of cause and effect [715.25], the arising of empty things from empty things, which is a nonimplicative negation that is free from the two extremes [716], is ascertained in meditation by means of the eight similes [of illusion]. Moreoever, it is sufficient to ascertain in meditation by means of a single suitable simile among the eight. In the *Sūtra of the Śākya Producing Joy* (*Shākya dga' skyes kyi mdo*), the specific enumeration and order of the eight similes are explained, and therefore it not necessary to explain them, as the eight are clarified elsewhere.

In this way, as the nature of this dependently arising cause and effect does not occur without conditions, it is [716.5] free from the extremes of annihilation. As an intrinsic nature does not transfer, it is free from the extremes of permanence. Therefore it is an emptiness in which existence and nonexistence are not at all established. [Cause and effect] cannot be called the same, so they are free from being a singularity, and they cannot be called different, so they are free from multiplicity. As cause and effect are not at all established as a singularity or multiplicity, it is an emptiness that is devoid of singularity and multiplicity.

[Query:] What is this appearance that is empty?

[Reply:] This appearance is not an appearance that is construed as a cause by being established by existence or intrinsic nature. It is an appearance by an accumulation of mistaken causes and conditions. It is an erroneous appearance that is like perceiving hair in space by one who has blurred vision. In this way [716.10], the nature of dependently arisen cause and effect is an emptiness that is free from the two extremes. Although empty, it appears through unceasing conditions. Although not established from the very beginning, it erroneously appears as appearances. In this way, as the erroneous cause is a cause and effect that cannot be called the same or different, it is free from the two extremes. This principle of cause and effect being called neither the same nor different and being free from the two extremes is the characteristic of cyclic existence. As it is without mind and imputed, this teaches the selflessness of the person. As cause and effect cannot be called the same or different, [716.15] being free from the two extremes, it principally appears in the small text on the [two] realities as indicating the selflessness of persons and things. The spiritual friend teaches both, the two types of selflessness.

Geshé Phuchungwa[600] states that the two previous characteristics from the base characteristic are, although an imputed name, harmonious [the back folio of the manuscript is missing at this point—JA].

Only this system establishes mistaken obscurations, the cause and effect of cyclic existence, from the perspective of the own-nature of erroneous cause and effect. In this way, the real condition (*gshis*) of mistaken obscuration is a mere appearance that is free from the two extremes, correct obscuration. The real condition of correct obscuration [716.20] is ultimate reality, a thing free from the two extremes, a nonappearance, selflessness. In this way, four characteristics of mistaken conventionals are taught.

[c. Objects Indicated by the Words "Correct Obscuration" and "Mistaken Obscuration" (*yang dag pa'i rdzob dang log pa'i rdzob kyi sgra'i don*)]

Now, [I will discuss] the objects [indicated by] words of correct conventionals and mistaken conventionals. Regarding this, (1) the objects [indicated by] conventional words, (2) the correct and mistaken objects [indicated by] words, and (3) the objects [indicated by] the words of reality (*bden pa*) and obscuration (*rdzob*) are the three [topics].

[i. Objects Indicated by Conventional Words (*kun rdzob kyi sgra'i don*) (716.23–717.1)]

(1) A conventional in actuality is produced having relied on causes and conditions. A conventional in actuality is not established and is not an existent [entity]. A conventional in actuality is a mere designation. Afterward, the imputation and the imputed object are said to be conventional. This is suitable as mistaken conventional [reality]. It is unreal, since it is not suitable [717] as a correct conventional. I will not write in detail regarding this conventional object [indicated by] words, as it may be understood elsewhere.

[ii. Correct and Mistaken Objects Indicated by Words (*yang dag pa dang log pa'i sgra'i don*)]

(2) The correct and mistaken objects [indicated by] words: as all conventional realities are erroneous, not different from an illusion, how can it be mistaken as correct? Although not distinct from an illusion, good or bad arises like an illusion erroneously. Mistaken obscuration is an illusion of ignorance, an appearance of ignorance. Since it is an appearance of ignorance, it is an erroneous illusion and mistaken [717.5] illusion. Since it is an erroneous, mistaken illusion of ignorance, as it occurs through other forces of mistaken karma and mental afflictions, it is an illusion that is not independent. Correct obscuration, as it arises from the conditions of discerning awareness, is an illusion of pristine awareness, a nonerroneous illusion, an unmistaken illusion, an illusion possessing mastery. Since mistaken conventions are appearances that are ignorant, erroneous, mistaken, it is contrary to ultimate reality, [to] the nature of reality (*chos nyid*). Since mistaken conventions are appearances of mistaken ignorance, as it is contrary to ultimate reality, obscuring the ultimate [717.10], it is called "mistaken" (*log pa*). Since correct obscuration is an appearance of

discerning awareness, it is not contrary to ultimate reality. It does not obscure realizing ultimate reality. As correct obsuration is a harmonious cause for realizing the ultimate, since it is not at all possible to realize the ultimate, which is the goal (*upeya*), when free from correct conventionals, it is called "correct" (*yang dag pa*). It is not a result that is produced by a producer. Cause and effect is subsequently established.

What is called a "cause and effect of subsequent relation" (*rjes su 'brel pa'i rgyu 'bras*) in another way is mutually inclusive of a mistaken convention, ignorance, and mistaken appearances. Nonexistent, false, unreliable, since even a little bit of reliability does not exist [717.15], it is called "mistaken" (*log pa*). Correct conventionals are appearances of discerning awareness. The attainments after the supermundane level are appearances of pure mundane wisdom.[601] Since they are suitable[602] as real, undeceiving, and reliable, they are called "correct." These sayings are the only harmonious teaching that are perpetually unmistaken.

Geshé [Ratna] has stated that mistaken conventionals, appearances as the two extremes, are like a person with blurred vision seeing hairs in the sky. Since a nonexistent [entity] appears, the nonexistent [entity] is understood as false; it is said to be deceptive, as it is understood as deceptive, it is not reliable [717.20], nor is it trustworthy. The conditioned cycle of mistaken conventionals—this appearance of oneself, sentient beings, and the worldly environment—since it is nonexistent, false, deceptive, and not at all reliable or trustworthy, all falsities are equally false.

[Query:] What is the point of reason of the falsity, as it is the basis that all sentient beings rely on for life and their life spans?

[Reply:] For this, as it is not at all reliable, since it is impermanent, it is false. As the base is false, the supported is false. This is like the Yorpo [people] who, as the audience of a properous king who enjoys wealthy surroundings [717.25], discard accomplishments since they are not reliable, [718] are impermanent, and are false. The cause that is impermanent casts out a maturation. Misbehavior is turned back since it is exhausted. By exhausting and turning back the cause, the result is reverted. The sayings of Geshé Ratna [Chakriwa] are unmistaken.

For this meaning, the thirteenth chapter of the *Mūlamadhyamakaśāstra*, the chapter on *Tattva*,[603] states,

> The Bhagavan has said that that which has a deceptive nature is false. All conditioned things have a deceptive [718.5] nature; therefore they are false.[604]

Therefore, the text states that "these are false," and a sūtra of the *śrāvaka*s states,

> Whatever dharma is deceptive, that is false. Monks, it is like so, the undeceptive dharma is *nirvāṇa*, the supreme reality.[605]

Thus, as it states, because conditioned things are deceptive, they are established as false. The deceptive is said to not exist; the false is said to not exist. As both are not reliable, one may object that "since it is deceptive, one is not able to establish that it is false." In reply to that, deceptive and falsity are not synonyoms. If, as you say, the deceptive and the false are both completely nonexistent, [718.10] that nonexistence is not suitable to be termed deceptive and false, since one will not [be able to] posit a conventional that is deceptive and false. For example, since a rabbit's horn does not at all exist, a rabbit's horn cannot be posited as deceptive and false. For this meaning,

> If there is a deceptive dharma, what is false with respect to that deceptive dharma?[606]

Therefore one cannot say that the deceptive and the false do not exist at all. One can say that the deceptive mistakenly appears, since it is erroneous. One can say that a falsity, an imputation of the two extremes, is empty of intrinsic nature. When one says that this cycle of conditioned existence, this imputation into two extremes, is empty of intrinsic nature because it is erroneous [718.15] and mistakenly appears, as a deceptive dharma is able to be established as false, the Bhagavan teaches that a dharma is deceptive in order to realize emptiness. The Bhagavan taught that emptiness is entirely an imputation.[607] Therefore this conditioned cycle does not exist, as it is like a person with blurred vision seeing hair in the sky. Since it is empty of intrinsic nature, which is imputed, it is false; as it mistakenly appears, it is deceptive; since it is impermanent, it is not trustworthy nor is it at all reliable. In this way, it is deceptive because it is [718.20] impermanent. Because it is deceptive, it is false, and because it is impermanent, it is false. Because it is deceptive, it is false. Both qualities occur. An erroneous mistake and impermanence are a single nature but different conceptual isolates.[608] As impermanence and the mistaken are a single nature, the Lord [Atiśa] stated that "a painful effect arises from an impermanent cause; it is painful due to impermanent causes, painful due to impermanent conditions." Along these lines, the Ācārya Āryadeva stated,

> From among the four,[609] certainly what is impermanent is harmful,
> [and] that which is harmful is not understood; therefore all that is
> impermanent will arise as suffering.[610]

[718.25] Rather than a permanent phenomenon being blissful when unmistaken, it is impermanent since it is erroneous. The suffering that is erroneous is not at all suitable to be reliable [719] or trustworthy, therefore it is impermanent and suffering. Since it is impermanent and suffering, it is deceptive (*slu ba*). Furthermore, since it is impermanent and suffering, it is false (*rdzun*). As it is deceptive, it is false. Therefore, since all falsities are equally false, they are called "mistakes" (*log pa*). In establishing this meaning, a great number of texts are in agreement.

Correct conventional reality, an appearance free from the two extremes, exists through abiding with a nature that is like an illusion. That object itself, [719.5] when construed as an object for an awareness that is after the supermundane level, is an appearance that is realized to be nonexistent, as it is produced like an illusion. An appearance of pristine awareness (*rig pa ye shes kyi snang ba*), since it is an appearance that is unerroneous and unmistaken, it is said to be "nondeceptive" (*mi slu ba*). As the cause is unceasing, the result is unceasing. Since the ripening of karma is banished and since it is not overturned when resources are exhausted, it is called "trustworthy" (*yid brtan du rung ba*).

[Query:] Well then, by destroying captivation with appearances at the time of meditative equipoise, an entity without appearance, an object that is selfless, is construed as an actual object having an own-character. What is this appearance that occurs having arisen from meditative equipoise after the supermundane level? [719.10]

[Reply:] That is called "the level due to latencies of ignorance" (*ma rig pa'i bag chags kyi sa*). The unafflicted misknowledge is established as an object of only the nature of dharma, which does not engage in the flow of cyclic existence. By existing in the continuum of a bodhisattva, it occurs as an appearance after [postmeditative equipoise].

[Query:] Well then, since the appearance of ignorance is not possible to be unmistaken, how is undeceiving acceptable?

[Reply:] When classifying the very appearance that is of the supermundane postmeditative state, there are two: an isolate of appearances and an isolate of realization. The isolate of appearance is an appearance of unafflicted misknowledge. [719.15] Since it is not possible for the appearance of ignorance to be unmistaken, all obscurations are proclaimed to be erroneous, a conventionality like an illusion. Appearances of pristine awareness emerge from the isolate of realization. The wisdom that is established on the supermundane path construes dharmas as actually being objects that are nonappearances whose own-character consists of selfless entities. In attaining potency in meditative equipoise, one gains mastery in the postmeditative state through subduing the brilliant appearance of ignorance, and appearances are realized as unproduced like an illusion. The mind is an appearance that is free from the two extremes. The mind is an appearance [719.20] that is not at all established. The appearance of pristine awareness that occurs as a single nature of appearance and emptiness emerges and, because it is a nonmistaken and unerroneous appearance, and since an appearance of ignorance that is nonmistaken and unerroneous is not possible, there is not the fault of stating something deceptive that is not feasible. In this way, when devoid of means, correct conventional reality, there is not a method for realizing the goal—ultimate reality.

Having relied on appearances, it is necessary to perform activities that exhaust immeasurable obscurations and gather immeasurable collections [of merit]. One must produce immeasurable virtuous qualities in the mental continuum. Furthermore, one or two aeons [of activities] [719.25] are not sufficient, and many aeons of practice are necessary. As all that occurs having relied on appearances, [720] the means, appearances, are especially necessary for bodhisattvas. Therefore a bodhisattva does not abandon for the sake of mental afflictions. Regarding this, as it is said, "The body, which is like a great city, is beneficial for a field of fruit. It is beneficial for a field of sugar. Likewise, the mental afflictions of a bodhisattva are beneficial for the bodhisattva's great awakening."

When abandoning mental afflictions, the means, correct conventional reality, stops appearances. When wisdom [720.5] is devoid of means, one falls into the Inferior Vehicle. Therefore an eighth-stage bodhisattva, having been taught by all the buddhas of the ten directions, first produces fortitude (*spro ba*):

> "Son of good family, it is good for you to be endowed with the patient endurance for the unproduced. We awakened to complete buddhahood through being endowed with the patient endurance for the unproduced."
>
> [The buddhas] confer a second round of advice: "However, you who are endowed with the patient endurance for the unproduced, we have pure qualities like this that you do not see. One should put forth effort and exertion for the sake of attaining [720.10] virtuous qualities like these."

Furthermore, you should look again and again to pacify, perfectly pacify, fully pacify these sentient beings of cyclic existence who are unpeaceful, extremely unpeaceful, completely unpeaceful. The bodhisattva accumulates the collections for the purpose of attaining virtuous qualities, and by cultivating compassion for sentient beings, attains the tenth power of a bodhisattva. The scope of knowledge must be extensive, as reality is extensive. As the bodhisattva realizes the utmost extent of reality exactly as it is, she or he is irreversible from the Inferior Vehicle. If that is not the case, the irreversible [bodhisattva], being devoid of method [720.15], being devoid of wisdom, takes possession of the afflictions as it taught in the *Daśabhūmikasūtra*. If it is like this at the time of the eighth stage, what is the purpose of the vision [of emptiness] after that point? Therefore, when devoid of the means, correct conventional reality, there is no method at all that realizes the goal, ultimate reality. Ārya Nāgārjuna states from the *Prajñāmūla*:

> Conventional reality functions as a means, and ultimate reality functions as the goal. Those who do not understand the difference between the two have a bad understanding and get a bad rebirth.[611]

The two [realities] are explained [720.20] as cause and effect. The Ācārya Candrakīrti states:

> There is no means of finding peace for those outside the system of Ārya Nāgārjuna. They have fallen from *correct conventional* reality, and having fallen, will not be able to achieve liberation.[612]

The Ācārya Ārya [Bhāviveka] states from the *Tarkajvālā*:

> Without the stairway of correct convention, a wise man cannot ascend to the top of the palace of reality.[613]

The Ārya *Prajñāpāramitāsaṃcayagāthā* states:

> Without method, devoid of wisdom, one falls to the level of a *śrāvaka*. [720.25]

The Lord [Atiśa], the sole lord, states from his *Bodhipathapradīpa*:

> Wisdom devoid of means, and means, as well, devoid of wisdom, [721] are taught as bondage. Therefore one should refrain from giving up either.[614]

Therefore, Geshé Ratna Chakriwa has stated:

> If the means does not dependently arise, that is, the stairway of correct conventional reality, the three individuals who go along the stages of the path will not occur.

Therefore, since the appearance that appears under the power of ignorance is subdued by the power of wisdom, the appearance of pristine wisdom that unmistakenly and nonerroneously appears is nondeceptive.

[Query:] Well then, [721.5] as a bodhisattva who resides on the levels plunders appearances in meditative equipoise and [perceives] only reality, from where do his appearances occur?

[Reply:] His postmeditative-state appearances arise through the force of the obstructions to omniscience consisting of unafflicted misknowledge (*nyon mongs pa can ma yin pa'i mi shes pa'i shes bya'i sgrib pa*).[615]

[Query:] Is there a distinction or not between seeing reality in meditative equipoise while on the path of vision or path of meditation established during the ten stages or seeing reality at the time of buddhahood?

[Reply:] Indian *paṇḍita*s are in disagreement regarding this. There is not a distinction in meditative equipoise. There is a distinction in the postmeditative state, as there is a system [of interpretation] that asserts [721.10] distinctions in abandonment, virtuous qualities, and postmeditative realization within the ten [bodhisattva] levels. Furthermore, there is a system [of interpretation] that asserts a distinction in meditative equipoise. Many great Tibetan spiritual masters (*bod kyi dge bshes chen po rnams*) are also in disagreement on this issue. However, there is not a distinction in seeing only reality.

[Query:] Nevertheless, when reality is perceived in the meditative equipoise of the path of vision, are all the obscurations for omniscience eliminated or not? It is not suitable for them to be eliminated. If [one is not] not eliminating [obsurations], it is not suitable to see reality. If one sees reality even while not eliminating [obscurations], then what do obscurations obstruct? Therefore at what point are obscurations posited?

[Reply:] While in the meditative equipoise of the path of vision, [721.15] there is not a fault for repeatedly generating the path of vision that sees the reality that is not different from the reality of [bodhisattvas] on the ten stages and the omniscient knowledge of a buddha. Although one does not [completely] eliminate the obscurations for omniscience on the ten stages, this is not contrary to seeing reality. While in the meditative equipoise that sees reality, obscurations are negated. It is not suitable for path of cultivation [obscurations] to be eliminated when negating obscurations while in meditative equipoise on the path of vision. As elimination is completed earlier, cessation (*'gag pa*) and elimination (*spong ba*) are not synonyms.

There is not both analytical cessation and nonanalytical cessation.[616] One does not eliminate through nonanalytical cessation [721.20] apart from eliminating by analytical cessation. Obscurations removed by seeing at the time of meditative equipoise in the path of vision occur as analytical cessation.

Although path of cultivation obscurations are not capable of being eliminated by special insight, through the distinctive power of meditative serenity (*śamatha*), obscurations for omniscience on the ten [bodhisattva] levels are subdued and negated due to nonanalytical cessation.[617] By negating through subduing all mistakes, one sees reality. However, since it is nonanalytical cessation, although subjugated in meditative equipoise, since they are not eliminated, the postmeditative-state appearances of a bodhisattva who resides on the [bodhisattva] levels occurs because of unafflicted misknowledge [721.25]. As the obscuration is [subjugated] due to nonanalytical cessation, [722] since it is not negated or eliminated by seeing reality, it is not contradictory for both [analytical cessation and nonanalytical cessation] to not obscure reality.

[Query:] Since reality on the path of vision in meditative equipoise is not distinguished from reality as construed as an actual object on the path, what is the reason for not eliminating at that time the obscurations of the ten [bodhisattva] levels?

[Reply:] There are two types of obscurations to perceiving reality: those eliminated by seeing and those eliminated by cessation. Although there is not a distinction in reality, since [obscurations] are eliminated by [the path of] cultivation, they are not eliminated at the time of [the path of] vision. For example, although the sun does not have distinctions, the moisture at the time of its arising is [722.5] not drinkable. After some delay, it is drinkable, so the foolish say. Although there are not distinctions in merely seeing reality, one is not able to eliminate previous obscurations. When they arise vast and small for reality, they are eliminated later.

[Query:] Is vast and small not feasible, since reality has one taste?

[Reply:] Although the space of a window and great space both have the single taste of space, the space of a window is construed as small and great space is construed as vast, since one is a discerned object and the other does not have a limit. Therefore it is not contrary for [space] to arise vast and small. One may say that since it does not abide [722.10] as an object with the position of reality, vast and small is not feasible for a single taste.

[Query:] Although vast and small does not exist for reality, vast and small arises for realization. The realization of the vastness of reality is due to the realization of the subject's vastness, as it is the awareness to its utmost extent (*ji snyed pa'i ye shes*) and the awarenes of things exactly as they are (*ji lta ba'i ye shes*).

[Reply:] That is not feasible. Although there are different dharmas, there are not differences in reality (*chos nyid, dharmatā*) for all the dharmas, and, as they are of one taste, when reality of one dharma is realized, the reality for all dharmas is mastered.[618] If it is not like that, there will be multiple final realities. It is true that if one does not gather a great amount of the collections of merit with the means of correct conventional reality, it is useless [722.15] to produce an awareness for this. Moreover, superimpositions are not cut at one time. Superimpositions are gradually cut. Therefore, like the vastness of the subject, the vastness of realizing reality eliminates the obscurations that were not able to be previously eliminated.

The *Knowing the Meaning of Reality* (*De nyid kyi don shes*)[619] explains that:

> Nine middle and great obscurations to be eliminated in the path of cultivation are eliminated by nine middle and great antidotes of wisdom, while the nine small of the nine small obscurations to be eliminated are eliminated by the great of the great wisdom antidotes.

Therefore, as the realization of reality occurs in great and small realizations, those who do not have special advice, the commentators who make distinctions in the elimination of objects to be eliminated should be understood as mistaken when they state that, "like the example with space, there is a distinction in the elimination of objects to be eliminated through [722.20] long or short duration."

Although great and small realizations occur, as like the space of a window and great space, or sugar and the taste of sugar, the single taste of reality does not occur at one time. Therefore, not eliminated by seeing, the object to be eliminated by meditation is sustained by realization that increases through meditation. As the goal will occur through increasing the accumulation of merit as the means while increasing realization, it should be understood that the goal, ultimate reality, is not realized if one is devoid of the means: correct conventional reality. As it is not contrary to realizing the ultimate, as it is not obscured, it is called "correct." [723] Furthermore, because it is nondeceptive, it is real and reliable. Alternatively, since it is reliable, it is real. For as long as space abides and for as long as existence abides, the two results of the compatibility of experience, both the intermediate and final [results], [i.e., higher rebirth and final liberation], are nondeceptive. If a cause is not eliminated, an effect is not eliminated. Cause and effect are true at all times and unceasing. As maturation and the lineage of causal concordance is unceasing [723.5] and true, it is trustworthy or reliable,[620] [and] the virtue of a bodhisattva is inexhaustible. The reason of inexhaustible [bodhisattva virtues] will be indicated below. In this way, since correct conventional reality exists, is true, nondeceptive, and reliable, it is called "correct" (*yang dag pa*). The explanation of the objects [indicated by] words of correct conventionals and mistaken conventionals is concluded.

[iii. Objects Indicated by the Words "Reality" or "Truth" and "Obscuration" (*bden pa'i sgra'i don te rdzob kyi sgra'i don*)]

(3) Now, the objects [indicated by] the words "reality" or "truth" will be explained. Regarding this, there are two: objects [indicated by the] words of mistaken conventional realities/truths and objects [indicated by the] words of correct conventional realities/truths.

[1) Objects Indicated by Mistaken Conventional Reality (*log pa'i kun rdzob bden pa'i sgra don*)]

As mistaken appearances, ignorance, and mistaken conventionals are like a person with blurred vision seeing hairs in the sky [723.10], they are nonexistent, false, erroneous, and mistaken. All falsities are equally false as false. For this, how is it feasible to use the words "true" or "real"? In this regard, there is not even a little reason for establishing the perception as real or true. However, from the perspective of mere falsity, it is said to be "true" or "real." Whereas from the correct perspective, it is not said to be "true" or "real" but is only established as "true" or "real" in a false, erroneous, or mistaken perspective. Since each and every result arises as a result of a cause, nondeceptively it is called "true/real." As it is true/real as the cause and effect of cyclic existence, [723.15] it is true/real as karma and effects, and it serves as a continuum by the method of the four effects, that is, the retributive effect (*vipākaphala*), the predominant effect (*adhipatiphala*), the correlative effect (*niṣyanda-phala*), and the effect caused by human action (*puruṣakāraphala*). As the four effects are produced by a single cause, one experiences a place of rebirth due to karma, as cyclic existence does not occur without a cause or due to a nonconcordant cause. It is true/real as experienced by performed actions. It is not suitable to take on others' [karmic actions], since unperformed actions are not experienced. Since [a karmic cause] is not lost until the effect of that karma is issued, it is called "true/real." One's object of action and portion of karmic action are true/real for as long as one has not produced the path of vision [723.20]. This cause and effect of cyclic existence, although nonexistent, is erroneously and mistakenly perceived because it is a mistaken appearance of ignorance for as long as the path of vision is not produced. Therefore this erroneous appearance that is unceasing is true/real from the perspective of mere falsity, or the erroneous "I." What is the purpose of the path if it does not exist? As cause and effect are nondeceptive [, it is taught that,]

> I always teach emptiness that eliminates eternalism and nihilism.
> *Saṃsāra* is like a dream and an illusion, and karma vanishes not.[621]

The Lord [Atiśa] has said,

> One should not be attached to negative deeds even for a moment.
> Keep watch until the sun of suchness [723.25] arises.

Avadhūtipa, the guru of Lord [Atiśa] has stated,

> For as long as self-grasping is not exhausted, the most subtle of subtle karmic actions should be understood to yield a result.

[Query:] How long does this self-grasping for oneself exist?

[Reply:] It all exists as a measure of oneself existing. Consequently, this mistaken appearance is unceasing, and as there is unceasing cause and effect that is mistaken up until producing the path of vision that sees the suchness of all things, cause and effect is true/real. As long as the path of vision is not produced, mistakes are unhindered. As long as mistakes are uninterrupted, the path of vision [724.5] is not produced.

[Query:] What hinders this mistaken appearance?

[Reply:] If these mistaken appearances were nonimplicatively negated for a mere kalpa of destruction through reasonings that are free from singularity and multiplicity, it would be useless, as these appearances for the duration are not interrupted, since uninterrupted cause and effect is true from the perspective of falsity; what is the purpose of the path if it does not exist? Consequently, if one belittles cause and effect when it is construed as emptiness, the Ācārya Nāgārjuna [724.10] has taught that:

> If their view of emptiness is wrong, those of little wisdom will be hurt, like a wrongly held snake, or a spell wrongly cast.[622]

Furthermore, the Ācārya himself has also stated,

> If reality is not well understood, it causes ruin for the unintelligent, as the person sinks into the impurity of nihilistic views. Other fools who have [the] pride of being a master do not understand it

properly, and therefore fall head down into the Hell of Avīci, being ruined by their criticism.[623]

[Query:] Well then, what ceases this appearance?

[Reply:] In order for this [appearance] to cease, the cause must cease. The causes must cease, which are three: karma, mental afflictions, and ignorance. The force of previous ignorance is destroyed by wisdom. [724.15] The afflictions are pressed down and refuted by means of the three trainings. They are drawn out from the roots. By purifying the obstructions of karma by means of the four opponent powers,[624] it is not necessary to overturn the effect, this mistaken appearance, as it ceases by itself. For example, when the form of a mongoose appears in a mirror, however much one wipes the mirror the mongoose is not overturned. By wiping the own-form of the mongoose, the mirror-form of the mongoose loosens its own bonds[625] and is cut off. The force of the spell of ignorance should be overcome with wisdom. It should be vanquished with the three wisdoms of hearing, reflection, and meditation.

To explain [the wisdom arising from] hearing further: [724.20] one relies on the spiritual friend who has skill in means, the one appropriate characteristic, for the unmistaken advice of the lineage of achieving the dharma. For one who practices the stages of the path, without the dependent-arising of the means, the stairway of correct conventional reality will not occur, that is, the stages of the path of the three types of individuals. The wisdom that is attained uniquely like this, [by] the means of mind training in the unmistaken meaning of the two realities, is reflective knowledge that is construed as the object of understanding. Training in a mode that completely purifies through meditative knowledge achieves certainty that cuts mistaken and great proliferations. Through eradicating [724.25] the four[626]—the ignorance that mistakes the impermanent for the permanent, the ignorance that mistakes suffering for happiness, the ignorance that is deluded for great, extensive means, and the ignorance that is deluded toward suchness—the wisdom of the profound [725] in this life occurs as antidote to the three poisons, to the afflictions of rebirth that depend on the four [ignorances], and to apprehending oneself and the entirety of cyclic existence as substantially existent.

One should repent, confess, and purify negative karmic actions that create the five [types of rebirth]. From this point onward, by training in moral practices that do not take life, on the lesser and middling path of accumulation one eliminates [negative karmic actions] by means of undermining the afflictions. One cuts off the [negative] path by knowledge derived from reflection (*bsam shes*) in both the lesser and middling path of accumulation [725.5]. The path of accumulation integrates meditative serenity (*śamatha*) and special insight (*vipaśyanā*) through producing in the mental continuum the essence of great concentration (*mahāsamādhi*). Since own-character (*rang gi mtshan nyid*) is not construed as an actual object in the path of preparation, special insight during the path of preparation—including the four, peak, patience, [heat,] and highest mundane dharma, and the fifth, the great path of accumulation—apart from realizing in a general manner the suchness of all things, is unable to eliminate the mental afflictions from the root. Through moistening the mental continuum with meditative serenity, in eliminating the previous causes of the afflictions, the training of the mind in special insight "hits the [afflictions] right on the head." When realizing in a general manner [725.10] the essencelessness of things in the path of accumulation and the path of preparation, the causes of subsequent relations and the indirect causes tend toward producing the actual path of vision [in perceiving] reality, tend toward the afflictions being stopped; when refuting the innate afflictions, by clearly realizing reality, the supreme wisdom removes [the afflictions] from the root. As it is said, "the path that will arise completely eliminates their obscurations."[627]

In this way, the wisdoms that arise from hearing, reflection, and meditation, by destroying the previous force of ignorance, enable one's own continuum to arise in three trainings. That is no different from the four opponent powers in refuting conditioned existence from the three: ignorance, afflictions [725.15], and craving. Through refuting the five mistaken causes, one attains liberation by exhausting the proclaimed seven effects of suffering, karma, and afflictions. Therefore, throughout the time when the stains of mistaken appearance are not refuted, the path of vision will not be produced. For example, as the nature of space is pure from the beginning, it is like not seeing the nature of space throughout the time that one is not free from previous obscuring overlays (*sgrib g.yogs*). In being free from previous obscuring overlays, space is self-luminous. Through overturning the mistaken cause, the effect, the mistaken appearance, spontaneously unfolds and reality [725.20] from the perspective of self-luminous, supreme all-knowing wisdom, exalted in all objects of knowledge, produces the path of vision that directly produces the nonappearance of things, the pure appearance of nonappearance, final reality. When, from the perspective of seeing reality like space, karma does not exist, the ripening of karma does not exist, the experiencer of experiencing karma does not exist, the agent who makes karma does not exist, the bonds of karma loosen. For the duration of not refuting the cause and effect of mistakes, cause and effect manifested from the perspective of mere deluded perception or false perception is true for as long as one has not produced the path of vision. As long as the path of vision is not produced, by not refuting the mistaken cause, [725.25] the mistaken appearance of the effect is not negated. Through not refuting mistaken appearances, through not actually [726] perceiving reality for the duration of not producing the path of vision, as mistaken appearances are all that exists as a measure of existence, what is the purpose of the path if it does not exist? Therefore, the principle of cause and effect is true. No matter how much one meditates on emptiness, by not actually perceiving emptiness other than merely construing it as an object due to an inclination toward perverse concordances (*rjes su mthun la phyin ci log* ≈ *anukūlā viparyastā*), it is useless to overturn mistaken appearances. As it is true from the perspective of mere falsity for as long as mistakes are not reversed, what is the purpose if the path does not exist? Even though one may meditate that holding fire with the hand is empty [726.5], one does not reverse the burning of the hand, as the phenomenon is true from the viewpoint of confusion. Therefore it is true from the viewpoint of confusion, but not true in the correct perspective, as it is false, refuted when producing the path of vision. For this reason, because it is refuted, the mistaken appearance is false. However, since it is true from the perspective of mere falsity, what is the purpose if the path does not exist? Therefore the greatness of repeatedly meditating on cause and effect has been earnestly advocated by Geshé Ratna. The explanation of the objects [indicated by] the words "mistaken conventional reality" is concluded.

[2) Objects Indicated by Correct Conventional Reality (*yang dag kun rdzob bden pa'i sgra don*)]

[726.10] The objects [indicated by] the words "correct conventional reality": the nature of correct conventional reality is mere appearance, the mind that is free from the two extremes for what is imputed as two extremes. Although the mind of mistaken conventional reality has form as mere appearance, it is the mind that is free from the two extremes that realizes correct conventional reality. Although realizing one's own mind as free from the two extremes, by not refuting the condition of ignorance, since one's own mind appears, the appearance appears by the force of unafflicted ignorance. Since the unmistaken is not possible for appearances of ignorance, all conventionals are like mistaken illusions [726.15]. In this way, the correct conventional aspect of appearance is an imputation.

[Query:] Well then, what is the reason for positing correct conventionals as true?

[Reply:] Since cause and effect is undeceiving, it is posited as true. The Ācārya Ārya Nāgārjuna states,

> As for extremely subtle entities, those who regard them with nihilism, lacking precise knowledge, do not perceive the meaning of conditioned arising.[628]

When that is true/real, the cause and effect of purification, the path, and *nirvāṇa* is true/real.

[Query:] How is it true/real?

[Reply:] Since the cause is undeceiving for each individual effect, it is true.

[Query:] At what time is it true/real? [726.20]

[Reply:] Since it is undeceiving for as long as space abides, for as long as existence abides, and for temporary and ultimate [results, i.e., higher rebirth and awakening], it is true for all time. Just as the mode of relating cause and effect as true, in this way, until buddhahood, it occurs as a continuum of effects of compatibility of experiences through the mode of five effects.[629]

The Protector Maitreya has stated:

> Being a fit vessel known as maturing; having power due to sovereignty therein, inclination, growth, and purification: these are the results in order.[630]

[The five effects are] the retributive effect, the predominant effect [726.25], the correlative effect, the effect caused by human action, and the separation effect. [727] The stairway of correct conventional reality, the stages of the path of the three individuals, does not dependently arise without skillful means. Through meditation that establishes realization in the path, realizing dependent-arising, and through the jewel of faith, the condition that purifies the turbidity of the mind, [one understands that] all things are produced in the manner of a reflection. The two accumulations of the path practiced in meditation and in postmeditation are the indivisibility of the two realities. That nonduality produces the five effects. The continuum of the body endowed with leisure and fortune is the retributive effect from both the path of accumulation [727.5] and the path of preparation. That path has a twofold result of mastery (*dbang gi 'bras bu*) through the force that is enhanced by maturation: the afflictions that are to be eliminated, the small-part antidote, [and] the jewel of the mind that aspires for awakening [consisting of] indivisible means and wisdom, arises very strong naturally.

The correlative effect is that one becomes respectful through faith and conviction in the spiritual friend and scriptural collection (*sde snod*) that indicates the path. One becomes joyful, having faith and conviction in that path. The effect caused by human action, that path is produced [727.10] in the continuum and is a path in which that to be eliminated (*spang bya*) and the one who eliminates (*spong byed*) are eliminated as a duality. The characteristic of the path is the development of a mind whose nature is motivated by compassion without concern for oneself. The object of reality of wisdom must view the two realities as indivisible. That path is twofold, having the conventional aspiration for awakening as its characteristic. When enhanced through viewing the object of reality of wisdom, both the lesser and middling path of accumulation are distinguished as paths of [wisdom arising from] hearing and [wisdom arising from] reflection.

One reflects that all things [727.15] are like space at the time of meditative equipoise based on the condition of the spiritual friend endowed with skillful means. Through considering that [all things] are not different from the eight similes of illusion in the postmeditative state, one cuts off mistaken elaborations and spontaneously generates certainty regarding the nature of the two realities. This is not awareness [that arises through] meditation. As it is awareness [that arises through] reflection, mindful awareness understands the five aggregates in the lesser path of accumulation to be unproduced like an illusion. The four foundations of mindfulness are wisdom that arises from reflection that ascertains [things] as unproduced. The mind that aspires for buddhahood for the sake of others, without relying on a rigid heart, like being clothed in love, is the lesser path of accumulation. [727.20] Although the foundations of mindfulness of reflective awareness understands [things] as unproduced, as it is verbal [knowledge], it produces the lesser- and middling-level patience that is concomitant with verbal conviction (*sgra'i rjes su 'gro ba'i bzod pa ≈ ghoṣānugāya kṣānti*). The Protector Maitreya states,

> Through indisposition, through being craving's cause, through being the object, and through removing ignorance—the aim of meditating on the foundations of mindfulness is to bring an understanding of the [nobles'] four truths.[631]

Awareness [that arises through] reflection is analagous to a fire spreading through a forest. The increase of awareness [that arises through] reflection, based on an ascertainment, through the wisdom arising from reflection, of the object of the two realities in the middling path of accumulation, produces a greater patience that is concomitant [727.25] with verbal conviction. The wisdom that arises from reflection that views the object of wisdom in both meditation and in the postmeditative state, [728] supported with diligence, thoroughly completes virtuous qualities in one's mental continuum. Through accomplishing both aspects of the aspiration for awakening, the path that gathers both accumulations increases the production [of virtuous qualities] that have not been produced in the mental continuum. The mode that undermines the accumulation of nonvirtue prompted by the three poisons, [and] the mental afflictions that are to be eliminated, which places effort and exertion on eliminating what has been produced, what has not yet been produced, and the unproduced in the mental continuum, is known as elimination in a manner that undermines the afflictions through [728.5] special self-discipline (*lhag pa'i shi la ≈ adhiśīla*). Since the awareness [arising from] reflection is firm, it is like meeting a familiar person from a previous occasion or like snow falling in a lake.[632] However, since it is not awareness [arising from] meditation, it is still verbal [knowledge], not actual knowledge. As it is verbal, it becomes a cause that is related to realization before the path of vision.

As the predominant effect, the correlative effect, and the effect caused by human action occur up until the middling path of accumulation, they exist as awarenesses [that arise from] reflection as verbal knowledges. Although verbal, since it is firm, one applies effort in not forgetting, while afflictions have been produced, to aggressively eliminate by applying antidotes [728.10] to forceful causes of previous afflictions. Special self-discipline is among the three trainings. The [wisdoms arising from] hearing and reflection are among the three types of wisdoms. In this way, one eliminates the five faults[633] through pure discipline and wisdom [that arises from] reflection, [and] the afflictions are undermined and eliminated by means of the special discipline that occurs up to and including the middling path of accumulation.

Relying on the eight remedies, illusion-like concentration arises.[634] The greater path of accumulation, the four legs of miraculous action,[635] thus the nature of concentration is produced in the mind. The three wisdoms, the three trainings, all meditative serenity and special insight is contained within. [728.15] One directly sees an emanation body (*sprul pa'i sku*), the prediction of hearing the Dharma occurs. Through attaining the *dhāraṇī* of not forgetting the hearing of the Dharma from a Tathāgata, one attains a concentration called "Stream of Dharma." In regard to attaining a concentration like this, the *Mahāyānasūtrālaṃkāra* states,

> Then one attains the extensive special instructions of the stream of dharma in order to attain meditative serenity, special insight, and wisdom.[636]

This exists in the greater path of accumulation, as it is clearly explained in the chapter on the [Bodhisattva] Sadāprarudita in the commentary on the [*Perfection of Wisdom in*] *Eight Thousand Lines*. Further, meeting with the noble spiritual friend is fitting, like a mother hen caring for her son [728.20]. With the teaching of the conventional aspiration for awakening, the altruistic intention (*lhag pa'i bsam pa*) increases more and more, like the waxing moon. One has a genuine conventional aspiration for awakening that is not motivated by being hard-hearted. One ascertains through awareness [arising from] reflection that conventional reality is like an illusion and ultimate reality is like space.

The awareness that arises from meditation, due to realizing external characteristics (*phyi'i mtshan nyid*), sometimes clear, sometimes unclear, like the sun obscured by clouds, generates compassion naturally for sentient beings who are understood to be like one's mother, and the love that is produced by seeing the suffering of mother-like sentient beings in cyclic existence, remembering to repay their kindness—both are causes [728.25]. The *Prajñāmūlamadhyamakakārikā* states:

> Accordingly, when emptiness is realized, the mind no doubt will become [729] joyful for the purpose of others.[637]

The conventional mind that aspires to awake is influenced by the greatness of emptiness and the great compassion that perceives the suffering of mother-like sentient beings without concern for oneself. The realization of the awareness [that arises in] meditation that is not yet clear has the general characteristics of the conventional [reality] of wisdom that is like an illusion and ultimate [reality] that is like space. The twofold aspiration for awakening, as wisdom and compassion are not separated, has the predominant effect, the correlative effect, and the effect [729.5] caused by human actions that completes virtuous qualities. The separation effect is devoid of the eight worldly concerns[638] in the path of accumulation. They are eliminated in a manner that undermines them through the awareness [arising from] reflection up to and including the middling path of accumulation. This [stage] is called "being devoid of the eight worldly concerns (*lo ka chos brgyad dang bral*)," since they do not exist, [and] as they are eliminated by meditative serenity as a forceful previous cause in the greater path of accumulation.

In this way, meditating on the two realities in the path of accumulation based on the condition of the spiritual friend endowed with skillful means becomes a subsequent cause of realization after the path of vision. A stable path of accumulation brought to completion [729.10] produces the path of preparation. The meditative equipoise in both [the stage of] heat (*drod, ūṣman*) and peak (*rtse mo, mūrdha*) is a meditation that possesses the five governing powers (*dbang po lnga*),[639] and has wisdom that arises in meditation that without distinction understands that things are like space and in the post-meditative state are like the eight similes of illusion. However, [the wisdom] arises with interruptions due to discordant factors. As the two wisdoms of patience (*bzod pa, kṣānti*) and highest mundane dharma (*chos mchog, laukikāgradharma*) are not disturbed by discordant factors, there are the five strengths.[640] In this way, the nature of the five powers and five strengths in the path of preparation clearly sees in a general manner the reality of the two realities. Although clearly seeing, since it does not see actual [reality], it is like seeing an illusory elephant. The general manner [729.15] of seeing with an awareness [that arises in] meditation serves as a cause that is concordant with actual seeing in the path of vision but is not an actual cause. The clear realization that has the general characteristics of the two realities in the path of preparation is a predominant effect, the correlative effect, and the effect caused by human action. The separation effect is like the function of the third casually concordant and is devoid of apprehended object (*gzung ba*, *grāhya*) and apprehending subject (*'dzin pa*, *grāhaka*) in the path of preparation. The apprehended object at the stage of heat and peak is realized in a general manner to lack intrinsic existence. The apprehending subject at the stage of patience and highest mundane dharma realizes in a general manner the lack of intrinsic existence without explicitly realizing specifically characterized phenomena.

[Query:] Well then [729.20], as it is taught that "without an apprehended object there is not an apprehending subject,"[641] when realizing that the apprehended object lacks intrinsic existence at the stages of heat (*drod*) and peak (*rtse mo*), what is the purpose of realizing that the apprehending subject also lacks intrinsic existence? What of the commentators who are without the advice of the practice lineage?

[Reply:] Among both the apprehended object and apprehending subject of external objects (*phyi don gyi gzung 'dzin*) and the apprehended object and apprehending subject of internal awarenesses (*nang shes pa'i gzung 'dzin*), all the apprehended objects and apprehending subjects of external objects that are said to be realized as lacking intrinsic existence should be understood as erroneous. Although an apprehending subject is unestablished when the nature of a functioning entity apprehended as an object does not exist, other than a realization being produced gradually when produced in the mind, what is the purpose if the path does not exist? [729.25]. One would not gather the accumulations and the objects to be known are useless to produce an awareness.

Although the three trainings (*bslab pa gsum*), the three wisdoms (*shes rab gsum*), [730] and both meditative serenity and special insight are complete in the path of preparation, as it is not actually other than a reflection of special insight, the wisdom of the lesser path of meditation is not able to eliminate mistakes from the root. The higher training of the mind, possessing the power of meditative serenity, eliminates the afflictions in a nondiscursive manner; the afflictions are eliminated at the root by not having a direct cause.

When clearly seeing suchness, in a general manner it is considered to occur through producing the path of vision [730.5] that directly sees the specific character of suchness (*de kho na nyid rang gi mtshan nyid*). At that time mental afflictions do not exist in the mental continuum, as they dissipate at the time of making effort.[642]

One hears the Dharma from an emanation body. Among the two, interpretable and definitive meaning, the interpretable meaning is important, as those to be guided by an emanation body are below the path of preparation. The special discipline of mind is known as "the means of rising above the afflictions." In dependence on the condition of the spiritual friend endowed with skillful means, the recognition of wisdom in a general manner of suchness in meditation and in the postmeditative state—nonforgetfulness through the way of mindfulness, [and] the wisdom of the path of preparation, which has the nature of the five governing powers and the five strengths [730.10] that were without cause before the worldly mind was expanded through the conviction of faith and one-pointedness through concentration—serves as the indirect cause that transmits the realization of final reality in the path of vision. An actual cause is not made. The wisdom of the preparatory analytical factors (*nges 'byed kyi ye shes*; *nirvedhabhāgiya*) is a realization that contacts general suchness, because there is a factor to be eliminated in the path of vision. Therefore it is a cause that transmits but is not a direct cause that is causally concordant.

[Query:] Well then, how is the effect of compatibility of experience (*rnam smin rgyu mthun*) indirect?

[Reply:] The effect of compatibility of experience is established as an imputation. It is not truly characterized. If it is the case that it exists, there would be the fault of actually seeing final reality in the path of preparation, similar with the cause of the compatibility of experience. Therefore it is said to be an indirect cause.

Moreover, [730.15] even though the object of apprehension is a generic image, as the conceived object has own-character, it is called a causally concordant cause (*rgyu mthun gyi rgyu*) without contradiction, so therefore it is called a causally concordant cause. In this way, the causally concordant is imputed. Although conception conceives own-character through the apprehended general object, it is actually a mistaken conceptualization. As mistakes are erroneous mistakes that are not suitable as casually concordant causes or direct causes of suchness, it is an indirect cause. At the end of the path of preparation, the path of vision is produced where the initial retributive effect is to be born as a conquering cakravartin king in Jambudvīpa. In the state of meditative equipoise when the predominant effect, the correlative effect [730.20], and the effect caused by human action is established, the superior all-knowing wisdom that distinguishes objects of knowledge imputes the actual suchness of the two realities. In both meditative equipoise and the postmeditative state, the suchness that has a single taste of both realities is recognized by wisdom, not forgotten by mindfulness (*dran pa*), clarified by concentration. The worldly mind is uninterrupted through effort (*vīrya*). With uncontaminated mental bliss and feelings of joy, one apprehends single-pointedly inseparably from that wisdom. Pliancy (*shin du sbyangs pa*) is suitable as activity for the object of observation. The path of vision that actually realizes the own-character of the two realities, which is achieved together with equanimity (*btang snyoms*) [730.25], produces in the mental continuum the nature [731] of the seven factors of awakening.[643] The *Yuktiṣaṣṭikā* states,

> If, after the awareness of reality, there is any particular here, imputing any sort of creation in anything, however subtle, such an unwise individual does not see the meaning of arising from conditions.[644]

This indicates that Ācārya Nāgārjuna accepts a single instant of wisdom. Candrakīrti clearly explains this in his commentary to the *Yuktiṣaṣṭikā*.[645] The Lord [Atiśa] also accepts a single instant.

The separation effect [731.5] is devoid of the defilements to be eliminated by insight in the path of vision, as the reasoning eliminates the defilements on the path of vision at the root. The system of eliminating defilements is identified as an uncommon system of the Great Vehicle in which "the path that arises eliminates its obscurations," as detailed in the previous explanation.

"The path that negates eliminates their obscurations"[646] are those who assert to eliminate through a manner in which the defilement to be eliminated and the antidote do not abide together. Attachments to things are not reached, and this is asserted by those of the Small Vehicle. The system of eliminating defilements [731.10] should be understood as eliminated according to what was asserted in the previous section. What is an obscuration when seeing final reality that is inseparable from erroneous defilements? Through obscuring it is called "an obscuration." It is like not seeing the pure nature of space that is inseparable from the five obscuring overlays. Along these lines, the path of meditation in the ten levels has two [bodies], a body of maturation and a mental body for each individual [level]. The result of maturation on the second level is that one is born as a great cakravartin king who possesses the seven jewels that conquer over the four continents. On the third level, one is born as [an] Indra king of gods. On the fourth level, [731.15] one is born as a lord who is free from the extremes. On the fifth level, one is born as a lord of Tuṣita Heaven. On the sixth level, one is born as a lord of the Heaven of Enjoying Emanation.

On the seventh level, one is born as a king of the Heaven of Controlling Others' Emanations. On the eighth level, one is born as Brahmā, master of one thousandfold. On the ninth level, one is born as Mahābrahmā, master of an intermediate second intermediate one thousandfold. On the tenth level, one is born as a great king among the five lineages of the pure places [among the form-realm heavens].

The predominant effect, the correlative effect, the effect caused by human action, the path of meditation whose nature is the noble eightfold path [731.20] increases realization by means of being extended and familiarized in dependence on the three results, the predominant effect, the correlative effect, the effect caused by human action, and actually seeing final reality arises during the ten [bodhisattva] levels.

The wisdom that recognizes the mind of awakening as indivisible wisdom and compassion is correct view (*yang dag pa'i lta ba, samyakdṛṣṭi*). A heroic mind that is mentally conditioned to meditate is correct intention (*yang dag pa'i rtog pa, samyaksaṃkalpa*), the mindfulness of not forgetting. The one-pointed concentration for indivisible reality, the worldly mind of interrupted exertion, these qualities destroy corrupt livelihood, and as inseparable wisdom and compassion lives without contempt for others, it is correct livelihood (*yang dag pa'i 'tsho ba, samyagājīva*). The nonpassing [731.25] from the mind of awakening, which is inseparable wisdom and compassion, is the correct path, the aim of activity (*yang dag pa'i lam las kyi mtha*, i.e., *samyak-karmānta*, right action). The afflicted cause [732], which arises as faulty, nonvirtuous, or neutral speech, never passes beyond in either the meditative state or postmeditative state from the mind of awakening that is inseparable wisdom and compassion that eliminates that cause. All speech taken up at any time, by being spoken with an uncontaminated virtuous quality, a mind of awakening that is inseparable wisdom and compassion, is called correct speech (*yang dag pa'i ngag, samyag-vāc*). One imputes the name of the effect from the cause. In the context of the mind of awakening that is enhanced by the five—wisdom, the heroic mind, mindfulness, concentration, and diligence; [732.5] the three—the correct aim of activity, [correct speech], and correct livelihood are not established in all situations. In this way, the path of meditation gradually produces the nature of the noble eightfold path construed as an actual object that has the own-character of the suchness of the two realities (*bden pa gnyis kyi de kho na nyid rang gi mtshan nyid*). The result of separation is free from the defilements to be eliminated by the path of meditation. This has been previously pointed out in detail.

The system of the indirect retributive effect (*rnam smin*) and the correlative effect (*rgyu mthun*): the system of the indirect retributive effect is primarily construed in terms without ascertainment. The indirect system of the fourth correlative effect is ascertained [732.10] in a similar manner. The predominant effect, the correlative effect, the effect caused by human action—the antidote is established from the factor of wisdom that cognizes the suchness of the two realities. The separation effect is concordant with the relations of a small affliction to be eliminated. A correlative effect has two [types], an effect of experience that resembles the cause (*myong ba rgyu mthun*) and the four that are effects of action that resemble the cause. By counting the stages of the path that rely on the cause, there is the grouping of the continuity.

[Query:] Well then, isn't there a great contradiction between the retributive effect and the correlative effect?

[Reply:] It is essential that the retributive effect does not produce the path of vision. It is essential that the correlative effect is produced after the path of vision. The retributive effect is up to not producing [732.15] the path of vision, for when entering into leisureless states (*akṣana, mi khom pa'i gnas*) [of rebirth], someone in the world is harmed by worldly qualities; the patience of the unproduced that arises from a retributive effect is a deceptive action, an essential point of the retributive effect. However, since all virtuous roots created by bodhisattvas must be correlative effects with mind training, retributive effects are not suitable for mind training.

[Query:] Well then, what should be done about retributive effects?

[Reply:] Through correlative effects purifying the good heart, retributive effects are implicitly established like flowers being cut at the same time as a horse race. However, as there is no way to reach maturation until the path of vision is produced, [732.20] an essential point is to protect the pure vows that have been taken and make pure aspirational prayers (*smon lam*).

[Query:] Well then, are aspirational prayers not suitable since they are objects of retributive effects?

[Reply:] Aspirational prayers do not become objects for retributive effects because the casually concordant patience for the unproduced is nondeceptive. When offering up aspirational prayers that are apprehended as harmoniously produced with maturation, the correlative effect is mind training. The essential point is that correlative effects are up until producing the path of vision. Even while retributive effects may proceed and cause one to arrive at lower states of rebirth, as supermundane qualities are not invalidated by worldly qualities, nonattachment to the suffering of misfortune naturally [732.25] occurs as the patience for the unproduced is not deceptive. Therefore, bodhisattvas, through the power of aspirational prayers for the sake of sentient beings, [733] take birth even in lower states of rebirth. In this way, important correlative effects are produced after the path of vision. How it is true/real has been indicated.

[Query:] At what time is it true/real?

[Reply:] It is true/real for as long as space abides and for as long as existence abides, since the result in this interval of time from the path of accumulation up through the ten stages until the final result of attaining the three bodies [of a buddha] performing miraculous deeds in cyclic existence for the sake of sentient beings is not refuted.

> [733.5] I do not pass into nirvāṇa, the dharma does not disappear,
> both are faulty like the moon in a vessel of water.

The term of the common locus is "correct conventional reality" and, as it is correct and conventional, it is also true/real. It is correct because it exists, is true/real, nonerroneous, and nonmistaken. It is conventional since it is produced by causes and conditions. It is true/real as well, since the causes of purification have nondeceptive individual results. For as long as space abides, for as long as existence abides, [733.10] causes for both temporary and ultimate [results] are not refuted. As the result is not refuted, since it is nondeceptive, it is reliable. As it is proper to be trustworthy, it is true/real. Since a cause for each and every effect that is nondeceptive at all times is real, inexhaustible bodhisattva roots of virtue are nonmistaken causes whose effects are not reverted. Inexhaustible bodhisattva roots of virtue are endowed with highly distinguished qualites of the Great Vehicle. They are inexhaustible because of extensively accomplished compassion. They are inexhaustible due to the profundity of accomplished wisdom in which conventionally things are produced like illusions, while ultimately they are without appearance, [733.15] having a selfless nature, like space.

[Query:] Well then, as they are emptiness, how can it be feasible for them to increase while being inexhaustible?

[Reply:] Although ultimately there is no increase while meditating on emptiness, conventionally there is a great amount of increase.

[Query:] Well then, how can the profound, as it is an object of wisdom, be conventionally exhausted, since it is not exhausted in the ultimate?

[Reply:] Since the conventional is adorned with lacking intrinsic existence, it is not exhausted. In this way, because it consists of compassion and wisdom, it is endowed with the distinction of increase and the inexhaustible.

When observing correlative effects and observing retributive effects, [733.20] to cast out maturation and exhaust benefit is contrary to overturning the result by exhausting the cause. Through observing the correlative effect, by casting out the effect, the cause increases and further external increase intensifies internal increase. The greatest external increasing is a result of "+a sho" and "+a da."[647] The increase of the support of internal awareness is even more extensive. As a single cause produces four or five effects, the increase of correlative effects exists as mere causes but is called "an observation of correlative effect" (*rgyu mthun la dmigs*). What is called "a correlative dedication" (*rgyu mthun du bsngos*) is observed as a correlative effect and is an entity that distinctively increases.

[Query:] Well then, [733.25] how is it viewed that dedication as a cause of completing the two accumulations is observed as a correlative effect and the dedication [734] to attain the effect, the three bodies [of a buddha], is observed as a retributive effect?

[Reply:] The three bodies that are imputed as a retributive effect are actually characterized as a correlative effect. As there is no way to increase from the final cause that attains the three bodies [of a buddha], the two accumulations are completed. The Ācārya Nāgārjuna states:

> The form body of the buddhas arises from the collection of merit.
> The body of Dharma, briefly, O King, arises from collected wisdom.[648]

In brief, as wisdom and compassion are accomplished, [734.5] the correlative effect completes the two accumulations. Since it is inexhaustible and increases through dedication to attain the result, the three bodies [of a buddha], the meaning is that the perfections of method are explained as inexhaustible through dedicating roots of virtue for awakening. Dedication is to be construed like this.

[Query:] Well then, by not overturning the cause, the time period of the ten stages of a bodhisattva and the final stage of buddhahood, as it is true by being nondeceptive in all times temporally and ultimately for as long as space exists and for long as existence exists, do buddhas and bodhisattvas experience rebirth and death or not?

[Reply:] A buddha does not.

[Query:] Well then, what about *nirvāṇa*?

[Reply:] That is true, yet hidden, due to the faults of those to be trained. For the sake of those to be trained, the mode of *nirvāṇa* is displayed. But actually, *nirvāṇa* does not exist.

> I do not pass into *nirvāṇa*; dharma does not disappear. Both are faulty like the moon in a vessel of water.

This explains the fault of those to be trained.

> A buddha does not pass into *nirvāṇa* and dharma does not disappear. The mode of *nirvāṇa* is displayed [734.15] to sentient beings for the sake of their training.[649]

This explains the purpose regarding those to be trained. Since the mode of *nirvāṇa* is for the sake of sentient beings, as the cause is nonmistaken, the effect to be proven is nonmistaken. That is the nonmistaken effect. In this way, *nirvāṇa* does not actually exist other than displaying the mode of *nirvāṇa*. Regarding this, the chapter on awakening from the *Uttaratantra* states that

> having infinite causes, having an inexhaustible number of sentient beings, being endowed with miraculous powers, and wisdom, governing all the elements, destroying the demon of death, representing nonsubstantiality, the lord of the world is permanent.[650]

Displaying the mode of *nirvāṇa* [734.20] is an appearance to trainees, but there is not an intrinsic appearance of birth and *nirvāṇa*.

[Query:] Well then, what about birth and death for bodhisattvas?

[Reply:] Intrinsically established birth and death does not exist. The birth and death of mere appearance exists. The *Uttaratantra* states:

> As they have perceived reality as it is, they are beyond the five [realms of] rebirth. As they are embodiments of compassion, they display birth, death, aging, and sickness.[651]

[Query:] Well then, what is the difference from buddhas?

[Reply:] Buddhas are appearances for the sake of those to be trained, while the birth and death of bodhisattvas who abide on the ten levels are their own appearance.

[Query:] Well then, [734.25] since there is the death of own appearance, as it is nondeceptive at all times, is it not feasible for it be true/real?

[Reply:] Through attaining potency and ability in meditative equipoise, [735] afterward there is true understanding. Although birth and death appear, it is understood as lacking intrinsic existence, similar to how memory of fortune that appears in a dream is understood to lack intrinsic existence. Birth and death are eternalist and nihilist beliefs.

[Query:] As a bodhisattva who abides on a level is liberated from cyclic existence in refuting those views, as birth and death are not at all substantially established, as they are undeceiving at all times, how is it feasible for them to be true/real?

[Reply:] Although birth and death do not intrinsically exist [735.5], the birth and death of own appearance exists as mere appearance; since the cause is not overturned, the effect is not overturned.

[Query:] Since it is nondeceptive at all times, isn't it feasible for it to be true/real?

[Reply:] For that, there is not a mistaken effect due to a mistaken cause, since there is not an independently existent cause; a mistaken or unmistaken cause is not subsequently construed, therefore there is no fault. The post-meditative appearances of bodhisattvas who reside on the levels are appearances of discerning awareness. Mere appearances that are free from the two extremes are understood to be like illusions, illusions of wisdom, awareness. Since suchness is nonmistaken and nonerroneous, [735.10] it is an independent cause. Attaining the ten levels of a bodhisattva is connected in all existences to attaining mastery in the transference between birth and death. Because it is subsequently construed as a mistaken or unmistaken cause, it is not a cause that exists independently. Therefore there is no fault.

[Query:] Well then, a bodhisattva who abides on a [spiritual] level (*sa*, *bhūmi*) negates mental afflictions and contaminated karma, and since it is said that "for one who has seen reality there is not projecting [activity], [and] for one who is free from craving there is not coming into existence,"[652] although attaining mastery, there is an appearance since it is an appearance of conditions, and therefore it is not feasible to take rebirth.

[Reply:] There is not a contradiction. Although destroying the connections of the [735.15] latencies of contaminated karma and afflictions, a bodhisattva, having relied on the mastery of birth by being accomplished in skillful means and wisdom, connects to existence with compassion by the force of the roots of virtue, does not transmigrate without conditions and skillful means, possesses the condition of a level of latencies of ignorance, [and] possesses the afflictions of a subtle conception attached to true existence of object and perceiver of the essence of things. With that conception, [a bodhisattva] has uncontaminated karma, which has joy in body and speech, taken in all places. He substitutes taking hold of craving with compassion, [735.20] takes up a mental body, and inconceivably transmigrates. As with all things, the appearances of mind are not essentially established as mind but are understood as the mere appearances of conditions. Wisdom is accomplished by being unpolluted with the connections to existence and the faults of existence. With skill-in-means, with a nature that is an appearance of mind, birthless like a reflection, having the nature of space, the appearances due to conditions are indicated as transmigrating through birth and death. This appearance of conditions through transforming the cause by attaining mastery in rebirth will not become a nonindependent illusion. Therefore, when one has the power to transform the cause, [735.25] since it is an independent illusion, because there is not a result overturned by a mistaken cause, [736] since it is nondeceiving at all times, it is not contradictory to be true/real.

[Query:] Well then, is there birth and death for the ordinary individual bodhisattva who resides on either the lesser, middling, or great path of accumulation or the path of preparation?

[Reply:] There is.

[Query:] Well then, how is that feasible if it is nondeceiving at all times?

[Reply:] In reply to that, when a cause is not refuted, an effect is not refuted. The manner in which both the isolated factor of nondeceiving at all times and the isolated factor of birth and death occurs are different. In not refuting the cause and effect of cyclic existence [736.5], of mistaken appearance of erroneous ignorance, birth and death occurs for the ordinary individual bodhisattva. When that does not occur, it passes as supermundane because it is free from the faults of cyclic existence. Although a supermundane cause is an unmistaken cause, there are the two faults of becoming a mistaken effect. Therefore, by not refuting the cause—igorance, karma, and mental afflictions—an effect is not able to overturn the suffering of cyclic existence. For this very reason, the ordinary individual bodhisattva has birth and death by not being free from the faults of cyclic existence; the appearance [736.10] is from the perspective of mistaken conventional reality. From the perspective of correct conventional reality, although there is birth and death for the ordinary individual bodhisattva, there is not essentially established birth and death, as it is birth and death of mere appearance since the cause has not been refuted.

[Query:] Well then, what is the difference from a bodhisattva who resides on the [spiritual] levels?

[Reply:] The bodhisattva who resides on the levels, having mastery over the cause, is an independently existent illusion and is characterized by correct conventional reality. The ordinary individual bodhisattva, not having mastery over the cause, is a nonindependent illusion that is characterized by mistaken conventional reality [736.15] because he is one who imputes correct conventional reality.

[Query:] Well then, how is possible for there to exist nonintrinsic birth and death as well as birth and death that is mere appearance?

[Reply:] The ordinary individual bodhisattva, although all things are unproduced, sees own-characteristics. She or he clearly sees the general characteristic for an object that is actually unproduced. It is like, for example, seeing a great illusory elephant. Although one clearly sees an illusory elephant, there is not an actual [elephant]. The bodhisattva who resides on the greater path of accumulation and path of preparation eliminates through invalidating conceptions that impute a self in two aspects. [736.20] Although there are latencies, by eliminating the actual cause, the two aspects of selflessness are actually seen. That is the way it is.

So much as that, the conceptualization that imputes the two extremes of permanence and nihilism does not occur because one realizes that birth and death are not essentially established and one refutes views for the two extemes. As birth and death are realized to lack intrinsic existence, in not refuting causes and conditions, appearances are understood as mere appearances. Therefore, it is stated that "there is birth and death that is the mere appearance of appropriate manifestations (*rang snang gi snang ba tsam*)." On this very topic [736.25] Ācārya Nāgārjunapāda has stated:

> Just as an illusory elephant appears to be born and perish, in actual reality, [737] there is neither birth nor perishing. Likewise, for a similar reason in the world, although it appears to arise and perish, in actual reality, there is not production and cessation.[653]

[Query:] Although the mere appearance of birth and death exists, as the cause is not overturned, the effect is not overturned, [and] since the effect at all times is nondeceiving, how it is feasible to be true/real?

[Reply:] Mistaken conventional reality accumulates causes and conditions due to imputing into the two extremes. In not refuting the suffering of cyclic existence, an effect due to imputing into two extremes, [737.5] birth and death that is essentially established is an appearance from the perspective of mistaken conventional reality.

From the perspective of correct conventional reality, appearances as birth and death, the suffering of cyclic existence, are effects of mere appearance arising from causes and conditions of mere appearance. Although there is not intrinsic birth and death, there is birth and death of mere appearance, which is understood as the mere appearance of conditions. While accepting a continuity of happiness from happiness and a partial concordance of that while not attaining mastery over the cause, when taking rebirth, by not overturning the cause, the effect is not overturned. [737.10] It is true/real, as it is nondeceptive at all times.

[Query:] Well then, there is not an actual experience of the meaning in meditation, as it is cut off by hearing and reflection. One produces the patience that is concordant with verbal conviction in the the lesser and middling path of accumulation, because one produces realization in a general manner of the lack of intrinsic existence, as there exists birth and death that is intrinsically established. Since it is not overturned, an effect is not overturned; how is it not true, as it is nondeceptive at all times?

[Reply:] At the time of residing in the prison of the six samsaric destinies, for one on the path lower than the highest mundane dharma, birth and death appear to be intrinsically established. [737.15] In not refuting mistaken conventional reality's cause and effect of cyclic existence, there are appearances from the perspective of mistaken appearances of ignorance. For appearances of discerning awareness, from the perspective of correct conventional reality, birth and death are not intrinsically established; that is construed as an object of understanding for [the wisdom arising from] study. Having cut the elaborations of the two extremes of reflective awareness, when ascertaining as mere appearance that is free from the two extremes, the essence of permanence is destroyed. The awareness [arising from] reflection is indicated as mere appearance that is free from the two extremes. When the experience occurs, like encountering a person one has previously met,[654] by refuting the extremes of permanence and annihilation, [737.20] birth and death is understood as mere appearance and is not understood to be intrinsically established.

Although it appears as birth and death by a mistaken cause, it is understood as mere appearance and ascertained as not intrinsically established as the continuity of happiness from happiness. Since it is mundane, although not attaining mastery over rebirth, one takes rebirth just as one offers up aspiration prayers and according to one's desires. Since it is merely a concordant factor with a powerful illusion, as the effect is not overturned since the cause is not overturned, it is feasible to be true/real at all times.

In these conditions, when there are not appearances of transmigrating birth and death, although a mistaken illusion of cyclic existence, the effect is overturned and [737.25], since it is free from the suffering of cyclic existence, there is the fault that it will become supermundane.

[738] Therefore, as a mistaken cause does not refute an effect, [there are] erroneous appearances of cyclic existence and of death, from the highest mundane dharma and below, [and] appearances [after the path of vision are] understood as mere appearance, the continuity of happiness from happiness, birth as one desires, and they are undeceiving at all times: it is true/real because if the cause is not overturned the effect will not be overturned. The explanation of the object [indicated by] the words "true/real of correct conventional reality" [is] present at all times.

In this way, the nature, characteristics, and objects [indicated by] [738.5] the words "correct conventional reality" have been explained in detail in order to describe correct conventional reality. A brief account of the preceding explanation of conventional reality is concluded.

[2. Explanation of Ultimate Reality (*don dam bden pa bshad pa*)]

The characteristics of ultimate reality: it is without characteristics since it is inexpressible due to being beyond referents (*tha snyad kyi yul*) and not being an object of words or thoughts. One cannot attain the meaning through teaching.

> I bow down to the mother of the Victors of the three times, [738.10] the Perfection of Wisdom, who is ineffable, inconceivable, unutterable, unborn, unceasing, the essence of space, in the scope of individually intuited awareness.[655]

Lord Atiśa has stated, "The realm of reality, the nonconceptual abode, is pristine wisdom (*jñāna*)." Thus conventional expressions are exhausted, but the pristine wisdom that realizes this is not asserted.

The pure nature is the realm of reality. One negates through examining with reasoning to attain the antidote. Through overturning all causes without exception, the effect, appearance, loosens its own bonds.[656] All things within cyclic exisence and *nirvāṇa* are included within one's own mind.[657] When the mind loosens its own bonds, there are not two minds. When this single mind loosens its own bonds, any remainder does not appear. There is not at all an appearance other than [738.15] the mere loosening of its own bonds. When appearance occurs as a single cause, there is the loosening of its own bonds. Because there is not even the mere convention of the two realities of loosening its own bonds, the *Sarvadharmaprakṛti-asaṃbhedanirdeśasūtra* states:

> When the realm of reality is taken as authoritative, then there is neither conventional reality nor ultimate reality.[658]

In this regard, as one is not able to arrive directly at the ultimate through words because it lies outside conventional discourse, *The Sūtra on the Teaching of the Licchavi Vimalakīrti* states:

> The Son of the Victorious One did not say anything at all. In not speaking, he made an extensive explanation. Why? Because there is not anything at all that serves as an object of expression for that.[659] [738.20]

A praise composed by the Ācārya Nāgārjuna, the *Stutyatītastava* (*'das par bstan pa*), states:

> For the sake of eliminating all views, O Protector, you taught [things] as empty. In this regard, as that is imputed, you did not declare it to be substantial, O Protector.[660]

As all appearances and imputations do not pass beyond the mind, when the mind unloosens its bonds, even saying "the mind unloosens its bonds" is not established. If it is established, as it does not pass beyond appearances and imputations, the mind would not loosen its own bonds. It would be a sphere of loosening its own bonds with intrinsic nature. That is [738.25] negated when examined with reasoning. When the mind overturns the cause by the antidote, it unloosens its own bonds of great ignorance, [the mind and] the very ignorance itself both become one taste in [739] becoming the realm of reality. There are no differences in loosening its own bonds. It is without characteristics, as it is not at all established. If a characteristic existed, that which is characterized and the characteristic would be established. If it is the case that a cause is established or a cause occurs, a mind would loosen its own bonds by not passing beyond the conventional reality of the mind's great ignorance. A *sūtra* states,

> All these are false, imaginary notions; one falsely imagines that the nonreal is real, that the inexistent is existent, that things that are not produced [739.5] and unborn are real and produced.[661]

As it is not at all established from the perspective of the mind loosening its own bonds, it is free from all characteristics. As it is not established, the characteristic of ultimate reality cannot be posited or defined. A sūtra states,

> Mañjuśrī, there is nothing at all seen in the essence of awakening.

Not produced of causes and conditions, as things are nonappearances, selfless, the mind unloosens itself. The Lord Atiśa has stated,

> Not reliant on a cause that is produced, not in contact with a condition that is established, its own-nature appears as unobserved, that is said [739.10] to be ultimate reality.

The Ācārya Āryadeva has stated,

> He who has no position stating existence, nonexistence, and [both] existence and nonexistence cannot ever be criticized.[662]

> This wisdom that sees the nature of all things is the very same wisdom that is explained as awareness, that should be cultivated nonconceptually.[663]

Thus it is in accordance with not establishing the thesis "the emptiness that is free from the two extremes." Even the wisdom that realizes this is not established, as it is like a fire that arises from two sticks rubbed together, and having burned, the fire itself subsides.[664] [739.15] At that time, all cognition and objects of cognition are pacified, and the mind unloosens its own bonds as the great darkness of elaborations disappear. [At that time,] all things are nonappearances without appearance; [they are] pure appearances, like the center of pure space. As it does not conventionally exist, ultimate reality does not have characteristics. Therefore one cannot teach "this is the characteristic of ultimate reality."

[Query:] Well then, if one is not able to teach ultimate reality, how will buddhahood be gained in not understanding through the absence of understanding and not meditating in the absence of meditating?

[Reply:] The Ārya Nāgārjuna has stated:

> Without relying on conventions, the ultimate [739.20] meaning cannot be taught. Without relying on the ultimate meaning, *nirvāṇa* will not be attained.[665]

Thus [ultimate reality] is to be taught through mere conventions. In this way, although the actual ultimate cannot be indicated, it is suitable to indicate an ultimate conventionally. The Ācārya himself does not accept a thesis. He utilizes only nonimplicative negations.

[Query:] Well then, is this nonimplicative negation an ultimate?

[Reply:] Any dharma that is nonimplicatedly negated is not established. There is not anything other than merely the loosening of the bonds of delusion. Therefore, since a thesis is not accepted [739.25], [Nāgārjuna states:]

> If I had any thesis, then I would suffer from this fault. [But as I have no theses,] I alone am without fault.[666]

[Query:] If a thesis is not accepted even conventionally [740], then how is the [ultimate] conventionally indicated?

[Reply:] It is indicated by means of nonimplicative negation.

The *Prajñāmūla* states:

> Not known through others, peaceful, unelaborated by elaborations, without differentiation, without conceptual thought: these are the characteristics of reality.[667]

[740.5] Five characteristics of ultimate reality are taught: individually intuited knowledge (*so so rang gis rig par bya ba*), the pacification of all general and specific characteristics, inexpressible as it is beyond all speech and thought, all things within cyclic existence and *nirvāṇa* have the single taste of suchness, and all conceptions that are imputed cease.[668] The *Small Middle-Way Dependent-Arising* states:

> There is nothing at all to be removed here. There is nothing to be established.[669]

The appearances of various stains of reified errors are like a person with distorted vision seeing hairs in space. Since they are not known from the very beginning, as there is nothing to remove, the text says, "there is nothing at all to be removed here." Since phenomena do not exist as appearances, are selfless, actually abide, and are established from the beginning like space, by way of [740.10] awarenesses, antidotes, and the path, what is previously nonexistent is later achieved, [and] as it is impossible to establish, the text says, "There is nothing to be established."

As appearances of phenomena do not exist, they are selfless objects. One may think it is unnessary to establish since it is an ever-present fact, and one may wonder if it is neccesary to remove, since this appearance, as various stains of reified errors, is not known to exist from the beginning. The pristine wisdom of the realm of reality is a selfless object, a dharma without appearance, like space, an ever-present object to oneself. Since it is like space, [and] it is proper to achieve, it should be achieved without conceptuality. [740.15] These appearances as various stains of reified errors, since they are not known to exist from the beginning, are suitable to remove. [They are] also necessary to remove since they are actual obstructions. The Lord Atiśa has stated:

> Speaking about someone with distorted vision who sees hair in the sky—there is no difference between one with distorted vision and all beings.

For example, an old woman struck with eye disease had a son who went for trade in another kingdom.[670] A daughter-in-law offered to cook rice gruel for the old woman. The old woman saw the bowl full of hair, [and thought that she] would become sick by eating. The son returned, [and asked,] What is it old mother? [The old woman replied,] "This wife of yours, it would be better if I die [740.20] than being offered a bowl full of hair. I will go away from such as this." The son, thinking this was true, spoke to his wife. [The wife stated,] "Son, you yourself brought and cooked the rice gruel." The son, thinking it would be better, [decided to] destroy the rice gruel that was full of hair. At that time, the son understood [the old woman] to be ensnared by the distorted vision of eye disease. Showing the cooked rice gruel to the mother, [he asked,] "Does this hair exist or not exist?" [She replied,] "It exists." [The son replied,] "Well then, I will dig a hole and bury the rice under the ground, not showing it to other people." Then a skillful doctor was summoned. Medicine to cure sickness was ingested. [740.25] By applying external medicine that clears away distorted vision in the eye, the old woman became free of the distorted-vision eye disease. Then the mother [741], prompted to consider the existence or nonexistence of hair in the rice gruel that had upset her, saw that the hair did not exist. The disease of the old woman was the dirt in her eyes. As the hair in the cooked rice did not actually exist, it is suitable to establish that the hair did not exist. The old woman's eye disease of distorted vision, which saw hair in cooked rice as existent, must also be established as mistaken and defiled. Likewise the realm of reality, pristine wisdom that is selfless, is suitable to realize as an ever-present object. [741.5] It also must be realized nonconceptually. Again, in the example, since the error of seeing hair was obviously momentary, it is suitable to remove. As one's vision is obscured from seeing the hair as nonexistent, and since the bowl full of hair is a mistaken perception, it is necessary to clear away the obstruction. Likewise, appearances as various stains of reified mistakes are suitable to remove since they are not known to exist from the beginning. It is necessary to remove the actual obstruction. In this way, in stating, "There is nothing at all to be removed here, there is nothing to be established," the [741.10] characteristic of ultimate reality is shown to be neither removed nor established. The natural state of ultimate reality is suitable to achieve; it must be achieved.

[Query:] When removing mistakes, how are they removed?

[Reply:] It is said, the method that removes mistakes and realizes ultimate reality is being correct for true reality. The realm of reality, a naturally pure object, is the true state of things. When viewing these, one views with the supreme all-knowing wisdom that distinguishes objects of knowledge.

[Query:] How is it that [741.15] one views just as it is the object of reality?

[Reply:] All things should be viewed as nonappearance, without appearance, a pure appearance like the center of the pure sky. When viewing having relied on method, one views through relying on the context of correct conventional reality that does not occur without the dependent-arising of the method of the stages of the path of the three types of individuals. On the stages of the path one has theoretical understanding through the wisdom that arises from hearing. [One] has ascertainment through the awareness that arises through reflection. Through the awareness that arises from meditation, by meditating one-pointedly, by practicing the conditions of the three wisdoms for the stages of the path of the three individuals, the staircase of correct conventional reality [741.20], which does not occur without the dependent-arising of method, like applying medicine that removes distorted vision for cataracts, one opens the eyes of the three wisdoms by removing cataracts and the distorted vision of ignorance by applying the eye medicine of the three wisdoms. The appearance of discerning awareness appears, and through method, the staircase of correct conventional reality, the stages of the path occur as antidotes to the three poisons of the afflictions. Then, one's own mind appears as path consciousness of the three roots of virtue indivisible from the path of accumulation. It is like ingesting medicine that demolishes disease [741.25]. Through purifying mental afflictions and karma that exist in the mental continuum, through overcoming the causes [742], the effects, and the erroneous and mistaken appearances of suffering that take rebirth, in loosening these bonds they are cut. This is like loosening the bond of hairs by being free from the distorted vision of eye disease. In this way, [in] seeing, through the three wisdoms and through relying on method, the stairway of correct conventional reality, and by overturning the cause, the effect of mistaken appearance loosens its own bonds, and there is the natural clear appearance of the object of nonappearance, selflessness. It is like, for example, the natural clear appearance of space after the five overlays of space have been removed [742.5]. In this way, the mere loosening of the mind's own bonds is called "seeing reality."

The benefit of realizing the ultimate: "When seeing reality, one is liberated."[671] One is liberated from karma, afflictions, and rebirth; as the Ācārya Nāgārjuna has stated, "Liberation is by exhausting karma and afflictions."[672]

[Query:] Well then, as it is sufficient to meditate on only emptiness, lower meditations do not have any purpose, the Ācārya Nāgārjuna states:

> One is liberated by exhausting karma and mental afflictions. Karma and afflictions are [742.10] fabricated by elaborations from conceptuality, and those come to cessation in emptiness.[673]

[Reply:] Because it is the stairway of correct conventional reality and because the stages of the path of the three individuals does not occur without the dependent-arising of method, the Ācārya Bhāviveka has stated,

> Without the stairway of correct convention, a wise man cannot ascend to the top of the palace of reality.[674]

The Ācārya Nāgārjuna has also stated,

> To those who seek reality, at first, one should state, "Everythings exists." When they have understood reality [742.15] and have become detached, one then later declares things as isolated (*viviktatā*).[675]

In this way, just that meaning that clarifies the characteristic of ultimate reality and demonstrates that it is not established is also stated by Candrakīrti:

> The mistaken natures that are conceived as hairs and so forth due to distorted vision will be seen correctly by one with clear vision. It should be understood that suchness of reality is the same.[676]

While hair descends from the sky for one with distorted vision, when seeing with clear vision the true nature of the hair, the hair is not seen at all according to the four extremes of existence, nonexistence, both [existence and nonexistence], and neither [existence nor nonexistence]. [742.20] The pure nature of the hair is seen. There is not a difference between the appearance as hair and the pure nature of the hair. The mistaken cause—ignorance, karma, and afflictions—appears as various stains of reified error.

When the mistaken causes—ignorance, karma, and the afflictions—are purified, the stains of the reified errors are, like the hair after seeing is purified of distorted vision, [seen as] pure by nature and seen as the mere loosening of its own bonds, [and] the extremes of existence or nonexistence do not appear. The error and the pure nature of error [742.25] are not different. Therefore, by seeing the hair, one sees the suchness of the hair. By seeing the error as naturally pure [743], one sees the suchness of the error. That which is produced under the power of distorted vision appears in the aspect of hair to one with distorted vision. Likewise, that which is produced by the power of aspiration is conceived as manifold by the trainees' mind. Therefore whatever entity is produced from self, other, both, without a cause, or from a deity, that is produced from the power of conditions.

The Lord Atiśa [743.5] has stated:

> There is no difference between one with distorted vision who sees hair in the sky and those with distorted conceptuality who see

> the world. One should meditate on all entities without exception as imputed with conceptuality, whose nature is equivalent to the sky.[677]

This teaching by way of the example of hair appearing for one with the distorted vision of mistaken appearance is of great importance for Ācārya [Nāgārjuna] and Candrakīrti, [spiritual] father and son, the sole deity Lord [Atiśa], and the above-mentioned spiritual teachers.

When searching for the intrinsic nature of the appearance that is like seeing hair in the sky of one with distorted vision, the mere not finding of it is the loosening of its own bonds. [743.10] In regard to elaborations on the characteristics of ultimate reality, *The Small Text on the Realities* states:

> In that [ultimate reality], there is neither seeing nor seer, but peace without beginning or end. (v. 7cd) [Reality is] devoid of entity and nonentity, free from conceptions, free from objects, without support, without basis, without coming or going, unexemplified, (v. 8) ineffable, invisible, unchanging, and unconditioned.[678]

The very same text also states:

> When the conventional that appears is analytically examined just as it is, nothing whatsoever is found. The unfindable is itself the ultimate and the nature of reality abiding from the beginning.[679]

[Query:] When the appearances of the nature of reality are loosened [743.15], what is this appearance?

[Reply:] As it is merely the appearance of conditions when it is produced by causes and conditions, in this way the conventional is established as appearance. Although it does not intrinsically exist, the causes and conditions are not refuted.

[Query:] One may think: Is it suitable for there to be an appearance of conditions when there is not intrinsic existence?

[Reply:]

> If it were impossible to establish it, by whom would the moon in water and the like be produced?[680]

Although not intrinsically existent, it is not contrary for things to be produced by causes and conditions.

[Query:] One may wonder if the reversal of cyclic existence comes about this way.

[Reply:]

> If the continuance of conditions is interrupted, it does not arise even conventionally.[681]

Thus, since the cause is overturned, one does not create mistaken cyclic existence. In regard to the characteristic of ultimate reality [743.20], the Ācārya Akṣayamati states:

> When the entity that one conceives "it does not exist" is not known, then how would the negation, without any support, remain before the mind?[682]
>
> When neither an entity nor nonentity remain before the mind, then, because there is no other aspect [to observe], the [mind] is pacified without any apprehension.[683]

As it is taught:

> When the object of negation is not established, the negation will not be established, and when the object is not established, the subject is not established.[684]

The *Yuktiṣaṣṭikā* states:

> With no basis and no object of observation, with no root and no foundation, totally arisen from the cause [743.25]—ignorance; bereft of beginning, middle, and end, essenceless—like a plantain [tree]—resembling [744] a fairy city, an unbearable city of confusion, the universe appears like an illusion.[685]

With these words, it is taught that the Ācārya Nāgārjuna, at the time of producing the path of vision in the great city of Saketa [Ayodhya], stated, "I see the nature of things that is ultimate reality, the unmistaken seeing of pristine wisdom."

As the governing condition (*bdag po'i rkyen* ≈ **adhipatipratyaya*) is [not][686] established for the six sense faculties, it is has no basis. As the observed object condition (*dmigs pa'i rkyen* ≈ **ālambanapratyaya*) is not established in the object, there is no object of observation. [744.5] As the causal condition (*rgyu'i rkyen*) does not establish a basis-of-all, there is no root. As the consciousness that is produced by these three [conditions] is not established, there is no foundation. If a basis exists, the universe (*'gro ba ≈ jagat*) exists. As [a basis] does not exist, [the universe] does not exist; a continuum is established for the universe. Because this universe that passes on (*'gro du 'gro ba*) is produced from causes and conditions, it lacks intrinsic existence.

[Query:] How does it lack intrinsic existence?

[Reply:] The text states "bereft of beginning, middle, and end." Unproduced in the beginning, without foundation in the middle, without cessation at the end, the mind loosens its own bonds.

[Query:] If there is not intrinsic existence, what is it that appears?

[Reply:] The text states, "totally arisen from the cause—ignorance." This appearance, the effect of ignorance, appears from the errors of one's own mind [744.10]. As this appearance is an appearance due to conditions, it lacks intrinsic nature. Furthermore, ignorance appears as mistaken errors, but non-errors do not appear. Since it is like a person with distorted vision who sees hairs in the sky, there is not intrinsic nature.

[Query:] One may think, how do we know that this mistaken appearance of the six types of transmigrators [in cyclic existence], which arises from the cause of ignorance, is true/real if it arises from a cause of ignorance?

[Reply:] This mistaken appearance of the six types of transmigrators [in cyclic existence], because it is perceived as having an essence even though it is essenceless, like the essence of a plaintain tree, arises from the cause of ignorance. Furthermore, this mistaken appearance of the universe resembles a fairy city. [744.15] Because it appears as real when it is unreal, it arises from the cause of ignorance. The text states, "Essenceless—like a plantain [tree]—resembling a fairy city." Due to ignorance, since there arises a city of mistaken appearance of transmigrators through the cause of confusion, the text states, "unbearable city of confusion." Since it is difficult to overturn the arising of harm and difficult for one to realize being obscured by the darkness of ignorance, it is unbearable. It is deceitful (*ma rungs ba*). Because any comfort that exists disintegrates, it is unbearable. Karma is deceitful (*las ma rungs pa*). As it abides with suffering that disintegrates, [744.20] and due to afflictions, there is not comfort; it is unbearable.

Alternatively, to expain the three one by one. Buddhas and bodhisattvas who perceive the supreme, who are devoid of mistaken ignorance, perceive this mistaken appearance of the universe, which appears as real and having an essence, as unproduced like an illusion. As the Ācārya Nāgārjuna teaches that the universe is perceived [in a manner] similar to [the perception of] an illusion, the text states, "the universe appears like an illusion." In this way, because the universe is dependently produced, it lacks intrinsic nature.

[Query:] One may think, because [the universe] arises from the cause of ignorance and is a mistaken appearance [744.25], it is not established that buddhas and bodhisattvas perceive [the universe] as unproduced, like an illusion. What about Ācārya Nāgārjuna? [745]

[Reply:] He has taught, "As for me, it is perceived accordingly."

Therefore with respect to which is it empty? The true nature of one's own mind is empty. As it is said, "There is nothing at all to be removed here. There is nothing to be established."

> Whether it is suitable that a buddha arises or does not arise, the true nature of dharma remains as suchness.[687]

Further, a sūtra states: "There is not thought; the nature of thought is clear light."[688]

[Query:] Of what is it empty?

[Reply:] One's own mind itself is empty of this appearance [745.5] of various stains that are reified mistakes. The *Ratnāvalī* explains that one should understand that the minds of existence are minds of great ignorance. As the mind itself appears as all things within cyclic existence and *nirvāṇa*:

> Appearances as mere appearance are empty and elemental forces are only ignorance. The instrinsic nature of entities does not exist. The speculative reasoning that becomes conceptual thought when cultivated as mere imputation does not intrinsically exist and is without cognition. Entities do not exist and the basis-of-all does not exist. These are conceived by childish beings.[689]
>
> Self-awakened buddhas and buddhas [745.10] and mental afflictions are imputed. The continuum of the person, aggregates, and conditions does not abide. The principal, God, and a creator are conceived from the mind only. All things do not exist with intrinsic natures. The thoroughly afflicted and liberation are not as they appear. There is not nonexistence, there is not existence. This true nature of things that is nonarising is neither an existent nor a nonexistent.[690]

Therefore, this mistaken mind is empty.

[Query:] How is it empty?

[Reply:] It is empty from the very beginning. It is empty of a past limit, empty of a future limit. It is empty of any entity that is produced, perdures, or perishes. [745.15] This is an entity that is neither existent nor nonexistent. As it said, "All things are empty of intrinsic nature."

> The body produced by the elements is bound by the mind. The elements are active without the mind. Therefore protect the mind at all times. Buddhas arise from a calm and pure mind.[691]

The nature of things that is the mind unloosening its own bonds is suchness at the time of understanding and complete realization. Since it is suchness also at the time of nonunderstanding and mistaken realization, an intrinsic nature does not arise during realization or nonrealization. Nonexistence is not fabricated as existent. The mind unloosening its own bonds is suchness. [745.20] Therefore it is empty from the very beginning. The nature of emptiness is like space. The *Bodhicittavivaraṇa* states,

> Sentient beings who are devoid of support have the mark of space. The cultivation of space is the cultivation of emptiness.[692]

In the *Chapter on Bodhisattva Sadāprarudita*, the Bodhisattva Dharmodgata (*chos 'phags*) taught that "cultivating space is cultivating the perfection of insight." Space is free from aspects, without position, extremes, or a middle, and [745.25] what is called space is an object not established in any way. Likewise, when the mind loosens its own bonds, a dual mind does [746] not exist. When this single [mind] loosens its own bonds, all things are without elaborations and abide not established at all. When there is a single accomplishment, the mind loosens its own bonds. In this way, from the perspective of the mind loosening its own bonds, as it is free from all aspects of positions, extremes, and without a middle, the example is like space.

> Sentient beings call that "seeing space." Through examining this meaning of how to see space, in this manner, the Tathāgata [746.5] indicates seeing dharma as well. [This type of] seeing is not relatable through another example. One who sees in this manner sees all things.[693]

All examined characteristics and conceptual thought without exception are negated, and all objects, subjects, emptiness, and the wisdom that realizes [emptiness] do not pass beyond one's own mind. When the mind unloosens its own bonds, as all cognitions and that which is cognized loosens its own bonds, there is nothing other than the loosening of the bonds and being free from all conventions.

> For the sake of eliminating all views, O Protector, you taught [things] as empty. [746.10] In this regard, as that is imputed, you did not declare it to be substantial, O Protector. You are not pleased by asserting empty, nonempty, [and] both. There can be no argument about that—this is the action of your great utterance.[694]

Rubbing two sticks together, fire arises, and having burned, the fire itself subsides. That to be examined is not established, the wisdom that realizes is not established, and the mind loosens its own bonds with the disappearance of the darkness of elaborations. The purpose of emptiness is to unobstructedly care for sentient beings. The Ācārya Nāgārjuna states:

> [746.15] Accordingly, when yogis cultivate emptiness, the mind no doubt will become joyful for the purpose of benefitting others.[695]

The nature of things with wisdom is seen as space and one unobstructedly cares for sentient beings of the three spheres of existence. By way of the remembrance of kindness, in dependence on gratitude, one cultivates love, compassion, and the mind of awakening. By realizing emptiness, a state of compassion arises in oneself for sentients beings who have not realized, and one unobstructedly cares for sentient beings.

The purport of this principle is that one exhausts all karmic obscurations by means of the four powers and through offering up the unbearable [746.20] sickness of sentient beings. Applying oneself in the uncorrupted vows that have been taken, [uncorrupted in] not even the least bit of a sesame husk,[696] and in dependence on gathering the two accumulations without being satisfied, one should repeatedly practice meditation. When dedicating the roots of virtue to great awakening, one apprehends the great nonobjectifying insight (*mi dmigs pa'i shes rab*), and because one apprehends the result, this is called energetically offering up various aspirational prayers. As it is said:

> Although one is powerless to benefit others, one perpetually thinks of them. One who has the [altruistic] thought for others [746.25] engages in the purpose of helping others.

One should have the earnest desire to help others. The purpose of realizing emptiness [747] is to eliminate the two obscurations, as the two obscurations must be eliminated.

From the perspective of the present moment, cultivating emptiness is a factor as an antidote to the three poisons of the afflictions. One must not turn into a vessel that apprehends things as substantially existent, a friend of the afflictions. In intensifying the determination to meditate with a small amount of endurance, to see oneself as doing well when going astray and degenerating is a mistake. It is vital to turn toward the Dharma. Through cultivating emptiness, emptiness may or may not become an antitdote for the afflictions. [747.5] The vital point is to pay attention to one's own mind.

> O Fearless One, what need to tell you more? This is the real beneficial advice: The vital point is to tame your mind, for, as the Buddha taught, mind is the root of dharma.[697]

Abolish the two obscurations by meditating on emptiness, as one is unable to eliminate [them] from the root by any other way of abolishing. This sevenfold [meditation posture, meditating] on emptiness, cultivates the quality of loosening the bonds of one's own mind, and realizes the nature of things without anything being removed or anything being established. As it is said in this context:

> Here, what exists to remove? There is not anything at all to establish. [747.10]

[III. Three Wondrous Qualities of Practice (*ngo mtshar can gyi spyod pa gsum*)]

Atiśa has taught that the stairway of correct conventional reality, which does not occur without the dependent-arising of method, the stages of the path of the three individuals, this advice of meditating on the two realities as indivisible, has three wondrous qualities of practice.

The great bodhisattvas who reside on the levels, like Avalokiteśvara or Mañjuśrī, in meditative equipoise, realize all things are like the center of space. With postmeditative awareness they realize all things are like the eight similes of illusion. If one thinks that the deeds of bodhisattvas [747.15] are not suitable, as it is pointless to perform exhalted deeds, the great waves of activity of nonretrogressing bodhisattvas do not forsake the vividness of the sense faculties. This engagement in not forsaking the purity of ancillary practices is wondrous.

In this way, the stairway of correct conventional reality, which does not occur without the three individuals, this advice that cultivates the two realities as indivisible, realizes in meditative equipoise [that things] are like space, and in the postmeditative state realizes [that things] are like illusions. Turning away from the contempt that cause and effect do not exist, one does not waste even a strand of hair of one's deeds, [747.20] as cause and effect is not feasible if intrinsically established. Although not at all established, as it is free from the two extremes, as this mere appearance of the mind is an appearance through conditions, the appearance is not an object of negation by reasoning. The appearance, by not negating, is an unnegated cause. What is the purpose of the path if it does not exist? Cause and effect is nondeceptive. Thus this engagement with persevering in cause and effect coming into being is even more wondrous than the previous point.

Cause and effect is true even though it does not intrinsically exist. It is not practical to posit cause and effect if it is intrinsically established. [747.25] It is like the eight similes of illusion that, even though they do not intrinsically exist, are appearances due to conditions. This appearance, [748] although it does not intrinsically exist, is an appearance of conditions. As cause and effect are feasible since it is a mere appearance, it is realized in meditative equipoise to be like space. Through realizing in the postmeditative state [that things] are like illusions, one generates an acute ascertainment of causality, and by renouncing contempt for effects, one comes to a uniquely characterized earnest engagement with causality. This is a wondrous practice. Precisely this meaning has been stated by Ācārya Nāgārjuna:

> One's own body to be given away does not produce wonder, [748.5] but having understood this dharma as empty, to state "the effect of karma exists" is even more wondrous than wonder, even more amazing than amazement.[698]

Through mind training that emptiness is like an illusion, if having little concern for causes and effects, misunderstanding arises. This is to indulge in musings (*rtog pa skye ba*) and deprecate the meaning with worldly wrong views. It is to view wrongly and obliterate wholesome roots of virtue. It is like an arrow shot downward to the hell-beings of Avīci Hell and the Hell of Intense Heat. [748.10] Demons emerge by cultivating emptiness. When thinking to perform fabricated actions, one accumulates very frightful, unwholesome deeds. The one seeking liberation and omniscience dies not even hearing the name of the higher heavenly realms. The *Prajñāmūla* states,

> If their view of emptiness is wrong, those of little wisdom will be hurt. Like a wrongly held snake, or a spell wrongly cast.[699]

The *Madhyamaka Ratnāvalī* states:

> If this doctrine is not well understood, it causes ruin for unskillful people, since they also sink into the impurity of nihilism.[700] [748.15]

By considering cause and effect to be true/real even though it lacks intrinsic existence and is similar to an illusion, one produces a special conviction that is earnestly attached to cause and effect. This is a wondrous quality of practice.

Moreover, those *ārya śrāvakas* and *pratyekabuddhas* who enter into the sphere of peace, being exhorted with rays of light by the exalted minds of buddhas and bodhisattvas, produce the mind for awakening, and having gathered the two accumulations, have great joy in attaining buddhahood. As it is taught:

> Although not continually hindered to transmigrate in hell, the levels of *śrāvakas* [748.20] and *pratyekabuddhas* are blocked from unsurpassable awakening [of full buddhahood].

Thus, even though it is extremely difficult, they become irreversible and, gathering the accumulations, produce the mind [for awakening] and attain buddhahood. This is an especially great wondrous quality. On this point the Ācārya Nāgārjuna has stated:

> As long as these *śrāvakas* are not exhorted to become buddhas, for that long they reside with bodies of wisdom arrogantly intoxicated with concentration. When exhorted, they joyfully pursue the welfare of sentient beings in various forms, and expanding their merit and wisdom [748.25], they will attain the awakening of buddhahood.[701]

Therefore, cultivating the stairway of correct conventional reality, which does not occur [749] without the dependent-arising of means, the stages of the path of the three types of individuals, meditating on the faults of cyclic existence, having seen cyclic existence to be like a prison, a wild forest, a whirlwind of fire, or an executioner's sword consumed with flames, distress and deep sickness occurs for the entirety of cyclic existence and one is taught to have an uncommon mind stricken with terror (*'jigs shing skrag pa ≈ bhayabhīta*). [As Nāgārjuna states:]

> Give up your efforts trying to stop all this [749.5], as if your hair or clothes had just caught fire. Just do your best to not be born again. No greater goal or need is there than this.[702]

Distressed with cyclic existence and suffering through the desire to attain liberation and *nirvāṇa*, an individual of stable mind, a being of middling capacity[703] who has the great armor of effort, who has communicated with the spiritual friend endowed with skillful means, who has himself experienced the suffering and wandering in endless cyclic existence since it is exactly the same suffering experienced by all sentient beings, one has intense compassion, and *śrāvakas* also have merely that compassion. [749.10] Meditating on account of the basis of equanimity, one meditates on the faults of acting for one's own welfare and the benefits of acting for the welfare of others. Holding from the base [sentient beings as like one's] mother, one cultivates gratitude to bring benefit many times to all mother-like sentient beings. Through viewing sentient beings as one's own mother, their great kindness is inconceivable; from the perspective of mistaken perception, there is no escape. By meditating without a method for enduring, from the perspective of suffering, an awareness of gratitude emerges that considers that it is necessary to benefit others in response to that extremely unbearable [suffering] [749.15] by considering how one may benefit [them]. In considering that worldly happiness is of no benefit, one trains the mind in love that desires to establish [beings] in unsurpassable happiness. In the desire to establish that, as it is necessary to liberate [them] from suffering, one trains the mind in compassion that aspires to liberate [them]. Since one is powerless to liberate sentient beings from suffering unless attaining buddhahood, one trains the mind in the jewel-like mind of awakening that aspires to attain buddhahood for the welfare of sentient beings. When that has been stabilized, with great compassionate awareness that does not have concern for oneself but is only for the welfare of others, the armor of effort arises and [749.20] one states, "These worldly powerless afflictions are unable to achieve one's own purpose; this is their single essence." This is pride due to karma. This great pride that is like a beloved only son arises, and the recollection that does forget sentient beings at any time considers them [to be] like one's parents. One who considers carrying the burden of beings must have armor for the great burden of sentient beings. That supreme being goes slowly, [in] a lineage of making a hundredfold effort for the various bonds of oneself and others, [749.25] a hundredfold greater armor than the armor of effort of *śrāvakas* previously taught arises, and one's awareness becomes concerned only with the welfare of others. [750] When accustomed to a lineage like this, taking joy to pacify the suffering of others, one even enters into Avīci Hell like a goose into a lake of lotuses.[704] The *śrāvakas* and *pratyekabuddhas* who dwell in the sphere of peace, exorted by the light from the heart-minds of buddhas and bodhisattvas, generate the aspiration for awakening, gather the accumulations, and then attain buddhahood. In indicating the being of middling capacity—having seen cyclic existence to be like an executioner brandishing a flaming sword [750.5], [one] arrives at seeking peace and happiness for oneself. Changing one's mind for the welfare of others is extremely difficult, for one is harmed by the suffering of cyclic existence. *Śrāvakas* and *pratyekabuddhas* are not harmed by the suffering of cyclic existence.

Well then, training the mind to not turn back on difficulties in dependence on the condition of the spiritual friend endowed with skillful means, having the great compassion that engages in only the welfare of others without concern for oneself, this is a greater wonder than even the previous [wonders]. In this way is the second wondrous practice.

Further, bodhisattvas who reside on the levels, the great beings, Avalokiteśvara, [750.10] Mañjuśrī, and so forth, in meditative equipoise realize that all things are like space. In postmeditative awareness, through realizing [that all things] are not different than the eight similes of illusion, through previously cultivated compassion for sentient beings without realization, without concern for themselves, having gone into the hell realms, [bodhisattvas] accomplish welfare in hell, [and] having gone into the realm of hungry ghosts, accomplish welfare for hungry ghosts. Likewise they accomplish [the welfare of others] in all six realms of rebirth. These bodhisattvas realize that the basis of cyclic existence is intrinsically empty (*rang stong pa*) and like an illusion. Erroneous, mistaken cyclic existence, a burning fire of suffering [750.15], is unnessary to engage in and is not a place for engagement. That bodhisattva who engages in the welfare of sentient beings while not turning back is a great wonder. The Ācārya Nāgārjuna states:

> The goal of awakening, like a fruit, arises from the seed, the mind of awakening, made firm by the root of compassion. The cultivations of the Conqueror's children, by means of cultivating these practices firmly, casting away even the bliss of concentration, in not enduring the suffering of others they enter into even Avīci Hell.[705]

The same text also states:

> With thoughts to protect sentient beings, taking rebirth in the swamp of conditioned existence, [750.20] like a lotus in mud, untainted by the faults of conditioned existence, in this, the Conqueror's children, such as Bhadra, with the fire of wisdom scorch the mental afflictions like kindling, but nevertheless are moistened with compassion.[706]

That is a great wonder. More than that, my two realities, by cultivating the stairway of correct conventional reality, which does not occur without the dependent-arising of the means, the stages of the path of the three individuals, in dependence on love, compassion, and the mind of awakening, one states:

> They are bound by not being liberated from the extent of their own bonds. As they do not overturn [them] because they are harmed by suffering and incapable, in [750.25] liberating all sentient beings from the suffering of cyclic existence, I must establish them in unsurpassable [751] awakening.

Thus, having taken the spiritual friend and the Three Jewels as witnesses, one engages in an uncommon degree of pledges from the depths of one's heart. This is an even greater wonder than the previous [wonders]. This is able to be harmed by suffering. The great bodhisattvas are not harmed by suffering. They have potency in carrying out actions for the benefit of others. They actualize the essential nature of all things.

[IV. Conclusion (*mjug gi don bshad pa*)]

In this way, my stages of the path, [751.5] this special advice on the two realities, due to its wonders, is endowed with the threefold analysis. This is a speech by Atiśa.

Part 3
How Mādhyamikas Meditate

5. Atiśa's *Special Instructions on the Middle Way* (*Madhyamakopadeśa*)

THE FOLLOWING CHAPTERS examine, and furnish translations for, the *Madhyamakopadeśa* of Atiśa, along with an Indian commentary by Prajñāmukti, the *Madhyamakopadeśavṛtti*, and a more extensive Tibetan commentary by an anonymous Kadampa author, entitled *Collection of Special Instructions on the Middle Way*.[707] The *Madhyamakopadeśavṛtti* is translated in its entirety for the first time in English,[708] and the *Collection of Special Instructions on the Middle Way* is identified for the first time as a commentary on Atiśa's *Madhyamakopadeśa*, as well as being an initial English translation. These three texts document the theory and practice of Madhyamaka during the early eleventh to twelfth century in Tibet as well as India. Although all three texts were composed in Tibet, the base text by Atiśa and the brief commentary (*vṛtti*) by Prajñāmukti were written by Indian authors initially in Sanskrit, while the *Collection of Special Instructions on the Middle Way* is by a Tibetan author. There are distinctions between how a text written by an Indian Buddhist was commented on by an Indian commentator such as Prajñāmukti, who was a contemporary of Atiśa, and by a later Tibetan commentator who belonged to the early twelfth-century lineage of Kadampa followers of Atiśa. In brief, Prajñāmukti is concise and to the point, providing the reader explanatory glosses on most of the words and phrases found in Atiśa's basic text. The anonymous Kadampa commentator, on the other hand, provides extended explanations to unpack the overall doctrinal meaning of Atiśa's text. The anonymous Tibetan author cites a number of well-known Kadampa figures with idiomatic Tibetan expressions in addition to referencing Indian Buddhist authors and sūtras.

The *Madhyamakopadeśa* is a brief text on the practice of Madhyamaka in meditation. The term *upadeśa* (special instructions) in the title of Atiśa's basic text has a long history in Indian Buddhism and different connotations over the centuries. As Étienne Lamotte has remarked in his study of the *Mahāprajñāpāramitāśāstra* (1970, 3: vii–viii), *upadeśa* is the name of the twelfth and last member of the "twelve-membered" word of the Buddha (*dvādaśāṅgabuddhavacana*) and generally signifies "instruction" or "teaching." A number of scholastic Indian Buddhist texts preserved in the Chinese Tripiṭaka have *upadeśa* in their title, such as the *upadeśa*s on the *Saddharmapuṇḍarīka* (Toh 1519, 1520), attributed to Vasubandhu. The Tibetan Tengyur has dozens of texts containing *upadeśa* in their titles. Atiśa wrote and translated several texts with *upadeśa* in the title, such as the *Sūtrārthasamuccayopadeśa* (*Mdo'i sde'i don kun las btus pa'i man ngag*, Toh 3957) and the *Ekasmṛtyupadeśa* (*Dran pa gcig pa'i man ngag*, Toh 3928). The term *upadeśa*, translated into Tibetan as either *gdams ngag* or *man ngag*, generally means, as Kapstein (1996, 275) notes, "the immediate, heartfelt instructions and admonitions of master to disciple concerning directly liberative insight and practice." The *Madhyamakopadeśa* is therefore special guidance or instructions concerning the practice of Middle Way philosophy. Several different lineages of this type of instruction and practice on Madhyamaka were brought into Tibet. Atiśa's lineage of the *Madhyamakopadeśa* was commented on at least up until the thirteenth century; Kyotön Mönlam Tsultrim (1219–99) wrote a brief text on this topic entitled *Explanation of Lord [Atiśa's] Middle Way Special Instructions* (*Jo bo rje'i dbu ma'i man ngag gi bshad pa*). Another lineage of similar instructions, *Guidance on the Great Middle Way* (*Dbu ma chen po'i khrid*), was brought into Tibet by Dawa Gyaltsen (twelfth century) (Kapstein 1996, 282). Chim Namkha Drak (1210–85), a Kadampa author, also wrote a commentary on this lineage of instruction entitled *Guidance on the Middle Way* (*Dbu ma'i khrid*), different from Atiśa's lineage. Other lineages of Middle Way practice instructions also existed in Tibet, and this genre of Middle Way instructions influenced later Tibetans scholars such as Rendawa Shönu Lodrö (1349–1412) and Tsongkhapa Losang Drakpa (1357–1419), who composed their own Middle Way guidance instructions (*dbu ma'i khrid*). The historical relations between these lineages is a topic for future reaseach. For now, Atiśa's *Madhyamakopadeśa* and its earliest known Indian and Tibetan commentaries are the focus.

Atiśa's *Special Instructions on the Middle Way*

Special Instructions on the Middle Way, along with *Entry to the Two Realities*, are considered by traditional Gelukpa historians to be the two foremost textual teachings (*gzhung*) on the view (*lta ba*) within Atiśa's works.[709] An early Kadampa commentary on *Entry to the Two Realities*, attributed to Naljorpa Sherap Dorjé (ca. 1125), who was a direct disciple of Sharawa Yönten Drak, understands *Special Instructions on the Middle Way* to be a text on meditation (*sgom pa*).[710] Be that as it may, most all traditional sources mention that this teaching was given by Atiśa in Lhasa at the request of Ngok Lekpai Sherap. Sources state that, based on Ngok Lekpai Sherap's request for Madhyamaka teachings (*dbu ma'i chos*), Atiśa and his translator-disciple Naktso Lotsāwa Tsultrim Gyalwa then translated Bhāviveka's *Tarkajvālā* (*Rtog ge 'bar ba*)[711] commentary to his *Madhyamakahṛdayakārikās* at Lhasa's main temple, the Trulnang Tsuglakhang. In addition to this translation, Atiśa is said to have composed the greater and lesser *Special Instructions on the Middle Way* (*Dbu ma'i man ngag che chung*). The "greater" special instructions is a reference to *Open Basket of Jewels*, while the "lesser" is the *Madhyamakopadeśa* (*Special Instructions on the Middle Way*). However, as discussed in chapter 1, according to the colophon of the canonical version of *Open Basket of Jewels*, this work was written in the great temple of Vikramaśīla, under the patronage of King Devapāla. The colophon to the so-called short *Special Instructions on the Middle Way* does mention that it was composed in the main temple of Lhasa and that Atiśa and Tsultrim Gyalwa translated and edited the text together. Therefore *Open Basket of Jewels* was composed first in India and then *Special Instructions on the Middle Way* was composed years later in Tibet. As *Special Instructions on the Middle Way* has similar content to some sections of *Open Basket of Jewels*, Atiśa may have composed *Special Instructions of the Middle Way* as a brief instruction based on extracts from the latter work. Atiśa may have used both texts to give lectures on Madhyamaka during his time in Lhasa.

Special Instructions on the Middle Way is Atiśa's advice for self-transformation through the practice of Madhyamaka. The brief text provides instructions for how Mādhyamikas meditate. In Tibetan catalogs the Sanskrit title is *Madhyamakopadeśa*, even though the reconstructed Sanskrit title in all Tibetan versions is *Madhyama-upadeśa*, instructions on the Middle or the Center. *Potowa's Middle Way*[712] explains that while all four major traditions of the Buddha teach a Middle Way, the instructions of Atiśa concern the Middle Way between the two extremes of existence and nonexistence based on the framework of the two realities. The instructions of the *Madhyamakopadeśa*, after formulaic statements regarding the languages of translation, the translator's homage, and the author's homage, may be analyzed as consisting of instructions on cultivating the three wisdoms of learning, reflection, and meditation within the context of meditative equipoise and postmeditative wisdom construed through the purviews of conventional and ultimate reality.[713] The instructions conclude with brief statements on the status of buddhahood after one attains the vajra-like concentration.

The first paragraph of *Special Instructions on the Middle Way*, from the sentence beginning "Conventionally, all things" to the sentence ending "something the size of the tip of a hair that is split a hundred times cannot be grasped," according to both Prajñāmukti and our Kadampa commentator indicates the training in the wisdoms of hearing and reflection in relation to conventional reality and ultimate reality. The instructions indicate that this exercise initially takes place at the level of the deluded whose vision is narrow—ordinary individuals who cannot understand the two realities nor cognize emptiness. At the level of reflection, karmic cause and effect are considered real as they appear. The phrase "as it appears" (*ji ltar snang ba*) occurs in Atiśa's *Entry to the Two Realities* (v. 21) and is found in works attributed to Bhāviveka and Jñānagarbha, as well as Śāntarakṣita.[714] The works of Atiśa and the Kadampa commentaries will repeatedly stress that appearances from causes and effects are perceived as real at the level of conventional reality until reaching the path of vision. *Special Instructions of the Middle Way* then mentions that, when the conventional as it appears is examined with the great reasons or reasonings, one gains an ascertainment (*niścaya*) that nothing, not even minute things, can be grasped, or, as the Kadampa commentary explains, are established. The great reasons refers to four reasons that Atiśa explains in his *Bodhimārgapradīpapañjikā*[715] and also in *A General Explanation*. The latter text clarifies that these reasons are based on the reasoning of dependent-arising and that all four reasons are accepted as consequences that nonimplicatively negate the intrinsic existence of things but do not negate the mere appearance of causes and effects. The mere appearances that arise from causes and effects are overturned through antidotes cultivated while practicing the path. Atiśa's *General Explanation* specifies that the object of negation of reasoning is a conceived object based on conceptualization that imputes things as either existent or nonexistent. The object negated by reasoning consists of conceptual thought that imputes objects as existing with own-character (*ad* 708.20–709.1). *General Explanation* offers an early distinction between objects negated by an antidote while implementing the path and objects negated by reasoning when searching out the inherent existence of something. Thus Atiśa in the first paragraph indicates the "reasoning at the level of reflection" (*yukti-cintā-mayī*) stage of this spiritual exercise of Madhyamaka meditation.

The second paragraph beginning with the phrase "While sitting in a cross-legged position" through to "for as long as the enemies or thieves of phenomenal marks[716] and conceptual thought does not arise" indicates how to cultivate the wisdom arising from meditation (*bhāvanāmayī-prajñā*). The stages of meditation are indicated in this and the following paragraph of *Special Instructions on the Middle Way*, including the application, the actual practice, and what occurs in the postmeditative state. In this dense paragraph,

Atiśa instructs that while seated cross-legged one should contemplate two kinds of entities: material and nonmaterial. The classification of entities into two kinds is mentioned in Candrakīrti's *Pañcaskandhaprakaraṇa*[717] and also in the *Madhyamakaratnapradīpa*[718] in its instructions on rough or "gross yoga" (*rags pa'i rnal 'byor*). The *Collection of Special Instructions on the Middle Way* commentary on this point provides the details that one should practice in solitude and outlines the corporeal details of body posture, where to place the eyes, and how to set one's mouth, as well as the time length for meditation sessions.

Atiśa's instruction therefore begins with contemplating material and then nonmaterial entities. Prajñāmukti and our Kadampa commentator indicate that this contemplation is to be carried out by examining with reasoning and that these two kinds of entities include all objects of knowledge. For Madhyamaka thinkers like Atiśa, reasoning "designates, in a restrained sense, the fundamental principle or proposition that enounces the law of causality discovered by the Buddha that has issued by inductive reasoning, proceeding to a direct and personal experience."[719] Atiśa does not explicitly state if reasoning is a valid cognition or not, but he does demonstrate in his works his understanding of reasoning as a weapon that dissolves conceptual thought. Prajñāmukti, the author of the Indian commentary on *Special Instructions on the Middle Way*, states that "Reasoning is a valid cognition that invalidates" (D, 122b), while the early Kadampa author of the *Collection of Special Instructions on the Middle Way* claims (folio 10a) that "reasoning" is neither a direct perception nor an inference. Be that as it may, the scope of reasoning for these scholars applies to the investigation of the ultimate ontological status of things and not their mere appearance, which, according to Atiśa, is unexamined.

Based on this understanding of reasoning, one examines material things, that is, things imputed to consist of collections of atoms, analytically breaking them down and performing a merelogical analysis based on their directional parts. The commentators provide examples of this reasoning procedure from the works of Śrīgupta, Śāntarakṣita, and Jñānagarbha. Through this reasoning procedure one ascertains that material things are not established and they no longer appear after being dissolved through reasoned analysis. The instructions then turn toward examining nonmaterial entities, which is, namely, the mind, and includes the four aggregates other than form.

Special Instructions on the Middle Way instructs that the mind has no color or shape, is free of unity and multiplicity, and is unproduced and unestablished. Yet at the same time the mind has a luminous nature. These instructions are close to those that Atiśa gives in *Open Basket of Jewels*, where he emphasizes that "the mind is without color, without form, by its own-nature clear light, and unarising from the beginning."[720] This same sequence of qualities is cited in the *Madhyamakaratnapradīpa*.[721] *Open Basket of Jewels* cites Nāgārjuna's *Bodhicittavivaraṇa* and the *Aṣṭasāhasrikā prajñāpāramitā* to support its claims about the mind being luminous and unestablished.[722] *Collection of Special Instructions on the Middle Way* also emphasizes that the mind has a natural luminosity and is naturally unproduced. The commentary stresses that the mind is not made to have these qualities due to analytical procedures but that the mind is luminous and empty by nature.[723]

The *Kāśyapaparivarta* (§98) and possibly other sūtras such as the *Mañjuśrīnairātmyāvatārasūtra* influenced Atiśa in his discussion about the mind.[724] However, what is of interest about Atiśa is that he gives these *Special Instructions on the Middle Way*, as well as in portions of *Open Basket of Jewels*, in his own formulation and integration of Buddhist sūtras and *śāstras*.

Atiśa then indicates that just as material and nonmaterial entities do not have any nature and are not established, "wisdom itself, without appearance and luminous, is not established with any nature at all." Atiśa compares the reasoning process to two sticks, which after rubbing together and generating a fire, burn up and become nonexistent. Although Atiśa does not state his textual source, he draws this example from the *Kāśyapaparivarta*,[725] which is cited in the *Madhyamakaratnapradīpa*. Kamalaśīla also cited this sūtra in his *Bhāvanākrama* and *Avikalpapraveśadhāraṇīṭīkā* as an example to illustrate that although the analysis of reality is indeed the nature of conceptual thought, it will nevertheless be consumed by the fire of correct wisdom produced by it.[726]

In his longer *Open Basket of Jewels* Atiśa states that "the wisdom of individual analysis (*so sor rtog pa'i shes rab*) itself turns into clear light." Prajñāmukti is even clearer in his *Madhyamakopadeśavṛtti*, where he describes how the wisdom that individually discriminates negates itself at the culmination of the analytical process in meditation.[727] These passages indicate that, for Atiśa and his followers, reasoning is a conventional process that dissolves itself when seeking to establish the existence of an object. Analytical reasoning that dissolves itself is, for Atiśa, philosophy that is preparatory for wisdom, more specifically, for nonconceptual wisdom, *nirvikalpa-jñāna*. The texts suggest a difference between *prajñā*, or discernment, at the level of learning and reflection utilizing reasoning (*rigs pa'i shes rab*), and the nonconceptual gnosis that comprises *jñāna*. *Collection of Special Instructions on the Middle Way* contains a number of reasonings, derived from Jñānagarbha's *Satyadvayavibhaṅga*, that leads the reader through merelogical forms of analysis to dissolve conceptual thought that reifies things and their relations.

Analysis dissolving conceptual thought while meditating generates other factors as well. Atiśa notes that in this process faults to achieving concentration, such as laxity and excitement, are eliminated. As *Potowa's Middle Way* (330.6) explains, in emptiness the faults of laxity and excitement are no longer established. The aim is to achieve a nonconceptual realization in which awareness does not apprehend anything at all. All recollection (*dran pa, smṛti*) and mental engagement (*yid la byed pa, manasikāra*) are also eliminated, indicating that concepts that objectify the past and the future are abandoned. The *Madhyamakaratnapradīpa*, in outlining its *bhāvanākrama* chapter, also advocates that *bhāvanā* should be cultivated to free oneself from *smṛti* and *manasikāra*.[728] The attainment of a state of nonconceptuality is advocated in a number of Mahāyāna Buddhist texts. However, unlike other meditation practices imported into Tibet, such as the Great Completion (*rdzogs chen*) or the practitioners of nonmentation (*amanasikāra*), which advocate nonmind and nonmentation in their spiritual exercises, *Collection of Special Instructions on the Middle Way* emphasizes that Atiśa's instructions "develop nonconceptual concentration in a way that cuts off attachment by means of not finding when searching through reasoning [13b]." The technique of not finding when searching through reasoning is mentioned in Atiśa's *Entry to the Two Realities* (v. 21), and as Tillemans notes, "There is a quasi-consensus amongst [Madhyamaka] commentators on . . . unfindability under analysis."[729] The point in Atiśa's special instructions is that this unfindability eliminates attachment and other negative afflictions. The instructions then prescribe that consciousness should reside in this nonconceptual state resulting from analysis for as long as the enemies or thieves of phenomenal marks and conceptual thought do not arise. *Collection of Special Instructions on the Middle Way* (13b) explains that phenomenal marks and conceptual thought are cognitive objects that scatter awareness away from nonconceptual concentration.

Atiśa's instructions in the third paragraph briefly explain the process of slowly arising from meditation and conducting postmeditative virtuous activities. In a comparable citation in *Open Basket of Jewels*, Atiśa states:

> In this manner, for a long time and with humility, the bodhisattva should continuously practice the teachings previously explained, even when not in contemplation, [and] at the time of meditative stabilization should cultivate the space-like *vajra-samādhi* previously explained. When one has a little clarity toward the ultimate mind of awakening, and not does not feel one's own body as existent, one should pacify the defilements a little, and view all worldly activities and verbal conventions, all inner and outer objects, as like

misty vapor (*ban bun lang long*) with subtle form. Then a vast, pervasive, smooth, light, joyful, and blissful awareness will occur.[730]

Collection of Special Instructions on the Middle Way provides more details describing the precise way that one should arise from meditation as well as the activities that one should perform. After devoted practice for a long time, one will be able to perceive reality. Atiśa states that bodhisattvas see reality in meditative equipoise and then in the postmeditative state perceive things like illusions based on the *Avikalpapraveśadhāraṇī*. Direct perception of reality in meditative equipoise causes one to lessen one's attachment to objects in the postmeditative state and the texts provide the example of seeing objects like illusions to illustrate that one no longer perceives things as substantially existent.

The final paragraph of instructions, beginning with the phrase "From the point of time when," indicates achieving the state of buddhahood through attaining the vajra-like concentration (*vajropama-samādhi*). The vajra-like concentration is also mentioned in Atiśa's *Open Basket of Jewels*, indicating the point when one has attained buddhahood. At this juncture, for Atiśa, based on Candrakīrti's understanding of the state of being a Buddha, all mind and mental factors are cut off and one has fully transformed into the realm of reality, being directly fused with the *dharmakāya*. Because of dwelling in the *dharmakāya*, directly fused with reality for as long as space endures, a Buddha does not possess subsequent attainment. Atiśa's understanding of the state of buddhahood is emphatically based on the texts of Nāgārjuna, and his Kadampa commentators indicate that this is also the system of Candrakīrti. But the implications of the last paragraph of instructions, in brief, is that the cultivation of the Mahāyāna's Middle Way is a spiritual exercise that is practiced in this lifetime, as well as in future lifetimes, until one attains buddhahood for the sake of all beings.

Translation of the *Madhyamakopadeśa, Special Instructions on the Middle Way*[731]

In the Indian language: *Madhyamakopadeśa.*
In the Tibetan language: *Dbu ma'i man ngag ces bya ba*
[*Special Instructions on the Middle Way*].
I bow down to the Protector of the World.

I bow down to that supreme holy person,
whose light rays of speech
opens the lotuses of the hearts
of all the deluded like me without exception.

The special instructions of the Mahāyāna's Middle Way are as follows: Conventionally, all things, from the perspective of the deluded whose vision is narrow, including all presentations of cause and effect and so forth, are real according to how they appear. Ultimately or actually, when the conventional as it appears is closely examined and clarified by the great reasonings, one should thoroughly understand with certainty that even something the size of the tip of a hair that is split a hundred times cannot be grasped.

While sitting in a cross-legged position on a comfortable seat, [contemplate] for a while as follows: there are two kinds of entities, material and nonmaterial. In this regard, material entities are collections of minute particles. When these are closely examined and broken up according to their directional parts, not even the most subtle [part] remains and they are completely without appearance. Nonmaterial is the mind. In regard to this, the past mind has ceased and perished. The mind of the future has not yet arisen or occurred. Even the mind of the present is extremely difficult to examine: it has no color and is devoid of shape, since it is similar to space, it is not established, and since it is free of unity and multiplicity, unproduced, and having a luminous nature and so forth, when it is analyzed and examined with the weapon of reasoning, one realizes that it is not established.

In this way, when those two are not established as having any nature at all and do not exist, the very wisdom that individually discriminates is not established either. For example, through the condition of fire occurring by rubbing two sticks together, the two sticks are burned up and become nonexistent. Just as the very fire [D96a1] that has burned subsides by itself, likewise when all specific and generally characterized things are established as nonexistent, wisdom itself, without appearance and luminous, is not established with any nature at all. All faults such as laxity and excitement and so forth are eliminated. In this interval of meditation, consciousness does not conceptualize, does not apprehend anything at all. All recollection and mental engagement is eliminated. Consciousness should reside in this way for as long as the enemies or thieves of phenomenal marks and conceptual thought do not arise. When you wish to arise, slowly release from the cross-legged position and stand up. Then, with a mind that sees all things like illusions,[732] do as many virtuous deeds as you are able with body, speech, and mind.

Accordingly, when one practices with devotion, for a long time and uninterruptedly, then those with good fortune will see reality in this very life and all things will be directly realized, effortlessly and spontaneously, like the center of space. Through the attainment [of wisdom] after [meditation], all things are understood to be like illusions and so forth. From the point of time onward when the vajra-like concentration has been realized, [buddhas] will not have any subsequent attainment, as they are settled in meditative equipoise at all times.

I will not speak here regarding the reasonings and scriptures that make statements such as, "If it is not like that, what is the difference from bodhisattvas?" Through the power of gathering the accumulations and making aspiration prayers for countless aeons for the welfare of others, [buddhas] will become just as those who are to be taught wish [them to be]. There are many scriptures and reasonings [on this topic], but I will not elaborate on them here.

The [text] called *Special Instructions on the Middle Way*, composed by the paṇḍita Dīpaṃkaraśrījñāna, is completed. The Indian master himself and the great editor translator and monk, Tsultrim Gyalwa, translated, edited, and set the final version at the Trulnang temple in Lhasa.

6. Prajñāmukti's *Commentary on Special Instructions on the Middle Way* (*Madhyamakopadeśavṛtti*)

PRAJÑĀMUKTI'S *Madhyamakopadeśavṛtti* is a commentary on the base text of Atiśa's *Madhyamakopadeśa* that provides glosses on individual words and phrases in the text, as well as cites various sūtras and *śāstras* to clarify points of Atiśa's concise teaching. Prajñāmukti furnishes important glosses for *apratiṣṭhita-nirvāṇa* and *madhyamaka*, among others. However, as Prajñāmukti's commentary also glosses words and phrases that are not found in the currently extant text of Atiśa's *Madhyamakopadeśa*, he may have utilized an earlier version for his comments. Be that as it may, Prajñāmukti notes (D, 122a) that he considers Atiśa's Madhyamaka to be Apratiṣṭhānavāda (*rab tu mi gnas par smra ba*). Prajñāmukti's commentary provides responses to questions regarding the relationship between the two realities and the interpretation of a Buddha's awakening that completely lacks any conceptuality. The understanding that it is impossible for a buddha to have any conceptual knowledge, based on Mahāyāna Buddhist sūtras and supported by Candrakīrti's *Madhyamakāvatāra* exegesis, is a vital point in the Madhyamaka system of Atiśa and his early Kadampa followers.[733] Along these lines, Prajñāmukti will mention several times conventional valid cognition (*tha snyad kyi tshad ma*), implying that it has applicability merely in a worldly transactual context.

Commentary on the Special Instructions on the Middle Way is the only work in the Tibetan Tangyur by Prajñāmukti. The colophon mentions that he was an Indian preceptor (*upādhyāya*) and that he translated the text with Tsultrim Gyalwa. He was most likely a member of the entourage that accompanied Atiśa during his journeys throughout Tibet. In the following translation I have highlighted in bold print words and phrases that reference Atiśa's *Special Instructions on the Middle Way.*

Translation of the *Madhyamakopadeśavṛtti* (*Dbu ma'i man ngag ces bya ba'i 'grel pa*).[734]

[116b7] In the Indian language: *Madhyamakopadeśavṛītti.*

In the Tibetan language: *Dbu ma'i man ngag ces bya ba'i 'grel pa.*
[In English: *Commentary on Special Instructions on the Middle Way.*]
I bow down to the Lord of the World (Lokeśvara).

[117a1] Having paid homage to the bodhisattva,
as a cause for increasing wholesome qualities
and eliminating the suffering of beings,
I will clarify the Middle Way Special Instructions.

Those who sink in the mud of *saṃsāra*
due to mistaken conceptuality
through relying on the path of special instructions
will achieve perfect awakening.

I will explain just a little of the special instructions.

Regarding this, "**whose light rays of speech**" and so forth is stated at the beginning as a homage to the object that possesses virtuous qualities. The intention [of the homage] is for the most excellent Ācārya himself to understand the ultimate itself, to pacify obstacles of interruption, and to make a commitment to explain [the instructions]. This verse indicates two condensed intentions. Offering worship through paying homage and offering worship by declaring virtuous qualities, the excellent object of other virtuous qualities is conceived as one's own purpose. The purpose for others is cause and result. For this, the text "**whose light rays of speech**" indicates the most excellent cause. "**Opens the lotuses of the hearts of all the deluded like me without exception**" indicates the most excellent effect. The text "**supreme holy person**" indicates the end point of one's own purpose. The [plural marker] *rnams* indicates many.[735] "**Bow down**" are words of paying homage.

I will now explain the meaning of the ancillaries. "**Whose**" is a word for an agent, or as a general term clearly applies to only a buddha as a support having abandoned other objects. This section makes offering by paying homage and worship to the qualities of a buddha. It is like saying "oh pretty one" as a general phrase to interact with a cow for the purpose of obtaining milk. "**Light rays of speech**" indicates the light rays of body, speech, and mind. Like white, red, or blue light, or the light of the sun and moon, the light when the sun rises clears away great black darkness, opens up flowers [117b] and so forth, ripens various medicines and fruits, pacifies the misery of touching cold frost and so forth, creates happiness for sentient beings who feel warmth, clarifies the path and what is not the path, as well as unclear objects, and subdues the brilliance of other lights, such as stars and so forth. In a similar fashion, the light of the teaching of the inconceivable Dharma that liberates by means of the body, speech, and mind of the Bhagavan, eliminates the darkness of misknowledge of sentient beings, opens up the lotus of the mind, completely ripens the unripened continuum, pacifies the harm of demons and so forth, pacifies the suffering of all sentient beings, establishes [them] in unsurpassable happiness, abandons and eliminates bad views, and subdues the brilliance of the maturing light of gods and so forth. Furthermore, it is also indicated by saying "eclipsing and so forth."[736] The text "**light rays**" demonstrates the activity of the agent. "**Opens**" indicates the action that is done. "**Me and so forth**" is easy to understand as the Ācārya himself and so forth. "**Deluded**" means not directly realizing the meaning of suchness. The text states "**all . . . without exception**" because the compassion of the Bhagavan is not of limited scope but pervades everywhere and is engaged in for the purpose of [benefiting] all [sentient beings].

"**Opens the lotuses of the hearts**" means that the heart functions as the support of the mind and is the designated place of support. Therefore it is like saying "opens the lotuses of the minds." Moreover, the mind is like a lotus. A lotus when seen produces joy and is a source for various kinds of scents and colors as well as honey and so forth. Although it rises from mud, it is untainted by the mud and is distinctively sublime. Likewise the mind is the place for various kinds of joys and affections, provides the taste of the coemergent nectar, [118a1] is the source of precious awakening, and, although it has adventitious stains, it is luminous by nature and pure. Further, "it is considered pure, just as water, gold, and space are pure"[737] and "the nature of the mind is the Buddha and one should not seek the Buddha elsewhere."[738] The text "**opens**" is likened to how a lotus blossom opens, as the mind is expanded to the five aspects of knowledge. Further, "One who apprehends, recites, practices, studies, and writes with respect to others, their awareness blossoms as a lotus by sunlight."[739] It is also taught that "if he has not applied himself to the five sciences,[740] even the supreme saint will never arrive at omniscience. Therefore he makes effort in those [sciences] in order to criticize and care for others as well as for the sake of his own knowledge."[741] "**Supreme holy person**" indicates that his nature consists of perfect and complete abandonment and wisdom as well as having the nature of the three bodies. "**I bow down to that**" indicates making homage and the virtuous actions of body, speech, and mind.

The text directly teaches the special instructions. "**The special instructions of the Mahāyāna's Middle Way are as follows**" are summarized and indicated through the cause, which is the three wisdoms of study, reflection, and meditation. With respect to this, **vehicle** (*yāna*) is the vehicle of cause and the vehicle of effect, and the cause is going from this path of the bodhisattvas. Vehicle is further explained in the manner of the vehicle of mantra and in the vehicle of the perfections, as explained by others. The vehicle of the effect has the nature of the three bodies[742] because it is to be traversed. **Great** (*mahā*) means the magnanimity of wisdom and compassion and so forth. In this regard, it is taught "great in giving, great in mind, great in power."[743] In that, great wisdom understands all things to be like an illusion and [118b] is not attached to anything at all. Great compassion connects means and wisdom continuously for the benefit of sentient beings and is the path of the bodhisattvas. As wisdom, compassion, and so forth are small, it is called the "Small Vehicle."[744] With respect to this, it is taught that "without method, disconnected from wisdom, one falls into being a *śrāvaka*." Therefore a *śrāvaka* falls to the extreme of *nirvāṇa* and, by directly perceiving *nirvāṇa* with the remnant of the aggregates and then without the remnant of the aggregates, forsakes the benefiting of sentient beings. Ordinary individuals fall to the extreme of *saṃsāra* and experience various sufferings. Bodhisattvas abandon these extremes. With great wisdom they do not abide in the extreme of *saṃsāra*, with great compassion they do not abide in the extreme of *nirvāṇa*—this is called the "nirvāṇa that does not abide (*apratiṣṭhita*) in the two extremes." Moreover, for nonabiding *nirvāṇa*, it is taught that "the means of achieving [the state of] lord of the world depends on a continuum that has indivisible emptiness and compassion, [and] this is explained by all the buddhas." Therefore the Great Vehicle (*mahāyāna*) is wisdom and compassion. "**Middle**" means free from all extremes, and "middle" has the meaning of heart/essence. With regard to the word and the ultimate meaning, the "real middle" will be explained below [in the discussion] with respect to the two realities. The word "middle" (*dbu ma*) is a sound that expresses middle and is only a designated term for abandoning the two extremes. The "**special instructions** of this" signifies something greatly cherished, and as one realizes great meaning with little effort, therefore it is special instructions. "**To meditate**"[745] signifies practice and will be explained below. "**From beginningless time**"[746] signifies *saṃsāra* without beginning and without end. The clinging to things as real means to fixate on something as truly existent, like subjects and objects and so forth. "**To posit the two realities**"[747]—some teach that in reality they are *one and nondifferentiated*. If [the two realities] were identical, just as conventionalities are abandoned, so the ultimate also would be abandoned; just as conventionalities have differences, [119a] so too the ultimate would have differences; just as the conventionalities are defiled, so too the ultimate would be defiled.[748] If [ultimate reality and conventional reality] were different, they would not be the real nature (*chos nyid*) and the possessor of the real nature *(chos can)*, and [realization of ultimate reality] would not overcome the marks of conditioned things; cultivation of the path would also be meaningless.[749] For this reason, [the two realities] can neither be called the same nor different. A detailed explanation is taught from other sources. Moreover, if it is asked why, it is said, "The defining characteristic of the conditioned realm and of the ultimate are free from identity and difference. Those who conceptualize identity and difference are improperly oriented."[750] Further, the meaning is briefly summarized by teaching that the two realities are liberated from identity and difference, like the whiteness of conch shells and so forth.[751]

To explain in detail the elements of the text: "**Conventionally, all things**" and so forth indicates that through the wisdom that arises from study and reflection, one trains in the method of the two realities. "**Conventional**" means deluded awareness that is obscured in regard to the object of reality, just as it is explained elsewhere.[752] "**All things**" means all without exception and is easy to understand. "**The deluded whose vision is narrow**" are those who do not see reality. "**From the perspective of**" means what is applied with the thought of attachment. "**Cause and effect and so forth**" are the aggregates, elements, sense-spheres, and so forth. "**According to how they appear**" means that they are pleasing when unexamined, appearing while having no self-nature. Along these lines, it is taught, "Convinced that impermanent things are like the moon's reflection in water, neither true nor false, one is not carried away by philosophical views."[753] "**Real**" means that it is real in terms of causal efficiency, real as mere appearance, and when examined is not established as real. Along these lines, it is taught, "When examined by reason, [something] is not real. Otherwise it is real. Therefore how can it be contradictory for the very same entity to be both real and unreal?"[754] "**Ultimately**" [119b] is correct wisdom, and since it is undeceiving in reference to a real object, since it issues forth a holy result, and since it is to be sought after, it is the utmost, and that, although pleasing when examined, it is not established. "**The conventional as it appears**" are external and internal entities. "**The great reasonings**": as reasoning is that which is not deceptive in the proof of what is to be proven, reasoning actually understands if [something] exists connected with natures other than conventional valid cognition. **Great** means to rely on conventional reasoning, such as smoke and so forth, and those reasonings are great, as they are undeceptive regarding conventional objects. Here, it is great because it is undeceptive regarding the object of reality, subjugates all distinctions of entities, pacifies all demons of wrong views, and negates all the extremes of conceptual proliferations. For that reason it is taught that "the emptiness of all the Victorious Ones definitely eliminates all views."[755] "**By the [great reasoning]s**" indicates four types [of reasoning]. In this regard, "that which is dependently arisen is without cessation, without production,"[756] and "not arisen from self, nor from another, nor from both or without a cause do any things ever exist anywhere,"[757] and "many do not produce one, many do not produce many, one does not produce many, and one does not produce one,"[758] and "those entities postulated as real by Buddhist and non-Buddhist schools do not have in reality intrinsic nature because they possess neither a single nor a plural nature, like a reflection."[759] This is merely a single fraction of formal reasoning. A more extensive explanation is in other [texts]. Eradicating movement is by distinguishing the directional parts that when examined may consist of sixteen or ten parts and so forth. "**Something the size of the tip of a hair that is split a hundred times**" is a measurement that is extremely subtle. "**To thoroughly understand**" indicates that through the wisdom of study and reflection, one should train in the method of the two realities for all dharmas. Furthermore, the preliminaries of training [120a] are the wisdoms [arising from] study and reflection, and having studied and reflected, one then meditates. Further, this is indicated by stating: "For those of great learning the happy place of aging and growing old is in the inner purity of the forest,"[760] and "previously having sought correct knowledge."[761]

Now the stages of meditating on the special instructions will be indicated. Special instructions has been explained earlier. Meditation has three aspects: the application, the actual [session of practice], and the postconcentrative state. "**Sitting in a cross-legged position on a comfortable seat**" indicates the application of concentration while resolving not to abandon any sentient being, and with immeasurable great effort having the intention to achieve great awakening. "**[Contemplate] for awhile as follows: there are two kinds of entities**" is to examine. "**Material and nonmaterial entities**": [these two types of entities] encompass all entities and a third alternative is eliminated as it is a contradiction [to postulate an alternative] for defining characteristics that stand in a relation of mutual exclusion. "**In this regard, material entities**" indicates that material entities are not established, and further, are accepted as cause and effect. The cause is the four elements that are subtle atoms, and furthermore, by observing many parts, a singular partless [atom] is not established. In not establishing a singularity, a multiplicity is also not established, nor is multiplicity the nature of one and so forth. In this way, in examining the singular and the multiple, other alternatives are not established. As it is explained, "There is not an entity that has a classification other than singularity or multiplicity, since these two [classifications] stand in the relation of mutual exclusion."[762] In this way, when subtle atoms are not established, the material that is the result is also not established, similar to when there is not a seed, a sprout is refuted. Furthermore, "In this way, because a creator does not exist, substantial entities and so forth are eliminated."[763] The text "**completely without appearance**" indicates that appearances are phenomenal marks and means that phenomenal marks do not occur since they are the cause of bondage. Now, since the phenomenal marks of the mind are themselves taught not to be observed, the text mentions "**nonmaterial entities.**" [120b] Regarding that, since causal efficiency is momentary, the momentary may be subdivided; furthermore, **the past** does not exist since it is a perished entity. If something exists, it will be right now in **the present. The future** does not exist since is it an unproduced entity. If something exists, it would not change in the future, as it is in the present. Therefore, the text states "**the mind of the present is extremely difficult to examine.**" "**Difficult to examine,**" since when it is searched for it does not exist as an observable object. "**It has no color and is devoid of shape**" means that is it devoid of blue, gold, and so on, and long, short, and so forth. "**Free of unity and multiplicity**" means, as explained elsewhere, that it is unable to withstand analysis through [the relations of] unity and multiplicity. "**Unproduced,**" since existence and nonexistence are unproduced. "**Having a luminous nature**"—since with respect to itself it is nonconceptual and free from defilements, it is naturally luminous. "**And so forth**" indicates that it is like an illusion since it is devoid of being produced from the four extremes, devoid of being produced from itself, from another, from both, or without a cause, and in reality has passed beyond the extremes of existence and nonexistence. "**With the weapon of reasoning**" indicates that reasoning itself cuts through and splits things apart, similar to a weapon. The *Jñānālokālaṃkāra* states, "I pay homage to the buddhas who continually have purified all dharmas, who are omniscient for all dharmas in not finding the mind, through not having an object of observation."[764] "**One realizes that it is not established**" by understanding of the application. "**In this way, when those two are not established**" indicates [that one realizes] through concentration. "**Those two**" are material and nonmaterial entities. "**Not established**" means not established ultimately and negates other conceptual thoughts. "**The very wisdom that analyzes is not established either**" negates the cognition itself. Since wisdom is a particular aspect of an entity (*dngos po'i bye brag*), when an entity is not established, the very wisdom itself is also not established, just like when a tree is not established the wood and so forth are negated. [121a] As it is said, "In this regard, a fire that burns fuel, having burned its fuel, does not remain." Furthermore, according to the principle summarized above, when mind is not established, then mental factors are also not established, like the sun and its rays of light. As it is said, "Because the mind is refuted in this way, the mental factors are also eliminated."[765] The text "**For example, through the condition of fire occurring by rubbing two sticks together**" is explained by means of scripture (*āgama*). The wisdom that analyzes is like a fire, and all conceptual thought is taught to be like firewood. As it is said, "All the dharmas of beings are asserted to be the firewood of consciousness. Those will become pacified when burned by the fire of analysis" and "through burning all nonvirtuous conceptual thought in the fires of analysis." "**All specific and generally characterized things**": Generally characterized things are empty, selfless, and so forth. The specific character of things is happiness, anguish, and so forth. "**Wisdom itself**" is the very wisdom of meditative equipoise. "**Freedom from hatred**"[766] means to be devoid of the conceptual thoughts of self and other. Furthermore, it is taught: "When not subsequently perceiving consciousness, objects of knowledge, or self, then because phenomenal marks do not emerge, one's concentration is firm, one does not get up."[767] "**Luminosity**" because it is naturally pure. "**Free from extremes**" signifies being free from permanence, annihilation, and so forth. "**Not established at all**" is due to not being established through [reasonings like] neither-one-nor-many and so forth. "**All faults such as laxity and excitement and so forth**" are faults of concentration. Furthermore, laxity is internal lethargy. Excitement is mental distraction. "And so forth" indicates other phenomenal marks. "**In this interval**" indicates an interval of meditative equipoise. "**Does not apprehend anything at all**" means to be free from the concepts of apprehended object and apprehending subject. "**All recollection and mental engagement are eliminated**" means that one abandons the concepts that objectify the past and the future. [121b] One abandons pleasant forms and so forth. "**Enemies of conceptual thought or enemies who steal, or like thieves**" indicates that [phenomenal marks] are enemies since they scatter the treasure of concentration, and therefore these should be abandoned by the spy-watcher of conscientiousness. Further, as it is said, "Fasten the wayward elephant-like mind with recollection's rope to the post of the [meditation] object; then gradually bring it under control using the hook of wisdom."[768] Conventionally, this is like stopping the bristling of bodily hair when perceiving a large fire.[769] Therefore it is unreasonable to generate dual appearances when accumulating the two collections [of merit and wisdom].

[Query:] If the Bhagavan is like a master of an illusion who understands illusion as illusion and attachment to reality does not arise, is reality nonmistaken?

[Reply:] In that case, those who adhere to a self cognize the self as a permanent self; *śrāvakas* as well cognize entities as real entities; and those who adhere to Mind Only cognize self-cognizing consciousness (*rang rig, svasaṃvedana*) as the ultimate that is the nonmistaken reality, as it has been said.

[Query:] If the self and so forth are entities that do not abide as objects of knowledge, and since they are invalidated by a valid cognition and are not established by a valid cognition, as they are only mere imputations, apprehending them would be mistaken, but as a mere illusion that is established by valid cognition and not invalidated by valid cognition, would not cognition according to that fact not be mistaken?

[Reply:] That is unreasonable. The object of knowledge of nonerroneous wisdom that abides like an illusion is not anywhere established, and the objects of knowledge of nonmistaken knowledge do not abide, like [the objects of] diseased vision and so forth.

[Query:] If it is the case, if not understanding the conventional just as it appears, [does that mean] the wisdom of total omniscience would not occur? In that case, since illusory elephants, [the objects of] diseased vision, and so forth would not appear to the direct perception of faultless sense-faculties, there would not be direct perception. Therefore it is unreasonable for the wisdom that abandons mistakes to be false. When there is false appearance, then even the wisdom itself would be mistaken, like cognizing water in a mirage.

[Response:] If it is not like that, then an object would be a real entity and any cognition [122a] would not be mistaken. Therefore how can phenomenal marks of dual appearance occur for final complete wisdom? Dual appearances and mistaken phenomenal marks are different as mere names but are not different objects. As it said in a sūtra, "Subhūti, forms are phenomenal marks, sounds are phenomenal marks." Furthermore, "The *samādhi* of the buddhas, the great sages, and the Conqueror's children has abandoned phenomenal marks. Phenomenal marks are for those of the world"[770] and so forth.

[Query:] If it is the case through fear, the fright of worry, the conventional is nonexistent, when the conventional does not appear through wisdom, would the appearance be evident?

[Reply:] That is unreasonable. By illuminating the nonappearance, since there is no entailment, there would not be an ascertainment. It is like the double moon, [the objects of] diseased vision, and so forth that do not appear to the cognition of faultless sense-faculties. That cognition does not illuminate them. When examined by insight and wisdom, since any dharma, truth, falsity, existence, or nonexistence does not abide, it is called "non-abiding Madhyamaka."

As it is said, "those whose intellect transcends existence and nonexistence and does not abide [in any extremes] realize the meaning of 'condition,' which is profound and nonperceived."[771] This also explains the stages of study and reflection. Contrary to this [understanding], because all conventionalities abide as objects of conventional valid cognition, [they] are not refuted. **Concentration** is one-pointedness of mind on an object of observation and it has unhindered power as a cause to immediately achieve the inconceivable three bodies [of a buddha]. "**When one has realized** [the vajra-like concentration] **onward**" means that from the point of attaining perfect complete buddhahood onward, since it is identical with awakening, although there are distinctions of wisdom, the realm of reality (*dharmadhātu*) is naturally one. Although the Ganges, Sindhu, Pakṣu, and so forth are different rivers, they are naturally one with the great ocean. As it is said, "Separate lineages are not proper, because the *dharmadhātu* does not have distinctions. [122b] The divisions are declared by distinguishing the supported dharmas."[772] "**[Buddhahood] does not have a postcontemplative state**"[773] because phenomenal marks no longer occur. "**[At all] times**" means before, after, and so forth. "**In meditative equipoise**" signifies not wavering from the realm of reality. As it is said, "The Great Nāga is concentrated when he walks. The Great Nāga is concentrated when he stands."[774]

"**If it is not like that**" means if it is the case that the phenomenal marks of dualistic appearance occur. "**Without difference**"[775] means without difference from abiding in the path of training while not abandoning the proliferation into mistaken notions of apprehended object and apprehending subject, and because [one's status] will not be totally the same as awakening, it is unacceptable as the phenomenal marks of dual appearance will occur. As it is said, "Awakening, the characteristic [of which is similar to that] of space, is due to the abandonment of all phenomenal marks (*mtshan ma*)."[776] Furthermore, since it is taught that "Subhūti, wisdom does not have an object. If there exists an object for wisdom, then wisdom will not be understood," how can phenomenal marks occur?

One may think, "As there will be the continuous appearance of wisdom when dual appearances no longer occur, then the making of aspirational prayers and the gathering of the accumulations is pointless." Here, the statement "**for the welfare of others**" indicates that the two buddha bodies of form occur from the nonconceptual state and perform inconceivable deeds for the purpose of sentient beings. Although not having conceptuality, it is not contradictory for the aims of sentient beings to occur. It is like waves emerging from the ocean, like light emerging from the sun, and like wishes and hopes being made possible from a wish-fulfilling jewel. Compared to other [things], the example of a stupa and so forth, although not having conceptual thought, are indicated to arise for the welfare of sentient beings. "**Reasonings**" are valid cognitions that invalidate. "**Scriptures**" are the word of the Buddha. "**I will not speak here**[777] signifies having concern with being too verbose. "**Welfare of others**" means mundane and supermundane benefit. "**Countless aeons**" signifies beyond calculation. "**The accumulations**" means the benefit of the cause, which is the accumulation of merit and wisdom. "**Making aspiration prayers**" [123a] is for the welfare of others. "**Those who are to be taught**" [that is, these instructions are] for the eyes and so forth of pure minds. "**Just as those . . . wish**" means whichever [teaching] will appear as the essence of whichever discipline, and in accordance with various reasonings, will be exactly according to the inclination. As it is said, "Living beings of various aspirations are awakened by various practices. Even when they are not devoted to the instructions of the profound teaching, they should not be rejected. Suchness is inconceivable."[778] Actually, the Bhagavan does not have a buddha body and so on and does not have phenomenal marks of dual appearance. Moreover, [a buddha] never departs from the realm of reality and remains in a nonconceptual state. As it is taught, "Whoever sees me as visible matter . . ."[779] Therefore, the dharma body is just like space. Although any distinctions of boundary, center, various colors, and so forth do not exist in space, sentient beings conceptualize multiple distinctions of boundaries, center, blue, and yellow.

[Query:] If it is the case that the form body and so forth does not have conceptual thought, then how can it be suitable to carry out the welfare of sentient beings?

[Reply:] The meaning of this has already been explained. Even though the sun does not have conceptual thought, various rays of light emerge from it and illuminate things. The very disk of the sun is not light rays. If the disk of the sun itself were light rays then it would remain in the inside of a house and so on, and the very object and the disk itself would be different. The light rays themselves are not the disk of the sun. If the light rays themselves were, then they would remain in space itself and would not illuminate all entities. Therefore even though the light rays are not the sun disk, the light rays emerge from it and illuminate all entities. For this reason, since a sūtra states, "The Buddha is like space and sentient beings are like a mountain," it is inconceivable.

The intention of Dīpaṃkara [123b] is difficult to measure and
the great meaning of Madhyamaka is not an object of the intellect.
Prajñāmukti has clearly described the special instructions
for the purpose of teaching those without knowledge who wish
for an explanation.

May one who has attained the merit of this virtue
attain the status of awakening
from having the precious teaching stay in the world;
remaining for as long as the earth, water, fire, wind, and space.

The commentary to the *Special Instructions on the Middle Way* composed by the Paṇḍita Prajñāmukti is concluded. The Indian preceptor (*upādhyāya*) Prajñāmukti himself and the monk Tsultrim Gyalwa translated, corrected, and edited [the text].

7. *Collection of Special Instructions on the Middle Way*: A Kadampa Commentary

THIS CHAPTER consists of a translation of an anonymous Kadampa commentary on Atiśa's *Special Instructions on the Middle Way* entitled *Collection of Special Instructions on the Middle Way.*[780] The Kadampa author of this commentary was affliated with the monastic center of Radreng, founded by Dromtönpa Gyalwai Jungné, also known as Geshé Tönpa, in 1056/57. The author explicitly mentions Radreng three times (folios 1b, 4a1, 14a). The commentary preserves a tradition of Atiśa's Madhyamaka that was upheld at Radreng during the late eleventh to twelfth centuries. The author mentions a number of Kadampa figures in the commentary, such as Gönpawa Wangchuk Gyaltsen, Potowa Rinchen Sal, Naljorpa Jangchup Rinchen, and Chengawa Tsultrim Bar, who were all affliated with Radreng at some point in their lives.

Collection of Special Instructions on the Middle Way contains a number of important historical anecdotes, linguistic points, and philosophical discussions. In terms of historical anecdotes, the commentary notes in its beginning section that Atiśa had a dispute with Ratnākaraśānti (ca. 970–1030), traditionally considered to be one of Atiśa's teachers. Tibetans usually mention a pious story of King Lha lama Yeshé Ö offering his head's weight in gold as ransom for Atiśa to come to Tibet (see Schaeffer, Kapstein, and Tuttle 2013, 176–81), but the *Collection of Special Instructions on the Middle Way* anecdote presents an alternative view from Atiśa's side, indicating a disagreement based on the fact that the Yogācāra Ratnākaraśānti did not approve of Atiśa's teaching of Madhyamaka. A traditional biography of Atiśa attributed to Dromtönpa Gyalwai Jungné (2012b, 45–46) states that Atiśa first received Madhyamaka teachings under the tantric yogi Avadhūtipa, with whom he studied for seven years. The biography mentions that Atiśa learned the Madhyamaka principles of subtle cause and effect under Avadhūtipa, a point specifically mentioned in *Collection of Special Instructions on the Middle Way* (folio 7b). Atiśa's study of Madhyamaka under Avadhūtipa is also supported by the colophon to the *Sūtrasamuccayasañcayārtha*, which mentions that he received the special instruction (*upadeśa*) regarding the view of nonabiding Middle Way (*apratiṣṭhita* [*madhyamaka*] *darśana*) under Avadhūtipa.[781] After study under Avadhūtipa, Atiśa learned the Yogācāra-Madhyamaka system under Ratnākaraśānti based on this teacher's commentary to the *Aṣṭasāhasrikāprajñāpāramitā*. However, this caused Atiśa to be aware of clear differences between Avadhūtipa's Madhyamaka and the Yogācāra-Madhyamaka, giving Atiśa strong faith in the Madhyamaka system of Candrakīrti.[782]

Indeed, *Collection of Special Instructions on the Middle Way*, in commenting on Atiśa's *Special Instructions on the Middle Way*, elaborates on Candrakīrti's system of Madhyamaka where mind, mental factors, and conceptuality are "cut off" in the state of buddhahood. The text advocates a faith-based Madhyamaka based on Mahāyāna sūtras rather than *śāstras,* placing emphasis on scriptural authority rather than valid cognition (folios 4a2, 5b1–7). Along these lines, the Kadampa author will directly cite, or refer to, the Madhyamaka works of Nāgārjuna (nine times), Āryadeva, Śrīgupta (twice), Jñānagarbha (twice), Śāntarakṣita (three times), Bhāviveka, and Candrakīrti (twice) without mentioning any divisions between them. The commentary exhibits an understanding of Madhyamaka thinkers as not being in conflict with one another. Unexpectedly, the author will cite Dharmakīrti's *Pramāṇavārttika* as proof for the reasoning that things do not arise without a cause, as found in the first chapter of Nāgārjuna's *Mūlamadhyamakakārikā*. The Kadampa author, like other Indian and Tibetan scholars between the eleventh and thirteenth centuries, may have considered Dharmakīrti as a Mādhyamika (Steinkellner 1990).

In the translation that follows, the text that corresponds to Atiśa's *Special Instructions on the Middle Way* is bolded. The paragraph divisions correspond to the sections marked with a double *shad* in the manuscript where the content of the commentary is differentiated.

[1A] Collection of Special Instructions on the Middle Way

[Manuscript mistakenly reads: *Collection on the Two Realities* (*bden gnyis kyi 'bum*)]

[1b] I pay homage to the omniscient one
who liberates from all faults and
who is adorned with all virtuous qualities;
a friend of all sentient beings.

I will speak a bit about the Dharma teaching of the Lord [Atiśa] to inspire faith in the faithful. May it consist for others in three [aspects of being] practical, an exposition, and equal in collections [of merit and wisdom]. It is not Tibetans who accuse Lord [Atiśa]. There are many who rely on the Secret Mantra, and it is not suitable as an object of explanation to study to collect [merit and wisdom]. Even all the sayings of the Hymn of Practice (*spyod pa'i glu*) and the Vajra Hymn (*rdo rje'i glu*) are completion-stage practices that rely on the Secret Mantra. There may be a small precipice in the single purpose in all those [Secret Mantra teachings], so this Dharma teaching is all. Although there are many systems of positing the two realities, for the followers of Radreng Monastery, this Dharma teaching is sufficient, as it is comparable to all [others]. An abundance of useless talk has no purpose. Among the three purposes formerly stated in the Indian language, only gratitude (*byas pa gzo' ba*) is essential to writing this text, as with writing other works. [This text] was written by Lord [Atiśa], as his own guru, Serlingpa, wrote a letter that requested Atiśa to provide a means of defining the Madhyamaka system of the two realities. Since it is written and taught with respect, [this text] is established as a pure source. The Madhyamaka [thought] of Atiśa is due to the kindness of Avadhūtipa, whom [Atiśa] served and followed for seven years. Since [Atiśa] had great reverence for Serlingpa, it is [due to] previous karma that [he] apprehended the Madhyamaka view of a sharp-minded paṇḍita like him. The teaching that it is beneficial to cultivate a forceful elimination of the conceptual elaborations of cognizer and cognized is unacceptable. At the onset, [Atiśa] did not have great reverence for Śāntipa. Later, when [Śāntipa] heard him [i.e., Atiśa] among Tibetans, like a bull, stating that "the proper object of meditation is that all things do not have inherent existence," [Śāntipa] was not pleased. It is said that Lord [Atiśa], immediately upon initiating a discussion of Madhyamaka, was thrown out because [Śāntipa] was annoyed. For the benefit of quickly apprehending the language, *svad tya* is "reality" (*bden pa*), *dho ya na* is "two," and *a ba ta ra na* is "to enter." In the future, the text of the Indian language will be a seed of the condition for quickly apprehending the meaning of the text, having met with and encountered the Sanskrit language (*saṃ kri ta'i skad*). The system of assigning the title is like [what is related in] "the story of the ravishment of Sītā and the killing of Karwa (*mkhar ba*)."[783] The actual *Entrance to the Two Realities*: with regard to all the pronouncements of the Buddha being grouped into two realities, there is the mistaken conventional, since the activity of an object, or the measure of its appearance, is empty, and the correct conventional, which has causal efficacy as a measure of its appearance, being some thing (*chos can*) that is pleasing when unexamined, a dependent-arising for affliction and purification that arises and ceases. As it comes from India as a Dharma teaching for the world [2a1], it is a subject that is known in India. Moreover, it is written with gratitude by Atiśa. As this *Entrance to the Two Realities* was written as a letter for the sake of students in future generations, when one has created conditions to encounter Dharma teachings to practice, even when one encounters Dharma teachings under the conditions of dwelling in harm, one should understand the teachings with gratitude and kindness. [This teaching] should be understood as created for the benefit of the world. When the previous spiritual teacher (*bla ma*), in the process of protecting [this teaching], was passing away, he stated: "I am protecting this [teaching], with the loss of life or letting go the force of life, having taken to entrust this [teaching] to you." This is just as it was spoken at the time of the passing of Geshé Tönpa when he handed [the teaching] over to another spiritual teacher. If the teaching is not handed over like this, not a single word of the spoken transmission of that spiritual teacher will be granted. One should meditate, supplicate, make offerings, pay homage, rely on the spiritual teacher with respectful faith, establish aspirational prayers to meet [the spiritual teacher] from here on in future lifetimes, staying at ease in not seeking out other spiritual teachers. Likewise, when making prayers throughout this lifetime, do not become satisfied. From here on, when reflecting on something like reality, having met with a superior one, having held previous thoughts, other oral instructions will come into being as meditation. In dependence on that high approach, moreover, make offerings and request at once: "For me, may I be able to have complete strength. Formerly, with respect to that, since I had disbelief I was incapable of receiving previous blessings. Even future blessings may be impossible, as unwholesome negativities have increased."

Potowa has said, "Now, everyone is like a bull who is determined to stray from the path when the owner of a young bull seeks out the young bull after it has gone down a path. The bull stops, then continues on his way while being pursued, having turned away from the owner. The neighbors recognize that [the bull] desires to go back to its home again. While straying from the path, [the bull] is carried away by a robber and killed. We will be similar to the bull, so we must try to reside in a straightforward manner, not straying from the path. [The bull] did not listen, and having strayed from the path, was killed by a robber. When the chick of a grouse does not completely die, the other chicks will protect the dying chick when dwelling in the same nest. The chick's wings are not fully formed and it jumps from the nest in an untimely manner. While the chick is limping around, a hawk and weasel will eat it. We are also like this as we sit up in the nest. When we have an untimely fall, the hawk and weasel will carry us away. Not listening, everyone will be carried away by the hawk and weasel. [2b1] Similarly, everyone who dwells in this way will likewise be slaughtered by the robber, carried away by the hawk and weasel."

All three brothers and Geshé Tönpa having passed away, the paṇḍita himself went, and having listened to the last testament of Geshé Tönpa, all those individuals did not stretch the heart of expectation to exist longer than before we disciples achieved the purpose of the teaching. In general, this action of listening to the last testament is of special, great importance for a trustworthy source for Dharma to be established as a pure source, similar to what was previously stated above. The benefit of learning the language quickly: at that time the king and his ministers classified Indian texts according to a rule, since scholars and translators would benefit enormously even by understanding merely this much of the Indian language title with the aim of understanding the translation.[784] That which is taught as *ma-dha-ma*, that which is said as *mahā-ma-ka*, has the meaning of "the middle"; *+u-pa dhe-sha* is called "special instruction"; and *na-ma* has the meaning of "what is called." In the future, a translator will be unable to obtain pure knowledge by relying on merely this Indian language title, yet even now, the Indian title is repeated in order to produce familiarity with the Sanskrit language in the future by creating predispositions to understand the text. The meaning of the title [*Special Instructions on the Middle Way*]: Outsiders accept a self or a person to exist, and since they assert cause and effect, truth, and the [Three] Jewels to not exist, they fall into the extremes of either superimposition or deprecation. Two of our own schools and the Yogācāra—since they assert both a subject and object, the dependent nature (*paratantra*), and mere representation as substantially established—are said to fall to the extreme of superimposition. When one upholds the two realities by being free from the two extremes, it is the *Middle Way*. It is *Special Instructions* because, the basic text being easy to understand, one is able to comprehend the meaning of the two realities by [the wisdoms of] hearing and contemplation, and one can directly realize the meaning through meditation. Furthermore, Ācārya [Nāgārjuna] has taught:

> To those who seek reality, at first
> one should state, "Everythings exists."
> When they have understood things and become detached,
> one can then later declare things as isolated (*viviktatā*).[785]

Āryadeva has stated:

> At first overturn nonvirtue;
> midway, one should overturn [the notion of] "self";
> in the end one should overturn everything.
> One who understands in this way is wise.[786]

Since all these teachings are special instructions, first for this life, and for after that as well, by accumulating actions for this [life], one comes to understand that there is the experiencing of happiness and suffering, and one has faith, which is confidence in impermanence and karmic causes and effects. Since a similar point has been established from the *Ratnāvalī*, it is essential that one does not [3a1] deprecate conventional reality and that one overturns nonvirtue. Then, through offering up awareness that accumulates virtue, and through relying on special instructions of the guru, one will understand the conditions of the successive relations of previous karma and its results, and one will understand that even the rebirths among the five lineages of transmigration do not have even a mere moment of happiness apart from suffering. By realizing the faults of all of conditioned existence, one will have disgust and detachment. The cause that establishes existence with its faults is both karma and mental afflictions. The root of karma and the root of mental afflictions is the view of a self. The view of a self is not held when merely establishing some self; rather, holding a self occurs when mistaking it for the collection of the aggregates and so forth. Since the aggregates and so forth are incompatible with the characteristics of a self, until one understands the nature of selflessness, one should overcome the self and eliminate superimposing the nature of a self on the aggregates.

Then, at the time of wandering in infinite cylic existence consisting of a successive continuum of cause and effect, as it is the case that all sentient beings are one's mother, all sentient beings who are construed as one's mother, who are deluded with respect to the two realities, who suffer as a self in existence by the force of delusion, one relies on great compassion in desiring to establish all sentient beings in complete buddhahood, the everlasting liberation from the suffering of cyclic existence. Wishing to set sentient beings in that [state of liberation], one realizes the goals of aspiring to awakening, compassion, and love that wishes to attain that [state of liberation], as well as detachment from the achievement of one's own liberation. Since it is necessary to summon up the causes for achieving the result of complete buddhahood, realize all the uncommon points of the causes—the six perfections—and without attachment to them, make firm the methods, including concentration. One will be unable to abandon the view of a self if one has not abandoned apprehending dharmas as substantially existent (*chos kyi dngos por 'dzin pa*). Even if one is able to eliminate the view of a self, if one does not meditate on all dharmas as unproduced, because one does not eliminate the obscurations for objects of knowledge, and therefore does not attain total omniscience, one must eliminate the extreme of superimposition that is devoid of the essence of dharmas and reverse any apprehension [of things] as real by relying on ultimate reality.

Ascertaining the characteristics of the two realities through listening and contemplation is called "view." At the time of meditating on reality, sitting in a cross-legged posture on a comfortable seat [3b1], while practicing, ascertain the unproduced by means of examining by reasoning, by determining all entities, and by cutting off duality. One should understand that even knowledge, through the force of unestablished objects of knowledge, itself becomes pacified. At the time of actual practice, having cleared away the faults of laxity and excitement, one should be established in the nonconceptual nature [of meditation] for as long as the enemies or robbers of phenomenal marks and conceptuality do not arise. After [meditation], bearing in mind that all dharmas are like an illusion, one should make effort in the collection of merit by means of the pure activity of the three spheres [of agent, action, and object]. In this way, by practicing with devotion, for a long time, and uninterruptedly, at the time of seeing reality, in both meditation and after [meditation], one directly realizes the aims of the two realities. These very aims are to become gradually accustomed to, and traverse, the ten [bodhisattva] stages, and through vajra-like concentration one will abandon without exception the most subtle latencies of apprehending things as real, and from that point on one will make manifest the highest limit of reality (*yang dag pa'i mtha'*). Abiding in this very condition of meditative equipoise at all times, the awakened activities (*'phrin las*), which achieve the aims of sentient beings by the impelling force of previous accumulations and aspirational prayers, gradually take rebirth as a continuum of a person that uninterruptedly occurs exactly according to the good fortune of those to be trained.

Having imputed this as the special instructions of the Middle Way, similar words are set in letters in a book and are the general meaning of terms that appear to the mind. The translator's homage is naturally pure when contemplating **Lord Avalokiteśvara**. Since all buddhas are lords of the world, contemplating in this way is in harmony with the *śāstra*, and since the *Pitāputrasamāgamasūtra* states, "The Tathāgata has realized both the conventional and the ultimate. The objects to be known are exhausted here in the two realities," it is only omniscience that understands the two realities exactly as they are. Generally, it is an appropriate aim (*skab su bab pa'i don*) to pay homage to only Mañjuśrī in Madhyamaka treatises. Ācārya Nāgārjuna, having declared an homage to omniscience in both the *Mūlamadhyamakakārikā* and the *Ratnāvalī*, dwells in the middle. The *Yuktiṣaṣṭika* and so forth all pay homage to the feet of Gautama. The purpose of paying homage is so that obstacles will not occur and that the composition will be completed. Having established a translation in Tibetan, the composition of the translator will be completed. Up to the present time, the translation is to provide an oral explanation of the teaching.

[4a1] It is said that a person from Lhasa views a person from Radreng (*rwa dreng ba*) in the desire for a deity and that the view is only desire for a deity. Likewise, those who are on the Mahāyāna path, since the path is undertaken in order to realize the two realities, undertake and supplicate through paying homage, worshipping, and offering to actualize omniscience with the mind and to cut through all karmic obscurations that impede realizing the two realities. Other than realizing the two realities through the blessings of [these activities] when supplicating, one is not able to discern the meaning of the two realities through logic.

The homage statement of the treatise itself, from "**One who**" through to "**supreme holy person**": since the buddha has become the chief or supreme of all, he is the supreme of two-legged beings, the omniscient one, who himself has stated, "I am the supreme in this world." Since his **light rays of speech** are likened to a rising sun, the Lord himself is mentioned by stating, "**like me and so forth.**" The buddha clears away the darkness of **delusion in its entirety** without prejudice in the distinctions of sentient beings, the multitude gathered in the midst. According to a scholar who has an extensive commentary on entering the Abhidharma, "heart" is explained as mental consciousness (*yid kyi rnam shes*). It is a meaning that consciousness abides in the heart or in the center, and the darkness that deludes objects of knowledge, the two realities, is produced within the sphere of that [mental consciousness], and since the wisdom that opens the mind to objects of knowledge, the two realities, is produced within the sphere of that [mental consciousness], it is only reasoning. Atiśa states, "I bow down to the **supreme holy person**" who extensively makes joy in opening his mouth to one closed to the two realities at the lotus of the mental consciousness of the heart. Generally when praising a complete, perfect buddha, one praises the three qualities of cause, effect, and awakened activity, but here instead, by stating "**supreme holy person,**" both the final end of abandonment which is wisdom, the result, and the awakened activity of speech are praised. [4a7]

How is the **lotus of the heart** opened up by clearing away the darkness of **delusion**? Prior to the Buddha arriving in the world, all the world was darkened by the darkness of delusion. He taught the Dharma when he arrived [in this world] to the fortunate ones who dwelled in the central land [of India]—the cause and effect consisting of affliction and purification, or the meaning of the two realities, which opens up the lotus of the heart and clears away the darkness of delusion. Then gradually including all of Tibet, [4b1] for the humans who had acccumulated merit, the Buddha Sarvārthasiddhi—"He who achieves all aims"—immediately spoke two verses and so forth. Forty-nine days after awakening, in Ba-ra-na-se [Varanasi], he turned the wheel of dharma of the four truths, and by teaching at first their characteristics, the Noble Kun-shes go'u-di [Ārya Ājñātakauṇḍinya] saw the Dharma. Three times [the Buddha] asked, "Do you perfectly understand the Dharma?" and hearing the response "I understand," gave him the name of "all-knowing" (*kun-shes* = *ājñāta*). Responding twice that "suffering should be understood," arhatship was realized by the five others who understood the Dharma. Replying thrice that "I realize suffering is to be known, and now that which is to be known does not exist," the six became arhats; the five [disciples] were five [arhats] and the sixth was the Buddha. The teachings taught gradually may be grouped into the twelve limbs and the two or three *piṭakas*. In his final words at the time of the final *nirvāṇa*, the Teacher gave the *prātimokṣa*, the teaching of the four applications of mindfulness gathered in the three basket collections as the group of six monks themselves had trained. "I truly reside in having done what is to be done, my relics are mere grains and I have given the twelve limbs without disinction." The Buddha having passed, the *saṃgha* asked the noble Ānanda, "Where was it that the Blessed One expounded the *Turning the Wheel of the Dharma Sūtra*? Child of the Sugata, speak! One of great wisdom, speak!" In this way the teaching and collections exist through a continuous lineage up to the present day.

In regard to **clearing away the darkness of delusion and opening the lotus of the heart**, uncommonly [the Buddha] dwells, opening up the lotus of the heart and clearing away delusion by expounding innumerable teachings while in Tuṣita Heaven or in the womb of the Mother. **Delusion** includes all misknowledge, mistaken consciousness, and doubt. From among these, the greatest, mistaken consciousness, is solely to view other lifetimes as nonexistent. The protector of all beings, the characteristics of the Three Jewels will thereby become mistaken. Even when other lifetimes are said to exist, [they are thought to] occur without a cause or are caused by a creator like Iśvara and so forth. One then accepts the occurrence from a discordant cause. Permanence, happiness, and purity [5a1] are mistaken as a self, one upholds sentient beings as adversaries, and one has attachment to all dharmas as substantially existent entities and so forth. In order to clear these delusions away, the Buddha gives preliminary Dharma teachings: all beings die, and except for the three [types] of arhats, all will take rebirth. He teaches *The Sūtra on Impermanence* and so forth to clear away initial delusion. In this way, the teaching produces an awareness that seeks out a place of refuge due to fear and terror, based on a definite understanding of the endless cycle of birth and death. At that time, it is only the speech of the Buddha that **opens up the lotus of the heart,** having cleared away delusion by the greatness of the [Three] Jewels as a place of refuge. By that [speech], one is protected from the hostilities of this life by principle blessings, and in this manner one is protected from the lower realms of rebirth up through the Inferior Vehicle by principle scriptural teachings that **open up the lotus of the heart and clear away the darkness of delusion**. The magnificent Buddha qualities of the Buddha himself and the bodhisattvas who dwell on the tenth stage and teach later are like this, but an *ācārya* never knows all, according to Geshé Tönpa.

[5a4] Then, through the force of being protected from the three lower realms of rebirth by the teaching transmission, in all rebirths one experiences happiness and suffering, and one takes rebirth in accordance with just one's accumulated karma. Even though, having performed contaminated virtuous deeds, one takes rebirth in happy realms of rebirth, all that has a deceptive quality that is impermanent—even its intrinsic nature is nothing other than a mistaken happiness for suffering. Therefore is it necessary to meditatively cultivate an uncontaminated path that wishes to attain transcendance from the suffering of existence. One understands that by meditatively cultivating an uncontaminated path, one achieves everlasting liberation from cyclic existence, although one does not attain buddhahood but merely one's own liberation. It is nothing but shameless to achieve merely one's own liberation, having abandoned sentient beings, who are considered as one's kinsmen, and who suf-

fer in cyclic existence. All sentient beings at the time of intoxication, who are punished by the stream of birth and death in limitless cyclic existence, are my mother. Through firm, great compassion for all sentient beings, considered as [one's] mother, who experience various sufferings in cyclic existence, I produce the mind that aspires [to and] solemnly promises great awakening for the sake of sentient beings. As one understands the necessity of engaging in the cause based on a wish to attain the result, one ascertains and practices the defining features of the cause, the five perfections. Having relied on conventional reality [5b], one **clears away the darkness of delusion and opens the lotus of the heart**, abandoning the extreme of deprecation. In this way, even being accustomed to the factors of method that rely on conventional reality, if one does not realize ultimate reality, whose meaning is the unproduced, complete omniscience will not be attained and all obstructions without exception will not be abandoned.

The *Noble Perfection of Wisdom Sūtra* and the *Sūtra That Teaches All Things Do Not Arise* and so forth settle the meaning of the unproduced, and by **clearing away the darkness of delusion and opening the lotus of the heart** for ultimate reality, one abandons the extreme of superimposition, comprehending exactly as they are the meaning of the two realities. Since it is only complete omniscience, the only point of relevance is to bow down to that [omniscience]. An *ācārya* who perceives the truth of reality construes as authoritative only that [omniscience] itself. It is said that the special instruction of paying homage to complete omniscience was made at the time of translating the Vinaya. The collected bits of scriptural authority in the *Vinayasūtra* provide many contradictory answers by examining contradiction and noncontradiction based only on oral scriptural authority. However many answers to objections occur throughout the *Abhidharmakośaṭīkā* and the *Commentary to the Great Dependent-Arising*, they are settled only by scriptural oral authority (*āgama*, *lung*). Bhāviveka, even when ascertaining the meaning of the profound, does not settle it merely by withered logic but reaches a conclusion only through scriptural oral authority. Geshé Tönpa has stated that the meaning of the unproduced is taught later in a similar way by buddhas and bodhisattvas who reside on the tenth stage, but that *ācārya*s do not know this. In the guru's [Geshé Tönpa] last words at the time of his passing, the other disciples searched [for a teacher], and he said, "Since a spiritual friend to be entrusted to you alone does not appear in Tibet, for your mutual support take the *sūtrapiṭaka* as your spiritual friend."[787] Thus in special instructions that do not rely on the Buddha's scriptural authority, any intelligent person would not be confident nor go along the path. [Scriptural statements say,] "The view is indicated by seeing" and "see the Buddha," which is to produce a view that realizes the abiding nature from his scriptural oral tradition but that is not realized by logic.

[5b8] The practical purpose is, as previously mentioned, to cut off hindrances, and moreover to produce a genuine intellectual understanding that increases in all future rebirths. Arising from the blessings of the Buddha, study, contemplate, and meditate at all times. [6a] As when the Lord [Atiśa] argued with [non-Buddhist] outsiders, the force of faith is an unbiased mind. The obstacles appearing to a small man are produced by his bad intelligence. These appearances are overturned when paying homage, worshipping, and supplicating omniscience. Through relying on conventional reality, one is said to abandon the extreme of deprecation and is said to enter the Middle Way. The actual **Middle Way special instructions**, the **Middle Way special instructions of the Great Vehicle,** is said to be this and so forth. Generally, even the schools from among the four great Buddhist traditions, along with those who are considered outsiders, superimpose, since a self and so forth does not exist. Some followers of the Great Vehicle state that my assertion that the self of a person does not even conventionally exist is falling to the extreme of deprecation. They rely on the mere dharma of subject and object, the experience of happiness or suffering arising from carrying out virtuous or nonvirtuous actions. They attain liberation by cultivating the uncontaminated path, and assert that the cause and effect of affliction and purification is all that exists, and that is said to be the Middle Way, free from the two extremes, [for them]. The Yogācāra state that outsiders [non-Buddhists] accept the self and that the Sautrāntika assertion that the material elements, and that which arises from the material elements, are the apprehended object, and that the six groups of consciousness that apprehend them are substantially existent, is a superimposition. [The Yogācārins also state] that Madhyamakas who assert that the dependent nature of mere cognition does not exist at all is a deprecation [of the dependent nature]. That is according to the way the *Madhyāntavibhāga*[788] states it: "Because [false imagining] exists, because [duality] does not exist, and because [false imagining] exists [in relation to emptiness, and emptiness in relation to false imagining]. And this is the middle path." [For Yogācārins,] the dependent nature exists as mere cognitive representation, and since the apprehended object and apprehending subject, the imagined nature, does not exist, the perfect nature, reality that is empty of the imagined nature in the dependent-nature, does exist. They say only this is called the middle path. In this particular sense, the **Middle Way special instructions of the Great Vehicle** is mentioned.

[6a7] **Conventionally** all dharmas exist just in the manner they are presented, and through the principle that states[789] "that which is the real nature of the conventional is considered the same as the ultimate," however, ulti-

mately the conventional itself, **something the size of the tip of a hair that is split a hundred times,** does not exist when examined by reason. In this way, since the expression "two realities" is free from the two extremes of deprecation and superimposition, by extension it is called Middle Way, and "special instructions" is like as before. In this way, the introduction (*gleng bslang ba*, **upodghāta*) of the treatise is indicated and the "purpose-connection" (*dgos 'brel*) is taught in four parts. [6b] The subject matter (*brjod bya*, *abhideya*) is the two realities. The purpose (*dgos pa*, *prayojana*) is to realize the [two realities] by [the wisdoms arising from] hearing and contemplation. The purpose of the purpose (*dgos pa'i dgos pa*, *prayojanaprayojana*) is to integrate means and wisdom by relying on the two realities. In the time period after seeing reality, those on the tenth [stage] directly realize the two realities. At the time of final buddhahood, one abides only in the nature of meditative equipoise and will uninterruptedly appear only as the good fortune of beings and for the aims of others. The relation (*'brel pa*, *sambandha*) is the relation between the purpose and the treatise. The relation between the purpose of the purpose and the purpose is in the manner of the means (*thabs*, *upaya*) and that which arises from the means (*thabs las byung ba*, *upeya*).[790] [6b3] At first, when settling the characteristics of the two realities by hearing and thinking, "**conventionally**" and so forth the four truths are certainly grouped within the two realities, but in this regard the great number of expressible existents have been sorted into five. The two words the sūtras use for the two realities are not grouped or are not incomplete. Regarding this, *kun* has the meaning of "all" or "the limits," and *rdzob* is in the Shangshung language. Since *rdzob* has the meaning of "false," the meaning of *kun rdzob* is "all is false or obscured" ("all-obscured", i.e., the conventional). "**All dharmas**" includes the aggregates, elements, and sensory media, or all that is afflicted and that which is to be purified. All that is construed **from the perspective of** the ordinary individual, **one with narrow vision** who habitually clings to things as substantially existent. [Ordinary individuals] think that, "an intrinsic nature must be present for the worldly relation of cause and effects of actions." [6b5] Generally, the conventional is not at all existent other than **cause and effect.** "**True just as it is established**" is true as measured and apprehended as real by those of narrow vision, but that nature is a false object, as mentioned before:

> Whatever is near and other, that appearance does not exist and is like a reflection. Artificial is the essence, that's just how it is.

In this manner, the object is a mere **appearance** dependent on similar causes and conditions. It is, for example, like a reflection that appears in dependence on mere similarity with an object in a mirror. Here Chengawa[791] and Naljorpa

Chenpo[792] say that is it like the legend regarding foolish talk in the language of pigeons. For a person of narrow vision, the very appearance of an object is an incompatible inferior appearance.

The *Śikṣāsamuccaya* states "all is true for all that is false." In the section that investigates the water element, the water itself that appears for as long as twenty eons, as spoken in the *Abhidharmakośa*, does not accord with how water is spoken of in the world. [7a1] Whenever the conventional is asserted as the mind, it is the **appearance** of the ordinary mind. When construed through the force of existent external objects, all incompatible appearances, as a measure of appearance, are true, but since that which is established as substantial does not exist, it is called "false." It is false since it is not established substantially, and in the section on activity of the *Perfection of Wisdom*, it states that everything, all dharmas from form up through omniscience, are indicated by conventional transactions. For as long as one does not abandon clinging to things as real, and the mountain-like [notion] of "I," the occurrence of causes and effects, the accumulation of causes and conditions, are undeceiving and undeniably occur, as they are not distinct [7a3] from being established as substantially existent and as real in the purview of one with narrow vision. It is called "conventional reality," and by the force of delusion for both cause and effect and the meaning of "suchness," the delusion for the cause and effect and karma and its effects, which produce the three lower realms of rebirth from sinful unvirtuous actions, does not exist for the object of suchness. By the force of delusion, through contaminated virtue, one has the cause and effect of rebirth among gods and humans, and through the freedom from delusion by understanding all existence as suffering, one generates detachment.

For the purpose of abandoning the cause of that [suffering] by taking up the two trainings, one attains one's own liberation through the cause and effect of the Inferior Vehicle (*theg dman*, *hīnayāna*). The training of a bodhisattva who is impelled by the aspiration to awaken (*bodhicitta*), who produces [the aspiration] spontaneously and continually for the benefit of all sentient beings who pervade the limits of space, is the cause and effect of the Great Vehicle (*theg chen*, *mahāyāna*). The six or eight types of consciousness of ordinary individuals and the wisdom of *ārya*s are all due to the cause and effect of birth from four conditions [that are perceived] as real along with their appearances. The appearances to sentient beings in hell of the four levels of red-hot irons and so forth; the appearances of skeletons, pus, and blood, and so forth for hungry ghosts; the appearances to animals, those who abide in and are scattered throughout the outer oceans and continents; the appearances to humans among the four continents; the appearance of the six types of desire-realms gods; the appearances that arise at certain times of the mansions of the brahmā-realm gods of the first concentration up through the individual mansions of the gods of the fourth concentration; and even all the appearances of the pure fields, the extremely pure fields of the buddhas, are **from the perspective of one with narrow vision**. Therefore, since it is true [from this perspective], the Buddha did not contradict teaching the world [the appearances of cause and effect]. [However,] it is said that the correct teaching is nothing [7b] whatsoever. Therefore, those who elaborate by differentiating the ultimate as emptiness, and who then, throughout existence, conventionally apprehend [things] as real, [understand] that by taking life sentient beings are reborn as hell-beings, hungry ghosts, or animals; that when one is reborn as a human, one issues forth the maturations of harmonious life and sickness and so forth; that when one abandons the taking of life, one is reborn as a god or human among the happy realms. Moreover, through issuing forth the maturation of long life and little sickness, one places trust in all that is said about abandoning nonvirtue and persevering in virtue, having relied on conventional reality. The great vital point is that one is free from the extreme of deprecation.

The spiritual teacher of Lord [Atiśa], Avadhūtipa, bestowed on Lord [Atiśa] the special instruction on nonarising. According to the nature [of this teaching], as long as one has not exhausted the view of a self, it is not suitable to belittle or waste even the most subtle action. The yogi who has attained the great power of concentration, the scholar *paṇḍita* who is a great master, the elders (*sthavira*) of the *saṃgha*—one should not belittle them, thinking, this one has merely attained concentration, this one is merely a scholar, and these are merely elders. Great supersensory powers see much in understanding that this fault and this belittling leads to rebirth now as a hell-being in this place, now a hungry ghost in that place, and so forth. Geshé Tönpa said, "O followers of the Elder [Atiśa], great pretension is inappropriate."[793] Entities are emptiness. One should imagine in meditation that one's hands are placed in a fire with nothing to help one. Since it is both the burned and the burner, the hand scorched by fire is said to be reality. Generally after attaining confidence, when one belittles, that is deceptive. It occurs without volition by the force of the afflictions. Relying on regret when engaging in practice, it is possible to not produce an effect. [7b6] Therefore, for as long as one does not exhaust the view of a self, [for all beings,] from a cattle herdsman up to one training in the the five knowledges, all appears as agreeable. It is real as merely that appearance. By this principle, all your rebirths are understood to be like an illusory person. One on the first [bodhisattva] level that comes after seeing reality, by cognizing the fundamental nature of the conventional—the rebirths of the three lower realms, the rebirths of the two happy realms, attaining the liberation of a *śrāvaka* or *pratyekabuddha* by training in the three trainings, obtaining buddhahood that performs actions for the purpose of all sentient beings who pervade the extent of the sky, the training of a bodhisattva that is impelled by the aspiration to awaken, the consciousness and wisdom that arises from the four conditions, and all the former appearances of these—although the **appearances** exist, they are not fixated on as truly existent and are understood to be like an illusion. Since they are understood as being like an illusion after attaining the first ground onward, it is proper to send out a hundred emanations instantaneously. Appearances are never at all suitable if substantially established.

There are different tenets for whether appearances exist or do not exist for one in reality or on the Buddha level. If they exist, there is not any invalidation from mere evanescent appearances. In this way, through vajra-like concentration, postmeditative appearances are not accepted and there is only meditative stabilization on reality from this point onward that abandons without exception the subtle latencies of grasping things as real. Therefore, while the fundamental nature of the aggregates and so forth is like an illusion, the childish apprehend them as real, having relied on a delusive basis, from which occurs the view of a self and being bound in *saṃsāra* by the misknowledge that is deluded in regard to reality. The fundamental reality of the conventional is like an illusion, and one should study, reflect, and repeatedly contemplate like Sangphuwa, who repeatedly diminished the grasping of things as real. Once on the path of vision, since one realizes that the fundamental nature is like an illusion, it is just like being taken by the hand. The ultimate (*don dam*) or the real (*yang dag pa*) is the highest of objects and the undeceiving object, or, it is the ultimate since it is the object of holy wisdom. When construing the unfabricated way things are, through the principle that "when the conventional that appears is analytically examined just as it, nothing whatsoever is found. The unfindable is itself the ultimate."[794] The text says, "**when the conventional as it appears,**" and the very nature of this is nonarising. By examining with **the great reasonings**, that which is the nature is realized. If the conventional is substantially established, it has no benefit, since the ultimate is unproduced. Relying on a conventional reality that is substantially established is the source of all faults.

[8a7] For this, **reasoning,** when construed at the base of all production and cessation, is called "dependent-arising" (*rten 'brel gyi gtan tshigs, pratītyasamutpādahetu*); "one and the many" (i.e., *gcig du bral gyi gtan tshigs, ekānekaviyogahetu*) is the second reasoning. By dividing production and cessation into three there are four [reasonings altogether]: the reasoning of dependent-arising, the diamond splinters (*rdo rje gzegs ma'i gtan tshigs, vajrakaṇahetu*), and the reasoning of the production and cessation of the four limits (*mu bzhi skye 'gog gi gtan tshigs, catuṣkoṭyutpādapratiṣeddhahetu*).[795] For this, generally,

since the production and cessation of existence or nonexistence in terms of effects and causes, when examined by the three times [of past, present, and future], is not suitable to produce a result, it is called "dependent-arising." The Ācārya [Nāgārjuna] teaches that since cause and effect occur only through mutual dependence, [8b1] there will be an effect only in dependence on a previous cause, and just as an effect is dependent on a former cause, the cause and effect is fabricated and does not have an independent nature, and this is regarded as the reasoning of dependent-arising.

[8b1] To refute the arising of the existent and nonexistent, Nāgārjuna states in his *Śūnyatāsaptati*:

> The existent cannot be produced, since it is [already] existent;
> the nonexistent cannot be produced, since it is nonexistent.[796]

Since they [existence and nonexistence] are incompatible dharmas, there is not both either. Because birth does not exist, permanence and cessation do not exist. The Sāṃkhyas assertion is clarified by the condition of a single existent effect from the beginning, and our own school, the Vaibhāṣika, claim that a future effect is presently pulled along by the condition of a single existent cause; since this present existence is accepted as coming along from the past, the three times are substantially established and both [cause and effect] are accepted as an existent that is already produced. The majority of others assert production as nonexistent. The *Catuḥśataka* unanimously condemns this assertion. Further, not including most of the sūtras, [some] accept the existent as produced. For all of these views, the *Śūnyatāsaptati* (v. 4) states:

> The existent cannot be produced, since it is [already] existent;
> the nonexistent cannot be produced, since it is nonexistent;
> since they are incompatible dharmas,
> there is not both [existence and nonexistence].

The *Madhyamakāvatāra* states that it is not acceptable by reasoning that:

> Pillars and so forth as
> ornaments of houses are meaningless
> to those who assert an effect as existent
> and to those who assert an effect as nonexistent."[797]

By being established as existent, it is unnecessary for an existent to be produced. Since there does not exist a time of being nonproduced when it is produced having a nature that is already established, there would be endless production. When supported by a cause that is existent, since a nonexistent production would not occur, there would be pointless production. By the reasoning that states, "even by one hundred million causes a nonexistent will not be subject to change,"[798] even a cause with great power is not able to produce a nonexistent. It will be like the production of a rabbit's horn, when produced from a cause that is nonexistent. Since existence and nonexistence are contradictory dharmas that are not possible, it is not acceptable to produce something that is both [existent and nonexistent]. How is it acceptable to produce something that is both [existent and nonexistent] if there is a nonexistent effect for a cause that is existent? When examining whether something exists through production or exists without production, the existent as a cause itself is not established, and since a cause is posited having relied on an effect, it is not acceptable for existence through the cause itself with a nonexistent result, and since there is a consequence for the faults of both, both are not possible. When examining from the point view of the cause, Nāgārjuna states,

> Not arisen from self, nor from another,
> nor from both or without a cause
> do any things ever exist anywhere.[799]

Arising is not acceptable from itself, from other, from both [itself and other], or without a cause. First, arising is not necessary if established from itself because when arising is established it would be endless, and because when independent entities like seeds [9a] and so forth themselves are [already] produced, consciousness, sprouts, and so forth would be without a cause. When [the effect] itself is not established, [a cause] will not obtain even its own conventional [status], as it would be unsuitable as a cause because of similarity with what is produced. Through the reasoning that:

> It is not even from other,
> the other is other in dependence on the other.
> Without the other,
> the other would not be other.[800]

Since an effect is not itself established, it is not established as an otherness that is related to that. This is because when an other is produced from an other, then everything would be produced from everything. An effect does not exist from either a permanent or impermanent other. A permanent [other] is not acceptable as an effect, as it would be produced either gradually or instantaneously. It would be impermanent if produced gradually, and if instantaneously, all effects would be perceived at one time. One is not able to assert an established effect because successively perceived impermanance is not suitable as a cause, because things of the past from among the three times would not arrive, disintegratedness and production would not exist. Since imputation would not occur concurrently in the present, cause and effect would be pointless. Since the consequence of both faults [of a permanent or impermanent other] and both [permanent and impermanent other] are contradictory dharmas that are not acceptable, an effect is not established from both [a permanent and impermanent other].

In the view of production from the condition of one's own seed or cause, from the perspective's "produced from an other condition" and "it is produced of itself," since it is produced from an other, production would be from both [one's own cause and an other]. For the Sāṃkhyas, since a preexistent effect exists from the beginning, it is eliminated by conditions that exist from the perspective of the effect existing from the beginning. If it is from itself and if there are other causal conditions, how can it be [produced from] both? The condition of the seed and the sprout is not itself established because the relation is one of cause and effect, as the former and latter are different. Likewise, since the conditions themselves are not established, as both product and nonproduct are different, one is not released from the previous defect of the consequence of both faults.

> Because that which is causeless does not depend on anything else, it
> would be either permanently existent or permanently nonexistent.
> Things occur intermittently because they are dependent.[801]

This reasoning [indicates] there is not arising without a cause. For those who advocate causeless arising, [let us ask]: Who is cut by a sharp thorn? Who draws the colorful tail of the peacock? Who makes the stem, leaves, and flowers of the lotus, if all these arise without a cause? These questions refute those who advocate causeless arising. Since an object is without distinction if it is causeless, the qualities of a peacock would exist for a crow and so forth. The qualities of a lotus would exist for a willow, a rhododendron bush, and so forth. [9b] Since Jñānagarbha states in his *Two Realities* that "many do not produce one, many do not produce many, one does not produce many, and one does not produce one,"[802] production is not acceptable when examined from the four extremes [of existence, nonexistence, neither, or both]. Conventionally, production is only fundamental for the arising of one effect from a collection of many causes and conditions, while ultimately production is not acceptable. Although many potencies exist as a cause for the faculties, objects, appearances, and mental engagements, because it is not agreeable for cause and effect, as there is only a single quality of consciousness that is the effect, a single effect will be causeless. Would there not be the arising of many effects by many causes, since there is arising that has the immediately preceeding condition similar to the cause, the eye faculty, and the apprehension of form and the self, which cognizes the consciousness that is an effect from the object such as form? Accordingly, the nature of the consciousness and realization and so forth would either be one or many. If you ask would it be one, is it one as the nature of a single consciousness or many distinct [consciousnesses]? If according to the former, there would be the previous fault of one arising from many, and if according to the latter, there would be many visual consciousnesses. If there are many, an arising of the nature and so forth would be realized by many conditions, but if consciousness is not produced, consciousness would be causeless. Furthermore, when many causes produce many effects, is each and every effect that is produced applied to all the causes or is each and every cause applied to each and every effect? If according to the former, there would be the fault of producing one by many, and if according to the latter, there would be the fault of producing one by one. If the cause, the faculty of the eye itself, produces later a concordant of its own type and eye consciousness is produced, does one [cause] produce many [effects]? Accordingly, is the faculty that produces a concordant type and the faculty that produces consciousness an identical or distinct nature? Is it identical? Accordingly, it is not suitable for many natures of an effect to arise from the single nature of a cause. If the faculties are distinct, there would be many [effects] that are produced from many [causes]. Furthermore, if the nature of the cause did not exist apart from the one, many qualities for the effect would arise, and cause and effect would be discordant. Many effects would be without a cause, and by a single cause many effects would be produced either simultaneously or gradually. If according to the former, all the effects, many simultaneously, would be cognized at one time, and when according to the latter, there would occur the fault of producing many [effects] by many [causes]. What if one cause produced only one effect? Accordingly, would the sense-faculty at the time of producing a single effect produce only that which accords with its own type, or would it produce only a consciousness? If according to the former, by not producing consciousness, all sentient beings would obtain the status of matter at the first moment. [10a] If according to the latter, by interrupting what is concordant with its own type in the two kinds of moments, all sentient beings would become deaf and blind, and so forth. Both cause and effect, when examined by [the reasoning of the] one and many, are not established. Śāntarakṣita, in his *Madhyamakālaṃkāra*, at first analyzes the self and so forth, determining that they are not suitable as entities, as they do not have causal efficiency to produce an effect when empty. If causally efficient, is it instantaneous or gradual? It is not the former, since all effects are cognized successively. It is not the latter, as existing sequentially for the effect, [and] as the cause through consequence is impermanent, a permanent and unitary effect would also degenerate. Likewise, with respect to directional parts, do they exist differently or do they exist in singularity?

> [It is claimed that] the atom in the center is in contact with [the other atoms forming one particle], or that it is surrounded [by them with intervals remaining in between], or that it is in nondimensional contiguity [with them, being neither contact nor intervals between them].[803]

> [However], if some say, [the atom in the center] entirely faces one atom in the front and also entirely faces another atom, then how can there be gross things like earth, water, and so forth?[804]

Through such reasoning, by having various parts, the form aggregate is not established as a unity. In this way, many is not established as well, [and] since many is not established, the support and the object are not established. The five sense-doors, consciousness, are not established, and since those are not established, the mind as soon as it stops is not established, and since that is not established, the consciousness of the mind is not established, and in this way, since the sixfold collection of consciousness does not establish the mind, the mental factors such as happiness, which are unified with those, are also not established. In this way, since form, mind, and mental factors are not established, the nonassociated factors that are determined on the status of those are not established. Thus, since the aggregates are not established, the elements and the sensory-spheres are not established, and mere cognitive representations, by the reasoning of the many aspects and the nondifferentiated, are not established as a unity. The unconditioned, space, and so forth, since they are connected with forms having various parts, are not established as a unity. If the unconditioned is not an object of knowledge, then it is established as not having an intrinsic nature. If it is an object of knowledge, since knowledge is connected successively, the unconditioned also would be impermanent and would be established as many; therefore it is not established as a unity. The *Madhyamakālaṃkāra* states:

> When any entity is examined, no unity is found in it. Where there is no unity, plurality cannot be found either.[805]

Thus by this reasoning the many is also not established, and the Ācārya [Nāgārjuna] states:

> Because the aggregate of form is only a name, space also is only a name. Without the elements [10b] how can forms exist? Therefore even [form] is also only a name.[806]

Thus space is not substantially established and that nature is suitable. The Madhyamaka *Pañcaskandhaka* asserts the unconditioned to be four, including space, the two cessations, and suchness. The unconditioned itself is also established as lacking inherent existence. In this way, when examined by settling dependent-arising, **even something the size of the tip of a hair that is split a hundred times cannot be grasped.** That is established, and afterward all that exists is sharply examined like this. The Ācārya [Nāgārjuna] states:

> When an explanation is made through emptiness, whoever claims a fault about it, all of that is not designated a fault, as that is equivalent to what is to be proven.
> When there is an argument about emptiness, whoever gives an answer, none of that is not a answer, as that is equivalent to what is to be proven.[807]

The *Madhyamakāvatāra* (6.68a–c) states:

> Since their giving such and such a reply is seen as similar to this, and that thesis . . .[808]

In this way, this teaching is comprehensive in regard to everything. Through hearing and reflection the two realities are ascertained just like this.

[10b4] The text discusses meditation itself when it states "**on a comfortable seat**" and so forth. First, just as it is taught in the *Bodhipathapradīpa*, through having conviction in the karmic principal of cause and effect, one does not disregard even the most subtle transgression. One should stay with the factors of method to the extent that one can achieve the five perfections through being impelled by the aspiration to awaken. With a single teaching, with even a mere incense bowl as the object of meditation, one should practice the concentration on emptiness. In this way, when following the factors of method at the time of cultivating wisdom, it is necessary to remain in solitude for the acquisition of meditative serenity (*zhi gnas, śamatha*). All worldly activities are to be settled, as one is incapable [of settling them] while remaining in solitude.

If a bit [of worldly activity] occurs during solitude, that is not satisfying. As the Kam[809] say, as soon as one closes the eyes, it would not do to remember all the lower worldly activities. As the elements of solitude have few activities, one must not have any activities that are not meditation. Furthermore, by having few desires and being easily satisfied, the conditions concordant with meditation, one will be easily satisfied with the bare necessities. One should keep distant from the place of one's birth, abandoning kinsmen. Just as when teaching in fives the accumulation of special insight, [11a] ascertain well the characteristics of the two realities through studying and contemplation, as well as the well-received special instruction of cultivating special insight in accordance with the spiritual friend.

At first, one should have compassion by considering sentient beings as one's parents who are confused in the meaning of the two realities and who, through the power of apprehending nonexistent things, wander in *saṃsāra* and are differentiated by various sufferings that do not [actually] exist. All sentient beings have previously discarded the ability to realize the meaning of the two realities as well as the ability to cultivate the meaning of nonarising as a means to eliminate apprehending things as real. Pay homage, worship with offerings, confess transgressions, and supplicate in order to manifest all the buddhas and bodhisattvas who reside in the ten directions and all the Three Jewels. The *Bhāvanākrama* states that all the activities of the path of activity, including greater and lesser external actions, should be well done. Sit on a comfortable seat cross-legged or in a half-cross-legged pose; the path of activity is the method for being able to remain [in meditation] for a long time. Remember to keep the body very straight, as one should be fully directed toward the object of meditation. One should place the nose and the navel as one would cast a line. One should bend in front slightly to the left and right. Place the teeth and lips as usual and set the tongue against the upper front teeth. Do not keep the eyes wide open nor closed, but rather in the path of activity; set [the eyes] at a mere four-fingers width at the tip of one's nose, as mentioned in the middle *Bhāvanākrama*.

As for mental applications such as impermanence and so forth on the path of application, do freely as you like. It is suitable to lie down or rest on one's back even on a road. Consider spreading ten fingers out on one's chest. Then examine the [object] with reasoning. This is the special instructions. One goes astray by forcing the breath by using a mantra as a method for mental stability as one would remain in meditation as if everything is existent. Examine with reasoning all objects of knowledge; entities and nonentities are two [distinct] classifications. Nonexistent unconditioned entities are not necessary to negate, as they are nonentities. Others' imputations of a self of a person and so forth, or the appearances to one's own mind, since appearances are actually empty, are not substantially established and are not objectified externally, internally, or something other than that.

Efficacious entities are exhausted as merely two [categories, material and nonmaterial]. Regarding that, material entities, from the perspective of the aggregates, is the aggregate of form, and there are four forms of cause. The forms of result include five faculties and five objects, which makes ten. When counted together, [11b] this makes fourteen forms. As the forms of cause and effect are classified into two categories, they are not established as a unity. The elements that pertain to a cause are distinguished as four, and are not established as a unity. Each individual element is not independently established, even though it is not included with the other three. Even something solid is not established as a unity when distinguished by directional parts. Resultant forms are not established as a unity when distinguished into sense faculties and objects. Since there are five [sense faculties] and five [sense objects], each one individually is not established as a unity when distinguished by directional parts. The eight substances of subtle atoms are soundless. Possessing the sense of touch is the ninth substance. Through the principle called the "tenth substance for another faculty," there is a dissimilar substance of an atom. The four elements from the four sense-organs [and] the four substances according to the atoms of color, odor, taste, and tangible object makes eight. Since the body sense-power pervades everywhere, the ninth substance is those atoms. [11b4] The eye and so forth have an individual atomic substance, which makes ten, and they are grouped as the tenth. One should closely view the atoms of an existent sound. The body sense-power has nine or ten atoms. The objects not consisting of the sense-powers are eight or nine. If consisting of eight or nine, the objects are not established as a unity, as each individual atom when divided by directional parts will become either six or ten. The measure of a subtle atom: the most subtle [atom] in the dust mote of a sunbeam will become a little more than two hundred thousand atoms by six distinctions of stages from an "ox particle."[810] With respect to a subtlety such like this, when distinguished by six or ten directions, it is extremely subtle without remainder and does not appear as an object of the mind. In this way, as the aggregate of form is not established, the elements and the sensory-spheres that have form are also not established because the ten elements and sense-spheres that possess form in regard to the aggregate of form itself are posited as ten.

[11b6] The name basis of **nonmaterial entities** is the aggregates, and that itself is posited on the side of the seven elements of mind, the sensory-sphere of the mental (*manāyatana*), and the element (*dhātu*) and sensory-sphere (*āyatana*) of dharma. Grouped together, all awarenesses are called "**mind**." It

is clear to designate mental factors in the context of the mind so that one does not think to group things beyond [mind and mental factors] when examining the status of those two. Furthermore, the unestablishment of that which has form is not established as mentioned before, but when examining the nature of that itself, the past and so forth will change into the three times [of past, present, and future] and the mind is asserted by all as impermanent.

Furthermore, in general, since it is the special instructions to break things down from the coarse at first, from previous rebirths up to the present [life] and future rebirths from here on make three. [12a] Then this [life] itself is gradually broken down into years, months, days, and moments. Here, in terms of the very moment itself, the past and the future are nonexistent. Candrakīrti teaches that since everything is impermanent, there is nothing other than mere cause and effect. Since cause and effect is mere dependence, it is conventional, but is itself not at all ultimately established. Here the present moment is **extremely difficult to examine.** Nonmaterial entities **do not have color,** like white and so forth, and are **free from shapes,** like a square and so forth. When nonmaterial entities have such a nature, apart from being devoid of touch that obstructs, since such entities are not established as having a material nature, they are not established, like space. In another way, nonmaterial entities are devoid of unity and multiplicity. When considering an object of mental awareness called "mind" for all awarenesses, and classifying that into mind (*sems*) and mental factors (*sems las byung ba*), mind is not established as a unity. This applies to mental factors also, for the feeling that is produced as the nature of experience, the perception that apprehends phenomenal marks, and the conditioning factors that are produced as the nature of effort and exertion may be classified into three and are not established as a unity. The mind [12a4] has the nature of ideation, and feeling itself when classified at its base has three types. Through classifying, those three types of feeling being produced among the assembly of six types of consciousness that are distinguished into eighteen types of sensory awareness that are not established as a unity. There are even more types of awareness than that when classified according to the apprehension of phenomenal marks. Even more than that, when produced as the nature of effort and striving, the conditional factors are like the trunk of a plantain tree. Consciousness also, from among six or eight types, is various when divided for the object for each and every one of the sensory organs. Since it observes the accumulation of consciousness for the five organs, the consciousness of the eye perceives various colors and shapes up to the bodily consciousness perceiving various objects of touch. Since mental consciousness has the nature to perceive the various eight conditioned dharmas and eight unconditioned dharmas and so forth, that which is called an aggregate is not established as singular. If one asserts that the mental factors do not exist and that consciousness exists as one group, the *Ratnāvalī* states:

> If the instant has a final moment, we must assume that it has the other two moments as well, namely, the initial and the middle; but inasmuch as the instant consists of three moments, the world cannot have the duration of the instant (I.69). Again, beginning, middle, and end must be considered to be like the instant, namely, each one divided into three moments; the condition of being beginning, middle, and end [is not existent by itself nor by another.][811]

Thus consciousness is not established as a unity and is accepted by all as being momentary. From this it is necessary to accept an end point. [12b] Further, since the beginning is dependent on a middle, segments of time become three. When contemplating each and every one of the three segments of time as momentary, by the same reasoning the three will each have three, making nine segments of time. At any rate, the measure of a instant is taught as one finger snap in the refutation of sixty-two [views] from [Candrakīrti's] *Catuḥśatakaṭīkā*. In other [texts], that to be refuted is one hundred twenty or three hundred sixty. It is worthless to examine the momentary down to this extent, as it occurs without an intrinsic nature. In another way, it is unproduced when examined by the five reasonings that refute production. Alternatively, there is natural luminosity, and by breaking down through these reasonings, [the mind] is not made empty, but since it is naturally unproduced, when it is not elaborated by elaborations or not conceptualized by concepts of "this is form," "this is not form," "low and excellent," "large and middle-sized," and so forth, the mind is called "**luminous**."

> Abiding, arising, and ceasing, existence and nonexistence, low, middle, and superior—the Buddha spoke of these under the power of wordly transactions, not under the power of reality.[812]

How is the mind accepted as naturally luminous? Through the principle that it is unsuitable to consist of adventitious defilements. The nature of the mind is luminosity, and that itself is also called the "element of sentient beings" or the "essence of the Tathāgata (*tathāgatagarbha*)." Since all conceptual elaborations are adventitious defilements, that luminous nature may be actualized through study and reflection in purifying the adventitious defilements. [12b6] This teaching is similar to Yogācāras who teach that it is considered pure, just as water, gold, and space are pure. In this way, **when analyzed and broken down by the weapon of reasoning**, objects of knowledge, from the perspective of either having form or not having form, are not at all established, since **the very wisdom that individually discriminates** is not established. This illustration is suitable, as form, experience, and so forth are **specific characteristics**. The **general characteristics** of all conditioned things is that they are impermanent, the general characteristics of all contaminated things is that they are suffering, and the general characteristic of all things is that they are selfless and so forth. Since all things are unestablished, the very wisdom of that is without appearance. Since the wisdom itself in the interval of refuting is without appearance, as an object of mind it does not exist. However, since the final relation is said to not be established at all in the explanation of reality, material entities, nonmaterial entities, and the very wisdom itself are naturally unestablished. The explanation of **luminosity** means that it is free from the extremes of elaboration and it is free from all the eight extremes of elaboration, such as distinctions of dharmas like cessation and production and so forth.

[13a1] In this way, having settled the mind at the time of application, one eliminates the faults of **laxity and excitement** from being established in the nonconceptual state at the time of meditative equipoise. **Laxity** is not having control over the mind in practice by being overcome with sleepiness, lethargy, and so forth. In going to sleep, one arises from sleep not apprehending the object of meditation. Laxity is taught in divisions of "great" and "middling," like entering nondarkness, like blinking one's eyes, and like a blind person. **Excitement** is being totally scattered to other objects of meditation, a distraction derived from attention being scattered to other virtues.

Eradicating those: By meditating on entities that are clear and bright, laxity passes away. When hardship occurs, select an antidote to both laxity and excitement, just as Śāntideva has taught that one should meditate on only the remembrance of death. One should sprinkle water on the face if one has gone to sleep, or, hearing a great noise, it is suitable to recite the stories of a father's death. Meditating on only emptiness is said to be like a great medicine that eradicates all unharmonious positions. To summarize in brief, emptiness eradicates all other faults of meditation, like the five faults and the five obscurations. Moreover, during meditative equipoise when any knowledge or objects of knowledge are not at all established, even objects of knowledge, material entities, nonmaterial entities, and wisdom itself are not cognized. [13a6] Anything whatsoever is nonconceptual. The apprehended object and apprehending subject, or the obstruction and the antidote, are also nonconceptual. One applies the following words as a cause of the nonconceptual, or in another way, by not apprehending anything at all, **memory** does not exist, and through not comprehending anything, one abandons all **mental activity** and stands firm.

As for this, the practitioners of the Great Completion (*rdzogs chen*), the practitioners of nonmentation (*amanasikāra*), and those who enter instantaneously assert that [meditation] is merely being without memory and mental attentiveness, which overturns the scattering of knowledge for the object. Just as one will not be free from the fear of demons by meditating that demons are not in the castle, likewise one will not be free from the fear of apprehending things as real. As previously mentioned, it is necessary to develop nonconceptual concentration in a way that cuts off attachment by means of not finding when searching through reasoning. [13b] It is like when an intelligent person, having hoisted up a lamp, through searching but not finding, is free from the fear of a demon. Distinguishing phenomenal **marks** include the five objects of form and so forth; the three times, persons, and the distinguishing marks of women make ten. Many more occur in the section on signlessness as a door of liberation in the *Perfection of Wisdom* sūtras. Of concern at present—the grasping of material phenomenal marks, nonmaterial marks, and wisdom or even conceptuality, the conceptuality of the obscuration and the antidote. A **phenomenal mark** is an object that scatters [the mind] like **a thief** who sneakingly steals nonconceptual concentration. **Conceptuality** is a coarse object that is like an enemy by scattering the actual nonconceptual concentration. One should abide in the nonconceptual state, being free from these [phenomenal marks and conceptions]. When they arise, through eradicating before the grasping at phenomenal marks and the very object of conceptuality, one will train in the nonconceptual mental continuum for objects of knowledge not yet accomplished. This section, which brings forth the [teachings of the] Ācārya [Nāgārjuna], was bestowed by the Lord [Atiśa] to Sangphuwa.

[13b3] Then, if one decides to go beyond one hour and twenty minutes and so forth for the duration of the [meditation] session, one should rise up when the body and mind become fatigued. If one does not know the time, one should do the right amount [of meditation] according to one's teacher or superior. A sudden interruption is unnacceptable for the mind in meditation. It is unnacceptable to sit again in the same seat after [immediately] going away from the meditation. One should sit down continually in meditation without being suddenly interrupted [and] when there is adequate focus on the object of meditation. When rising from the meditation mat, make a clap. Since harm or sickness may occur, and the body and mind may be harmed, just as Gönpawa and Potowa have done, extend all the limbs, rub all the muscles smoothly, and with a pleasant and pliable body rise up and go. Moreover, the cross-legged posture should be disrupted by rising in the same way.

The way things are should be examined, as previously, by oneself, and meditate just as if there is indeed nonproduction. However, one should dedicate the roots of virtue for perfect buddhahood to the extent of reaching all the things grasped as real by sentient beings [13b7] by projecting compassion for sentient beings who wander in *saṃsāra* by the force of not cognizing [things as unproduced]. At the time of meditation, having closed the door or covered the window, sit in meditation. Having arisen [from meditation], it is said that one should not eat in the field or give mother's milk to a calf or grass to a horse. For all fields and commerce and so forth, it will not do to ask if they are accomplished or not accomplished. [14a] This is to get distracted with imputing imputations, whereas all phenomena are like an illusion; mental engagement and so forth is like thick mist or like a rainbow. As much as possible, one should do virtuous acts and so forth for the two collections or the six perfections by body, speech, and mind by the method of threefold perfect purity [of agent, action, and object]. One should dedicate as much as one achieves for the purpose of complete awakening. As in the interval on emptiness, it is taught that afterward [things] are like an illusion. Generally, since this is settled after the unmistaken treasure of meditative equipoise, it is necessary to weaken attachment for this life after meditative equipoise on impermanence. It is necessary to shun evil and increase virtue after meditative equipoise on the relations of cause and effect. In this manner, one should ascertain all meditations with postcontemplative knowledge. Both quantities of postcontemplative knowledge and meditative equipoise can be purified in Radreng. Later on both quantities can even exist in all places.

Postcontemplative knowledge is in disagreement with the entire world. One should uphold a majority of harmonious practices of a bodhisattva, which is taught from all the sūtras and *śāstras* of the Mahāyāna, and rejoice in altruism for others—Potowa has [discussed] this. Right now in one's own state of meditative equipoise, cultivate only the aspect of integration. In the postconcentrative state of this lifetime, there is not another aspect that is desired. Just a few persons greatly invoke mindfulness **in this lifetime**; the extremes of the head and shoulder are like one who hears that leads a blind person. The great majority of people do not live apart from desirable things, in addition to food, clothing, and dear ones, like relatives. The beginner should create as much virtue as possible when unable to subdue everything; doing as much as possible for each [meditative] fixation with respect to different factors during each individual juncture will become meaningful. Finally, it is necessary to offer aspirational prayers and cultivate devotion, completely engaging in what is necessary to achieve complete buddhahood. Having done so, by meditating on emptiness, one will surely become a master, and it will serve as an antidote to all unfavorable conditions. One's conduct in the postconcentrative state produces multiple virtues in one's own mental continuum and one will nourish sentient beings. In cultivating emptiness alone, which does not nourish beings, one will not cognize suchness, and even if cognizing, it will be from the point of view of a *śrāvaka*.

[14a8] In this way, the measure of **devotion**, in the *Śikṣāsamuccaya*—just as one wishes for a cool water source in a burning house, by gathering the evil spirit of grasping things as real or through the darkness of delusion, [14b] all mother-like sentient beings accumulate various bad actions and have extensive passionate attachment. One wanders in cyclic existence, which is everywhere like a house blazing. Then, emerging from that state by cultivating the understanding of nonproduction, by great devotion one thinks that grasping things as real is to be avoided, but that is not to experience the undegenerated essence. Moreover, when not falling into scattering while meditating for as long as one is able and **for a long time**, one is said to reach the boundary at the point of the fundamental state of awakening, the essence. Futhermore, it is necessary to employ both meditative equipoise and posterior practices continuously for multiple years, months, days, or even for an instant. After eliminating unceasing evil deeds, it is necessary to have a basis of meditation. Then, at that time, unconscientious behavior will be eliminated. With solid, erroneous predispositions, not to abandon the taste of alcohol would not do; it is just like pursuing a cooked, rotten fish while not knowing the pure portions. It is necessary to be unconcerned even in the time interval after meditation.

From the point of view of **those with** incalculable **good fortune**, who have done what is needed, even the Noble Sadāprarudita's great good fortune[813] was mainly through practicing the factors of method. At the time of Geshe Shönjung (*gzhon 'byung*) arriving at Radreng, saying that there exists the special instructions for obtaining the accomplishment of the Great Seal (*mahāmudrā*) in this very lifetime for all individuals, Potowa [taught that] the fortune of accomplishing the Great Seal **in this very lifetime** is not [innately] produced like our own complexions. Rather, it is said to be produced on the ground of one's own [effort], like the eighteen different craftsman of the great city of the central land and those skilled in the five topics of science and so forth. The understanding of all phenomena is said to be the only thing that counts. Reality is again said to be the only single truth, the only object of the unproduced. It is just suchness. The worldly meditate on the state of nonproduction emerging dimly as substantially existent and that does not pass beyond the conventional itself. All seeing is seeing false conventionalities.

Meditative equipoise and the exact perception of the bodhisattva's postconcentrative state, from the point of seeing reality onward, are precepts of the *Saṃdhinirmocana[sūtra]*. Called the **center of the sky** by being free from extremes, there does not exist a center that has a reference point. It is an example illustrating that nothing at all is established. The other eight examples of an illusion [15a] and so forth exist as mere appearances from collecting and assembling. The establishment of a real nature is an example that is established as nonexistent. Geshé Tönpa widely taught that correct conventional activities are said to be mundane postconcentrative appearances. Since it is likewise, **the postmeditative attainment** after seeing reality realizes the true nature of the conventional. Through the blessing of the Buddha, all the eight examples of illusion, along with the plaintree, come forth as a means to understand the meaning of nonproduction. After the teachings have subsided, all those who are incapable are taught the [analogy of the] echo from this moment on as a measure of disappearance.

[15a2] "**From the point of time when**" indicates to ascertain the meaning at the level of a Buddha. The text states that the **concentration** is like the example of a **vajra.** Just as the vajra destroys all entities while itself remaining indestructible, likewise when attaining this concentration all the latencies of apprehending things as real are destroyed while the apprehension of things as real is unable to create a nature that apprehends things as real. The teaching of Candrakīrti asserts that, from this point on, all movements of mind and mental factors are perpetually cut off. This system of thought does not assert the activity of postconcentrative attainment other than meditative equipoise. Even if accepting postconcentrative attainment, alternations [between meditative equipoise and postconcentrative attainment] are not accepted. The object of meditation of meditative equipoise at all times is taught to be reality. The *Daśabhūmikasūtra*, by means of questions and answers, teaches that the meditative equipoise is only for the welfare of sentient beings. The meaning is that by the first moment of exalted wisdom in the second moment of attaining the vajra-like concentration through the principle "that totally pervades the sphere of objects of knowledge," all objects of knowledge just as they are (*ji lta ba, yathāvad-bhāvika*) and to their utmost extent (*ji snyed pa, yāvad-bhāvika*) are spontaneously realized just as they are. After that, the meaning of abiding is shining like a great sun that never declines.

We settle buddhahood awkwardly only in the Buddha level. Buddhahood is understood as merely *nirvāṇa* for the Sautrāntikas in not having a continuum of utmost highest wisdom. One is unable to measure [a continuum] that has entered into the stabilizing on the meditation of cessation, since at the time buddahood is only the meditative equipoise that does not posses subsequent knowledge. It would not do to understand that state of meditative equipoise as a time opposite from that of blinking the eyes or deep sleep. [15b] In following Mahāyāna sūtras, one proceeds with faith alone on the qualities of the Buddha level. However, buddhahood is not realized from the *śāstras*. Since even the lords of the tenth stage are said not to realize [things] other than the sun among the clouds or merely the space of a needle's eye, how could we realize [reality] by stating only what is picked out by our own conceptuality? At the time of asking Geshé Tönpa whether a continuum of wisdom was possessed or not and whether subsequent attainment was possessed or not at the level of a buddha, [he replied:] "I say that I have not known awakening indivisibly and exactly as it is because it has not been known previously by anyone other than a buddha himself." Therefore it is suitable for the Buddha to be the source of one's own refuge if one is ill at ease in the world. It is suitable even if ill at ease with the particular thought in mind to save sentient beings in order to attain buddhahood. Acting for the benefit of sentient beings is suitable whether or not it is suitable for there to be a continuum of wisdom or whether or not subsequent attainment is suitable. This is like the conceptual thought that precedes the preparation for wisdom. Furthermore, acting for the benefit of sentient beings is said to be exclusively projected at the time of generating the initial aspiration thought [for awakening].

[As regards the text] "**if it is not so that there is not subsequent attainment on the level of a buddha, then what is the distinction with a bodhisattva?**" and similar words, it may be that this teaching is not indicated in reasoning and scripture, but since the activity of subsequent attainment is a quality of training to be done, it is taught only in the sūtras of reasoning themselves. Isn't it deceiving sentient beings, who are entertained at first, by cutting off the benefit to others when abiding on the ground of only permanent meditative equipoise? How does the benefit to others arise? The benefit arises as follows. At first, by generating compassion, one produces the altruistic aim to benefit sentient beings. Then the accumulations are gathered solely for the benefit/welfare of sentient beings. Aspirational prayers are also made solely for the benefit/welfare of [sentient beings]. From the perspective of a buddha who is practicing for sentient beings, one does not achieve the benefit/welfare of sentient beings from the power of meditative equipoise itself. Furthermore, from the beginning of buddhahood, because of the ability to completely accomplish the welfare of sentient beings until sentient beings are exhausted, [the Buddha's] appearance and disappearance does not exist and [he] comes forth spontaneously, independent of exertion. Therefore there is also not forgetting. There is forgetfulness when it is necessary to rely on effort and exertion. In this way, from the purview of a buddha, there is not conceptuality. This does not conflict with the forces of the fortune of sentient beings who are different due to outward actions and actions based on the five sense objects into differences of higher and lower. From the *Tathāgatotpattisambhāvasūtra*:

> When the orb of the sun arises initially, it reflects on the elevated mountain peaks, [16a] then gradually it reflects heroically in all the deep forests and in the lower areas, as it is taught that the activities of the buddha level are in every way a system of deeds for the benefit of others. Through the qualities of the Tathāgata and his inconceivable wisdom: some are in the circle of attendents; some are inclinded toward becoming a monk of the Tathāgata and are known to renounce the family; some become monks; some practice austerities; some proceed to the seat of awakening; some understand him to sit at the seat of awakening; some understand that he conquers over Māra; some know that he manifests buddhahood; some understand that he is requested to turn the wheel of dharma by Brahmā and so forth; some understand that he turns the wheel of dharma; some hear him give a discourse on the *Śrāvaka* Vehicle; some hear him give a discourse on the *Pratyekabuddha* Vehicle; some hear him give a discourse on the Great Vehicle; some see a sixfold-tall Tathāgata; some instantly hear him from far away; some see him in the body of a Tathāgata hundreds of thousands of *niyutas* of *koṭis* long; some see him as a golden-colored Tathāgata; some see him as the color of a precious wish-fulfilling jewel; some understand him to pass into complete *nirvāṇa*; some understand him to achieve complete *nirvāṇa*; some understand him to be inclined to engagement; some understand him as one incorruptible body; some understand him to establish relics of a Tathāgata; some understand him to mature ten years after attaining complete buddhahood; some understand him to pass ten years in his complete *nirvāṇa*; some understand him to arrive at the terrace of awakening; some understand the teaching of Bhagavan Śākyamuni to disappear; some understand ten, twenty, thirty, forty, or hundreds of thousands of *niyutas* of *koṭis* of eons since his complete *nirvāṇa*; some understand an ineffable number of aeons since Bhagavan Śākyamuni's buddhahood. The Tathāgata perpetually grows in these activities through the force of considering the welfare of sentient beings nonconceptually, without conceptuality, even more so in a spontaneous, nonconceptual manner.[814]

The *Avataṃsakasūtra* states:

> Mañjuśrī, it is as follows: [16b] For example, there is an ocean that is five thousand *yojana*s in size. A bird sits at the edge [of the ocean], as [there] it is suitable to drink. There are some lotus-leaf coverings. With respect to this [scenario], a man has a thousand-spoked-wheel iron chariot. The chariot is drawn speedily by a strong horse who is like a *garuḍa* bird, the axles do not touch the water when pulled by the horse, and the lotus petals are not injured when the chariot is drawn in this way. A poisonous snake springs forth from the ocean. Instantly, in the moments of the chariot turning, [the snake] encircles the chariot seven times. In the moment of the poisonous snake encircling the chariot one time, the monk Ānanda explains and understands ten qualities of ten Dharmas. In the moment of Ānanda's explaining a single Dharma, the monk Śāradvatipūtra understands in a single moment one thousand aspects of Dharma. In the single moment in which Śāradvatipūtra explained the aspects of Dharma, the monk Maudgalyāyana passes through eighty thousand world-realms. In the moment in which Maudgalyāyana passes through a world-realm, in that moment, the Tathāgata instantly teaches everywhere and spontaneously in a nonconceptual manner, easily through the realm of reality (*dharmadhātu*), in world-realms of the ten directions to the limits of the realm of space, in each and every world-realm in all the ocean of galaxies, in each and every continent, to each and every hair on your head. Furthermore: dying and passing from the realm of Tuṣita; entering the womb; being born; being received by Indra and Brahmā; [16b6] arranging a dwelling place; taking seven steps; looking in the ten directions; making a great lion's roar; training in arts, crafts, athletics, and all the five sciences; being taught in the stages of royalty; sporting in the retinue of female attendents; going forth to the forest grove; tending toward omniscience; departure from home; taking up the homeless life; performing austerities; forsaking the eating of food; departing to and entering the seat of awakening; conquering over Māra; awakening into buddhahood; viewing with his eyes unblinking at the tree of awakening; being requested to teach by great Brahmā; turning the wheel of dharma; going to the divine realms; providing different aspects to the object of complete awakening; [17a] the turning the wheel of the law; giving the name of the eon, the measure of time, the array of the retinue, the man-

ner in which the arrangement of the buddha-field is purified; the activity and aspiration of the mind for awakening, the perfections, grounds, [and] supersensory knowledges, the patiences, the dhāraṇīs, the concentrations, the liberations; the offerings for that; the immeasurable objects of dharma of the bodhisattvas and the tathāgatas; the different engagements in the immeasurable cloud of dharma; the ripening of sentient beings; the different aspects of setting forth skillful means; emanating great miraculous emanations; indicating the great complete *nirvāṇa*; distributing solid relics in a single body; teaching at all times during the flourishing of the practices of Dharma; the conflicts, the diminishment, and even disappearance of the holy Dharma. All the practices in the places of non-Buddhists, even in the entire succession of previous rebirths, by teaching continuously through blessings to the limit of eons until the end of time, on each and every mere hair, from the ten directions the very momentary object up through each and every hairpore, the *tathāgatas* in the three times, all along with the oceanic assembly of bodhisattvas, all the extensive array of buddha qualities, all the arrays of the abodes of the lineages of sentient beings, the extensively designated sensory-spheres of the lineage of sentient beings, all of the extensively arranged, perfectly established activities of bodhisattvas, and all the extensive arrangement of the object of a *tathāgata* are instantly taught in a nonconceptual, spontaneous manner. All the extensive array of omnipresent, continuous blessings to the limit, until the end of time, he teaches down to the mere measure of a hair, in that very moment, through ten directions, instantly teaching spontaneously and nonconceptually in all realms of sentient beings without exception, every sentient being without a body, all sentient beings with a body, and other distinctions of shape, color, voice, language, and different aspects of teaching Dharma and so forth. [17b] Through the force of the thoughts of other sentient beings, he teaches in all ways continuously through blessings to the limit until the end of time. Mañjuśrī, it is as follows, at midnight of the fifteenth day of the waxing phase of the moon, the arising of the orb of the moon over Jambudvīpa is seen in places in front of all women, children, and young maidens. The orb of the moon, nonconceptually without thought yet spontaneously, arises like this, having unshared qualities that are nonconceptual. Likewise, all sentient beings, just as they resolve and just as they are to be trained, are seen to dwell in front of the Tathāgata. The tathāgatas,

> nonconceptually, without thought yet spontaneously, arise with such deeds through the unshared qualities of a Buddha.[815]

Thus the benefit is illustrated through all sides. Although there are many scriptures and reasonings for completely ascertaining the meaning of the two realities and ascertaining the level of a buddha, here I will not elaborate. As the special instructions of meditating on the meaning of nonproduction are taught in the manner of pointing out [the moon] with a finger, therefore they are only instructions of the Middle Way.[816] This is in accordance with engaging in the teachings of the methods of the nonconceptuality of nonproduction in all the secret mantra texts. Teaching using another terminology is sometimes difficult to understand. Entering the spindle of that terminology leads to a great abyss that is unsuitable for meditation.

> Through illuminating the special instructions of the Middle Way,
> whatever virtue I have have obtained,
> may all beings become omniscient
> through entering the path of the Middle Way.

[18a] In cutting off all affairs [of worldly life], one does not meet with evil friends. In meeting with good friends through proper measures, one should greatly progress in the protective commitments that one has promised. One should mainly refrain from material things of this life such as food, clothing, and so forth. However, do not fall into decay. Whatever dharma has been produced in the present that is unfinished should not diminish. One should be greatly concerned about faulty moral virtue and spoiled vows. May it be auspicious.

Appendix of Translated Passages

1. *Atiśa's Bodhisattvacāryavatārabhāṣya*

[The following passage is an excerpt from Atiśa's *Bodhisattvacāryāvatārabhāṣya*, a summary on Śāntideva's *Bodhicaryāvatāra*, where Atiśa directly addressed the controversial topic of the status of gnosis at the level of a buddha.]

> The Dharma body (*dharmakāya*) is the level of buddhahood where gnosis (*jñāna*) has been cut off. To understand that the continuum of gnosis is cut off: that gnosis while in the phase of the Dharma body does not substantially exist according to the view of permanence, nor does it not exist at all according to the view of annihilation. Both [permanence and annihilation] are not acceptable. In brief, within present cyclic existence, the continuum of conceptual knowledge is not acceptable as a singular cause to experience [the Dharma body]. Through eliminating all conceptual thought of the subject that apprehends and for the object that is apprehended, it is said that "the nonexistence of the object of observation itself is pacified." That is called the Dharma body. It is for these reasons [that the *Bodhicaryāvatāra* states],
>
> When neither an entity nor nonentity remain before the mind, then, because there is no other aspect [to observe], the [mind] is pacified without any apprehension.[817]
>
> To further understand that the continuum of gnosis is cut off, the Ācarya Akṣayamati asked Ārya Mañjuśrī, "Noble One, is this continuum of conceptual knowledge discerned within a buddha's gnosis?" [Mañjuśrī replied,] "Even that gnosis is not apprehended." Therefore, [the *Bodhicaryāvatāra* states,]
>
> "The ultimate is not within the range of the intellect. Mind and words are conventional."[818]

In this way, this continuum of present knowledge is taught not to experience [the ultimate]. The Ācārya asked, "If there is not an object of mind for the ultimate, how will [the ultimate] be experienced?" [Mañjuśrī replied,] "When sought out from the purview of those with limited vision, it is the experience of nonexistence. It is for this reason that one explains ultimate reality with synonyms such as 'internal emptiness, external emptiness, internal and external emptiness, the emptiness of emptiness, great emptiness.'"

[The Ācārya said,] "In that case, the synonym for those of limited vision is emptiness and one then wonders if that which is construed as ultimate reality is changeless and stable and separately exists as one." [Mañjuśrī replied,] "Since it is taught that the ultimate is emptiness, one states, 'It is devoid of even the gnosis that realizes the ultimate.' In brief, when all the conceptual thoughts of those with limited vision disappear, by being devoid of sentient beings, their objects, their activities, and so forth, gnosis is cut off."

[The Ācārya asked,] "If realization does not exist for the benefit of beings, since gnosis has been cut off, how would that be suitable, as even the two form bodies [of a buddha] would not occur? How can they exist according to individual karma and good fortune?"

[Mañjuśrī replied,] "[The two bodies] appear to bodhisattvas, *śrāvakas*, *pratyekabuddhas*, and ordinary individuals even though nonconceptual wisdom does not exist, [as the *Bodhicaryāvatāra* 9.35 (Tib. 36 states,] 'As the wishing-gem and the magical tree fulfill desires, so the body of the Conqueror appears because of those to be disciplined and his vow.'"

[The Ācārya asked,] "Well then, as the appearance is totally based on merit, when there is a precious jewel such as that, the jewel and so forth are nonconceptual. If the blessings of a nonconceptual buddha do not exist, what is the meritorious fortune of individual sentient beings, *śrāvakas*, *pratyekabuddhas*, and bodhisattvas? If merit is not accumulated, then there is not an appearance."

[Mañjuśrī replied,] "That is not [the case]. For example, when the form of the moon appears in clear water, if the water does not exist, then the appearance of the moon does not exist. If the moon does not exist, the cause for the appearance in the water does not exist. Similar to this example, if the bodhisattvas and so forth do not exist, the appearance of the form body does not exist. Like the moon, if the Buddha does not exist, the cause for the occurrence of the form body does not exist. In this way, therefore, although there is not conceptual thought, when the conditions are gathered by training on the path, all the activities are accomplished through observing sentient beings as an object and then, due to previous aspirational prayers, the form bodies appear while not having conceptuality and accomplish owing to the force of previous aspirational prayers. For example, previously as a brahmin, Mañju[śrī] constructed a snake-healing pillar, thinking to benefit others. Accordingly, the brahmin perished after constructing [the pillar], and [the pillar] benefits others, although it does not have conceptual thought in its benefits. Likewise, although the perfect Buddha does not have gnosis that realizes, by the force of previous aspirational prayers, the form bodies [appear] in accord with the aim of sentient beings and the wishes of bodhisattvas and so forth. In this way, it is an essential point for both [sentient beings and bodhisattvas]. The precious jewel and so forth are examples of only nonconceptuality. Therefore this is explained as a correct example, [when the *Bodhicaryāvatāra* states,][819]

'As a snake charmer perishes after having completed a pillar [of healing], even a long time after his perishing, it still cures the effect of poison: So also the Conqueror-pillar, having been completed by conformity to the Way of Awakening, does all that is to be done, even when the Bodhisattva has disappeared.'"[820]

2. *Atiśa's Bodhimārgapradīpapañjikā*

[The following passage is an excerpt from Atiśa's *Bodhimārgapradīpapañjikā*, indicating key Madhyamaka standpoints discussed in the Introduction.]

[1] When one examines reality, all things that appear and all tenets and so forth that are imputed are accepted as being mistaken and false.

[2] For example, a diseased eye, owing to defects, sees sewing-needles, hairs, two moons, or a mass of bees. They exist for an awareness that apprehends them in that way.

[3] For example, through the force of sleep and one's habitual tendencies, one experiences happiness, suffering, forms, and so forth. They exist for an awareness that apprehends them in that way.

[4] Likewise, from beginningless time, the diseased eye of ignorance with its defects experiences external and internal entities. They exist for an awareness that apprehends them in that way.

[5] Also, from beginningless time, in the great, deep sleep of ignorance comes the dream of the four types of habitual tendencies. They are experienced when apprehended in that way.

[6] When one examines the ultimate sense, the real nature of things is unable to be established as existent or nonexistent by those mistaken conceptions.

[7] For example, with an unfit, diseased eye one is unable to state that hair in one's vision does not exist. When the diseased eye becomes fit, one is unable to say that the hair in one's vision exists.

[8] For example, when one wakes from the sleep of ignorance, one is unable to say one sees a dream. As long as one does not wake up, one is not able to say the dream does not exist.

[9] When one recovers from diseased vision, and when one awakens from sleep, the hair in one's vision, the dream and so forth, [and] the awareness that apprehends them in that way no longer exist.

[10] Likewise, when one recovers from the diseased vision of ignorance or the deep sleep of ignorance, all appearances and imputations and the awareness that experiences them no longer exist.

[11] In proclaiming whether the continuum is interrupted or unceasing, for someone who posits existence, the continuum ceases; in reality, that does not exist, the childish analysis suddenly comes to end.

[12] However, the Ācārya Śāntideva did not claim here that the continuum ceases; in his exposition on nonexistence and the continuum ceasing, his special instructions state:[821]

[13] There is nothing at all to be removed here. There is nothing to be established. Reality should be perceived as it is, and one who sees reality becomes liberated.[822]

[14] Some of our own and others' schools have established that things exist. Others state that things do not exist.

[15] When one analyzes reality, existence and nonexistence do not exist as real limits. They are not able to be established anywhere.

[16] Those outside the lineage of spiritual teachers, although establishing existence, nonexistence, permanence, annihilation, and so forth with their inferential knowledge, will grow weary and not reach their goal.

[17] Why did Dharmakīrti, Dharmottara, and so forth compose many treatises? Scholars wrote [them] in order to refute the objections of non-Buddhists.

[18] Thus valid cognition is unnecessary for cultivating ultimate reality. I have already mentioned this elsewhere.[823] For the time being, it is not necessary to speak about it here.

[19] Therefore one should cast aside texts of logic that are mainly concerned with inference and one should cultivate the special instructions of the lineage based on the explanatory tradition of the Ārya Nāgārjuna.

[20] Reality (*tattva*) that is free from the four extremes—neither existent, nor nonexistent, nor both existent and nonexistent, nor even neither [existent nor nonexistent]—is known by the Mādhyamika.[824]

[21] The Mādhyamika realize reality that is liberated from the four alternatives: neither eternal, nor annihilated, nor both eternal and annihilated, nor even neither [eternal and annihilated].

[22] Gone beyond what corresponds to existence and nonexistence, eliminating permanence and annihilation, released from knowledge and object of knowledge; this is the tradition of the Great Middle Way.

[23] Those concerned with inference speak of existence, nonexistence, permanence, annihilation, and so forth, [and] do not

pursue reality; their knowledge amounts to nothing more than reification and deprecation.

[24] For example, gold, sky, water, and so forth have pure natures, yet the faults that appear to be associated with them should not be pursued.

[25] Eliminate reification and deprecation and cultivate only the reality that definitely liberates from all imputations while not residing in any tenets.

[26] Meditate on only the special instructions of the lineage of the Ārya Nāgārjuna, Āryadeva, Candrakīrti, Bhavya, and Śāntideva.

[27] If there is no one of the lineage, then repeatedly study the texts composed by them.

[28] All things have the door of "A," from the beginning unproduced, unceasing, naturally *nirvāṇa*, pure by nature.

[29] Even if one sees, the sight does not exist; the seer, what is seen, and the awareness of seeing do not exist at all. The Sage is always in meditative equipoise.

[30] When eliminating all conceptual thought and abiding in the realm of reality (*dharmadhātu*), arising and entering are unacceptable for the gnosis of great yoga.

[31] Therefore I do not accept meditative equipoise and the post-meditative state for buddhahood. [Those two] are while abiding on the [bodhisattva] stages, as explained from the *Avikalpapraveśadhāraṇī*.

[32] As I have not expanded on this point here, one must repeatedly request [its explanation] by making offerings and veneration to a spiritual teacher who understands my text.

[33] By following after Bodhibhadra, who holds the lineage descending from Ārya Nāgārjuna predicted by the Omniscient One, refrain from holding any tenet whatsoever.

Table of Tibetan Transliteration

Amé Naljorpa Jangchup Rinchen	A mes Rnal 'byor pa Byang chub rin chen (aka Naljorpa, Naljorpa Chenpo)
Ānandagarbha	Kun dga' snying po
Ba	Rba
Bangtön Jangchup Gyaltsen	Bang ston Byang chub rgyal mtshan
Barak	Sba rag
Bhikṣu *Paiṇḍapātika of Java	Dge slong Bsod snyoms pa Ya ba dwi pa
Chakdar Tönpa	Phyag dar ston pa
Chakri Gongkhawa	Lcags ri Gong kha pa
Chakriwa	Lcags ri ba
Changkya Rölpai Dorjé	Lcang skya Rol pa'i rdo rje
Chapa Chökyi Sengé	Phywa pa Chos kyi seng ge
Chengawa Tsultrim Bar	Spyan snga ba Tshul khrims 'bar
Chim Namkha Drak	Mchim Nam kha' grags
Chimphu	'Chims phu
Chomden Rikpai Raldri	Bcom ldan rig pa'i ral gri
Danma	Lda ma
Dawa Gyaltsen	Zla ba rgyal mtshan
Denma	'Dan ma

Dergé	Sde dge
Dokham	Mdo khams
Domé Tsongkha	Mdo smad tsong kha
Drakpa Gyaltsen	Grags pa rgyal mtshan
Drangkha Berchung	’Phrang kha ber chung
Dren	’Dren
Drepung	’Bras spungs
Dring	’Bring
Dring Yeshé Yönten	Bring Ye shes yon tan
Drok Jhosé Dorjé Bar	’Brog Jo sras rdo rje ’bar
Drokmi Śākya Yeshé	’Brog mi Shākya ye shes
Dromtönpa	’Brom ston pa
Dromtönpa Gyalwai Jungné	’Brom ston Rgyal ba’i ’byung gnas
Dusum Khyenpa	Dus gsum mkhyen pa
Gampopa	Sgam po pa
Gampopa Sönam Rinchen	Sgam po pa Bsod nams rin chen
Gargewa	Mgar dge ba
Gelukpa	Dge lugs pa
Geshé	Dge bshes
Geshé Chakdar	Dge bshes Phyag dar
Geshé Kawa	Dge bshes Ska wa
Geshé Naljorpa	Dge bshes Rnal ’byor pa
Geshé Tönpa (=Dromtönpa)	Dge bshes Ston pa
Gö Lotsāwa Shönu Pal	’Gos lo tsā ba Gzhon nu dpal
Gönpawa	Dgon pa ba

Gönpawa Wangchuk Gyaltsen	Dgon pa ba Dbang phyug rgyal mtshan
Gya Chakri Gongkawa Jangchup Pal	Rgya Lcags ri gong kha ba Byang chub dpal
Gya Lotsāwa	Rgya Lo tsā ba
Gya Tsöndrü Sengé	Rgya Brtson 'grus seng ge
Gyal	Rgyal
Gyalsé Thokmé Sangpo	Rgyal sras Thog med bzang po
Gyamar Jangchup Drak	Rgya dmar ba Byang chub grags
Gyaphip	Rgya phibs
Ja Dülzin Tsöndrü Bar	Bya 'Dul 'dzin Brtson 'grus 'bar
Jampai Lodrö	Byams pa'i blo gros
Jangchup Ö	Byang chub 'od
Jayülwa Shönu Ö	Bya yul ba Gzhon nu 'od
Jowo	Jo bo
Kachu	Kva chu
Kadampa	Bka' gdams pa
Kagyüpa	Bka' rgyud pa
Karma Tenkyong Wangpo	Kar ma Bstan skyong dbang po
Kawa Shākya Wangchuk	Ka ba Shā kya dbang phyug
Kham	Khams
Khutön Tsöndrü Yungdrung	Khu ston Brtson 'grus g.yung drung
Khyung Gochan	Khyung mgo can
Kyirong	Skyi rong
Kyotön Mönlam Tsultrim	Skyo ston Smon lam tshul khrims
Lachen Gongpa Rabsel	Bla chen dgong pa rab gsal

Langri Thangpa Dorjé Sengé	Glang ri thang pa Rdo rje seng ge
Lechen Kunga Gyaltsen	Las chen Kun dga' rgyal mtshan
Lha Lama Yeshé Ö	Lha bla ma Ye shes 'od
Lhading	Lha sdings
Lhatsun Jangchup Ö	Lha btsun Byang chub 'od
Lumé	Klu mes, Slu mes
Lumé Sherap Tsultrim	Klu mes Shes rab tshul khrims
Mapja Jangchup Tsöndrü	Rma bya Byang chub brtson 'grus
Mangyul	Mang yul
Metsun Yönten Sherap	Sme btsun Yon tan shes rab
Mikyö Dorjé	Mi bskyod rdo rje
Milarepa	Mi la ras pa
Naktso Lotsāwa Tsultrim Gyalwa	Nag tsho lo tsā ba tshul khrims rgyal ba
Naljorpa	Rnal 'byor pa
Naljorpa Amé Jangchup	Rnal 'byor pa A mad byang chub
Naljorpa Chenpo Jangchup Rinchen	Rnal 'byor pa chen po Byang chub rin chen
Naljorpa Sherap Dorjé	Rnal 'byor pa Shes rab rdo rje
Nam	Gnam
Neusurpa Yeshé Bar	Sne'u zur pa Ye shes 'bar
Ngari	Mnga' ris
Ngawang Losang Gyatso	Ngag dbang blo bzang rgya mtsho
Ngok Lekpai Sherap (aka Sangphuwa)	Rngog Legs pa'i shes rab
Ngok Loden Sherap	Rngog Blo ldan shes rab
Nyantso	Nyan tsho

Nyené Yönten	Nye gnas yon tan
Nyethang	Snye thang
Nyethang Ö	Snye thang 'od
Nyukrumpa	Snyug rum pa
Nyukrumpa Tsöndrü Gyaltsen	Snyug rum pa Brtson 'grus rgyal mtshan
Paltsek	Dpal brtsegs
Patsap Nyimadrak	Spa tshab Nyi ma grags
Phenyul	'Phan yul
Phuchungwa	Phu chung ba
Phuchungwa Shönu Gyaltsen	Phu chung ba Gzhon nu rgyal mtshan
Potowa Rinchen Sal	Po to ba Rin chen gsal
Purang	Pu hrang
Radreng	Rwa sgreng, Ra sgreng, Ra sgyeng
Rak	Rag
Ratna Chakriwa	Ratna lcag ri ba
Rendawa Shönu Lodrö	Red mda' ba Gzhon nu blo gros
Rinchen Sangpo	Rin chen bzang po
Rongpa Gargewasel	Rong pa 'Gar dge ba gsal
Samyé	Bsam yas
Sangphu (monastery)	Gsang phu
Sangphu Neuthok	Gsang phu Ne'u thog
Sangphuwa (aka Ngok Lekpai Sherap)	Gsang phu ba
Sedur	Se rdur
Serlingpa	Gser gling pa

Setön Drachan Dzin	Se ston Sgra gcan 'dzin
Setsun Wangchuk Shönu	Se btsun Dbang phyug gzhon nu
Shang Chenpo	Zhang chen po
Shang Nanam Dorjé Wangchuk	Zhang sna nam Rdo rje dbang phyug
Shang Wangchuk Gön	Zhang Dbang phyug mgon
Shangshung	Zhang zhung
Shangthak Sakpa	Zhang thag sag pa
Sharawa Yönten Drak	Sha ra ba Yon tan grags
Sönam Tsemo	Bsod nams rtse mo
Sölnak Tangboché	Sol nag thang po che
Songtsen Gampo	Srong btsan gam po
Tholing	Mtho lding
Thuken Chökyi Nyima	Thu'u bkwan Chos kyi nyi ma
Tölungpa Rinchen Nyingpo	Stod lung pa Rin chen snying po
Tongten Nago	Stong bstan na mgo
Trathok	Skra 'thog
Tré	Spras
Trichok	Khri mchog
Trulnang	'Phrul snang
Trulnang Tsuglakhang	'Phrul snang gtsug lag khang
Tsang	Gtsang
Tsöndrü Gyaltsen	Brtson 'grus rgyal mtshan
Tsöndrü Sengé	Brtson 'grus seng ge
Tsongkhapa Losang Drakpa	Tsongkhapa Blo gzang grags pa
Tsultrim Gyalwa	Tshul khrims rgyal ba
Ü	Dbus

Üpa Losal	Dbus pa blo gsal
Uru Jang	Dbu ru byang
Yarlung	Yar lung
Yeshé Dé	Ye shes sde
Yokzong (aka Yongzok Naljorpa)	Yog rdzong (Yongs rdzogs rnal 'byor pa)
Yorpo	G.yor po

Abbreviations

AA	*Abhisamayālaṃkāra* (Stcherbatsky and Obermiller 1929)
AAA	*Abhisamayālaṃkārālokā* (Wogihara 1932–35)
AK	*Abhidharmakośa* (Pradhan 1975)
AKBH	*Abhidharmakośabhāṣya* (Pradhan 1975)
AKV	*Abhidharmakośavyākhyā* (Wogihara 1971)
AS	*Abhidharmasamuccaya* (Rāhula 2001)
BCA	*Bodhicaryāvatāra* by Śāntideva (Vaidya 1960)
BCAP	*Bodhicaryāvatārapañjikā* by Prajñākaramati (Vaidya 1960)
BMPP	*Bodhimārgapradīpapañjikā* by Atiśa (Sherburne 2000)
BPP	*Bodhipathapradīpa* by Atiśa (Eimer 1978)
BV	*Bodhicittavivaraṇa* by Ācārya Nāgārjuna (Lindtner 1997b)
D	Tsultrim Rinchen, *Bstan 'gyur (sde dge)*, 1982–85
MA	*Madhyamakāvatāra* by Candrakīrti (La Vallée Poussin 1907–12)
MĀ	*Madhyamakāloka* by Kamalaśīla
MABH	*Madhyamakāvatārabhāṣya* by Candrakīrti (La Vallée Poussin, 1907–12)
MAK	*Madhyamakālaṃkāra* by Śāntarakṣita (Ichigō 1985)
MAV	*Madhyamakālaṃkāravṛtti* by Śāntarakṣita (Ichigō 1985)
MAP	*Madhyamakālaṃkārapañjikā* by Kamalaśīla (Ichigō 1985)
MAS	*Madhyamakārthasaṃgraha* by Bhāviveka (Lindtner 1981)
MAU	*Madhyamakālaṅkāropadeśa* by Ratnākaraśānti
MHK	*Madhyamakahṛdayakārikā*, by Bhāviveka (Lindtner 2001)
MMK	*Mūlamadhyamakakārikā* (La Vallée Poussin 1903–13)
MRP	*Madhyamakaratnapradīpa* by Bhavya or Bhāviveka
MSA	*Mahāyānasūtrālaṃkāra* (Lévi 1983)
MSABH	*Mahāyānasūtrālaṃkārabhāṣya*, by Vasubandhu (Lévi 1983)
MVK	*Madhyāntavibhāgakārikā* by Maitreya (Pandeya 1999)
P	Peking Tengyur
PP	*Prasannapadā* by Candrakīrti (La Vallée Poussin, 1903–13)
PPU	*Prajnāpāramitopadeśa* by Ratnākaraśānti

PV	*Pramāṇavārttikakārikā* by Dharmakīrti (Miyasaka 1971–72)
SDA	*Satyadvayāvatāra* by Atiśa (*Entry to the Two Realities*)
SDV	*Satyadvayavibhaṅga* by Jñānagarbha (Eckel 1987)
TBRC	Tibetan Buddhist Resource Center
Toh	*A Complete Catalogue of the Tibetan Buddhist Canons* (Hakuju et al. 1934)
TS	*Tattvasaṃgraha* by Śāntarakṣita, cited by verse number (Shastri 1968)
TSP	*Tattvasaṃgrahapañjikā* by Kamalaśīla (Shastri 1968)
VV	*Vigrahavyāvartanīkārikā* (Yonezawa 2008)
VVV	*Vigrahavyāvartanīvṛtti* (Johnston and Kunst 1978)
YSV	*Yuktiṣaṣṭikavṛtti* (Scherrer-Schaub 1991)

Notes

1. Wangchen Lhamo et al. 2006–15. Hereafter referred to as *Collected Works of the Kadampas.*
2. See Smith 2004, 364–81.
3. Yeshé Döndrup's *Treasury of Gems: Selected Anthology of the Well-Uttered Insights of the Teachings of the Precious Kadam Tradition* does not refer to of the content found in the *Collected Works of the Kadampas.*
4. The footnotes throughout the translations document the older readings of the Kadampa manuscripts as well as the variant readings that differ from those in the Tengyur. See Apple 2013, 226–67; and Apple 2016 for the orthographic characteristics that date the physical manuscripts utilized in this book to the late seventeenth century.
5. This is a short work explaining Atiśa's *Special Instructions of the Middle Way* according to the lineage of Potowa Rinchen Sal and his spiritual son Sharawa Yönten Drak (in vol. 19 of *Collected Works of the Kadampas*, 317–34).
6. *Rnal 'byor pa shes rab rdo rje mdzad pa'i bden gnyis kyi rnam par bshad pa* (in vol. 21 of *Collected Works of the Kadampas*, 513–625).
7. Dromtönpa Gyalwai Jungné et al. 2014.
8. Matsumoto (1990) and Yoshimizu (1993) have demonstrated the uniqueness of Tsongkhapa's and his Gelukpa followers' understanding of Madhyamaka thought. Ruegg (2010) has argued against Matsumoto's analysis. However, the recent Kadampa manuscript evidence favors Matsumoto's and Yoshimizu's conclusions (see Apple 2013 and 2015a).
9. As noted in Eimer 1982, 47n1, and in Sopa et al. 2001, 24n2, the form Atiśa is derived from the Sanskrit *atiśaya*, "eminent, superior" (Tib. *phul* [*du*] *byung* [*ba*]), rather than the Sanskrit *ati* + *īśa*, "the great Lord," which is not permitted by the rules of Sanskrit grammar. Tibetans often refer to Atiśa as *jo bo*, "Lord." Note, as well, that early biographies depict the teacher Serlingpa as referring to Dīpaṃkaraśrījñāna as "*adhi sha*" (≈ Adhīśa) (Chim Namkha Drak 2012a, 97.7, 107.10, 161.21, 162.17, 164.9, 173.1). However, in Naktso's biography (2014, 399.2, 399.5), his name is already attested as Atiśa. See Kano 2016b, 98n8, on the name Adhīśa.
10. In general, *madhyamaka* (*dbu ma*) refers to the system of religious thought and practice and *mādhyamika* (*dbu ma pa*) designates the adherents or followers of the system. See May 1979, 472; and Tillemans 2016, 14n1, on the distinction between the terms.
11. All Buddhists consider themselves followers of the Middle Way (*madhyamapratipad*) in that they follow a path of practice advocated by the Buddha that avoids the extremes of self-indulgence and self-mortification. Buddhists also follow a Middle

Way, outlined by the Buddha in discourses such as the *Kaccāyanagottasutta*, between the extremes of permanent existence and nihilistic nonexistence based on the Buddha's teaching of the eightfold path and dependent-arising (*pratītyasamutpāda*). After the Buddha's life, different traditions of Buddhist thought arose, each with their own understanding of the Middle Way. As demonstrated throughout this book, Atiśa follows a Middle Way based on the teachings of the second-century Buddhist thinker Nāgārjuna. In brief, this tradition avoids the extreme of eternalism (*śāśvatānta*) and the extreme of annihilationism (*ucchedānta*) based on the teaching of two realities, ultimate reality (*paramārthasatya*) and conventional reality (*saṃvṛtisatya*), construed through a multifaceted understanding of dependent-arising and emptiness (*śūnyatā*). Atiśa's understanding of Nāgārjuna's thought is complex and multifaceted in that it involves Buddhist spiritual factors such as meditation, nonconceptuality, and an emphasis more on faith than systematic reasoning. Atiśa's Middle Way is more than just a philosophy analogous to features in modern analytical philosophy. Rather, as indicated throughout this book, Atiśa's vision of the Middle Way comprises a whole way of life more in line with Pierre Hadot's conception of philosophy as a way of life. On Nāgārjuna's thought as a way of life, see Apple 2010.

12. The term *kadam* (*bka' gdams*) has a broad semantic range that refers to the *ka* (*bka'*), "sacred word or speech," that is taken as *dam* (*gdams*), advice or instruction. As an epithet, *kadampa* (*bka' gdams pa*) distinguishes its followers as "those who understand the sacred words of the Buddha in terms of Atiśa's instructions" (Jinpa 2008, 2). The term became popular for Atiśa's followers after the founding of Radreng. See section below on the "Early Contemplative Community of Radreng." On traditional understandings of the term "Kadampa," see Jinpa 2008, 2, 7–8; and Iuchi 2016, 3n1.
13. Eimer 1979, 2: 6: "having travelled throughout this great central land of India, the south, Kasmir, Bengal, and the Golden Island [Sumatra], for each system of Dharma [he studied] he had innumerable teachers (*rgya gar yul dbus chen po 'di dang lho dang kha che za hor gser gling nas gling la sogs par byon nas / chos lugs re re la yang bla ma dpag tu med pa mnga' /*)."
14. See Sanderson 2009, 87–108, for the location and size of Vikramaśīla as well as related manuscript and archeological evidence. Uddaṇḍapura is also known as Odantapurī.
15. Phuntsok Tseten 2011, 5–8.
16. Jitāri (ca. 1000), also Jetāri (Tib. *dgra las rnam rgyal*). As noted by Tucci (1956, 249–52) and Ruegg (1981, 100n312), it appears that there are two masters under this name, one who lived in the early ninth century and the other ca. 1000. The later one is said to have been a teacher of both Atiśa and Ratnākaraśānti.
17. Cf. Sherburne 2000, index s.v. Bodhibhadra.
18. *Bodhimārgapradīpapañjikā* (D 282a2–3): *'phags pa klu sgrub kyi man ngag gis dngos grub brnyes nas 'phags pa 'jam pa'i dbyangs kyi gnang ba 'thob pa / mngon par shes pa brnyes pa / rgyud thams cad dang mdo thams cad dang / 'dul ba'i lung ma lus pa'i dgongs pa dus gcig tu thugs la gsal ba bden pa gzigs pa des na gcig nas gcig tu brgyud pa'i bla ma ni dpal byang chub bzang po 'di yin pas 'di'i rjes su 'brang bar bya'o //*. Cf. Sherburne 2000, 247; and Miyazaki 2007a, 78.
19. Cf. Dromtönpa Gyalwai Jungné 2012a, 230.16–18: *'di bla ma dam pa rig pa'i khu byug ces bya ba / slob dpon chen po zla ba grags pa la dngos su slob pa'i mkhas grub chen po de lags mod / shes sam a ti sha'i bla ma yin zer //* (Decleer 1997b, 171).

20. See Schaeffer 2007 on multiple persons with the name Avadhūtipa, and Tatz 1988 on problematic historical accounts of Avadhūtipa.
21. *Sūtrasamuccayasañcayārtha*, extended colophon not in Dergé Tengyur but in *Bstan' 'gyur gser bris ma*, vol. 118 [*a*], 513a: *lha khang ke ru'i khyams smad kyi ban de bdag gyis zhus te gdams ngag dang bcas te gnang ngo / jo bo'i bla ma a wa dhū ti pas rab tu mi gnas pa'i lta ba dang / las mtha' sems bskyed pa'i cho ga dang / mdo kun las btus pa'i don man ngag tu byas pa 'di gsum stabs gcig tu gnang ba lags so //*. Cf. Chattopadhyaya 1967, 462.
22. Note that the title page and first folios of the *Bden gnyis kyi 'bum*, "Collection on the Two Realities," was either wrongly copied or misplaced, and should be the first folio that precedes the content of the manuscript currently entitled *Dbu ma'i man ngag gi 'bum*, "Collected of Madhyamaka Special Instruction," whose actual content is a brief commentary on Atiśa's *Entry to the Two Realities*. In brief, the title page and first folios of *Bden gnyis kyi 'bum* and *Dbu ma'i man ngag gi 'bum* were switched at some point in their history and I have corrected the manuscripts' titles based on their corresponding content.
23. For activities in the Vajrāsana area, see Eimer 1979, 1: 196–205, §§137–69, and for Vikramaśīla Monastery, see Eimer 1979, 1: 205–13.
24. The Tibetan tradition records that the top scholars at Vikramaśīla, or at monasteries in places such as Bodhgayā, held positions of stature at the entry gates of the monastery where they were known as "gatekeeper masters" (*mkhas pa sgo*). As Kano (2016b, 55n44 and 72n4) discusses, the Indic origins of the ambiguous notion of "gatekeepers" at Buddhist monasteries is not presently well understood.
25. According to Lechen Kunga Gyaltsen (2003, 97), Atiśa spent thirteen years in Tibet, including the first three at Ngari, four years in [places] other than Ü-Tsang, and six years in Nyethang (*de ltar na jo bos mnga' ris su lo gsum / dbus gtsang gzhan du lo bzhi / snye thang du lo drug ste / bod du lo bcu gsum 'gro ba'i don mdzad nas / . . .*). See also Chattopadhyaya 1967, 330–66; and Vetturini 2013, 89.
26. *The Blue Annals* (Roerich 1976, 251). Atiśa met Dromtönpa in 1044 when he was preparing to return to India while residing at a place called Rgyal zhing of Purang (cf. Gö Lotsāwa Shönu Pal 1984, 308.1–3: *de nas rgya gar du 'byon par chas te / pu hrangs kyi rgyal zhing zhes par bzhugs pa'i tshe 'brom gyis mjal ba yin te /*).
27. The verses of the letter are preserved in *Spiritual Biography of Geshé Tönpa* (Chim Namkha Drak 2012b, 176a6–178a2 [note that the number 178 is used twice in the manuscript, cf. Eimer 2008, 383n25]; Chim Namkha Drak 2012a, 145.4–147.3; and Ja Dülzin Tsöndrü Bar 2014, 336.4–11). The letter mentions Lha btsun Bodhirāja; Ye shes blo gros; three with the name Ka ba; two with the name Dmigs byed dge bshes; twelve Rjes slob dpal ldan; the two Ring lugs chen po, Kaba and Gar mi; Kun phan dbang phyug rgyal mtshan; Sha kya gzhon rgyal ba'i sras; and Legs pa'i shes rab. The letter was handed over to Shang Wangchuk Gön for delivery to Geshé Kawa (Eimer 1979, 2: 226–29, §282).
28. Van der Kuijp 1987; Vose 2009, 44; and Hugon 2016, 293–95.
29. Vitali 2004, 132.
30. Sørensen and Hazod 2007, 402.
31. Atiśa's early disciples, Khutön Tsöndrü Yungdrung, Ngok Lekpai Sherab, and Dromtönpa Gyalwai Jungné, received their early Buddhist education, including the study of Madhyamaka, in Khams 'dan ma. On the early education of these Kadampa

masters, see Iuchi 2008 and 2013; Minyak Gönpo et al. 1996–2000; Khujuk 2004, 86; and Chim Namkha Drak 2012b, 168a5–179b5.

32. Chim Namkha Drak 2012b, 172b4; Davidson 2005, 100; and Vetturini 2007, 90.
33. Chim Namkha Drak 2012b, 168a5ff.; Roerich 1976, 251–53; and Iuchi 2013, 218–21.
34. Ja Dülzin Tsöndrü Bar 2014, 337.19–22: *khu ston brtson 'grus g.yung drung zhes pa slu mes thams cad kyi gnas brtan mdzad pa / dam pa'i chos mngon pa la shin tu mkhas pa de /*; see also Eimer 1979, 2: 233–34, §286; and Chim Namkha Drak 2012a, 149.1; cf. Roerich 1976, 255.
35. Roerich 1976, 324; Ngok Lekpai Sherab (Rngog Legs pa'i shes rab) should not be confused with Lochung Lekpai Sherab (Lo chung Legs pa'i shes rab), born in Purang, who was a disciple of Lochen Rinchen Sangpo (958–1055) and went to India; see Kramer 2007, 34. For a brief biography of Lochung Lekpai Sherab, see Tsering Gyalpo 2006, 468–69.
36. Ja Dülzin Tsöndrü Bar 2014, 340.12–13; Eimer 1979, 2: 241–43, §294; and Chim Namkha Drak 2012a, 152.20–153.1: . . . *dge shes rnal 'byor pa chen po yul mdo khams smad / gdung yung / mtshan byang chub ces pa /* . . .
37. Lechen Kunga Gyaltsen 2003, 207–8.
38. Chim Namkha Drak 2012a, 152.1–2: *se ston sgra bcan 'dzin gyis nyi ma bdun rjes su 'brang nas dbu ma'i lta ba dri ba mdzad /*; Phuntsok Tseten 2011, 82: *se ston sgra gcan 'dzin gyis nyi ma bdun ring rjes su 'brangs nas dbu ma'i lta ba sogs dri ba zhus.*
39. Ja Dülzin Tsöndrü Bar 2014, 343.11–14; Eimer 1979, 2: 251–52, §303; Chim Namkha Drak 2012a 157.11–15; Phuntsok Tseten 2011, 87.
40. *Bram ze chen po* refers to Saraha the Brahmin. Cf. Chim Namkha Drak 2012a, 65.20.
41. Ja Dülzin Tsöndrü Bar 2014, 343.15–22; Eimer 1979, 2: 252, §304. Cf. Chim Namkha Drak 2012a, 65.20.
42. Ja Dülzin Tsöndrü Bar 2014, 343.22–344.1: *de nas khu ston gyis kva chur spyan drangs nas khu ston rngog ston gnyis kyis zhus nas dbu ma rig pa'i tshogs drug gsung /*. Chim Namkha Drak 2012a, 157.15–17: */ de nas ka chur byon te khu rngog gnyis kyis zhus nas dbu ma rigs pa'i tshogs drug gsungs /*. Phuntsok Tseten 2011, 87.
43. See Lessing and Wayman 1968 on this classification, as well as Ruegg 2010, 113–14.
44. A curriculum is suggested below based on Dromtönpa's biography; see the section below on "The Early Contemplative Community of Radreng."
45. Ja Dülzin Tsöndrü Bar 2014, 346.15–20; Chim Namkha Drak 2012a, 161.5–12; Phuntsok Tseten 2011, 91. Cf. Davidson 2005, 111. See Kano 2014 on Atiśa and Naktso's translation of the *Uttaratantra*.
46. For an account of the fracas between Khutön and Tibetan members of Atiśa's entourage, including Dromtönpa and Amé Naljorpa Janchup Rinchen, see Eimer 1979, 2: 259–66, §312–§18.
47. Ja Dülzin Tsöndrü Bar 2014, 349.10; Chim Namkha Drak 2012a, 164.17–165.1; Phuntsok Tseten 2011, 90.
48. See Eimer 1979, 2: 268–70, §321; Chim Namkha Drak 2012a, 167.
49. Sørensen et al. 2007, 2: 599, 663.
50. Van der Kuijp 1987, 105.
51. Ja Dülzin Tsöndrü Bar 2014, 353.2–7: *yang rngog gis zhu sna mdzad nas dbu ma'i chos zhus pas dbu ma rtog ge la 'bar ba gsungs / de'i man ngag che chung gnyis bla ma nyid kyis mdzad nas dge bshes rnal 'byor la gzigs su phul bas / nged la lkog tu ji ltar khrid pa bzhin du bris nas 'dug cung zab grags gsungs / de lo tstsha bas bsgyur nas de'i gsham na*

/ ra sa 'phrul snang gtsug lag khan chen du / sha' kya dge slong rngog btsun legs she yis / gsol ba btab nas yi ger bkod pa yin/ bya ba de jo bo'i gsung yin //. Chim Namkha Drak 2012a, 169.1–8.

52. See Huanhuan and van der Kuijp 2014 for the historical and philological issues in the Tibetan translation of this text and other works of Bhāviveka.
53. The reconstructed Sanskrit title is *Ratnakaraṇḍodghāṭamadhyamakopadeśa* (Toh 3930). A critical edition of the Tibetan and Japanese translation of this work is found in Miyazaki (2007b).
54. The Sanskrit title is *Madhyamakopadeśa* (Toh 3929; also 4468). *Jo bo rje dpal ldan a ti sha'i rnam thar bka' gdams pha chos* (Dromtönpa Gyalwai Jungné 2012c, 1691.8): *yang rngog gis zhus sna mdzad dbu ma'i chos zhus pas / dbu ma rtog ge 'bar ba gsungs / de'i man ngag che chung gnyis mdzad nas rnal 'byor pa la gzigs su phul bas / nged la lkog tu khrid pa bzhin du bris 'dug cung yang zab drags gsung / de lo tsā bas bsgyur ba'i zhabs na / ra sa 'phrul snang gtsug lag khang chen du / / shākya'i dge slong rngog btsun legs shes yis / / gsol ba btab nas yi ger bkod pa yin / / zhes pa jo bo'i gsung yin /. Bka' gdams chos 'byung gsal ba'i sgron me //* (2003, 148): *lha sar . . . rngog gis dbu mdzad pa'i bod ston kha cig la rim pa'i cho ga rgyas par gnang / rtog ge 'bar ba bsgyur ba'i zhu ba phul / jo bos gnang nas nag tshos tshang bar bsgyur / de'i zhar la dbu ma'i man ngag kyang mdzad //. The Blue Annals* (Gö Lotsāwa Shönu Pal 1984, 1: 316.15–17): *der rngog gis lo paṇ la zhu ba phul nas / rtog ge 'bar ba bsgyur / de'i man ngag tu dbu ma'i man ngag che chung gnyis mdzad //.*
55. Chim Namkha Drak 2012a, 177.8–18.
56. Chim Namkha Drak 2012a, 178.
57. Eimer 1979, 2: 306, §360: *dge bshes ston pas jo bo la zla grags lugs kyi rtog pa phul bas / jo bos phyag thal mo shar phyogs su sbyar nas da lta rgya gar shar phyogs na lta ba 'di kho na 'dzin /.* Also cited in Thuken Chökyi Nyima's *Grub mtha' shel gyi me long* and Changkya Rölpai Dorjé's *Grub mtha'i rnam gzhag chen mo* (see Losang Chökyi Nyima 2009, 108, 433n371).
58. Naktso completed the translation with the Indian Kṛṣṇapaṇḍita (Hopkins 2008, 238, note b).
59. Eimer 1979, 2: 319–20, §378.
60. Eimer 1979, 2: 321, §380; Chim Namkha Drak 2012a, 188.12–14.
61. Eimer 1979, 2: 321, § 381.
62. Chim Namkha Drak 2012a, 199.20–200: . . . *dgung lo bdun cu rtsa gnyis bzhes pa'i dus su snye thang du shing pho rta'i lo'i dbyug gu'i tshes bco brgyad la dga' ldan du gshegs so/.* For Atiśa's rebirth in Tuṣita, see Chattopadhyaya 1967, 375, 383, 388. Vetturini (2007, pt. 1, 71) reconstructs the name as Gaganāmala. Vetturini (2007, pt. 2, 107): *dga' ldan du rje btsun byam pa'i drung du / lha'i bu nam mkha' dri ma med pa zhes bya bar gyur te / bka' gdams glegs bam las / bskal bzang 'di la rje bstun byams pa'i rjes su rgyal ba seng ge 'byon par gsungs pa de jo bo rje yin par bzhed do /.* Vetturini notes ZLNp 46a, rNrG 94b, and rNrGya 83a 4.4 as historical references for the account of Atiśa's rebirth in Tuṣita. Eimer 1979, 1: 353; Eimer 2003, 24.
63. Ja Dülzin Tsöndrü Bar 2014, 386.13–21; Eimer 1979, 2: 367–68, §426; Chim Namkha Drak 2012a, 210.8–19; Sørensen et al. 2007, 404.
64. Davidson 2005, 111–12; Eimer 1979, 2: 367–68, §426.
65. See Iuchi 2016 and *Spiritual Biography of Geshé Tönpa* (*Dge bshes ston pa'i rnam thar*, Chim Namkha Drak 2012b), for an early Tibetan history of Radreng.

66. This summary is paraphrased from *Spiritual Biography of Geshé Tönpa* (Chim Namkha Drak 2012b, 180a6–182a3).
67. Chim Namkha Drak 2012b, 182a3–182a5: [182a3] *de'i rjes la dge bshes ston pa dang / rnal 'byor pa chen po* [182a4] *dang dgon pa pa dang shes rab rdo rje dang byams pa'i blo gros dang / khri mchog dang stong btsan dang phyag dar dang yog rdzong dang / nye gnas yon tan 'bar dang / jo bo'i thugs* [182a5] *dam nas zhes yan chad byon te me pho spre'u'i lo ra sgyeng du chags phab po / de yang dang po ldan ma'i yul yin pas ldan skad du ra sgyeng / bod skad du chu mi ring mo zhes bya ba yin skad /.*
68. Lechen Kunga Gyaltsen 2003, 162.5–12: *khams pa sku mched bzhir grags pa . . .*
69. Chim Namkha Drak 2012b, 185a1–6); for the residences and sponsors, see *Rwa sgreng gi bshad pa* (Iuchi 2016, 101–2).
70. *Spiritual Biography of Geshé Tönpa* (Chim Namkha Drak 2012b, 193a1–4): *chos pha rol du phyin pa brgyad stong mdo 'grel char gnyis / nyi khri tshar gcig /* [193a2] *'grel chung mngon rtogs; pa nya tsi ka gsung / bslab btus ra sgyeng du ye ma gsung gu rar gcig gsungs / spyod 'jug lam sgron sgom rim* [193a3] *la sogs pa mang du gsung/ sems tsam kun las btus dang theg bsdus dang phran yang mang du gsungs / dbu ma shar ba gsum ka gsungs snang* [193a4] *pa mang du gsungs skad /.*
71. *The Blue Annals* (Roerich 1976, 265; Cheng du 324.4–6): */ 'brom de ni snags mtshan nyid gnyis ka'i yon tan shin tu che ste / gsang sngags ni spas te cher ma gsung la / mtshan nyid la ni brgyad ston pa dang brgyad stong 'grel chen dang / 'grel chung dang / nyi khri snang ba la sogs pa dang /.* The account continues, mentioning that 'Brom-ston corrected the translation of a tantra as well: *sngags kyi yang ye shes grub pa la 'gyur mcos mdzad snang /.*
72. *Dbu ma'i man ngag gi bshad pa, Pu to yab sras kyi lugs* (*Potowa's Middle Way*) 2006, 318.2.
73. *The Blue Annals* (Roerich 1979, 265; Gö Lotsāwa Shönu Pal 1984, 324.7–10): *kho bo'i dbu ma'i lta ba ci yang ma yin pa bya ba yin gsung ste / don med par dgag pa ste / chos kyi grags pas / med par dgag pa ni ci yang ma yin pa'i phyir ro / zhes gsung pa bzhin no /.* "('Brom-ston-pa) [would] say that his Madhyamaka position was [that ultimate reality] is nothing at all, the non-implicative negation of an object, for Dharmakīrti said, 'non-implicative negation means that it is nothing.'" Gö Lotsāwa Shönu Pal (1392–1481) records that the basis of Dromtönpa's statement is from Dharmakīrti. Indeed, Dharmakīrti's discussion of impermanence (*anityatā*) in the *Pramāṇavārttikasvavṛtti* does mention nonimplicative negation (Miyasaka 1971–72, 144.20–146.1 *ad* k.274, 277: *vināśasya akiṃcittvāt . . . na bhavatīti ca prasajyapratiṣedha*). However, the manuscript evidence in the following chapters indicates that Dromtönpa's position for employing nonimplicative negation was based on Atiśa's understanding of Nāgārjuna and Candrakīrti.
74. See Chim Namkha Drak 2012b, 189b1; 190b6–191a1; Lechen Kunga Gyaltsen 2003, 528–30; and see Vetturini 2013, 118–20, for additional sources on Phuchungwa. *The Blue Annals* (Roerich 1979, 264; Gö Lotsāwa Shönu Pal 1984, 1: 323.6–7): *phu chung ba la ni 'phags pa'i bden ba bzhi las brtsams pa'i chos mang du bshad /.*
75. See *Spiritual Biography of Geshé Tönpa* (Chim Namkha Drak 2012b, 189b2; 190b5–6); *The Blue Annals* (Roerich 1976, 264; Gö Lotsāwa Shönu Pal 1984, 1: 323.2–6): *spyan snga la chos kyi phung po stong phrag brgyad cu rtsa bzhi yo ma btub pa kun kyi skad yin / khyod rang stong pa nyid kho na legs par bsgroms gsung /.* See also Vetturini 2013, 123–24.

76. *Spiritual Biography of Geshé Tönpa* (*dge bshes ston pa'i rnam thar*, 190b4); *The Blue Annals* (Roerich 1976, 264; Gö Lotsāwa Shönu Pal 1984, vol. 1): *po ta ba la gdams pa bstan pa tsam gyis thugs la ji lta ba bzhin du 'khrungs /.* See also Vetturini 2013, 120–22.
77. *Spiritual Biography of Geshé Tönpa* (*dge bshes ston pa'i rnam thar*, 196b1): *dge bshes ston pa 'das nas sku mched gsum gyis rnal 'byor pa gang 'og la chos 'brel tsam mdzad nas sgrub pa kho na mdzad de / de yan chad la ra sgyeng pa'i dge ba'i bshes gnyen zhes gleng ba lags skad /.*
78. *Spiritual Biography of Geshé Tönpa* (*dge bshes ston pa'i rnam thar*, 191a3–4): *a me byang chub ni dben pa bas tshogs rang thugs dam 'phel 'phel tsam byung pas rnal 'byor chen por gtags /.*
79. Eimer 1979, 2: 347, §407; Ja Dülzin Tsöndrü Bar 2014, 18–20: *rnal 'byor pa chen pos jo mo'i* [read *jo bo'i*] *chos mang du mkhyen / de yang bden pa gnyis dang las kha tshar ba la rtsal thon / dam tshig gsum pa bkod pa dang 'jam dpal 'gro ba'i zhal gzigs /.* Lechen Kunga Gyaltsen 2003, 11: *Jo bo'i slob ma bden gnyis la shin tu mkhas pa ni rnal' byor pa chen po yin . . . /.* Lechen Kunga Gyaltsen 2003, 208.3–7: *de la rnal 'byor pa chen pos jo bo'i chos mang du mkhyen kyang / jo bo'i bzhed pa'i bden gnyis la 'brom ston pa las kyang mkhas par grags / las kha tshar la rtsal thon / dam tshig gsum bkod rgyal po dang 'jam dpal bgro ba mdzad pa'i zhal gzigs /.* Also Lechen Kunga Gyaltsen 2003, 319.19–20. *The Blue Annals* (Roerich 1976, 265; Gö Lotsāwa Shönu Pal 1984, vol. 1): *jo bo'i bzhed pa'i bden pa gnyis la 'brom ston pa las kyang khong mkhas zer /.*
80. *Spiritual Biography of Geshé Tönpa* (Chim Namkha Drak 2012b, 196a6–196b1) states thirteen years, whereas *The Blue Annals* (Roerich 1976, 265) mentions fourteen years as abbott.
81. *Spiritual Biography of Geshé Tönpa* (*dge bshes ston pa'i rnam thar*, 196b1–2).
82. On Poto Monastery, see Roesler and Roesler 2004.
83. *The Blue Annals* (Gö Lotsāwa Shönu Pal 1984, 1: 323.2–4): *spyan snga la ni chos kyi phung po stong phrag brgyad cu rtsa bzhi yo ma btub pa kun gyi skad yin / khyod rang stong pa nyid kho na legs par bsgoms gsung /.* Lechen Kunga Gyaltsen 2003, 319.8–12: *yang ston pa'i zhal nas/ jo bo ba nyon mongs pa brgyad khri bzhi stong gi gnyen por chos kyi sgo mo brgyad khri bzhi stong gsungs pa de ma ma btub pa rnams kyi las yin/ khyod rang stong pa nyid bsgoms dang sman dpa' bo chig thub lta bu yin gsungs nas gdams pa zab mo rnams gnang /.*
84. Lechen Kunga Gyaltsen 2003, 319.19–320.1: *rnal 'byor pa chen po de bden pa gnyis dang las kha tshar la ston pa bas kyang ci zhib tsam tu byung / dgon pa pa de sgom skyon sel ba dang chos zab mo thams cad la ston pa bas kyang ci zhib tsam du byung / rnal 'byor pa shes rab rdo rje de grub mtha' la ston pa bas kyang ci zhib tsam du byung bas mya ngan rdog po re re sangs gsungs /.*
85. As cited in Deroche 2011, 144n19: *bod kyi dbu ma'i lta ba'i 'chad nyan dar tshul blo gsal mig 'byed* ; 2004, 124: *spyan snga bas jo bo'i bden gnyis la 'jug pa zhes pa 'chad nyan rgya cher mdzad pa gang ltar skabs der jo bo rje'i bden gnyis la 'jug pa zhes pa'i bshad rgyun ches dar ba ni spyan snga ba'i bka' drin las byung bar bshad do /.*
86. As Iuchi (2012, 60) notes, based on the earliest known Tibetan work focused on Radreng, "Rwa sgreng monastery seemed to have been on a decline during Po to ba's tenure. 'Brom Shes rab me lce states, on 19b4–5, that there was no abbot for *sixty-five* years after Po to ba [emphasis added]."
87. On Sangphu Neuthok overtaking Radreng within thirty years of its founding as the

center stage of early Kadampa monastic seats, see Davidson 2005, 279; Sørensen and Hazod 2007, 685; Hugon 2016, 291–93.

88. The *General Explanation* (chap. 4 *ad* 703.25) mentions both Ngari and Radreng (*mnga' rigs pa ra sgreng pa ni . . .*).

89. Sanskrit manuscripts of these texts have recently been recovered from Lhasa (Franco 2015).

90. *Sugatamatavibhaṅgakārikā* (*Bde bar gshegs pa gzhung rnam par 'byed pa'i tshig le'ur byas pa*), Toh 3899 (also 4547), vol. *a*, 7b.5–8a4; Shirasaki 1978; and Shirasaki 1985.

91. According to Shirasaki 1978, Jitāri did not criticize the *nirākāra* theory of cognition.

92. *Bodhicittotpādasamādānavidhi* (*Byang chub kyi sems bskyed pa dang yi dam blang ba'i cho ga*), Toh 3968 (also 4493), vol. *gi*, 241b6–245a2.

93. See Ruegg 1981, 109, on the four extremes in Madhyamaka; see Ruegg 1977; and Ruegg 2000, 139–47.

94. Mimaki 1976, 206: *'dir dbu ma pa de dag kyang kun rdzob rnam par gzhag pa gnyis te / snang ba la mi 'jal ba ni slob dpon bha bya la sogs pa dang / snang ba'i dngos po ji lta ba ma yin gyi nang gi shes pa kho na sna tshogs su snang bar smra ba slob dpon zhi ba 'tsho la sos pa'o /*. Cf. Mimaki 1982, 376n78: "Ici Mi pham développe ou simplifie l'explication du *JSSN* de Bodhibhadra, en introduisant à la manière tibétaine ce qui n'existait pas littéralement dans le commentaire de Bodhibhadra. C'est surtout l'emploi du terme Yogācara[-mādhyamika] qui est ici typiquement tibétain. En effet, le terme Yogācāra-mādhyamika, avec sa contre-partie Sautrāntika-mādhyamika, a été inventé par des auteurs tibétains tels que Ye śes sde etc. au début du 9e siècl, et ne se trouve pas dans les textes indiens avant cette date."

95. Dromtönpa Gyalwai Jungné 2012a, 15.10–12; Dromtönpa Gyalwai Jungné 2014, 12.6; Jinpa 2006, 43.

96. */ rmi lam sgyu 'dra rang bzhin spros dang bral / / sems nyid ma bcos ye nas* {*rang bzhin,* 2012a} *gnyug ma'i ngang / / gang gi* {*gis*] *'di gnyis blo la ma bsams na / / 'khor ba'i 'dam du bying bar 'gyur ro ang / / rgyal bu don dam mnyam bzhag nam mkha' 'dra / / rjes thob sgyu 'dra las 'bras bsam par rigs / / bla mas zab mo'i chos de bstan pa na / / sbyor ba'i lam brnyes dpa' ba'i ting 'dzin thob //*. Dromtönpa Gyalwai Jungné 2012a, 15.17–16.3; Dromtönpa Gyalwai Jungné 2014, 12.12–16; English translation Jinpa 2006, 43–44.

97. */ de tshe rje la rtogs pa 'di phul ba / / kho bos ting 'dzin gcig la mnyam bzhag tshe / / nam mkha' sprin dang bral ba ji bzhin du / / gsal la dwangs la rtog pa* {*rnyog pa,* 2012a} *mi gda' na / / bla ma chos kyi gnas lugs de lags sam / / de nas ting 'dzin de las sad pa na / / snang yang zhen pa med par sems can dran / / rdzun yang phra zhib las la bag yod thob / / bla ma bdag gi nyams de ma 'khrul lam //*. Dromtönpa Gyalwai Jungné 2014, 12.16–21; Dromtönpa Gyalwai Jungné 2012a, 16.3–8; English translation Jinpa 2006, 44.

98. *Bden gnyis spyi bshad*, 703.21: *jo bo'i zhal nas / a ba dhu ti ba dang lo bdun 'grogs / a ba dhu ti ba la thos / rig pas bde / slob dpon klu sgrub kyi gzhung dang mthun / jo mo sgrol mas lung bstan nga'i 'di 'phags pa'i bzhed pa ma nor ba yin gsungs /*.

99. *Bden gnyis spyi bshad*, 723.25–724.1: *jo bo'i bla ma +a va dhu ti ba'i zhal nas ji srid du bdag tu 'dzin pa ma* [724] *zad kyi bar du las phra'i phra bas 'bras bu 'byin par shes par bya gsungs /*.

100. See Jinpa 2008, 274.

101. "The [one who teaches] karmic cause and effect" (*las rgyu 'bras pa*). Eimer 1979, 2: 191, §253; Ja Dülzin Tsöndrü Bar 2014, 323.8–9; Chim Namkha Drak 2012a, 129.10–11.

102. Atiśa uses the terms "mere cognitive representation" (*vijñaptimātra*) and "mind only" (*cittamātra, sems tsam pa*) as synonyms for Yogācāra. Note, however, that the term *cittamātra* is found in Mahāyāna sūtras such as the *Daśabhūmikasūtra* and is interpreted differently by Mādhyamikas and Yogācaras. See below, "The Questioning of Atiśa in Western Tibet." See Buescher 2008 for Yogācāra as a doxographic category from the sixth century onward. Also Schmithausen 2014 for the genesis of Yogācāra-Vijñānavāda.
103. Atiśa lists in *Open Basket of Jewels* two Vasubandhus, an earlier one among *śrāvaka* Sautrāntika and one under Yogācāra.
104. Mimaki 1976, 188–89. Cf. Kajiyama 1966, 147n412: *grāhyagrāhakanirmuktaṃ vijñānaṃ paramārthasat.*
105. The Sanskrit terms for the two kinds of Yogācārins—*sākārajñānavādin* and *nirākāravādiyogācāra*—are found in Advayavajra's *Tattvaratnāvalī* (Moriyama 2014, 341n4). In addition, sources in Tibetan often employ the terms *rnam bden pa* (**satyākāravādin*), "those who maintain images are real," and *rnam brdzun pa* (**alīkākāravādin*), "those who maintain images are false" (see Funayama 2007, 188–92). I have provided the exact terms that appear in the texts throughout this book.
106. Dromtönpa Gyalwai Jungné 2014, 53.22–56.5.
107. Note that Devamati is the name of the monk mentioned in verse 28 of the *Satyadvayāvatāra* (see chap. 2).
108. Dromtönpa Gyalwai Jungné 2014, 54.16–17: */ mdang gsum gnyid kyis log pa'i rmi lam na / / sgyu ma mkhan gyis glang po gnyis sprul te/ /glang po gcig gis glang po gcig bsad na / / bsad dam shi 'am sgyu ma nyid yod dam /.*
109. Ibid., 54.18–20: */ rmi lam rdzun gyi sgyu ma mkhan pas ci / / de'i sprul pa'i glang po'i shi bsad ci / / dī paṃ rmi po'i shes pa dper len nam / / glang po gnyis kyi shes pa dpe ru len //.*
110. Ibid., 54.20–55.2: */ rmi bzhin pa yi shes pa bden 'dzin yin / / sad pa'i shes pa snang yang zhen pa chung / / yul la wal le pa tsam dper len gyi / / rmi bzhin log pa'i dpe don cha gcig yin / / sad shes yang dag dpe don cha gcig yin /* [55.1] */ glang po'i gzung 'dzin don dam dpe don yin / / 'on kyang bzung 'dzin lta bur snang ba ni / / ming tsam kun rdzob yin gyi don dam min //.*
111. Ibid., 55.5–55.15: */ bden zhen can la log pa'i dpe don 'grig / / rang rgyud pa la snang tsam kun rdzob bde / / skyes bu mchog la ming tsam kun rdzob 'thad / / ye nas gnas pa'i gnas lugs don dam mchog / rmi lam rmis pa'i yul gyi glang po gnyis / / shes pa yin na med pa 'am gsum du 'gyur / / min na sems tsam pa ni ci zhig mchis / / gal te sad tshe yul med shes yod na / / shes pa de ni mdang gi shes pa'am / / sngar med snang 'dra blo bur ba cig yin /* [55.10] */ gal te shes pa sngar gyi de nyid na / / nang par 'gal zhing sngar gyi yin pa nyams / / gal te snang 'dra blo bur ba nyid na / / 'o na glang po gnyis kyang cis mi ring / / des na yul dang yul can mi mnga'i bar / / glang po'i glang po yul du byas pa ltar / / sems dang yul 'di gcig min tha dad min / / yul dang yul can gzhi nas mi gnas pa / / de ni don dam yin par chos nyid smra //.*
112. Ibid., 55.15–21: */ sa lu la brten myu gu 'byung ba na / / dang po myu gu med par kun gyis shes / / sa bon de la brten pa tshul tsam na / / de'i tshe na myu gu yod min zhing / / myu gu'i tshe na sa bon 'gags gyur te / / brten pa yod kyang brten pa por med phyir / / dus mnyam mi srid 'di ni stong nyid de / / rang la mthu med gzhan brten nang tshugs bral / / 'di ni ye nas gnas pa'i chos nyid yin //.* Cf. *Satyadvayāvatāra*, v. 21d: */ ye nas gnas pa'i chos nyid do /.*
113. Ibid., 56.1–3: */ chos kyi gnas lugs dbu mar ma shes par / / mkhas kyang phyi rol nyid na*

gnas pa yin / / 'di ltar chos de yongs su rtogs pa dang / / ngang zhugs dus mnyam rten 'brel chen po yin //.

114. On the seed and sprout example in Madhyamaka discourse, see Candrakīrti's MA (vv. 9–11) and MABH (83–85), and the *Prasannapadā* (MacDonald 2015, 94–97).

115. Chim Namkha Drak 2012a, 81.20; Ja Dülzin Tsöndrü Bar 2014, 276.9–12.

116. Ja Dülzin Tsöndrü Bar 2014, 250.10–14: The Lord [Atiśa] first upheld the view of False Aspectarian Mind Only of the Guru Ratnākaraśānti and having discarded that, then upheld the view of the system of Ācārya Nāgārjuna. In casting away the view, Lord [Atiśa] made a great offering to the Guru Ratnākaraśānti. He was not pleased as the view upheld by the student should be the same. These are used up as being good views (*jo bo dang po ni bla ma rad na ^a ka ra shan ti'i sems tsam rnam rdzun pa'i lta ba 'dzin pa la de bor nas slob dpon klu sgrub kyi lugs kyi lta ba 'dzin pa yin / lta ba 'bor ba la jo bos bla ma rad na ^a kar shan ti pa la 'bul ba chen po cig byas / des kyang ma mnyes slob ma bya ba lta ba 'dzin pa gcig dgos pa yin gsungs/ de rnams lta ba rnam par dag pa yin byas su zad /*).

117. Chim Namkha Drak 2014, 69: *nga'i bla ma shanti ba brgyad stong pa gsungs tsa na dbu mar bshad pa thams cad re re nas sun phyung bas / nga'i dbu ma'i lta ba de nyid gsal btab ba bzhin du song / rnal* [69.15] *'byor spyod pa'i dbu ma shin tu gsal bar gyur/ nga zla ba grags pa'i lugs la shin du dad pa yin gsungs /.*

118. Ruegg 1981, 123; Hayashi 1996.

119. See chapter 6 on Atiśa's presentation of mind as mere appearance. For Ratnākaraśānti's understanding of awareness as luminosity, see Yiannopoulos 2012 and Isaacson 2013 on Ratnākaraśānti's exegesis of *Yuktiṣaṣṭikā* (v. 34).

120. See Brunnhölzl 2011, 143–44, on Ratnākaraśānti and negation.

121. See Moriyama 2013, 6.

122. Yiannopoulos 2012, 191–92.

123. Chim Namkha Drak 2014, 67.8–12: *jo bo dang po bla ma ratna ā kara shānti pa'i lta byas sems tsam rnam brdzun 'dzin pa la phyis de bor nas slob dpon klu sgrub lugs kyi lta ba 'dzin pa yin / lta ba de 'bor ba la jo bos bla ma shānti pa la 'bul ba chen po byas kyang ma mnyes te / slob ma bya ba lta ba 'dzin pa cig dgos pa yin gsung skad do //.*

124. This episode is recorded or referenced in several Kadampa and Kagyüpa sources. The early Kadampa sources include Atiśa's *General Explanation* (chap. 4), the Kadampa commentary on Atiśa's *Satyadvayāvatāra* (chap. 3), biographies of Atiśa (Eimer 1979, 2: 191–94), the *Be'u bum sngon po 'grel pa* (n.d., 347–48), and the *Dpe chos rin po che spungs pa'i 'bum 'grel*. Kagyüpa sources include the Mkhas pa'i dga' ston (2006, 345) and Shes bya kun khyab. I have translated this episode from the *Jo bo chen po rje lha cig gi rnam par thar ba* (Ja Dülzin Tsöndrü Bar 2014).

125. See chapter 3. On the three texts of the "Easterners," see Mimaki 1982, 4–5; Eckel 1987, 15; Tauscher 1999, 387n2.

126. On the establishment of a network of monastic colleges during the Tibetan imperial period, see Uebach 1990.

127. See Ruegg 1981 and Decleer 1998 on this point.

128. Ruegg 1981, 89, briefly discusses the lineage of Śāntarakṣita's Madhyamaka.

129. On these points, see Keira 2004, 8–9.

130. Ja Dulzin Tsöndrü Bar 2014: */ khyed rang gang 'dod* [323.13] *gsungs / de la gtam rnying gi bzhin dbu ma sems tsam logs* {em. *sogs*} *gang 'dod pa la yang de 'dod gsungs / de la bsgrub byed kyi lung dang rigs pa 'di bdog ste / shin tu legs pa lags* [323.15] *zhes*

thams cad la gsungs / mnga' ris pa blo gros gsal ba zhes bya ba mnga' ris bskor gsum na blo rno ba gcig gis jo bo nyid kyi bzhed pa mi gsungs par kun la mthun par 'gyur snang pa ji ltar lags zhus pas / nga yang bud dha'i rjes su slob pa'i dge slong lags pas gdul bya'i bsam pa dang mthun par lan btab pa yin gsungs / yang sme btsun yon tan shes rab bya ba gcig gis jo bo nyid kyi bzhed pa ji ltar lags zhus pas / [323.20] *nga la 'dod pa med gsung pa la / don dam du bzhed pa mi mnga' yang / kun rdzob tu ji ltar bzhed pa lags pa gcig gsungs bar zhu phul bas / jo bo'i zhal nas/ rab rib can gyi skra shad ji ltar mthong ba ltar 'di dag thams cad de ltar gnas pa yin gsung* [324.1] *pa la / de nyid kyang ji ltar lags zhu ba ni med / kun dang mi mthun pa'i lta ba gcig yod par 'dug snyam yang jo bo la snang ba sel ba lag sam mi sel ba lags zhus pas / 'bras can la rab rib dag pa lta bu gcig yin gyi / khyed rang spyod dang gsungs //.*

131. On this issue in later Tibetan scholasticism, see Dreyfus and McClintock 2003 and Cabezón 2007.
132. See Ruegg 2000, 245 and note 20, for resources on this issue in the history of Indian and Tibetan Buddhist thought. For Śāntarakṣita's, Kamalaśīla's, and Jñānagarbha's positions on common establishment, see Tillemans 1990 and Keira 2004.
133. Yoshimizu 2013; MacDonald 2015.
134. Although Atiśa appears to follow Candrakīrti for his definitive understanding of Madhyamaka thought and practice, this does not mean that he excluded the thought of Bhāviveka, Śāntarakṣita, Kamalaśīla, Jñānagarbha, or others as a subbranch of Madhyamaka. As mentioned earlier, for an Indian Buddhist thinker like Atiśa in his time and place, Madhyamaka was an undifferentiated classification within the Buddhist tradition that consisted of a variety of different thinkers who each had specific characteristics, as well as noted characterizations by others, of their interpretation of Madhyamaka thought.
135. For Shangthak Sakpa on this issue, see Yoshimizu 2010, and for Chapa Chökyi Sengé's criticism, see Vose 2009, 149–64.
136. Śāntarakṣita, *Madhyamakālaṃkāravṛtti* (Toh 3885, vol. *sa*, 75a6): *kho bo yang mig la sogs pa'i shes pa la snang ba'i ngang can gyi dngos po ni mi sel mod kyi /.* Cf. Tillemans 1990, 43n96.
137. MAK 91 (Toh 3884, vol. *sa*, 56a6): *rgyu dang 'bras bur gyur pa yang / / shes pa 'ba' zhig kho na ste / / rang gi grub pa gang yin pa / / de ni shes par gnas pa yin //.* English translated Ichigo 1989, 220–21; cf. Eckel 1987, 21; Blumenthal 2009, 56.
138. Cited by Kamalaśīla both in his *Sarvadharmaniḥsvabhāvasiddhi* (Tillemans 2011, 152) and MAP.
139. Atiśa, following Nāgārjuna and Candrakīrti, seems to accept valid cognition (*pramāṇa*), or epistemic warrants, at the conventional level through mutual dependent designation, *but does not accept them as intrinsically established* on the conventional level as do Śāntarakṣita and Kamalaśīla. Atiśa's position on conventional valid cognition *(tha snyad kyi tshad ma)* is not clear, as it is only mentioned in passing by his commentators.
140. The phrase *rig pa'i shes rab* also appears in *A General Explanation*. Often translated as "reasoning consciousness," the use of the term in the eleventh-century Indo-Tibetan context may differ from later Tibetan scholastic usage found among Gelukpa exegetes. The term *rig shes* may be a contracted form of *rig pa'i shes rab*. Be that as it may, as Cabezón 1992, 461n481, 513n1089 notes, *rig shes* may refer to the inferential knowledge of emptiness, ultimate reality, or to the direct understanding of emptiness in

equipoised wisdom of an *ārya*. MacDonald 1988, 162, translates as "correct consciousness" in the context of the Kadampa Üpa Losal's fourteenth-century *grub mtha'*.

141. *Jo bo chen po rje lha cig gi rnam par thar ba* (Ja Dülzin Tsöndrü Bar 2014): *yang jo bo la rigs pa'i shes rab la chos can snang ngam mi snang zhus pas / rigs pa'i shes pa la chos can* [324.5] *mi snang ste med nas mi snang ba dang yul ma yin nas mi snang ba gnyis yin pa las / skabs 'dir rigs ngo nas chos can med nas mi snang ba yin gsungs / jo bo'i zhal nas khyed snang bar 'dod dam mi snang bar 'dod gsungs / snang bar 'dod zhus pas / bod chos can snang par 'dod pas bzod pa mdzod gcig gsungs /.*
142. English translation McClintock 2003, 147, 170n91: ... *chos can snang ba 'di la yang rang bzhin yang dag par sgro bstags pa dgag pa sgrub par byed kyi / chos can gyi rang gi ngo bo 'gog par ni ma yin pas mtshungs so //* (MAP *ad* MA 76–77). See also Tillemans 1990, 42n94.
143. For instance, MAK v. 75 and its corresponding comments in MAV and MAP.
144. On Kamalaśīla's arguments for inference utilizing Dharmakīrti, see Keira 2004.
145. *Jo bo chen po rje lha cig gi rnam par thar ba* (Ja Dülzin Tsöndrü Bar 2014): */ sangs rgyas pa'i sa na ye shes kyi rgyun mnga' 'am mi mnga' zhus pas / sangs rgyas ma myong cha med gsungs / de nas jo* [324.10] *bo'i zhal nas sgyu ma mkhan pos blong po bslus pa lta bu gcig yin gyis khyed rang spyod gsung bas / ye shes kyi rgyun mi mgna' bar bzhed par brtags nas thams cad rgyal pogs pa bzhin du gyur pa la / jo bo'i zhal nas khyed bod la nga'i dbu ma'i lta bas sems tsam bstan kyang mi bzod gsungs /.*
146. See Almogi 2009 on Śrīgupta and her comments regarding Śāntarakṣita and Kamalaśīla (156–57).
147. See Saito 1996, 261, on early Tibetan BCA commentaries.
148. *Bodhicaryāvatāra* 9.15ab: *pratyayānāṃ tu vicchedāt saṃvṛtyāpi na saṃbhavaḥ*; Tib. *rkyen rnams rgyun ni chad pas na // kun rdzob tu yang mi 'byung ngo.*
149. Note that the title of the work in the *Collected Works of the Kadampas* is "The Stages of How to Generate the Path in the Mental Continuum according to the Discourse of the *Bodhicaryāvatāra*." See Mochizuki 1999.
150. On this point, see Kano 2016a for Jñānaśrīmitra's view, and Yiannopoulos 2012 for Ratnākaraśānti's view.
151. See Williams 2009 for a translation and analysis of Śāntideva's *Bodhicaryāvatāra* (BCA v. 9.35–37), and Vose 2010b for later Tibetan debates on this issue among students of Ngok Loden Sherap and Chapa Chökyi Sengé, as well as an interpretation of the early Sakyapa hierarch Sönam Tsemo (Bsod nams rtse mo, 1142–82).
152. See Tillemans 1990, 64–66; Lindtner 1997a; and Ruegg 2002 on this topic.
153. Ja Dulzin Tsöndrü Bar 2014: 324.13: *yang jo bo'i zhal khyed dbu ma ba la sgyu ma ji ltar dper len zhes tshur smra ba la / bod ston rnams kyis rde'u shing bu la dmigs sngags btab* [324.15] *pas rta glang du snang ba de lta bu lags zhus pas / jo bo zhal 'dzum nag tings kyis mdzad nas/ bod ngan par thal de sems tsam man chad kyi lugs lags gsungs /.*
154. MAV *ad* MAK 52 (Toh 3885, vol. *sa*, 66b5–6): */ rnam par shes pa de ni don dam par na shel sgong dag pa lta bu ste / sngon po la sogs pa'i rnam pa'i byed brag tu gyur pa ma yin na / de lta bu de la yang thog ma med pa'i dus kyi phyin ci log gi bag chags smin pa'i* [66b6] *mthus rnams pa rnams snang ste sngags la sogs pas dkrugs pa'i mig can rnams la 'dzim pa'i dum bu la sogs pa rta dang glang po che la sogs par snang ba zhin no zhe'o.*
155. See Kajiyama 1978, 128ff.
156. Note Ichigō 1989 and Keira 2004 on this point. See also Jñānaśrīmitra's *Sākārasiddhi* and Ratnākaraśānti's PPU.
157. See Salvini 2015 for a detailed analysis on these points of Yogācāra thought.

158. *Jo bo chen po rje lha cig gi rnam par thar ba* (Ja Dülzin Tsöndrü Bar 2014: 324.16–19): *'o na dbu ma pa ji ltar bzhed zhus pas / dmigs sngag btab pa tsam gyis nam mkha' stong pa la rta glang la sogs sna tshogs su snang ba ltar 'di ltar sang ba 'di yang sna tshogs su snang ba tsam las 'khrul gzhi de lta bu kun rdzob tsam du yang mi bzhed pa lags gsungs /.*

159. This point is also made in *Sherab Dorjé's Explanation of Atiśa's Entry to the Two Realities*, Naljorpa Sherab Dorjé 2006, 37b7–8. On *prajñapti* in Madhyamaka discourse, see *Prasannapadā* (La Vallée Poussin 1903–13, 28nn1–2); May 1959; Tillemans 1990, 64nn40 and 363; Burton 1999; Arnold 2005.

160. See Candrakīrti's MABH *ad* MA 6.28 (Tib., La Vallée Poussin 1907–12, 107.5–108). French translation Louis de la Vallée Poussin, in *Le Muséon* 1910, 304–5. The passage is translated and discussed in Dunne 1996, 542–44. For Tsongkhapa's interpretation of this passage, which differs from Atiśa's understanding, see Hopkins 2008, 235–43, 325.

161. *Jo bo chen po rje lha cig gi rnam par thar ba* (Ja Dülzin Tsöndrü Bar 2014): */ jo bo ma byon* [324.20] *tsa na bod thams cad lta ba dbu ma zhes rtag bzhed pa la / jo bo byon nas dris tsa na thams cad dbu mar ma song bar nor nas sngang /.*

162. *Jo bo chen po rje lha cig gi rnam par thar ba* (Ja Dülzin Tsöndrü Bar 2014): [325.1] *de'i dus su ma snang sgom chen bya ba gcig gis ri rab kyi dpe bya ba ji ltar bzhed zhus pas / rgya gar du rgan mo gcig la bu shin tu byams pa gcig yod pas / khong tshong la 'gro ba'i shul du ma 'o rgyal gyis dogs nas kong rang gi chung ma la nga ma byung gi bar du nga'i ma 'di la bsnyen bkur legs pa shig gyis shig ces bslabs nas song / der mna' mas de* [325.5] *bzhin du byas pas rgan mo lto snum pas mig 'gribs te / zas tham cad skra shad du mthong bas rgan mo 'khrul te khong par sran zhugs / mna' ma la yi mug par gyur te / de nas bu 'khor ba dang rgan mos yus gsol / bus chung ma la de ji ltar yin byas pas chung ma na re ngas ni gus par byas mo rang mig 'khrul ba yin te / khyod rang gis zas byin cig zer / bus zas legs par g.yos pa gcig byin pas snga ma bzhin mthong / rgan mo na re mnga' ma* [325.10] *dang khyed kyang de ltar byed dam zer / bu na re de ltar ma yin khyed rang 'khrul ba yin pas zas de sbos cig zer nas sman pa mkhas pa bkug ste phyi'i sman dang / nang gi sman gyis mig gsos pas mig sos / de nas zas la skra shad med par shes pas khong pa'i nad rang bzhin gyis sos pa cig byung/ de bzhin du sde snod gsum gyi chos kyis phyi'i sgro 'dogs chod / bla ma dam pa'i gdam ngag gis nang gi sgro 'dogs chod pa yin gsungs pas /* [325.15] *bod ston thams cad spobs pa med cing ngo mtshar du gyur nas / chos 'di la rgya gar kha spu can* [325.16] *rang dgos par 'dug zer nas thams cad kyi the tshom chod do /.*

163. Davidson 1995, 293.

164. BMPP, Toh 3948; Sherburne 2000, 218–75. Some scholars, such as Eimer (1978, 46) and Ruegg (1989, 104), have doubted that the *Bodhimārgapradīpapañjikā* (Toh 3948) is Atiśa's own work, without a detailed justification. However, as Kragh (2015, 160n435) has recently noted, "the text speaks of Atiśa's guru Bhikṣu *Paiṇḍapātika of Java (Dge slong Bsod snyoms pa Ya ba dwi pa) as 'my teacher' (*bdag gi bla ma*), using the first-person pronoun. See D 3948, 289b1–2."

165. BMPP, Toh 3948, vol. *khi*, 282a: *sngar bkod pa'i gzhung de dag gi don ni 'di yin te /.* Note that this sentence does not appear in Sherburne's translation.

166. See chapter 4 where Atiśa provides an exegesis on this verse (at *Bden gnyis spyi bshad*, 740.5–20). The verse is also cited in Bhāviveka's MRP (Toh 3854, vol. *tsha*, 262a5). See Brunnhölzl 2014, 901–51 for selected Indian and Tibetan comments on *Uttaratantra* 1.154–55 and *Abhisamayālaṃkāra* 5.21.

167. See Conze 1975, 66, 67, 72, 164, 306, 314, 331, 430, 599, 689; Lamotte 1944, 1: 297n2.

168. Atiśa's *Stages* is virtually unknown to traditional and modern scholarship. The

twenty-two-folio work is contained within a larger one-hundred-folio cursive-script manuscript of twenty-six other minor works all devoted to Atiśa's stages of the path teachings. An annotation found on the first folio of Atiśa's *Stages* mentions that the work was composed by Atiśa for the benefit of his student Dromtönpa. Atiśa's *Lamp* is around three folios in length, but the *Stages* is almost seven times as long. I am preparing a full annotated translation of the work. See Apple 2017 for a brief overview of this important work.

169. Note that another copy of the manuscript was published in the PL480 Library of Congress program in 1973 as *Byang chub lam gyi rim pa: Writings of Lord Atiśa on the Theory and Practice of the Graduated Path.*
170. *Byang chub lam gyi rim pa* (**bodhipathakrama*): */ chos kun sems yin sems nyid mtha' bral te / dge sdig* [8a7] *rgyu 'bras sna tshogs mang po rnams / mi 'gag chad pa'i mtha' las nges par grol / 'khor 'das rgyu 'bras ji ltar snang gyur kyang / sems gyi rang bzhin cir yang ma grub pas / rtag pa'i mtha' las nges par grol ba yin / stong nyid rgyu 'bras dbyer med rang* [8b1] *gi sems / mtha' yi spros bral dbu ma chen po /.*
171. BMPP (Sherburne 2000, 260): *slob dpon zla grags kyang . . . 'dzam bu'i gling du lo bzhi brgyar bzhugs nas gzhan gyi don 'ba' zhig mdzad pa yin no /.*
172. See Ray 1996 on these points regarding long life spans in Buddhist culture and on Nāgārjuna's extraordinary long life span.
173. In the history of Madhyamaka, some Indian Buddhists posited an understanding of ultimate reality that is concordant with words (*paryāya*) and another type of ultimate reality that is completely beyond words and thoughts (*aparyāya*). Atiśa does not adhere to these classifications. See the commentary to SDA 3.3.
174. Scherrer-Schaub 1991, 221n398, 245n471.
175. Hadot 1998, 55–56, 88.
176. Atiśa will state four great reasons (*gtan tshigs chen po bzhi*) in his *Bodhimārgapradīpapañjikā* (Sherburne 2000, 230–36), including the reason refuting production according to the tetralemma (*mu bzhi skye 'gog gi gtan tshigs, catuṣkoṭyutpādapratiṣedhahetu*), the diamond-splinters reason (*rdo rje gzegs ma'i gtan tshigs, vajrakaṇahetu*), the reason of being neither one nor many (*gcig du bral gyi gtan tshigs, ekānekaviyogahetu*), and the reason consisting in dependent-arising (*rten 'brel gyi gtan tshigs, pratītyasamutpādahetu*). Atiśa leaves out the reason refuting the production of existent and nonexistent things (*yod med skye 'gog gi gtan tshigs, *sadasadutpādapratiṣedhahetu*) that is discussed by earlier Mādhyamikas like Kamalaśīla (Keira 2004, 13).
177. As Ruegg (2010, 262) notes, "The Samye debate was not between two homogenous and monolithic national traditions standing in opposition as Indian vs. Chinese Buddhism, but rather an opposition between two transmission traditions of Mo-ho-yen traced back to *Bodhidharma from Kāśyapa and that of Śāntarakṣita and Kamalaśīla traced back to Nāgārjuna."
178. See Mimaki 1982, 53: "Tous les termes utiles pour classer les sous-écoles des Mādhyamika, tels que Sautrāntika-mādhyamika, Yogācāra-mādhyamika, 'Jig rten grags sde spyod pa'i dbu ma pa, Svātantrika et Prāsaṅgika sont une invention des auteurs tibétains."
179. Brunnhölzl 2007, 370n397 (*Bodhipathapradīpapañjikā*, 280a.4–7). In *A General Explanation* the term "Great Madhyamaka" (*dbu ma chen po*) occurs twice (697.25, 699.19) and indicates the definitive understanding of Nāgārjuna's thought. The

term occurs five times in Atiśa's BMPP (Toh 3948, vol. *khi*, 258b4–7, 280a5–6, 280a7, 281a4–5, 283a1) and once in his *Sūtrārthasamuccyopadeśa* (Toh 3957, 305b2). According to Mochizuki's analysis (2007, 117–20), the expression is employed by Atiśa to integrate Madhyamaka and Yogācāra understandings of emptiness. Note though, that the MRP, which Atiśa used to teach Madhyamaka in India and had his disciples translate into Tibetan, explicitly refers to the thought of Nāgārjuna as "Great Madhyamaka" (Toh 3854, vol. *tsha*, 268a2–3, 277b4, 279a3). As van der Kuijp (1983, 37) notes, the term becomes a polemical one in early Tibetan scholasticism and its meaning is dependent on the context in which it is being used.

180. Note that Hopkins (1989, 12), in his discussion of two prominent Indian Madhyamaka thinkers, observes that "one might say that the evidence for a difference in the view of emptiness between Candrakīrti and Bhāvaviveka is so thin that even great Indian scholars did not notice it."

181. On this subclassification of Madhyamaka, see Napper 1989, 403–40; Ruegg 2000; Almogi 2009, 2010; and Vose 2010.

182. For Maitrīpāda's understanding of Madhyamaka, see Mathes 2015. On Maitrīpāda's dates, see Tatz 1988 and Kragh 2015, 70.

183. *Rnal 'byor pa shes rab rdo rjes mdzad pa'i bden gnyis kyi rnam par bshad pa*, 5a7: *dbu mar rtan la phab / dbu ma la yang phi rol don khas blangs kyi dbu ma dang / rnal 'byor spyod pa'i dbu ma dang / snang tsam dbu ma 3 (gsum) las* . . . ; 6a5: *snang tsam dbu ma ba ni /* . . . ; 34a: *klu grub kyi lta ba dbu ma chen po la gzhugs pa'i don du bstan pa'o //* . . .; 38a: *snang tsam ni klu grub kyi lugs te /* . . . ; 43b6–8: Likewise, the Vaibhāṣika, Sautrāntika, True-Aspectarian Sautrāntika, False-Aspectarian Sautrāntika, False-Aspectarian Yogācāra-Mādhyamika, Yogācāra-Mādhyamika, and the Māyopama[ādvayavāda Mādhyamika] have the ground of the Jambu continent, while the Great Madhyamaka of the Ācārya Nāgārjuna does not have more than the mere ground of the tip of a nail (*De bzhin* [43b7] *du bye brag du smra ba dang mdo sde pa / de bzhin du mdo sde pa dang rnam bden pa / rnam bdzun pa / de bzhin du rnam bdzun pa dang rnal 'byor spyod pa'i dbu ma / de bzhin du sbyor spyod pa'i dbu ma dang / sgyu ma lta bu ni 'jam bu kling gi sa tsam* [43b8] *yod pa yin la / slob dpon klu grub kyi dbu ma chen po ni / sen mo'i steng gi sa tsam las med pa yin no /*).

184. On Sangphu overtaking Radreng as the center stage of Kadampa monastic education within thirty years of Sangphu's founding in 1073, see Hugon 2016.

185. The following translation of the *Ratnakaraṇḍodghāṭamadhyamakopadeśa* (*Dbu ma'i man ngag rin po che'i za ma tog kha phye ba*) is based on Miyazaki's (2007b) critical edition of the Tibetan, which utilizes the Dergé *(sde dge)*, Choné (*co ne*), Golden Manuscript (*gser gyi lag bris ma*), Narthang (*snar thang*), and Peking Tengyurs. I have also adapted the section headings of Miyazaki's edition so as to facilitate a comparison between translations and editions of the text. In addition, I have noted important variants from Miyazaki's critical edition with a version of the text, the *Dbu ma'i man ngag rin po che za ma tog kha phye ba* (594–608.11; 793.23–807.25), recently published in the *Jo bo rje dpal ldan a ti sha'i gsung 'bum* (hereafter *Collected Works of Atiśa*), published by the Dpal brtsegs Group in Lhasa in 2006. For details on this Kadampa manusript, see Apple 2010.

186. Monier-Williams 1988, 254.

187. *Dharmadhātudarśanagīti* (*Chos kyi dbyings lta ba'i glu*), Toh 2314 (also 4475), vol. *zhi*, 254b7–260b5.

188. *Ratnakaraṇḍodghāṭa* (Toh 3930, vol. *ki*, 97b6–7; Miyazaki 2007b, 7): *de ltar rnal 'byor pa des nang du mnyam par gzhag pa na / don dam byang chub kyi sems bsgoms la / de las langs pa na kun rdzob byang chub kyi sems bsgoms pas stong pa snying rje chen po'i snying po can gyi byang chub kyi sems gnyis po brtan par bya'o /*. Cf. Wangchuk 2007, 257–58 and 258n125.

189. *Ratnakaraṇḍodghāṭa*, Toh 3930, vol. *ki*, 100b1–b3 (Miyazaki 2007b, 17): *de sbyang ba ni sems de dang po gang nas kyang ma 'ongs shing / tha ma gar yang mi 'gro ba / gang na yang mi gnas pa ste / kha dog med pa / dbyibs med pa / gzod ma nas ma skyes pa / tha mar mi 'gag pa / rang bzhin gyi stong pa / 'od gsal ba'i ngo bo yang nas yang du dran par bya'o / yang na byams pa dang / snying rje byang chub kyi sems de goms pas brtan par bya ba dang / shin tu byang bar bya ste / sems kyi skad cig re re la dran pa rgyun chags su bya ba dang / dran pa dang / shes bzhin dang / tshul bzhin du sems pa dang / bag yod pas gnas par bya'o /*.

190. Atiśa indicates the individuals within the lineage of Ācārya Nāgārjuna in several of his works. The *Bodhipathapradīpa* states, "Cultivate only the instruction of Ārya Nāgārjuna, Āryadeva, Candrakīrti, Bhavya, and Śāntideva (26), and if there is no one of that tradition, then study the texts composed by them over and over again" (Sherburne 2000, 250); *'phags pa klu sgrub 'phags pa'i lha / zla grags bha bya zhi ba'i lha / brgyud pa'i man ngag 'ba' zhig bsgom / gal te brgyud pa med gyur na / de dag rnams kyis bkod pa yi / gzhung rnams yang dang yang du blta* (*Bodhipathapradīpa*, P 327a5). The *Bodhipathapradīpa-pañjikā* states, "The nectar of Ārya Nāgārjuna's words filled up Āryadeva, Candrakīrti, Bhavya, and Śāntideva down to Bodhibhadra too; even on me a little has been sprinkled and thus with their four great proofs, I establish the non-arising of all phenomena; and following the steps of those Ācāryas of old, I will hold to the tenets of the great Middle Way" (Sherburne 2000, 237; cf. Lindtner 1981, 210); *'phags pa klu sgrub zhal gyi bdud rtsi des / arya de ba zla grag bha bya dang / zhi ba'i lha dang byang chub bzang po'i bar / tshim par gyur pa bdag la 'ng cung zhig 'thor / de ltar gtan tshigs chen po bzhi dag dis / chos rnams thams cad skyes med bsgrub byas te / sngon gyi slob dpon rnams kyis res 'brang nas / dbu ma chen po'i grub mthar gnas par bya /* (P 323b6–327a1). Also, the *Satyadvayāvatāra* states, "But who has [actually] 'understood' emptiness?—Nāgārjuna, who was predicted by the Tathāgata, [and his] disciple Candrakīrti who [also] saw the absolute truth (*dharmatāsatya*) (Lindtner 1981, 194); *stong nyid gang gis rtog shes na / de bzhin gshegs pas lung bstan zhing / chos nyid bden pa gzigs pa yi / klu sgrub slob ma zla grags yin / de las brgyud pa'i man ngag gis / chos nyid bden pa rtogs par 'gyur /* (Lindtner 1981, 191; cf. Sherburne 2000, 335). See also the *Dbu ma'i man ngag gi 'bum* (*Collected Works of Atiśa, Jo bo rje'i gsung 'bum*, 642–68), an early Kadampa commentary on Atiśa's *Satyadvayāvatāra*, where (658.19–20) "the special instructions only exist from the lineage derived from Ācārya Candrakīrti" (*slob dpon zla ba grags pa nas brgyud pa'i man ngag yod pa cig las gdam ngag tshul bzhin du mnos nas /*) and (658.22–23) "the special instructions of the lineage derived from Candrakīrti are the only Madhyamaka special instructions" (*zla ba grags pa las brgyud pa'i man ngag kyang dbu ma'i man ngag kho na yin te*).

191. *Collected Works of Atiśa* (*Jo bo rje'i gsung 'bum* 594.11), adds "those born from the womb" (*mngal las skyes po*).

192. *Piṇḍīkṛtasādhana*, v. 3 (La Vallée Poussin 1896, 1): *vikalpavāsanādoṣān jagattrayavimohakān / samabhivīkṣya tān dhīmān yogatantreṇa śodhayet /*.

193. Atiśa's Tibetan differs from the Tengyur. Cf. *Bodhicittavivaraṇa*, vv. 74–75 (Lindtner 1997b, 56–58): *gang dag pha dang ma dang ni / gnyen bshes gyur pas bdag la sngon / phan pa byas par gyur pa yi / sems can de dag rnams la ni / byas pa bzo bar gyur par bya / srid pa'i btson rar sems can ni / nyon mongs me yis gdungs rnams la / bdag gis sdug bsngal byin pa ltar / de bzhin bde ba sbyin par rigs /.*

194. The "four immeasurables" (*catvāry apramānāṇi*, Tib. *tshad med bzhi*), also known as the four "abodes of Brahma" (*brahmavihāra*), the contemplations of immeasurable love (*maitrī*), compassion (*karuṇā*), joy (*muditā*), and equanimity (*upekṣā*). *Mahāvyutpatti*, 1503–7.

195. Aspirations to liberate (*bsgrol ba*) beings, free (*dgrol ba*) them from obstacles, free them from great powerful suffering (*dbugs dbyung ba*), and to free those not passed beyond nirvāṇa (*mya ngan las bzla*).

196. *Collected Works of Atiśa* (*Jo bo rje'i gsung 'bum* 595.3), reads *til gyi gang bu* (heap of mustard seeds) rather than *til gyi ga'u ad* D 97a.

197. The six antidotes are (1) recitation of sūtras, (2) meditation on emptiness, (3) recitation of mantras, (4) making statues or paintings of buddhas, (5) making offering to buddhas or *stūpas*, and (6) recitation of the names of buddhas.

198. These comprise the seven-limbed (*saptāṅga*, *yang lag bdun*) prayer liturgy based on the *Samantabhadracārya-praṇidhāna*: praise (*vandana*), offering (*pūjanā*), confession (*pāpadeśanā*), rejoicing (*modanā*), requesting (*adhyeṣaṇā*) to turn the wheel of dharma, begging [the buddhas not to abandon beings] (*yācanā*), and dedication (*pariṇāmanā*); see Crosby and Skilton 1995, 9–13.

199. The five obstacles to be relinquished are laziness, forgetting the instructions, dullness and agitation, nonapplication, and overapplication. There are eight antidotes to these five; see *Madhyāntavibhāga*, IV.4–6ab (Pandeya 1999, 130–31): *kausīdyam avavādasya saṃmoṣo laya uddhavaḥ / asaṃskāro 'tha saṃskāraḥ pañca doṣā ime matāḥ / āśrayo 'thāśritas tasya nimittaṃ phalam eva ca / ālambane 'saṃmoṣo laya-uddhatyānubuddhyanā / tadapāyābhisaṃskāraḥ śāntau praśaṭhavāhitā /.*

200. Eight similes of illusion (*aṣṭamāyopamā*, Tib. *sgyu ma'i dpe brgyad*). The eight are said to be a twinkling star (*skar mar*), optical illusion (*rab rib*), lamp (*mar me*), dream (*rmi lam*), flash of lightning (*glog*), moon in the water (*chu zla*), mirage (*smig rgyu*), and cloud (*sprin*). See Ruegg 1966, 99n2.

201. *The Collected Works of Atiśa* (*Jo bo rje'i gsung 'bum*, 595.21), reads *de ltar* rather than *de dag*.

202. "Divide into four portions" is explained by Atiśa in his *Caryāsaṃgrahapradīpa* (Sherburne 2000, 349): "Divide your food into four parts: first give pure food gifts to the gods, then scatter generous offerings to the guardians of the dharma, and after your own food and drink, give what remains to all creatures" (*zlas la cha bzhir bgo bya ste / dang po lha la bshos gtsang dbul / de rjes chos kyi srung ma la / gtor ma shin tu rgya chen gtang / rang gis zos shing 'thungs pa yi / lhag ma 'byung po kun la sbyin /*).

203. Cf. *Bodhicittavivaraṇa* (Lindtner 1997b, 32): *byang chub sems dpa' gsang sngags kyi sgor spyad pa spyod pa rnams kyis de ltar kun rdzob kyi rnam pas byang byang chub kyi sems smon pa'i rang bzhin can bskyed nas / don dam pa'i byang chub kyi sems bsgom pa'i stobs kyis bskyed par bya ba yin pas . . . /.* Translation (33): "When a bodhisattva, having practiced a course by way of mantras, has thus produced the bodhicitta that in its relative aspect has the nature of aspiration, he must by means of meditational development produce the absolute bodhicitta."

204. *Bodhicittavivaraṇa*, v. 73 (Lindtner 1997b, 56): *de ltar stong pa nyid 'di ni / rnal 'byor pa yis bsgom byas na / gzhan gyi don la chags pa'i blo / 'byung bar 'gyur ba the tshom med /.*

205. *Collected Works of Atiśa* (596.8) adds: "the object of attainment called 'awakening' is nothing at all" (*de byang chub ces bya'i thob par bya ba ni ci yang med de /*).

206. Cf. Miyazaki (8n6), *Vairocanābhisaṃbodhi*, Toh 494, vol. *tha*, 226b7–227a1: *byang chub nam mkha'i mtshan nyid do kun tu rtog pa thams cad spangs /.*

207. Cf. *Ratnaguṇasaṃcayagāthā*, 15.3cd (Obermiller 1937, 57): *na ca bodhi skandha vimṛśitva parāmṛśeyā ye ādikarmaka na deśayitavyaṃ evaṃ /.*

208. *The Collected Works of Atiśa* (596.16); the verse up to this point is missing.

209. *Guhyasamāja*, 2.3–4 (Matsunaga 1978, 10): *sarvabhāvavigataṃskandhadhātvāyatana-grāhyagrāhakavarjitam / dharmanairātmyasamatayā svacittam ādyanutpannaṃ śūnyatābhāvam /.*

210. *The Collected Works of Atiśa* (596.17–18) differs: *sha ra dva ti'i bu gang sems ma yin pa de ni sems med pa'o / gang sems med pa de ni sems med pa'o / gang sems med pa de ni rang bzhin gyis 'od gsal ba'o /.* Cf. *Aṣṭasāhasrikā* (Wogihara 1932, 38): *tac cittam acittam / prakṛtiś cittasya prabhāsvarā /.*

211. *Bodhicittavivaraṇa*, v. 43 (Lindtner 1997b, 46). The Tibetan of this verse differs from the following canonical version in Toh 1800: *mdor na sangs rgyas rnams kyis ni / gzigs par ma gyur gzigs mi 'gyur / rang bzhin med pa'i rang bzhin can / ji ltar bur na gzig par 'gyur /.* Buddhas not perceiving the mind goes back to *Kāśyapaparivarta* §98 (Vorobyova–Desyatovskaya 2002, 35): *cittaṃ hi kāśyapa sarvabuddhair na dṛṣṭaṃ na paśyaṃti na paśyiṣyanti na drrakṣyanti /.*

212. Miyazaki 2007b, 9n13; *Jñānasārasamuccaya*, v. 33abc. Sanskrit located in *Tattvaratnāvalī* (Shastri 1927, 17): *cittaṃ niścitya bodhena abhyāsaṃ kurute yadā / tadā cittaṃ na paśyāmi* (*kva gataṃ kva sthitaṃ bhavet*)*/.*

213. *The Collected Works of Atiśa* (*Jo bo rje'i gsung 'bum* 596.22) add: *'phags pa phung po gsum pa'i mdo las kyang.*

214. "Endowed with all excellent features" (*sarvākāravaropetā śūnyatā*; trans. Wangchuk 2007, 210) is an important concept in Tathāgatagarbha and Vajrayāna traditions. This expression is discussed by Ruegg 1981, 84, 97, 98.

215. *Bodhicittavivaraṇa*, v. 2. Atiśa's Tibetan of this verse differs from the following version in Lindtner 1997b, 32: *sangs rgyas rnams kyi byang chub sems / bdag dang phung sogs rnam rig gi / rtog pa rnams kyi ma bsgribs pa / rtag tu stong nyid mtshan nyid bzhed /.*

216. Compare *Sāgaramatiparipṛcchā*, Toh 152, vol. *pha*, 58b7–59a1 (Miyazaki 2007b, 10n16): *blo gros rgya mtsho theg pa chen po par 'gyur ba'i chos gcig ste / chos gcig gang zhe na / 'di lta ste / byang chub kyi sems brjed pa med cing bag yod pa ste / blo gros rgya mtsho 'di ni theg chen po sdud par 'gyur ba'i chos gcig go /.*

217. Compare *Bodhisattvagocaropāyaviṣayavikurvāṇanirdeśa*, Toh 146, vol. *pa*, 87a7–b5 (Miyazaki 2007b, 11n17): *rigs kyi bu chos bcu gnyis dang ldan pa'i rigs kyi bu' am rigs kyi bu mo bla na med pa yang dag par rdzogs pa'i byang chub tu sems skye bar 'gyur ro / bcu gnyis gang zhe na / 'di lta ste /*: (1) *rang bzhin gyis rgya chen po la mos shing dman pa la mos pa med pa yin /* (2) *rang bzhin gyis snying rje'i spyod yul dang ldan zhing dkar po'i rang bzhin can yin /* (7) *bcos ma ma yin pa'i lhag pa'i bsam pa'i spyod yul dang ldan zhing yi dam la brtan pa yin /* (10) *tshogs shin tu bsags shing spyad pa legs par spyad pa yin /* (5) *sangs rgyas 'byung ba legs par bsnyen bkur zhing dkar po'i chos legs par yongs su bsdus pa yin /* (6) *lus dang ngag dang yid kyi las kyi mtha' kha na ma*

tho ba med pa dang ldan zhing sdig pa'i las thams cad bor ba yin / (3) *sdig pa'i grogs po thams cad yongs su spangs shing dge ba'i bshes gnyen la brten pa yin /* (4) *ji ltar smras pa de bzhin du byed cing slu ba med pa yin /* (8) *bged pa'i ngang tshul can yin zhing ro bro ba rnams la ma zhen ma chags pa mang ba yin /* (9) *de bzhin gshegs pa'i byin gyi rlabs kyis byin gyis brlabs shing bdud kyi byin gyi rlabs dang bral ba yin /* (11) *sems can thams cad la yang dang yang snying rje chen po yang dag par 'jug pa yin /* (12) *bdog pa thams cad yongs su gtong zhing ma chags pa'i sems dang ldan pa yin te / (rigs kyi bu yon tan gyi chos bcu gnyis po de dag dang ldan pa'i rigs kyi bu'am rigs kyi bu mo bla na med pa yang dag par rdzogs pa'i byang chub tu sems skye ste /.*

218. *Bodhisattvabhūmi* (Dutt 1996, 10): *catvāro hetavaḥ katame / gotrasampad bodhisattvasya prathamo hetuś cittasyotpattaye / buddhabodhisattvakalyāṇamitraparigraho dvitīyo hetuś cittasyotpattaye / sattveṣu kāruṇyaṃ bodhisattvasya tṛtīyo hetuś cittasyotpattaye / saṃsāraduḥkhād duṣkaracaryāduḥkhād api dīrghakālikād vicitrāt tīvrān nirantarādabhīrutā caturtho hetuś cittasyotpattaye /.*

219. This most likely refers to the *Sūtra of the Three Heaps* (*Triskandhakasūtra,* Dergé 384), used for the confession of downfalls and featuring thirty-five buddhas of confession. The "three heaps" or three sections referred to in the title are (1) confession of sin (*pāpadeśanā*), (2) rejoicing at merit (*puṇyānumodanā*), (3) and requesting instruction from a buddha (*buddhādhyeṣaṇā*).

220. *The Collected Works of Atiśa* (*Jo bo rje'i gsung 'bum* 598.8): "the excellence of the special instructions for the individual" (*rten gdam nga gi khyad par dang /*).

221. *Abhidharmakośa*, 4.32 (Pradhan 1975, 216): *buddhasaṃghakarān dharmān aśaikṣān ubhayāṃs ca saḥ / nirvāṇaṃ ceti śaraṇaṃ yo yāti śaraṇatrayam /.*

222. The Three Jewels of (1) ultimate truth are the emptiness or *śūnyatā* of the Buddha, Dharma, and Saṃgha; the Three Jewels (2) in front of oneself are the physical representations of the Three Jewels; and the Three Jewels (3) of realizations (*mngon par togs pa*) are realizations attained on the path.

223. Miyazaki 2007b, 14n20 notes that this citation is not in the *Karuṇāpuṇḍarīka*. Cf. *Tathāgatajñānamudrāsamādhi*, Toh 131, vol. *da*, 240a7–b7: *de ci'i phyir zhe na byams pa rnam pa bdun gyis byang chub sems dpa' byang chub tu* [240b1] *sems skyed do / bdun gang zhe na / 'di lta ste /* (1) *sangs rgyas bcom ldan 'das rnams kyis byang chub sems dpa' byang chub tu sems skyed pa dang /* (2) *dam pa'i chos rnam par 'jig pa'i dus na dam pa'i chos yongs su bsrung ba'i phyir byang chub sems dpa' byang chub tu sems skyed pa dang /* (3) *sdug bsngal sna tshogs kyis yongs su gzir ba'i sems can gyi khams mthong nas snying rje chen po skyes te byang chub sems dpa' byang chub tu sems bskyed pa dang /* (4) *byang chub sems dpas byang chub sems dpa' byang chub tu sems bskyed pa dang /* (5) *bsti stang du byas te sbyin pa bzang po yid du 'ong ba byin nas / byang chub sems dpa' bdag nyid byang chub tu sems bskyed pa dang /* (6) *gzhan yang byang chub tu sems bskyed pa mthong nas byang chub sems dpa' byang chub tu sems bskyed pa dang /* (7) *de bzhin gshegs pa'i sku'i mtshan dang dpe byad bzang po'i rgyan sna tshogs kyi yon tan bsngags pa yongs su rdzogs pa thos nas byang chub sems dpa' byang chub tu sems bskyed pa ste / byams pa rnam pa bdun po de dag gis byang chub sems dpa' byang chub tu sems bskyed do / byams pa de la gang byang chub sems dpa' sang rgyas bcom ldan 'das rnams kyis byang chub tu sems bskyed pa gang yin pa dang / gang dam pa'i chos rnam par 'jig pa'i dus na dam pa'i chos yongs su bsrung bar bya ba'i phyir byang chub sems dpa' byang chub tu sems bskyed pa gang yin pa dang / gang sdug bsngal sna tshogs kyis yongs su gzir ba'i sems can gyi khams mthong nas sems can thams cad la snying rje chen po skyes te /*

byang chub sems dpa' byang chub tu sems bskyed pa gang yin pa dang / byams pa sems bskyed pa 'di gsum ni sangs rgyas bcom ldan 'das rnams kyi byang chub bsrung ba yin te / myur du bla na med pa yang dag par rdzogs pa'i byang chub las phyir mi ldog par 'gyur ro /.

224. *Daśadharmakasūtra*, 168a1–7 (Miyzaki 2007b, 15n21). Cited in the *Śikṣāsamuccayasūtra* (Bendall 1971, 8): *yathā daśadharmakasūtre deśitaṃ / iha kulaputra bodhisatvo gotrasthaḥ sann anutpāditabodhicittaḥ tathāgatena vā tathāgataśrāvakeṇa vā saṃcodyamānaḥ saṃvedyamānaḥ samādāpyamāno 'nuttarāyāṃ samyaksaṃbodhau bodhicittam utpādayatîdaṃ prathamaṃ kāraṇaṃ bodhicittôtpādāya / saṃbodher vā bodhicittasya vā varṇaṃ bhāṣyamāṇaṃ śrutvânuttarāyāṃ samyaksaṃbodhau cittam utpādayatîdaṃ dvitīyaṃ kāraṇaṃ / sa satvā . . . naśaraṇān advīpān dṛṣṭvā kāruṇyacittam upasthāpya yāvad anuttarāyāṃ samyaksaṃbodhau cittam utpādayatîdaṃ tṛtīyaṃ kāraṇaṃ bodhicittôtpādāya / sa tathāgatasya sarvâkāraparipūrṇatāṃ dṛṣṭvā prītim utpādyânuttarāyāṃ samyaksaṃbodhau cittam utpādayatîdaṃ caturthaṃ kāraṇam iti /.*

225. *Mahāyānasūtrālaṃkāra*, 4.7 (Lévi 1911, 14): *mitrabalāt hetubalān mūlabalāc chrutabalāc chubhābhyāsāt / adṛḍhadṛḍhodaya (uktaś cittopādaḥ parākyānāt) /.*

226. *Bodhisattvabhūmi* (Dutt 1966, 9.12): *tasya khalu cittasyotpādaḥ caturbhiḥ pratyayaiś caturbhir hetubhiś caturbhir balair veditavyaḥ.*

227. See Sparham 1987 regarding debates on the relation of *bodhicitta* to mental factors (*caitta*) such as desire.

228. *Collected Works of Atiśa* (599.13) has the archaic *ji snyed du mgon po byam pa'i zhal snga nas /.*

229. *Abhisamayālaṃkāra*, 1.18ab (Stcherbatsky and Obermiller 1929, 4): *cittotpādaḥ parārthāya samyaksaṃbodhikāmatā /.*

230. Compare with *Akṣayamatinirdeśa* (Braarvig 1993, 20): *bstun pa sha ra dva ti'i bu byang chub sems dpa' rnams kyi dang po sems bskyed pa yang mi zad pa'o / de ci'i phyir zhe na / ma 'dres pa'i phyir ro / sems de ni nyon mongs pa thams cad dang ma 'dres par skyes so / theg pa gzhan la 'dod pa med pas sems de ni ma 'brel bar skyes so /.* Also BMPP *ad* 250b7–251b6.

231. See *Special Instructions on the Middle Way*, part 3.

232. Cf. Atiśa's *Bodhisattvamaṇyāvali* (Mochizuki 1999, 79).

233. *Ten Great Blessings of the Vajra Banner* (*Rdo rje rgyal mtshan gyi bsngo ba chen po bcu*) is chapter 30 of the *Buddhāvataṃsakasūtra* (Mochizuki 1999, 79).

234. *Bodhicittavivaraṇa*, vv. 74–75. Atiśa's Tibetan of these verses differs from the following version in Lindtner 1997b, 56–58: *gang dag pha dang ma dang ni / gnyen bshes gyur pas bdag la sngon / phan pa byas par gyur pa yi / sems can de dag rnams la ni / byas pa bzo bar gyur par bya / 74 / srid pa'i btson rar sems can ni / nyon mongs me yis gdungs rnams la / bdag gis sdug bsngal byin pa ltar / de bzhin bde ba sbyin par rigs /.*

235. *Bodhisattvasaṃvaraviṃśaka*, v. 18c, Toh 4081, vol. *hi*, 167a4: *byams la lan du phan mi 'dogs /.* Cf. Tatz 1985, 29: "Not to repay a good turn."

236. *Aṣṭasāhasrikāprajñāpāramitā* (Wogihara 1932, 117–18): *tasmān mātṛsaṃjñā pitṛsaṃjñā putrasaṃjñā duhitṛsaṃjñā bodhisattvena mahāsattvena sarvasattvānām antike yāvad ātmasaṃjñā utpādayitavyā / yathā ātmā sarveṇa sarvaṃ sarvathā sarvaṃ sarvaduḥkhebhyo mocayitavyaḥ evaṃ sarvasattvāḥ sarveṇa sarvaṃ sarvathā sarvaṃ sarvaduḥkhebhyo mocayitavyā iti / evaṃ ca sarvasattveṣu saṃjñā utpādayitavyā mayaite sarvasattvā na parityaktavyāḥ / mayaite sarvasattvāḥ parimocayitavyā apari-*

māṇato duḥkhaskandhāt / na ca mayaiteṣu cittapradoṣa utpādayitavya antaśaḥ śataśo 'pi chidyamāneneti / evaṃ hi bodhisattvena mahāsattvena cittam utpādayitavyam.

237. *Collected Works of Atiśa* (600.25) adds: "engaging with an angry mind" (*khro ba'i sems kyis rjes su 'jug /*).

238. These are bodhisattva downfalls listed in the *Bodhisattvasaṃvaraviṃśaka*, Toh 4081, vol. *hi*, 166b4–5: (v. 7ab) *gzhan gyis bsags kyang mi nyan par / khros nas gzhan la 'tshog pa dang /* (167a1, v. 13c) *pha rol shad kyis 'chags pa spong /* (13ab) *gshe la lan du gshe la sogs / khros pa rnams ni yal bar 'jog /*. Tatz 1985, 28.

239. The five sins of immediate retribution (*ānantaryakarma*) are killing one's father, mother, or an arhat, drawing the blood of a buddha, and creating a schism in the monastic community. See Silk 2007.

240. *Cittaviśuddhiprakaraṇa*, v. 32 (Patel 1949, 3): *dvādaśayojanavyāsaṃ cakraṃ vai śirasi bhramat / bodhicittaṃ samutpādya apanītam iti śrutiḥ.*

241. Miyazaki 2007b, 21n37; cf. *Catuḥśataka*, 6.11; Sanskrit text is found in the *Subhāṣitasaṃgraha* (Bendall 1903, 385): *glāne putre viśeṣeṇa mātā 'rtā jāyate yathā / asatsu bodhisattvānāṃ viśeṣeṇa dayā tathā /.*

242. Cf. *Madhyamakahṛdaya* 3.296cd, 297a, 301ab (Lindtner 2001, 41): *aśokaḥ śokasaṃtaptaṃ prekṣate duḥkhitam jagat /* 296 */sa tadā karuṇādreṇa lokam ālokya cakṣuṣā /* 297ab */pepīḍyamānaḥ kṛpayā taddhitādhānadīkṣitaḥ /* 301 a /. For comments on these verses, see Eckel 1992, 27–28, 174–76; and Eckel 2008, 45–46.

243. Cf. *Gaganagañjaparipṛcchā*, Toh 148, vol. *pa*, 323a7–b1: *sems can rnyed dang 'dod gnas pa / tshul khrims 'chal* [323b1] *ba mthong nas su / de yi 'gro ba cir 'gyur zhes / mchi ma'ang rab tu 'byung bar gyi /*. Cited in the *Śikṣāsamuccaya*, 45.15–16: *dṛṣṭvā duḥśīlasatvāṃś cecchālobhapratiṣṭhitān / aśrupātaṃ kariṣyāmo gatiḥ kāndhasya bhāvitā /.*

244. English translation Dunne and McClintock 1997, 69; *Ratnāvalī*, 5.82 (Hahn 1982, 160): *ye pāpāni cikīrṣanti sarvalokeṣu vartataḥ / vārayeya*[*ṃ nirābādhaṃ*] *tān sarvān yugapat sadā /.*

245. *The Collected Works of Atiśa* (*Jo bo rje'i gsung 'bum* 601.18) cites from the *'phags pa blo gros mi zad pa'i mdo.*

246. *Pratibhānamatiparipṛcchā*, Toh 151, vol. *pa*, 339a3 (Miyazaki 2007b, 22n42): (*kun tu thogs pa med pa'i 'od zer rnams kyis*) *sems can thams cad bdag dang 'dra zhing bu gcig pa'i byis pa dang 'dra bar mthong ba dang /.*

247. The Tibetan here differs from the Sanskrit. Cf *Mahāyānasūtrālaṃkāra*, 13.22 (Lévi 1907, 89): *yathā kapotī svasutātivatsalā svabhāvakāṃstānupaguhya tiṣṭhati / tathāvidhāyaṃ pratigho virudhyate suteṣu tadvatsakṛpe 'pi dehiṣu /*. See Thurman et al. 2004, 172.

248. *Śrīparamādyamantrakalpakhaṇḍa*, Toh 488, vol. *ta*, 173b–34: *ci srid 'khor ba'i gnas su ni / mkhas mchog 'dug par 'gyur ba'i tshe / de srid mtshungs med sems can don / mya ngan mi 'da' byed par nus /*; cf. *Adhyardhaśatikā*, v. 1 (Tomabechi 2009, 23): *yāvat saṃsāravāsasthā bhavanti varasūrayaḥ / tāvat sattvārtham atulaṃ śakyā kartum anirvṛtāḥ /*. Also cited in the *Bodhipathapradīpapañjika* (Sherburne 2000, 267).

249. The four means of gathering disciples (*bsdu ba'i dngos po, saṃgrahavastu*) are generosity (*dāna*), kind words (*priyavāditā*), beneficial acts (*arthacaryā*), and sympathy (*samānārthatā*). *Mahāvyutpatti*, 924–28.

250. Also known as the five sciences (*pañcavidyā*): linguistic science (*śabda*), logical science (*hetu*), "inner" science (*adhyātma*), medical science (*cikitsā*), and the science

of fine arts and crafts (*śilpakarmasthāna*). *Mahāvyutpatti*, 1554–59. See Gold 2007, 11–16, 20–24.

251. Cf. *Kāśyapaparivarta* §4 (Vorobyova-Desyatovskaya 2002, 6): *na jīvitārthe anṛtaṃ vadanti bhāṣaṃti vācaṃ sada arthayuktāṃ māyāya ṣāṭṭhyena ca nitya varjitā adhyāśayena sada satva paśyati ·bodhāya ye prasthita śuddhasatvā śāsteti tān manyati bodhisatvān varṇaṃ ca teṣāṃ bhaṇate caturdiśaṃ śāstāra saṃjñāṃ sad upasthapitvā yāṃś cāpi satvān paripācayati anuttare jñāne samādapeti cāpieteṣu dharmeṣu pratiṣṭhitānāṃ cittam na bodhāya kadāci muhyati.*

252. Miyazaki 2007b, 25n48, *Avalokiteśvaraparipṛcchāsaptadharmaka*, Toh 150, vol. *pa*, 331a7–b2: *rigs kyi bu byang chub tu sems bskyed ma thag pa'i byang chub sems dpas chos bdun la bslab par bya ste / bdun gang zhe na / 'di lta ste / rnam par tog pas kyang 'dod pa la sten par mi byed na dbang po gnyis sbyor ba lta smos kyang ci* [331b1] *dgos / tha na rmi lam gyi nang du yang mi dge ba'i bshes gnyen bsten par mi byed pa dang / bya dang 'dra ba'i sems kyis yongs su 'dzin pa med par bya ba dang / thabs dang shes rab la mkhas pas nga rgyal dang / ngar 'dzin pa med par bya ba dang / dngos po dang dngos po med pa spangs nas stong pa nyid kyi rnam par thar pa brtan po dang ldan par bya ba dang / yang dag par bden pa ma yin pa'i kun du rtog pa'i shes pa sgyu ma dang / rmi lam dang 'dra bar 'khor ba las mngon par dga' bar bya ba ma yin pa dang / rgyu dang 'bras bu la skur bag dab par mi bya ba ste /.*

253. Atiśa cites two half-verses in inverse order from the *Bodhicaryāvatāra* (5.26cd, 25cd), making it difficult to determine the subject of the citation. The Sanskrit of the regular order of the half-verses is as follows (Vaidya 1960, 57): *sacchidrakumbhajalavanna smṛtāvavatiṣṭhate* / 5.25cd / / *asaṃprajanyadoṣeṇa bhavanty āpattikaśmalāḥ* / 5.26 /.

254. *Śikṣāsamuccaya*, 27c–d (Bendall 1971, 356): *apramādāviyojanāt / smṛtyātha samprajanyena yoniśaścintanena ca.*

255. *Bodhisattvasaṃvaraviṃśaka*, Toh 4081, vol. *hi*, 166b7: (v. 10c) *chos 'dod pa la sbyin mi byed /* (167a3, v. 17dc) *dgos pa'i grogs su 'gro mi byed / nad pa'i rim gro bya ba spong /* (166b7, v. 11b) *sems can don la bya ba chung /*. See Tatz 1985, 28–29.

256. *Kāśyapaparivarta* §3 (Vorobyova-Desyatovskaya 2002, 4–5): (*caturbhiḥ kāśyapa dharmaiḥ samanvāgatasya bodhisatvasya bodhicittaṃ muhyati katamaiś caturbhiḥ*) *yad utācāryaguru dākṣiṇīyavisaṃvādanatayā pareṣam akokṛ{i}tye kaukṛtyaupasaṃhāraṇatayā mahāyānasaṃprasthitānāṃ ca satvānām avarṇāyaśakīrtiśabdaślokaniścāraṇataya māyāṣāṭṭhyena ca param upacarati nādhyāśayena ebhiḥ kāśyapa caturbhiḥ dharmaiḥ samanvāgatasya bodhisatvasya bodhicittaṃ muhyati.*

257. Miyazaki 2007b, 28n56, *Sarvapuṇyasamuccayasamādhi*, Toh 134, vol. *na*, 101a4–7.

258. I have translated this seemingly out of place sentence at the location where it occurs in the manuscript.

259. Cf. *Aṣṭasāhasrikā* (Wogihara 1935, 832): *syāt khalu punaḥ kauśika śakyeta trisāhasramahāsāhasre lokadhātau tulyamāne palāgreṇa pramāṇaṃ grahītum, na tve va kauśika tasya kulaputrasya vā kuladuhitur vā bodhisattvasya mahāsattvasyānumodanāsahagatasya cittotpādasya puṇyapramāṇaṃ grahītuṃ /.*

260. The preceding irregular sequence of citation follows the order given in the Tibetan.

261. *Bodhicaryāvatāra*, 4.9 (Vaidya 1960, 44): *yo 'pyanyaḥ kṣaṇamapyasya puṇyavighnaṃ kariṣyati / tasya durgatiparyanto nāsti sattvārthadhātinaḥ /.*

262. Citation not identified.

263. *Mahāyānasūtrālaṃkāra*, 3.7 (Lévi 1907, 11): *kleśābhyāsaḥ kumitratvaṃ vidhātaḥ paratantratā / gotrasyādīnavo jñeyaḥ samāsena caturvidhaḥ /.*

264. Cf. *Abhisamayālaṃkāra*, 4.6, 7abd (Stcherbatsky and Obermiller 1929, 18): *kṛtādhikārā buddheṣu teṣūptaśubhamūlakāḥ / mitraiḥ sanāthāḥ kalyāṇair asyāḥ śravaṇabhājanam / buddhopāsanasaṃpraśnadānaśīlādicaryayā / (udgrahadhāraṇādīnāṃ) bhājanatvaṃ satāṃ matam /.*

265. *Mahāyānaprasādaprabhāvanā*, Toh 144, vol. *pa*, 15a6–b3 (Miyazaki 2007b, 34n66): *rigs kyi bu 'di la byang chub sems dpa' rnams kyi theg pa chen po'i phyir theg pa chen po la dad pa'i bag chags byang chub sems dpa'i gnas la rje su 'brang ba de ni 'di ltar rjes su 'brang ste / 'di lta ste / 'gro 'am 'dug gam nyal lam gnyid kyis log gam / ra ro'am / smyos kyang rung ste / rtag tu theg pa chen po la dad pa de dang ldan par 'gyur ro / byang chub sems dpa' tshe rabs gzhan du rjes te / theg pa chen po la dad pa de brjed du zin kyang dman pa skal pa mi mnyam pa'i sems bskyed* [15b] *pa'i tshul can ma yin pas / bshes gnyen ngan pa nyan thos dang rang sangs rgyas dang 'dre bas kyang 'phrog par mi 'gyur na / gzhan mu steg can gyi lta 'phrogs par ga la 'gyur / theg pa chen po'i phyir theg pa chen po la dad pa'i rkyen chung ngu zhig rnyed pas kyang myur ba dang / shas che ba dang / rgyun gyis theg pa chen po'i phyir theg pa chen po la dad pa skyed do / de'i theg pa chen po'i phyir theg pa chen po la dad pa'i bag chags rjes su 'brel pa de yang tshe rabs tshe rabs su rnam par 'phel te / bla na med pa yang dag par rdzogs pa'i byang chub kyi bar du 'gyur ro /.*

266. *Bodhicaryāvatāra*, 1.9–10 (Vaidya 1960, 7–8): *bhavacārakabandhano varākaḥ sugatānāṃ suta ucyate kṣaṇena / sanarāmaralokavandanīyo bhavati smodita eva bodhicitte / 9 / aśucipratimām imāṃ gṛhītvā jinaratnapratimāṃ karoty anarghāṃ / rasajātam atīva vedhanīyaṃ sudṛḍhaṃ gṛhṇata bodhicittasaṃjñaṃ / 10 /.*

267. *Bodhicaryāvatāra*, 1.17 (Vaidya 1960, 12–13)*: bodhipraṇidhicittasya saṃsāre 'pi phalaṃ mahat / na tv avicchinnapuṇyatvaṃ yathā prasthānacetasaḥ /.*

268. *Bodhicaryāvatāra*, 1.19 (Vaidya 1960, 13): *tataḥ prabhṛti suptasya pramattasy āpy anekaśaḥ / avicchinnāḥ puṇyadhārāḥ pravartante nabhaḥsamāḥ /.*

269. *The Collected Works of Atiśa* (*Jo bo rje'i gsung 'bum*, 607.14–15) adds this line: *de gnyis kyi phan yon ni spyod pa la 'jug pa dang / sdong po bkod pa dang /.*

270. Miyazaki 2007b, 36n72; *Kudṛṣṭinirghātana*, v. 3 (Shastri 1927, 1): *parārthasaṃpad buddhānāṃ phalaṃ mukhyatamaṃ matam / buddhatvādi yad anyat tu tādarthyāt phalam iṣyate /.* Cited in the *Ekasmṛtyupadeśa*, D (3928), vol. *ki*, 95a6–7; see Sherburne 2000, 416–17.

271. Miyazaki 2007b, 37n73; cf. *Māyopamasamādhi*, Toh 130, vol. *da*, 227a7–b2: *rigs kyi bu de ltar de bzhin gshegs pa 'od dpag med yongs su mya ngan las 'das nas dam pa'i chos nub ma thag pa'i mtshan mo* [227b1] *reng 'char ba'i dus kyi tshe byang chub sems dpa' sems pa' chen po spyan ras gzigs dbang phyug rin po che du ma'i bkod pa'i byang chub kyi shing drung du 'dug nas bla na med pa yang dag par rdzogs pa'i byang chub mngon par rdzogs par 'tshang rgya'o / de mngon par rdzogs par sangs rgyas nas 'od zer kun nas 'phags pa'i dpal brtsegs rgyal po zhes bya bar 'gyur ro /.*

272. Miyazaki 2007b, 37n74; cf. *Tathāgatācintyaguhyanirdeśa*, Toh 47, vol. *ka*, 166b4–167a1.

273. The following lines explain how Atiśa construes Mañjuśrī to be an Ādibuddha, an "all-pervasive lord" who pervades all buddha families and who pervades different systems. This accords with the role of Mañjuśrī in the *Mañjuśrī-nāmasaṃgīti* (Davidson 1981). For a similar discussion of how Mañjuśrī appears according to the different systems of *śrāvaka*, *pāramitā*, and *tantra* based on the exegesis of Rong-zom-pa, see Almogi 2009, 125–28, 127n307.

274. Vajratīkṣṇa is a *hṛdaya* deity in the *Sarvatathāgatatattvasaṃgraha* (Tribe 2016, 84n94).
275. *The Collected Works of Atiśa* (*Jo bo rje'i gsung 'bum* 608.8) reads: *dpal gshin rje' gshed kyi rgyud kyi lha'i 'khor lo mdzad pa dang* /.
276. Unlike Vilāsavajra in his commentary to *Mañjuśrīnāmasaṃgīti* (Tribe 2016), Atiśa does not make a distinction between the esoteric and bodhisattva forms of Mañjuśrī. Note that the *Collected Works of Atiśa* (*Jo bo rje'i gsung 'bum* 608.11) first section ends at this point and begins again at 793.23; see Apple 2010.
277. At this point and in section 3.2, although the numbers are not exactly the same, Atiśa refers to the extensive activities of bodhisattvas in twenty-seven forms listed in the *Abhisamayālaṃkāra* (8.40b, *dharmakāyasya karmedam saptaviṃśatidhā matam*) and in thirty-two forms (*dvatriṃśadākāraṃ bodhisattvakarma*) listed in the *Ratnagotravibhāga* (see Mathes 2008, 308–12).
278. *Collected Works of Atiśa* (*Jo bo rje'i gsung 'bum* 794.10) adds: *gang gis sems can gtses na nga la gtses pa yin* /.
279. *Sattvārādhanagāthā*, Toh 1125, vol. *ka*, 74b7–75a1 (Miyazaki 2007b 39n75): *chung ma dag dang bu dang 'byor dang rgyal srid chen po dang / sha rnams dang ni khrag dang tshil dang mig dang lus rnams kyang / gang la brtse ba'i dbang du byas nas nga yis yongs btang ba / des na de la gnod pa byas* [75a1] *na ngag la gnod byas 'gyur* /.
280. See Ohnuma (2007) regarding the giving away of the body in Indian Buddhist literature.
281. *Bodhisattvabhūmi* (Dutt 1966, 223): *tatrādhimukticaryāvihāriṇāṃ sarvākārasūpacitakuśalamūlānāṃ* [*samāsataḥ samyagbodhisattvacaryāniryātānāṃ bodhisattvānāṃ*] *tac cittam utpadyate/.*
282. *Collected Works of Atiśa* (*Jo bo rje'i gsung 'bum*, 794.21) adds: *rje btsun.*
283. *Collected Works of Atiśa* (*Jo bo rje'i gsung 'bum*, 794.24) adds: *rigs kyi bu.*
284. *Collected Works of Atiśa* (*Jo bo rje'i gsung 'bum*, 795.1) adds: *bla ma.*
285. "Great" is missing from *Collected Works of Atiśa* (*Jo bo rje'i gsung 'bum* 795.5).
286. *Mahāvairocanābhisaṃbodhi*, Toh 494, vol. *tha*, 153a5: *rgyu ni byang chub kyi sems so / rtsa ba ni snying rje chen po'o* /. Cf. *Bhāvanākrama* I: *tad eta sarvajñajñānaṃ karuṇāmūlaṃ bodhicittahetukam* /.
287. *Collected Works of Atiśa* (*Jo bo rje'i gsung 'bum* 795.8) adds: *dam pa'i chos spong ba dang* /.
288. *Vairocanābhisaṃbodhi*, Toh 494, vol. *tha*, 220b5–7 (Miyazaki 2007b, 40n78): *'dus ma byas pa'i tshul khrims kyi phung po bla na med pa de bzhin gshegs pas bsngags pa la gnas te / 'dus byas kyi tshul khrims la thabs dang shes rab kyis yongs su zin par spyod cing / ltung ba'i rtsa ba bzhi ni srogs gyi phyir yongs su nyams par mi bya'o / bzhi gang zhe na / 'di lta ste/ dam pa'i chos spong ba dang / byang chub kyi sems gtong ba dang / ser sna byed pa dang / sems can la gnod pa byed pa'o* /.
289. Miyazaki 2007b, 98n74, notes the five impure conditions of degenerate time (*pañcakaṣāyāḥ*): the impurity of life (*āyuḥ*), the impurity of view (*dṛṣṭi*), the impurity of defilements (*kleśa*), the impurity of beings (*sattva*), and the impurity of time (*kalpa*) (*Mahāvyutpatti*, 2335–40).
290. The three types of impermanence are changeability, disintegration, and separation.
291. The four powers consist of the power of the support (*rten gyi stobs*), the power of anti-

dote (*gnyen po kun spyod kyi stobs*), the power of regret (*rnam par gsun 'byin pai stobs*), and the power of turning away from future faults (*nyes pa las slang ldog pa'i stobs*).

292. *Collected Works of Atiśa* (*Jo bo rje'i gsung 'bum*, 795.20) reads: *byams dang snying rje skyed pa'i sa /*.

293. *Tarkajvālā, ad Madhyamakahṛdaya* 2.5, Toh 3856, vol. *dza*, 51a7–b3 (Miyazaki 2007b, 42n80): *'bras bu la re ba'i zhags pas bcings pa'i blo gros can dag zhing tshol bar yang byed la / gang gzhan dag gis bkres pa la sogs pa'i sdug bsngal nye bar zhi bar bya ba tsam kho na la dmigs nas snod la mi rtog par snyoms par sbyin pa sbyin par byed pa des chos nyid mnyam par yang rtogs par 'gyur te / ji skad du gzhon nu chos gcig gis byang chub sems dpa' myur du bla na med pa yang dag par rdzogs pa'i byang chub mngon par rdzogs par 'tshang rgya ste / 'di lta ste sems can thams cad la sems myam pa nyid do zhes bya ba dang / de bzhin du gal te byang chu sems dpa' 'di snyam du de bzhin gshegs pa ni bdag gi yon gnas yin gyi dud 'gro ni ma yin no snyam du sems na / byang chub sems dpa'i chos su mi 'gyur ro zhes bya ba la sogs pa gsung pa lta bu'o /*.

294. *Collected Works of Atiśa* (*Jo bo rje'i gsung 'bum*, 796.11) reads: *yang dag pos ni bskyed par bya /*.

295. *Jñānasiddhi*, 8.24cd, 25d, 26ab (Samdhong Rinpoche et al. 1987, 120): *samyak cittam samutpādyaṃ samatvaṃ sarvadehiṣu* / 24cd / *viṣamatvaṃ yadā sthitam* / 25d / *na tad utpadyate jñānam ādimadhyāntavarjitam* / 26ab.

296. The eight worldly concerns (*aṣṭalokadharma*) are gain (*lābha*), loss (*alābha*), pleasure (*sukha*), misery (*duḥkha*), praise (*praśamsā*), degradation (*nindā*), fame (*yaśa*), and infamy (*ayaśa*). Mahāvyutpatti, 2341–48.

297. The ten virtues are abstaining from killing, stealing, sexual misconduct, lying, plus abstention from slanderous, harsh, or frivolous speech, abstention from covetousness, malevolence, and false views.

298. "*Chos thams cad mnyam pa nyid*" is missing from *Collected Works of Atiśa* (*Jo bo rje'i gsung 'bum* 796.3).

299. *Śikṣāsamuccaya*, v. 4ab (Bendall 1971, 17), 5a (Bendall 1971, 34): *ātmabhāvasya bhogānāṃ trydhvavṛtteḥ śubhasya ca* / 4ab / *paribhogāya satvānām* / 5a /.

300. Cf. *Madhyamakahṛdaya* 2.3 (Lindtner 2001, 5): *ṛjunā hatamānena manasā tattvadarśinā / paradoṣekṣaṇāndhena svadoṣāpattibhīruṇā* /. See Miyazaki 2007b, 44n83; Gokhale 1972, 43.

301. *Mūlāpattisaṃgraha*, v. 4 (Lévi 1929, 266): *maitrītyagena sattveṣu caturthī kathitā jinaiḥ / bodhicittaṃ dharmamūlaṃ tasya tyāgāc ca pañcamī* /.

302. This verse is missing from the *Collected Works of Atiśa* (*Jo bo rje'i gsung 'bum*, 797.8).

303. The seven treasures of noble beings (*ārya*) are faith (*śraddha*), morality (*śila*), listening (*śruta*), generosity (*tyāga*), sense of shame (*lajjin*), dread of blame (*āpatrāpya*), and insight (*prajñā*). *Mahāvyutpatti*, 1565–72.

304. The six recollections (*ṣaḍanusmṛti*) are on the Buddha, Dharma, Saṃgha, śila, tyāga, devatā. *Mahāvyutpatti*, 1148–54.

305. The eight illuminations of the bodhisattva are *smṛti*, *manas*, *caryā*, *dharma*, *jñāna*, *satya*, *abhijñā*, and *apratihatajñāna*.

306. *Collected Works of Atiśa* (*Jo bo rje'i gsung 'bum*, 797.13) reads: *gsum*, "three."

307. *Collected Works of Atiśa* (*Jo bo rje'i gsung 'bum*, 797.17) reads: *dul bar byed* rather than *gnas par bya*.

308. Cf. *Ratnaguṇasaṃcayagāthā*, 16.6 (Obermiller 1937, 61): *niryāyanāya iha icchati*

buddhajñāne samacitta sarvajagatī pitṛ mātṛsaṃjñā / hitacitta maitramana eva parākrameryā akhilārjavo mṛdugirāya parākrameryā /.

309. The stories related to Apalāla, a nāga king, and Āṭavaka (Pali, Āḷavaka), a demon of the wilderness, take place during the Buddha's lifetime and involve narratives that illustrate the value of having faith and keeping one's commitments. See Strong 1992, 26–28, concerning Apalāla. For information on Āṭavaka, see Duquenne 1983, 610a–640b.

310. *Collected Works of Atiśa* (*Jo bo rje'i gsung 'bum*, 797.22) adds: *dbugs rgyu ba mi tshor ba dang /* .

311. *Ratnaguṇasaṃcayagāthā*, 17.2 (Obermiller 1937, 62): *nānātvasaṃjñavigatā gira yuktabhāṇī.*

312. These consist of mindfulness with regard to body (*kāya*), feeling (*vedanā*), mind (*citta*), and things (*dharma*). *Mahāvyutpatti*, 952–56.

313. The four miraculous powers are supernormal powers related to determination (*chanda*), discernment (*mīmāṃsā*), diligence (*vīrya*), and samādhi. *Mahāvyutpatti*, 966–70.

314. The five faculties are faith (*śraddhā*), energy (*vīrya*), mindfulness (*smṛti*), concentration (*samādhi*), and insight (*prajñā*). *Mahāvyutpatti*, 976–81.

315. The five powers are faith (*śraddhā*), energy (*vīrya*), mindfulness (*smṛti*), concentration (*samādhi*), and insight (*prajñā*). *Mahāvyutpatti*, 982–87.

316. *Collected Works of Atiśa* (*Jo bo rje'i gsung 'bum* 798.6) reads: *de kho na nyid kyi don.*

317. *Collected Works of Atiśa* (*Jo bo rje'i gsung 'bum* 798.9) adds: *sa bcu pa'i bar du.*

318. The bodisattva's eighfold brilliance (*aṣṭākāro bodhisattvāvabhāsaḥ*) consists of memory (*smṛti*), the intellect (*mati*), understanding, phenomena (*dharma*), knowledge, truth (*satya*), supernormal powers (*abhijñā*), and accomplishment (*pratipatti*). See Mathes 2008, 304–5; Takasaki 1966a, 152.

319. The four *alaṃkāras* of the bodhisattva are morality (*śīla*), concentration (*samādhi*), insight (*prajñā*), and *dhāraṇī*. See Takasaki 1966a, 152n88.

320. Sixteen "compassions" are translated by Mathes (2008, 307), from 'Gos lo-tsā-ba gzhon nu dpal's commentary to the *Ratnagotravibhāga*, as compassion that "takes the form of wishing [that sentient beings] may be free from [the following defects]: (1) various views, (2) the four errors, (3) the notion of mine, (4) the five hindrances, (5) the attachment to the objects of the six sense spheres, (6) seven[fold] pride, (7) straying from the noble path, (8) lack of independence, (9) anger, (10) being influenced by sinful friends, (11) lacking the potential of the noble ones, (12) mistaken views, (13) a view of a self caused by ignorance, (14) being seized by the executioner [in the hire] of the skandhas, (15) being tied in the noose of Māra, and (16) straying from the higher realms and liberation." See also Takasaki 1966a, 152n88.

321. In the previous three items listed, Atiśa is referring to the qualities of the sixtyfold process of purifying the buddha element (*buddhadhātoḥ ṣaṣṭyākāraviśuddhipari karmaguṇāḥ*), as found in the *Ratnagotravibhāgavyākhyā*; see Mathes 2008, 304, 535n1670. According to Gö Lotsāwa Shönu Pal, Atiśa and Naktso translated the *Ratnagotravibhāga* before Ngok Loden Sherap (Mathes 2008, 162). See Kano (2014) on Atiśa and Naktso's translation of the *Ratnagotravibhāga*.

322. Cf. *Avikalpapraveśadhāraṇī*, Toh 142, vol. *pa*, 3b4–6: *byang chub sems dpa' sems dpa' chen po rnam par mi rtog pa'i dbyings la rab tu gnas pas ni shes bya dang khyad par med pa rnam par mi rtog pa'i ye shes kyis chos thams cad nam mkha'i dkyil dang mtshungs*

par mthong ngo / rnam par mi rtog pa'i rjes las thob pa'i shes pas ni chos thams cad sgyu ma dang / smig rgyu dang / rmi lam dang / mig yor dang / brag cha dang / gzugs brnyan dang / chu zla dang / sprul pa dang mtshung par mthong ngo /.

323. *Collected Works of Atiśa* (*Jo bo rje'i gsung 'bum*, 798.15) reads: *rnam par mi rtog pa mthar phyin pa.*

324. *Collected Works of Atiśa* (*Jo bo rje'i gsung 'bum*, 798.19) reads the last line as: *'dren pa rnams ni chos nyid gzigs /.* For a discussion on these verses, see Almogi 2009, 252n46. Cf. *Vajracchedikā*, §26, vv. 1–2ab (Conze 1957, 56–57): *ye māṃ rūpeṇa cādrākṣur ye māṃ ghoṣeṇa cānvaguḥ / mithyāprahāṇaprarṭā na māṃ drakṣyanti te janāḥ / 1 / dharmato buddho draṣṭavyā dharmakāyā hi nāyakāḥ /.*

325. Miyazaki 2007b, 47n91: "Not identified in the *Vajramālā*, but cf. *Piṇḍīkṛtasādhana*, v. 43cd, 44ab (La Vallée Poussin 1896, 3): *vijñānaskandham āyāti vijñānaṃ ca prabhāsvaram / sanirvāṇaṃ sarvaśūnyaṃ ca dharmakāyaś ca gadyate/.*"

326. Miyazaki 2007b, 47n93: "Not found in the *Lokottara-parivarta*. Cf. *Buddhāvataṃsaka*, D (44) *ka* 81b5: *yang dag sang rgyas chos kyi sku / rnam dag nam mkha' 'dra ba ste /.*"

327. *Prajñāpāramitāpiṇḍārtha*, v. 1ab (Tucci 1947, 56): *prajñāpāramitā jñānam advayaṃ sā tathāgataḥ /.*

328. *Prajñāpāramitāstotra*, vv. 2–3 (Lamotte 1949, 1060): *ākāśam iva nirlepāṃ niṣprapañcāṃ nirakṣarām / yas tvāṃ paśyati bhāvena sa paśyati tathāgatam / 2 / tava cāryguṇāḍhyāyā buddhasya ca jagadguroḥ / na paśyanty antaraṃ santaś candracandrikayor iva / 3.*

329. *Collected Works of Atiśa* (*Jo bo rje'i gsung 'bum*, 799.3) reads: *chos rnams kun la mi ngas pa* rather than *dge chos kun la mi gnas par.*

330. *Paramārthastava*, v. 8 (Tola and Dragonetti 1985, 20): *asthitaḥ sarvadharmeṣu dharmadhātugatiṃ gataḥ / parāṃ gaṃbhīratāṃ prāpto gaṃbhīrāya namo 'stu te /.*

331. *Acintyastava*, v. 42ab (Tola and Dragonetti 1985, 18): *buddhānāṃ sattvadhātoś ca tenābhinnatvam arthataḥ /.*

332. *Paramārthastava*, v. 3 (Tola and Dragonetti 1985, 19): *anutpannasvabhāvena utpādas te na vidyate / na gatir nāgatir nāthāsvabhāvāya namo 'stu te /.*

333. *Vajrajñānasamuccaya*, Toh 447, vol. *ca*, 286a2 (Miyazaki 2007b, 49n101): *ji srid du zhi ba la sogs pa'i las kyis sems can gyi don mi byed pa de srid du yang dag pa'i mtha' la rab tu gnas par 'gyur ro /.*

334. Atiśa is claiming that Asaṅga asserts that on the absolute level gnosis does not exist at the stage of a buddha. This claim relates to the controversy surrounding the existence of gnosis at the stage of a buddha between the various adherents of Yogācāra and Madhyamaka philosophical systems. See the chapter in Almogi (2009, 142–59) on "the mental element of the absolute and Yogācāra theories of knowledge."

335. Miyazaki, 50n103: "Not in the *Vajramālā*." But cf. *Piṇḍīkṛtasādhana*, v. 45 (La Vallée Poussin 1896, 4): *paramārthamaṇḍalaṃ hy etan nirābhāsam alakṣaṇam / paramārthasatyanāmāpi sarvatathāgatālayaḥ /.*

336. *Collected Works of Atiśa* (*Jo bo rje'i gsung 'bum*, 799.19) reads: *chos nyid skye med nyid la ni / thugs gnas sang rgyas yin par gsungs*, whereas the canonical (Miyazaki 2007, 50) reads: *chos nyid skye ba med pa ni / thub gnas sangs rgyas yin par gsung /.* Cf. *Triśaraṇasaptati*, v. 22ab (Sørensen 1986, 28): *chos rnams dngos med nyid la ni / blo gnas sangs rgyas yin par bshad /.*

337. Cf. *Bodhicittavivaraṇa*, v. 31 (Lindtner 1997b, 42): *'das pa gang yin de ni med / ma 'ongs pa ni thob pa min / gnas phyir gnas ni yongs gyur pa / da lta ba la ga la yod /.*

338. *Pañcakrama*, 6.15c, 16abd (La Vallée Poussin 1896, 47): *yuganaddhaṃ vadec chāntaṃ [svāpabodhavivarjitam] / 15 / samādhānāsamādhānaṃ yasya nāsty eva sarvathā / [yuganaddhe sthito yogī] bhāvābhāvavivarjitaḥ / 16 /.*

339. See Almogi 2009, 300n6, for a discussion of this verse. *Timira* (*rab rib*) means literally "darkness," and may refer to the darkness of the eyes or a certain type of eye disease. The version here differs slightly from the canonical. Cf. *Laṅkāvatāra*, 2.168, 169 (Nanjio 1923, 109)*: āryo na paśyati bhrāntiṃ nāpi tattvaṃ tadantare / bhrāntir eva bhavet tattvaṃ yasmāt tattvaṃ tadantre / 168 / bhrāntiṃ vidhūya sarvāṃ hi nimittaṃ jāyate yadi / saiva tasya bhaved bhrāntir aśuddhaṃ timiraṃ yathā / 169 /.*

340. This terse citation implies that the *dharmadhātu* is equated with *svayaṃbhūjñāna* (self-arisen gnosis) and is undivided in reality but has five aspects that appear according to the purview of the person to be trained (*vineya*, *gdul bya*). The five aspects of the *dharmadhātu* that appear follow a schemata of five gnoses: (1) the mirror-like gnosis (*samatājñāna*), (2) the gnosis of equality (*samatājñāna*), (3) discerning gnosis (*pratyavekṣaṇajñāna*), (4) the gnosis of performing activities (*kṛtyānuṣṭhānajñāna*), and (5) the gnosis [that equates to] the *dharmadhātu* (*dharmadhātujñāna*). On the multiple gnoses of a buddha, see Almogi 2009, 114–18.

341. *Niraupamyastava*, v. 24 (Tola and Dragonetti 1985, 14): *na te 'sti manyanā nātha na vikalpo na ceñjanā / anābhogena te loke buddhakṛtyaṃ pravartate /.* Miyazaki 2007b, 53n109, *Kudṛṣṭinirghātana*, v. 2 (Shastri 1927, 1): *na te 'sti manyanā nātha na vikalpo na veñjanā / anābhogena te loke buddhaktyaṃ pravartate /.*

342. Miyazaki 2007b, 53n110, *Kudṛṣṭinirghātana*, v. 4 (Shastri 1927, 1): *cintāmaṇir ivākampyaḥ sarvasaṃkalpavāyubhiḥ / tathāpi sarvasattvānām aśeṣāśāprapūrakaḥ /.* Cited in the *Madhyamakaratnapradīpa* (D 3854, vol. *tsha*, 286b1) as well.

343. *Niraupamyastava*, v. 9 (Tola and Dragonetti 1985, 13): *sattvasaṃjñā ca te nātha sarvathā na pravartate / duḥkhārteṣu ca sattveṣu tvam atīva kṛpātmkaḥ /.*

344. Miyazaki 2007b, 54n112, *Kudṛṣṭinirghātana*, v. 3 (Shastri 1927, 1): *parārthasaṃpad buddhānāṃ phalaṃ mukhyatamaṃ matam / buddhatvādi yad anyat tu tādarthyāt phalam iṣyate /.*

345. This verse is also cited in the *Guhyasamājatantravivaraṇa* (*Dpal gsang ba 'dus pa'i rgyud kyi 'grel pa*, Toh 1845, vol. *ji*, 161b.1–244a.7), attributed to Thagana.

346. Cf. *Svādhiṣṭhānakramaprabheda*, vv. 56–57, Toh 1805, vol. *ngi*, 114a4–6: */ gang zhig gser dngul dang ni nor bu dung dang shel bye ru/ bai durya dang zangs dang 'dzin mo steng sogs yang dag gnas / nam mkha' ngos nas ri bong can gyi gzugs ni gcig shar bas / / de la rnam par 'jug pas shin tu gsal bar gang byas ltar / / rang dngos sna thogs gzugs can zag med gang/ 'jig rten kun khyab sgyu ma'i rang bzhin nyid / / rnam pa sna tshogs 'gro ba'i sdir gnas pa'i / / sems mgon rdo rje de yang de bzhin no /.* Skt. (Pāṇḍey 1990, 24).

347. *Mahāyānasūtrālaṃkāra*, 9.16 (Lévi 1907, 36): *yathodabhājane bhinne candrabimbaṃ na dṛśyate / tathā duṣṭeṣu sattveṣu buddhabimbaṃ na dṛśyate /.* Thurman et al. 2004, 80.

348. Atiśa's version of these verses differs from that found in the Tengyur. Cf. *Ratnāvalī*, 4.94cd, 95, 96 (Hahn 1982, 128–30): *buddho 'vadat tathā dharmaṃ vineyānāṃ yathākṣamam / 94 / keṣāṃcid avadad dharmaṃ pāpebhyo vinivṛttaye / keṣāṃcit puṇyasiddhyarthaṃ keṣāṃcid dvayaniśritam / dvayāniśritam ekeṣāṃ gambhīraṃ bhīrubhīṣaṇam / śūnyatākaruṇāgarbham ekeṣāṃ bodhisādhanam / 96 /.* For the English of the Tengyur version, see Dunne and McClintock 1997, 71.

349. *Collected Works of Atiśa* (*Jo bo rje'i gsung 'bum* 801.22) is missing this line of the verse.

350. Cf. *Lalitavistara*, 25.1 (Vaidya 1958, 286): *gambhīra śānto virajaḥ prabhāsvaraḥ prāpto mi dharmo hy amṛto 'saṃskṛtaḥ / deśeya cāhaṃ na parasya jāne yan nūna tūṣṇīpavane vaseyam /.*

351. Atiśa's version of these verses differs from that found in the Tengyur. Cf. *Ratnāvalī*, 1.74 (Hahn 1982, 30): *sarvajña iti sarvajño budhais tenaiva gamyate / yenaitad dharmagāmbhīryaṃ novācābhājane jane /.* For the English of the Tengyur version, see Dunne and McClintock 1997, 20.

352. *Collected Works of Atiśa* (*Jo bo rje'i gsung 'bum* 802.14) adds: *drug rnams.*

353. *Collected Works of Atiśa* (*Jo bo rje'i gsung 'bum,* 803.8) states: *yang de dag gi thad du.*

354. Missing from *Collected Works of Atiśa* (*Jo bo rje'i gsung 'bum,* 803.11).

355. Missing from *Collected Works of Atiśa* (*Jo bo rje'i gsung 'bum,* 803.12).

356. This summary is also found in the *Madhyamakaratnapradīpa*, Toh 3854, vol. *tsha*, 286b6–287a2: *de bzhin du 'phags pa sbrin chen po'i mdo las kyang / ji skad du / lha'i bu dag bskal pa brjod du med pa'i ngon du de bzhin gshegs pa klu rigs sgron ma'i chos kyi rgyal po'i brtson 'grus chen po'i klu yum bstan pa 'dzin pa / blon po dam pa'i chos kyi mdzod 'dzin pa / rgyal po dang blon po gnyis sangs rgyas* [287a1] *kyi ring bsrel gyi gtam byas shing / rgyal pos legs par bshad pas dus der 'khor thams cad ngo mtshar skyes nas bcom ldan 'das la zhus pa / rgyal po 'di zab mo la mkhas pa'o zhes zhus pas / bcom ldan 'das kyis rgyal po'i yon tan rgyas par gsung te /.*

357. Miyazaki 2007b, 61n120 notes that this is a summary of *Mahāmegha*, Toh 232, vol. *wa*, 180–181b1. This summary is also found in the *Madhyamakaratnapradīpa*, Toh 3854, vol. *tsha*, 287a2–4.

358. Cf. *Mahāmegha*, Toh 232, vol. *wa*, 187a5–7 (Miyazaki 2007b, 61n121): *bcom ldan 'das kyis stsal pa / lha'i bu dag nga 'das pa'i 'og lo brgya phrag mang po 'das pa na lho phyog kyi rgyud du mkhar gyi rgyal po bde spyod ches bya ba 'byung bar 'gyur te / de'i tshe lo brgyad cu na dam pa'i chos nub par 'gyur ba'i lhag ma tsam du lus pa'i dus la bab pa de'i tshe nga'i nyan thos 'byung bar 'gyur te / dam pa'i chos kyang 'byin par 'gyur / chos kyi 'khor lo yang bskor bar 'gyur / theg pa chen po yang gzhan dag la rgyas par 'chad par 'gyur ro /.* This summary is also found in the *Madhyamakaratnapradīpa*, Toh 3854, vol. *tsha*, 287a4–5.

359. Cf. *Mahāmegha*, Toh 232, vol. *wa*, 187b5–188a3 (Miyazaki 2007b , 62n122): *bcom ldan 'das kyi bka' stsal pa/ mthong na dga' ba dri za'i rgyal po dge slong de lung bstan pa nyon cig / de ni nga la dpen pa dang / nga'i bstan pa 'byung bar byed cing khur chen po khyer ba dang / nga'i shākya gzhon nu yin te / mthong na dga' ba dri za'i rgyal po nga 'das pa'i 'og tu lho phyogs kyi rgyud du drang srong byi bo zhes bya ba'i yul 'khor du bsod nams ldan gyi grong khyer bye ma chen po zhes byas ba 'byung ste / grong de'i 'bab chu mdzes 'byor ces bya ba de'i byang phyogs kyi 'gram du 'byung bar 'gyur ro / der rje'u rigs chen po rnam par dag pa 'bra go can zhes bya ba'i sa'i phyogs su 'byung bar 'gyur te / shākya'i rigs gzhon nu lid tsa byi'i bu gzhon nu 'jig rten thams cad kyis mthong na dga' ba de nga'i chos 'byung bar bya ba'i phyir lid tsa byi'i bu 'jig rten thams cad kyis mthong na dga' ba byang chub sems dpa'i mi mchog de der rigs chen por skye bar* [188a1] *'gyur te / de'i pha ma dang gnyen sde rnams kyis nga'i ming de'i ming du 'dog par 'gyur ro / 'bra go can gyi rje'u rigs chen po'i rigs kyang de bzhin gshegs pa'i rigs yin par blta'o / de'i tshe drang srong byi bo'i yul 'khor yang 'byor cing rgyas las skyes bo mang pos gang bar 'gyur ro / de bzhin gshegs pa dang ming 'thun pa'i khye'u de yang skye bo thams cad kyi snying du sdug par 'gyur zhing skye bo mang po thams cad kyi bkur*

bar 'gyur ro / gang gi tshe khye'u de rab tu byung ba na tshang pa mtshungs par spyod pa'i 'khor dang / dge slong gi tshogs rnams khrid de / rang gi srog dang bsdos nas dam pa'i chos ston cing / de bzhin gshegs pa'i spyod pa 'byung bar byed de / mchog tu dga' ba spyod par 'gyur ro /. A summary is also found in the *Madhyamakaratnapradīpa*, Toh 3854, vol. *tsha*, 287a5–b2.

360. *Collected Works of Atiśa* (*Jo bo rje'i gsung 'bum*, 804.21) adds: *lus kyis mngon sum du byas pa'o /*.

361. Cf. *Mahāmegha*, Toh 232, vol. *wa*, 188b2–6 (Miyazaki 2007b , 62n123): *dge bsnyen gyi sde tshan dang / dge bsnyen ma'i sde tshan de dag ni sangs rgyas 'byung ba dang phrad par 'gyur / dam pa'i chos la yang nan tan du sgrub par 'gyur mod kyi / 'on kyang mthong na dga' ba dri za'i rgyal po nga'i nyan thos kyi tshig la yid ches pa'i sems can de dag ni nyung ste / shin tu phal cher ni mos par mi 'gyur ro / mthong na dga' ba dri za'i rgyal po rnam pa bzhi dang ldan na nga'i nyan thos de bzhin gshegs pa dang ming 'thun pa'i dge slong gi tshig la yid ches par 'gyur te / bzhi gang zhe na / sngon gyi mthar yang yang dag par rdzogs pa'i sangs rgyas snga ma rnams las zab mo brtan pa'i chu'i rgya mtsho'i dus tshod kyi ting nge 'dzin 'di thos pa dang / dge ba'i bshes gnyen gyis yongs su gzung ba dang / lhag pa'i bsam pa la zhugs shing dge ba'i rtsa ba nye bar brtan pa dang / rgya chen po la mos pa lus kyis mngon sum du byas pa ste / mthong na dga' ba dri za'i rgyal po rnam pa bzhi pa de dag gis na nga'i nyan thos kyi tshig la yid ches par 'gyur ro / gang dag yid mi ches pa de dag thams cad ni bdud kyis byin gyis brlabs pa'i mi gti mug can yin par rig par bya'o / sems can gang dag mos par 'gyur ba de dag ni sangs rgyas mang pos yongs su gzung ba yin par rig par bya'o /*. A summary is also found in the *Madhyamakaratnapradīpa*, Toh 3854, vol. *tsha*, 287b2–b4.

362. Cf. *Mahāmegha*, Toh 232, vol. *wa*, 189b4–5 (Miyazaki 2007b, 62n124): *dge slong de la sems can gang dag gis bsnyen bskur byas pa de dag gis ni 'das pa dang / ma byon pa dang / da ltar byung ba'i de bzhin gshegs pa thams cad la bskal pa grangs med par bsnyen bkur byas pa yin no /*.

363. Cf. *Mahāmegha*, Toh 232, vol. *wa*, 190a6 (Miyazaki 2007b, 63n125): *de ni mtha' mar 'byung bar 'gyur la / de dang 'dra ba'i sems can gzhan med de mi srid /*.

364. *Collected Works of Atiśa* (*Jo bo rje'i gsung 'bum*, 805.3) reads: *de'i steng la sangs rgyas bdun po'i gcig 'byung ngo /*.

365. Cf. *Mahāmegha*, Toh 232, vol. *wa*, 190a7–b3 (Miyazaki, 63n126): *rigs kyi* [190b1] *bu khyod legs kyis rigs kyi bu nga'i nyan thos kyi che ba nyid nyon cig / rigs kyi bu bskal pa bzang po 'di 'das te / sangs rgyas stong yongs su mya ngan las 'das pa'i 'og tu bskal pa drug cu rtsa gnyis su sangs rgyas 'byung bar mi 'gyur te / rang sangs rgyas bye ba phrag 'bum 'byung bar 'gyur ro / rigs ki bu bskal pa drug cu rtsa gnyis po de dag 'das nas sangs rgyas gzhan bdun 'byung bar 'gyur ro / de nas bdun pa yongs su mya ngan las 'das pa de'i tshe de'i dus na 'jig rten gyi khams 'di 'jig rten gyi khams mngon par dang ba zhes bya bar 'gyur te / 'jig rten gyi khams mngon par dang ba der bcom ldan 'das de bzhin gshegs pa dgra bcom pa yang dag par rdzogs pa'i sangs rgyas ye shes 'byung gnas 'od ces bya bar 'gyur ro /*.

366. *Mañjuśrīmūlakalpa*, 53.449cf, 450ad (Śāstri 1925, 616–17): / *nāgāhvayo nāma sau bhikṣuḥ / jīved varṣaśatāni ṣaṭ* / 53.449 / *māyūrī nāmato vidyā siddhā / niḥsvabhāvārthatattvavit* / 53.450 /.

367. *Laṅkāvatārasūtra*, 10.164c, 165abc (Nanjio 1923, 286): *mahāmate nibodha tvaṃ / dakṣiṇāpathavedalyāṃ bhikṣuḥ śrīmān mahāyaśāḥ / nāgāhvayaḥ sa nāmnā tu*.

368. *Laṅkāvatārasūtra*, 10.166cd (Nanjio 1923, 286): *āsādya bhūmiṃ muditāṃ yāsyate 'sau sukhāvatīm* /.

369. *Pradīpodyotanaṭīkā,* chap. 17 (Chakravarti 1984, 229): *evaṃ śrīnāgārjunapāda-bhāṭṭārakānuprāptasvakārthaḥ / pratyātmavedyaṃ mahāvajradharasamādhiṃ loke pratipādya devamanuṣyasukham atikramya tīrthikaśrāvakapratyekabuddhadhyān asamādhisamāpattisukham atikramya utpādabhaṅgarahitaṃ sarvākāravaropetam āsecanakavigrahaṃ daśabalavaiśāradyādibuddhālaṅkṛtaṃ tathāgatakāyaṃ prati-labhya sukhāvatīṃ gatvāṣṭaguṇaiśvaryānvito viharati /.*

370. Cf. *Caryāmelāprakapradīpa* (Wedemeyer 2007, 446–47): *anenaîva krameṇa / bhagavān śrī-śākyasiṃhaḥ sarva-tathāgatair acchaṭā-śabdaiḥ saṃcodite sati / āsphānaka-samādher vyutthāya bodhimūle niṣadyârddharātra-samaye prabhāsvaraṃ sākṣāt-kṛtvā / māyopamasamādhinā vyutthāya janebhyo dharma-cakraṃ pravartitavān / tad ārabhya yāvat saddharmo 'sthāt tāvad guru-vaktrād guru-vaktraṃ saṃkrāmati (yoga-yugma-viśva-viśuddhi-rahasyābhisambodhi-kramaḥ saṃkrāmatîti*)/; Tibetan Toh 1803, vol. *ngi,* 90a2–4: *rim pa 'di nyid kyis bcom ldan 'das dpal shākya thub pa la de bzhin gshegs pa thams cad kyis se gol gyi sgras bskul bar gyur pas mi g.yo ba'i ting nge 'din las bzhengs te / byang chub kyi shing drung la bzhugs nas mtshan phyed kyi dus su 'od gsal ba mngon du mdzad de / sgyu ma lta bu'i ting nge 'dzin las bzhengs nas / 'gro ba rnams la chos ston par mdzad pa yin no / dengs nas brtsams te / dam pa'i chos ji srid gnas pa de srid du bla ma'i kha nas bla ma'i khar brgyud pa yin no /.*

371. In Sarvāstivādin accounts of the bodies of a buddha, the maturation body (*vipākakāya*) is related to the form body (*rūpakāya*). See Lamotte 1988, 689–90. See also Bhavya's *Tarkajvālā* (Toh 3856, 103a7–b1, referenced in Almogi 2009, 243n20), which cites Vajrasena as explaining the maturation body as the *rūpakāya,* which is supported by the *dharmakāya,* and whose sphere of activity is Akaniṣṭha heaven (*'phags pa rdo rje sdes ni gzugs kyi sku 'og min gyi spyod yul can chos kyi sku'i gzhi la brten pa ni rnam par smin pa'i sku zhes bshad do*).

372. *Collected Works of Atiśa* (*Jo bo rje'i gsung 'bum,* 806.18) adds: *nā ro pa.*

373. Compare with *Bodhipathapradīpa* and *Pañjikā* (D 290b; Sherburne 2000, 300–303), where these two empowerments are forbidden to those who are celibate.

374. This verse is cited in the *Bsam gtan mig sgron* of gNubs-chen Sangs-rgyas ye-shes from a tantra called *Spyi bcings*; see Karmay 2007, 110.

375. Miyazaki (2007b, 68n136); cited from the *Nayatrayapradīpa* (Toh 3797, vol. *tsu,* 16b3–4) and the *Tattvaratnāvalī* (8): *ekārthatve 'py asaṃmohāt bahūpāyād aduṣkarāt / tīkṣṇendriyādhikārāc ca mantraśāstraṃ viśiṣyate /.* Also cited in the *Bodhimārgapradīpapañjikā* (Toh 3948, vol. *khi,* 286b3–4; Sherburne 2000, 280–81).

376. This verse is missing from *Collected Works of Atiśa* (*Jo bo rje'i gsung 'bum* 807.16).

377. Missing from *Collected Works of Atiśa* (*Jo bo rje'i gsung 'bum,* 807.24).

378. Chim Namkha Drak 2014, 122.11–13: . . . *rgya gar du bhri ka ma la shi lar bden pa gnyis la 'jug pa dang / de'i 'grel pa dang / . . .*

379. *Rnal 'byor pa shes rab rdo rjes mdzad pa'i bden gnyis kyi rnam par bshad pa,* 7a8 (roman 531): *dngos kyi dgos pa ni / bla ma gser kling ba'i lta ba bsgyur ba'i ched yin te / jo bo nyid . . .* Unfortunately, folio side 7b is missing, which contains the remainder of the commentary on this specific point.

380. Cf. *Madhyamakaratnapradīpa* (Lindter 1981, 170).

381. The first folio of the actual manuscript is entitled *A Collection of Special Instructions on the Middle Way* (*Dbu ma'i man ngag gi 'bum*). However, the title page and first folios of the manuscript *Collection on the Two Realities* (*Bden gnyis kyi 'bum*) were either wrongly copied or misplaced, and should be the first folio that precedes the

content of the manuscript currently entitled *A Collection of Special Instructions on the Middle Way* (*Dbu ma'i man ngag gi 'bum*), whose actual content is a brief commentary on Atiśa's *Satyadvayāvatāra*. In brief, the title page and first folios of *Bden gnyis kyi 'bum* (*Collection on the Two Realities*) and *Dbu ma'i man ngag gi 'bum* (*Collection of Special Instructions on the Middle Way*) were switched at some point in their history and I have corrected the titles based on their corresponding content. I have kept the actual title of the given manuscript in the notes.

382. *A Collection of Special Instructions on the Middle Way* (*Dbu ma'i man ngag gi 'bum*, 1b3): *dge bshes dgon pa 'di gzigs nas nga la a ti shas gdam ngag gnang ba bzhin tu 'di na bris nas . . .*

383. As cited in Deroche 2011, 144n19, from the *Bod kyi dbu ma'i lta ba'i 'chad nyan dar tshul blo gsal mig 'byed* by Khu byug Bka' mgon (b. 1966) (2004, 124): *spyan snga bas jo bo'i bden gnyis la 'jug pa zhes pa 'chad nyan rgya cher mdzad pa gang ltar skabs der jo bo rje'i bden gnyis la 'jug pa zhes pa'i bshad rgyun ches dar ba ni spyan snga ba'i bka' drin las byung bar bshad do /.*

384. See Sørensen 1999, 178–179n4; and Sørensen et al. 2007. We note here that all of these figures—Potowa, Chengawa Tsultrim Bar, Neusurpa, Sharawa, as well as Patsap Nyimadrak—were from areas within Phen yül (see Sørensen et al. 2007, 153–70), and that the regional and clan-based affiliations of these individuals may have shaped their textual orientation against other competing monastic-regional communities such as Sangphu. It may well be the case that Patsap Nyimadrak was sent to Kashmir to translate the Madhyamaka texts that had been trasmitted by Atiśa in his teachings on the *Satyadvayāvatāra* while in Tibet.

385. Śāntarakṣita (MAK, v. 64) and Jñānagarbha (SDV, v. 12) qualify correct conventions according to appearances that have causal efficiency (*don byed nus pa, arthakriyā*) (see following notes), while Nāgārjuna (VVV) and Candrakīrti (CŚṬ XIII) refer to dependent-arisings that are suitable to perform actions (*bya ba byed pa, kriyākaraṇa*). See Yoshimizu 1997 and Ruegg 2002, 174–78.

386. MAK, v. 64 (Toh 3884, vol. *sa*, 51a4): *ma brtags gcig pu nyams dga' zhing / / skye dang 'jigs pa'i chos can pa / / don byed pa dag nus rnams kyi / / rang bzhin kun rdzob pa yin rtogs //.* "Some thing that is pleasing only as long as it is not examined, that arises and ceases to exist, and that is capable of causal efficiency—this nature is realized to be conventional reality."

387. SDV, v. 12 (Tib., Eckel 1987, 163; Eng., Eckel 1987, 79): "Correct and incorrect relative [realities] are similar in appearance, but they are distinguished by their ability or inability to produce effective action."

388. MRP (Toh 3854, vol. *tsha*, 260a2): *chu shing gi ni phung po bzhin / / ma brtags nyams dga'i mtshan nyid can / / rgyu las skyes dang don byed nus / / tshul rol mthong ba'i kun rdzob yin / /.* Adopted from Lindtner (1981, 170): "The [correct] conventional reality of those with limited vision, is, however, like the pith of a plantain (*kadalīskandha*): When you do not examine it, it affords pleasure, and it is causally produced and efficient." For Jñānagarbha's *Satyadvayavibhaṅgakārikā*, see Eckel 1987, 79.

389. MHK 3.7 and 3.12–13, along with *Tarkajvālā* (Iida 1980, 60–68).

390. See also the *General Explanation* (chapter 4) for the exegesis of Nāgārjuna's *Dharmadhātustava* (vv. 30–33).

391. See Introduction; also Almogi 2009; and Vose 2010b, 301–12.

392. *Bden gnyis gsal ba'i sgron me* (1518–84), as found in Deroche 2011, 161–62: *'jig rten*

mchog man chad kyi so so skye bo'i blo la snang tshad tsam log pa'i kun rdzob tu 'gro ste / log shes kyis bsgrub pa yin pa'i phyir ro / log shes kyi snang ba la log pa and yang dag gnyis med de / de gnyis ka log pa'i kun rdzob yin pas / gnyis ka lam du mi 'gro ba'i phyir yang dag pa'i sgra mi 'jug go / sa dang po yan chad kyi rjes thob gyi snang ba de thams cad / yang dag pa'i kun rdzob ces bya ste / snang ba tsam zhig ma 'gags pas kun rdzob yin la / de nyid brdzun pa la brdzun par mngon sum du gzigs shing / de nyid gzigs pa phyin ci ma log pa yin pas lam du 'gro ba'i phyir na yang dag kun rdzob yin no /.

393. *Tarkajvālā,* Toh 3856, vol. *dza*, 60b.4–5: *don dam pa ni rnam gnyis te / de la gcig ni mngon par 'du byed pa med par 'jug pa 'jig rten las 'das pa zag pa med pa spros pa med pa'o / / gnyis pa ni mngon par 'du byed pa dang bcas par 'jug pa bsod nams dang ye shes kyi tshogs kyi rjes su mthun pa dag pa 'jig rten pa'i ye shes zhes bya ba spros pa dang bcas pa ste /.*

394. See commentary at folio 7b2.

395. Also known as the five sciences (*pañcavidyā*): linguistic science (*śabda*), logical science (*hetu*), "inner" science (*adhyātma*), medical science (*cikitsā*), and the science of fine arts and crafts (*śilapakarmasthāna*). *Mahāvyutpatti*, 1554–59. The "inner" science is the study and practice of the Buddha's teachings. See Gold 2007, 11–16, 20–24. The MSABh (Thurman et al. 2004, 141) mentions: "In specific, he should investigate logic and linguistics in order to criticize those who have no faith in that (universal vehicle)." And (253): "In the second (science, i.e., logic), it is to understand faults (in practice and communication) and refute the arguments of others."

396. See Chattopadhyaya 1967, 495. *Vādanyāyaprakaraṇa* (*Rtsod pa'i rigs pa zhes bya ba'i rab tu byed pa*), Toh 4218, vol. *che*, 326b.4–355b.5, translated by Jñānaśrībhadra and Dge ba'i blo gros, rev. Dīpaṅkara and Dar ma grags pa.

397. A statement written later occurs in the *Bodhimārgadīpapañjikā* (Toh 3948, vol. *khi*, 282b4–6; P 326b5–8): *yang dag nyid la rnam dpyad na / / yod ces pa dang med ces pa / / yang dag mtha' la de dag med / / de bas gang yang bsgrub mi nus / / bla ma'i brgyud pa 'bral ba dag / / rjes su dpag pa'i shes rab kyis / / yod med rtag chad sogs bsgrubs kyang / / ngal 'gyur don la reg mi 'gyur / / chos grags chos mchog la sogs pas / / gzhung mang byas pa ji lta bu / / mu stegs rgol ba bzlog pa'i phyir / / mkhas pa rnams byis byas pa yin / / de bas don dam bsgom pa la / / tshad mas dgos pa med do zhes / / bdag gis gzhan du bkod pas na / / re zhig 'dir ni brjod mi dgos / / de bas rjes dpag gtsor byed pa'i / / rtog ge'i gzhung rnams dor byas la / / 'phags pa klu sgrub gzhung lugs kyi / / brgyud pa'i man ngag bsgom pa bya //.* Apple translation: "When one analyzes reality, real extremes such as 'existence' and 'nonexistence' do not exist. In this way, one is unable to establish anything at all. Those who are separated from the lineage of gurus, even when establishing existence, nonexistence, permanence, annihilation, and so forth through the discernment by means of inference, will become exhausted and not reach their goal. Why did Dharmakīrti, Dharmottara, and so forth compose many treatises? The scholars composed them in order to refute the objections of Tīrthikas. In this way, I wrote elsewhere, 'such valid means of knowledge are unnecessary for cultivating the ultimate.' It is not necessary to explain it here. Therefore one should discard texts of speculative reasoning that are primarily concerned with inference and one should cultivate the special instructions of the lineage of the textual system of the Noble Nāgārjuna."

398. Thurman (1984), and more recently Kapstein (2013, 282), have suggested: "In Atiśa's view, because Buddhism's dialectially savy Brahmanical opponents were a product

of the Indian cultural sphere, and not at all present in Tibet, the study of *pramāṇa* for the Tibetans was a mere distraction that served no good purpose at all." In other words, Atiśa did not stress *pramāṇa* in Tibet because there were no non-Buddhists in Tibet who argued utilizing *pramāṇa*. See Sherab Dorjé's commentary, which mentions two ways that Buddhists dealt with opponents: through debate or through the use of miracles.

399. As McClintock (2008, 33) notes, "[Āgamāśritānumāna . . .] is not considered a separate pramāṇa, but is a way of allowing scriptures to be introduced as evidence into arguments under very specific conditions: namely, when the topic in question is an epistemically remote entity (atyantaparokṣadharma) and when the scriptural passage in question can be shown not to be in conflict with perception or inference."

400. *Prasannapadā* (La Vallée Poussin 1903–13, 75.6–7; MacDonald 2015, 1: 275): *sākṣād atīndriyārthavidām āptānāṃ yad vacanaṃ sa āgamaḥ /*. English translation Eltschinger 2014, 208.

401. See *Collection on the Two Realities* translation at verse 27.

402. *Rnal 'byor pa Shes rab rdo rjes mdzad pa'i bden gnyis kyi rnam par bshad pa*, 54b5–8: [54b5] . . . *legs par brtags pas zhes bar bya'i zhes bya ba ni / gzhal bya mngon sum pa dang 'gal ba med pa / lkog gyur la rjes* [54b6] *dpag dang mi 'gal ba / shin tu lkog du gyur pa lung dang 'gal ba med par nyams su blang zhes pa'o // de nyid la sangs rgyas kyis: dge slong dag gam mkhas rnams kyis // bsregs bcad bdar ba'i gser bzhin du / legs par brtags la* [54b7] *nga'i bka' // blang bar bya'i gus phyir min zhes gsungs so // 'on na gong du tshad ma mi dgos par bshad pa dang 'gal zhe na / gong du des chos nyid dngos su mi rtogs zhes bshad pa yin / 'di ni re zhig gzhal bya gtan la 'bebs* [54b8] *pa'i dbang du byas nas bstan pas mi 'gal lo // . . .*

403. Followers of Dharma (*dharmānusārin*) and followers of faith (*śraddhānusārin*) are defined in the AK (4.29), AS (Rāhula 2001, 202–3), and AA (1.23). See Apple 2008. The classification is also followed by Kamalaśīla in the *Tattvasaṃgrahapañjikā* (see McClintock 2010, 300).

404. The meaning of "profound" (*zab mo'i don*, *gambhīrārtha*), as noted by Scherrer-Schaub (1991, 207n355), signifies the "deep" understanding of dharmas that is a nonunderstanding, free of discursive knowledge, and peaceful. Scherrer-Schaub identifies four senses of profound (*zab mo*, *gambhīra*): (1) dependent-arising (YSV, P 4a8: *rten cing 'brel par 'byung ba zab mo*), (2) to the profound Dharma that the Buddha had discovered at the time of his awakening, (3) to *nirvāṇa*, and (4) to emptiness (*śūnyatā*). The meaning of profound as emptiness is explicity stated by Candrakīrti in the MA (La Vallée Poussin 398.10–14): The profound is emptiness, the other qualities are the vast. Through knowing the ways of the profound and the vast, these qualities will be attained (*zab mo stong pa nyid yin te / / yon tan gzhan rgya che ba'o / / zab dang rgya che'i tshul shes pas / / yon tan 'di dag 'thob par 'gyur //* [12.34]).

405. *Satyadvayāvatāra*: / *rgya gar skad du / sa tya dwa ya'a ba ta' ra / bod skad du / bden pa gnyis la 'jug pa //*.

406. Tib. *tshu rol thong ba'i tshad ma*. The Sanskrit equivalents for *tshu rol thong ba* are *arvāgdarśana, arvāgdṛś*, or *aparadarśana*. As noted by Keira (2004, 94), Kamalaśīla explains in his *Tattvasaṃgrahapañjikā* that people of narrow vision (*tshu rol thong ba*) have three types of direct perception—sense cognition (*indriyajñānam*), mental [cognition](*mānasaṃ*), and reflexive cognition (*ātmasaṃvedana*), but such people

do not have *yogipratyakṣa*, which directly understands emptiness (*śūnyatā*). Atiśa and the Kadampa commentary will repeatedly mention that the direct perception and inferences of those with narrow vision cannot understand the two realities nor cognize emptiness.

407. *Satyadvayāvatāra*: *thugs rje chen po la phyag 'tshal lo /.*

408. This statement provides supporting evidence for Jan Nattier's (2003, 26–27) hypothesis that opening formulas of salutation were a relatively late development in India.

409. *Satyadvayāvatāra*, v. 1 (Ejima 1983, 361): *sangs rgyas rnams kyis chos bstan pa / / bden pa gnyis la yang dag brten / / 'jig rten kun rdzob bden pa dang / / de bzhin don dam bden pa'o // 1 //.* Cf. MMK 24.8, Tib. (vol. *tsa*, 14b7–15a1): *sangs rgyas rnams kyis chos bstan pa* [15a1] *bden pa gnyis la yang dag brten / 'jig rten kun rdzob bden pa dang / / dam pa'i don gyi bden pa'o //*; Skt. (La Vallée Poussin 1907–12, 492.4–5): *dve satye samupāśritya buddhānāṃ dharmadeśanā / lokasaṃvṛtisatyaṃ ca satyaṃ ca paramārthataḥ //.* See Lindtner 1981, 196n1, for further references.

410. As noted by Newland and Tillemans (2011, 5–11), the Buddhist notion of "two realities" was initially based on examining the Buddha's teachings. Note here that the text does not classify the two realities based on objects of knowledge (*jñeya*), which becomes standard in later Tibetan doxographical exegesis through citation of the *Pitāputrasamāgamasūtra* (P 760. 16, vol. 23; Toh 60, vol. *nga* (*dkon brtsegs*)), found in Śāntideva's *Śikṣāsamuccaya* (Toh 3940, vol. *khi*, 142b.2 [Skt. in Bendall 1971, 256]): *etāvaccaitat jñeyam / yaduta saṃvṛtiḥ paramārthaśca /*; English translation in Bendall and Rouse 1971, 236; or in Prajñākaramati's *Bodhicaryāvatārapañjikā* (Vaidya 1960, 177). See Mimaki 1982, 138–40.

411. The four points mentioned here are often referred to in Tibetan as the four seals (*phyag rgya bzhi*), which, along with taking refuge (*skyab 'gro*) in the Three Jewels, are the criteria for defining a Buddhist. The Seals of the Law (*dharmamudrā* or *dharma-uddāna* in Sanskrit) are mentioned in Ekottara-āgama and the *Sāgaranāgarājaparipṛcchā* (Dergé no. 155), among other texts. See Mizuno and Sekimori 1996, 121–34.

412. Atiśa lists four great Nikāya ordination lineages and eighteen Nikāyas in his *Bodhimārgapradīpapañjikā* (Dergé no. 3948). The four great Nikāya lineages are the Mahāsaṃghika, Sarvāstivāda, Sthaviravāda, and Sammatīya. See Sherburne 2000, 123–25; and Skilling 2004, 140.

413. Five bases of knowables (*shes bya'i gzhi lnga*, Skt. *pañcavastu*) consist of form (*rūpa*), mind (*citta*), mental factors (*caitasika*), conditioned forces dissociated from thought (*cittaviprayuktasaṃskāra*), and unconditioned factors (*asaṃskṛtadharma*). They are listed in AKBH (Pradhan 1975, 52.20–21; La Vallée Poussin 1923–31, I, 144) and glossed in the AKV (123.8–14) as *pañcavastu*. The expression *pañcavastu* becomes a preferred mode of classifying dharmas among Tibetan doxographers (Mimaki 1982, 58–82, 138–39).

414. See *Mahāyānasūtrālaṃkāra* 18.83–92.

415. On the Vātsīputrīya ordination lineage, see Thiện Châu 1999. On the Vātsīputrīya theory of person and Vasubandhu's critique, see Duerlinger 1997.

416. See Mimaki 1980, 155. As stated in AK (2.55–56a), the Sautrāntika posits fourteen conditioned forces dissociated from thought ([*sems*]*mi ldan pa'i 'du byed,* [*citta*] *viprayuktasaṃskāra*): (1) possession (*thob pa, prāpti*), (2) nonpossession (*ma thob pa, aprāpti*), (3) group homogeneity (*skal mnyam, nikāyasabhāga*), (4) ideationlessness

(*'du shes med pa ba, āsaṃjñika*), (5) ideationless attainment (*'du shes med pa'i snyoms 'jug, āsaṃjñisamāpatti*), (6) cessation attainment (*nirodhasamāpatti*) (7) vital faculty (*jīvitendriya, srog gi dbang po*), characteristics (*mthan nyid, lakṣaṇa*) of (8) arising (*skye ba, jātilakṣaṇa*), (9) persistence (*gnas pa, sthiti*), (10) decay (*rga ba, jarā*), and (11) of cessation (*mi rtag pa, anityatā*), as well as collections (*tshogs, kāya*) of (12) words (*ming, nāma*) (13) phrases (*tshig, pada*), and (14) syllables (*yi ge, vyañjana*).

417. Mimaki (1992, 24–33) translates and notes Üpa Losal's (Dbus pa blo gsal's) doctrinal positions of Yogācāras who posit eight groups of consciousness, those who maintain six groups (*rnam par shes pa tshogs drug du smra ba, *ṣaḍvijñānakāyavādin*), and those who maintain a single consciousness ([*rnam par shes pa tshogs*] *gcig du smra ba, *ekavijñānakāyavādin*).

418. Tib. *bye brags tu smra bas rnam med du kye bar 'dod la / mdo sde bas rnam bcas su skye bar 'dod de //.* This statement appears to be an early and basic Tibetan classification for what became known among later doxographers, such as Changkya Rölpai Dorjé (Lcang skya Rol pa'i rdo rje, 1717–86), as the way that different Sautrāntika systems posit how one consciousness can understand variegated objects. See Klein 1991, 160–63; and Keira 2004, 190n329.

419. Cf. *Yuktiṣaṣṭikāvṛtti* on stanza 5cd (Scherrer-Schaub 1991, 36): The truth of cessation "by worldly conventions is called ultimate reality because it is not deceiving to the world. That which is a deceptive compositional thing is not ultimate reality. The [other] three truths, because they are deceptive to childish beings, since they appear to exist intrinsically owing to having the character of compositional things, are established as conventional realities" (*de'i bdag nyid du 'jig rten la mi bslu ba'i phyir 'jig rten gyi tha snyad kyis don dam pa'i bden pa zhes bshad do / / bslu ba 'dus byas gang yin pa de ni don don dam pa'i bden pa ma yin no / / bden pa gsum ni 'dus byas kyi mtshan nyis de ngo bo nyid yod par snang bas byis pa rnams la bslu ba'i phyir kun rdzob kyi bden par rnam par bzhag go //*).

420. Cf. *Madhyamakāvatārabhāṣya* at MA 5.1 (La Vallée Poussin 1907–12, 70.15–71.7): "In this way, how can another four nobles' truths exist differently from the two realities? I shall explain. Although it is indeed like that, nevertheless, in order to indicate each one of the properties of cause and result to be accepted and to be abandoned, here the four nobles' truths are described. In this regard, the portion that is to be abandoned is the thoroughly afflicted. Its result is the truth of suffering. The cause is [71] the truth of arising. The portion that is to be accepted is purification. Its result is the truth of cessation. The cause of attaining that is the truth of the path. In this way, the truths of suffering, arising, and the path are included within conventional reality. The truth of cessation has the intrinsic nature of ultimate reality. Likewise, whatever other truths there are should be ascertained as included only within either of the two realities" (*de phyir bden pa gnyis las tha dad par 'phags pa'i bden pa bzhi po gzhan ga la yod ce na / bshad pa / gal te yang de lta yod mod kyi / de lta na yang blang bar bya ba dang spang bar bya ba dag re re'i rgyu dang 'bras bu'i dngos po bstan par bya ba'i phyir / / 'dir 'phags pa'i bden pa bzhi bsnyad do / / de la spangs bar bya ba'i phyogs ni kun nas nyon mongs pa'o / / de'i 'bras bu ni sdug bsngal gyi bden po'o / / rgyu ni kun* [71] *'byung gi bden pa'o / / blang bar bya ba'i phyogs ni rnam par byang ba yin la / de'i 'bras bu ni 'gog pa'i bden pa'o / / de thob pa'i rgyu ni lam gyi bden pa'o / / de la sdug bsngal dang kun 'byung dang lam gyi bden pa ni kun rdzob kyi bden pa'i khongs su gtogs so / / 'gog pa'i bden pa ni don dam pa'i bden pa'i rang gi ngo bo'o / / de bzhin*

du bden pa gzhan gang cung zad cig yod pa de yang ci rigs par bden pa gnyis kyi khongs su gtogs pa kho nar nges par bya'o //).

421. *Yum gyi man ngag* refers to the *Prajñāpāramitopadeśa* (*Shes rab kyi pha rol tu phyin pa'i man ngag*, Toh 4079, vol. *hi*, 133b.7–162b.1, trans. Zhi ba bzang po and 'Gos Lhas btsas) of Śāntipa, aka Ratnākaraśānti. The Kadampa author must be referring to the discussion of the two realities at D 143b5: *gnyi ga la yang rnam pa gsum gsum ste*. . . See Katsura 1976, 486, §3.5.

422. Cf. *Madhyamakopadeśa* (*Dbu ma'i man ngag*, Toh 3929, vol. *ki*), 95b3–4: *kun rdzob tu* [95.4] *chos thams cad tshu rol mthong ba'i ngor byas nas / rgyu 'bras la sogs pa rnam par bzhag pa thams cad ji ltar snang ba bzhin du bden pa yin la //*.

423. Tib. *sgyu ma'i don byed nus pa tsam*. Although causal efficacy (*don byed nus pa*, *arthakriyāsamartha*) is associated with the work of Dharmakīrti—*Pramāṇavarttika* (3.3ab), *Hetubindu* (3.14), *Nyāyabindu* (1.14–15)—it may be the case that the Kadampa author is referring to the type of causal efficacy (i.e., *kāryakriyāsamartha*) that is argued by Nāgārjuna in the *Vigrahavyārtanī* (v. 2 and commentary, reply vv. 22–23) emphasizing dependent-arising illustrated through the example of the "illusory person" (*māyā-puruṣaḥ*). See Westerhoff 2010, 46–53.

424. *Satyadvayāvatāra*, v. 2 (Ejima 1983, 361): *kun rdzob rnam pa gnyis su 'dod / log pa dang ni yang dag go // dang po gnyis te chu zla dang / / grub mtha' ngan pa'i rtog pa'o // 2 //*. Cf. BCAP (1960, 171) *ad* BCA 9.2: *sā ca saṃvṛtirdvividhā lokata eva / tathyasaṃvṛtirmithyāsaṃvṛtiśceti / tathā hi kiṃcit pratītyajātaṃ nīlādikaṃ vasturūpamadoṣavadindriyairūpalabdhaṃ lokata eva satyam / māyāmarīcipratibimbādviṣu pratītya samupajātamapi doṣavadindriyopalabdhaṃ yathāsvaṃ tīrthikasiddhāntaparikalpitaṃ ca lokata eva mithyā //*.

425. Eight similes of illusion (*aṣṭamāyopamā*, Tib. *sgyu ma'i dpe brgyad*). The eight are said to be a twinkling star (*skar mar*), optical illusion (*rab rib*), lamp (*mar me*), dream (*rmi lam*), flash of lightning (*glog*), moon in the water (*chu zla*), mirage (*smig rgyu*), and cloud (*sprin*). See Ruegg 1966, 99n2.

426. *Satyadvayavibhaṅgakārikā*, v. 12: *snang du 'dra yang don byed dag / nus pa'i phyir dang mi nus phyir / / yang dag yang dag ma yin pa'i* {Eckel *pas*} */ / kun rdzob kyi ni dbye ba byas* (Tib., Eckel 1987, 163).

427. *Ratnāvalī*, 1.54a–b (bold Kadam manuscript; Hahn 1982, 22): ***ji ltar smig rgyu chu 'dra yang*** {Hahn, *ba*} */ / **chu min** don du ma yin pa*; Skt. *marīcis toyasadṛśī yathā nāmbho na cārthataḥ*.

428. *Yuktiṣaṣṭikā*, v. 45 (variant readings Scherrer-Schaub 1991, 15): *gang rten* {*brten*} *nas dnogs po rnams / /chu yi zla ba lta bur ni / yang dag ma yin log min par/ /'dod pa de dag lhas* {em. *ltas*} *mi phrogs* {var. *'phrogs*} *//*. The reading in 45a, *rten*, follows the paracanonical edition of Pa tshab's translation.

429. Sāṃkhya (Tib. *grangs can pa*) philosophy enumerates twenty-five principles (*tattvas*), including (1) consciousness (*puruṣa*), (2) primal nature (*prakṛti*), (3) intellect (*buddhi*), (4) ego (*ahaṃkāra*), (5) mind (*manas*), (6–10) five sense-capacities (*buddhīndriyas*), (11–15) five action-capacities (*karmendriyas*), (16–20) five subtle elements (*tanmātras*), and five gross elements (*mahābhūtas*). See Larson 1998.

430. In Vaiśeṣika philosophy, the understanding of six categories (*padārtha*), consisting of substances (*dravya*), qualities (*guṇa*), motion (*karma*), universals (*sāmānya*), particulars (*viśeṣa*), and inherence (*samavāya*), lead to the supreme bliss (*niḥśreyasa*) of liberation (*mokṣa*). See Keira 2004, 188.

431. *Satyadvayāvatāra*, v. 3 (Ejima 1983, 362): *ma brtags gcig pu nyams dga' ba'i / skye ba dang ni 'jig pa'i chos / / don byed nus dang ldan pa ni / / yang dag kun rdzob yin par 'dod // 3 //*. Cf. *Madhyamakālaṃkāra*, v. 64 (Ichigō 1985, cxxv, 13–16). See Eckel 1987, 137–38; De Jong 1989, 209–11.
432. De Jong (1989, 211) notes that the expressions *avicāraramaṇīya* and *avicāraikaramaṇīya* become commonly used among Buddhist texts from the eighth century. He mentions that the expression is employed in the works of Śāntarakṣita, Haribhadra, Prajñākaramati, and Atiśa. It is not clear which Sautrāntika or Yogācāra texts the author is basing his claim on.
433. In accounts of Atiśa's early arrival in Western Tibet, he is said to have taught that "the especially profound Dharma is only karmic casuality" (Eimer 1979, 2: 190: *jo bo'i zhal nas / chos zhin tu zab pa las rgyu 'bras kho na yin*). Cf. Vetturini 2007, 65–66.
434. Cf. *Dharmadhātu-stava (Chos kyi dbyings su bstod pa)*, Toh 1118, vol. *ka*, 64b7–65a1, vv. 30–31: [30] *ji ltar ri bong mgo yi rwa / / brtags pa nyid de med pa ltar / / de bzhin chos rnams thams cad kyang / / brtags pa nyid de yod ma yin //* [31] *// phra rab rdul gyi ngo bo yis / / glang gi rwa yang dmigs* {*yod*, N, P} *ma yin / / ji ltar sngon bzhin phyis de bzhin / de* {65a} *de la ci zhig brtag par bya //*. "Just as horns on a rabbit's head do not exist and are only imagined, likewise, all things do not exist and are only imagined. As they are not made of solid atoms, the horns of an ox do not exist either. Just as before so it is after, what is to be imagined there?"
435. *Satyadvayavibhaṅgakārikā*, v. 2: *bden gnyis rnam dbye shes pa dag / thub pa'i dka'* {*em. bka'*} *la rmongs te / de dag ma lus tshogs bsags nas / / phun tshogs pha rol 'gro ba nyid /* (Tib., Eckel 1987, 155). English translation adapted, with slight changes, from MacDonald 1988, 96.
436. This brief statement by the Kadampa author points toward different Mādhyamika approaches to debate and discussion. For a number of Mādhyamika thinkers (Nāgārjuna, Buddhapālita, Candrakīrti), the proper approach is to employ apagogic reasoning (Ruegg 2000, 137) that points out the internal contradictions of asserting any form of intrinsic nature through statements that adduce undesired consequences (*prasaṅgāpādana = thal ba bsgrub pa*). For Candrakīrti, this technique results simply in the negation of another's thesis (*parapratijñāpratiṣedhamātra-phala*) (Ruegg 2000, 251; Vose 2010a, 560). This point regarding procedure and proof will become one basis among several for later Tibetan scholars to differentiate Thal-'gyur-ba (Prāsaṅgika) and Rang-rgyud-pa (Svātantrika) Madhyamaka systems.
437. "Easterners" (*shar ba dag*) refers in later Tibetan traditions (post-thirteenth century) to the so-called Three Eastern Svātantrika-Madhyamaka (*rang rgyud shar gsum*) works of Śāntarakṣita's *Madhyamakālaṃkāra,* Kamalaśīla's *Madhyamakāloka*, and Jñānagarbha's *Satyadvayavibhaṅga* (Mimaki 1982, 4–5; Eckel 1987, 15; Tauscher 1999, 387n2). Note that the Kadampa author does not use the term *rang rgyud* (Svātantrika), as this work does not know of any classifications of Madhyamaka traditions.The Kadampa author makes reference to the "enumerated ultimate" (*rnam grangs kyi don dam = paryāya-paramārtha*). As Mimaki (1982, 160–61) points out, the term *paryāya-paramārtha* does not appear in the works of Jñānagarbha, Śāntarakṣita, or Kamalaśīla. However, the equivalent of this term, *don dam pa dang mthun pa ['i don da pa (= paramārthānukūla[paramārtha]*), was known to these authors. The counterpart term, *rnam grangs ma yin don dam (= aparyāyaparamārtha)*, does appear in Śāntarakṣita's *Satyadvayavibhaṅgapañjikā*. Both *paryāya-paramārtha*

and *aparyāyaparamārtha* appear in the *Madhyamakārthasaṃgraha* v. 4 attributed to Bhāviveka. Ruegg (2010, 157) and Del Toso (2011) argue that this work is not by the Bhāviveka who wrote the *Madhyamakahṛdayakārikā* and *Tarkajvālā*, and most likely dates to the eighth-century time period of Jñānagarbha. Along these lines, Del Toso (2011, 354–55) demonstrates that both *paryāya-paramārtha* and *aparyāyaparamārtha* also appear in the eighth-century *Sarvayānālokaviśeṣabhāṣya* attributed to Subhūtighoṣa. See also Macdonald 1988, 94; Tauscher 1988.

438. *Satyadvayāvatāra*, v. 4 (Ejima 1983, 362): *dam pa'i don ni gcig nyid de / / gzhan dag rnam pa gnyis su 'dod / cir yang ma grub chos nyid de / / gnyis dang gsum sog ga la 'gyur / / 4 / /.*

439. Cf. *Saddharmapuṇḍarīka*. Skt. (Kern and Nanjio 1908–12, 39.13–40.15): *ekakṛtyena śāriputraikakaraṇīyena tathāgato 'rhan samyaksaṃbuddho loka utpadyate . . . yad idaṃ tathāgatajñānadarśanasamādāpanahetunimittaṃ sattvānāṃ tathāgato 'rhan samyaksaṃbuddho loka utpadyate / . . . ekam evāhaṃ śāriputra yānam ārabhya sattvānāṃ dharmaṃ deśayāmi yad idaṃ buddhayānaṃ / na kiṃcic chāriputra dvitīyaṃ vā tṛtiyaṃ vā yānaṃ saṃvidyate / sarvatraiṣā śāriputra dharmatā daśadigloke / . . .*" With a single duty, Śāriputra, with a single task the Tathāgata, the *Arhat* and Perfectly Awakened One, appears in the world . . . Namely, in order to inspire living beings to the mental vision of a tathāgata (*tathāgatajñādarśana*), the Tathāgata, the *Arhat* and Perfectly Awakened One, appears in the world . . . With reference to only a single vehicle, Śāriputra, I teach the Dharma for living beings, namely, the vehicle of the buddhas. Śāriputra, there is not any second or third vehicle. This, Śāriputra, is the True Law everywhere in the worlds of the ten regions." English translation Zimmermann 1999, 156 (with minor corrections for clarity).

440. Cf. *Yuktiṣaṣṭikāvṛtti* (Scherrer-Schaub 1991, Tib., P 14b7–15a3, 50–51): *de ltar na chos shes pas skad cig gcig la rten cing 'brel par 'byung ba mthong bas sngon ma mthong ba'i lta bar bya ba gzhan mi srid do . . . sde pa kha cig ni mthong ba'i lam skad cig ma bco lngar mi 'dod kyi / mngon par rtogs pa gcig tu zad par 'dod do // de dag gi 'dod pa dang bshad pa 'di mi 'gal lo . . . de khon na ni ngo bo gcig pur zad do . . . /.* "Therefore, since the cognition of dharmas sees dependent-arising in one moment, it is not possible that other previously unperceived [truths remain] to be seen . . . Some schools do not accept fifteen moments on the path of vision, but assert that realization culminates in a single instant; their claim and our explanation are not incompatible . . . Reality has a single essence."

441. The immutable perfected nature (*'gyur ba med pa'i yongs su grub pa, avikāra-pariniṣpatti*) and the unmistaken perfected nature (*phyin ci ma log pa'i yongs su grub pa, aviparyāsapariniṣpatti*) are mentioned at *Madhyāntavibhāga* 3.11cd (Pandeya 1999, 95): *nirvikarā'viparyāsapariniṣpattito dvayaṃ /.* See O'Brien 1954, 230. The *Madhyāntavibhāgakārikā* (*Dbus dang mtha' rnam par 'byed pa'i tshig le'ur byas pa*) was translated into Tibetan by Jinamitra, Śīlendrabodhi, and Ye shes sde. Dbus pa blo gsal mentions this distinction at folios 90a5–6 (Mimaki 1982).

442. *Satyadvayāvatāra*, v. 5 (Ejima 1983, 362): *bstan pa'i tshig gis sbyor ba yis / skye med 'gag med sogs pas mtshon // don dam thad dad med tshul gyis / / chos can med cing chos nyid med / / 5 //.*

443. The example of mistaking fingers pointing at the moon for the moon itself as analogous to mistaking conceptual instruction for nonconceptual reality is from the *Laṅkāvatārasūtra* 6.3. Skt. (Nanjio 1923, 223–24): "As the childish grasp the

finger-tip and not the moon, so those who are attached to the letter do not know the reality of my [teaching]" (*aṅgulyagraṃ yathā bālo na gṛhṇāti niśākaram / tathā hy akṣarasaṃsaktas tattvaṃ vetti na māmakam / /*).

444. *Satyadvayāvatāra*, vv. 6–7ab (Ejima 1983, 362): *stong pa nyid la thad dad ni / / cung zad yod pa ma yin te / / rtog med tshul gyis rtogs pas na / / stong nyid mthong zhes tha snyad gdags // 6 // ma mthong ba nyid de mthong bar / / shin tu zab pa'i mdo las gsungs //* 7ab. Cf. *Prasannapadā* (La Vallée Poussin 1903–13, 265.4); *Madhyamakāvatārabhāṣya* (La Vallée Poussin 1907–12, 110.13).
445. *Dharmasaṃgīti* (Toh 238, vol. *zha*, 68b6): *bcom ldan 'das chos thams cad ma mthong ba ni yang dag pa mthong ba'o /*. *Śikṣāsamuccaya* (Bendall 1971, 264.1–2): *adarśanaṃ bhagavan sarvadharmāṇāṃ darśanaṃ samyagdarśanam iti*. Also *Bhāvanākrama I* (Tucci 1958, 212.2–3): *tathā coktam sūtre / katamaṃ paramārthadarśanam / sarvadharmāṇām adarśanam iti //*. See MacDonald 1988, 159; Tauscher 1988, 484n8; Keira 2004, 70, 71, 100, 103.
446. Actually from the *Vajracchedikā*. For a discussion on these verses, see Almogi 2009, 252n46. Cf. *Vajracchedikā*, §26, vv. 1–2ab (Conze 1957, 56–57): *ye māṃ rūpeṇa cādrākṣur ye māṃ ghoṣeṇa cānvayuḥ / mithyāprahāṇaprasṛtā na māṃ drakṣyanti te janāḥ / 1 / dharmato buddhā draṣṭavyā dharmakāyā hi nāyakāḥ //*.
447. *Prajñāpāramitāratnaguṇasaṃcayagāthā* 7.3 (Yuyama 1976, 167): *gang tshe 'dus byas 'dus ma byas dang dkar nag chos / / shes rab rnam par bshigs nas rdul tsam mi dmigs tshe / / 'jig rten dag na shes rab pha rol phyin grangs 'gro / nam mkha' gar gang la'ang chung zad mi gnas de dang 'dra* {3d follows Tib. Recension B (Yuyama 1976, 3n3d). Recension A, 3d, reads: *mi gnas pa ji yang med pa bzhin*} *// 3 //*. Skt. (Yuyama 1976, 35–36): *yada dharma saṃskṛta asaṃskṛtakṛṣṇaśuklā aṇumātru no labhati prajñā vibhāvamānaḥ / tada prajñapāramita gacchati saṃkhya loke ākāśu yatra na pratiṣṭhitu kiṃ ci tatra // 3 //*. Tibetan Recension B is the early ninth-century translation of Vidyākarasiṃha and Dpal brtsegs. As Yuyama (1976, xxxiii) notes, the *Prajñāpāramitāratnaguṇasaṃcayagāthā* is listed as *'phags pa sdus pa tshigs su bcad pa* ≈ *Āryasaṃcayagāthā* in the ninth-century *Dkar chag ldan dkar ma* catalog.
448. *Prajñāpāramitāratnaguṇasaṃcayagāthā*. Tib. 12.9 (Yuyama 1976, 171): *nam mkha' mthong zhes sems can tshig tu rab brjod pa / /nam mkha' ji ltar mthong ste don 'di brtag par gyis / /de ltar chos mthong ba yang de bzhin gshegs pas bstan / /mthong ba dpe gzhan gyis ni snyad par nus ma yin /* (underlined portions differ from the critical edition). Skt. 12.10 (Yuyama 1976, 52): *ākāśadṛṣṭu iti sattva pravyāharanti khanidarśanaṃ kutu vimṛṣyata etam arthaṃ / tatha dharmadarsanu nidiṣṭu tathāgatena na hi darśanaṃ bhaṇitu śakya nidarśanena // 10 //*.
449. This is a reference to Atiśa's meeting with hierarchs of Ngari after first arriving in Tibet and being questioned on his view of Madhyamaka. The *Dbu ma'i man ngag* reference may be the earliest extant mention of this event.
450. The following sentences are a paraphrase of Candrakīrti's discussion found in chapter 6 (6.29–6.31) of the *Madhyamakāvatārabhāṣya* (La Vallée Poussin 1907–12, 109–11). The example of eye disease is also found in the *Yuktiṣaṣṭikāvṛtti ad* verse 10. As Mimaki (1979, 181) discusses, early Kadampa commentators often do not distinguish between a root text and commentary when citing or paraphrasing a text.
451. *Ratnāvalī*, 1.52–53 (Hahn 1982, 22): *thag ring nas ni mthong ba'i gzugs / / nye ba rnams kyis gsal bar mthong / / smig rgyu gal te chu yin na // nye ba rnams kyis cis mi mthong // 52 // ji ltar ring ba rnams kyis ni / / 'jig rten 'di ni yang dag mthong // de ltar*

de dang de {*nye*, Hahn} *rnams kyis / / mi mthong mtshan med smig rgyu bzhin /*. Skt: *durād ālokitaṃ rūpam āsannair dṛśyate sphuṭam / marīcir yadi vāri syād āsannaiḥ kiṃ na dṛśyate / /* 52 *// dūrībhūtair yathābhūto loko 'yaṃ dṛśyate tathā / na dṛśyate tadāsannair animitto marīcivat //* 53 *//*.

452. *Satyadvayāvatāra*, vv. 7cd–9 (Ejima 1983, 363): *de la mthong dang mthong byed med / / thog ma tha ma med zhi ba //* 7 *// dngos dang dngos med rnam par spangs / / rnam par rtog med dmigs pa bral / /gnas pa med pa gnas med pa / / 'gro 'ong med cing dpe dang bral //* 8 *// brjod du med bltar med pa / / 'gyur ba med pa 'dus ma byas / / rnal 'byor pa yis de rtogs na / / nyong mongs shes bya'i sgrib pa spangs //* 9 *//*.

453. *Satyadvayavibhaṅgakārikā*, v. 9cd (Eckel 1987, 161): *dgag bya yod pa ma yin pas / / yang dag tu na bkag med gsal //*. Translation from van der Kuijp 1991, 404.

454. The Kadampa text reads: *yod pa dmigs pa ma yin na / / med gang gis yin par 'gyur /*. This most likely represents an old Tibetan translation of *Mūlamadhyamakakārikā* 5.6ab, which was intially translated by Jñānagarbha and Klu'i rgyal mtshan. The Tengyur translation, a revision by Sumati, Pa tshab nyi ma grags, Kanaka, and De nyid, reads (Toh 3824, vol. *tsa*, 4a4–5): *dngos po yod pa ma yin na / / dngos med gang gi yin par 'gyur /*. Skt. (La Vallée Poussin 1903–13, 132.5–7): *avidyamāne bhāve ca kasyābhāvo bhaviṣyati*

455. Cited from the *Śūnyatāsaptati* (Lindtner 1997b, 100–101): *dngos po med par ngos med min* (20a) */ dngos dang dngos med cig par* {*car*, Lindtner} *min* (19a) *//*.

456. Tib. *tshul bzhin ma yin pa'i yid la byed pa*; Skt. *ayoniśo manaskāraḥ*.

457. Cf. *Vajracchedikā prajñāpāramitā* §7 (Harrison and Watanabe 2006, 117): *asaṃskṛtaprabhāvitā hy āryapudgalāḥ*. See also Apple 2008, 65; Ruegg 1989, 37.

458. *Ārya Akṣayamatinirdeśasūtra*, Kadampa citation: *don dam pa'i bden pa gang la sems rgyu ba yang med na / yi ge'i rgyu ba lta smos kyang ci dgos*. Braarvig's edition (1993, 1:73.3–4) reads: *don dam pa'i bden pa ni: gang la sems kyi rgyu ba med pa ste / yi ge lta ci smos /*. Cited in *Prasannapadā* (La Vallée Poussin 1903–13, 374.2): *paramārthasatyaṃ katamat / yatra jñānasyāpy apracāraḥ kaḥ punar vādo 'kṣarāṇām*. Tibetan translation by Mahāsumati and Pa tshab nyi ma grags (Toh 3860, vol. *'a*, 120a3–4): *don dam pa'i bden pa gang zhe na / gang la sems kyi rgyu ba yang med na / yi ge rnams la lta smos kyang ci dgos*.

459. The five eyes (*pañcacakṣu, spyan lnga*) are fleshly matured (*māṃsavaipākika*), divine (*divya*), wisdom (*prajñā*), dharma, and buddha eyes. The five eyes are one of the special instructions for bodhisattvas in the *Abhisamayālaṃkāra* 1.22; see Apple 2008, 59–60.

460. *Satyadvayāvatāra*, v. 10 (Ejima 1983, 363): *mngon sum dang ni rjes su dpag / / sangs rgyas pa yis de gnyis gzung / / gnyis pos stong nyid rtogs so zhes / tshul rol mthong ba'i rmongs pa smra //*.

461. *Satyadvayāvatāra*, v. 11 (Ejima 1983, 363): *mu stegs nyan thos rnams kyis kyang / / chos nyid rtogs par thal bar 'gyur / / rnam rig pas lta smos ci dgos / / dbu ma pa la mi mthun med //*.

462. *Satyadvayāvatāra*, v. 12ab (Ejima 1983, 363): *des na grub mtha' thams cad kyang / tshad ma 'jal phyir mthun par 'gyur //*.

463. Cf. Opponent's objection cited in *Vigrahavyāvartanī* vv. 5–6 (Yonezawa 2008): *pratyakṣeṇa hi tāvad yady upalabhya vinivartayasi bhāvān / tan nāsti pratyakṣaṃ bhāvā yenopalabhyante // anumānaṃ pratyuktaṃ pratyakṣeṇāgamopamāne ca / anumānāgamasādhyā ye 'rthā dṛṣṭāntasādhyāś ca //*. Westerhoff (2010, 21–22)

translation: "5. If you deny objects after having apprehended them through perception, that perception by which the objects are perceived does not exist. 6. Inference, testimony, and likeness are refuted by perception, as well as the objects to be established by inference, testimony, and example." Nāgārjuna's reply occurs in *Vigrahavyāvartanī* vv. 29–30, for which see Ruegg 2000, 115–33.

464. Cf. *Nyāyabindu* 2.10–11: *trirūpāṇi ca trīṇy eva liṅgāni // anupalabdhiḥ svabhāvaḥ kāryaṃ ceti //*. See Keira 2004, 52–64.

465. The textual sources for the author's statement are not clear. The eleven types of nonperception are mentioned in Dharmakīrti's *Nyāyabindu* 2.31: "And that (i.e., *anupalabdhi*) is of eleven kinds according to difference of the formulation" (*sā ca prayogabhedād ekādaśaprakārā*). The Tibetan translation of the *Nyāyabindhu* (*Rigs pa'i thig pa*) was by Gzhan la phan pa bzang po and Blo ldan shes rab (twelfth century). Dharmottara's commentary, the *Nyāyabinduṭīkā* (*Rigs pa'i thigs pa'i rgya cher 'grel pa*), was initially translated by Jñānagarbha and Dharmāloka (ninth century) and then revised by Sumatikīrti and Blo ldan shes rab (twelfth century).

466. *Mahāyānasūtrālaṃkāra* 1.12 (Lévi 1907, 5): *niśrito 'niyato 'vyāpī sāṃvṛtaḥ khedavān api / bālāśrayo matas tarkas tasyāto viṣayo na tat // 12 //*. MSA, Phi, 2b2: *rtog ge rten cing ma nges la // ma khyab kun rdzob skyo* {*skye,* Dergé} *ba can // byis pa la ni brten par 'dod // de phyir de dag* {*ni,* Dergé} *de'i yul min //*. Lévi 1911, 11: "La Dialectique a un soubassement; elle n'a rien de définitif; elle manque d'extension, elle est contingente; elle se fatigue; elle a pour Fond les esprits puérils; clone le Grand Véhicule n'est pas son domaine."

467. Tib: *so sor rang gis rig*; Skt. *pratyātmavedya*. MABH (La Vallée Poussin 1907–12, 108.16–19): *sangs rgyas rnams kyi don dam pa ni rang bzhin nyid yin zhing / de yang slu ba med pa nyid kyis don dam pa'i bden pa yin la, de ni de rnams kyi so so rang gis rig par bya ba yin no //*. "The ultimate of the buddhas is self-nature itself, and further, as it is only nondeceptive, it is the ultimate truth; it is an object to be cognized by themselves individually." MABH (La Vallée Poussin 1907–12, 306.17), citing *Ratnamegha: rigs kyi bu don dam pa ni brjod du med cing zhi ba 'phags pa rnams kyis so so rang gis rigs par bya'o /*. "Son of good lineage, the ultimate is inexpressible and peace, the object of the Noble Being's personal knowledge." PP, 493.10: *sa hi paramārtho 'parapratyayaḥ śāntaḥ pratyāmavedya āryāṇāṃ sarvaprapañcātītaḥ //*. Also note Nāgārjuna's *Dharmadhātustava,* vol. *ka*, 64b6, vv. 29, 46, and 56. See Kapstein 2000.

468. *Satyadvayāvatāra*, vv. 12–13 (Ejima 1983, 363–64): *des na grub mtha' thams cad kyang / tshad mas 'jal phyir mthun par 'gyur / / rtog ge thams cad mi mthun pas / / tshad mas gzhal ba'i chos nyid kyang // 12 // mang po nyid du mi 'gyur ram / / mngon sum rjes dpag dgos pa med / / mu stegs rgol ba bzlog pa'i phyir / / mkhas pa rnams kyis byas pa yin // 13 //*.

469. The names Bhavya, Bhāvaviveka, and Bhāviveka, as attested in Indian sources or reconstructed from Tibetan and Chinese sources, generally refer to the well-known Madhyamaka author who lived in the sixth century. However, the authorship of works ascribed to this name are not always clear (see Ruegg 2010, 145–58). As Ruegg (2010, 159 n1) notes, the preferred forms of this author's name is Bhāviveka or Bhavya.

470. *Satyadvayāvatāra*, v. 14 (Ejima 1983, 364): *lung las kyang ni gsal po ru / / rtog bcas rtog pa med pa yi / / shes pa gnyis kyis mi rtogs shes / / slob dpon mkhas pa bha bya gsung //*.

471. Krasser (2004; 2011) notes that Dignāga's aim in composing the *Pramāṇasamuccaya*

was not only to establish his own *pramāṇa*s and refute the faults of the others, but also to turn outsiders away from their mistaken views (2004, 134): "I composed this [work] in order to turn those who are inclined toward (*źen pa rnams*) the assumptions of the outsiders away from them, because they are without essence as the valid cognitions (*pramāṇa*), and their objects (*prameya*) [as taught by them] are not arranged properly. However, by [doing] that much (*iyatā*) I do not aim at their introduction into the teaching of the Tathāgata, because his teaching is not in the realm of logic. But those being turned away [from the assumptions of the outsiders] can easily understand [*dharmatā*], as it is absent/remote [from their teaching] and present [in his teaching]."

472. The author is pointing out, following Atiśa, that the two realities are not able to be realized through the wisdom which arises from hearing (*śrutamayī prajñā*) or the wisdom which arises from thinking or reflection (*cintāmayī prajñā*). For Atiśa and his direct followers, the two realities are realized through the wisdom that arises during meditation (*bhāvanāmayī prajñā*). On *cintāmayī prajñā* in Dharmakīrti's thought see Eltschinger 2009, 2010.

473. *Rigs pa* (Skt. *yukti*) is polysemous in Buddhist discourse. See Scherrer-Schaub 1991, 221n398, 245n471: "*yukti* designates, in a restrained sense, the fundamental principle or proposition that enounces the law of causality discovered by the Buddha that has issued by inductive reasoning, proceeding a direct and personal experience." See Scherrer-Schaub 1981; Ruegg 2010, 169; Eltschinger 2010; Nance 2007.

474. Cf. *Tarkajvālā ad Madhyamakahṛdaya* 3.285 (Eckel 1992, 167): "Conceptual cognition is inferential cognition because [inference] has to do with concepts [that come] from imagination and memory. Nonconceptual cognition is perceptual cognition because it grasps particulars." See *Madhyamakahṛdaya* 5.104–14; and *Tarkajvālā* (Eckel 2008, 295–98). See also *Madhyamakahṛdaya* 8.104 (Lindtner 2001, 91): *savikalpāvikalpā ca yadā buddhir nivartate / dhiyām aviṣaye tasmin prapañcopaśamaḥ śivaḥ //.* Tib: *rtog bcas rtog pa med pa las / gang tshe blo ni log gyur pa / / de tshe blo ni yul med phyir spros pa nyer shi ba nyid //.* "When conceptual and non-conceptual cognition cease, then there is the peaceful cessation of proliferations which are not an obect of the mind." Cf. *Madhyamakahṛdaya* 3.265: *nirvikalpārthaviṣayā nirvikalpāpi dhīr mṛṣā / anātmādi svabhāvatvāt tadyathā savikalpadhīḥ /* "A nonconceptual cognition as an object is false, even though it is nonconceptual, because it is a [cognition of] no-self and so forth, like a conceptual cognition." See Qvarnström 1989, 95; Nakamura 1983, 205–6.

475. *Satyadvayāvatāra*, vv. 15–16ab: *stong nyid gang gis rtogs shes na / / de bzhin gshegs pas lung bstan zhin / / chos nyid bden pa gzigs pa yi / / klu sgrub slob ma zla grags yin / / de las brgyud pa'i man ngag gis / / chos nyid bden pa rtogs par 'gyur //.*

476. *Laṅkāvatārasūtra* (Nanjio 1923, 286), 10.164c, 165abc: *mahāmate nibodha tvaṃ / dakṣiṇāpathavedalyāṃ bhikṣuḥ śrīmān mahāyaśāḥ / nāgāhvayaḥ sa nāmnā tu.*

477. *Laṅkāvatārasūtra*, 10.166cd (Nanjio 1923, 286): *āsādya bhūmiṃ muditāṃ yāsyate 'sau sukhāvatīm //.*

478. *Dbu ma'i man ngag* reads (10a6–10b1): *li tsa byi gzhon nu sems can thams cad kyi* {*kyis*, La Vallée Poussin} *mthong na dga' ba zes bya ba 'di ni /* {om. /, LVP} *nga mya ngan las 'das nas lo bzhi brgya lon pa na /* {om. /, LVP} *klu zhes bya ba'i dge slong du 'gyur* {*gyur*, LVP} *nas nga'i bstan pa rgyas par rab tu bstan te / mthar gyi sa rab tu dga'* {*dang*, LVP} *ba'i od ces bya ba'i 'jig rten gyi khams su de bzin gshegs pa dgra bcom pa*

yang dag par rdzogs pa'i sangs rgyas {insert *ye shes*, LVP} *'byung gnas 'od ces bya bar 'gyur ro* //. The author is citing the *Mahāmegha* from the *Madhyamakāvatāra*, as the citation from the canonical sūtra differs. See *Madhyamakāvatāra* (La Vallée Poussin 1970, 76–77). For the extensive citation of the *Mahāmegha* by Atiśa and comparative notes, see Apple 2010, 174–78.

479. *Madhyamakāvatāra* 6.4–5a (La Vallée Poussin 1907–12, 78.2–6): *Dbu ma'i man nga gi 'bum* reads: *so so'i skye bo'i dus na yang* {*na'ang*, LVP} *stong pa nyid thos nas / nang du rab du dga' ba yang dang yang du 'byung zhing* {*om. zhing*, LVP} // *rab tu dga' ba las 'byung ba'i mchi mas mig brlan zhing / lus kyi ba spu ldang ba skyes bar* {*om. skyes bar* LVP} *'gyur ba* {*gyur pa*, LVP} *gang yin pa* {insert / /, LVP} *de la rdzogs pa'i sangs rgyas kyi* {*blo yi*, LVP} *sa bon yod*. The Kadampa author's reading follows a recension close to the translation of Pa tshab nyi ma grags, although not exactly, and the readings may represent a paraphrase from memory or even an early, pre-Tengyur version of Pa tshab's translation. The variants for Nag tsho tshul khrim's translation differ. See Ruegg 1969, 115–16, for another variant reading of this verse in Tsongkhapa's *Gser phreng* as well as the extant Sanskrit.

480. *Yuktiṣaṣṭikā*, v. 1. *Dbu ma'i man nga gi 'bum* reads: *gang blo yod dang med pa las* // *rnam par 'das shing mi gnas pa* // *de dag zab mo dmigs med pa'i* {var. *yi*} / /*rkyen gyi don la rnam par bsgsoms* //. The citation of this verse is from the Tibetan translation by Ye shes sde (ninth century) of the commentary, the *Yuktiṣaṣṭikāvṛtti* of Candrakīrti. The Tibetan translation by Pa tshab nyi ma grags of the this verse from the *Yuktiṣaṣṭikā* differs. See Scherrer-Schaub 1991, 7, 24–25. The verse is preserved in Sanskrit in the *Sekoddeśaṭīkā* (Scherrer-Schaub 1991, 116n42): *asti-nāsti-vyatikrāntā buddhir yeṣāṃ nirāśraya / gambhīras tair nirālambaḥ pratyayārtho vibhāyate* //. The commentary to this verse in the *Yuktiṣaṣṭikāvṛtti* (Scherrer Schaub 1991, 24; P 4a6–7) mentions that "those who have meditated on emptiness in previous lives, as they have understood dependent-arising and have the seed for the vision of emptiness, have great power" (*gang dag 'das pa'i srid pa na stong pa nyid la goms pa de dag rten cing 'brel par 'byung ba rtogs shing stong pa nyid mthong ba'i sa bon yod pa'i phyir mthu che ba yin te* //).

481. Unable to identify claim in the *Pañcaskandhaprakaraṇa* (Lindtner 1979).

482. The Kadampa author is mostly likely referring to the mahāsiddha Dhobīpa, "The Washerman." See Schroeder 2006, 81, plate 28.

483. In this section the Kadampa author is drawing a parallel between a statement from the *Prasannapadā* and his current situation in eleventh-century Tibet. The author is paraphrasing several verses from what De Jong (1962) calls Candrakīrti's *Madhyamakaśāstrastuti* that are found between the end of the twenty-seventh chapter and colophon in the Tibetan translation of the *Prasannapadā* (Toh 3860, vol. *'a*, 198b5–200a4) and in the Sanskrit of the Tucci mansucript. The verses (7–8) that are paraphrased are as follows: "(7.) But Nāgārjuna, the son of the Jina, having cut his head [off] and giving it out of compassion to the man who came to ask him, went to the heaven of Sukhāvatī. For a long time the books he composed and also the multitude of his disciples have disappeared. Now that the sun of truth has set, his doctrine is by no means clear. (8.) Today most men only excel at grasping the meaning established by metaphors. They have moved away from the right path and are intoxicated by drinking the wine of reasoning. The doctrine of the Buddha is troubled because they have forsaken the awakening to reality proclaimed by the Omniscient

One. Blessed is the one who rejects the doubt, if only for a moment—and penetrates into emptiness. Tib.: (7.) *dbu ni don du gnyer ba 'ongs la thugs rjes dbu ni bcad de stsal mdzad nas / / bde ba can du rgyal ba'i sras po klu sgrub gshegs par gyur pa des mdzad pa'i / / gzhung rnams dang ni slob ma'i tshogs de dag kyang dus mang zhig na nyams pa gyur / / de nyid nyi ma nub pas deng sang gzhung lugs gsal po de ni gang na'ang med / /* (8.) *da ltar 'jig rten phal cher rtogs pas sbyar ba'i don tsam la ni mkhas gyur la / / dam pa'i lam las ring zhing rtog ge'i chang 'thungs pa yis myos pa dang / / sangs rgyas gzhung lugs thams cad mkhyen pas gsungs pa'i de nyid bral zhing 'khrugs pa'i tshe / / gang zhig skad cig tsam yang yid gnyis bsal nas stong nyid rtogs te skal bar ldan //.* Skt.: (7.) *āyātāya śiro 'rthine karuṇayā protkṛtya dattvā śiraḥ saṃyāte tu sukhāvatiṃ jinasute nāgārjune tatkṛtāḥ / granthāḥ śiṣyagaṇāś ca te 'pi bahunā kālena nāśaṃ gatās tattvārke 'stamite 'dhunā na hi mataṃ spaṣṭaṃ tad asti kvacit //* (8.) *utprekṣāracitārthamātranipuṇe dūraṃgate satpathād unmatte 'tha nipīya tarkamadirām loke 'dhunā bhūyasā / /sarvajñoditatattvabodharahite bauddhe mate vyākule dhanyo 'sau kṣaṇam apy apāsya vimatiṃ yaḥ śūnyatāṃ gāhate //.*

484. The Kadampa author assumes that Nāgārjuna and Candrakīrti were teacher and student within their purported long lifetimes. The early Tibetan biographies of Atiśa gloss Nāgārjuna as one who lived six hundred years (*lo drug brgya bzhugs*) and Candrakīrti as one who lived four hundred years (*lo gzhi brgya bzhugs*). See Eimer 1979, 2: 12.

485. Tib. *dbu ma'i lta ba = madhyamakadarśana*. Ruegg (1981, 1n3, 2n6, 3; 2000, 133–36) notes the difference between *dṛṣṭi* and *darśana* in the works of Nāgārjuna and Candrakīrti. See also Huntington 2003, 75–77, on Candrakīrti's use of *darśana*.

486. Ruegg (2010, 337) notes that Rig pa'i khu byug (*Vidyākokila) is often listed in the Madhyamaka lineage between Candrakīrti and Dīpaṃkaraśrījñāna and is purported to have been a teacher of the latter.

487. *Satyadvayāvatāra*, v. 16c–e: *chos nyid phung po brgyad khri dang / / bzhi stong gsung pa thams cad ni / / chos nyid 'di la gzhol zhing 'bab //.*

488. *Mahāyānasūtrālaṃkāra* 16.14 (Lévi 1907, 101): *pūrvottaraviśrayataścotpattestatkra meṇa nirdeśaḥ / hīnotkarṣasthānādaudārikasūkṣmataścāpi //.* Thurman et al. (2004, 195): "They are taught in their order because the latter arises dependent on the former, they have progressively superior status, and they grow progressively subtle."

489. Van der Kuijp 1992 discusses the lineage of this tantra among early Kadampas from Atiśa.

490. *Satyadvayāvatāra*, v. 17ab (Ejima 365, v. 16bc): *stong nyid rtogs pas grol 'gyur gyi / / sgom pa lhag ma de don yin //.*

491. The Tibetan here follows the earlier *Bodhicaryāvatāra* translation of Sarvajñādeva and Paltsek Rakṣita (ca. 800), perhaps providing a clue that our anonymous author was writing before the canonical Tibetan translation of Sumatikīrti and Blo ldan shes rab (eleventh–twelfth centuries). The Tibetan translation by Sarvajñādeva and Paltsek Rakṣita, *Byang chub sems dpa'i spyod pa la 'jug pa*, as edited in Saito (2000), from St. 628, 629, and 630. Page 49.4–7 reads: ***bsdog pa 'di dag thams chad kyang / / bdag dang bzhan gyi shes rab don*** */ de bas mya ngan 'das pa dang / / bde ba 'dod pas shes rab skyed //.* The Tibetan Tengyur translation of Sumatikīrti and Blo ldan shes rab (eleventh–twelfth centuries), *Byang chub sems dpa'i spyod pa la 'jug pa*, in Toh 3871, vol. *la*, 1b1–40a7 reads: */ /* ***yan lag 'di dag thams cad ni / / thub pas shes rab don du gsungs*** */ / de yi phyir na sdug bsngal dag / / zhi bar 'dod pas shes rab bskyed //.*

"All these ancillaries the Sage has taught for the sake of wisdom; so he that seeks to still suffering must cultivate wisdom."

492. *Ratnāvalī* v. 2.25 (Hahn 1982, 49.17–20): *de phyir ji srid ngar 'dzin pa / / sel ba'i chos 'di ma shes pa / de srid sbyin dang tshul khrims dang / / bzod pa'i chos la gus par mdzod //.* Skt.: *tasmād yāvad avijñāto dharmo 'haṃkāraśātanaḥ dānaśīlakṣamādharme tāvad ādaravān bhava // 25 //.*

493. *Ratnāvalī* v. 1.5cd (Hahn 1982, 3.20–23): *'di gnyis gtso bo shes rab ste / /'di sngon 'gro ba dad pa yin /.* Skt. *prajñā pradhānaṃ tv anayoḥ śraddhā pūrvaṃgamāsya tu.*

494. Tib.: *thams cad mkhyen pa'i ye shes* {insert *de,* Dergé} *ni snying rje'i rtsa ba can* {*byung ba,* Dergé} *yin / / byang chub kyi sems kyi rgyu las byung ba yin / / thabs kyi* {*kyis,* Dergé} *mthar phyin pa yin //.* Skt.: *sarvajñajñānaṃ karuṇāmūlaṃ bodhicitta-hetukam upāyaparyavasānam.* Cited from the *Vairocanābhisaṃbodhitantra* three times by Kamalaśīla, *Bhāvanākrama* I (Tucci 1958, 196), *Bhāvanākrama* II (Toh 3916, vol. *ki*, 42a7–b1, 55b1).

495. *Madhyamakahṛdayam* 1.33 (Lindtner 2001, 4): *sasaddharmapradīpo hi praṇaṣṭāṣ-ṭākṣaṇaḥ kṣaṇaḥ / saphalīkaraṇīyo'yaṃ mahāpurūṣacaryayā // 33 //.*

496. *Śikṣāsamuccaya,* v. 9 (Bendal 1902, xli): ***samāhito yathābhutaṃ prajānāti iti ava-dan muniḥ** śamāc ca na calec cittaṃ bāhya ceṣṭā nivartanāt;* Tib.: ***mnyam gzhag yang dag ji bzhin du / shes par 'gyur zhes thub pas gsungs** phyi rol g.yo ba bzlog pa yis / sems ni zhi las mi g.yo 'gyur //.*

497. *Satyadvayāvatāra,* v. 17c–f (Ejima 1983, 365): *yang dag kun rdzob khyad bsad nas / / stong pa nyid la goms byed na / / kun rdzob rgyu 'bras dge sdig sogs / / 'jig rten pha rol bslus par 'gyur //.*

498. The five sins of immediate retribution (*ānantaryakarma*) are killing one's father, mother, or an arhat, drawing the blood of a buddha, and creating a schism in the monastic community. See Silk 2007.

499. The four powers consist of the power of the support (*rten gyi stobs*), the power of anti-dote (*gnyen po kun spyod kyi stobs*), the power of regret (*rnam par gsun 'byin pa'i stobs*), and the power of turning away from future faults (*nyes pa las slang ldog pa'i stobs*).

500. The Kadampa author's Tibetan of citation of *Vigrahavyāvartanī* verse 70 is: *su la stong nyid 'di srid pa / de la chos rnams thams cad srid* (ab) . . . *su la stong nyid mid srid pa / de la chos rnams srid pa med* (cd). This may be a citation from the early translation of Jñānagarbha and Paltsek (ca. 800). It differs from the canonical Tibetan (Lindtner 1997b, 229), the revised Tibetan translation of Jayānanda and mDo sde dpal (twelfth century), which is: *gang la stong pa nyid srid pa / / de la don rnams thams srid / / gang la stong nyid mi srid pa / / de la ci yang mi srid do //.* The Sanskrit is (Lindtner 1997b, 217): *prabhavati ca śūnyateyaṃ yasya prabhavanti tasya sarvārthāḥ / prabhavati na tasya kiṃ cin na prabhavati śūnyatā yasya //.*

501. *Satyadvayāvatāra,* v. 18 (Ejima 1983, 365): *cung zad thos pa la brten te / / rnam par dben don mi shes shing / / mi gang bsod nams mi byed pa / / skyes bu tha shal de dag brlag / / stong pa nyid la blta nyes na / / shes rab chung ldan phung bar 'gyur //.* As noted by Lindtner 1981, 198n18, v. 18a–d resembles *Yuktiṣaṣṭikā* 31 (Scherer-Schaub 1991, 12–13): *rnam par dben don mi shes la / / thos pa tsam la 'jug byed cing / / gang rnams bsod nams mi byed pa / / skyes bu tha shal de dag brlag //.* Scherrer-Schaub (1991, 246n474) points out that this verse is cited in the *Madhyamakālaṃkārapañjikā* of Kamalaśīla (Ichigō 1985, 278–79). Lindtner 1981, 202n29 references a related stanza from the *Subhāṣitasaṃgraha* (vol. 23, pt. 2, 46): *evam ajñātatattvā ye śrutamātrāvalambinaḥ*

/ / naiva kurvanti puṇyāni hatās te buddhaśāsane //. Note that 18ef is the same as Tibetan *Mūlamadhyamakakārikā* 24.11ab: *stong pa nyid la blta nyes na / / shes rab chung ldan phung bar 'gyur*; Skt.: *vināśayati durdṛṣṭā śūnyatā mandamedhasam.*

502. *Śikṣāsamuccaya* (Skt., Bendall 1971, 327; Eng., Bendall and Rouse 1971, 291): *mālyavataṃsaka mālya vitānāḥ* . . . Citation is from the *Ārya ratnôlkādhāraṇī*. Also cited by Atiśa in the *Bodhipathapradīpapañjikā* (Sherburne 2000, 46).

503. *Satyadvayāvatāra*, v. 19 (Ejima 1983, 365–66): *slob dpon zla grags 'di skad du* {om. Ejima} *// thabs su gyur pa kun rdzob bden pa dang / / thabs las byung ba don dam bden pa dag / gnyis po'i dbye ba gang gis mi shes pa / / de dag log par rtogs pas ngan 'gror 'gro // 19 //*. *Madhyamakāvatāra*, 6.80 (La Vallée Poussin 1907–11, 175.3–6): *tha snyad bden pa thabs su gyur pa dang / / don dam bden pa thabs byung gyur pa ste / / de gnyis rnam dbye gang gis mi shes pa / / de ni rnam rtog log pas lam ngan zhugs // 6.80 //*. Cited in the *Subhāṣitasaṃgraha* (Bendall 1903, 396.7–10): *upāyabhūtaṃ vyavahārasatyam upeyabhūtaṃ paramārthasatyam / tayor vibhāgaṃ na paraiti yo vai mithyāvikalpaiḥ sa kumārgayātaḥ //*. As noted by Lindtner (1979, 89n13), this verse is also cited in the *Bodhisattvayogācāracatuḥśatakaṭīkā*, chap. 3 (Peking bstan 'gyur, vol. 98, *dbu ma Ya* 63a.1–2).

504. *Satyadvayāvatāra*, v. 20 (Ejima 1983, 365, vv. 20–21): *tha snyad la ni ma brten par / / dam pa'i don ni rtogs mi 'gyur / / yang dag kun rdzob rnams kyi skas / / med par yang dag khang chen gyi / steng du 'gro bar byed pa ni / / mkhas la rung ba ma yin no /*. The latter part corresponds with *Madhyamakahṛdaya* 3.12 (Toh 3855, vol. *dza*, 4a4): */ yang dag kun rdzob rnams kyi skas / / med par yang dag khang pa yi / / steng du 'gro bar bya ba ni / / mkhas la rung ba ma yin no // 12 //*. Skt. (Lindtner 2001, 8): *tattvaprāsādaśikharārohaṇaṃ na hi yujyate / tathyasaṃvṛtisopānam antareṇa yatas tataḥ // 12 //*.

505. *Mūlamadhyamakakārikā* 24.10cd (Toh 3824, vol. *tsa*, 15a2): *dam pa'i don ni ma rtogs par / / mya ngan 'das pa thob mi 'gyur /* Skt. (La Vallée Poussin 1903–13, 494.13): *paramārtham anāgamya nirvāṇaṃ nādhigamyate //*.

506. See Stein and McKeown 2010, 200, for references to the Tengyur and Dunhaung manuscript Tibetan versions of this verse from the *Prajñāśataka*. The Sanskrit for this verse is not extant. I do not have access to the critical edition of Hahn (1990).

507. *Satyadvayāvatāra*, v. 21 (Ejima 1983, 365): */ kun rdzob ji ltar snang ba 'di // rigs pas brtags na 'ga' mi rnyed // ma rnyed pa nyid don dam yin / ye nas gnas pa'i chos nyid do /*. On the "conventional that appears just as it is," see Eckel 1987, 110–11n7. The phrase *ji ltar snang ba = yathādarśana* also occurs in the *Madhyamakārthasaṃgraha* attributed to Bhāviveka; see Del Toso 2011, 360. The term *yathādarśana* may be a contracted form of *yathānudarśana* found in Dharmakīrti's *Pramāṇavarttika* 3.357ab, for which see Keira (2004, 38–46); Tillemans (2015, 2016).

508. The first half of the citation is found in the *Madhyamakaratnapradīpa* v. 9 (Toh 3854, vol. *tsha*, 261a): ***kun rdzob 'di ltar snang ba' di*** */ / rigs pas brtags na 'ga' mi rnyed / / ma rnyed pa nyid don dam yin / / de phyir kun rdzob shes par bya /*. Cf. Lindtner 1981, 173. The second half of the citation is from the *Madhyamakāvatāra* v. 28a (La Vallée Poussin 1907–12, 107): ***gti mug*** *rang bzhin sgrib phyir kun rdzob ste /*. However, the Kadampa author cites the half-verse as ***ma rig*** *rang bzhin sgrib phyir kun rdzob ste /*. This may reflect the use of an earlier translation of the *Madhyamakāvatāra* by the Kadampa author.

509. *Dbu ma'i mang ngag* reads *rdo rje zegs ma = rdo rje gzegs ma*; Skt. *vajra-kaṇa*. The

"diamond-splinters" reason (*rdo rje gzegs ma'i gtan tshigs= vajrakaṇahetu*) is one of five reasons for the nonexistence of any intrinsic nature of entities. See Keira 2004, 10–13; Mimaki 1982, 217–21. Atiśa will state four great reasons (*gtan tshigs chen po bzhi*) in his *Bodhimārgapradīpapañjikā* (Sherburne 2000, 230–36), including the reason refuting production according to the tetralemma (*mu bzhi skye 'gog gi gtan tshigs, catuṣkoṭyutpādapratiṣedhahetu*), the diamond-splinters reason (*rdo rje gzegs ma'i gtan tshigs, vajrakaṇahetu*), the reason of being neither one nor many (*gcig du bral gyi gtan tshigs, ekānekaviyogahetu*), and the reason consisting in dependent-arising (*rten 'brel gyi gtan tshigs, pratītyasamutpādahetu*). Atiśa leaves out the reason refuting the production of existent and nonexistent things (*yod med skye 'gog gi gtan tshigs, *sadasadutpādapratiṣedhahetu*) that is discussed by earlier Mādhyamikas like Kamalaśīla (Keira 2004, 13). See chapter 7 at folio 8a7 for an early Tibetan understanding of Atiśa's four great reasons.

510. See *Madhyamakāvatāra* 6.35. On the unfindable in Madhyamaka discourse, see T. Tillemans 2007, 509.

511. *Mūlamadhyamakakārikā* 1.1 (Toh 3824, vol. *tsa*, 1a3–2b1): *bdag las ma yin gzhan las min / / gnyis las ma yin rgyu med min / / dngos po gang dag gang na yang / / skye ba nam yang yod ma yin //*. La Vallée Poussin 1903–13, 12.13): *na svato nāpi parato na dvābhyāṃ nāpy ahetutaḥ / utpannā jātu vidyante bhāvāḥ kva cana ke cana //* 1 //.

512. Citation from *Śūnyatāsaptati* v. 4. Kadampa text reads: *yod pa yod pa'i phyir mi skye / / med pa med pa'i phyir mi skye /*. This citation does not match what is preserved in the Tengyur and may preserve an earlier Tibetan edition. Lindtner's critical edition (1997b, 94) of the *Śūnyatāsaptatikārikā* reads: *yod phyir yod pa skye min te / / med phyir med pa skye ma yin /*. The verse within the *Śūnyatāsaptativṛtti* reads (Lindtner 1997b, 177): *yod pa yod phyir skye ma yin / / med pa med pa'i phyir ma yin //*. See also Tola and Dragonetti 1987, 11.

513. *Satyadvayāvatāra*, v. 22ab (Ejima 1983, 366, v. 23ab): *rgyu rkyen dag gis bskyed pas na / / kun rdzob ji ltar snang ba grub //*.

514. *Satyadvayāvatāra*, vv. 22cd–23 (Ejima 1983, 366, vv. 23cd–24abcd): *gal te grub mi rung na / / chu zla la sogs su yis bskyed // 22 // des na rgyu rkyen sna tshogs kyis / / bskyed pas snang ba tham cad grub / / rkyen rnams rgyun ni chad gyur na / / kun rdzob tu yang mi 'byung ngo // 23 //*. Lindtner (1981, 198n23) notes last two lines from *Bodhicaryāvatāra* 9.15ab: *pratyayānāṃ tu vicchedāt saṃvṛtyāpi na saṃbhavaḥ*; Tib. (9.13).

515. As studied by Vose (2010b), this statement is related to the Tibetan interpretation of *Bodhicaryāvatāra* 9.15ab and a Buddha's awareness of appearances. The interpretation of this verse develops into distinct classifications of Madhyamaka in eleventh-to-thirteenth-century Tibet. Ngok Loden Sherap's student Gyamar Jangchup drak posits two Mādhyamika groups: "those who assert that wisdom has its continuum cut" and "those [who assert] that wisdom does not have its continuum cut." For the first group, Gyamar states: "Some Mādhyamikas assert that since all awareness is mistaken, when mistake is exinguished awareness itself does not exist and thus wisdom has its continuum cut; "even conventionally" wisdom does not exist" (Vose 2010b, 305). A similar statement to this concerning what a Buddha perceives will be interpreted as a Prāsaṅgika position by Sönam Tsemo (1142–82). Vose (2010b, 313) also notes that Sönam Tsemo's younger brother Drakpa Gyaltsen discusses divisions within "utterly non-abiding" Madhyamaka in terms of "Continuum Cutting Utterly Non-Abiding [Mādhyamikas] (*rgyun chad rab tu mi gnas pa*)" and "Union Utterly Non-Abiding [Mādhyamikas] (*zung 'jug rab tu mi gnas pa*)."

516. *Satyadvayāvatāra*, v. 24 (Ejima, 1983, 367, v. 25): */ de ltar lta bas ma rmongs shing / / spyod pa shing tu dag gyur na / / gol ba'i lam du mi 'gro shing / / 'og min gnas su 'gro bar 'gyur // 24 //.*
517. Unidentified citation.
518. *Suhṛllekha*, v. 50a. See Klong-chen ye-shes-rdo-rje and Nāgārjuna 2005, 46–47: *phung po 'dod rgyal las min dus las min / / rang bzhin las min ngo bo nyid las min / / dbang phyug las min rgyu med can min te / / mi shes las dang sred las byung rig mdzod //.* "The aggregates are not a simple whim, from neither time nor nature do they come, nor by themselves, from God, or without a cause; their source, you ought to know, is ignorance, from karmic deeds and craving have they come."
519. *Pratītyasamutpādahṛdayakārikā*, v. 4 (Jamieson 2000, 49): *Dbu ma'i man ngag: 'gro kun rgyu dang 'bras bu ste / / 'di na* {var. *la*} *sems can gzhan* {om. *gzhan*} *ci yang med / stong pa kho na'i chos rnams las / / stong pa'i chos rnams 'byung bar* {var. *ba*} *zad /.* Skt.: *hetuphalañca hi jagat prajñaptiṃ vihāya anyo nāsti kaścidiha sattvaḥ / śūnyebhya eva śūnyā dharmāḥ prabhavanti dharmebhyaḥ.* See La Vallée Poussin 1913, 122–24; Gokhale 1955; Sastri 1968; Lindtner 1982.
520. *Satyadvayāvatāra*, v. 25 (Ejima, 1983, 367, v. 26): *tshe ni yun thung shes bya'i rnam pa mang / / tshe yi kyang ji tsam mi shes pas / / ngang pa chu la 'o ma len pa ltar / rang gi 'dod pa dang la blang bar gyis // 25 //.* Also cited by Atiśa in his *Bodhipathapradīpa* (Sherburne 2000, 236–37) with slight difference in the Tibetan.
521. Also known as the five sciences (*pañcavidyā*): linguistic science (*śabda*), logical science (*hetu*), "inner" science (*adhyātma*), medical science (*cikitsā*), and the science of fine arts and crafts (*śilapakarmasthāna*). Mahāvyutpatti, 1554–59.
522. *Mahāyānasūtrālaṃkāra* 11.60 (Lévi 1907, 70): *vidyāsthāne pañcavidhe yogam akṛtvā sarvajñātvaṃ naiti kathaṃcit paramāryaḥ / ity anyeṣāṃ nigrahaṇānugrahaṇāya svājñārthaṃ vā tatra karoty eva sa yogam.* See Gold 2007, 109.
523. For the simile of the goose that can separate milk out of water, see *Mahāyānasamgraha*, chap. 1, v. 49.
524. This sentence refers to the practice of pulse reading in traditional Tibetan medicine.
525. Tib. *skyes bu gsum gyi rim pa sbyang ba.* This refers to the typology of training discussed in Atiśa's *Bodhipathapradīpa* (vv. 2–5) that is followed by Kadampa and later by Gelukpa traditions. These consist of persons of small scope (who seek higher rebirth), intermediate scope (who seek individual liberation), and great scope (who seek buddhahood for the sake of all beings). See Sherburne 2000, 5, 27–31.
526. "Four-three-twelve" (*bzhi gsum bcu gnyis*) is a special expression found in Kagyüpa (Bka' brgyud) works. See, for example, Losang Chökyi Nyima 2009, 136.
527. *Satyadvayāvatāra*, v. 26 (Ejima 1983, 367, v. 27): *tshu rol mthong ba'i rmongs pa dag gis ni / bden gnyis gtan la dbab par mi nus kyang / / bla ma rnams kyi gsung la brten nas ni / klu sgrub lugs ki bden gnyis bkod pa 'di // 25 //.*
528. *Satyadvayāvatāra*, v. 27 (Ejima 1983, 367, v 28): *gser gling rgyal po'i ngor byas 'di la ni / / gal te ding sang skye bo dad gyur kyang / / legs par brtags la blang bar bya ba yi / / dad pa tsam dang gus pa tsam gyis min // 27 //.* Translated by Lindtner 1981, 196.
529. MSA 8.9ab (Lévi 1907, 29): ***sudharmatāyuktivicāraṇāśayo viśeṣalābhaḥ parapakṣadūṣaṇam*** */ punaḥ sadā māranirantarāyatā ahāryatāyāḥ paripākalakṣaṇam // 9 //.* Tib. (Toh 4020, vol. *phi*, 7b7–8a1): *chos bzangs rigs pas rnam dpyad bsam pa can // rtag tu bdud kyi bar chad byed pa med / khyad par rnyed dang gzhan gyi phyogs sun 'byin // mi 'phrogs yongs su smin pa'i mtshan nyid do //.* Lévi (1911, 62): "Tendance à critiquer les Raisonnements sur la bonne Idéalité, profit tout-particulier,

affaiblissement de l'Aile adverse, impuissance perpétuelle des Démons à faire obstacle, tel est l'Indice de la Per-maturation d'Inébranlabilité."

530. *Satyadvayāvatāra*, v. 28 (Ejima 1983, 368, v. 29): *gser gling rgyal po gu ru pha la yis / dge slong de ba ma ti btang gyur nas / / de yi ngor byas bden gnyis la 'jug 'di / / ding sang mkhas pa rnams kyis brtags par rigs // 28 //.*
531. The mental purification method of "exchanging self and others" (*parātma-parivārtana, bdag dang gzhan du brje ba*) is considered a private practice of Atiśa and his principal disciples and is based on the eighth chapter of the *Bodhicaryāvatāra* (8.120–31); see Sweet 1996. The Kadampa author is also influenced by the *Bodhicaryāvatāra* (10.51) in his dedication to arrive at the "stage of delight" (*pramuditāṃ bhūmiṃ*).
532. *Collected Works of Atiśa* (751): *+a ti shas gsungs pa yin no /.* I cite the page and line number of the 2006 edited version of the text throughout my analysis and translation of the work, noting any differences with the manuscript's facsimile (2009).
533. *Collected Works of Atiśa* (697): *'di jo bo'i gsung dngos min /.*
534. See chapter 1 for translation; see also Miyazaki 2007b, 7 and Apple 2010, 126–27, for philological details.
535. See Krasser 2011b and Del Toso 2014 for the characteristics of oral notes taken by students of Bhāviveka.
536. In the analysis of texts, the principle of embarrassment is "when an author reveals, in the course of a discussion, something that is quite unflattering to the group or the position that he or she represents . . ." (Nattier 2003, 65–66). The following statements are unlikely to have been advocated by a Tibetan author who was *polemically writing* on Atiśa's thought. Rather, the statements are a record of what was *orally transmitted* by Atiśa without his awareness of their unflattering content.
537. See Mimaki 1992, 32–33, on the doxographic position of bodhisattvas who maintain a single mental consciousness, and Brunnhölzl 2007, 380–82, note 342, for the historical complexities of classifying this position by Tibetan Buddhist doxographers after the eleventh century.
538. See Ruegg 2000 for a historical overview of the reception of Madhyamaka in Tibet and notes (9,17) on Indo-Madhyamaka lineages. Jackson (1985) describes early Madhyamaka studies among the Sa-skya-pa and also provides lineages lists for Tsongkhapa and Mkhas grub that demonstrate that the Madhyamaka teachings for these figures descend from Patsap Nyimadrak.
539. According to Lechen Kunga Gyaltsen (2003, 97), Atiśa spent thirteen years in Tibet, including the first three at Ngari, four years in places other than Ü-Tsang, and six years in Nyethang (*de ltar na jo bos mnga' ris su lo gsum/ dbus gtsang gzhan du lo bzhi/ snye thang du lo drug ste/ bod du lo bcu gsum 'gro ba'i don mdzad nas / . . .* See also Chattopadhyaya 1967, 330–66; and Vetturini 2013, 89.
540. Lechen Kunga Gyaltsen (2003, 132–33): */ de'i du su dge bsnyen rnam pa gnyis skad pa / pu rangs gyi rgya brtson 'grus shes rab dang / ljang dar ma blo gros gnyis kyis lo chen la jo bo'i bde mchog zhus pas ma gnang . . . de nas dge bsnyen gnyis pos dbus su byon / de'i dus na rgya lcags ri gong kha ba de lha sa na bskor ba mdzad cing bzhugs //.*
541. Mikyö Dorjé (2004, 9b, [*pha dgu*, 9.3]): */ brgyud tshul gnyis pa ni / slob dpon klu / ārya de ba / zla grags / rig pa'i khu byug che chung sogs nas jo bo a ti sha / dge ba'i bshes gnyen ston pa chen po / de sras spyan snga ba dang bya yul pa sogs bka' gdams kyi bla ma du ma la rje sgam po pas gsan pa dang / yang na pu to ba nas drang srong chen po sha ra*

ba / des dpal ldan du gsum mkhyen pa / de phyin 'dra'o //. Ruegg, 1988, reprinted in Ruegg 2010, 337.

542. Lechen Kunga Gyaltsen 2003, 11.4–20: *bden pa gnyis kyi 'khrid kyis ni shin tu phra ba'i chos kyi bdag med pa la 'khrid par mdzad pa yin no / / jo bo'i slob ma bden gnyis la shin tu mkhas pa ni rnal 'byor pa chen po yin la / des dge bshes stod lung pa dang / spyan snga rnal 'byor gyi dbang phyug gnyis la gsungs / spyan sngas kyang stod lung pa dang / bya yul ba gnyis la lkog chos su mdzad do / / des na bden pa gnyis la mkhas par gyur pa ni stod lung pa chen po yin / des bden pa gnyis po tshogs su'ang gsungs / lkog chos su yang bstan / brtsams chos kyang mang du mdzad pa las / bden gnyis kyi brtsams chos phal che ba btsan gro dgon pa'i gtsug lag khang gi sgrom du bzhugs / de'i slob ma khyung kham gyis gtsang du byon te / bden gnyis kyi chos mang du gsungs te man ngag kyang dar bar mdzad / sangs rgyas dbon gyis mdzad pa'i bden gnyis kyi bshad pa'ang rgyas bsdus mang du yod par snang / gzhan yang stod lung pa dang / bya yul ba'i man ngag gnyis ka mnga' ba / phu dang bka' gdams pas bden gnyis kyi yig 'jog mang du mdzad te / de rnams ni lta ba'i man ngag go //*.

543. The system of the "five paths" is one the best-known among path schemes found in Buddhist literature. The system is associated with Abhidharma traditions, although its exact historial beginnings are not clear. The five paths are (1) the path of accumulating the provisions (*tshogs lam, saṃbhāramārga*), (2) the path of preparation (*sbyor lam, prayogamārga*), (3) the path of vision (*mthong lam, darśanamārga*), (4) the path of meditation (*sgom lam, bhāvanāmārga*), and (5) and the path of no more training (*mi slob pa'i lam, aśaikṣamārga*).

544. *A General Explanation's* citation of twelve of Nāgārjuna's works are as follows (noted according to 2006 printed edition): *Pratītyasamutpādavyākhyākārikā* (700.15, 715.22, 726.18, 740.8), *Dharmadhātustava* (702.2), *Mūlamadhyamakakārikā* (705.15, 718.2, 724.10, 739.20, 740.1, 742.10, 748.10), *Yuktiṣaṣṭikā* (707.16, 709.17, 711.10, 731.1, 742.15, 743.25), *Suhṛllekha* (707.18, 747.5, 749.4), *Vigrahavyāvartanī* (708.22, 739.28), *Cittavajrastava* (710.1, 745.17), *Mahāyānaviṃśikā* (711.15), *Bhāvanākrama* (711.18, 745.10), *Ratnāvalī* (724.12, 734, 748.13), *Bodhicittavivaraṇa* (728.25, 745.20, 746.15, 748.5, 748.22, 750.16), and *Stutyatītastava* (738.20, 746.10).

545. See chapter 1, section 5, "The Teachings of Nāgārjuna."

546. I have translated *rab rib* (*timira, taimira*) as "eye disease" and *rab rib can* (*taimirika*) as "one with eye disease" throughout, although as recently suggested by Higgins (2013, 125n318), *rab rib* describes the optic condition known as myodesopsia, or "floaters." *General Explanation* (particularly 740.7–743.8) repeatedly employs this parable based on the works of Candrakīrti (e.g., MABH *ad* MA 6.29) and Atiśa's works and sayings. *General Explanation* also states that Nāgārjuna discusses *timira*, although the only work attributed to Nāgārjuna that mentions *timira* is his *Bhāvanākrama* (Lindtner 1992, 268–69).

547. In *General Explanation* the term "Great Madhyamaka" (*dbu ma chen po*) occurs twice (697.25, 699.19) and indicates the definitive understanding of Nāgārjuna's thought. The term occurs five times in Atiśa's BMPP (D 258b4–7, 280a5–6, 280a7, 281a4–5, 283a1) and once in his *Sūtrārthasamuccyopadeśa* (D 3957, 305b2). According to Mochizuki's analysis (2007, 117–20), the expression is employed by Atiśa to integrate Madhyamaka and Yogācāra understandings of emptiness. Note though, that the MRP, which Atiśa used to teach Madhyamaka in India and had his disciples translate into Tibetan, explicitly refers to the thought of Nāgārjuna as "Great Madhyamaka" (D 268a2–3, 277b4, 279a3). As van der Kuijp (1983, 37) notes, the

term becomes a polemical one in early Tibetan scholasticism and its meaning is dependent on the context in which it is being used.

548. The classifications "Consequentialist" (*thal 'gyur ba*, **prāsaṅgika*) and "Autonomist" (*rang rgyud pa*, *svātantrika*) were not current at the time of the composition and transmission of the *General Explanation*. Dreyfus and Tsering (2010, 393–94) have found evidence in recently recovered works of Patsap Nyimadrak for the term *thal 'gyur ba* (**prāsaṅgika*). The term *svātantrika* (*rang rgyud pa*) occurs in the work of Jayānanda (*Madhyamakāvatāraṭīkā*, D 281b6, 282a3, 337a8, 337b6; Nagashima 2004, 65), but this is several decades after the time of the *General Explanation*. Tibetan historical accounts mention that after Patsap returned from India his teachings on **prāsaṅgika* did not initially gain followers (Lang 1990). The accounts mention that Sharawa Yönten Drak sent his disciples to study Madhyamaka under Patsap. A recently published manuscript of a *lam rim* by Sharawa (2014) does not utilize these classifications of Madhyamaka in its articulation of the two realities, which is mainly based on the works of Śāntarakṣita and Kamalaśīla. The earliest occurrence of the term *thal 'gyur ba* (**prāsaṅgika*) I have so far noted among works in the Bka'-gdam-pa gsung-'bum is found in the *grub mtha' chen mo* of Ja Chékawa Yeshé Dorjé (Bya 'chad kha ba ye shes rdo rje, 1101–75); see Kapstein 2009 for preliminary remarks on this text. This may indicate that Patsap's Madhyamaka teachings spread slowly outside his circle of direct disciples, such as Shangthak sakpa (Yoshimizu 2005), and that the classificaton *thal 'gyur ba* (**prāsaṅgika*) (which is not used by Shangthak sakpa) did not gain traction in Tibet until the mid-twelfth century.

549. *A General Explanation's* understanding of ultimate reality challenges the prevalent modern refrain that "the ultimate truth is that there is no ultimate truth" (Siderits 2007, 182), followed by numerous contemporary interpretations of Indian Madhyamaka.

550. In this series of citations, the author misattributes a citation from Candrakīrti's *Madhyamakāvatāra* to Nāgārjuna's *Prajñāmūla*, as well as a citation from Bhāviveka's *Madhyamakahṛdaya* to the *Tarkajvālā*. Note, however, that the name *Tarkajvālā* was used for the verses alone based on the colophon of the Sanskrit manuscript of the MHK (Lindtner 2001, 110). In citing Candrakīrti's *Madhyamakāvatāra* (6.79), the author gives the significant variant reading "They have fallen from correct conventional reality" (*de ni yang dag kun rdzob bden las nyams*) rather than "They have fallen from the realities, conventional and suchness" (*de dag kun rdzob de nyid bden las nyams*).

551. The term *śuddhalaukika* appears in Vasubandhu's *Viṃśikāvṛtti* (*ad* v.17cd) as well as in Sthiramati's *Mahāyānasūtrālaṃkāravṛttibhāṣya* (D'Amato 2009, 43–44). See Makransky 1997, 97–100, 351–53, 444–45, for an overview of this concept in classical Yogācāra works; see Arnold 2003, 31, for Vasubandhu's remarks; and see Schmithausen 2015, 54–56, on Hsüan-tsang's *Ch'eng wei shih lun* regarding this concept in Yogācāra thought.

552. *Bden gnyis spyi bshad dang / bden gnyis 'jog tshul*. The editors of the dbu-can version (2006, 697) have added the phrase, "This is not actually spoken by the Lord [Atiśa]" (*'di jo bo'i gsung dngos min*), which is not found in the facsimile of the manuscript.

553. *Madhyamakāvatāra* 6.25 (La Vallée Poussin 1907–12, 104.4–7). Kadampa text citation differs: *gnod pa med pa'i dbang po drug rnams kyis / / gzung ba gang zhig 'jig rten*

gyis rtogs te / / lo ka {Poussin, *'jig rten*} *nyid la* {*las*} *bden yin lhag ma ni / / lo ka* {LVP, *'jig rten*} *nyid la* {*las*} *log pa rnam par gzhag /*. Skt. (Li 2012, 6; 2014): *vinopaghātena yad indriyāṇāṃ ṣaṇṇām api grāhyam avaiti lokaḥ / satyaṃ hi tal lokata eva śeṣaṃ vikalpitaṃ lokata eva mithyā //*.

554. *Satyadvayavibhaṅgakārikā*, v. 12ab, Eckel (1987, 79, Tib. 163): *snang du 'dra yang don byed dag / nus pa'i phyir dang mi nus phyir /*.

555. *zag pa med pa'i dge ba'i rtsa ba gsum* ≈ *anāsravāṇi kuśalamūlāni triṇī*. Candrakīrti's *Pañcaskandhaprakaraṇa* (Lindtner 1979, 124–25) discusses the three roots of virtue (*dge ba'i rtsa ba sum*) as nonattachment (*ma chags pa, alobha*), nonhatred (*zhe sdang med pa, adveṣa*), and nonignorance (*gti mug med pa, amoha*). Uncontaminated roots of virtue (*anāsravāṇi kuśalamūlāni*) are discussed in the *Prajñāpāramitā* literature. However, it is not clear what exactly constitutes the three uncontaminated roots of virtue mentioned in the text.

556. Eight similes of illusion (*aṣṭamāyopamā*, Tib. *sgyu ma'i dpe brgyad*). The eight are said to be a twinkling star (*skar mar*), optical illusion (*rab rib*), lamp (*mar me*), dream (*rmi lam*), flash of lightning (*glog*), moon in the water (*chu zla*), mirage (*smig rgyu*), and cloud (*sprin*). Discussed in Atiśa's *Open Basket of Jewels*; see also Ruegg 1966, 99n2.

557. *Madhyamakāvatāra* 6.28. Kadampa citation matches La Vallée Poussin (1907–12, 107.1–4): *gti mug rang bzhin sgrib phyir kun rdzob ste / des gang bcos ma bden par snang de ni / kun rdzob bden zhes thub pa des gsungs te / / bcos mar gyur pa'i dngos ni kun rdzob tu'o /*. Translation in Huntington 1989, 160; Dunne 1996, 541–42; Skt., BCAP, 171 (Li 2014): *mohaḥ svabhāvāvaraṇād dhi saṃvṛtiḥ satyaṃ tayā khyāti yad eva kṛtrimam / jagāda tat saṃvṛtisatyam ity asau muniḥ padārthaṃ kṛtakañ ca saṃvṛtiḥ //*.

558. The two types of karmic actions, mental formations (*saṃskāra, 'du byed*) and becoming (*bhava, srid pa*), are mentioned in Nāgārjuna's *Pratītyasamutpādahṛdayakārikā*, vv. 2–3.

559. "Gradual stages of the path of the three kinds of individuals" (*skyes bu gsum lam rim*). Atiśa in his BPP (vv. 2–5) and BMPP (D 242a–243a) outlines three types of persons: the individual of narrow scope (*adhamapuruṣa, skyes bu chung ngu*) who seeks the pleasures of *saṃsāra*, the individual of middling scope (*madhyamapuruṣa, skyes bu 'bring*) who seeks peace from *saṃsāra* (i.e., *śrāvakas* and *pratyekabuddhas*), and the individual of superior scope (*mchog*) who seeks to end the suffering of others (i.e., *bodhisattvas*).

560. A hierarchical model in which awarenesses are ranked higher and lower based on the understanding that yogic awareness invalidates the awareness of ordinary individuals is found in Candrakīrti (MA 6.30) and Śāntideva (BCA 9.3–4ab); see Wangchuk 2009, 232–33.

561. *med na mi 'byung ba, avinābhāva*; Cf. Bhāviveka, *Prajñāpradīpa ad* 13.4cd (Nietupski 1996, 118n61).

562. Bhāviveka is the first known Mādhyamika to use "nonimplicative negation" (*prasajyapratiṣedha, med dgag pa*) and "implicative negation" (*paryudāsapratiṣedha, ma yin par dgag pa*) to distinguish two types of negation (Ames 2003, 51). *Prasajyapratiṣedha* is a simple negation of a proposition without any further implications. *Paryudāsapratiṣedha* implies the opposite of what is negated (see Nietupski 1996, 108n14 for references). In the *Prajñāpradīpa* (D 48b), Bhāviveka states that

such nonimplicative negations are employed "to establish nonconceptual wisdom (*nirvikalpakajñāna*), which is endowed with all cognizable objects (*jñeyaviṣaya*), by negating the net of all conceptual constructions (*kalpanā*)" (Ames 2003, 51).

563. Nāgārjuna, *Pratītyasamutpādahṛdayakārikā* 4cd (Jamieson 2000, 49): *stong pa kho na'i chos rnams las // stong pa'i chos rnams 'byung bar zad //*. Skt., BCAP (Vaidya 1960, 172, 248): *śūnyebhya eva śūnyā dharmāḥ prabhavanti dharmebhyaḥ*. MRP (Toh 3854, vol. *tsha*, 272a1).

564. Text emended to *brjod byed* (signifier) from *brjod bya* (signified) for consistency with earlier section.

565. *Dharmadhātustava*, Toh 1118, vol. *ka*, 64b7–65a2, vv. 30–33ac: [30] *ji* {Bka'-gdams text *ri*} *ltar ri bong mgo yi* {*mgo'i*} *rwa / / brtags* {*btags*} *pa nyid de med pa ltar / / de bzhin chos rnams thams cad kyang / / brtags* {*btags*} *pa nyid de yod ma yin /* [31] */ phra rab rdul gyi ngo bo yis / / glang gi rwa yang dmigs* {*yod*, Kadam, N, P} *ma yin / / ji ltar sngon bzhin phyis de bzhin / de* {65a} *la ci zhig brtag par bya /* [32] *brten* {*rten*} *nas 'byung bar gyur pa dang / / brten* {*rten*} *nas 'gag par 'gyur bas na / / gcig kyang yod pa ma yin na / / byis pa ji ltar rtog par byed /* [33] */ ri bong ba glang* {missing *glang*} *rwa yi dpes / / ji ltar bde gshegs chos rnams nyid / / dbu ma nyid du sgrub par byed /*. Skt. (Kano 2015, 192): [30] *yathā śaśaviṣāṇaṃ hi kalpyamānaṃ na vidyate / tathā hi sarvadharmeṣu kalpitaṃ naiva vidyate //* [31] *paramāṇurajaḥ kin tu goviṣāṇaṃ na vidyate / yathā pūrvaṃ tathā paścāt tasya kiṃ kalpyate budhaiḥ //* [32] *pratītyotpadyate caiva pratītya ca nirudhyate / ekasya sambhavo nāsti kathaṃ bālair vikalpyate //* [33] *śaśagośṛṅgadṛṣṭāntāv ubhau kalpitalakṣaṇau / madhyamāṃ pratipadyeta yathā sugatadharmatā //*. See also Liu 2015, 14–15; Brunnhölzl 2007.

566. *don dam rtog ge'i yul min par / / rgyal ba sras bcas nges par bzhed / / tshad ma tha snyad pa nyid du / / mkhas pa thams cad 'dod pa yin //*. Unidentified verse.

567. See *Vigrahavyāvartanī* (vv. 30–32) and *Vigrahavyāvartanīvṛtti* (Toh 3832, vol. *tsa*, 128b6; Bhattacharya 1978, 15–16).

568. *Satyadvayāvatāra*, vv. 15–16ab: *stong nyid gang gis rtogs shes na / / de bzhin gshegs pas lung bstan zhin / / chos nyid bden pa gzigs pa yi / / klu sgrub slob ma zla grags yin / / de las brgyud pa'i man ngag gis / / chos nyid bden pa rtogs par 'gyur / /*.

569. See chap. 1, section 5.2, "Nāgārjuna's Predicted Buddhahood," for citations from these texts as sources for the Buddha's prediction of Nāgārjuna.

570. Rongpa Gargewasel (Rong pa 'Gar dge ba gsal, eleventh century) was a lay disciple of Atiśa who received the teachings of the *brāhmaṇa* Jitāri and other teachings from Atiśa in Mang yul, Chim, Nyethang, and Samyé (Vetturini 2013, 24, 98).

571. Ratna Chakriwa (Ratna Lcags ri gong kha ba Byang chub dpal) most likely refers to Gya Chakri Gongkawa Jangchup Pal, an eleventh-century Kadampa master who was one of Gampopa's teachers.

572. Kadampa author cites old Tibetan version of MMK 15.1–2, which matches *Akutobhayā* but differs from Tengyur, and reads: *ngo bo nyid ni rgyu rkyen las / 'byung ba rigs pa ma yin te / rgyu dang rkyen las byung ba'i / ngo bo nyid ni byas par 'gyur / / ngo bo nyid ni byas pa zhes / / ji lta bur na 'thad par 'gyur / / ngo bo nyid ni bcos min zhing / / gzhan la ltos pa yod ma yin /*. Tengyur (Huntington 1986, 386–87) reads: */ rang bzhin rgyu dang rkyen las ni / / 'byung bar rigs pa ma yin* <u>*no*</u> */ /rgyu dang rkyen las* <u>*gang byung ba'i*</u> */ / r*<u>*ang bzhin byas pa can du*</u> *'gyur / /* <u>*rang bzhin*</u> *byas* <u>*pa can zhes byar*</u> */ / ci ltar bur na* <u>*rung bar*</u> *'gyur / /* <u>*rang bzhin dag ni*</u> *bcos min* <u>*dang*</u> */ / gzhan la ltos pa* <u>*med pa yin*</u> */*. Skt. (La Vallée Poussin 1903–13, 259–60): *na saṃbhavaḥ svabhāvasya*

yuktaḥ pratyayahetubhiḥ / hetupratyayasaṃbhūtaḥ svabhāvaḥ kṛtako bhavet //15.1// svabhāvaḥ kṛtako nāma bhaviṣyati punaḥ katham / akṛtrimaḥ svabhāvo hi nirapekṣaḥ paratra ca // 15.2 //.

573. Actually from *Laṅkāvatāra* II, v. 138 (Tib. D 88b7, P 97b3–4); Skt. II.140 (Nanjio 1923, 84): *na hy atrotpadyate kiṃ cit pratyayair na nirudhyate / utpadyante nirudhyante pratyayā eva kalpitāḥ //.* Cited by Śāntarakṣita MAK (see Ichigo 1989, 155, 227–28n7. Mimaki 1982, 167–69n458).
574. In the following section the author explains that the reasoning of dependent-arising (*rten 'grel gyi rigs pa*) contains within it both the four reasonings (*yukticatuṣṭayam*) found in the MSABH *ad* MSA 19.46 and the four great reasons (*hetu*) of the Madhyamaka mentioned in MAS v. 6 (Lindtner 1981, 200n14) and explained by Atiśa in his BPP and BMPP (see following note).
575. Atiśa in his *Bodhipathapradīpa* (Toh 3947, vol. *khi*, 240a5–7) and the *Bodhipathapradīpapañjikā* (Toh 3948, vol. *khi*, 279a3–280a4; Sherburne 2000, 229–36) outlines "four great reasons" *(gtan tshigs chen po bzhi)* proving emptiness, that is, (1) the reason refuting production according to the tetralemma (*mu bzhi skye 'gog gi gtan tshigs*; *catuṣkoṭyupādapratiṣedhahetu*), (2) the "diamond-splinters" reason (*rdo rje gzegs ma'i gtan tshigs*; *vajrakaṇahetu*), (3) the reason of being neither one nor many (*gcig du bral gyi gtan tshigs*; *ekānekaviyogahetu*), and (4) the reason consisting in dependent origination (*rten 'brel gyi gtan tshigs*; *pratītyasamutpādahetu*). However, in the following sentences the Kadampa author includes the reason refuting the production of existent things and nonexistent things (*yod med skye 'gog gi gtan tshigs*; **sadasadutpādapratiṣedhahetu*) in place of the reason refuting production according to the tetralemma.
576. An inference that is known to others (*gzhan la grags pa'i rjes dpag*), or an other-acknowledged inference (*paraprasiddhānumāna*), is an inference in which the subject and reason are established for the opponent but not for the Mādhyamika (Yoshimizu 2013, 419). The term *gzhan la grags pa'i rjes dpag* is found in Shangthak Sakpa's *dBu ma tshig gsal gyi ti ka* (twelfth century; Yoshimizu 2014, 53) and also in the work of Mapja Jangchup Tsöndrü (d. 1185) (Doctor 2014, 138–39). This occurrence in *A General Explanation* may be the earliest recorded in Tibetan Madhyamaka literature and suggests that it was a term employed by Atiśa. The concept is formative for later Tibetans to formulate the so-called distinction between (*thal 'gyur ba*, **prāsaṅgika*) and *rang rgyud pa* (*svātantrika*); see Dreyfus and McClintock 2003.
577. As noted by Pascale Hugon (personal communication), this paragraph may be the earliest extant mention of four types of consequence used by Mādhyamikas. The four types of consequence are (1) consequences that composes contradictions (*'gal ba brjod pa'i thal 'gyur*, **virodhacodanāprasaṅga*), (2) the inference that is known to others (*gzhan la grags pa'i rjes dpag*; see previous note), (3) [the evidence that is] not established due to the equivalance with what is being established (*bsgrub bya dang mtshungs pa'i ma grub pa*), and (4) equivalence of the reason (Kadam manuscript reads *mgo bsgre ba*, in later Tibetan commentaries the term is *'go snyom*). I thank Pascale Hugon for suggestions in revising my translation.
578. These four reasonings are from texts affiliated with Maitreya-Asaṅga (Wangchuk 2009, 217–18) and are elucidated in the MSABH based on MSA 19.43–46 (Eltchinger 2010, 567–74).

579. *Yuktiṣaṣṭikā*, v. 1. Kadampa manuscript reads: *gang blo yod dang med pa las / / rnam par 'das shing mi gnas pa / / de dag zab mo dmigs med pa'i* {var. *yi*} / / *rkyen gyi don la rnam par bsgsoms* /. The citation of this verse is from the Tibetan translation by *Ye shes sde* (ninth century) of the commentary, the *Yuktiṣaṣṭikāvṛtti* of Candrakīrti. The Tibetan translation by Patsap Nyimadrak of this verse from the *Yuktiṣaṣṭikā* differs. See Scherrer-Schaub 1991, 7, 24–25. The verse is preserved in Sanskrit in the *Sekoddeśaṭīkā* (Scherrer-Schaub 1991, 116n42): *asti-nāsti-vyatikrāntā buddhir yeṣāṃ nirāśraya / gambhīras tair nirālambaḥ pratyayārtho vibhāyate* /. The Tibetan of the verse is also cited in MRP (D 274b1–2).

580. *Suhṛllekha* (v. 112), Klong chen ye shes rdo rje 2005, 70–71. Kadampa manuscript reads: *rten cing 'brel par 'byung 'di rgyal ba yin* {Tengyur *yi*} / /*gsung gi mdzod kyi gces pa zab mo ste* / / *gang gis 'di ni yang dag mthong des* / / *des ni sangs rgyas* {Tengyur *sangs rgyas de nyid*} *rig pa rnam mchog mthong* //.

581. *Satyadvayāvatāra* (SDA) v. 16ab (Ejima 1983, 365): *de las brgyud pa'i man ngag gis / / chos nyid bden pa rtogs par 'gyur* / /.

582. Mapja Jangchup Tsöndrü (d. 1185) (see Doctor 2010, 438; 2014, 33), and later Tsongkhapa (1357–1419) in his *Lam rim chen mo* (Cutler et al. 2002, 203; Tsongkhapa 1985, 651), make a distinction between objects negated by the path (*lam gyi dgag bya*) and objects negated by reason (*rigs pa'i dgag bya*).

583. *Vigrahavyāvartanī*, v. 63. Kadampa citation: *dgag bya ci'ang med pas na* / / *nga* {Tengyur *da*} *ni ci yang mi 'gog go* / *de phyir 'gog par byed do zhes* / <u>*khyod ni nga la skur ba 'debs*</u> /. Jñānagarbha and Paltsek Rakṣita, *Rtsod pa bzlog pa'i 'grel pa* (Tibetan translation of *Vigrahavyāvartanīvṛtti*), in Toh 3832, vol. *tsa*, 121a4–137a7: *dgag bya ci yang med pas na* / / *da ni ci yang mi 'gog go* / / *de phyir 'gog par byed do zhes* / / *skur pa de ni khyod kyis btab* //. Bhattacharya 1978, 41: *kiṃ cānyat / pratiṣedhyāmi nāhaṃ kiṃcit pratiṣedhyam asti na ca kiṃcit / tasmāt pratiṣedhayasīty adhilaya eṣa tvayā kriyate* // 63 //.

584. See Tillemans 2004 and Tanji 2000 on superimpositions (*samāropa*) that are refuted by Mādhyamikas. Note, however, that in *A General Explanation* things themselves are either deceptive appearances that perpetuate *saṃsāra* or mere appearances that are necessary falsities (*mṛṣā*) that lead to awakening (*bodhi*).

585. *Caryāgīti* (*spyod pa'i glu*) (Toh 1496, vol. *zha*, 215b6–7): *rab rib can gyis* {Tengyur, *ji ltar*} *mkha' la skra mthong* {*dang*} / *rnam rtog lo ka pa rab rib* {*rab rib 'jig rten*} *mthong la khyad par med* / *rnam rtog skyes pa mkha' dang mnyam pa'i rang bzhin du* / {*rnam rtog* <u>*rang bzhin*</u> *mkha' dang mnyam pa'i rang bzhin du*} *btags pa'i dngos po ma lus pa dag bsgom par bya'o* {*brtags pa'i* <u>*rang bzhin*</u> *ma lus pa dag bsgom par* <u>*gyis*</u>}. See also Sherburne 2000, 408–9.

586. *Yuktiṣaṣṭikā* vv. 37–38. The Kadampa text preserves the old Tibetan translation: *ma rig rkyen gyis lo ka zhes* / /*'di ltar rdzogs pa'i sangs rgyas gsungs* / / *de phyir lo ka 'di dag kyang* / / *rnam par rtog par cis mi 'thad* / / *ma rig 'gag par gyur na ni* / / *gang rnams 'gag par 'gyur ba rnams* / / *de dag mi shes kun btags par* / / *ci'i phyir na gsal mi 'gyur* //. Tengyur (Loizzo 2007, 329–31): *ma rig rkyen gyis* <u>*'jig rten*</u> *zhes* / / *'di ltar rdzogs pa'i sangs rgyas gsungs* / / *de phyir* <u>*'jig rten*</u> *'di dag kyang* / / *rnam par rtog par cis mi 'thad* / / *ma rig 'gag par gyur na ni* / / *gang rnams 'gag par 'gyur ba rnams* / / *de dag mi shes kun btags par* / / *ci yi phyir na gsal mi 'gyur* //. Lindtner (1997b, 117) differs: *'jig rten ma rig rkyen can du* / / *gang phyir sangs rgyas rnams gsung pa* / / *'di yi phyir*

na 'jig rten 'di / / rnam rtog yin zhes cis mi 'thad / / ma rig 'gags par gyur pa na / / gang zhig 'gog par 'gyur ba de / / mi shes pa las kun brtags par / / ji lta bu na gsal mi 'gyur //.

587. *Cittavajrastava*, vv. 3–4. Kadampa author slightly differs from Tengyur: *sems rtog pa ni bo de ste / / sems ni 'gro ba lnga po yin / / bde dang du kha mtshan nyid dag / / sems las ma gtogs cung zad med / / 'gro ba kun gyi mthong thos rnams / / cung cad* [710.1] *bsgom pa'i rnam pa gang / / de kun sems kyi dra ba ru / / de nyid gsungs pas bstan pa yin //*. Tib. (Tola and Dragonetti 1985, 37): [3] *sems thob pa ni byang chub ste / sems ni 'gro ba lnga po yin / bde dang sdug bsngal mtshan nyid dag / sems las ma gtogs cung zad med //* [4] *'gro ba kun gyis mthong ba rnams / cung zad bsgom pa'i rnam pa yang / de kun sems kyi dra ba ru / de nyid gsung bas bstan pa yin //.*

588. This statement seems out of place in the manuscript.

589. Atiśa's system establishes the cognition of mind in a similar manner to *satyākāravadins*, but these cognitions are accepted only as mistaken conventional reality. This is comparable to Candrakīrti, who adapts the Sautrāntika *ākāra* theory on the conventional level for the sake of supporting his own views (MacDonald 2009, 151).

590. *Yuktiṣaṣṭikā*, v. 34. Kadampa manuscript reads: *'byung pa che la sogs bshad pa / / rnam par shes su yang dag 'du / de shes pas na 'bras 'byung na / / log par rnam btags ma yin nam //*. Tengyur (Scherrer-Schaub 1991, 74) reads: *'byung ba che la sogs bshad pa // rnam par shes su yang dag 'du / / de shes pas ni 'bral 'gyur na / / log par rnam brtags ma yin nam //.* Skt. (Scherrer-Schaub 1991, 253): *mahābhūtādi vijñāne proktaṃ samavarudhyate / tajjñāne* {or, *taj jñāne*} *vigamaṃ yāti nanu mithyā vikalpitaṃ //.* See Scherrer-Schaub 1991, 254–55; Loizzo 2001, 506; Shulman 2009, 160–61; Isaacson 2013.

591. The author is most likely referring to BV verses 22, 23, 25, 27. See Lindtner 1997a, 120–21; 1997b, 40–41; and Ruegg 2002, 202–4. See van der Kuijp 2014, 117–42, for the recensions and reception of the BV in Tibet.

592. *Mahāyānaviṃśikā* vv. 19–20 (Jamieson 2000, 45), Kadampa citation: [19] / *'di dag thams cad sems tsam zhes* {Tengyur *ste*} / / *sgyu ma lta bur gnas pa yin / / dge dang mi dge'i las rnams kyi* {*mi dge las rnams kyis*} / / *de yi* {*yis*} *bzang ngan skye ba rnams* / [20] / *sems kyi 'khor lo 'gag pa yis / / chos rnams thams cad 'gag pa nyid / / de phyir chos nyid bdag med cing / / des na chos nyid rnam par dag /*. Skt. (Tucci 1956, v. 18 [= v. 19]): *cittamātram idaṃ sarvaṃ māyākāravad utthitam / tataḥ śubhāśubhaṃ karma tato janma śubhāśubham //.*

593. *Bhāvanākrama* (Toh 3908, vol. *ki*, 4a, vv. 54–55bd), Kadampa author citation: *sems tsam la ni brten nas su / / phyi rol don la mi rtog* {Tengyur *rtag*} *go / / de bzhin nyid mig gnas nas nam* {*ni*} / / *sems tsam las ni 'das par bya / / snang ba med las bzlas* {*'da'*} *par bya / / snang med gnas pa'i rnal 'byor pas* {*pa*} / / *de'i* {*de yis*} *theg pa chen po mthong /*. Skt. (Lindtner 1992, 273): [54.] *cittamātraṃ samāruhya bāhyam arthaṃ na kalpayet / tathatālambane sthitvā cittamātram atikramet //* (= *Laṅkāvatārasūtra* X, v. 256) [55bd] [missing *a*] *nirābhāsam atikramet / nirābhāsasthito yogī mahāyānaṃ sa paśyati* (= *Laṅkāvatārasūtra* X, v. 257). Also cited in MRP (Toh 3854, vol. *tsha*, 280a3–4) from *Laṅkāvatārasūtra*.

594. Similar examples are found in Candrakīrti's MA (v. 12.2), MABH (D, vol. *'a*, 330a3–5), and PP (La Vallée Poussin 1907–12, 375.1–6).

595. Atiśa appears to accept the position of "consciousness as one group" (**ekavijñānakāya*) as correct conventional reality. This position and the example of the monkey in a window are mentioned in the later *Blo gsal grub mtha'* as the Yogācāra standpoint

of "those who maintain a single consciousness" (*rnam par shes pa tshogs gcig tu smra ba, *ekavijñānakāyavādin*) (see Mimaki 1992, 32–33).

596. This example seems to be influenced from Nāgārjuna's *Dharmadhātustava*, vv. 5–7. See Kano 2015, 184; Liu 2015, 8–9; Brunnhölzl 2007, 219–21.

597. Among the twelve links of dependent-arising (*pratītyasamutpāda*), the five causes refer to the three afflictions (ignorance [*avidyā*], craving [*tṛṣṇā*], and grasping [*upādāna*]) along with the two types of karmic actions (mental formations [*saṃskāra*] and becoming [*bhava*]) that give rise to the seven effects of suffering (consciousness [*vijñāna*], name and form [*nāmarūpa*], the six sense media [*ṣaḍāyatana*], touch [*sparśa*], feeling [*vedanā*], birth [*jāti*], aging and death [*jarāmaraṇa*]) mentioned in the *Pratītyasamutpādahṛdayakārikā*, vv. 2–3.

598. Naljorpa Chenpo Jangchup Rinchen was a direct disciple of Atiśa and later became abbot of Radreng Monastery after Dromtönpa Gyalwai Jungné.

599. Cf. *Pratītyasamutpādahṛdayakārikā* 4cd (Jamieson 2000, 49): *stong pa kho na'i chos rnams las / stong pa'i chos rnams 'byung bar zad //*; Skt. BCAP (Vaidya 1960, 171): *śūnyebhya eva śūnyā dharmāḥ prabhavanti dharmebhyaḥ //*. Lindtner (1981); MRP (Toh 3854, vol. *tsha*, 272a1).

600. Pho {or Phu} chung ba gzhon nu rgyal mtshan (1031–1106).

601. *dag pa lo ka ba'i ye shes kyi snang ba* [*dag pa 'ji rten pa'i ye shes* ≈ *śuddhalaukikajñāna*]. The *śuddhalaukikajñāna* is discussed by Bhāviveka in his *Tarkajvālā* (Toh 3856, vol. *dza*, 60b4–5). This agrees with Dromtönpa Gyalwai Jungné's understanding of correct conventional reality (see chapter 3).

602. Text emended to "suitable" (*rung ba*) from "unsuitable" (*mi rung ba*).

603. *Rtsa ba'i shes rab kyi brtag pa bchu gsum pa de kho na nyid brtag pa'i rab tu byed pa*. Note that this chapter of the MMK is called *Tattva* in the commentaries of the *Akutobhayā*, Buddhapālita, and Bhāviveka (Nietupski 1996, 133n2; Katsura and Siderits 2013, 137), whereas Candrakīrti identifies the chapter as *saṃskāra parīkṣā*.

604. MMK 13.1. The Kadampa citation matches the verse as preserved in the *Akutobhayā* (Huntington 1986, 372): *chos gang slu ba de brdzun zhes / / bcom ldan 'das kyi de skad gsung / / 'du byed thams cad slu ba'i chos / / des na de dag brdzun pa yin //*. Tengyur differs: / <u>*bcom ldan 'das kyis chos gang zhig*</u> / / <u>*bslu ba de ni brdzun zhes gsungs*</u> / / *'du byed thams cad bslu ba'i chos / / des na de dag brdzun pa yin //*. Skt. (La Vallée Poussin 1903–13, 237.9–10): *tan mṛṣā moṣadharma yad bhagavān ity abhāṣata / sarve ca moṣadharmāṇaḥ saṃskārās tena te mṛṣā //*.

605. *chos gang bslu ba de ni rdzun pa'o / / dge slong dag 'di lta ste / mi bslu ba'i chos mya ngan las 'das pa de ni bden pa'i mchog go*. The citation of the sūtra is from the *Akutobhayā* (Huntington 1986, 372). Variant forms of the citation are found in the commentaries of Buddhapālita, Bhāviveka (*Prajñāpradipā*, Toh 3853, vol. *tsha*, 147b2–7), and Candrakīrti (Huntington 1986, 203).

606. MMK 13.2ab (Toh 3824, vol. *tsa*, 8a3). Kadampa citation: *gal te slu chos gang yin pa / / de rdzun* {Tengyur, *brdzun*} *de la ci zhig slu //*. Skt. (La Vallée Poussin 1903–13, 238.13–239.7): *tan mṛṣā moṣadharma yad yadi kiṃ tatra muṣyate*.

607. *Bden gnyis spyi bshad* (2006, 718): *des na slu ba dang rdzun pa gtan med la mi zer te / slu ba ni 'khrul nas log par snang ba la zer / rdzun pa ni mtha' gnyis su* <u>*btags pa de ngo bo nyid kyis stong pa la*</u> *zer / 'dus byas kyi tsakra 'di la mtha' gnyis su rnam par btags pa 'di ngo bo nyid kyis stong ste 'khrul zhing* [718.15] <u>*log par snang ba'i*</u> *phyir zer ba na / slu ba'i chos kyis rdzun pa bsgrub nus pas* <u>*bcom ldan 'das kyis slu ba'i chos*</u> *zhes gsungs pa de*

stong pa nyid rtogs par byed pa yin pas na / bcom ldan 'das kyis de gsungs pa / stong nyid yongs su btags pa yin zhes gsungs so /. This section is a paraphrase from the *Akutobhayā* attributed to Nāgārjuna (Huntington 1986, 373): *gal te bslu ba'i chos zhes gsung pa gang yin pa de rdzun pa yin na ni med pa'i don yin par 'dra bas de la cig zhig bslu bar 'gyur / 'di ltar bslu ba ni log par snang ba yin la rdzun pa ni rnam par gtags pa'i ngo bo nyid stong pa yin pas med'i don ma yin pa'i phyir bslu ba'i chos kyis rdzun pa bsgrub tu rung ngo // de'i phyir bcom ldan 'das kyis bslu ba'i chos zhes bya ba de gsungs pa ni stong pa nyid yongs su ston par byed pa yin par shes par bya'o //*.

608. The well-known phrase "single nature but different conceptual isolates" (*ngo gcig ldog pa tha dad*) is utilized by a number of Tibetan thinkers in discussing the two realities; see for instance Hopkins 2008, 105–7.

609. Among the four *viparyāsa* (*caturviparyāsa*, "four errors"), perceiving the impermanent as permanent (*anitye nityasaṃjña*), perceiving the selfless as having a self (*anātmanyātmasaṃjñā*), perceiving the impure as pure (*aśucau śucisaṃjñā*), perceiving suffering as happiness (*duḥkhe sukhasaṃjñā*).

610. *Catuḥśataka* 2.25. Kadampa author citation differs from Tengyur: *bzhi pa'i nang nas mi rtag pa la nges par gnod / / gang la gnod yod de go med / / de phyir mi rtag gang gi kun / / du kha skye bar 'gyur ba yin //*. Tengyur (Lang 1986, 38): *mi rtag pa la nges par gnod / / gang la gnod yod de bde min / / de phyir mi rtag gang yin pa / / thams cad sdug bsngal zhes byar 'gyur / /*. Skt. (Lang 1986, 38): *anityasya dhruvā pīḍā pīḍā yasya na tat sukham / tasmād anityaṃ yat sarvaṃ duḥkhaṃ tad iti jāyate / /*.

611. The cited verse is actually from the *Satyadvayāvatāra*, v. 19 (Ejima 1983, 365–66): *thabs su gyur pa kun rdzob bden pa dang / / thabs las byung ba don dam bden pa dag / / gnyis po'i dbye ba gang gis mi shes pa / / de dag log par rtogs pas ngan 'gror 'gro //19//*. This version is also cited in the MRP (Toh 3854, vol. *tsha*, 261a2–3) and attributed to Candrakīrti. Compare *Madhyamakāvatāra* 6.80 (La Vallée Poussin 1907–12, 175.3–6): *tha snyad bden pa thabs su gyur pa dang / / don dam bden pa thabs byung gyur pa ste / / de gnyis rnam dbye gang gis mi shes pa / / de ni rnam rtog log pas lam ngan zhugs // 6.80 //*. Cited in the *Subhāṣitasaṃgraha* (Bendall 1903, 396.7–10): *upāyabhūtaṃ vyavahārasatyam upeyabhūtaṃ paramārthasatyam / tayor vibhāgaṃ na paraiti yo vai mithyāvikalpaiḥ sa kumārgayātaḥ //*. As noted by Lindtner (1979, 89n13), this verse is also cited in the *Bodhisattvayogācāracatuḥśatakaṭīkā*, chap. 3 (Peking bstan 'gyur, vol. 98, *dbu ma Ya* 63a.1–2).

612. Kadampa citation of *Madhyamakāvatāra* 6.79: */ arya klu sgrub zhags kyi lugs las ni / / phyi rol gyur pa zhi ba'i thabs ma yin / de ni yang dag kun rdzob bden las nyams / / de nyams gyur pas thar pa grub yod min //*. Reading from the Tengyur reading differs (La Vallée Poussin 1907–12, 175.15–9, v. 6.79): */ slob dpon klu sgrub zhabs kyi lam las ni / / phyi rol gyur la zhi ba'i thabs med do / / de dag kun rdzob de nyid bden las nyams / / de las nyams pas thar pa 'grub yod min /*. Note the reading *yang dag kun rdzob* instead of *de dag kun rdzob*. This important variant is also found in Dharmakīrtiśrī's *Abhisamayālaṃkāradurbodhālokā* (Toh 3794, vol. *ja*, 142a) citation of the *Madhyamakāvatāra* (6.79c): *de ni kun rdzob yang dag bden las nyams /*. Dharmakīrtiśrī (aka Serlingpa) was Atiśa's teacher and Atiśa translated this work in western Tibet. Skt. (Li 2014): *ācāryanāgārjunapādamārgād bahirgatānāṃ na śivābhyupāyaḥ / bhraṣṭā hi te saṃvṛtitattvasatyāt tad bhraṃśataś cāsti na mokṣasiddhiḥ //*.

613. Actually from Bhāviveka's *Madhyamakahṛdaya* 3.12 (Toh 3855, vol. *dza*, 4a4): /

yang dag kun rdzob rnams kyi skas / / med par yang dag khang pa yi / / steng du 'gro bar bya ba ni / / mkhas la rung ba ma yin no // 12 //. Skt. (Lindtner 2001, 8): *tattvaprāsādaśikharārohaṇaṃ na hi yujyate / tathyasaṃvṛtisopānam antareṇa yatas tataḥ // 12 //*. Also in *Satyadvayāvatāra*, v. 20bcd (Ejima 1983, 365, vv. 20–21).

614. *Bodhipathapradīpa* (Toh 3947, vol. *khi*, 40a2, v. 43): */ thabs dang bral ba'i shes rab dang / / shes rab bral ba'i thabs dag kyang / / gang phyir 'ching ba zhes gsungs pas / / de phyir gnyis ka spang mi bya /*. Sherburne 2000, 12.

615. Obstructions to omniscience consisting of unafflicted misknowledge (*nyon mongs pa can ma yin pa'i mi shes pa'i shes bya'i sgrib pa*) are mentioned in Bhāviveka's *Tarkajvālā* (Eckel 2008, 334, 345). The phrase "unafflicted misknowledge" (*nyon mongs pa can ma yin pa'i mi shes pa ≈ akliṣṭāvidyā*) occurs in the *Tarkajvālā*. Both Bhāviveka and Candrakīrti discuss this type of obstruction, although Bhāviveka's *Prajñāpradīpa ad* MMK 18.5 uses the term *kun nas nyon mongs pa ma yin pa'i ma rig pa* (*akliṣṭājñāna*) and Candrakīrti's *Triśaraṇasaptati* (v. 47) mentions (*akliṣṭājñāna*, *mi shes nyon mongs min*), while MABH *ad* MA 6.28 (La Vallée Poussin 1907–12, 107.19–108.1) mention *śrāvakas*, *pratyekabuddhas*, and *bodhisattva*s who eliminate afflicted ignorance (*nyon mongs pa can kyi ma rig pa*).

616. Note that the Kadampa author uses *so sor rtog pa'i 'gog pa* for *so sor brtags pa'i 'gog pa* (*pratisaṃkhyānirodha*) and *'rtag* {*brtag*} *min gyi 'gog pa* as an abbreviation for *so sor brtag min gyi 'gog pa* (*apratisaṃkhyānirodha*).

617. Differs from Tsongkhapa's understanding of the role of serenity in the meditative process. See Cutler et al. 2002, 3: 99–110.

618. The principle of "realizing one" to "realize all" is found in *Catuḥśataka* 8.16 and cited in the PP and MMK 4.9 (La Vallée Poussin 1903–13, 128.4). See McClintock 2000, 225–44. *Ekarasa* (*ro gcig*) is a synonym of nondiversity and an epithet of emptiness (Scherrer-Schaub 1991, 227n415; PP 375.7). *A General Explanation* (740.5) correlates *anānārtham* (MMK 18.9) with "all things within *saṃsāra* and *nirvāṇa* have the single taste of suchness."

619. The Tengyur does not have a text by this title, but the reference is most likely to a citation from an Abhidharma commentary.

620. Text emended from "unreliable."

621. *Laṅkāvatārasūtra* 2.137. Kadampa Tibetan: *'khor ba rmi lam sgyu 'dra dang / rtag dang chad pa spangs pa'i rtags* [*sic!*] *stong pa nyid bshad kyang / las ni rnam par mi 'jig go*. Tengyur (Toh 107, vol. *ca*, 135a): *'khor ba rmi lam sgyu 'dra dang / / rtag dang chad pa spangs pa nyi / / rtag tu stong pa nyid bshad kyang / / las ni rnam par mi 'jig go /*. Skt. (Nanjio 1923, 76): *deśemi śūnyatāṃ nityaṃ śāśvatocchedavarjitām / saṃsāraṃ svapnamāyākhyaṃ na ca karma vinaśyati /*.

622. MMK 24.11; Kadampa Tibetan matches *Akutobhayā* (Huntington 1986, 520) but differs from Tengyur (Toh 3824, vol. *tsha*, 15a2): *stong pa nyid la blta nyes na / / shes chung rnams phung par byed* {Tengyur: *'gyur*} */ / ci* {*ji*} *ltar sbrul la bzung* {*gzung*} *nyes* {*nyi*} *dang / / rigs* {*rig*} *sngags nyes par bsgrubs pa bzhin /*. Skt. (La Vallée Poussin 1903–13, 495.1–2): *vināśayati durdṛṣṭā śūnyatā mandamedhasam / sarpo yathā durgṛhīto vidyā vā duṣprasādhitā / /11 //*.

623. *Ratnāvalī*, chap. 2, vv. 19–20. Kadampa Tibetan differs from Tengyur (Hahn 1982, 47): [19] */ chos nyid* {Tengyur: *'di*} *log par shes gyur na / / mi mkhas rnams ni chud kyang zad* {*za*} */ / gzhan yang* {*'di ltar*} *med par lta ba yis* {*yi*} */ / mi gtsang der ni bying bar 'gyur / /* [20] *gzhan du* {*yang*} *de ni log bzung bas* {*nas*} */ / blun*

pa mkhas pa'i nga rgyal can / / spong bas ma rungs las dag gis {bdag nyid can} / / mnar med par ni spyi'u tshugs 'gro //. Skt. (Hahn 1982, 47): [19] / *vināśayati durjñāto dharmo 'yam avipaścitam / nāstitādṛṣṭisamale yasmād asmin nimajjati / /*[20] *aparo 'py asya durjñānān mūrkhaḥ paṇḍitamānikaḥ / pratikṣepavinaṣṭātmā yāty avīcim adhomukhaḥ // //.*

624. The four opponent powers consist of the power of the support (*rten gyi stobs*), the power of antidote (*gnyen po kun spyod kyi stobs*), the power of regret (*rnam par gsun 'byin pa'i stobs*), and the power of turning away from future faults (*nyes pa las slang ldog pa'i stobs*).
625. The Kadampa text reads *sgrog rang dhal*, which I have taken to be equivalent to *sgrog rang bdal* or *sgrog rang grol* found in the works of Gampopa.
626. These differ from the standard list of the four errors (*viparyāsa*).
627. This principle is cited in Kong sprul blo gros mtha' yas (1813–99), *Shes bya mtha' yas pa'i rgya mtsho*. See *The Treasury of Knowledge: Books Nine and Ten—Journey and Goal* (Barron 2011, 86).
628. Nāgārjuna, *Pratītyasamutpādahṛdayakārikā*, v. 6. Kadampa citation differs from Tengyur (Jamieson 2000, 51, 61, 91; Scherrer-Schaub 1987, 108n42): *shin tu phra ba'i dngos la yang / / gang gis chad par rnam btags* {Tengyur, *brtas*} *pa / / rnam par mi mkhas de yis ni / / rkyen las byung ba'i* {*'byung ba'i*} *don ma mthong /.* MRP (Toh 3854, vol. *tsha*, 272a2; P 342a5–342a6) matches Kadampa citation. The verse is similar to *Yuktiṣaṣṭikākārikā* 12.
629. Five effects, the five kinds of fruition: correlative effect (*rgyu mthun gyi 'bras bu, niṣyandaphala*), predominant effect (*bdag po'i 'bras bu, adhipatiphala*), effect caused by human action (*skyes bu byed pa'i 'bras bu, puruṣakāraphala*), retributive effect (*rnam smin gyi 'bras bu, vipākaphala*), and separation effect (*bral ba'i 'bras bu, visaṃyogaphala*).
630. *Madhyāntavibhāga* 4.16cd–4.17ab (Toh 4021, vol. *phi*, 43b4). Kadampa author reads: *snod gyur rnam par smin brjod pas* {Tengyur: *dang*} */ / de'i* {*de yi*} *dbang gi* {*gis*} *stobs dang ni / / 'dod dang 'phel dang rnam dag dang* {*ste*} */ / de dag 'bras bu go rim bzhin //.* Skt. (Nagao 1964, 57): *bhājanatvaṃ vipākākhyaṃ balan tasyādhipatyataḥ //* [4.16] *rucir vṛddhir viśuddhiś ca phalam etad yathākramaṃ /.* See D'Amato 2012, 169–70.
631. *Madhyāntavibhāga*, chap. 4, v. 1 (Toh 4021, vol. *phi*, 43a2). English translation based on Engle (2009, 143). Kadampa author citation slightly differs from Tengyur: *gnas ngan len dang* {Tengyur *phyir*} *sred rgyu'i phyir / / dngos po'i phyir* {*gzhi yi phyir*} *dang ma rmongs phyir / / bden pa bzhi la 'jug bya bas / / dran pa nye bar bzhag pa sgoms* {*bsgoms*}. Skt. (Nagao 1964, 56): *dauṣṭhulyāt tarṣahetutvād vastutvād avimohataḥ / catuḥsatyāvatārāya smṛtyupasthānabhāvanā /.*
632. These analogies are cited by Gampopa in his notes on his teachings from Chakriwa (Lcags ri ba). See Sherpa 2004, 199.
633. The five faults (*nyes pa lnga, pañcadoṣā*) in developing quiescence (*śamatha*) listed in *Madhyāntavibhāga* (4.4): (1) laziness (*kausīdya, le lo*), (2) forgetting the instruction (*avavādasammosa, gdams ngag brjed pa*), (3) laxity (*laya, bying ba*) and excitement (*uddhata, rgod pa*), (4) nonapplication (*asamskāra, 'du mi byed pa*), and (5) overapplication (*samskāra, 'du byed pa*). Atiśa discusses these as well as the eight remedies (see following note) in *Open Basket of Jewels* and BMPP (Toh 3948, vol. *khi*, 275a; Sherburne 2000, 205–6).

634. The eight remedies (*'du byed brgyad, aṣṭaprahāṇasaṃskārāḥ*) to attaining *samādhi* are found in the *Madhyāntavibhāgabhāṣya* (Nagao 1964, 51–52): faith (*dad pa, śraddhā*), aspiration (*'dun pa, chanda*), exertion (*brtson 'grus, vyāyāma*), pliancy (*shin sbyangs, prasrabdha*), mindfulness (*smṛti, dran pa*), awareness (*saṃprajanya, shes bzhin*), attention (*sems pa, cetanā*), and equanimity (*btang snyoms, upekṣā*).

635. Four legs of miraculous action (*rdzu 'phrul gyi rkang pa bzhi*): determination, discernment, diligence, and *samādhi*, which are perfected on the greater path of accumulation.

636. *Mahāyānasūtrālaṃkāra*, chap. 14, v. 3 (Toh 4020, vol. *phi*, 19a1–2). Kadampa author differs from Tengyur: *de tshe chos kyi rgyun la ni / / zhi gnas dang ni lhag mthong dang* {Tengyur: *sangs rgyas rnams las zhi gnas dang*} */ / ye shes yangs pa thob bya'i phyir / / gdams ngag rgya che thob par 'gyur* {*rnyed par 'gyur*} *zhes so /*. Skt. (Lévi 1907, 90): *dharmasrotasi buddhebhyo 'vavādaṃ labhate tadā / vipulaṃ śamathajñānavaipulyagamanāya hi /*.

637. Kadampa citation is actually a verse based on *Bodhicittavivaraṇa* (v. 73); it is missing *pāda* c, and differs: *de ltar stong pa nyid rtogs na /* [missing c] */ blo ni gzhan don la dga' ba / / 'gyur ba nyid du the tsom med /*. *Bodhicittavivaraṇa*, v. 73 (Lindtner 1997b, 56): *de ltar stong pa nyid 'di ni / rnal 'byor pa yis bsgom byas na / gzhan gyi don la chags pa'i blo / 'byung bar 'gyur ba the tshom med /*. This verse is also cited in Atiśa's *Open Basket of Jewels*.

638. Eight worldly dharmas (*aṣṭalokadharma, 'jig rten gyi chos brgyad*): (1) gain (*lābha, rnyed pa*), (2) loss (*alābha, ma rnyed pa*), (3) fame (*yaśa, snyan pa*), (4) infamy (*ayaśa, mi snyan pa*), (5) slander (*nindā, smad pa*), (6) praise (*praśamsā, bstod pa*), (7) pleasure (*sukha, bde ba*), and (8) misery (*duḥkha, sdug bsngal*). *Mahāvyutpatti*, 2341–48.

639. Five governing powers (*dbang po lnga, pañcendriya*): faith (*dad pa, śraddhā*), energy (*brtson 'grus, vīrya*), mindfulness (*dran pa, smṛti*), concentration (*ting nge 'dzin, samādhi*), and wisdom (*shes rab, prajñā*).

640. Five strengths (*stobs lnga, pañcabala*) are a transmutation of the five governing powers of faith (*dad pa, śraddhā*), energy (*brtson 'grus, vīrya*), mindfulness (*dran pa, smṛti*), concentration (*ting nge 'dzin, samādhi*), and wisdom (*shes rab, prajñā*).

641. Vasubandhu, *Triṃśikā* 28d (Toh 4055, vol. *shi*, 3a1–2): [*nam zhig shes pas dmigs pa rnams / mi dmigs de yi tshe na ni / rnam par rig pa tsam la gnas /*] *gzung pa med pas de 'dzin med /*. Skt. (Anacker 2005, 423): [*yadālambanaṃ vijñānaṃ naivopalabhate tadā / sthitaṃ vijñānamātratve*] *grāhyābhāve tadagrahāt //*.

642. Manuscript is not clear at this point and the translation is not definite.

643. Seven factors of awakening (*byang chub kyi yan lag bdun, bodhyaṅga* [Edgerton 1953, 403]): mindfulness (*dran pa, smṛti*), investigation (*chos rab du rnam par 'byed pa, dharmapravicaya*), energy (*brtson 'grus, vīrya*), joy (*dga' ba, prīti*), pliancy (*shin du sbyangs pa, praśrabdhi*), concentration (*ting' dzin, samādhi*), and equanimity (*btang snyoms, upekṣā*). The author has listed wisdom (*shes rab*) for investigation.

644. *Yuktiṣaṣṭikā* 11cd–12. Kadampa text differs from Tengyur (Scherrer-Schaub 1991, 47–48), cited from the *Yuktiṣaṣṭikāvṛtti* with slight differences: *chos shes de'i* {Tengyur *de yi*} *'og tu ni / / 'di la bye brag dbye yod na / / shin du phra ba'i dngos la yang / / gang gi* {*gis*} *skye bar rnam brtags pa / / rnam par mi mkhas de yin* {*yis*} *ni / / rkyen las byung ba'i don ma mthong /*. See Loizzo 2007, 158–59, 283.

645. See Scherrer-Schaub 1991, 172–77, and Loizzo 2007, 158–62, on this point in Candrakīrti's *Yuktiṣaṣṭikāvṛtti*. Note that the "single instant of wisdom" (*ye shes*

skad gcig ma) is also accepted by Bhāviveka in his MHK 1.6, *Tarkajvālā* (*ad* 3.273); see Eckel 1992, 160.

646. Tib: *'gag par 'gyur ba'i lam gyi ni / de'i sgrib pa rab tu spong /*. Cf. *Abhidharmakośa* 6.77cd (Pradhan 1975, 389.9): *nirudhyamāno mārgas tu prajahāti tadāvṛtim //6.77//*. Tib. (La Vallée Poussin 1923–31, 4: 300): *'gag par 'gyur ba'i lam gyis ni / de yi sgrib pa rab tu spang //* ("c'est périssant que le Chemin cause l'abandon de l'obstacle").

647. *phyi'i 'phel che shos +a sho dang +a da'i 'bras bu yin ste*. The practices these results reference are not clear.

648. *Ratnāvali*, 3.12–13. Kadampa author differs from Tengyur: */ sangs rgyas rnams kyi gzugs sku ni / / pu nya tshogs las byung ba yin / / chos kyi sku ni mdo bsdus na / rā dza ye shes tshogs las 'khrungs //*. Tengyur (Hahn 1982, 74): *sangs rgyas rnams kyi gzugs sku ni / bsod nams tshogs las byung ba ste / chos kyi sku ni mdor bsdu na / rgyal o ye shes tshogs las 'khrung //*.

649. *Suvarṇaprabhāsa* 2.30. Kadampa citation differs from Kangyur (Toh 557, vol. *pha*, 6a5): *sangs rgyas mya ngan mi 'da' zhing* {Kangyur: *yong mi 'da'*} */ / chos kyang nub par ma gyur te* {*mi 'gyur te*} */ / sems can rnams ni gdul ba'i phyir* {*yongs su smin mdzad phyir* }*/ / mya ngan 'das pa'i tshul bstan to* { *yongs su mya ngan 'da' ba ston*} */*. Skt. (Bagchi 1967, 9): *na buddhaḥ parinirvāti na dharma parihīyate / sattvānāṃ paripākāya parinirvāṇaṃ nidarśayet //*. This verse is also cited by Jñānagarbha and Haribhadra; see Inagaki 1977, 141.

650. *Mahāyānottaratantraśāstra*, chap. 2, v. 62. Kadampa citation differs from Tengyur (Toh 4024, vol. *phi*, 64b7–65a1): {Tengyur: *dang po la ni tha ma gnas /*} *rgyu mtha' yas dang / sems can zad med dang / tshe* {*brtshe*} *dang 'phrul dang / mkhyen dang / phun tshogs ldan chos kyi dbang phyug 'chi ba'i bdun* {*bdud*} *bcom dang / / ngo bo med phyir lo ka* {*'jig rten*} *mgon pa rtag* {*mgon pos brtag*} *//*. Skt. (Johnston 1991, 156–57): *hetvānantyāt sattvadhātvakṣayatvāt kāruṇyarddhijñāna-saṃpattiyogāt / dharmaiśvaryān mṛtyumārāvabhaṅgān naiḥsvābhāvyāc chāśvato lokanāthaḥ //*. Takasaki 1966a, 332, *kārikā* 12, v. 62.

651. *Mahāyānottaratantraśāstra*, chap. 1, v. 68. Kadampa author differs from Tengyur (Toh 4024, vol. *phi*, 57b4): *ji bzhin yang dag mthong ba'i phyir / / skye ba lnga rnams las gyur kyang* {Tengyur, *skye sogs rnams las 'das gyur kyang*} */ / snying rje'i bdag nyid skye ba dang / / 'chi dang rga dang na bar ston /*. Skt. (Johnston 1991, 115): *janmamṛtyujarāvyādhīn darśayanti kṛpātmakāḥ / / jātyādivinivṛttāś ca yathābhūtasya darśanāt //*. Takasaki 1966a, 244, v. 68.

652. Kadampa citation from Vasubandhu's *Pratītyasamutpādādivibhaṅgabhāṣya*, Toh 3995, vol. *chi*, 52b4, with minor difference: */ bden pa mthong la 'phen pa med / / sred dang bral la* {Tengyur *sred pa bral na* } *'byung ba med //*.

653. Cited in Dhārmikasubhūtighoṣa's *Bodhisattvacaryāsaṅgrahapradīparatnamālā* (Toh 3936, vol. *ki*, 338a): */ ji ltar sgyu ma'i glang po la / / skye dang 'jig pa gnyis* {Tengyur, *nyid*} *snang yang / / de la don gyi yang dag tu / / skye dang 'jig pa gnyis* {Tengyur, *nyid*} *med ltar / / de bzhin sgyu 'dra'i lo ka* {*'jig rten*} *la / / skye dang 'jig pa gnyis* {*nyid*} *snang yang / / de la don gyi yang dag tu* {*dam pa'i don du skye ba dang*} */ / skyes ba dang ni 'gag pa med* {*'jig pa nyid ni yod ma yin*} */*. Similar to *Acintyastava*, v. 30. From the standpoint of ultimate reality, there is neither arising (*utpāda*) nor cessation (*nirodha*). See Scherrer-Schaub 1991, 200–201, *Mahāyānaviṃśikā* (v. 2ab), MRP (Lindtner 1981, 171).

654. Kadampa phrase found in the collected works of Gampopa (Sherpa 2004, 199).

655. *smra bsam brjod med shes rab pha rol phyin / / ma skyes ma 'gag nam mkha' i ngo bo nyid / / so so rang rig ye shes dpyod yul ba / / dus gsum rgyal ba' i yum la phyag 'tshal lo //.* As noted by Phuntsho (2005, 229n28), "although this verse is attributed to Rāhulabhadra by Tibetan scholars, it does not appear in the *Prajñāpāramitāstotra*." Rather, a related verse is found in Ānandagarbha's (Kun dga' snying po) *Shes rab kyi pha rol tu phyin pa' i dkyil 'khor gyi cho ga zhes bya ba, Prajñāpāramitāmaṇḍalavidhināma* (Toh 2644, vol. *ju*, 254b4–5: */ smra bsam brjod med* [254b5] *shes rab pha rol phyin / / ma skyes mi 'gag nam mkha' i ngo bo nyid / / so so rang rig ye shes spyod yul ba / / dus gsum rgyal ba' i yum la skabs su mchi //.* The verse is attributed by Gampopa to Nāgārjuna in his *Collected Works*. On Rahulabhadra's *Prajñāpāramitāstrotra* (*Sher phyin bstod pa*), see Lamotte 1949, 2: 1060–65; Lopez 1988, 147; Kapstein 2000, 111.
656. The Kadampa text reads *sgrog rang dhal*, which I have taken to be equivalent to *sgrog rang bdal, sgrog rang grol* (Kragh 2015, 40), *sgrog rang gdal* (Jackson 1994, 152), *sgrog rang brdal* ("loosens its own bonds," Martin 1992, 302n30).
657. Atiśa's understanding that all things are within one's own mind is stated in the BMPP (Toh 3948, vol. *khi*, 285a; Sherburne 2000, 261), based on instructions from his teacher Bodhibhadra: "All things are contained in the mind, and the mind is contained in the body, make effort to release the body into the realm of reality" (*chos thams cad sems la bsdus shing / sems kyang lus la bsdus la / lus kyang chos kyi dbyings su btang ba*). In the *Sayings of the Kadam Masters* (*Bka' gdam kyi skyes bu dam pa rnam kyi gsung bgros thor bu pa rnams*, 3b2–3), Atiśa states: "There is nothing in this world of appearance and everyday convention that does not come into being except from one's own mind. The mind, too, is an empty awareness, and recognition of it [i.e., the empty mind] as the nonduality of awareness and emptiness is the *view*" (*'di ltar snang tshod grags tshod 'di thams cad rang gi sems las ma byung ba med/ sems rig pa stong pa yin/ de rig stong gnyis med du rtogs pa de lta ba yin*; translation Jinpa 2013, 26).
658. *Chos kyi dbyings rang bzhin dbyer med par bstan pa' i mdo* (*Sarvadharmaprakṛti-asaṃbhedanirdeśasūtra*). Atiśa cites this text in the *Bodhipathapradīpapañjika* (Sherburne 2000, 254–55). Also cited in the *Madhyamakaratna-pradīpa* (Lindtner 1981, 169).
659. This is a paraphrase of the dialogue between Mañjuśrī and Vimalakīrti found in the *Vimalakīrtinirdeśa*, chap. 8, §33 (English, Thurman 1976, 77). Tib. (Study Group on Buddhist Literature 2004, 350): *legs so legs so / / rigs kyi bu / 'di ni byang chub sems dpa' rnams kyi gnyis su med par 'jug pa yin te / de la yi ge dang / sgra dang / rnam par rig pa' i rgyu ba med do //.* Skt. (Study Group on Buddhist Literature 2004, 350): *sādhu sādhu kulaputra ayaṃ bodhisatvānām advayadharmamukhapraveśo yatra nāk ṣararutaravitavijñaptipracāraḥ //.*
660. *Stutyatītastava* (*'das par bstan pa*), v. 9 (Mitrikeski 2010, 189–90); Kadampa author citation differs from Tengyur: *lta ba thams cad spangs pa' i phyir / / mgon po khyod kyi* {Tengyur, *kyis*} *stong par bstan* {*gsungs*} */ / de la yongs su brtags pas te* {*de yang yongs su btags pa ste*} */ dngos su mgon po khyod mi bzhed //.*
661. The *Saddharmapuṇḍarīkasūtra* (13.20), as cited in the *Yuktiṣaṣṭikāvṛtti ad* kārikā 3 (Scherrer-Schaub 1991, 130; Loizzo 2007, 138–39). Skt. (Kern and Nanjio 1908–12, 281.11–12): *viparītasaṃjñī hi ime vikalpitā asantasantā hi abhūtabhūtataḥ / anusthitāś cāpi ajātadharmā jātātha bhūta viparītakalpitāḥ //.*
662. *Catuḥśataka* 16.25; translation from Ruegg 2010, 50n40. Kadampa author differs

from the Tengyur (Lang 1986, 150): *yod dang med dang yod med dang* {Tengyur: *me zhes*} / *phyogs ni gang na yang* {*gang la phyogs ni*} *yod min pa* / / *dus ring btags kyang de la ni* {*de la yun ni ring po na'ang*} / / *brgal bar nus pa ma yin no* {*klan ka brjod pa nus ma yin*} //. Skt. (Lang 1986, 150): *sad asat sadasac ceti yasya pakṣo na vidyate / upālambhāś cireṇāpi tasya vaktuṃ na śakyate //.*

663. *Bodhipathapradīpa*, v. 54, with one major variant, the Kadampa author reads: / *gang gi rang bzhin mthong ba ni* / instead of the Tengyur, *gang gi rang bzhin ma thong bzhing* / (Sherburne 2000, 16–17, 241).

664. This analogy is explained in Atiśa's *Madhyamakopadeśa*.

665. *Mūlamadhyamakakārikā* 24.10. Kadampa citation matches *Akutobhayā* (Huntington 1986, 520) but differs from Tengyur (Toh 3824, vol. *tsa*, 15a2): *tha snyad la ni ma brten par* / / *dam pa'i don ni bstan mi nus* / / *dam pa'i don la ma brten par* {Tengyur: *ni ma rtogs par*} / / *mya ngan 'das pa thob mi 'gyur* //. Skt (La Vallée Poussin 1903–13, 494.13): *vyavahāram anāśritya paramārtho na deśyate / paramārtham anāgamya nirvāṇaṃ nādhigamyate //.*

666. *Vigrahavyāvartanī* 29. The Kadampa author leaves out 29c: *nga la dam 'ga' yod na* / *des na nga la skyon re yod* / [missing 29c] / *nga ni skyon med kho na* //. Tengyur (Toh 3832, vol. *tsa*, 128b2–3): *ngas dam bcas 'ga' yod* / / *des na nga la skyon de yod* // *nga la dam bcas med pas na* / / *nga la skyon med kho na yin* //. Skt. (Bhaṭṭacharya 1978, 23): *yadi kācana pratijñā syān me tata eṣa me bhaved dośa nāsti ca mama pratijñā tasmān naivāsti me doṣaḥ.*

667. *Mūlamadhyamakakārikā* 18.9. Kadampa differs from Tengyur: *gzhan yin rkyen min zhi ba ste* / / *spros pa rnams kyi ma spros pa* / / *tha dad don min rnam mi rtog* / / *'di ni yang dag mtshan nyid do* //. Tengyur (Toh 3824, vol. *tsa*, 11a3–4): *gzhan las shes min zhi ba dang* / / *spros pa rnams kyis ma spros pa* // *rnam rtog med don tha dad med* / / *de ni de nyid mtshan nyid do* //. Skt. (La Vallée Poussin 1903–13, 372.12–13): *aparapratyayaṃ śāntaṃ prapañcair aprapañcitam / nirvikalpam anānārtham etat tattvasya lakṣaṇam //.*

668. These five characteristics are based on the exegesis of MMK 18.9 found in the *Akutobhayā* attributed to Nāgārjuna (Huntington 1986, 438). Note that *A General Explanation* comments on the five characteristics in order of the Tibetan translation of the verse, *tha dad don min* (*anānārtha*) before *rnam mi rtog* (*nirvikalpa*).

669. The text *dbu ma rten chung* (an abbreviation also used by Gampopa) refers to the *Pratītyasamutpādahṛdaya* (*Rten cing 'brel bar 'byung ba'i snying po*) of Nāgārjuna (v. 7ab): *'di la bsal bya ci yang med* / / *gzhal bar bya ba gang yang med* /. The verse is cited in Atiśa's BMPP (282b; Sherburne 2000, 248 [Tibetan only]) in a series of stanzas attributed to his teacher Bodhibhadra. The verse is also found in the MRP and *Abhisamayālaṃkāra* 5.21 = *Ratnagotravibhāga*. See Takasaki 1966a, 300; Wangchuk 2007, 199–200, no. 11; *Kāyatrayastotranāmavivaraṇa* (*Sku gsum la bstod pa shes bya ba'i rnam par 'grel pa*, Toh 1124, D72a3).

670. The story, attributed to Atiśa, is found in the *Jo bo rje dpal ldan a ti sha'i rnam thar bka' gdams pha chos* (Dromtönpa Gyalwai Jungné 2012c, 131–32). See the section "The Questioning of Atiśa in Western Tibet" in the Introduction to this book.

671. *Pratītyasamutpādahṛdayakārikā*, v. 7d (Jamieson 2000, 52, 91): *yang dag mthong na rnam par grol* /.

672. See following note on *Mūlamadhyamakakārikā* 18.5.

673. *Mūlamadhyamakakārikā* 18.5. Kadampa citation slightly differs from Tengyur (Toh 3824, vol. *tsa*, 11a1): */ las dang nyon mongs pa zad nas* {Tengyur *pas*} *thar / / las dang nyon mongs rnam rtog las / / de dag spros pas spros pa ste* {*ni*} */ / stong pa nyid kyi* {*kyis*} *'gags par 'gyur /*. Skt. (La Vallée Poussin 1903–13, 349.15–350.5): *karmakleśakṣayān mokṣaḥ karmakleśā vikalpataḥ / te prapañcāt prapañcas tu śūnyatāyāṃ nirudhyate / /*.

674. *Madhyamakahṛdaya* 3.12 (Toh 3855, vol. *dza*, 4a4): */ yang dag kun rdzob rnams kyi skas / / med par yang dag khang pa yi / / steng du 'gro bar bya ba ni / / mkhas la rung ba ma yin no / / 12 / /*. Skt. (Lindtner 2001, 8): *tattvaprāsādaśikharārohaṇaṃ na hi yujyate / tathyasaṃvṛtisopānam antareṇa yatas tataḥ / / 12 / /*.

675. Kadampa citation of *Yuktiṣaṣṭikā*, v. 30, slightly differs from Tengyur: *de nyid '<u>tshol la</u> thog mar '<u>di</u> / / thams cad yod ces brjod par bya / / don <u>dam</u> rtogs shings chags med nas / / <u>de'i</u> 'og tu dben pa'o /*. *Yuktiṣaṣṭika*, verse 30: *de nyid tshol la thog mar ni / / thams cad yod ces brjod par bya / / don rnams rtogs shing chags med nas / de yi 'og tu dben pa'o //*. Loizzo 2007, 180 (Eng.), 318 (Tib). Skt. (Lindtner 1997b, 174): *sarvam astīti vaktavyam ādau tattvagaveṣiṇaḥ / paścād avagatārthasya niḥsaṅgasya viviktata*.

676. *Madhyamakāvatāra* 6.29 (La Vallée Poussin 1907–12, 109.6–9); Kadampa author citation: *rab rib mthu yis skra shad la sogs pa* {LVP: *pa'i*} *// ngo bo log pa gang zhig rnam brtags pa / / de'i bdag nyid gang zhig mig dag pas* {*de nyid bdag nyid gang du mig dag pas*} */ mthong de de nyid de bzhin 'dir shes kyis /*. Skt. (Li 2012, 6; 2014): *vikalpitaṃ yat timiraprabhāvāt keśādirūpaṃ vitathaṃ tad eva / yenātmanā paśyati śuddhadṛṣṭis tat tattvam ity evam ihāpya avaihi / /*.

677. *Caryāgīti*, v. 10 (Sherburne 2000, 408–9), Kadampa author citation: *rab rib can gyi* {Tengyur *gyis* } {*ji ltar*} *mkha' la skra mthong dang / / rnam rtog rab rib lo ka* {*'jig rten*} *mthong la khyad par med / / rnam rtog skyes pa'ang mkha' dang* {*rnam rtog rang bzhin mkha' dang*} *mnyam pa'i rang bzhin du / / brtags pa'i dngos po* {*rang bzhin*} *ma lus pa dag sgom par bya'o* {*bsgom par gyis*} *//*.

678. *Satyadvayāvatāra*, vv. 7cd–9 (Ejima 1983, 363; Apple 2013, 300): *de la mthong dang mthong byed med / / thog ma tha ma med zhi ba // 7 // dngos dang dngos med rnam par spangs / / rnam par rtog med dmigs pa bral / / gnas pa med pa gnas med pa / / 'gro 'ong med cing dpe dang bral // 8 // brjod du med bltar med pa / / 'gyur ba med pa 'dus ma byas /* [*/ rnal 'byor pa yis de rtogs na / / nyong mongs shes bya'i sgrib pa spangs // 9 //*].

679. *Satyadvayāvatāra*, v. 21 (Ejima 1983, 365): */ kun rdzob ji ltar snang ba 'di / / rigs pas brtags na 'ga' mi rnyed / / ma rnyed pa nyid don dam yin / ye nas gnas pa'i chos nyid do /*. See chapter 3 on the "conventional that appears just as it is."

680. *Satyadvayāvatāra*, v. 22cd (Ejima 1983, 366, vv. 23cd–24abcd): *gal te grub mi rung na / / chu zla la sogs su yis bskyed // 22 //*.

681. *Satyadvayāvatāra*, v. 23cd (Ejima 1983, 366): */ rkyen rnams rgyun ni chad gyur na / / kun rdzob tu yang mi 'byung ngo // 23 //*. Lindtner (1981, 198n23) notes the last two lines from *Bodhicaryāvatāra* 9.15ab: *pratyayānāṃ tu vicchedāt saṃvṛtyāpi na sambhavaḥ*; Tib. (9.13).

682. *Bodhicaryāvatāra* 9.34. The Kadampa author's citation of verse 34 does not match the Tengyur (Toh 3871, vol. *la*, 32a3–4) or Dunhuang (Saito 1993, 52.14–17, differences are underlined): *gang tshe gang zhig med do zhes / / brtag bya'i dngos po <u>ma rig pa</u> / / de tshe <u>bkag pa rten bral ba</u> / / <u>blo'i bdun du gnas mi 'gyur</u> /*. Skt. (Vaidya 1960, 198): *yadā na labhyate bhāvo yo nāstīti prakalpyate / tadā nirāśrayo 'bhāvaḥ kathaṃ tiṣṭhen mateḥ puraḥ // 34 //*.

683. *Bodhicaryāvatāra* 9.35. The Kadampa author's citation of verse 35 closely matches the

Tengyur (Toh 3871, vol. *la*, 32a4) but differs from the Dunhuang (Saito 1993, 52.18–21): *gang tshe dngos dang dngos med dag / blo'i mdun na mi gnas pa / / de tshe rnam pa gzhan med pas / / dmigs pa med pas rab tu zhi /*. Skt. (Vaidya 1960, 199): *yadā na bhāvo nābhāvo mateḥ saṃtiṣṭhate puraḥ / tadānyagatyabhāvena nirālambā praśāmyati // 35 //*. Matches citation by Atiśa in his BMDP (D 285a; Sherburne 2000, 263).

684. *dgag bya ma grub pas bkag pa mi 'grub pa dang / yul ma grub pas yul can ma grub pa'o /*. Similar to Jñānagarbha, SDV 9cd; Eckel 1987, 76. Patsap makes a similar point regarding that which is negated (Dreyfus and Tsering 2010, 402; Vose 2010b, 299n41).

685. *Yuktiṣaṣṭikā* 26–27 matches Tengyur verses preserved in the *Yuktiṣaṣṭikāvṛtti*. See Scherrer-Schaub 1991, 65, 222–23. English translation Loizzo 2007, 122.

686. The text is missing a negation marker at this point.

687. The *Śālistambasūtra, kārikā* 12cd (Schoening 1995, 2: 537, 594): *sangs rgyas byung ma byung rung* [12c] */ chos kyi 'di ni gnas pa yin*. See also Reat 1993, 33–34. Kadampa author citation differs: *sangs rgyas 'byung yang rung / ma byung yang rung ste / chos kyi chos nyid ni de bzhin nyid du gnas so /*. Similar to MRP (D 275b5–6) citation. Sanskrit quoted in Yaśomitra's *Abdhidharmakośavyākhyā* (Wogihara 1971, 293): *utpādād vā tathāgatānām anutpādād vā tathāgatānāṃ sthitaiveyaṃ dharmatā dharmasthititā dharmaniyāmatā tathatā avitathatā ananyatathatā bhūtatā satyatā tattvam aviparītatāviparyastatā*. See also *Laṅkāvatārasūtra* (Nanjio 1923, 143); *Prasannapadā* 40 (Ruegg 2002, 77); MA 6.222a–c; Cox 2000; Takasaki 1966b.

688. *Aṣṭasāhasrikā prajñāpāramitā*, 3: *taccittam acittam / prakṛtiś cittasya prabhāsvarā /*.

689. *Bhāvanākrama* of Nāgārjuna (Toh 3908, vol. *ki*, 2b4–5; Lindtner 1992, 269–70, vv. 21–22c). Kadampa reading differs from Tengyur: *snang yang snang tsam na stong ste* {Tengyur, *no equivalent*} / [21] *ma* {*rnam*} *rig tsam du 'byung ba rnams / / dngos po'i rang bzhin yod ma yin/ rtog par 'gyur ba'i rtog ge pa / / brtags pa tsam du bsgom pa na /* [22] *rang bzhin med cing rnam rig med / / dngos po med cing kun gzhi med / /'di dag byis pas rab tu brtags / /*. Cf. *Laṅkāvatārasūtra* (Nanjio 1923, 275, 10.86[=3.52]): *prajñaptimātraṃ tribhavaṃ nāsti vastu svabhāvataḥ / prajñaptivastubhāvena kalpayiṣyanti tārkikāḥ / /* (Nanjio 1923, 276, 10.91[=3.48]) *na svabhāvo na vijñaptir na vastu na ca ālayaḥ / bālair vikalpitā hy ete . . .*

690. *Bhāvanākrama* of Nāgārjuna. Kadampa citation differs from Tengyur (Toh 3908, vol. *ki*, 3a2–3; Lindtner 1992, 270, vv. 28cd–31ab): *rang sangs rgyas dang sangs rgyas dang / / nyon mongs rnams kyang* {Tengyur, *nyan thos kyang ni*} *brtags pa yin / / gang zag rgyud dang phung po dang / / rkyen rnams gnas pa ma yin no / / gtso bo dbang phyug byed pa po* {*byed po rnams*} */ / sems tsam po las* {*la ni*} *rnam par brtags / / chos kun ngo bos*{*bo*} *yod ma yin / / kun nas nyon mongs med cing grol / / ji ltar snang ba de ltar med / / med pa ma yin yod ma yin* {*pa min*} */ /skye ba med pa'i chos nyid 'di* {*'di ni*} */ /yod dang med pa ma yin no/*. Cf. *Laṅkāvatārasūtra* (Nanjio 1923, 282, 10.132cd): *buddhāḥ pratyekabuddhāśca śrāvakāścāpi kalpitāḥ //* [10.133] */ pudgalaḥ saṃtatiḥ skandhāḥ pratyayā hyaṇavastathā / pradhānamīśvaraḥ kartā cittamātre vikalpyate //* [10.137] */ abhāvāt sarvadharmaṇāṃ saṃkleśo nāsti śuddhi ca / / na ca te tathā yathādṛṣṭā na ca te vai na santi ca //* (Nanjio 1923, 283, 10.144ab) *anutpannā hy amī dharmā na caivaite na santi ca //*.

691. *Cittavajrastava*, v. 7. Kadampa citation differs from Tengyur: *khams skyed lus ni sems kyis bcings / / sems med khams ni rnam par 'jug / de phyir sems ni kun tu bsrungs / / bde legs sems las sangs rgyas 'byung /*. Tengyur (Tola and Dragonetti 1985, 37): *khams*

bskyed sems ni lus kyis bcings / / sems med khams ni bde bar 'jug / de phyir sems ni kun tu bsrungs / / bde legs sems las sangs rgyas 'byung / /.

692. Kadampa citation of *Bodhicittavivaraṇa* (v. 51), close to Atiśa's citation in the BMPP (Sherburne 2000, 262): *dmigs pa dang* [*ni*] *bral ba'i sems*[*/*] *nam mkha'i mtshan nyid la gnas nas* {BMPP, *te*}*/ nam mkha' bsgom* {*sgom*} *par byed pa ni / stong nyid bsgom par byed pa yin* {BMPP, *stong pa nyid ni sgom pa'o*} */.* Tengyur (Lindtner 1997b, v. 51) differs: */ sems la dmigs pa med pa ni / / gnas pa nam mkha'i mtshan nyid yin / / de dag stong nyid sgom pa ni / / nam mkha' sgom par bzhed pa yin //.* See Mathes 2009, 16–17, for Kagyüpa commentary on this verse.

693. *Prajñāpāramitāratnaguṇasaṃcayagāthā*, Tib. 12.9 (underlined portions differ from the critical edition, Yuyama 1976, 171): *nam mkha' mthong zhes sems can tshig tu rab brjod de / / nam mkha' ji ltar mthong ste don 'di brtag par gyis / / de ltar chos mthong ba yang de bzhin gshegs pas bstan / / mthong ba dpe gzhan gyis ni bsnyad par nus ma yin /.* Skt. 12.10 (Yuyama 1976, 52): *ākāśadṛṣṭu iti sattva pravyāharanti khanidarśanaṃ kutu vimṛṣyata etam arthaṃ / tatha dharmadarsanu nidiṣṭu tathāgatena na hi darśanaṃ bhaṇitu śakya nidarśanena // 10 //.*

694. *Stutyatītastava* (*'das par bstan pa*), vv. 9–10 (Mitrikeski 2010, 189–90). Kadampa author citation differs from Tengyur: *lta ba thams cad spangs pa'i phyir / / mgon po khyod kyi* {Tengyur, *kyis*} *stong par bstan* {*gsungs*} */ / de la yongs su brtags pas te* {*de yang yongs su btags pa ste*}*/ dngos su mgon po khyod mi bzhed / /* [9] *stong dang mi stong bzhed ma lags / gnyis kar khyod dgyes ma lags te / de la brtsod pa ma mchis par / / khyod kyi gsung chen spyod pa lags* [10] *//.*

695. *Bodhicittavivaraṇa*, v. 73. Kadampa author citation differs from Tengyur: *de ltar rnal 'byor pa de yis / / stong pa nyid ni goms byas na / / blo ni gzhan don la dga' bar / / 'gyur ba nyid du the tshom med //.* This citation matches Atiśa's citation in *Open Basket of Jewels* (see chap. 1 of this book; also Miyazaki 2007b, 7; Apple 2010, 126–27). Tengyur (Lindtner 1997b, 56): *de ltar stong pa nyid 'di ni / rnal 'byor pa yis bsgom byas na / gzhan gyi don la chags pa'i blo / 'byung bar 'gyur ba the tshom med /.*

696. Atiśa also employs this analogy in *Open Basket of Jewels* (see chap. 1; and Apple 2010, 123).

697. *Suhṛllekha* of Nāgārjuna, v. 117 (Klong chen ye shes rdo rje and Nāgārjuna 2005, 72–73). Kadampa author differs from Tengyur: *bsnyems dang bral ba mang du gsol cing 'tshal* {Tengyur, *bral la ha cang ci 'tshal*} */ phan pa'i gdam ngag don po 'di lags so* {*te*} */ khyod kyis thugs dul mdzod cig bcom ldan gyis / sems ni chos kyi rtsa ba lags pa gsungs //.*

698. *Bodhicittavivaraṇa*, vv. 87cd–88; Kadampa Tibetan differs from Tengyur: *rang lus spyin par gtong ba 'di / / ngo mtshar skye ba ma yin gyi / / chos 'di stong par shes nas kyang / / las kyi 'bras bu yod ces pa / / ngo mtshar las kyang 'di ngo mtshar / / smad byung las kyang 'di smad byung /.* Matches citation in MRP (D 275b2–3). Tengyur (Lindtner 1997b, 62): *de dag rnams kyi rang lus dang / / nor rnams byin pa ngo mtshar min /87cd/ chos rnams stong pa 'di shes nas / / las dang 'bras bu sten pa gang / / de ni ngo mtshar bas ngo mtshar / / rmad du 'byung bas rmad du 'byung //.* This verse is also cited by Tsongkhapa (Hopkins 2008, 93).

699. MMK 24.11; Kadampa Tibetan differs from Tengyur (Toh 3824, vol. *tsa,* 15a2): *stong pa nyid la lta nyes na / / shes rab chung ldan* {Tengyur, *chung rnams*} *phung par 'gyur / / ji ltar sbrul* {*sprul*} *la gzung nyes dang / / rigs* {*rig*} *sngags log par* {*nyes par*} *bsgrubs*

pa bzhin /. Skt. (La Vallée Poussin 1903–13, 495.1–2): *vināśayati durdṛṣṭā śūnyatā mandamedhasam / sarpo yathā durgṛhīto vidyā vā duṣprasādhitā //11 //*.

700. *Ratnāvalī* 2.19; Kadampa author differs from Tengyur (Hahn 1982, 47.13–16): *chos 'di log par shes gyur na / / mi mkhas rnams kyi chud kyang za'* {Tengyur: *za*} */ gzhan yang med par blta ba'i* {*'di ltar med par lta ba yi*} */ / ming tsam* {*mi gtsang*} *der ni bying bar 'gyur //*. The Kadampa reading of *ming tsam* for *mi gtsang* may reflect misunderstanding through oral transmission or scribal error. Skt. (Hahn 1982, 46.13–16): *vināśayati durjñāto dharmo 'yam avipaścitam / nāstitādṛṣṭisamale yasmād asmin nimajjati //*.

701. *Bodhicittavivaraṇa*, vv. 95–96. Kadampa citation differs from Tengyur: *nyan thos de dag ji srid du / sangs rgyas rnams kyi ma bskul ba / / de srid ye shes lus kyis su / / ting 'dzin dregs pas myos te gnas / / bskul nas sna tshogs gzugs kyis su / / sems can don la dga' byed cing / / pu nya ye shes nyer spel nas / sangs rgyas bo dho thob par 'gyur //*. Tengyur (Lindtner 1997b, 64): *ji srid sangs rgyas kyis ma bskul / / de srid ye shes lus dngos can / / ting 'dzin myos pas rgyal 'gyur ba / / nyan thos de dag gnas par 'gyur //* 95 // *bskul na sna tshogs gzugs kyis ni / / sems can don la chags gyur cing / / bsod nams ye shes tshogs bsags nas / / sangs rgyas byang chub thob par 'gyur //*. A citation in the *Prasphuṭapadā* commentary of Dharmamitra (ninth century; Toh 3796, vol. *nya*, 83b) closely matches the Kadampa citation: *nyan thos de dag ji srid du / / sangs rgyas rnams kyis ma bskul ba / / de srid ye shes lus gcig gis / / ting 'dzin dregs pas myos te gnas / / bskul nas sna tshogs gzugs kyis ni / /sems can don la dga' byed cing / / bsod nams ye shes nyer 'phel nas / / sangs rgyas byang chub thob par 'gyur //*.

702. *Suhṛllekha* of Nāgārjuna, v. 104 (Klong chen ye shes rdo rje and Nāgārjuna 2005, 68–69). Kadampa author differs from Tengyur: *blo bur mgo'am gos la me shor nas* {Tengyur: *mgo'am gos la glo bur me shor na*} */ de dag phyir bzlog bya ba* {*bzlog phyir bgyi ba*} *btang nas kyang / / yang srid med par bgyi slad 'bad 'tshal te / de las dgos pa che mchog* {*de bas ches mchog dgos pa*} *gzhan ma mchis //*.

703. In Atiśa's gradual stages of the path (*lam rim*), a being of middling capacity or scope (*madhyamapuruṣa, skyes bu 'bring*) seeks peace from *saṃsāra* (i.e., *śrāvakas* and *pratyekabuddhas*).

704. The metaphor of diving into Avīci Hell as a goose dives into a lake of lotuses is found in Śāntideva's *Bodhicaryāvatāra* (8.107) and *Śikṣāsamuccaya* (360.8).

705. *Bodhicittavivaraṇa*, vv. 85–86. Kadampa citation differs from Tengyur: *bo dhe 'bras bu bzhin don ni / byang sems myu gu las byung bas / snying rje'i rtsa bas brtan par ni / rgyal ba'i sras kyi bsgom par bya / / brtan pa rnams kyis gar bsgoms pas / / bsam gtan bde ba'ang bor nas ni / / gzhan gyi du kha ma bzod pas / / mnar med par yang 'jug par byed gsungs //*. Tengyur (Lindtner 1997b, 60): *snying rjes brtan pa'i rtsa ba can / / byang sems myu gu las byung ba / / gzhan don gcig 'bras byang chub ni / / rgyal ba'i sras rnams sgom par byed //* 85 // *gang zhig bsgom pas brtan pa ni / / gzhan gyi sdug bsngal gyis bred nas / / bsam gtan bde ba dor nas kyang / / mnar med pa yang 'jug par byed //*.

706. *Bodhicittavivaraṇa*, vv. 89–90. Kadampa citation differs from Tengyur: *sems can skyabs pa'i bsam pa yis / / srid pa'i 'dam du skyes mod kyi / / pad 'dam la ni chu bzhin du / / srid pa'i skyon gyi de mi gos / / bzang po la rgyal sras rnams kyi / / 'di na ye shes me yis 'dis / / nyon mongs bud shing bsreg bzhin du / / 'on kyang thugs rjes brlan par mdzad //*. Tengyur (Lindtner 1997a, 62): *sems can bskyab pa'i bsam pa can / / de dag srid pa'i 'dam skyes kyang / / de byung nyid pas ma gos pa / / chu yi padma'i 'dab ma*

bzhin // 89 // *kun bzang la sogs rgyal ba'i sras* / / *stong nyid ye shes me yis ni* / / *nyon mongs bud shing bsregs mod kyi* / / *de lta'ang snying rjes brlan 'gyur cing* // 90 //.

707. As noted, the title page and first folios of the *Collection of Special Instructions on the Middle Way* (*Dbu ma'i man ngag gi 'bum*) and *Collection on the Two Realities* (*Bden gnyis kyi 'bum*) were switched at some point in their history and I have corrected the titles based on their corresponding content. I have kept the actual title of the given manuscript in the notes.
708. Tibetan critical editions of the *Madhyamakopadeśa* and *Madhyamakopadeśavṛtti*, along with annotated Japanese translations, may be found in Mochizuki 2002.
709. Lechen Kunga Gyaltsen 2003, 10: / *lta ba gtso bor ston pa ni jo bo nyid kyis mdzad pa'i bden pa gnyis la 'jug pa dang* / *dbu ma'i man ngag la sogs pa yin la* //. Texts on the "view" (*lta ba*), along with practice (*spyod pa*) and integration (*zung 'brel*), belong to the textual (*zhung*) lineage of teachings. The textual lineage belongs to a broader classification that includes advice (*gdams ngag*) and special instructions (*man ngag*).
710. *Sherab Dorjé's Explanation of Atiśa's Entry to the Two Realities* (*Bden gnyis kyi rnam par bshad pa*), 2b7): *sgom pa rtan la 'bebs pa'i dbang du byas na* / *dbu ma'i man ngag . . .*
711. See Huanhuan and van der Kuijp 2014 for the historical and philological issues in the Tibetan translation of this text and other works of Bhāviveka.
712. *Dbu ma'i man ngag gi bshad pa/ pu to yab sras kyi lugs*, 320.6–321.3.
713. On *samāhitajñāna* and *pṛṣṭhalabdhajñāna*, see Makransky 1997, 97–104; Almogi 2009, 163–171; Martini 2011, 151–52n37.
714. *Satyadvayāvatāra*, v. 21 (Ejima 1983, 365): / *kun rdzob ji ltar snang ba 'di* / / *rigs pas brtags na 'ga' mi rnyed* / / *ma rnyed pa nyid don dam yin* / / *ye nas gnas pa'i chos nyid do* //. On the "conventional that appears just as it is," see chap. 3.
715. Atiśa will state great four reasons (*gtan tshigs chen po bzhi*) in his *Bodhimārgapradīpapañjikā* (Sherburne 2000, 230–36), including the reason refuting production according to the tetralemma (*mu bzhi skye 'gog gi gtan tshigs, catuṣkoṭyutpādapratiṣedhahetu*), the diamond-splinters reason (*rdo rje gzegs ma'i gtan tshigs, vajrakaṇahetu*), the reason of being neither one nor many (*gcig du bral gyi gtan tshigs, ekānekaviyogahetu*), and the reason consisting in dependent-arising (*rten 'brel gyi gtan tshigs, pratītyasamutpādahetu*). Atiśa leaves out the reason refuting the production of existent and nonexistent things (*yod med skye 'gog gi gtan tshigs, *sadasadutpādapratiṣedhahetu*) that is discussed by earlier Mādhyamikas like Kamalaśīla (Keira 2004, 13).
716. Although *nimitta* (Tib. *mtsan ma*) is usually translated as "signs," in the context of Madhyamaka the term signifies some type of appearance such as phenomenal marks (Ruegg 2010, 54).
717. Lindtner 1979, 113: *chos la bdag med pa ni chos rnams kyi ngo bo nyid med pa'o* / / *de la mdor bsdu na chos ni rnam pa gnyis te* / *gzugs can dang gzugs can ma yin pa'o* / / *de la gzugs can la yang rnam pa gnyis te* / *'byung ba dang 'byung ba las gyur pa'o* / / *gang gzugs can ma yin pa la yang rnam pa gnyis te* / *'dus byas dang 'dus ma bya pa'o* // *de la gzug can ma yin pa 'dus byas la yang rnam pa gsum ste* / *sems dang sems las byung ba dang* / *sems dang mi ldan pa'o* // *gang yang zugs can ma yin pa 'dus ma byas pa ni*

rnam pa bzhi ste / nam mkha' dang / so sor brtag pa'i 'gog pa dang / so sor brtags pa ma yin pa'i 'gog pa dang / chos rnams kyi chos nyid do //.

718. MRP (Toh 3854, vol. *tsha*, 279a5–b2): *slob dpon zla ba grags pa'i zhal nas / dngos ni rnam pa gnyis te / gzugs can dang / gzugs can ma yin no // gzugs can ni gnyis te / 'byung ba dang / 'byung ba las gyur pa'o / / gzugs can ma yin pa'i chos ni gnyis te / 'dus byas dang / 'dus ma byas so // 'dus byas kyi chos ni gsum ste / sems dang / sems las byung ba dang ldan pa ma yin ba'o // 'dus ma byas kyi chos ni bzhi ste / so sor brtag pa'i 'gog pa dang / so sor brtags pa ma yin pa dang / nam mkha' dang / chos rnams kyi de bzhin nyid do zhes gsungs mod kyi / 'on kyang 'di dngos po'i chos bsdus par gyur na ni 'di ltar gnyis te/ gzugss can dang/ gzugs can ma yin pa'o //.*

719. Scherrer-Schaub 1991, 221n398, 245n471.

720. Tib. (Miyazaki 2007, 6): *sems ni kha dog med pa / dbyibs med pa / rang bzhin gyis 'od gsal ba/ gdod nas ma skyes pa'o /.*

721. MRP (Toh 3854, vol. *tsha*, 280a2).

722. See chap. 1, §1.

723. See chap. 7, Tib. *Bden gnyis kyi 'bum* (12b): *yang na rang bzhin gyis 'od gsal ba ste / rigs pa de dag gis bzhigs nas stong par byed pa ni ma yin gyi / rang bzhin skye ba med pa yin pas gzugs can dang de ma yin pa'am / dman pa dang gya nom pa'am / che 'bring la sogs pa'i spros pas ma spros shing rtogs pas ma rtogs pas na 'od gsal ba zhes bya ste //.*

724. Martini 2011, 151–52n37.

725. *Kāśyapaparivarta* (*'od srung gi le'u*, Toh 87, *dkon brtsegs*, vol. *cha*, 133a.7–133b.1): "Kāśyapa, it is as follows: For example, wind rubs together two sticks of wood, from that, fire emerges, and once arisen, the two sticks are consumed. Similarly, Kāśyapa, when one has correct individual analysis [of things, through its force] a noble being's faculty of wisdom arises. Once produced, correct individual analysis itself is consumed" (*'od srung 'di lta ste / dper na shing gnyis rlung gis drud pa / de las me byung ste / byung nas shing de gnyis sreg pa de bzhin du 'od srung yang dag par so sor rtog pa yod na 'phags pa shes rab kyi dbang po skye ste / / de skyes pas yang dag par so sor rtog pa de nyid sreg par byed do / / de la 'di skad ces bya ste / dper na shing gnyis rlung gis drud pa las / / ma byung nas ni de nyid sreg par byed / / de bzhin gshegs rab dbang po skyes nas kyang / / so sor rtog pa de nyid sreg par byed //*). Tibetan and Chinese edited by Staël-Holstein 1977 [1926], 102, §69. The Sanskrit of this passage is not extant, although a citation of Sthiramati is preserved in the *Madhyāntavibhagaṭīkā* (trans. Martini 2011, 147): Sthiramati's *Madhyāntavibhāgaṭīkā*: *tad yathā, Kāśyapa, kāṣṭhadvayaṃ pratītyāgnir jāyate iti jātaś ca samānas tad eva kāṣṭhadvayaṃ dahati. evam eva, Kāśyapa, bhūtapratyavekṣāṃ pratītyāryaṃ prajñendriyaṃ jāyate jātaṃ ca tām eva bhūtapratyavekṣāṃ dahatīti.* "Just as, Kāśyapa, from a pair of firesticks fire is born and, as soon as fire is born, it burns up that very couple of pieces of wood, exactly so, Kāśyapa, in dependence on analytical examination of reality the faculty of wisdom is born and, once it is born, it burns up exactly that very analytical examination of reality."

726. See Ruegg 1989, 94–95n179.

727. See chapter 6. *Madhyamakopadeśavṛtti* (Toh 3931, vol. *ki*, 120b7–121a1): *so sor rtog pa'i shes rab de nyid kyang mi 'grub ste zhes bya bas ni bdag nyid kyi rtog pa 'gog par byed do / / shes rab ni dngos po'i bye brag yin pas dngos po ma grub na shes rab de nyid*

kyang mi 'grub ste / shing ma grub na sha pa la sogs pa bkag pa bzhin no / / [121a] */ / de yang bsreg bya tshig pa'i me / / bsreg bya tshig nas mi gnas ltar / / zhes pa dang //.*

728. Ruegg 1989, 207.
729. Tillemans 2007, 509.
730. *Open Basket of Jewels,* chap. 1, §3.1.
731. *Madhyamakopadeśa,* Toh 3929, vol. *ki,* 95b1–96a.7.
732. Lit., "with an illusion-like mind."
733. See my Introduction on the late Indian subclassifications of Madhyamaka into Māyopamādvayavāda (Tib. *sgyu ma lta bu gnyis su med par smra ba*), "the strand that maintains that [things] are not two, inasmuch as they are like illusions," and Apratiṣṭhānavada, "the strand that maintains that all things have so substance whatsoever." See also Almogi 2010. See Newland 1992 for how Gelukpa authors utilize Prajñāmukti in interpreting the relationship between the two realities. See Dunne 1996 on Candrakīrti's understanding of the nonconceptual knowledge of a buddha.
734. *Madhyamakopadeśavṛtti,* Toh 3931, vol. *ki,* 116b.7–123b.2. Translated by the author and Tsultrim Gyalwa.
735. This indicates that Prajñāmukti's text states "bow down to **those** supreme holy persons."
736. Prajñāmukti cites the *Abhisamayālaṃkāra* and his text reads: *mog mog por mdzad dang*; AA I.8: "eclipsing and so forth, the paths of disciples and rhinoceroses, the path of vision of great beneficial qualities for this other [lives]." Skt. (Stcherbatsky and Obermiller 1929, 2): *śyāmīkaraṇatādīni śiṣyakhaḍgapathau ca yau / mahānuśaṃso dṛṅmārga aihikāmutrikairguṇaiḥ //.* Tib. I.8. (Stcherbatsky and Obermiller 1929, 3): *mog mog por byed la sogs* dang */ / slob ma bse ru'i lam gang dang / / 'di dang gzhan pa'i yon tan gyis // phan yon che ba mthong ba'i lam //.*
737. *Madhyāntavibhāgakārikā,* I.17cd (Pandeya 1999, 41): *abdhātukanakākāśaśuddhiva cchuddhiriṣyate.* Hoornaert, 2003, 157n 6: "The comparison of the intrinsically pure nature of the mind with the purity of water, gold, and space is used in, for example, MVK I.16, MSA XI.13, XIII.16, 18, YBh, T vol. 30, 70 I b28–c3, 748b 13–l 8." The parallel passage in PP quotes MVK I.16cd and MVK 1.21–22 (see Eckel 1985, 57–59).
738. A similar verse is found in the *Ātajñānamahāyānasūtra* (*'Phags pa 'da' ka ye shes shes bya ba theg pa chen po'i mdo,* "The Gnosis of the Moment of Passing Away"); see Jackson 2009, 5.
739. Unidentified verse: *gang zhig 'dzin dang 'don dang spyod pa dang / / gzhan la 'dri zhing thos pa 'dzin byed dang / / de yi blo ni nyi ma'i 'od zer gyis / / padma bzhin du rnam par kha 'byed do //.*
740. The five sciences (*pañcavidyā*): linguistic science (*śabda*), logical science (*hetu*), "inner" science (*adhyātma*), medical science (*cikitsā*), and the science of fine arts and crafts (*śilapakarmasthāna*).
741. Thurman et al. 2004, 141: "If he has not applied himself to the five sciences, even the supreme saint will never arrive at omniscience. Therefore, he makes effort in those (sciences), in order to criticize and care for others as well as for the sake of his own knowledge." MSA 11.60 (Lévi 1907, 70): *vidyāsthāne pañcavidhe yogamakṛtvā sarvajñatvaṃ naiti kathaṃcitparamāryaḥ / ityanyeṣāṃ nigrahaṇānugrahaṇāya svājñārthaṃ vā tatra karotyeva sa yogam //.* Tib. (Toh 4020, vol. *phi,* 15b4–5): *rig pa'i gnas lnga dag la mkhas par ma byas na / / 'phags mchos gis kyang thams cad mkhyen nyid mi 'gyur te / / de lta bas na gzhan dag tshar gcad rjes gzung / / bdag nyid kun shes bya phyir de la de brtson byed //.* French translation (Lévi 1911, 127): S'il ne s'est pas

appliqué aux cinq Sciences classiques, le Saint par excellence n'arrive absolument pas à l'Omniscience; aussi il y met son Application pour empêcher les autres, ou pour les seconder, ou pour reconnaître par soi-même.

742. The three bodies of a buddha are the emanation body (*nirmāṇakāya*), enjoyment body (*saṃbhogakāya*), and dharma body (*dharmakāya*).

743. *Ratnaguṇasaṃcayagāthā* I.18a (Yuyama 1976, 13; Conze 1975, 11): *mahadāyako mahatabuddhi mahānubhāvo*.

744. The text mentions the "Small Vehicle" (*theg pa chung*) as opposed to the more common Tibetan translation of "Inferior Vehicle" (*theg dman*) for *hīnayāna*.

745. Not in Atiśa's root text.

746. Not in Atiśa's root text.

747. Not in Atiśa's root text.

748. Translation of sentence based on Newland 1992, 68.

749. Translation also found in Newland 1992, 64.

750. *Saṃdhinirmocanasūtra* III.6; see Mathes 2008, 79. Also, Atiśa's *Dharmadhatudarśanagīti*, v. 35.

751. That is, the whiteness of the shell is neither one with nor different from the shell.

752. See Candrakīrti's *Madhyamakāvatāra* 6.28. Translation in *General Explanation*. See also Huntington 1989, 160; Dunne 1996, 541–42.

753. *Yuktiṣaṣṭikā*, v. 45 (Scherrer-Schaub 1991, 15): *gang rten* {*brten*} *nas dnogs po rnams / / chu yi zla ba lta bur ni / yang dag ma yin log min par / / 'dod pa de dag lhas* {em. *ltas*} *mi phrogs* {var. *'phrogs*} *//*. The reading in 45a, *rten*, follows the paracanonical edition of Patsap's translation.

754. *Satyadvayavibhaṅgavṛtti* (Eckel 1987, 172) slightly differs: *rigs pas brtags na bden ma yin / / de las gzhan du bden pa yin* {Prajñāmukti *ste*} *// des na gcig la bden nyid dang / / mi bden par ni ji ltar 'gal //* {Prajñāmukti *des na dngos po gcig nyid la / / bden dang bden ji ltar 'gal*}. See also Eckel 1987, 86.

755. Prajñāmukti, 119b3–4: *rgyal ba <u>kun kyi</u> stong <u>nyid ni</u> / / lta kun nges par <u>sel ba yin</u>.* MMK 13.8ab: Klu'i rgyal mtshan (ca. eighth century). Tibetan translation (Toh 3824, vol. *tsa*, 8a6): *rgyal ba <u>rnams kyis</u> stong <u>pa nyid</u> // lta kun nges par <u>'byung bar gsungs</u> /*. Skt. (Katsura and Siderits 2013, 145): *śūnyatā sarvadṛṣṭīnāṃ proktā niḥsaraṇaṃ jinaiḥ*.

756. MMK, dedicatory verse a, c: *anirodham anutpādam . . . yaḥ pratītyasamutpādaṃ . . .*

757. MMK, 1.1 (La Vallée Poussin 1903–13, 12.13–4): *na svato nāpi parato na dvābhyāṃ nāpy ahetutaḥ / utpannā jātu vidyante bhāvāḥ kva cana ke cana //*. Translated by MacDonald 2015, 2: 48. In the *Bodhipathapradīpapañjika* (Sherburne 2000, 234), cited as an example of diamond-particle proof.

758. Jñānagarbha, *Satyadvayavibhaṅgakārikā*, v. 14 (Eckel 1987, 80): *du mas dngos po gcig mi byed / / du mas du ma byed ma yin / / gcig gis du ma'i dngos mi byed / / gcig gis gcig byed pa yang min //.*

759. Śāntarakṣita, *Madhyamakālaṃkāra* 1 (Ichigō 1989, 191): *niḥsvabhāvā amī tattvataḥ svaparoditāḥ / ekānekasvabhāvena viyogāt pratibimbavat //*. Cited also in the *Bodhipathapradīpapañjika* (Sherburne 2000, 234). Proof that refutes identity and multiplicity.

760. Cited in Bodhibhadra's *Samādhisambhāraparivarta*, 81b (*ting nge 'dzin gyi tsogs kyi le'u zhes bya ba*), as from the *'Phags pa nyan thos kyi so sor thar pa'i mdo*.

761. *Madhyamakālaṃkāravṛtti* (P, 83b8–84a3; Toh 3885, vol. *sa*, 83a4–6).

762. *Madhyamakālaṃkāra* 62 (Ichigō 1989, 211): *gcig dang du ma ma gtogs par / /rnam*

pa gzhan dang ldan pa yi / / dngos po mi rung 'di gnyis ni / / phan tsun spangs te gnas phyir ro /.

763. Śrīgupta, *Tattvāvatāravṛtti* (*De kho na la 'jug pa'i 'grel pa*, Toh 3892, vol. *ha*, 40a2–3: */ de ltar rtsom byed med* [40a3] *pa'i phyir / / rdzas la sogs thams cad bsal //.*

764. Prajñāmukti's text reads: *sangs rgyas rnams kyis nam yang ni / / gtan du chos rnams thams cad dag / sems ma rnyed cing chos mkhyen pa / / dmigs mi mnga' la phyag 'tshal bstod //.* Cited in *Madhyamakāloka*, Toh 3887, vol. *sa*, 240b. Differs but close to *Jñānālokālaṃkāra* (Study Group on Buddhist Literature 2004, 154): *cittaṃ na labdhaṃ buddhehi atyantāya kadācana / sarvvadharmā ca sarvvajña nirālamba namo 'stu te // 30 //.*

765. Śrīgupta, *Tattvāvatāravṛtti* (*De kho na la 'jug pa'i 'grel pa*, Toh 3892, vol. *ha*, 40b–41a): *sems ni de ltar* [41a] *med pa'i phyir / / sems las byung ba rnams kyang bsal /* {Prajñāmukti reads *bkag pa'i phyir /* }.

766. This indicates that Prajñāmukti's text states "freedom from hatred"; the phrase is not found in Atiśa's root text.

767. Jñānagarbha, *Satyadvayavibhaṅgakārikā* (Eckel 1987, 101, v. 39; Tib., Eckel 1987, 187): *gang tshe shes dang shes bya dang / / bdag nyid rjes su mi mthong ba // de ni mtshan ma mi 'byung phyir // gnas pa brtan phyir mi bzheng so //.* Prajñāmukti citation differs: *gang tshe shes dang shes bya dag / / bdag nyid rjes su mi mthong bas / / de tshe mtshan ma mi 'byung phyir / / gnas pa brten phyir mi bzhengs so //.*

768. Bhāviveka, *Madhyamakahṛdayam*, 3.16. English translation Engle 2009, 91–92. Skt. (Lindtner 2001, 8): *nibadhyālambanastambhe smṛtirajjvā manogajam / unmārgacāriṇaṃ kuryāt prajñāṅkuśavasaṃ śanaiḥ.* Tib. (Toh 3855, vol. *dza* 4a6): *yid kyi glang po log 'gro ba / dmigs pa'i ka ba brtan po la / dran pa'i thag pas nges bcings nas / shes rab lcags kyus rim dbang bya //.* Prajñāmukti's citation differs in the first line: *sems kyi glang po log 'gro ba.*

769. Dergé erroneously reads *ma chen po.*

770. Cited from the *Vairocanābhisaṃbodhitantra.*

771. *Yuktiṣaṣṭikā*, v. 1 (Scherrer-Schaub 1991, 7). *Dbu ma'i man nga gi 'bum* reads: *gang blo yod dang med pa las / / rnam par 'das shing mi gnas pa / / de dag zab mo dmigs med pa'i* {var. *yi*} */ / rkyen gyi don la rnam par bsgsoms //.* The citation of this verse is from the Tibetan translation by *Ye shes sde* (ninth century) of the commentary, the *Yuktiṣaṣṭikāvṛtti* of Candrakīrti. The Tibetan translation by Patsap Nyimadrak of this verse from the *Yuktiṣaṣṭikā* differs. See Scherrer-Schaub 1991, 24–25. The verse is preserved in Sanskrit in the *Sekoddeśaṭīkā* (Scherrer-Schaub 1991, 116n42): *astināsti-vyatikrāntā buddhir yeṣāṃ nirāśrayā / gambhīras tair nirālambaḥ pratyayārtho vibhāvyate //.* The commentary to this verse in the *Yuktiṣaṣṭikāvṛtti* (Scherrer-Schaub 1991, 24; P, 4a6–7) mentions that "those who have meditated on emptiness in previous lives, as they have understood dependent-arising and have the seed for the vision of emptiness, have great power (*gang dag 'das pa'i srid pa na stong pa nyid la goms pa de dag rten cing 'brel par 'byung ba rtogs shing stong pa nyid mthong ba'i sa bon yod pa'i phyir mthu che ba yin te /*).

772. *Abhisamayālaṃkāra* I.39 (Stcherbatsky and Obermiller 1929, 6): *dharma-dhātor asaṃbhedāt gotrabhedo na yujyata / ādheyadharmabhedāt tu tadbhedaḥ pāragīyate //.* English translation Sparham 2006, 1: 84–85. Cited also in Atiśa's *Bodhipathapradīpapañjika* (Sherburne 2000, 116).

773. This corresponds to "[Buddhas] will not have any subsequent attainment" in Atiśa's text.

774. Tibetan reads: *glang chen bzhugs kyang mnyam par bzhugs / / glang chen bzhengs kyang mnyam par bzhengs* [em. *bzhugs*]. Cf. *Abhidharmakośabhāṣya ad* 4.12 (Pradhan 1975, 204): *caran samāhito nāgastiṣṭhannāgaḥ samāhitaḥ / svapan samāhito nāgo niṣaṇṇo 'pi samāhita //*. *Aṅguttara*, III. 346. Verse cited in full in MRP (Toh 3854, vol. *tsha*, 283a3): *glang chen bzhugs kyang mnyam par gzhag / glang chen bzhud kyang mnyam par gzhag / glang chen man la yang mnyam par bzhag / glang chen gzigs kyang mnyam par bzhag //*.

775. Different from Atiśa's text.

776. Prajñāmukti reads *mtshan ma* for *kun tu rtog pa*. Cf. Miyazaki 2007b, 8n6, *Vairocanābhisaṃbodhi* (Toh 494, vol. *tha*, 226b7–227a1): *byang chub nam mkha'i mtshan nyid do kun tu rtog pa thams cad spangs //*.

777. Different from Atiśa's text.

778. Cf. *Saṃvarodayatantra* 33, Tib. vv. 33abc–34a. Skt. (Tsuda 1974, 164–65): *nānādhimuktikāḥ sattvāś caryānānāvibodhitāḥ / nānānayavineyānām upāyena tu deśitāḥ // 32 // gambhīradharmanirdeśe nādhimuktikā yadi pratikṣepo na kartavyo 'cintyā sarvadharmatā // 33 //*.

779. "Whoever sees me as visible matter, whoever understands me as sound, has entered into a wrong path; that person will not see me. The buddhas are the *dharmakāya*; the 'leaders' see reality (*dharmatā*)." *Vajracchedikā*, §26, vv. 1–2ab (Conze 1957, 56–57): *yo māṃ rūpeṇa cādrākṣur yo māṃ ghoṣeṇa cānvaguḥ / mithyāprahāṇaprartā na māṃ drakṣyanti te janāḥ / 1 / dharmato buddho draṣṭavyo dharmakāyā hi nāyakāḥ //*.

780. As noted, the title page and first folios of the *Collection of Special Instructions on the Middle Way* (*Dbu ma'i man ngag gi 'bum*) and *Collection on the Two Realities* (*Bden gnyis kyi 'bum*) were switched at some point in their history and I have corrected the manuscripts' titles based on their corresponding content. I have kept the actual title of the given manuscript in the notes. For information on the manuscript of the *Bden gnyis kyi 'bum*, see Apple 2015, 21–23.

781. *Sūtrasamuccayasañcayārtha*, extended colophon not in Dergé Tengyur but in the *Bstan' gyur gser bris ma, mdo 'grel a*, 513r: . . . *lha khang ke ru'i khyams smad kyi ban de bdag gyi zhus te gdams ngag dang bcas te gnang ngo / jo bo'i bla ma a wa dhū ti pas rab tu mi gnas pa'i lta ba dang / las mtha' sems bskyed pa'i cho ga dang / mdo kun las btus pa'i don man ngag tu byas pa 'di gsum stabs gcig tu gnang ba lags so //*. Cf. Chattopadhyaya 1967, 462.

782. See Dromtönpa Gyalwai Jungné 2012b, 46.13–16: *nga'i bla ma shānti pa brgyad stong pa gsung tsa na dbu mar bshad pa thams cad re re nas sun phyung bas / nga'i dbu ma'i lta ba de nyid gsal btab pa bzhin du song / rnal 'byor spyod pa'i dbu ma shin tu gsal bar gyur / nga zla ba grags pa'i lugs la shin tu dad pa yin gsung //*.

783. This story relates to how the titles of texts should be composed. See De Jong 1972, 191; Roesler 2002, 447nn40, 41, 43.

784. The content of the manuscript now shifts to commenting on Atiśa's *Special Instructions on the Middle Way*.

785. *Yuktiṣaṣṭika*, v. 30 (Scherrer-Schaub 1991, 12): *de nyid tshol la thog mar ni / / thams cad yod ces brjod par bya / / don rnams rtogs shing chags med la / phyis ni rnam par dben pa'o //*. English translation Loizzo 2007, 180 (Tib. 318). Skt. (Lindtner 1997b, 110): *sarvam astīti vaktavyam ādau tattvagaveṣiṇaḥ | paścād avagatārthasya niḥsaṅgasya viviktata //*.

786. *Catuḥśataka*, chap. 8, v. 15. Kadampa text reads: *dang por bsod nams min las bzlog / bar du bdag las bzlog bya zhing / tha mar kun las bzog bya ba / / de ltar shes pa rigs par*

ldan //. Tib. (Lang 1986, 82): *bsod nams min pa dang por bzlog / bar du bdag ni bzlog pa dang / phyi nas lta ba kun bzlog pa / gang gis shes de mkhas pa yin //.* Skt. (Lang 1986, 82): *vāraṇaṃ prāg apuṇyasya madhye vāraṇam ātmanaḥ / sarvasya vāraṇaṃ paścād yo jānite sa buddhimān //.*

787. See Vetturini 2007, 108, for later historical accounts of this saying.

788. Cf. *Madhyāntavibhāga*, vv. 1–2 (Nagao 1964, 17–18): *abhūtaparikalpo 'sti dvayan tatra na vidyate / śūnyatā vidyate tv atra tasyām api sa vidyate // na śūnyaṃ nāpi cāśūnyaṃ tasmāt sarvam vidhīyate / sattvād asattvāt sattvāc ca madhyamā pratipac ca sā //.* Translation based on Mathes 2000, 197–97: "False imagining exists. Duality is not found in that. But emptiness is found there, [and false imagining] is found in relation to [emptiness] as well. Therefore, everything is taught as neither empty nor non-empty, because [false imagining] exists, because [duality] does not exist, and because [false imagining] exists [in relation to emptiness, and emptiness in relation to false imagining]. And this is the middle path."

789. Jñānagarbha's *Satyadvayavibhaṅgakārikā*, 17a (Eckel 1987, 87, Tib., 173): *kun rdzob de bzhin nyid gang yin // de nyid dam pa'i don gyis bzhed //.* Sanskrit in Haribhadra's AAA (Wogihara 1932, 407.25): *saṃvṛtes tathatā yaiva paramārthasya sā matā / abhedāt so 'pi ni nyāyo yathādarśanam āsthitaḥ //.*

790. This echoes the relationship between the two realities found in Atiśa's *Satyadvayāvatāra* and Candrakīrti's *Madhyamakāvatāra* (6.80). The *Satyadvayāvatāra*, v. 19 (Ejima 1983, 365–66; Apple 2013, 314): [The Ācārya Candrakīrti has stated as follows]: "Conventional reality functions as a means, and ultimate reality functions as the goal. Those who do not understand the difference between the two have a bad understanding and get a bad rebirth." *slob dpon zla grags 'di skad du* {om. Ejima} *// thabs su gyur pa kun rdzob bden pa dang / / thabs las byung ba don dam bden pa dag / gnyis po'i dbye ba gang gis mi shes pa / / de dag log par rtogs pas ngan 'gror 'gro //* 19 *//. Madhyamakāvatāra*, 6.80 (La Vallée Poussin 1907–11, 175.3–6): *tha snyad bden pa thabs su gyur pa dang / / don dam bden pa thabs byung gyur pa ste / / de gnyis rnam dbye gang gis mi shes pa / / de ni rnam rtog log pas lam ngan zhugs //* 6.80 *//.* Cited in the *Subhāṣitasaṃgraha* (Bendall 1903, 396.7–10): *upāyabhūtaṃ vyavahārasatyam upeyabhūtaṃ paramārthasatyam / tayor vibhāgaṃ na paraiti yo vai mithyāvikalpaiḥ sa kumārgayātaḥ //.* As noted by Lindtner (1979, 89n13), this verse is also cited in the *Bodhisattvayogācāracatuḥśatakaṭīkā*, chap. 3 (P, vol. 98 [*dbu ma Ya*], 63a.1–2).

791. Chengawa Tsultrim Bar was the youngest of the three Kadampa brothers, the other two being Potowa Rinchen Sal and Phuchungwa Shönu Gyaltsen.

792. This refers to Naljorpa Jangchup Rinchen, who was a direct disciple of Atiśa and later became abbot of Radreng Monastery after Dromtönpa Gyalwai Jungné.

793. Quoted in Tsongkhapa's *Lam rim chen mo* (Tsongkhapa 1985, 195); for the English, see Cutler and Newland 2000, 1: 251.

794. *Satyadvayāvatāra*, v. 21abc (Ejima 1983, 365): */ kun rdzob ji ltar snang ba 'di // rigs pas brtags na 'ga' mi rnyed // ma rnyed pa nyid don dam yin //.* See Apple 2013, 315–17.

795. The Kadampa author is following Atiśa's tradition of "four great reasons" (*gtan tshigs chen po bzhi*) as articulated in the *Bodhipathapradīpa* (Sherburne 2000, 15, 229–35). Atiśa's system of positing four reasons for proving emptiness is different from Kamalaśīla, who discusses five reasons (see Keira 2004, 10–13).

796. *Śūnyatāsaptati*, v. 4ab (Lindtner 1997b, 94): *yod pa yod phyir skye ma yin / med pa med pa'i phyir ma yin //.*

797. This citation is actually from Āryadeva's *Catuḥśataka* (11.15) rather than verses of the *Madhyamakāvatāra*. The manuscript reads (Lang 1986, 106): *'bras bu yod par gang 'dod dang / / 'bras bu med par gang 'dod la / / ka ba lasogs rgyan rnams ni* {Lang: *khyim gyi don du ka ba la*} */ / khyim gyi don du don med do* {*sogs pa'i rgyan ni don med 'gyur*} /. Skt. (Lang 1986, 106): *stambhādīnām alaṃkāro gṛhasārthe nirarthakaḥ / satkāryam eva yasyeṣṭaṃ yasyāsatkāryam eva ca //*. Howevever, the verse is found in Candrakīrti's *Madhyamakāvatārabhāṣya* (La Vallée Poussin 1907–12, 99.13–14), cited without source, indicating that early Tibetans may have attributed the verse to Candrakīrti.

798. *Bodhicaryāvatāra* 9.147 (Vaidya 1960, 272.30): *nābhāvasya vikāro 'sti hetukoṭiśatairapi //*.

799. *Mūlamadhyamakakārikā* 1.1. Toh 3824, vol. *tsa*, 1a3–2b1 (MacDonald 2015, 2: 48): *bdag las ma yin gzhan las min / / gnyis las ma yin rgyu med min / / dngos po gang dag gang na yang / / skye ba nam yang yod ma yin /*. Skt. (La Vallée Poussin 1904, 12.13): *na svato nāpi parato na dvābhyāṃ nāpy ahetutaḥ / utpannā jātu vidyante bhāvāḥ kva cana ke cana //* 1 //.

800. This verse is an old Tibetan translation of MMK 14.5, which reads: */ gzhan las kyang ma yin te / gzhan ni gzhan la bsten te gzhan / / gzhan min gzhan du mi ltar 'gyur /*. This version differs from the canonical Tibetan translation, which reads (Toh 3824, vol. *tsa*, 8b2): */ gzhan ni gzhan la brten te gzhan / / gzhan med par gzhan gzhan mi 'gyur / / gang la brten te gang yin pa / / de ni de las gzhan mi 'thad //*. Skt. (Katsura and Siderits 2013, 149–50): *anyad anyat pratītyānyan nānyad anyad ṛte 'nyataḥ / yat pratītya ca yat tasmāt tad anyan nopapadyate.*

801. *Pramāṇavārttika* 1.35. English translation Dunne 2004, 336–37. Skt. (PV 3.35, Miyasaka 1971–72, 118): *nityaṃ sattvam asattvaṃ vā 'hetor anyānapekṣaṇāt / apekṣāto hi bhāvānāṃ kādācitkatvasambhavaḥ //*. Tib. (Miyasaka 1971–72, 119): *rgyu med gzhan la mi ltos phyir / rtag tu yod pa'am med par 'gyur / dngos po rnams ni res 'ga' zhig / 'byung ba ltos pa las yin no //*. The verse is preserved in Candraharipa's *Ratnamālā*, Toh 3901, vol. *a*, 67a3–4.

802. See Jñānagarbha, *Satyadvayavibhaṅgakārikā* (v. 14, trans. Eckel 1987, 80).

803. *Madhyamakālaṃkāra* 11 (Ichigō 1989, 192–93; Skt. TS, v. 1989): *saṃyuktaṃ dūradeśasthaṃ nairantaryavyavasthitam / ekāṇvabhimukhaṃ rūpaṃ yang aṇor madhyavarttinaḥ //*.

804. *Madhyamakālaṃkāra* 12 (Ichigō 1989, 195; Skt. TS, v. 1990): *aṇvantarābhimukhyena tad eva yadi kalpyate / pracayo bhūdharādīnām evaṃ sati na yujyate //*.

805. *Madhyamakālaṃkāra* 61 (Ichigō 1989, 210–11; Skt. TS, v. 1995: *tad evaṃ sarvapakṣeṣu naivaikātmā sa yujyate / ekāniṣpattito 'nekasvabhāvo 'pi na sambhavī //*.

806. *Ratnāvalī* 1.99 (Hahn 1982, 38–39): *gzugs kyi dngos po ming tsam phyir / / nam mkha' yang ni ming tsam mo / / 'byung med gzugs lta ga la yod / / de phyir ming tsam nyid kyang yin //*. Skt.: *rūpasyābhāvamātratvād ākāśaṃ nāmamātrakam / bhūtair vinā kuto rūpaṃ nāmamātrakam apy ataḥ //*.

807. The Kadampa author cites an old Tibetan translation of *Mūlamadhyamakakārikā* verses 4.8 and 4.9 in inverse order that reads: *stong pa nyid skyis bshad byas tshe / / gang zhig skyon 'dogs smra byed pa / / de'i thams cad skyon btags min / / bsgrub par bya dang mtshung par 'gyur //* [4.9] *// stong pa nyid kyi brtsad byas tshe / gang zhig lan 'debs smra byed pa / / de'i thams cad lan btab min / / bsgrub par bya dang mtshung par 'gyur //* [4.8]. The Tibetan Tengyur reads 4.8 and 4.9 (Toh 3824, vol. *tsa*, 3b7–

4a1) as: / *stong pa nyid kyis brtsad byas te / / gang zhig lan 'debs smra byed pa / / de yis thams cad* [4a1] *lan btab min / / bsgrub par bya dang mtshungs par 'gyur //*[4.8] // *stong pa nyid kyis bshad byas tshe / / gang zhig skyon 'dogs smra byed pa / / de yis thams cad skyon btags min / / bsgrub par bya dang mtshungs par 'gyur //*[4.9]. MMK, Skt. 4.8–4.9 (La Vallée Poussin 1903–13, 127): *vigrahe yaḥ parīhāraṃ kṛte śūnyatayā vadet / sarvaṃ tasyāparihṛtaṃ samaṃ sādhyena jāyate // 8 // vyākhyāne ya upālambhaṃ kṛte śūnyatayā vadet / sarvaṃ tasyānupālabdhaṃ samaṃ sādhyena jāyate // 9 //*; Katsura and Siderits 2013, 56–57.

808. *Madhyamakāvatāra* 6.68a–c (La Vallée Poussin 1907–12, 159.6–7): *'di yis lan ni gang dang gang btab pa / / de dang de ni dam bcas* {LVP *bca'*} *mtshungs mthong nas* {LVP *mthong bas*}*//*.

809. According to Tsenlha Ngawang Tsultrim (Btsan lha ngag dbang tshul khrims, 1997, 3), Kam is a Tibetan clan name.

810. According to *Rangjung Yeshe Dictionary*, an "ox particle" (6) is a measure the size of seven {*lug rdul*} dust particles raised by a flock of sheep (5), a measure the size of seven rabbit particles {*ri bong gi rdul*} (4), a measure the size of seven water particles {*chu rdul*} (3), which are equal to seven *lcags rdul*, "iron particles" (2), a measure the size of seven minute particles {*rdul phran*} (1).

811. *Ratnāvalī* I.69–70abc (Hahn 1982, 28–29): *ji ltar skad cig mtha' yod pa / / de bzhin thog ma dbus brtag go / / de ltar skad cig gsum bdag phyir / / 'jig rten skad cig gnas pa min /* [I.69] */ thog ma dbus dang tha ma yang / / skad cig bzhin du bsam par bya / / thog ma dbus dang tha ma nyid //* [I.70abc]. Skt.: *yathānto 'sti kṣaṇasyaivam ādimadhyaṃ ca kalpyatām / tryātmakatvāt kṣaṇasyaivaṃ na lokasya kṣaṇaṃ sthitiḥ //* [69] // *ādimadhyāvasānāni cintyāni kṣaṇavat punaḥ / ādimadhyāvasānatvaṃ //*. English translation Dunne and McClintock 1997, 19.

812. *Śūnyatāsaptati* 1 (compare Lindtner 1997b, 94): *gnas pa dang* {Lindtner *'am*} *skye 'jig yod med dang* {Lindtner *dam*} */ dman dang khyad par can rnams ni* {Lindtner *dman pa'i am mnyam pa'am khyad par can*} */ sangs rgyas 'jig rten snyad dbang gis / gsung gi di nyid* {Lindtner *yang dag*} *dbang gis min //*.

813. The story of the bodhisattva Sadāprarudita (Tib. *rtag tu ngu*, "Ever Weeping") is found in the *Aṣṭasāhasrikāprajñāpāramitā*.

814. Unidentified citation from a Tibetan version of the *Tathāgatotpattisambhāvasūtra*, which is comparable to the thirty-seventh book of the *Avataṃsakasūtra* translated in Chinese in 699 CE (see Cleary 1993, 984–85).

815. Unidentified citation attributed to the *Avataṃsakasūtra*.

816. Just as one should not mistake a finger pointing at the moon for the moon itself, the special instructions on nonproduction should not be mistaken for the meditative realization of nonproduction.

817. *Bodhicaryāvatāra* 9.35. Skt. (Vaidya 1960, 199): *yadā na bhāvo nābhāvo mateḥ saṃtiṣṭhate puraḥ / tadānyagatyabhāvena nirālambā praśāmyati*. Tib. (Toh 3871, vol. *la*, 32a4): */ gang tshe dngos dang dngos med dag / / blo yi mdun na mi gnas pa / / de tshe rnam pa gzhan med pas / / dmigs pa med par rab tu zhi //*.

818. *Bodhicaryāvatāra* 9.2cd. Note that Atiśa's citation follows the earlier translation of the BCA. Tib. (Saito 1993, 2): *don dam blo'i spyod min / blo dang sgra ni kun rdzob yin //*. Tengyur translation (Toh 3871, vol. *la*, 31a1): *don dam blo yi spyod yul min / / blo ni kun rdzob yin par brjod //*.

819. *Bodhicaryāvatāra* 9.37–38. Skt. (Vaidya 1960, 200): *yathā gāruḍikaḥ stambhaṃ*

sādhayitvā vinaśyati / sa tasmiṃś ciranaṣṭe 'pi viṣādīn upaśāmayet / 37 / bodhicaryānurūpyeṇa jinastambho 'pi sādhitaḥ / karoti sarvakāryāṇi bodhisattve 'pi nirvṛte // 38 //. Tib (Toh 3871, vol. *la*, 32a5): */ dper na nam mkha' lding gi ni / / mchod sdong bsgrubs nas 'das gyur pa / / de 'das yun ring lon yang de / / dug la sogs pa zhi byed bzhin // 9.36 // byang chub spyod pa'i rjes mthun pas / / rgyal ba'i mchod sdong sgrub pa yang / / byang chub sems dpa' mya ngan las / / 'das kyang don rnams thams cad mdzad //.*

820. *Spyod 'jug 'khor lo lta bu lam rgyud la ji ltar skye ba'i rim pa bzhugs*, 861.3–862.16; Mochizuki 1999, 116–18, readings follow Kadampa manuscript unless indicated: */ rnam par grol ba'i ye shes mthong ba'i lam ni / chos kyi sku de ye shes rgyun chad pa sangs rgyas* [861.4] *kyi sa'o / / ye shes rgyun chad pa'i* [em. from *chad med pa'i*, Mochizuki 1999, 116] *go ba ni chos sku'i gnas skabs na ye shes de rtag par lta ba ltar dngos* [861.5] *por med kyang / chad par* [em. from *tshad par*] *lta ba ltar dngos med da'ang med pa / gnyis gar yang mi 'dod / mdor na da ltar* [861.6] *gyi 'khor ba rtog bcas kyi shes pa'i rgyun 'dis nyams su myong rgyu gcig mi 'dod / gzung 'dzin gyi rnam par* [861.7] *rtog pa thams cad phar spangs nas / dmigs pa med pa de nyid la rab tu zhi ba zhes bya / chos kyi sku zhes bya / de'i* [861.8] *phyir na / gang tshe dngos dang dngos med dag / blo'i mdun na mi gnas pa / / de tshe rnam pa gzhan med* [861.9] *pas / / dmigs pa med pas rab tu zhi / / zhes gsungs so / / yang ye shes rgyun chad pa'i go ba ni /* [861.10] *slob dpon blo gros mi bzad pas 'phags pa 'jam dpal la dris pa'i dus su'ang / 'phag pa lags de ltar gyi* [861.11] *shes pa rtog pa dang bcas pa'i rgyun 'dis sangs rgyas kyi ye shes la legs par dpyod dam / ye shes tsam yang* [861.12] *mi dmigs zhes dris pas / don dam blo'i spyod yul min / / blo dang sgra ni kun rdzob yin / / zhes gsung nas da* [861.13] *ltar gyi shes pa'i rgyun 'dis nyams su myong ba ma yin gsung ngo / / slob dpon gyis dris pa / don dam pa de'i blo'i* [861.14] *yul du mi 'gyur na ji ltar nyams su myong zhe na / tsho rol mthong ba'i ngos nas bstal bas* [em. from *bcol bas*, Mochizuki 1999, 116] *nyams su myong bo med* [861.15] *pa nyid do / / ci ste na rnam grangs kyi don dam pa'i bden pa bshad tsa na / nang stong* [Mochizuki 1999, 117] *pa nyid dang / phyi stong pa* [861.16] *nyid dang / phyi nang stong nyid dang / stong pa nyid stong pa nyid dang / chen po stong pa nyid los pa bshad pas / 'o na tshul* [861.17] *rol mthong ba'i rnam grangs rnams stong pa yin la / don dam pa'i bden pa bya ba nges nges po gcig las logs* [861.18] *na yod dam snyam pa la / don dam pa stong pa nyid ces gsungs pas / don dam du rtog pa'i ye shes tsam dang bral* [861.19] *bar bzhes pas na / mdor na tshul rol mthong ba'i rtog pa thams cad nub pas / sems can dang de'i don bya rgyu* [861.20] *la sogs pa dang yang bral bas na ye shes rgyun chad med zhes bya'o / / lon ye shes rgyun chad nas 'gro don gyi* [861.21] *rtogs pa'ang med na gzugs sku gnyis kyang mi 'byung bar rigs so zhe na / / so so'i las dang skal ba ji ltar yod* [861.22] *pa / byang chub sems dpa' dang / nyan rang dang / so so'i skye bo la sogs pa ma rtog pa'i ye shes med* [861.23] *bzhin du snang ste / yid bzhin nor bu dpag bsam shing / / ji ltar re ba yongs skong ba / / de bzhin gdul bya'i* [861.24] *smon lam gyis / / dbang gi rgyal ba'i skur snang ngo / / bces gsungs so / / 'o na nor bu rad na la sogs pa 'dra* [861.25] *na bsod nams kun gyi snang ba yin pas na nor bu la sogs pa ni rtog pa med sangs rgyas kyi byin rlabs med* [862.1] *na / sems can dang nyan rang dang byang chub sems dpa' so so'i bsod nams kyi skal bar 'dug go zhe na /* [862.2] *bsod nams ma bsags pa la ni snang ba med pas na'o / / ma yin te dper na chu dwangs ba la zla ba'i gzugs* [862.3] *rnyan shar ba'i dus su chu med na zla ba 'char ba med / / zla ba med na'ang chu nang du 'char rgyu med / dpe de* [862.4] *bzhin du 'dra ba'i byang chub sems dpa' la sogs pa med na'ang gzugs sku'i 'char ba med / zla ba dang 'dra* [862.5] *ba'i sangs rgyas med na'ang gzugs*

sku 'byung rgyu med / de bas na de ltar rtog pa med kyang [Mochizuki 1999, 118] *slob pa lam gyis* [862.6] *bsdus pa'i gnas skabs na / spyod pa thams cad yul sems can la dmigs nas bsgrubs pas sngon gyi smon* [862.7] *lam gyis rtog pa med bzhin du gzugs sku 'byung ste / de'ang sngon gyi smon lam gyi mthu btsan pa* [862.8] *las 'grub ste / dper na bram ze 'jam pas sngon nam mkha' lding gi sku brten gzhan la phan pa'i bsam pas* [862.9] *bsgrubs pas / de ltar bram ze bsgrub mkhan sngon 'das te phan par bya ba'i rtog pa med kyang phan pa bzhin du /* [862.10] *rdzogs pa'i sangs rgyas la de ltar rtogs pa'i ye shes mi mnga' 'ang / sngon gyi smon lam gyi mthus gzugs kyi* [862.11] *skus 'gro ba'i don byang chub sems dpa' la sogs pa'i bsam pa dang mthun par byed pas so de bas na* [862.12] *gnyis ka 'dzems pa gal che'o / / rin po che la sogs pa ni rtog pa med pa tsam gyi dpe yin no / / 'di yang dag* [862.13] *pa'i dper bshad pas na / / dper na nam mkha' lding gi ni / / mchod sdong bsgrubs nas 'das gyur* [862.14] *pa / / de 'das yun rings len pa des / / dug la sogs pa zhi byed bzhin / / byang chub spyod dang rjes 'mthun* [862.15] *pas / / rgyal ba'i chos sdong bsgrub pa yang / / byang chub sems dpa' mya ngan las / / 'das kyang don* [862.16] *rnams thams cad mdzad / / ces gsungs so /.*

821. Śantideva's verse on nonexistence and the continuum ceasing is found in *Bodhicaryāvatāra* 9: 150 (Tib., 149). Skt. (Vaidya 1960, 274): *evam na ca nirodho'sti na ca bhāvo'sti sarvadā / ajātam aniruddham ca tasmat sarvam idam jagat //*. Tib. (Toh 3871, vol. *la*, 36b4): *de ltar 'gag pa yod min zhing / dngos po'ang yod min de yi phyir / 'gro ba di dag thams cad ni / rtag tu ma skyes ma 'gag nyid //*. "Thus there does not exist cessation, and never does there exist entity. Therefore all this world (Tib. 'all these beings') is (Tib. 'always are') not arisen and not ceased."

822. The verse is also found in the MRP and *Abhisamayālaṃkāra* 5.21 (= *Ratnagotravibhāga* I.154) (Stcherbatsky and Obermiller 1929, 29): *nāpaneyamataḥ kiṃcidupaneyaṃ na kiṃcana / draṣṭavyaṃ bhūtato bhūtaṃ bhūtadarśī vimucyate //*. Tib. (Stcherbatsky and Obermiller 1929, 53): *'di la bsal bya ci yang med / / gzhag par bya ba cung zad med / / yang dag nyid la yang dag lta / / yang dag mthong na rnam par grol //*. See Takasaki 1966a, 300; Wangchuk 2007, 199–200, no. 11; *Kāyatrayastotravivaraṇa* (*sku gsum la bstod pa shes bya ba'i rnam par 'grel pa*, Toh 1124, D72a3).

823. See chapter 2, *Entry to the Two Realities* (*Satyadvayāvatāra*).

824. Compare *Sugatamatavibhaṅga*, v. 8 (Toh 3899, vol. *a*, 8a3; P 5296, vol. *ha*, 64b7–8): *yod min med min yod med min / / gnyis kyi bdag nyid du yang med / / mtha' bzhi dag las nges grol ba / / dbu ma de nyid mkhas pa 'dod //*. However, the same verse in the *Sugatamatavibhaṅgabhāsya* is translated differently (Toh 3900, vol. *a*, 60b3, P 5868, vol. *nyo*, 348b5–6): *yod min med min yod med min / / gnyi ga min pa'i bdag nyid min / / de nyid mtha' bzhi las grol ba / / dbu ma pa yis rtogs pa yin //*. Nagashima 2002, 171.

Bibliography

Indian Sources

Kangyur (Canonical Scriptures)

Adhyardhaśatikāprajñāpāramitā. The Perfection of Wisdom in One Hundred Lines. 'Phags pa shes rab kyi pha rol tu phyin pa'i tshul brgya lnga bcu pa. Toh 489, vol. *ka,* 133a6–139b6. English translation in Astley-Kristensen 1991. Sanskrit and Tibetan critical edition in Tomabechi 2009.

Akṣayamatinirdeśasūtra. The Teaching of Akṣayamati. 'Phags pa blo gros mi zad pas bstan pa zhes bya ba theg pa chen po'i mdo. Toh 175, vol. *ma,* 79a1–174b7. English translation in Braarvig 1993.

Aṣṭasāhasrikāprajñāpāramitā. The Perfection of Wisdom in Eight Thousand Lines. 'Phags pa shes rab kyi pha rol tu phyin pa brgyad stong pa. Toh 12, vol. *ka,* 1b1–286a6. Tibetan translation by Śākyasena, Jñānasiddhi, and Dharmatāśīla. Sanskrit in Wogihara 1932–35.

Avalokiteśvarapariprcchāsaptadharmakasūtra. Inquiry of Avalokiteśvara on the Seven Qualities. 'Phags pa spyan ras gzigs dbang phyug gis zhus pa chos bdun pa zhes bya ba theg pa chen po'i mdo. Toh 150, vol. *pa,* 331a2–331b5.

Avataṃsakasūtra or *Buddhāvataṃsakanāmamahāvaipulyasūtra. Sangs rgyas phal po che zhes bya ba shin tu rgyas pa chen po'i mdo.* Toh 44, vols. *ka* through *a.* Tibetan translation by Jinamitra, Surendrabodhi, and Ye shes sde. Revised by Vairocana.

Avikalpapraveśadhāraṇī. Incantation on Access to the Nonconceptual, 'Phags pa rnam par mi rtog par 'jug pa zhes bya ba'i gzungs. Toh 142, vol. *pa,* 1b1–6b1.

Bodhisattvagocaropāyaviṣayavikurvāṇanirdeśasūtra. The Sutra Teaching the Bodhisattvas' Miracles in Skillful Means. 'Phags pa byang chub sems dpa'i spyod yul gyi thabs kyi yul la rnam par 'phrul pa bstan pa zhes bya ba theg pa chen po'i mdo. Toh 146, vol. *pa,* 82a3–141b7.

Daśadharmakasūtra. The Ten Dharmas Sutra. 'Phags pa chos bcu pa zhes bya ba theg pa chen po'i mdo. Toh 53, vol. *kha,* 164a6–184b6.

Dharmasaṃgītisūtra. Perfect Gathering of Qualities Sutra. 'Phags pa chos yang dag par sdud pa zhes bya ba theg pa chen po'i mdo. Toh 238, vol. *zha,* 1b1–99b7. Tibetan translation by Mañjuśrīgarbha, Vijayaśīla, Śīlendrabodhi, and Ye shes sde.

Gaganagañjapariprcchāsūtra. The Inquiry of Gaganagañja Sutra. 'Phags pa nam mkha' mdzod kyis zhus pa zhes bya ba theg pa chen po'i mdo. Toh 148, vol. *pa,* 243a1–330a7.

Guhyasamājatantra. Guhyasamāja Root Tantra. Gsang 'dus rtsa rgyud. Toh 442, vol. *ca,* 90a1–148a6. Critical edition, Matsunaga 1978.

Jñānālokālaṃkāra or *Sarvabuddhaviṣayāvatārajñānālokālaṅkārasūtra. The Ornament of*

Light Awareness Sutra. 'Phags pa sangs rgyas thams cad kyi yul la 'jug pa'i ye shes snang ba'i rgyan zhes bya ba theg pa chen po'i mdo. Toh 100, vol. *ga,* 276a– 305a7. Tibetan translation by Surendrabodhi and Ye shes sde. Transliterated Sanskrit text collated with Tibetan and Chinese translations in Study Group on Buddhist Literature 2004.

Jñānamūdrasūtra. See *Tathāgatajñānamudrāsamādhisūtra.*

Karmāvaraṇapratiprasrabdhisūtra. Purification of Karmic Obscurations Sutra. 'Phags pa las kyi sgrib pa rgyun gcod pa zhes bya ba theg pa chen po'i mdo. Toh 219, vol. *tsha,* 297b5–307a6. Tibetan translation by Jinamitra, Dānaśīla, and Ye shes sde.

Karuṇāpuṇḍarīkasūtra. White Lotus of Compassion Sutra. 'Phags pa snying rje padma dkar po zhes bya ba theg pa chen po'i mdo. Toh 112, vol. *cha,* 129a1–297a7. Tibetan translation by Jinamitra, Surendrabodhi, Prajñāvarman, and Ye shes sde.

Kāśyapaparivartasūtra. Kāśyapa Chapter Sutra.'Phags pa 'od srung gi le'u zhes bya ba theg pa chen po'i mdo. Toh 87, vol. *cha,* 119b1–151b7. Romanized text and facsimiles in Vorobyova–Desyatovskaya 2002. English translation in Pāsādika 2015.

Kuśalamūlasaṃparigrahasūtra. Obtaining the Roots of Virtue Sutra. 'Phags pa dge ba'i rtsa ba yongs su 'dzin pa zhes bya ba theg pa chen po'i mdo. Toh 101, vol. *nga,* 1b1–227b7.

Lalitavistarasūtra. The Play in Full. 'Phags pa rgya cher rol pa zhes bya ba theg pa chen po'i mdo. Toh 95, vol. *kha,* b1–216b7. Tibetan translation by Jinamitra, Dānaśīla, Munivarman, and Ye shes sde. Sanskrit edition, Vaidya 1960.

Laṅkāvatārasūtra. The Descent into Laṅka Sutra. 'Phags pa lang kar gshegs pa'i theg pa chen po'i mdo. Toh 107, vol. *ca,* 56a1–191b7. Tibetan translation by 'Gos Chos grub. English translation in Suzuki 1932. Sanskrit edition, Nanjio 1923.

Mahāmegha. The Great Cloud Sutra. 'Phags pa sprin chen po. Toh 235 (also 657, 1063), vol. *wa,* 250a2–263a7. Tibetan translation by Jinamitra, Śīlendrabodhi, and Ye shes sde.

Mahāyānaprasādaprabhāvanasūtra. Cultivating Faith in the Mahāyāna Sutra. 'Phags pa theg pa chen po la dad pa rab tu sgom pa zhes bya ba theg pa chen po'i mdo. Toh 144, vol. *pa,* 6b6–34a3. Tibetan translation by Jinamitra, Dānaśīla, and Ye shes sde.

Mañjuśrīmūlatantra. The Root Tantra of Mañjuśrī. 'Phags pa 'jam dpal gyi rtsa ba'i rgyud. Toh 543, vol. *na,* 105a1–351a6. Tibetan translation by Kumārakalaśa and Shākya blo gros. Sanskrit text in Śāstri 1920–25.

Māyopamāsamādhisūtra. The Illusory Absorption. 'Phags pa sgyu ma lta bu'i ting nge 'dzin zhes bya ba theg pa chen po'i mdo. Toh 130, vol. *da,* 210b3–230b4. Tibetan translation by Surendrabodhi and Ye shes sde.

Pañcaviṃśatisāhasrikāprajñāpāramitā. The Perfection of Wisdom in Twenty-Five Thousand Lines. Shes rab kyi pha rol tu phyin pa stong phrag nyi shu lnga pa. Toh 9, vols. *ka* through *ga* (26–28). Sanskrit edition, Dutt 1934. English translation in Conze 1975.

Paramādyamantrakalpakhaṇḍa. A Section of the Chapter on Mantras of "The Glorious Supreme Prime." Dpal mchog dang po'i sngags kyi rtog pa'i dum bu. Toh 488, vol. *ta,* 173a1–265b7. Tibetan translation by Zhi ba 'od.

Prajñāpāramitāsaṃcayagāthā. The Verses That Summarize the Perfection of Wisdom. 'Phags pa shes rab kyi pha rol tu phyin pa sdud pa tshigs su bcad pa. Toh 13, vol. *ka,* 1b1–19b7. Tibetan translation by Vidyākarasiṃha and Dpal brtsegs. Sanskrit in Obermiller 1937. Sanskrit-Tibetan-English index in Conze 1960. Tibetan version in Yuyama 1976.

Pratibhānamatiparipṛcchāsūtra. The Inquiry of Pratibhānamati Sutra. Spobs pa'i blo gros kyi zhus pa zhes bya ba theg pa chen po'i mdo. Toh 151, vol. *pa,* 331b5–344a4. Tibetan translation by Prajñāvarman and Ye shes sde.

Saddharmapuṇḍarīkasūtra. White Lotus of the True Dharma Sutra. Dam pa'i chos padma dkar po zhes bya ba theg pa chen po'i mdo. Toh 113, vol. *ja*, 1b1–180b7. Tibetan translation by Surendrabodhi and Sna nam Ye shes sde. Sanskrit edition, Kern and Nanjio 1908–12.

Sāgaramatiparipṛcchāsūtra. Inquiry of Sāgaramati Sutra. 'Phags pa blo gros rgya mtshos zhus pa zhes bya ba theg pa chen po'i mdo. Toh 152, vol. *pha*, 1b1–115b7. Tibetan translation by Jinamitra, Dānaśīla, Buddhaprabha, and Ye shes sde

Sāgaranāgarājaparipṛcchāsūtra. Inquiry of the Nāga King Sāgara Sutra. 'Phags pa klu'i rgyal po rgya mtshos zhus pa zhes bya ba theg pa chen po'i mdo. Toh 154, vol. *pha*, 198a3–205a6. Tibetan translation by Jinamitra, Prajñāvarman, and Ye shes sde.

Śālistambanasūtra. The Rice Sprouts Sutra. Sa lu ljang pa zhes bya ba theg pa chen po'i mdo. Toh 210, vol. *tsha*, 116b2–123b1. Tibetan edition and English translation in Reat 1993. Indian commentaries in Schoening 1995.

Sarvapuṇyasamuccayasamādhisūtra. The Absorption That Encapsulates All Merit. Bsod nams thams cad sdud pa'i ting nge 'dzin zhe bya ba theg pa chen po'i mdo. Toh 134, vol. *na*, 70b2–121b7. Tibetan translation by Prajñāvarman and Ye shes sde.

Śatasāhasrikāprajñāpāmitāsūtra. The Perfection of Wisdom in One Hundred Thousand Lines. Toh 8, vol. *ka*, 1b1–a395a6. Chapters 1–12 in Ghosha 1902–13.

Śraddhābalādhānāvatāramudrāsūtra. The Seal of Engagement in Kindling the Power of Faith. 'Phags pa dad pa'i stobs bskyed pa la 'jug pa'i phyag rgya zhes bya ba theg pa chen po'i mdo. Toh 201, vol. *tsha*, 1b1–63a2. Tibetan translation by Surendrabodhi and Ye shes sde.

Suvarṇaprabhāsasūtra, or *Suvarṇaprabhāsottamasutrendrarājasūtra. The King of Glorious Sutras Called the Sublime Golden Light. Gser 'od dam pa mdo sde'i dbang po'i rgyal po'i mdo.* Toh 557, vol. *pha*, 1b1–62a7. Sanskrit text with English introduction in Bagchi 1967.

Tathāgatācintyaguhyanirdeśasūtra. The Teaching on the Unfathomable Secrets of the Tathāgatas. De bzhin gshegs pa'i gsang ba bsam gyis mi khyab pa bstan pa'i mdo. Toh 47, vol. *ka*, 100a1–203a7. Tibetan translation by Jinamitra, Dānaśīla, Munivarman, and Ye shes sde.

Tathāgatajñānamudrāsamādhisūtra. The Sutra on the Samādhi That Is the Seal of the Gnosis of the Tathāgatas. De bzhin gshegs pa'i ye shes kyi phyag rgya'i ting nge 'dzin gyi mdo). Toh 131, vol. *da*, 230b4–253b5. Tibetan translation by Jinamitra, Munivarman, and Ye shes sde.

Tathāgatotpattisambhāvasūtra. The Sutra on the Manifestation of the Tathāgata. De bzhin gshegs pa skye ba srid pa'i mdo. Part of the *Avataṃsaka* or *Buddhāvataṃsakanāmamahāvaipulyasūtra* (*Sangs rgyas phal po che zhes bya ba shin tu rgyas pa chen po'i mdo*). Toh 44, vol. *ga*, 75a–141b. Tibetan translation by Jinamitra, Surendrabodhi, and Ye shes sde. Revised by Vairocana.

Triskandhakasūtra. The Sutra of the Three Heaps. Phung po gsum pa'i mdo. Toh 284, vol. *ya*, 57a3–77a3. Tibetan translation by Ye shes sde.

Vairocanābhisaṃbodhi. The Complete Enlightenment of Mahāvairocana Tantra. Rnam par snang mdzad mngon par rdzogs par byang chub pa'i rgyud. Toh 494, vol. *tha*, 151b2–260a7. Tibetan translation by Śīlendrabodhi and Dpal brtsegs.

Vajracchedikā. The Diamond Sutra. Shes rab kyi pha rol tu phyin pa rdo rje gcod pa. Toh 16, vol. *ka*, 121a1–132b7. Tibetan translation by Śīlendrabodhi and Ye shes sde. Sanskrit in Conze 1957. Sanskrit and English in Harrison and Watanabe 2006, and Harrison 2006.

Vajrajñānasamuccayatantra. Compendium of Vajra Gnosis Tantra. Ye shes rdo rje kun las btus

pa zhes bya ba'i rgyud. Toh 447, vol. *ca,* 282a1–286a6. Tibetan translation by Jñānākara and Khu Dngos grub. Revised by Tshul khrims rgyal ba.

Vidyottamamahātantra. The Great Tantra of Supreme Knowledge. Rig pa mchog gi rgyud chen po. Toh 746, vol. *dza,* 1b1–237b7. Tibetan translation by Vidyākaraprabha and Dpal brtsegs.

Vimalakīrtinirdeśasūtra. The Teaching of Vimalakīrti Sutra. Dri med grags pas bstan pa'i mdo. Toh 176, vol. *ma,* 175a1–239b7. Tibetan translation by Chos nyid tshul khrims. Sanskrit collated with Tibetan and Chinese translations in Study Group on Buddhist Literature 2004. Translation in Thurman 1976.

Tengyur (Canonical Treatises)

Abhidharmakośabhāṣya by Vasubandhu. *Commentary on the Treasury of Higher Knowledge. Chos mngon pa'i mdzod kyi bshad pa.* Toh 4090, vol. *ku,* 26b1–258a7, continued in vol. *khu,* 1b1–95a7. Tibetan translation by Jinamitra and Dpal brtsegs rakshi ta. Sanskrit in Pradhan 1975. French translation, La Vallée Poussin 1923–31.

Abhidharmakośakārikā by Vasubandhu. *Treasury of Higher Knowledge. Chos mngon pa'i mdzod kyi tshig le'ur byas pa.* Toh 4089, vol. *ku,* 1b1–25a7. Tibetan translation by Jinamitra and Dpal brtsegs rakshi ta. Sanskrit in Pradhan 1975. French translation, La Vallée Poussin 1923–31.

Abhisamayālaṃkāra by Maitreya. [*Abhisamayālaṃkāraprajñāpāramitopadeśaśāstrakārikā*] *Ornament for Clear Realization. Shes rab kyi pha rol tu phyin pa'i man ngag gi bstan bcos mngon par rtogs pa'i rgyan zhes bya ba'i tshig le'ur byas pa.* Toh 3786, vol. *ka,* 1b1–13a7. Edited by Stcherbatsky and Obermiller 1929.

Abhisamayālaṃkāradurbodhālokā by Dharmakīrtiśrī. *Illumination of [Points] Difficult to Understand Commentary on the Ornament for Clear Realization. Mngon par rtogs pa'i rgyan ces bya ba'i 'grel pa rtogs par dka' ba'i snang ba zhes bya ba'i 'grel bshad.* Toh 3794, vol. *ja,* 140b1–254a7. P 5192, vol. 91. Tibetan translation by Dīpaṃkaraśrījñāna and Rin chen bzang po.

Abhisamayālaṃkārālokā Prajñāpāramitāvyākhyā by Haribhadra. *Illumination of the Ornament for Clear Realization That Explains the Perfection of Wisdom Sutra in Eight Thousand Verses. Shes rab kyi pha rol tu phyin pa brgyad stong pa'i bshad pa mngon par rtogs pa'i rgyan gyi snang ba.* Toh 3791, vol. *cha,* 1b1–341a7. Sanskrit edition, Wogihara 1932–35. English translation, Sparham 2006–12.

Acintyastava by Nāgārjuna. *Hymn to the Inconceivable. Bsam gyis mi khyab par bstod pa.* Toh 1128, vol. *ka,* 76b7–79a2.

Akutobhayā or *Mūlamadhyamakavṛttyakutobhayā,* attributed to Nāgārjuna. *Fearless: A Commentary on the Fundamental Verses on the Middle Way. Dbu ma rtsa ba'i 'grel pa ga las 'jigs med.* Toh 3829, vol. *tsa,* 29b1–99a7. Tibetan translation by Jñānagarbha and Klu'i rgyal mtshan. English translation, Huntington 1986.

Bhagavadratnaguṇasañcayagāthāpañjikā by Haribhadra. *Commentary on the Blessed Verses on the Accumulation of Precious Qualities. Bcom ldan 'das yon tan rin po che sdud pa'i tshigs su bcad pa'i dka' 'grel.* Toh 3792, vol, *ja,* 1a1–78a7.

Bhāvanākrama-1 by Kamalaśīla. *Stages of Meditation—1. Bsgom pa'i rim pa.* Toh 3915, vol. *ki,* 22a1–41b7. Sanskrit edition in Tucci 1958 (187–229).

Bhāvanākrama-2 by Kamalaśīla. *Stages of Meditation—2. Bsgom pa'i rim pa.* Toh 3916 (also 4567), vol. *ki,* 42a1–55b5. English translation, Goshima 1983 and Gyatso 2001.

Bhāvanākrama-3 by Kamalaśīla. *Stages of Meditation—3. Bsgom pa'i rim pa.* Toh 3917, vol. *ki*, 55b6–68b7. English translation, Sharma 1997.

Bhāvanākrama by Nāgārjuna. *Stages of Meditation. Bsgom pa'i rim pa.* Toh 3908, vol. *ki*, 1b1–4a3. Sanskrit and Tibetan edition in Lindtner 1992.

Bodhicaryāvatāra or Bodhisattvacaryāvatāra by Śāntideva. *Guide to the Bodhisattva Way of Life. Byang chub sems dpa'i spyod pa la 'jug pa.* Toh 3871, vol. *la*, 1b1–40a7. Sanskrit edition in Vaidya 1960.

Bodhicittavivaraṇa by Nāgārjuna. *Commentary on the Awakening Mind. Byang chub sems 'grel; byang chub sems kyi 'grel pa.* Toh 1800 (also 4556), vol. *ngi*, 38a5–42b5. Tibetan translation by Guṇākara and Rab zhi bshes gnyen. Revised by Kanakavarman and Pa tshab Nyi ma grags. English translation, Lindtner 1997.

Bodhimārgapradīpapañjikā by Dīpaṃkaraśrījñāna (Atiśa). *Commentary on the Difficult Points in the Lamp for the Path to Awakening. Byang chub lam gyi sgron ma'i dka' 'grel.* Toh 3948, vol. *khi*, 241a4–293a4. Tibetan translation by Atiśa and Tshul khrims rgyal ba. Translated and Tibetan edition, Sherburne 2000.

Bodhipathapradīpa by Atiśa. *Lamp for the Path to Awakening. Byang chub lam gyi sgron ma.* Toh 3947, vol. *khi*, 238a6–241a4. Edition and German translation, Eimer 1978.

Bodhisattvabhūmi by Asaṅga. *Bodhisattva Levels. Rnal 'byor spyod pa'i sa las, Byang chub sems dpa'i sa.* Toh 4037, vol. *wi*, 1b1–213a7. Sanskrit edition, Dutt 1966. English translation, Engle 2016.

Bodhisattvacaryāsaṅgrahapradīparatnamālā by Dhārmikasubhūtighoṣa. *Precious Garland: A Lamp of Summary Verses on the Bodhisattva Way of Life. Byang chub sems dpa'i spyod pa bsdus pa'i sgron ma rin po che'i phreng ba.* Toh 3936, vol. *ki*, 334a4–338b6. Tibetan translated by by Prajñākaravarman and Rin chen bzang po.

Bodhisattvacāryāvatārabhāṣya by Dīpaṃkaraśrījñāna (Atiśa). *Commentary on the Guide to the Bodhisattva Way of Life. Byang chub sems dpa'i spyod pa la 'jug pa'i bshad pa.* P 5872, *ngo mtshar bstan bcos*, vol. *nyo*, 462b2–463a4. Tibetan edition in Mochizuki 1999.

Bodhisattvasaṃvaraviṃśaka by Candragomin. *Twenty Verses on the Bodhisattva Vow. Byang chub sems dpa'i sdom pa nyi shu pa.* Toh 4081, vol. *hi*, 166b1–167a5. In Tatz 1985.

Caryāgīti by Dīpaṃkaraśrījñāna (Atiśa). *Song of Conduct. Spyod pa'i glu.* Toh 1496 (also 4474), vol. *zha*, 215a6–216b4. Tibetan translation by Vajrapāṇi and Chos kyi shes rab.

Caryāmelāpakapradīpa by Āryadeva. *Lamp of the Compendium of Practice. Spyod pa bsdus pa'i sgron ma.* Toh 1803, vol. *ngi*, 57a2–106b7. English translation, Wedemeyer 2007.

Catuḥśataka by Āryadeva. *Four Hundred. Bzhi brgya pa.* Toh 3846, vol. *tsha*, 1b1–18a7. Tibetan translation by Sūkṣmajāna and Pa tshab Nyi ma grags (last half of the eleventh century). Sanskrit in Lang 1986.

Cittavajrastava by Nāgārjuna. *Hymn to the Diamond of the Mind. Sems kyi rdo rje'i bstod pa.* Toh 1121, vol. *ka*, 69b5–70a2. Tibetan translation by Kṛṣṇa Paṇḍita and Tshul khrims rgyal ba.

Cittaviśuddhiprakaraṇa by Āryadeva. *Treatise on Mental Purification. Sems kyi sgrib pa rnam par sbyong ba zhes bya ba'i rab tu byed pa.* Toh 1804, vol. *ngi*, 106b7–112a3. Sanskrit and Tibetan edition, Patel 1949. English translation, Varghese 2008.

Dharmadhātudarśanagīti by Dīpaṃkaraśrījñāna (Atiśa). *Song of the Vision of the Realm of Reality. Chos kyi dbyings lta ba'i glu.* Toh 2314 (also 4475), vol. *zhi*, 254b7–260b5. Translated by Atiśa and Tshul khrims rgyal ba.

Dharmadhātustava by Nāgārjuna. *Praise of the Realm of Reality. Chos kyi dbyings su bstod pa.* Toh 1118, vol. *ka*, 63b5–67b3. Tibetan translation by Kṛṣṇa Paṇḍita and Tshul khrims rgyal ba. Sanskrit, Tibetan, and Chinese edition in Liu 2015. Annotated Japanese translation, Kano 2015.

Jñānasiddhināmasādhana by Indrabhūti. *The Sādhana for the Accomplishment of Wisdom. Ye shes grub pa zhes bya ba'i sgrub pa'i thabs.* Toh 2219, vol. *wi*, 36b7–60b6. Sanskrit and Tibetan in Samdhong Rinpoche et al. 1987.

Kramapraveśikabhāvanārtha by Vimalamitra. *The Meaning of Gradualist Meditation. Rim gyis 'jug pa'i sgom don.* Toh 3938, vol. *ki*, 340b7–358a7. Tibetan translation by Prajñāvarma and Ye shes sde.

Kudṛṣṭinirghāta, attributed to Advayavajra. *Lta ba ngan pa sel ba.* Toh 2229, vol. *wi*, 104a7–110a2. Sanskrit in Shastri 1927.

Madhyamakahṛdayakārikā by Bhāviveka. *Heart of the Middle Way. Dbu ma'i snying po'i tshig le'ur byas pa.* Toh 3855, vol. *dza*, 40b7–329b4. Sanskrit edition, Lindtner 2001.

Madhyamakahṛdayatarkajvālā by Bhāviveka. *Blaze of Reasoning Commentary on the Heart of the Middle Way. Dbu ma'i snying po'i 'grel pa rtog ge 'bar ba.* Toh 3856, vol. *dza*, 40b7–329b4.

Madhyamakālaṃkāra by Śāntarakṣita. *Ornament of the Middle Way. Dbu ma rgyan gyi tshig le'ur byas pa.* Toh 3884, vol. *sa*, 53a1–56b3. Tibetan translation by Surendrabodhi and Ye shes sde. Tibetan edition, Ichigō 1985. English translation, Blumenthal 2004.

Madhyamakālaṃkāravṛtti by Śāntarakṣita. *Commentary on the Ornament of the Middle Way. Dbu ma'i rgyan gyi 'grel pa.* Toh 3885, vol. *sa*, 56b4–84a1. Tibetan translation by Śīlendrabodhi and Ye shes sde. Tibetan edition, Ichigō 1985.

Madhyamakāloka by Kamalaśīla. *Illumination of the Middle Way. Dbu ma snang ba.* Toh 3887, vol. *sa*, 133b4–244a7. Tibetan translation by Śīlendrabodhi and Dpal brtsegs rakshi ta.

Madhyamakaratnapradīpa by Bhāviveka or Bhavya. *Jewel Lamp of the Middle Way. Dbu ma rin po che'i sgron ma.* Toh 3854, vol. *tsha*, 259b3–289a7.

Madhyamakāvatāra by Candrakīrti. *Introduction to the Middle Way. Dbu ma la 'jug pa.* Toh 3861, vol. *'a*, 201bl–219a7; P 5262, vol. *'a*, 245a2–264b8. Edited French translation, La Vallée Poussin 1907–12.

Madhyamakāvatārabhāṣya by Candrakīrti. *Commentary on the Introduction to the Middle Way. Dbu ma la 'jug pa'i bshad pa.* Toh 3862, vol. *'a*, 220b1–348a7. Edited French translation, La Vallée Poussin 1907–12.

Madhyamakopadeśa by Dīpaṃkaraśrījñāna (Atiśa). *Special Instructions on the Middle Way. Dbu ma'i man ngag.* Toh 3929 (also 4468), vol. *ki*, 95b1–96a7.

Madhyamakopadeśavṛtti by Prajñāmukti. *Commentary on the Special Instructions on the Middle Way. Dbu ma'i man ngag ces bya ba'i 'grel pa.* Toh 3931, vol. *ki*, 116b7–123b2.

Madhyāntavibhāgakārikā by Maitreyanātha. *Clear Differentiation of the Middle and Extremes. Dbus dang mtha' rnam par 'byed pa'i tshig le'ur byas pa.* Toh 4021, vol. *phi*, 40b1–45a6. Tibetan translation by by Jinamitra, Śīlendrabodhi, and Ye shes sde. Sanskrit in Pandeya 1999.

Mahāyānasūtrālaṃkārabhāṣya by Vasubandhu. *Commentary on the Ornament of Mahayana Sutras. Mdo sde'i rgyan gyi bshad pa.* Toh 4026, vol. *phi*, 129b1–260a7. Tibetan translation by Śākyasiṃha and Dpal brtsegs. Sanskrit and French translations, Lévi 1907. English translation, Thurman et al. 2004.

Mahāyānasūtrālaṃkārakārikā by Maitreya. *Ornament of Mahayana Sutras. Theg pa chen po mdo sde'i rgyan zhes bya ba'i tshig le'ur byas pa.* Toh 4020, vol. *phi*, 1b1–39a4. Tibetan translation by Śākyasiṃha and Dpal brtsegs. Revised by Parahita, Sajjana, and Blo ldan shes rab. Sanskrit and French translations, Lévi 1907. English translation, Thurman et al. 2004.

Mahāyānaviṃśikā by Nāgārjuna. *Twenty Verses on the Great Vehicle. Theg pa chen po nyi shu pa.* Toh 3833 (and 4551), vol. *tsa*, 137b1–138a7. Translation by Candrakumāra and Shākya 'od. Tibetan edition and English translation, Jamieson 2000.

Mahāyānottaratantraśāstra by Maitreya. *The Sublime Continuum of the Great Vehicle Treatise. Theg pa chen po rgyud bla ma'i bstan bcos.* Toh 4024, vol. *phi*, 54b1–73a7. Tibetan translation by Sajjana and Blo ldan shes rab. English translation and Sanskrit text, Johnston et al. 1991.

Mūlamadhyamakakārikā by Nāgārjuna. *Fundamental Verses on the Middle Way. Dbu ma rtsa ba'i tshig le'ur byas pa shes rab.* Toh 3824, vol. *tsa*, 1b1–19a6. Tibetan translation by Jñānagarbha and Cog ro Klu'i rgyal mtshan. Revised by Hasumati and Pa tshab Nyi ma grags. Revised again by Kanaka and Pa tshab Nyi ma grags. Sanskrit in La Vallée Poussin 1903–13. English translation, Katsura and Siderits 2013.

Mūlāpattisaṃgraha by Aśvaghoṣa. *Summary of Root Downfalls. Rtsa ba'i ltung ba bsdus pa.* Toh 2478, vol. *zi*, 179a6–179b5. Sanskrit fragment in Lévi 1929.

Nayatrayapradīpa by Tripiṭakamāla. *Lamp of the Three Modes. Tshul gsum gyi sgron ma.* Toh 3707, vol. *tsu*, 6b4–26b1.

Niraupamyastava, attributed to Nāgārjuna. *Praise to the Incomparable. Dpe med par bstod pa.* Toh. 1119, vol. *ka*, 67b3–68b4. Tibetan translation by Kṛṣṇa Paṇḍita and Tshul khrims rgyal ba. Sanskrit text with Tibetan version and Hindi translation in Namdol 2001. Tola and Dragonetti 1985.

Pañcakrama by Nāgārjuna. *Five Stages. Rim pa lnga pa.* Toh 1802, vol. *ngi*, 45a5–57a1. Tibetan translation by Śraddhākaravarman and Rin chen bzang po. Revised by Kamalagupta and Rin chen bzang po. Critical edition, Mimaki and Tomabechi 1994.

Paramārthastava by Nāgārjuna. *Praise of the Ultimate. Don dam par bstod pa.* Toh 1122, vol. *ka*, 70a2–70b2.

Piṇḍīkṛtasādhana by Nāgārjuna. *Condensed Sādhana. Sgrub pa'i thabs mdor byas pa.* Toh 1796, vol. *ngi*, 1b1–11a2. Sanskrit in La Vallée Poussin 1896.

Pradīpodyotanaṭīkā by Candrakīrti. *Bright Lamp Extensive Commentary. Sgron ma gsal bar byed pa zhes bya ba'i rgya cher bshad pa.* Toh 1785, vol. *ha*, 1b1–201b2. Tibetan translation by by Śraddhākaravarman, Rin chen bzang po, Śrījñānākara, and 'Gos Lhas btsas. Revised by Nag po and 'Gos Lhas btsas. Sanskrit in Chakravarti 1984. English translation, Wayman 1977.

Prajñāpāramitāmaṇḍalavidhi by Ānandagarbha. *A Maṇḍala Ritual for the Perfection of Wisdom. Shes rab kyi pha rol tu phyin pa'i dkyil 'khor gyi cho ga.* Toh 2644, vol. *ju*, 247a4–260a7.

Prajñāpāramitāpiṇḍārtha or *Prajñāpāramitāsaṃgraha* by Dignāga. *Condensed Meaning of the Perfection of Wisdom. Shes rab kyi pha rol tu phyin pa ma bsdus pa'i tshig le'ur byas pa.* Toh 3809, vol. *pha*, 292a4–294a7. Tibetan translation by Tilakakalaśa and Blo ldan shes rab. Sanskrit and English translation, Tucci 1947.

Prajñāpāramitāpiṇḍārthapradīpa by Dīpaṃkaraśrījñāna (Atiśa). *Lamp for the Condensed Meaning of the Perfection of Wisdom. Shes rab kyi pha rol tu phyin pa'i don bsdus sgron ma.* Toh 3804, vol. *tha*, 230b1–240a7. Tibetan translation by Atiśa and Tsḥul khrims rgyal ba.

Prajñāpāramitāstotra by Rāhulabhadra. *Praise to the Perfection of Wisdom. Shes rab kyi pha rol tu phyin ma'i bstod pa.* Toh 1127, vol. *ka*, 76a1–76b7. Sanskrit in Lamotte 1949.

Prajñāpāramitopadeśa by Ratnākaraśānti. *Special Instructions on the Perfection of Wisdom. Shes rab kyi pha rol tu phyin pa'i man ngag.* Toh 4079, vol. *hi,* 133b7–162b1. Tibetan translation by Zhi ba bzang po and 'Gos Lhas btsas.

Prajñāpradīpa by Bhāviveka. *Lamp of Wisdom.* Toh 3853, vol. *tsha,* 45b4–259b3; P 5253, vol. *tsha,* 53b3–326a6. Tibetan translation by Jñānagarbha and Cog ro Klu'i rgyal mtshan.

Prajñāpradipaṭīkā by Avalokitavrata. *Lamp of Wisdom Commentary.* Toh 3859, vol. *wa,* 1–287a7, *zha* 1–338a7, *za* 1–341a7; P 5259, vol. *wa,* 1–333a6, *zha* 1–394, 395, *za* 1406a8. Tibetan translation by Jñānagarbha and Cog ro Klu'i rgyal mtshan.

Pramāṇavārttika by Dharmakīrti. *Treatise on Valid Cognition. Tshad ma rnam 'grel gyi tshig le'ur byas pa.* Toh 4210, vol. *ce,* 94b1–151a7. Tibetan translation by Subhūtiśrīśānti and Dge ba'i blo gros. Sanskrit and Tibetan in Miyasaka 1971–72.

Prasannapadā by Candrakīrti. *Clear Words. Tshig gsal ba.* Toh 3860, vol. *'a,* 1b1–200a1. Tibetan translation by Mahāsumati and Pa tshab Nyi ma grags. Revised by Kanakavarman and Pa tshab Nyi ma grags. Sanskrit in La Vallée Poussin 1903–13.

Pratītyasamutpādādivibhaṅgabhāṣya by Vasubandhu. *Commentary on the Distinctions of Dependent Arising from the Beginning. Rten cing 'brel bar 'byung ba dang po'i rnam par dbye ba bshad pa.* Toh 3995, vol. *chi,* 1b1–61a7. Tibetan translation by Surendrākaraprabha and Nam mkha'.

Pratītyasamutpādahṛdayakārikā by Nāgārjuna. *Verses on the Essence of Dependent Origination. Rten cing 'brel bar 'byung ba'i snying po'i tshig le'ur byas pa.* Toh 3836 (also 4553), vol. *tsa,* 146b2–146b7. Tibetan edition and English translation, Jamieson 2000.

Ratnakaraṇḍodghāṭamadhyamakopadeśa by Dīpaṃkaraśrījñāna (Atiśa). *Open Basket of Jewels: Special Instructions on the Middle Way. Dbu ma'i man ngag rin po che'i za ma tog kha phye ba.* Toh 3930, vol. *ki,* 96b1–116b7. Tibetan edition, Miyazaki 2007b.

Ratnāvalī (*Rājaparikathāratnamālā*) by Nāgārjuna. *The Precious Garland. Rgyal po la gtam bya ba rin po che'i phreng ba.* Toh 4158, vol. *ge,* 107a1–126a4. Sanskrit, Tibetan, and Chinese in Hahn 1982. English translation, Dunne and McClintock 1997.

Samādhisambhāraparivarta by Bodhibhadra. *Chapter on the Equipment of Concentration. Ting nge 'dzin gyi tshogs kyi le'u.* Toh 3924, vol. *ki,* 79b7–91a6. Tibetan translation by Vinayacandrapa and Chos kyi shes rab.

Sattvārādhanagāthā or *Sattvārādhanastava* by Nāgārjuna. *Praise to Make Sentient Beings Happy. Sems can mgu bar bya ba'i tshigs su bcad pa* or *Sems can mgu bar bya ba'i bstod pa.* Toh 1125, vol. *ka,* 74b3–75b1.

Satyadvayāvatāra by Dīpaṃkaraśrījñāna (Atiśa). *Entry to the Two Realities. Bden pa gnyis la 'jug pa.* Toh 3902 (also 4467), vol. *a,* 72a2–73a7. English translations, Lindtner 1981, Sherburne 2000, and Apple 2013.

Satyadvayavibhaṅgakārikā by Jñānagarbha. *Verses on the Distinction between the Two Realities.* Toh 3881, vol. *sa,* 1–3b3. Tibetan translation by Śīlendrabodhi and Ye shes sde. Tibetan edition and English translation, Eckel 1987.

Satyadvayavibhaṅgavṛtti by Jñānagarbha. *Verses on the Distinction between the Two Realities Commentary.* Toh 3882, vol. *sa,* 3b3–15b1. Tibetan translation by Śīlendrabodhi and Ye shes sde.

Śikṣāsamuccaya by Śāntideva. *Compendium of Training. Bslab pa kun las btus pa.* Toh 3940, vol. *khi,* 3a2–194b5. Tibetan translation by Jinamitra, Dānaśīla, and Ye shes sde. Revised by Tilakakalaśa and Blo ldan shes rab. English translations, Bendall 1971, and Bendall and Rouse 1971.

Stutyatītastava by Nāgārjuna. *Praise of What Surpasses Praise. Bstod pa las 'das par bstod pa.* Toh 1129, vol. *ka*, 79a2–79b6. Tibetan translation by Tilaka and Pa tshab Nyi ma grags.

Subhāṣitasaṃgraha by anonymous author. *Compendium of Good Sayings.* Sanskrit in Bendall 1903–4.

Sugatamatavibhaṅga by Jītari. *Differentiating the Sugata's Texts. Bde bar gshegs pa gzhung rnam par 'byed pa'i tshig le'ur bya pa.* Toh 3899 (also 4547), vol. *a*, 7b5–8a4. Tibetan translations by Śāntibhadra and ['Bro Seng dkar] Shākya 'od.

Sugatamatavibhaṅgabhāsya by Jītari. *Commentary on Differentiating the Sugata's Texts. Bde bar gshegs pa gzhung rnam par 'byed pa'i bshad pa.* Toh 3900, vol. *a*, 8a4–66b7. Tibetan translations by Kanakaśrīmitra and Shes rab grags.

Suhṛllekha by Nāgārjuna. *Letter to a Friend. Bshes pa'i spring yig.* Toh 4182 (also 4496), vol. *nge*, 40b4–46b3. Tibetan translation by Sarvajñadeva and Dpal brtsegs rakshi ta. English translation, Klong chen ye shes rdo rje and Nāgārjuna 2005.

Śūnyatāsaptatikārikā by Nāgārjuna. *Seventy Stanzas on Emptiness. Stong pa nyid bdun cu pa'i tshig le'ur byas pa.* Toh 3827, vol. *tsa*, 24a6–27a1. Tibetan translation by Gzhon nu mchog, Gnyan Dar ma grags, and Khu. English translation, Lindtner 1997b.

Sūtrasamuccayasañcayārtha by Dīpamkaraśrījñāna (Atiśa). *Condensed Meaning of the Compendium of Sutras. Mdo kun las btus pa'i don bsdus pa.* Toh 3937, vol. *ki*, 338b7–340b7. Extended colophon in *Bstan' gyur gser bris ma*, vol. 118, vol. *a*, 510a–513a. Tibetan translation by Atiśa and Rgya Brtson 'grus seng ge.

Svādhiṣṭhānakramaprabheda by Āryadeva. *Stages of Self-Blessing. Bdag byin gyis brlab pa'i rim pa rnam par dbye ba.* Toh 1805, vol. *ngi*, 112a3–114b1. Tibetan translation by Śraddhākaravarman and Rin chen bzang po.

Tattvaratnāvalī by Advayavajra. *Precious Garland on Suchness. De kho na nyid rin po che'i phreng ba.* Toh 2240. vol. *wi*, 115a6–120a1. Sanskrit in Shastri 1927. English translation, Tatz 1990.

Tattvāvatāravṛtti by Śrīgupta (Dpal sbas). *Commentary on Entering to Reality. De kho na la 'jug pa'i 'grel pa.* Toh 3892, vol. *ha*, 39b4–43b5.

Triṃśikākārikā by Vasubandhu. *Thirty Verses. Tshig le'ur byas pa sum cu pa.* Toh 4055, vol. *shi*, 1b1–3a3. Tibetan translation by Jinamitra, Śīlendrabodhi, and Ye shes sde. English translation, Anacker 2005.

Triśaraṇagamanasaptati by Candrakīrti. *Seventy Stanzas on Going for Refuge. Gsum la skyabs su 'gro ba bdun cu pa.* Toh 3971 (also 4564), vol. *gi*, 251a1–253b2. Tibetan translation by Dīpaṅkaraśrījñāna (Atiśa) and Rin chen bzang po. English translation, Sørensen 1986.

Vajrayānamūlāpattisaṅgraha. See *Mūlāpattisaṃgraha.*

Vigrahavyāvartanīkārikā by Nāgārjuna. *The Dispeller of Disputes. Rtsod pa bzlog pa'i tshig le'ur byas pa.* Toh 3828, vol. *tsa*, 27a1–29a7. Tibetan translation by Jñānagarbha and Ska ba Dpal brtsegs. Revised by Jayānanda and Khu Mdo sde 'bar. Sanskrit transliteration and Tibetan translation, Yonezawa 2008. English translation, Johnston and Kunst 1978, and Westerhoff 2010.

Vigrahavyāvartanīvṛtti by Nāgārjuna. *Commentary on The Dispeller of Disputes. Rtsod pa bzlog pa'i 'grel pa.* Toh 3832, vol. *tsa*, 121a4–137a7. Tibetan translation by Jñānagarbha and Dpal brtsegs rakshi ta. English translation, Johnston and Kunst 1978, and Westerhoff 2010.

Yuktiṣāṣṭikāvṛtti by Candrakīrti. *Sixty Stanzas of Reasoning. Rigs pa drug cu pa'i 'grel pa.* Toh

3864, vol. *ya*, 1b1–30b6. Tibetan translation by Jinamitra, Dānaśīla, Śīlendrabodhi, and Ye shes sde. French translation, Scherrer-Schaub 1991. English translation, Loizzo 2007.

Tibetan Sources

Bden gnyis spyi bshad dang/ bden gnyis 'jog tshul (*General Explanation*), attributed to Atiśa Dīpaṃkaraśrījñāna. 2009. 124 folios, Roman number in *Bka' gdams gsung 'bum*, 64: 23–265. Chengdu: Si khron mi rigs dpe skrun khang. Also in *Jo bo rje dpal ldan a ti sha'i gsung 'bum* (*The Collected Works of Atiśa*), 697–751.

Bod kyi lo rgyus rnam thar phyogs bsgrigs bzhugs so. 2010. *Collected Works of Tibetan Histories and Biographies.* 60 vols. Xining: Mtsho sngon mi rigs dpe skrun khang. Compiled by Dpal brtsegs bod yig dpe rnying zhib 'jug khang. TBRC: W1KG10687.

'Bras spungs dgon du bzhugs su gsol ba'i dpe rnying dkar chag. 2004. 2 vols. Beijing: Mi rigs dpe skrun khang. TBRC: W28949.

Byang chub lam gyi rim pa: Writings of Lord Atiśa on the Theory and Practice of the Graduated Path. 1973. Ladakh, India: Thupten Tsering. TBRC: W1KG506.

Chim Namkha Drak (Mchims nam mkha' grags, 1210–85). 2007. *Dbu ma'i khrid.* In *Bka' gdams gsung bum phyogs bsgrigs thengs gnyis pa*, 31: 177–214. Khreng tu'u: Si khron dpe skrun tshogs pa / si khron mi rigs dpe skrun khang.

———. 2012a. *Jo bo rin po che rje dpal ldan a ti sha'i rnam thar rgyas pa yongs grags bzhugs so*, 41–217. Ziling: Mtsho sngon mi rigs dpe skrun khang.

———. 2012b. *Dge bshes ston pa'i rnam thar.* (*Spiritual Biography of Geshé Tönpa*). In *Bod kyi lo rgyus rnam thar phyogs bsgrigs*, 2: 351–424. Ziling: Mtsho sngon mi rigs dpe skrun khang.

———. 2014. *Jo bo rin po che rje dpal ldan a ti sha'i rnam thar rgyas pa yongs grags bzhugs so*, 65–205. In *Jo bo rje dpal ldan a ti sha'i rnam thar phyogs bsgrigs*. Lhasa: Bod ljongs mi dmangs dpa skrun khang.

Collected Works of the Kadampas. See Wangchen Lhamo et al. 2006–15.

Dbu ma bden gnyis kyi 'bum. 2006. 18 folios, in *Bka' gdams gsung 'bum phyogs bsgrigs glegs bam bcu dgu pa zhugs*, 335–69. Compiled by Dpal brtsegs bod yig dpe rnying zhib 'jug khang. Ziling: Krung go'i bod rig pa dpe skrun khang.

Dbu ma'i man ngag gi 'bum. 2006. In *Bka' gdams gsung 'bum phyogs bsgrigs glegs bam bcu dgu pa zhugs*, folio 1a–16a, Roman 371–401. Compiled by Dpal brtsegs bod yig dpe rnying zhib 'jug khang. Ziling: Krung go'i bod rig pa dpe skrun khang.

Dbu ma'i man ngag gi 'bum. 2006. In *Jo bo rje dpal ldan a ti sha'i gsung 'bum* (*The Collected Works of Atiśa*), 642–68.

Dbu ma la 'jug pa'i bsdus don. 2006. In *Bka' gdams gsung 'bum phyogs bsgrigs glegs bam bcu dgu pa zhugs*, 247–317. Compiled by Dpal brtsegs bod yig dpe rnying zhib 'jug khang. Ziling: Krung go'i bod rig pa dpe skrun khang.

Dromtönpa Gyalwai Jungné ('Brom ston pa rgyal ba'i 'byung gnas, 1005–64). 2012a. *'Brom ston pa rgyal ba'i 'byung gnas kyis mdzad pa'i jo bo rje'i rnam thar lam yig chos kyi 'byung gnas.* In Dromtönpa Gyalwai Jungné 2012c, 218–75.

———. 2012b. *Jo bo rin po che rje dpal ldan a ti sha'i rnam thar rgyas pa yongs grags bzhugs so.* In Dromtönpa Gyalwai Jungné 2012c, 41–217.

———. 2012c. *Jo bo rje dpal ldan a ti sha'i rnam thar bka' gdams pha chos.* Ziling: Mtsho sngon mi rigs dpe skrun khang.

———. 2014a. *Dpal ldan a ti sha'i rnam par thar ba chos kyi 'byung gnas zhes bya ba bzhugs so*. In Dromtönpa Gyalwai Jungné at al. 2014b, 1–64.

Dromtönpa Gyalwai Jungné et al. 2014b. *Jo bo rje dpal ldan a ti sha'i rnam thar phyogs bsgrigs*. Lhasa: Bod ljongs mi dmangs dpa skrun khang.

Gö Lotsāwa Shönu Pal ('Gos lo tsā ba Gzhon nu dpal, 1392–1481). 1984 [composed in 1476]. *Deb ther sngon po*. 2 vols. Edited by Dung dkar blo bzang 'phrin las. Chengdu: Si khron mi rigs dpe skrun khang.

Ja Dulzin Tsöndrü Bar (Bya 'dul 'dzin brtson 'grus 'bar, 1091–1166/1100–1174). 2014. *Jo bo chen po rje lha cig gi rnam thar ba zhugs so*, 245–39. In *Jo bo rje dpal ldan a ti sha'i rnam thar phyogs bsgrigs*. Lhasa: Bod ljongs mi dmangs dpa skrun khang.

Jo bo rje dpal ldan a ti sha'i gsung 'bum. 2006. (*The Collected Works of Atiśa* [works attributed to Atiśa and his early disciples]). Lhasa: Dpal brtsegs Group.

Jo bos rgyal srid spang nas thar pa ji ltar mdzad pa. 2012. In Dromtönpa Gyalwai Jungné, *Jo bo rje dpal ldan a ti sha'i rnam thar bka' gdams pha chos*, 1–26.

Khujuk (Khu byug). 2004. *Bod kyi dbu ma'i lta ba'i 'chad nyan dar tshul blo gsal mig 'byed*. Beijing: Krung go'i bod rig pa dpe skrun khang. TBRC: W28813.

Kyotön Mönlam Tsultrim (Skyo ston Smon lam tshul khrims, 1219–99). 2007. *Jo bo rje'i dbu ma'i man ngag gi bshad pa*. In Wangchen Lhamo et al., *Bka' gdams gsung bum phyogs bsgrigs thengs gnyis pa*, 50: 417–20.

Lechen Kunga Gyaltsen (Las chen kun dga' rgyal mtshan, 1432–1506). 2003. *Bka' gdams kyi rnam par thar pa bka' gdams chos 'byung gsal ba'i sgron me*. Lhasa: Bod ljongs mi dmangs dpe skrun khang.

Mikyö Dorjé (Mi bskyod rdo rje, 1507–54). 2004. *Dbu ma la 'jug pa'i rnam bshad dpal ldan dus gsum mkhyen pa'i zhal lung dwags brgyud grub pa'i shing rta /*. In *Gsung 'bum/_mi bskyod rdo rje*, 14: 3–978. Lhasa: n.p. TBRC: W8039.

Minyak Gönpo et al. (Mi nyag mgon po, Ye shes rdo rje, Thub bstan nyi ma, Dpal rdor, and Lha mo skyabs). 1996–2000. "Brom ston pa rgyal ba'i 'byung gnas kyi rnam thar mdor bsdus/ (1004/1005–1064)." In *Gangs can mkhas dbang rim byon gyi rnam thar mdor bsdus*, 2: 13–16. Beijing: Krung go'i bod kyi shes rig dpe skrun khang. TBRC: W25268.

Naktso Lotsāwa Tsultrim Gyalwa (Nag tsho lo tsā ba tshul khrims rgyal ba, 1011–64). 2014. *Jo bo'i rnam thar kha skong zur du gleng ba zur rtsam thor bu ba bzhugs so*. In Chim Namkha Drak, *Jo bo rje dpal ldan a ti sha'i rnam thar phyogs bsgrigs*, 393–408.

Naljorpa Sherab Dorjé (Rnal 'byor pa Shes rab rdo rje, ca. 1125). 2006. *Rnal 'byor pa Shes rab rdo rjes mdzad pa'i bden gnyis kyi rnam par bshad pa*. ([Naljorpa] *Sherab Dorjé's Explanation of Atiśa's Entry to the Two Realities*). In Wangchen Lhamo et al., *Bka' gdams gsung 'bum phyogs sgrig thengs dang po*, 21: 513–625.

Pawo Tsuklak Trengwa (Dpa' bo gtsug lag phreng ba). 2006. *Dam pa'i chos kyi 'khor lo bsgyur ba rnams kyi byung ba gsal bar byed pa mkhas pa'i dga' ston*. Beijing: Mi rigs dpe skrun khang.

Phuntsok Tseten (Phun tshogs tshe brtan). 2011. *Mnyam med jo bo rje dpal ldan a ti sha'i rnam par thar pa phyogs bsdus dad pa'i 'jug ngogs*. Beijing: Krung-go'i Bod rig pa dpe skrun khang.

Potowa's Middle Way. Dbu ma'i man ngag gi bshad pa, Pu to yab sras kyi lugs. 2006. In *Bka' gdams gsung 'bum phyogs bsgrigs glegs bam bcu dgu pa zhugs*, folio 1a–9a, Roman 317–34. Compiled by Dpal brtsegs bod yig dpe rnying zhib 'jug khang. Ziling: Krung go'i bod rig pa dpe skrun khang.

Sharawa Yönten Drak (Sha ra ba Yon tan grags, 1070–1141). 2014. *Dge ba'i bshes gnyen zhang sha ra ba yon tan grags kyis mdzad pa'i lam rim bzhugs so*. N.p.: Ser gtsug nang bstan dpe rnying 'tshol bsdu phyogs sgrig khang nas bsgrigs.

Tsenlha Ngawang Tsultrim (Btsan lha ngag dbang tshul khrims). 1997. *Brda dkrol gser gyi me long*. Beijing: Mi rigs dpe skrun khang.

Tsering Gyalpo (Tshe ring rgyal po). 2006. *Mnga' ris chos 'byung gangs ljongs mdzes rgyan zhes bya ba bzhugs so*. Lhasa: Bod ljongs mi dmangs dpe skrun khang.

Tsultrim Rinchen (Tshul khrims rin chen). 1982–85. *Bstan 'gyur (sde dge)*. 213 vols. Tibetan Buddhist Resource Center W23703. Delhi: Delhi karmapae choedhey, gyalwae sungrab partun khang. http://tbrc.org/link?RID=W23703.

Tsongkhapa Losang Drakpa (Tsong kha pa Blo bzang grags pa, 1357–1419). 1985. *Lam rim chen mo. Mnyam med tsong kha pa chen pos mdzad pa'i byang chub lam rim che ba*. Kokonor, Tibet: Mtsho ngon mi rigs dpe skrun khang.

Wangchen Lhamo (Dbyangs can lha mo), et al., eds. 2006–15. *Collected Works of the Kadampas. Bka' gdams gsung 'bum phyogs bsgrigs bzhugs so*. 120 vols. Chengdu: Si khron Dpe skrun Tshogs pa, Si khron mi rigs dpe skrun khang.

Yeshé Döndrup (Ye shes don grub bstan pa'i rgyal mtshan, 1792–1855). *Legs par bshad pa bka' gdams rin po che'i gsung gi gces btus legs bshad nor bu'i bang mdzod*. (*Treasury of Gems: Selected Anthology of the Well-Uttered Insights of the Teachings of the Precious Kadam Tradition*). Typeset edition. Kansu, China: Nationalities Press, 1995.

Yongzin Yeshé Gyaltsen (Yongs 'dzin Ye shes rgyal mtshan). 1980. *Dge bshes dgon pa ba'i rnam thar*. In *Lam rim bla ma brgyud pa'i rnam thar*, 1: 276–87. 'Bar khams: Rnga khul bod yig rtsom sgyur cus.

———. 1990. *Dpal ldan mgon pa ba'i rnam thar*. In *Lam rim bla ma brgyud pa'i rnam thar*, 1: 206–14. Lhasa: Bod ljongs mi dmangs dpe skrun khang.

Secondary Sources

Almogi, Orna. 2009. *Rong-Zom-Pa's Discourses on Buddhology: A Study of Various Conceptions of Buddhahood in Indian Sources with Special Reference to the Controversy Surrounding the Existence of Gnosis (Jñāna : Ye Shes), as Presented by the Eleventh-Century Tibetan Scholar Rong-Zom Chos-Kyi-Bzang-Po*. Tokyo: International Institute for Buddhist Studies of the International College for Postgraduate Buddhist Studies.

———. 2010. "Māyopamādvayavāda versus Sarvadharmāpratiṣṭhānavāda: A Late Indian Subclassification of Madhyamaka and Its Reception in Tibet." *Journal of the International College for Postgraduate Buddhist Studies* 14: 135–212.

Ames, William L. 2003. "Bhāvaviveka's Own View of His Differences with Buddhapālita." In *The Svātantrika-Prāsaṅgika Distinction: What Difference Does a Difference Make?* edited by Georges B. J. Dreyfus and Sara L. McClintock, 41–66. Boston: Wisdom Publications.

Anacker, Stefan. 2005. *Seven Works of Vasubandhu, the Buddhist Psychological Doctor*. 2nd rev. ed. Delhi: Motilal Banarsidass.

Apple, James B. 2008. *Stairway to Nirvāṇa: A Study of the Twenty Saṃghas Based on the Works of Tsongkhapa*. Albany: State University of New York Press.

———. 2010. "Atiśa's Open Basket of Jewels: A Middle Way Vision in Late Phase Indian Vajrayāna." *Indian International Journal of Buddhist Studies* 11: 117–98.

———. 2013. "An Early Tibetan Commentary on Atiśa's *Satyadvayāvatāra*." *Journal of Indian Philosophy* 41: 263–329.

———. 2015a. "A Study and Translation of Atiśa's *Madhyamakopadeśa* with Indian and Tibetan Commentaries." *Acta Tibetica et Buddhica* 7: 1–82.

———. 2015b. "Candrakīrti and the *Lotus Sutra*." *Bulletin of the Institute of Oriental Philosophy* 31.1: 97–122.

———. 2016. "An Early Bka'-gdams-pa Madhyamaka Work Attributed to Atiśa Dīpaṃkaraśrījñāna." *Journal of Indian Philosophy* 44: 619–725.

———. 2017. "Atiśa's Teachings on Mahāmudrā." *Indian International Journal of Buddhist Studies* 18: 1–42.

Arnold, Daniel A. 2003. "Verses on Nonconceptual Awareness: A Close Reading of *Mahāyānasaṃgraha* 8.2–13." *Indian International Journal of Buddhist Studies* 4: 9–49.

———. 2005. *Buddhists, Brahmins, and Belief: Epistemology in South Asian Philosophy of Religion*. New York: Columbia University Press.

Astley-Kristensen, Ian. 1991. *The Rishukyô: The Sino-Japanese Tantric Prajñāpāramitā in 150 Verses*. Tring, UK: Institute of Buddhist Studies.

Bagchi, S., ed. 1967. *Suvarṇaprabhāsasūtra*. Darbhanga, India: Mithila Institute.

Barron, Richard, trans. 2011. *The Treasury of Knowledge. Journey and Goal: An Analysis of the Spiritual Paths and Levels to Be Traversed and the Consummate Fruition State Books Nine and Ten*. Ithaca, NY: Snow Lion Publications.

Bendall, Cecil, ed. 1903–4. *Subhāṣitasaṃgraha. Subhāṣita-Saṃgraha. Le Muséon* vol. 4 (1903): 375–402; vol. 5 (1904): 1–46, 245–74. Louvain, Belgium: J. B. Istas.

———. 1971. *Çikshāsamuccaya: A Compendium of Buddhistic Teaching*. Bibliotheca Buddhica 1. St. Petersburg, Russia, 1897–1902. Reprint, Delhi: Motilal Banarsidass, 1971.

Bendall, C., and W. H. D. Rouse, eds. 1971. *Śikṣā Samuccaya: A Compendium of Buddhist Doctrine*. J. Murray: London, 1922. Reprint, Delhi: Motilal Banarsidass, 1971.

Bhaṭṭacharya, K. 1978. *The Dialectical Method of Nāgārjuna*. Delhi: Motilal Banarsidass.

Blumenthal, James. 2004. *The Ornament of the Middle Way: A Study of the Madhyamaka Thought of Śāntarakṣita*. Ithaca, NY: Snow Lion Publications.

———. 2009. "Dynamic and Syncretic Dimensions to Śāntarakṣita's Presentation of the Two Truths." *Asian Philosophy* 19.1: 51–62.

Braarvig, Jens. 1993. *Akṣayamatinirdeśasūtra*. Oslo: Solum Forlag.

Braarvig, Jens, et al., eds. 2006. *Buddhist Manuscripts in the Schøyen Collection*. Oslo: Hermes.

Brunnhölzl, Karl. 2007. *In Praise of Dharmadhātu: Nāgārjuna and the Third Karmapa, Rangjung Dorje*. Ithaca, NY: Snow Lion Publications.

———. 2011. *Prajñāpāramitā, Indian "gzhan stong pas," and the Beginning of Tibetan gzhan stong*. Vienna: Arbeitskreis für Tibetische und Buddhistische Studien, Universität Wien.

———. 2014. *When the Clouds Part: The Uttaratantra and Its Meditative Tradition as a Bridge between Sūtra and Tantra*. Boston: Snow Lion Publications.

Buescher, Hartmut. 2008. *The Inception of Yogācāra-Vijñānavāda*. Vienna: Verlag der Österreichischen Akademie der Wissenschaften.

Burton, David. 1999. *Emptiness Appraised: A Critical Study of Nāgārjuna's Philosophy*. Richmond, England: Curzon.

Cabezón, José Ignacio. 1992. *A Dose of Emptiness: An Annotated Translation of the sTong thun chen mo of mKhas-grub dGe-legs-dpal-bzaṅg*. Albany: State University of New York Press.

———. 2007. *Freedom from Extremes: Gorampa's "Distinguishing the Views" and the Polemics of Emptiness*. Boston: Wisdom Publications.

Cabezón, José Ignacio, and Roger R. Jackson, eds. 1996. *Tibetan Literature: Studies in Genre*. Ithaca, NY: Snow Lion Publications.

Chakravarti, Chintaharan (Cintāharaṇacakravartti), ed. 1984. *Guhyasamājatantra-pradīpodyotanaṭīkā-ṣaṭkoṭīvyākhyā*. Tibetan Sanskrit Works Series 25. Patna, India: Kashi Prasad Jayaswal Research Institute.

Chandra, Lokesh, ed. 1982. *Biography of Atiśa and His Disciple ḥBrom-ston*. New Delhi: International Academy of Indian Culture.

Chattopadhyaya, Alaka. 1967. *Atīśa and Tibet: Life and Works of Dīpaṃkara Śrījñāna in Relation to the History and Religion of Tibet*. Calcutta: Indian Studies, Past and Present.

Cleary, Thomas. 1993. *The Flower Ornament Scripture: A Translation of the Avatamsaka Sutra*. Boston: Shambhala Publications.

Conze, Edward, ed. and trans. 1957. *Vajracchedikā Prajñāpāramitā*. Serie Orientale Roma 13, edited by Giuseppe Tucci. Rome: Istituto Italiano per il Medio ed Estremo Oriente.

———, 1960. *Prajñā-pāramitā-ratna-guṇa-saṃcaya-gāthā: Sanskrit and Tibetan Text Edited by E. Obermiller*. Photomechanic reprint with a Sanskrit-Tibetan-English index by Edward Conze. The Hague: Mouton and Company.

———, trans. 1975. *The Large Sutra on Perfect Wisdom, with the Divisions of the Abhisamayālaṅkāra*. Berkeley: University of California Press.

Cowherds. 2011. *Moonshadows: Conventional Truth in Buddhist Philosophy*. Oxford: Oxford University Press.

Cox, Collett. 2000. "Whether Buddhas Arise or Do Not Arise: The Variant or Invariant Nature of Dependent Origination (*Pratītyasamutpāda*)." In *Felicitation Volume for Professor Junshō Katō*, edited by Toshihiro Wada, 580–64. Tokyo: Shunjusha.

Crosby, Kate, and Andrew Skilton. 1995. *The Bodhicaryāvatāra*. Oxford: Oxford University Press.

Cutler, Joshua W. C., and Guy Newland. 2000. *The Great Treatise on the Stages of the Path to Enlightenment*. vol. 1. Ithaca, NY: Snow Lion Publications.

Cutler, Joshua W. C., et al. 2002. *The Great Treatise on the Stages of the Path to Enlightenment* (*Lam rim chen mo*). vol. 3. Ithaca, NY: Snow Lion Publications.

D'Amato, Mario. 2009. "Why the Buddha Never Uttered a Word." In *Pointing at the Moon: Buddhism, Logic, Analytic Philosophy*, edited by M. D'Amato, J. L. Garfield, and T. J. F. Tillemans, 41–55. New York: Oxford University Press.

———, trans. 2012. *Maitreya's Distinguishing the Middle from the Extremes (Madhyāntavibhāga) along with Vasubandhu's Commentary (Madhyāntavibhāga-bhāṣya)*. New York: American Institute of Buddhist Studies.

Davidson, Ronald M. 1981. "The Litany of Names of *Mañjuśrī*: Text and Translation of the *Mañjuśrīnāmasaṃgīti*." In *Tantric and Taoist Studies (R. A. Stein Festschrift)*, edited by Michel Strickmann, 1–69. Brussels: Institut Belge des Hautes Études Chinoises (Melanges Chinois et Bouddhiques).

———. 1995. "Atiśa's *A Lamp for the Path to Awakening*." In *Buddhism in Practice*, edited by Donald S. Lopez Jr., 290–301. Princeton, NJ: Princeton University Press.

———. 2005. *Tibetan Renaissance: Tantric Buddhism in the Rebirth of Tibetan Culture*. New York: Columbia University Press.

Decleer, Hubert. 1996. "Master Atiśa in Nepal: The Tham Bahīl and Five Stūpas' Foundations according to the *'Brom ston Itinerary*." *Journal of the Nepal Research Centre* 10: 27–54.

———. 1997a. "Atisha's Arrival in Nepal." *Buddhist Himalaya: Journal of Nagarjuna Institute of Exact Methods* 8.1–2: 1–15.

———. 1997b. "Atiśa's Journey to Tibet." In *Religions of Tibet in Practice*, edited by Donald S. Lopez Jr., 157–77. Princeton, NJ: Princeton University Press.

———. 1998. "Death of the Translator Virya Siṃha." *Buddhist Himalaya: Journal of Nagarjuna Institute of Exact Methods* 9.1–2: 1–19.

De Jong, J. W. 1962. "La Madhyamakaśāstrastuti de Candrakīrti." *Oriens Extremus* 9: 47–56.

———. 1972. "An Old Tibetan Version of the Ramāyāṇa." *T'oung Pao* 58: 190–202.

———. 1989. "Review of Eli Franco, *Perception, Knowledge and Disbelief*." *Indo-Iranian Journal* 32: 209–12.

Del Toso, Krishna. 2011. "Il Madhyamakārthasaṃgraha di Bhāviveka: Introduzione, edizione del testo tibetano e traduzione annotata." *Escercizi Filosofici* 6: 347–65.

———. 2014. "Some Problems concerning Textual Reuses in the *Madhyamakaratnapradīpa*, with a Discussion of the Quotation from Saraha's *Dohākośagīti*." *Journal of Indian Philosophy*, 43: 511–57, doi:10.1007/s10781-014-9246-3.

Deroche, Marc-Henri. 2011. "Instructions on the View (*Lta khrid*) of the Two Truths: Prajñāraśmi's (1518–1584) *Bden gnyis gsal ba'i sgron me* (1518–1584)." *Revue d'Études Tibétaines* 22: 139–214.

Doctor, Thomas H. 2010. "In Pursuit of Transparent Means of Knowledge—The Madhyamaka Project of rMa bya Byaṅ chub brtson 'grus." *Journal of the International Association of Buddhist Studies* 32.1–2: 419–42.

———. 2014. *Reason and Experience in Tibetan Buddhism: Mabja Jangchub Tsöndrü and the Traditions of the Middle Way*. New York: Routledge.

Dreyfus, Georges B. J., and Sara L. McClintock. 2003. *The Svātantrika-Prāsaṅgika Distinction: What Difference Does a Difference Make?* Boston: Wisdom Publications.

Dreyfus, Georges, and Drongbu Tsering. 2010. "Pa tshab and the Origin of Prāsaṅgika." *Journal of the International Association of Buddhist Studies* 32.1–2: 387–418.

Duerlinger, James. 1997. "Vasubandhu's Philosophical Critique of the Vātsīputrīyas' Theory of Person." *Journal of Indian Philosophy* 25: 307–35.

Dunne, John D. 1996. "Thoughtless Buddha, Passionate Buddha." *Journal of the American Academy of Religion* 64: 525–56.

———. 2004. *Foundations of Dharmakīrti's Philosophy*. Boston: Wisdom Publications.

Dunne, John, and Sarah McClintock. 1997. *The Precious Garland: An Epistle to a King*. Boston: Wisdom Publications.

Duquenne, Robert. 1983. "Daigensui (Āṭavaka)." *Hobogirin* 6: 610a–640b.

Dutt, Nalinaksha. 1934. *The Pañcaviṁśatisāhasrikā Prajñāpāramitā*. London: Luzac.

———. 1966. *Bodhisattvabhūmi*. Patna, India: K. P. Jayaswal Research Institute.

Eckel, Malcolm David. 1987. *Jñānagarbha's Commentary on the Distinction between the Two Truths*. Albany: State University of New York Press.

———. 1992. *To See the Buddha: A Philosopher's Quest for the Meaning of Emptiness*. Princeton, NJ: Princeton University Press.

———. 2008. *Bhāviveka and His Buddhist Opponents: [Chapters 4 and 5 of Bhāviveka's Madhyamakahṛdayakārikā with Tarkajvālā Commentary]*. Cambridge, MA: Department of Sanskrit and Indian Studies, Harvard University.

Edelglass, William, and J. L. Garfield. 2009. *Buddhist Philosophy: Essential Readings*. New York: Oxford University Press.

Edgerton, Franklin. 1953. *Buddhist Hybrid Sanskrit Grammar and Dictionary*. New Haven, CT: Yale University Press.

Eimer, Helmut. 1977. *Berichte über das Leben des Atiśa (Dīpaṃkarásrījñāna): Eine Untersuchung der Quellen*. Wiesbaden: O. Harrassowitz.

———. 1978. *Bodhipathapradīpa: Ein Lehrgedict des Atiśa (Dīpaṃkaraśrījñāna) in der tibetischen Überlieferung.* Asiatische Forschungen 59. Wiesbaden: O. Harrassowitz.

———. 1979. *Rnam thar rgyas pa: Materialien zu einer Biographie des Atiśa (Dīpaṃkaraśrījñāna)*. Vol. 1, *Einführung, Inhaltsverzeichnis, Namensglossar*. Vol. 2, *Textmaterialien*. Wiesbaden: Harrassowitz.

———. 1982. "The Development of the Biographical Tradition concerning Atiśa (Dīpaṃkaraśrījñāna)." *Journal of Tibet Society* 2: 41–52.

———. 2003. *Testimonia for the Bstod-pa brgyad-cu-pa: An Early Hymn Praising Dīpaṃkaraśrījñāna (Atiśa)*. Lumbini, Nepal: Lumbini International Research Institute.

———. 2008. "Sources for the *Vita* of 'Brom ston rgyal ba'i 'byung gnas." In *Contributions to Tibetan Buddhist Literature*, edited by Orna Almogi, 377–92. Beiträge zur Zentralasienforschung 14. Halle (Saale), Germany: International Institute for Tibetan and Buddhist Studies.

Ejima, Yasunori. 1983. "Atīsha no Ni-shinri-setsu (Atīśa's Theory of the Two Truths)." In *Ryūju kyōgaku no kenkyū* (*Studies of Teaching of Nāgārjuna*), edited by Taishun Mibu, 359–91. Tokyo: Daizō Shuppan.

Eltschinger, Vincent. 2009. "On the Career and Cognition of Yogins." In *Yogic Perception, Meditation and Altered States of Consciousness*, edited by Eli Franco, 169–213. Beiträge zur Kultur- und Geistes-geschichte Asiens 65. Vienna: Verlag der Öster-reichischen Akademie der Wissenschaften.

———. 2010. "Studies in Dharmakīrti's Religious Philosophy: 4. The *Cintāmayīprajñā*." In *Logic and Belief in Indian Philosophy*, edited by Piotr Balcerowicz, 565–603. Warsaw Indological Studies 3. Delhi: Motilal Banarsidass.

———. 2014. *Buddhist Epistemology as Apologetics: Studies on the History, Self-Understanding and Dogmatic Foundations of Late Indian Buddhist Philosophy*. Vienna: Verlag der Österreichischen Akademie der Wissenschaften.

Engle, Artemus. 2009. *The Inner Science of Buddhist Practice: Vasubandhu's Summary of the Five Heaps with Commentary by Sthiramati*. Ithaca, NY: Snow Lion Publications.

———. 2016. *The Bodhisattva Path to Unsurpassed Enlightenment: A Complete Translation of the Bodhisattvabhūmi*. Boulder, CO: Snow Lion Publications.

Franco, Eli. 2009. "Introduction." In Franco and Eigner, *Yogic Perception, Meditation and Altered States of Consciousness*, 1–51.

———. 2015. "Jitāri on Backward Causation (*Bhāvikāraṇavāda*)." In *Buddhist Meditative Praxis Traditional Teachings and Modern Applications*, edited by K. L. Dhammajoti, 81–115. Hong Kong: University of Hong Kong Press.

Franco, Eli, and D. Eigner, eds. 2009. *Yogic Perception, Meditation and Altered States of Consciousness*. Vienna: Austrian Academy of Sciences.

Funayama, T. 2007. "Kamalaśīla's Distinction between the Two Sub-Schools of Yogācāra: A Provisional Survey." In *Pramāṇakīrtiḥ: Papers Dedicated to Ernst Steinkellner on the Occasion of His 70th Birthday*, edited by B. Kellner, H. Krasser, H. Lasic, M. T. Much, and H. Tauscher, 187–202. Vienna: Arbeitskreis für tibetische und buddhistische Studien.

Ghosha, P., ed. 1902–13. *Śatasāhasrikāprajñāpāmitāsūtra*. Bibliotheca Indica. voi 1 (chapters 1–12 of the *Śatasāhasrikāprajñāpāmitāsūtra*). Calcutta: Asiatic Society of Bengal.

Gokhale, V. V. 1955. "Der Sansktrit-Text von Nāgārjuna's Pratītyasamutpādahṛdayakārikā." In *Studia Indologica, Festschrift für Willibald Kirfel zur Vollendung seines 70*, vol. 3 of *Bonner Orientalische Studien*, edited by O. Spies, 101–6. Bonn: Lebensjahres.

———. 1972. "The Second Chapter of Bhavya's Madhyamakahṛdaya (Taking the Vow of an Ascetic)." *Indo-Iranian Journal* 14: 40–45.

Gold, Jonathan C. 2007. *The Dharma's Gatekeepers: Sakya Pandita on Buddhist Scholarship in Tibet*. Albany: State University of New York Press.

Goshima, K. 1983. *The Tibetan Text of the Second Bhāvanākrama*. Kyoto: Goshima Kiyotaka.

Guenther, Herbert V. 1959. *Jewel Ornament of Liberation*. London: Rider.

Gyatso, Tenzin. 2001. *Stages of Meditation, Root Text by Kamalashila*. Translated by Ven. Geshe Lobsang Jordhen, Losang Choephel Ganchenpa, and Jeremy Russell. Ithaca, NY: Snow Lion Publications. (English translation of the *Bhāvanākrama-2*).

Hadot, Pierre. 1998. *The Inner Citadel: The Meditations of Marcus Aurelius*. Cambridge, MA: Harvard University Press.

Hahn, Michael. 1982. *Nāgārjuna's Ratnāvalī*, vol. 1, *The Basic Texts (Sanskrit, Tibetan, Chinese)*. Indica et Tibetica 1. Bonn: Indica et Tibetica Verlag.

———. 1990. *Hundert strophen von der Lebensklugheit: Nāgārjunas Prajñāśataka*. Indica et Tibetica 18. Bonn: Indica et Tibetica Verlag.

Hakuju, Ui, Suzuki Munetada, Kanakura Yenshô, and Tada Tôkan, eds. 1934. *A Complete Catalogue of the Tibetan Buddhist Canons—Bkaḥ-ḥgyur and Bstan-ḥgyur (with an Index)*. Sendai: Tohoku Imperial University.

Harrison, Paul. 2006. "*Vajracchedikā Prajñāpāramitā:* A New English Translation of the Sanskrit Text based on Two Manuscripts from Greater Gandhāra." In Braarvig et al., *Buddhist Manuscripts in the Schøyen Collection*, 133–59.

Harrison, Paul, and Shogo Watanabe. 2006. "*Vajracchedikā Prajñāpāramitā*." In Braarvig et al., *Buddhist Manuscripts in the Schøyen Collection*, 89–132.

Hayashi, Keijin. 1996. "Ratnākaraśānti's Siddhānta Text—An Annotated Translation of *Triyānavyavasthāna*." *Asian Culture and Thought* (*Ronsō Ajia No Bunka To Shisō*), no. 5: 34–93.

Hayes, Richard. 2014. "Madhyamaka." *The Stanford Encyclopedia of Philosophy*, edited by Edward N. Zalta. Stanford, CA: Metaphysics Research Lab, Stanford University.

Heitmann, Annette L. 2004. *Nektar der Erkenntnis, Buddhistische Philosophie des 6. Jh.: Bhavyas Tarkajvālā I–III.26*. Aachen: Shaker Verlag.

Higgins, David. 2008. "On the Development of the Non-Mentation (*Amanasikāra*) Doctrine in Indo-Tibetan Buddhism." *Journal of the International Association of Buddhist Studies* 29.2: 255–303.

———. 2013. *The Philosophical Foundations of Classical rDzogs chen in Tibet: Investigating the Distinction between Dualistic Mind (sems) and Primordial Knowing (ye shes)*. Vienna: Arbeitskreis für Tibetische und Buddhistische Studien, Universität Wien.

Hoornaert, Paul 2003. "An Annotated Translation of *Madhyamakahṛdayakārikā/ Tarkajvālā* V.85–114." *Kanazawadaigaku bungakubu ronshū, Kōdōkagakkahen—Studies and Essays, Behavioural Sciences and Philosophy* 23: 139–70.

Hopkins, Jeffrey. 1989. "A Tibetan Delineation of Different Views of Emptiness in the Indian Middle Way School." *Tibet Journal* 14.1: 10–43.

———. 2007. *The Essence of Other-Emptiness*. Ithaca, NY: Snow Lion Publications.

———. 2008. *Tsong-kha-pa's Final Exposition of Wisdom*. Ithaca, NY: Snow Lion Publications.

Huanhuan, He, and Leonard W. J. van der Kuijp. 2014. "Further Notes on Bhāviveka's Principal Oeuvre." *Indo-Iranian Journal* 57: 299–352.

Hugon, Pascale. 2016. "Enclaves of Learning, Religious and Intellectual Communities in Tibet: The Monastery of gSang phu Ne'u thog in the Early Centuries of the Later Diffusion of Buddhism." In *Meanings of Community across Medieval Eurasia*, edited by Eirik Hovden, Christina Lutter, and Walter Pohl, 289–308. Leiden: Brill.

Huntington, C. W. 1986. "The Akutobhayā and Early Indian Madhyamaka." PhD diss., University of Michigan.

———. 1989. *The Emptiness of Emptiness: An Introduction to Early Indian Mādhyamika*. Honolulu: University of Hawai'i Press.

———. 2003. "Was Candrakīrti a Prāsaṅgika?" In Dreyfus and McClintock, *The Svātantrika-Prāsaṅgika Distinction*, 67–91.

Ichigō, Masamichi. 1985. *Madhyamakālaṃkāra of Śāntarakṣita: With His Own Commentary or Vṛtti and with the Subcommentary or Pañjikā of Kamalaśīla*. Kyoto: Kyoto Sangyō University.

———. 1989. "Śāntarakṣita's Madhyamakālaṃkāra." In *Studies in the Literature of the Great Vehicle: Three Mahāyāna Buddhist Texts*, edited by Luis Gómez and Jonathan A. Silk, 141–240. Ann Arbor: Collegiate Institute for the Study of Buddhist Literature and Center for South and Southeast Asian Studies, University of Michigan.

Iida, Shotaro. 1980. *Reason and Emptiness: A Study in Logic and Mysticism*. Tokyo: Hokuseido Press.

Inagaki, Hisao. 1977. "Haribhadra's Quotations from Jñānagarbha's *Anantamukhanirhāradhāraṇīṭīkā*." In *Buddhist Thought and Asian Civilization: Essays in Honor of Herbert V. Guenther on His Sixtieth Birthday*, edited by Leslie S. Kawamura and Keith Scott, 132–44. Emeryville, CA: Dharma Publishing.

Isaacson, Harunaga. 2013. "Yogācāra and Vajrayāna according to Ratnākaraśānti." In *The Foundation for Yoga Practitioners: The Buddhist Yogācārabhūmi Treatise and Its Adaptation in India, East Asia, and Tibet*, edited by Ulrich Timme Kragh, 1036–51. Cambridge, MA: Department of South Asian Studies, Harvard University.

Iuchi, Maho. 2008. "'Dan ma: The Place of the Second Diffusion of Buddhism in Eastern Tibet" [in Japanese]. *Indogaku bukkyōgaku kenkyū* [*Journal of Indian and Buddhist Studies*] 57.1: 465–57.

———. 2012. "A Note on the Relationship between the Bka' gdams pa School and Mi nyag/Xixia." *Journal of Tibetology* 8: 58–62.

———. 2013. "Early bka' gdams pa Masters and Khams 'Dan Ma: A Preliminary Study of Monasteries Related to Smṛtijñānakīrti." In *Tibet after Empire: Culture, Society and Religion between 850 and 1000*, edited by Christoph Cüppers, Robert Mayer, and Michael Walter, 215–24. Lumbini, Nepal: Lumbini International Research Institute.

———. 2016. *An Early Text on the History of Rwa sgreng Monastery: The Rgyal ba'i dben gnas Rwa sgreng gi bshad pa nyi ma'i 'od zer of 'Brom Shes rab me lce*. Harvard Oriental Series 82. Cambridge, MA: Harvard University Press.

Jackson, David Paul. 1985. "Madhyamaka Studies among the Early Sa-skya-pas." *Tibet Journal* 10.2: 20–34.

———. 1994. *Enlightenment by a Single Means: Tibetan Controversies on the "Self-Sufficient*

White Remedy" (dkar po chig thub). Vienna: Verlag der Österreichischen Akademie der Wissenschaften.

Jackson, Roger R. 2009. "Two Bka' 'gyur Works in Mahāmudrā Canons: The *Ārya-ātajñāna-nāma-mahāyāna-sūtra* and the *Anāvila-tantra-rāja*." *Journal of the International Association of Tibetan Studies*, no. 5 (December): 1–24.

Jamieson, R. C. 2000. *A Study of Nāgārjuna's Twenty Verses on the Great Vehicle (Mahāyāna-viṃśikā) and His Verses on the Heart of Dependent Origination (Pratītyasamutpādahṛdayakārikā), with the Interpretation of the Heart of Dependent Origination (Pratītya-samutpādahṛdayavyākhyāna)*. New York: Peter Lang.

Jinpa, Thupten. 2006. *Mind Training: The Great Collection*. Boston: Wisdom Publications.

———. 2008. *The Book of Kadam: The Core Texts*. Boston: Wisdom Publications.

———. 2013. *Wisdom of the Kadam Masters*. Boston: Wisdom Publications.

Johnston, E. H., et al., trans. 1991. [1950] *The Uttaratantra of Maitreya: Containing an Introduction, E. H. Johnston's Sanskrit Text, and E. Obermiller's English Translation*. Delhi: Sri Satguru Publications.

Johnston, E. H., and A. Kunst, eds. 1978. "The Vigrahavyāvartanī of Nāgārjuna with the Author's Commentary." In *The Dialectical Method of Nāgārjuna's Vigrahavyāvartanī*, edited by Kamaleswar Bhattacharya, 34–86. New Delhi: Motilal Banarsidass.

Kajiyama, Yūichi. 1965. "Controversy between the Sākāra- and Nirākāra-vādins of the Yogācāra School: Some Materials." *Journal of Indian and Buddhist Studies* 14.1: 418–29.

———. 1966. *An Introduction to Buddhist Philosophy: An Annotated Translation of the Tarkabhāṣā of Mokṣākaragupta*. Kyoto: Memoirs of the Faculty of Letters, Kyoto University.

———. 1978. "Later Mādhyamikas on Epistemology and Meditation. In *Mahāyāna Buddhist Meditation: Theory and Practice*, edited by Minoru Kiyota and Elvin W. Jones, 114–43. Honolulu: University of Hawai'i Press.

———. 1987. "Mādhyamika." In *The Encyclopedia of Religion*, edited by M. Eliade et al., 9: 71–77. New York: Macmillan.

———. 1999. *The Antarvyāptisamarthana of Ratnākaraśānti*. Tokyo: International Research Institute for Advanced Buddhology, Soka University.

Kano, Kazuo. 2008. "Rngog blo ldan shes rab's Topical Outline of the *Ratnagotravibhāga* Discovered at Khara Khoto." In *Contributions to Tibetan Literature. Proceedings of the Eleventh Seminar of the International Association for Tibetan Studies, Königswinter 2006. Beiträge zur Zentralasienforschung*, edited by O. Almogi, 127–94. Halle, Germany: International Institute for Tibetan and Buddhist Studies.

———. 2014. "Six Tibetan Translations of the *Ratnagotravibhāga*." *China Tibetology*, no. 2: 76–101.

———. 2015. "Text-Critical Remarks and Annotated Japanese Translation of the Sanskrit Text of the Dharmadhātustava Verses 1–51." *Indo ronrigaku kenkyū* 8: 177–201.

———. 2016a. "Jñānaśrīmitra on the *Ratnagotravibhāga*." *Oriental Culture*, no. 96: 7–48.

———. 2016b. *Buddha-Nature and Emptiness: rNgog Blo-ldan-shes-rab and a Transmission of the Ratnagotravibhāga from India to Tibet*. Vienna: Arbeitskreis für tibetische und buddhistische Studien, Universität Wien.

Kapstein, Matthew. 1996. "gDams ngag: Tibetan Technologies of the Self." In Cabezón and Jackson, *Tibetan Literature*, 275–89.

———. 2000. "We Are All Gzhan stong pas: Reflections on *The Reflexive Nature of*

Awareness: A Tibetan Madhyamaka Defence, by Paul Williams." *Journal of Buddhist Ethics* 7: 105–25.

———. 2009. "Preliminary Remarks on the Grub mtha' chen mo of Bya 'Chad kha ba Ye shes rdo rje." In *Sanskrit Manuscripts in China: Proceedings of a Panel at the 2008 Beijing Seminar on Tibetan Studies, October 13 to 17*, edited by Ernst Steinkellner in cooperation with Duan Qing and Helmut Krasser, 137–52. Beijing: China Tibetology Publishing House.

———. 2013. "'Spiritual Exercise' and Buddhist Epistemologists in India and Tibet." In *A Companion to Buddhist Philosophy*, edited by S. M. Emmanuel, 270–89. Chichester, UK: John Wiley & Sons.

Karmay, Samten Gyaltsen. 2007. *The Great Perfection (rDzogs chen): A Philosophical and Meditative Teaching of Tibetan Buddhism*. 2nd ed. Leiden: Brill.

Katsura, Shōryū. 1976. "A Synopsis of the Prajñāpāramitopadeśa of Ratnākaraśānti." *Indogaku Bukkyōgaku Kenkyū* 25.1: 38–41.

Katsura, Shōryū, and Mark Siderits. 2013. *Nāgārjuna's Middle Way: The Mūlamadhyamakākarikā*. Boston: Wisdom Publications.

Keira, Ryusei. 2004. *Mādhyamika and Epistemology: A Study of Kamalaśīla's Method for Proving the Voidness of All Dharmas: Introduction, Annotated Translations, and Tibetan Texts of Selected Sections of the Second Chapter of the Madhyamakāloka*. Vienna: Arbeitskreis für tibetische und buddhistische Studien, Universität Wien.

Kern, Hendrik, and Bunyiu Nanjio. 1977 [1908–12]. *Saddharmapuṇḍarīkasūtra*. Bibliotheca Buddhica 10. St. Petersburg, Russia: Académie Imperiale des Sciences, 1908–12. Reprint, Tokyo: Meicho-Fukyū-Kai, 1977. (Sanskrit edition of the *Saddharmapuṇḍarīkasūtra*.)

Klein, Anne C. 1991. *Knowing, Naming, and Negation: A Sourcebook on Tibetan Sautrāntika*. Ithaca, NY: Snow Lion Publications.

Klong chen ye shes rdo rje, and Nāgārjuna. 2005. *Nagarjuna's Letter to a Friend: With Commentary by Kangyur Rinpoche*. Ithaca, NY: Snow Lion Publications.

Kragh, Ulrich Timme. 2015. *Tibetan Yoga and Mysticism: A Textual Study of the "Yogas" of Nāropa and "Mahāmudrā Meditation" in the Medieval Tradition of Dags po*. Tokyo: International Institute for Buddhist Studies of the International College for Postgraduate Buddhist Studies.

Krasser, Helmut. 2004. "Are Buddhist Pramāṇavādins Non-Buddhistic? Dignāga and Dharmakīrti on the Impact of Logic and Epistemology on Emancipation." *Hōrin* 11: 129–46.

———. 2011. "Bhāviveka, Dharmakīrti and Kumārila." In *Chūgoku-Indo syūkyō-shi tokuni bukkyō-shi ni okeru syomotsu no ryūtsū-denpa to jinbutsu-idō no chiikitokusei* [Regional characteristics of text dissemination and relocation of people in the history of Chinese and Indian religions, with special reference to Buddhism], edited by T. Funayama, 193–242. *A Report of Grant-in-Aid for Scientific Research* (B) 19320010 (March). Mie, Japan: Faculty of Humanities, Mie University.

Kumagai, Seiji. 2011. "The Two Truths from Indian Buddhism to Tibetan Buddhism and Bon." In *The Two Truths of Bon*, 9–35. Kathmandu: Vajra Publications.

La Vallée Poussin, Louis de. 1896. *Études et textes tantriques: Pañcakrama*. Louvain, Belgium: J. B. Istas.

———, ed. 1903–13. *Mūlamadhyamakakārikās (Mādhyamikasūtras) de Nāgārjuna avec la Prasannapadā Commentaire de Candrakīrti*. Bibliotheca Buddhica 4, SI. St. Petersburg, Russia: Académie Impériale des Sciences.

———, ed. 1907–12. *Madhyamakāvatāra par Candrakirti*. Bibliotheca Buddhica 9, SI. St. Petersburg, Russia: Académie Impériale des Sciences.

———. 1910, 1911. "Madhyamakāvatāra, Introduction au Traité du Milieu de l'Ācārya Candrakīrti, avec le commentaire de l'auteur, traduit d'après la version tibétaine." *Le Muséon* (Louvain) XI (1910), 271–358; XII (1911), 235–328.

———. 1913. *Théorie des douze causes*. Ghent, Belgium: E. van Goethem.

———. 1923–31. *L'Abhidharmakośa de Vasubandhu*. 6 vols. Paris: J. B. Istas.

Lamotte, Étienne. 1944. *Le traité de la grande vertu de sagesse de Nāgārjuna (Mahāprajñāpāramitāśāstra)*. vol. 1. Louvain, Belgium: Bureaux du Muséon.

———. 1949. *Le traité de la grande vertu de sagesse de Nāgārjuna (Mahāprajñāpāramitāśāstra)*. vol. 2. Louvain, Belgium: Bureaux du Muséon.

———. 1988. *History of Indian Buddhism from the Origins to the Śaka Era*. Louvain-la-Neuve, Belgium: Université Catholique de Louvain.

Lang, Karen. 1986. *Āryadeva's Catuḥśataka: On the Bodhisattva's Cultivation of Merit and Knowledge*. Copenhagen: Akademisk Forlag.

———. 1990. "Spa-tshab Nyi-ma-grags and the Introduction of Prāsaṅgika Madhyamaka into Tibet." In *Reflections on Tibetan Culture: Essays in Memory of Turrell V. Wylie*, edited by L. Epstein and R. F. Sherburne, 127–41. Studies in Asian Thought and Religion 12. Lewiston, NY: Edwin Mellen Press.

Larson, Gerald James. 1998. *Classical Sāṃkhya: An Interpretation of Its History and Meaning*. 2nd rev. ed. Delhi: M. Banarsidass.

Lessing, Ferdinand, and Alex Wayman. 1968. *Mkhas grub rje's Fundamentals of the Buddhist Tantras. Rgyud sde spyi'i rnam par gzhag pa rgyas par brjod*. The Hague: Mouton.

Lévi, Sylvain, ed. 1983 [1907]. *Mahāyāna–Sūtrālaṅkāra: Exposé de la doctrine du Grand Véhicule selon le système Yogācāra*. Paris: Champion, 1907. Reprint (vol. 1 Sanskrit, vol. 2 French), Kyoto: Rinsen, 1983.

———. 1929. "Autour d'Aśvaghosa." *Journal Asiatique* 215: 255–87.

Li, Xuezhu. 2012. "Madhyamakāvatāra-kārikā." *China Tibetology* 18: 1–16.

———. 2015. "Madhyamakāvatāra-kārikā. Chapter 6." *Journal of Indian Philosophy* 43.1: 1–30, doi:10.1007/s10781-014-9227-6.

Lindtner, Christian. 1979. "Candrakīrti's *Pañcaskandhaprakaraṇa*: I. Tibetan Text." *Acta Orientalia* 40: 87–145.

———. 1981. "Atiśa's Introduction to the Two Truths, and Its Sources." *Journal of Indian Philosophy* 9: 161–214.

———. 1982. "The Pratītyasamutpādahṛdayakārikā—A Reply, in *Adversaria Buddhica*." *Wiener Zeitschrift für die Kunde Südasiens* 26: 167–94.

———. 1992. "The *Laṅkāvatārasūtra* in Early Indian Madhyamaka Literature." *Asiatische Studien* 46.1: 244–79.

———. 1997a. "Cittamātra in Indian Mahāyāna until Kamalaśīla." *Wiener Zeitschrift für die Kunde Südasiens* 39: 159–206.

———, ed. and trans. 1997b. *Master of Wisdom: Writings of the Buddhist Master Nāgārjuna*. rev. ed. Oakland, CA: Dharma Publishing.

———, ed. 2001. *Madhyamakahṛdayam of Bhavya*. Adyar Series 123. Chennai, India: Theosophical Society.

Liu, Zhen. 2015. *The Dharmadhātustava: A Critical Edition of the Sanskrit Text with the Tibetan and Chinese Translations, a Diplomatic Transliteration of the Manuscript and*

Notes. Beijing: China Tibetology Publishing House. Vienna: Austrian Academy of Sciences Press.

Loizzo, Joseph John. 2001. "Candrakīrti and the Moon-Flower of Nālandā: Objectivity and Self-Correction in India's Central Therapeutic Philosophy of Language." PhD diss., Columbia University.

———. 2007. *Nāgārjuna's Reason Sixty with Chandarkīrti's Reason Sixty Commentary*. New York: Columbia University Press.

Lopez, Donald S. 1987. *A Study of Svātantrika*. New York: Snow Lion Publications.

———. 1988. *The Heart Sūtra Explained: Indian and Tibetan Commentaries*. Albany: State University of New York Press.

Losang Chökyi Nyima. 2009. *The Crystal Mirror of Philosophical Systems: A Tibetan Study of Asian Religious Thought*. Translated by Geshe Lhundub Sopa et al. Edited by Roger R. Jackson. Boston: Wisdom Publications, in association with the Institute of Tibetan Classics.

MacDonald, Anne Elizabeth. 1988. *Blo gsal grub mtha'*. MA thesis, University of British Columbia.

———. 2009. "Knowing Nothing: Candrakīrti and Yogic Perception." In Franco and Eigner, *Yogic Perception, Meditation and Altered States of Consciousness*, 133–69.

———. 2015. *In Clear Words: The Prasannapadā, Chapter One*. 2 vols. Vienna: Austrian Academy of Sciences.

Makransky, John J. 1997. *Buddhahood Embodied: Sources of Controversy in India and Tibet*. Albany: State University of New York Press

Martin, Dan. 1992. "A Twelfth-Century Tibetan Classic of Mahāmudrā, *The Path of Ultimate Profundity: The Great Seal Instructions of Zhang*." *Journal of the International Association of Buddhist Studies* 15.2: 243–319.

Martini, Giuliana. 2011. "A Large Question in a Small Place: The Transmission of the *Ratnakūṭa* (*Kāsyapaparivarta*) in Khotan." *Sōka-Daigaku Kokusai bukkyōgaku kōtō kenkyūsho nenpō* (*Annual Report of the International Research Institute for Advanced Buddhology at Soka University*) 14: 135–83.

Mathes, Klaus-Dieter. 2008. *A Direct Path to the Buddha Within: Gö Lotsāwa's Mahāmudrā Interpretation of the Ratnagotravibhāga*. Boston: Wisdom Publications.

———. 2009. "The Role of the *Bodhicittavivaraṇa* in the Mahāmudrā Tradition of the Dwags po bka' brgyud." *Journal of the International Association of Tibetan Studies* 5: 1–31.

———. 2015. *A Fine Blend of Mahāmudrā and Madhyamaka: Maitrīpa's Collection of Texts on Non-Conceptual Realization (Amanasikāra)*. Vienna: Austrian Academy of Sciences.

Matsumoto, Shirō. 1990. "The Mādhyamika Philosophy of Tsong-kha-pa." *Memoirs of the Research Department of the Toyo Bunko* 48: 17–47.

Matsunaga, Yukei. 1978. *The Guhyasamāja Tantra: A New Critical Edition*. Osaka: Toho Shuppan.

May, Jacques. 1959. *Candrakīrti, Prasannapadā Madhyamakavṛtti (Commentaire limpide au traité du milieu): Douze chapitres, traduits du sanscrit et du tibétain en francais et accompagnés d'une introduction, de notes, et d'une édition critique de la version tibétaine*. Paris: Adrien-Maisonneuve.

———. 1979. "Chūgan." In *Hōbōgirin* 5: 470–93. Tokyo: École Française d'Extrême-Orient.

McClintock, Sara L. 2000. "Knowing All Through Knowing One: Mystical Communion or Logical Trick in the *Tattvasaṃgraha* and *Tattvasaṃgrahapañjikā*." *Journal of the International Association of Buddhist Studies* 23: 225–44.

———. 2003. "The Role of the 'Given' in the Classification of Śāntarakṣita and Kamalaśīla as Svātantrika–Madhyamikas." In Dreyfus and McClintock, *The Svātantrika-Prāsaṅgika Distinction*, 125–71.

———. 2008. "Rhetoric and the Reception Theory of Rationality in the Work of Two Buddhist Philosophers." *Argumentation* 22: 27–41.

———. 2010. *Omniscience and the Rhetoric of Reason: Śāntarakṣita and Kamalaśīla on Rationality, Argumentation, and Religious Authority*. Boston: Wisdom Publications.

Meinert, Carmen. 2003. "Structural Analysis of the *Bsam-gtan Mig Sgron*: A Comparison of the Fourfold Correct Practice in the *Āryavikalpapraveśanāmadhāraṇī* and the Contents of the Four Main Chapters of the Bsam-gtan Mig Sgron." *Journal of the International Association of Buddhist Studies* 26.1: 175–95.

Mimaki, Katsumi. 1976. *La réfutation bouddhique de la permanence des choses (sthirasiddhidūṣaṇa) et la preuve de la momentanéité des choses (kṣaṇabhaṅgasiddhi)*. Paris: Institut de Civilisation Indienne.

———. 1979. "Le chapitre du *Blo gsal grub mtha'* sur les Sautrāntika: Présentation et édition." *Zinbun: Memoirs of the Research Institute for Humanistic Studies, Kyoto University* 15: 175–210.

———. 1980. "Le chapitre du *Blo gsal grub mtha'* sur les Sautrāntika: Un essai de traduction." *Zinbun* 16: 143–72.

———. 1982. *Blo gsal grub mtha': Chapitres IX (Vaibhāṣika) et XI (Yogācāra) et chapitre XII (Mādhyamika)*. Kyoto: Université de Kyoto.

———. 1992. "Annotated Translation of the Chapter on the Yogācāra of the *Blo Gsal Grub Mtha'*, Part One." *Kyōtodaigaku-Bungakubu-Kenkyū-Kiyō* 31: 1–49.

———. 2000. "*Jñānasārasamuccaya* kk° 20–28: *Mise au point* with a Sanskrit Manuscript." In Silk, *Wisdom, Compassion, and the Search for Understanding*, 233–44.

Mimaki, Katsumi, and Toru Tomabechi, eds. 1994. *Pañcakrama: Sanskrit and Tibetan Texts Critically Edited with Verse Index and Facsimile Edition of the Sanskrit Manuscripts*. Tokyo: Centre for East Asian Cultural Studies for UNESCO.

Mitrikeski, Drasko. 2010. "Nāgārjuna's *Stutyatātastava* and *Catuḥstava*: Questions of Authenticity." *Modern Greek Studies* 14: 181–94.

Miyasaka, Yusho. 1971–72. *Pramāṇavārttikakārikā* (Sanskrit and Tibetan). vol. 2. *Acta Indologica* (Indo koten kenkyû). Narita: Naritasan Shinsho ji.

Miyazaki, Izumi. 2007a. "Atiśa (Dīpaṃkaraśrījñāna)—His Philosophy, Practice and Its Sources." *Memoirs of the Toyo Bunko* 65: 61–89.

———. 2007b. "Annotated Tibetan Text and Japanese Translation of the Ratnakarandodghaṭa-nāma-madhyamakopadeśa of Atiśa." *Memoirs of the Faculty of Letters, Kyoto University* (Department of Literature, Kyoto University) 46: 1–126. https://repository.kulib.kyoto-u.ac.jp/dspace/handle/2433/73130?mode=full.

Mizuno, Kōgen, and Gaynor Sekimori. 1996. *Essentials of Buddhism: Basic Terminology and Concepts of Buddhist Philosophy and Practice*. Tokyo: Kōsei Publishers.

Mochizuki, Kaie. 1999. "Zum *Bodhisattvacāryāvatārabhāṣya* des Dipaṃkaraśrījñāna." *Hokke-Bunka Kenkyū = Journal of Institute for the Comprehensive Study of Lotus Sutra* 25: 39–121.

———. 2002. "On the *Madhyamakopadeśa* of Dīpaṃkaraśrījñāna." *Bulletin of the Faculty of Buddhism, Minobusan University*, no. 3: 9–48.

———. 2007. "Is Dīpaṃkaraśrījñāna a Mādhyamika?" *Nagoya Studies in Indian Culture and Buddhism: Saṃbhāṣā* 26: 99–126.

———. 2015. "On the Ekasmṛtyupadeśa of Dīpaṃkaraśrījñāna and His View on Nāgārjuna." *Journal of Indian and Buddhist Studies* 63.3: 1307–14.

Monier-Williams, Monier. 1988. *A Sanskrit-English Dictionary*. New York: Oxford University Press.

Moriyama, Shinya. 2013. "Ratnākaraśānti's Criticism of the Madhyamaka Refutation of Causality." *China Tibetology*, no. 3: 53–66.

———. 2014. "Ratnākaraśānti's Theory of Cognition with False Mental Images (**alīkākāravāda*) and the Neither-One-nor-Many Argument." *Journal of Indian Philosophy* 42: 339–51.

Nagao, Gajdin Masato. 1964. *Madhyāntavibhāga-bhaṣya: A Buddhist Philosophical Treatise Edited for the First Time from a Sanskrit Manuscript*. Tokyo: Suzuki Research Foundation.

Nagashima, Jundo. 2002. "A Study of the Late Madhyamaka Doxography." PhD diss., University of Bristol.

———. 2004. "The Distinction between Svātantrika and Prāsaṅgika in Late Madhyamaka: Atiśa and Bhavya as Prāsaṅgikas." *Nagoya Studies in Indian Culture and Buddhism: Saṃbhāṣā* 24: 65–98.

Nakamura, Hajime. 1983. *A History of Early Vedānta Philosophy*. Delhi: Motilal Banarsidass.

Namdol, Ācārya Gyaltsen, trans. and ed. 2001. *Catuḥstavaḥ of Ācārya Nāgārjuna* [Sanskrit Text with Tibetan Version and Hindi Translation]. Sarnath, India: Central Institute of Higher Tibetan Studies.

Nance, Richard. 2007. "On What Do We Rely When We Rely on Reasoning?" *Journal of Indian Philosophy* 35.2: 149–67.

Nanjio, Bunyiu. 1923. *The Laṅkāvatāra Sūtra*. Bibliotheca Otaniensis Series 1. Kyoto: Otani University Press.

Napper, Elizabeth. 1989. *Dependent-Arising and Emptiness: A Tibetan Buddhist Interpretation of Mādhyamika Philosophy Emphasizing the Compatibility of Emptiness and Conventional Phenomena*. Boston: Wisdom Publications.

Nattier, Jan. 2003. *A Few Good Men: The Bodhisattva Path according to The Inquiry of Ugra (Ugraparipṛcchā)*. Honolulu: University of Hawai'i Press.

Newland, Guy. 1992. *The Two Truths in the Mādhyamika Philosophy of the Ge-luk-pa Order of Tibetan Buddhism*. Ithaca, NY: Snow Lion Publications.

Newland, Guy, and Tom J. F. Tillemans. 2011. "An Introduction to Conventional Truth." In Cowherds, *Moonshadows*, 3–22.

Nietupski, Paul. 1996. "The Examination of Conditioned Entities and the Examination of Reality." *Journal of Indian Philosophy* 24: 103–43.

Obermiller, E. 1937. *Prajñāpāramitā-ratna-guṇa-saṃcaya-gāthā*. Bibliotheca Buddhica 29. St. Petersburg, Russia: Imperial Academy of Sciences.

O'Brien, Paul Wilfred. 1953. "A Chapter on Reality from the Madhyantavibhagacastra." *Monumenta Nipponica* 9.1–2: 277–303.

Ohnuma, Reiko. 2007. *Head, Eyes, Flesh, and Blood: Giving Away the Body in Indian Buddhist Literature*. New York: Columbia University Press.

Pāṇḍey, Janārdan. 1990. "Durlabh Granth Paricaya." *Dhīḥ: A Review of Rare Buddhist Texts* 10: 3–24.

Pandeya, Ramchandra. 1999. *Madhyānta Vibhāga Śāstra, Containing the Kārikās of Maitreya, Bhāṣya of Vasubandhu, and Ṭīkā by Sthiramati*. Delhi: Motilal Banarsidass.

Pāsādika, Bhikkhu, ed. and trans. 2015. *The Kāśyapaparivarta*. New Delhi: Aditya Prakashan.

Patel, P. B., ed. 1949. *Cittaviśuddhiprakaraṇa of Āryadeva: Sanskrit and Tibetan Texts.* Santiniketan, India: Visva-Bharati Research Publications.

Phuntsho, Karma. 2005. *Mipham's Dialectics and the Debates on Emptiness: To Be, Not to Be or Neither*. London: RoutledgeCurzon.

Pradhan, Prahallad. 1975. *Abhidharmakośabhāṣya*. Patna, India: K. P. Jayaswal Research Institute.

Qvarnström, Olle. 1989. *Hindu Philosophy in Buddhist Perspective: The Vedāndatattvaviniścaya Chapter of Bhavya's Madhyamakahṛdayakārikā*. Lund, Sweden: Plus Ultra.

Rāhula, Walpola. 2001. *Abhidharmasamuccaya: The Compendium of the Higher Teaching (Philosophy)*. Translated by Sara Boin-Webb. Fremont, CA: Asian Humanities Press.

Ray, Reginald A. 1996. "Nāgārjuna's Longevity." In *Sacred Biography in the Buddhist Traditions of South and Southeast Asia*, edited by Juliane Schober, 129–59. Honolulu: University of Hawai'i Press, 129–59.

Reat, Noble Ross. 1993. *The Śālistamba Sūtra: Tibetan Original, Sanskrit Reconstruction, English Translation, Critical Notes (including Pāli Parallels, Chinese Version, and Ancient Tibetan Fragments)*. Delhi: Motilal Banarsidass.

Roerich, George N., trans. 1976 [1949]. *The Blue Annals*. New Delhi: Motilal Banarsidass.

Roesler, Ulrike. 2002. "The Great Indian Epics in the Version of Dmar ston Chos kyi rgyal po." In *Tibet, Past and Present: Religion and Secular Culture in Tibet*, edited by Blezer and Ardussi, 431–50. Leiden: Brill.

———. 2015. "As It Is Said in a Sutra: Freedom and Variation in Quotations from the Buddhist Scriptures in Early Bka'-gdams-pa Literature." *Journal of Indian Philosophy* 43.4–5: 493–510.

Roesler, Ulrike, and Hans-Ulrich Roesler. 2004. *Kadampa Sites of Phempo: A Guide to Some Early Buddhist Monasteries in Central Tibet*. Kathmandu: Vajra Publications.

Ruegg, David Seyfort. 1969. *La théorie du tathagatagarbha et du gotra: Études sur la sotériologie et la gnoséologie du bouddhisme*. Paris: École Française d'Extrême-Orient.

———. 1977. "The Use of the Four Positions of the Catuṣkoṭi and the Problem of the Description of Reality in Mahāyāna Buddhism." *Journal of Indian Philosophy* 5: 1–77.

———. 1981. *The Literature of the Madhyamaka School of Philosophy in India*. History of Indian Literature series. Wiesbaden: Harrassowitz.

———. 1988. "A Karma bKa' brgyud Work on the Lineages and Traditions of the Indo-Tibetan dBu ma (Madhyamaka)." In *Orientalia Iosephi Tucci Memoriae Dictata*, edited by G. Gnoli and L. Lanciotti, 1249–80. Rome: Istituto Italiano per il Medio ed Estremo Oriente.

———. 1989. *Buddha-Nature, Mind and the Problem of Gradualism in a Comparative Perspective: On the Transmission and Reception of Buddhism in India and Tibet*. London: School of Oriental and African Studies, University of London.

———. 2000. *Three Studies in the History of Indian and Tibetan Madhyamaka Philosophy*. Studies in Indian and Tibetan Madhyamaka Thought 1. Vienna: Arbeitskreis für Tibetische und Buddhistische Studien, Universität Wien.

———. 2002. *Two Prolegomena to Madhyamaka Philosophy: Candrakīrti's Prasannapadā Madhyamakavṛttiḥ on Madhyamakakārikā I.1, and Tsoṅ kha pa Blo bzaṅ grags pa / Rgyal Tshab Dar ma rin chen's Dka' gnad/gnas brgyad kyi zin bris: Annotated Translations*. Vienna: Arbeitskreis für Tibetische und Buddhistische Studien, Universität Wien.

———. 2010. *The Buddhist Philosophy of the Middle: Essays on Indian and Tibetan Madhyamaka.* Boston: Wisdom Publications.

Ruegg, David Seyfort, and Rin chen rnam rgyal. 1966. *The Life of Bu Ston Rin Po Che, with the Tibetan Text of the Bu Ston Rnam Thar.* Rome: Istituto Italiano per il Medio ed Estremo Oriente.

Saito, Akira. 1993. *A Study of Akṣayamati (= Śāntideva)'s Bodhisattvacaryāvatāra as Found in the Tibetan Manuscripts from Tun-Huang.* Project no. 02801005 (April 1990–March 1993). Mie, Japan: Faculty of Humanities, Mie University.

———. 1996. "Śāntideva in the History of Mādhyamika Philosophy." In *Buddhism in India and Abroad: An Integrating Influence in Vedic and Post-Vedic Perspective*, edited by Kalpakam Sankarnarayan, Motohiro Yoritomi, and Shubhada A. Joshi, 257–63. Mumbai: Somaiya Publications.

———. 2000. *A Study of the Dūn-huáng Recension of the "Bodhisattvacaryāvatāra." A Report of Grant-in-Aid for Scientific Research* (C) 09610021 (April 1997–March 2000). Mie, Japan: Faculty of Humanities, Mie University.

Salvini, Mattia. 2015. "Language and Existence in Madhyamaka and Yogācāra: Preliminary Reflections." In *Madhyamaka and Yogācāra: Allies or Rivals?* edited by Jay L. Garfield and Jan Westerhoff, 29–71. New York: Oxford University Press.

Samdhong Rinpoche, et al., eds. 1987. *Guhyādi-Aṣṭasiddhi-Saṅgraha.* Sarnath, India: Central Institute for Higher Tibetan Studies.

Sanderson, Alexis. 2009. "The Śaiva Age." In *Genesis and Development of Tantrism*, edited by Shingo Einoo, 41–349. Tokyo: University of Tokyo.

Sastri, N. Aiyasvami. 1968. "Nāgārjuna's Exposition of Twelve Causal Links." *Bulletin of Tibetology* 5.2: 5–27.

Śāstri, T. Gaṇapati, ed. 1920–1925. *Mañjuśrīmūlakalpa.* Trivandrum Sanskrit Series 70 (1920), 76 (1922), 84 (1925). Trivandrum: Oriental Institute and Manuscripts Library. https://archive.org/details/Trivandrum_Sanskrit_Series_TSS.

Schaeffer, Kurtis R. 2005. *Dreaming the Great Brahmin: Tibetan Traditions of the Buddhist Poet-Saint Saraha.* New York: Oxford University Press.

———. 2007. "Crystal Orbs and Arcane Treasuries: Tibetan Anthologies of Buddhist Tantric Songs from the Tradition of Pha Dam pa sangs rgyas." *Acta Orientalia* (Norway) 68: 5–73.

Schaeffer, Kurtis R., Matthew Kapstein, and Gray Tuttle. 2013. *Sources of Tibetan Tradition.* New York: Columbia University Press.

Scherrer-Schaub, Cristina. 1991. *Yuktiṣāṣṭikāvṛtti: Commentaire à la soixantaine sur le raisonnement ou du vrai enseignement de la causalité par le maître indien Candrakīrti.* Brussels: Institut Belge des Hautes Études Chinoises.

———. 1999. "Towards a Methodology for the Study of Old Tibetan Manuscripts: Dunhuang and Tabo." In *Tabo Studies II: Manuscripts, Texts, Inscriptions and the Arts*, edited by C. A. Scherrer-Schaub and E. Steinkellner, 3–36. Rome: Istituto Italiano per l'Africa e l'Orient.

———. 2002. "Enacting Words: A Diplomatic Analysis of the Imperial Decrees *(bkas bcad)* and Their Application in the *sGra sbyor bam po gñis pa* Tradition." *Journal of the International Association of Buddhist Studies* 25.1–2: 263–340.

Scherrer-Schaub, C. A., and George Bonani. 2002. "Establishing a Typology of the Old Tibetan Manuscripts: A Multidisciplinary Approach." In *Dunhuang Manuscript Forgeries*, edited by S. Whitfield, 184–215. London: British Library.

———. 2008. "Establishing a Typology of the Old Tibetan Manuscripts: A Multidisciplinary

Approach." In *The Cultural History of Western Tibet: Recent Research from the China Tibetology Research Center and the University of Vienna*, edited by Deborah E. Klimburg-Salter, Helmut Tauscher, Junyan Liang, and Yuan Zhou, 299–337. Beijing: China Tibetology Research Center.

Schmithausen, Lambert. 2014. *The Genesis of Yogācāra-Vijñānavāda: Responses and Reflections*. Tokyo: International Institute for Buddhist Studies of the International College for Postgraduate Buddhist Studies.

———. 2015. *On the Problem of the External World in the Ch'eng wei shih lun*. Tokyo: International Institute for Buddhist Studies. http://jairo.nii.ac.jp/0307/00000276. (Electronic edition with corrections and additions.)

Schoening, Jeffrey D. 1995. *The Śālistamba Sūtra and Its Indian Commentaries*. Vienna: Arbeitskreis für Tibetische und Buddhistische Studien, Universität Wien.

Schroeder, Ulrich von. 2006. *Empowered Masters: Tibetan Wall Paintings of Mahāsiddhas at Gyantse*. Chicago: Serindia Publications.

Sharma, Parmananda, trans. 1997. *Bhāvanākrama of Kamalaśīla*. New Delhi: Aditya Prakashan. (English translation of *Bhāvanākrama-3*.)

Shastri, Dwarikadas. 1968. *Tattvasaṅgraha of Ācārya Shāntarakṣita, with Commentary "Pañjikā" of Shri Kamalashīla*. Varanasi: Bauddha Bharati.

———. 1998. *Abhidharmakośa and Bhāṣya: With Sphutārthā Commentary of Ācārya Yaśomitra*. 2 vols. Varanasi: Bharati.

Shastri, Hara Prasad. 1927. *Advayavajrasamgraha*. Baroda, India: Oriental Institute.

Sherburne, Richard. 1983. *A Lamp for the Path and Commentary of Atisa*. Wisdom of Tibet Series 5. London: Allen & Unwin.

———. 2000. *The Complete Works of Atīśa Śrī Dīpaṁkara Jñāna: Jo-Bo-Rje: The Lamp for the Path and Commentary, Together with the Newly Translated Twenty-Five Key Texts (Tibetan and English Texts)*. New Delhi: Aditya Prakashan.

Sherpa, Trungram Gyaltrul Rinpoche. 2004. "Gampopa, the Monk and the Yogi: His Life and Teachings." PhD diss., Department of Sanskrit and Indian Studies, Harvard University.

Shirasaki, Kenjô. 1978. "The Sugatamatavibhaṅgabhāṣya of Jitāri." *Bulletin of Kobe Women's University* 17.1: 77–107.

———. 1985. "The Sugatamativibhaṅgabhāṣya of Jitāri (II), Chapter 4: Mādhyamika." *Kôbe Joshi Daigaku (Bungakubu) Kiyô* 18.1: 101–43.

Shulman, Eviatar. 2009. "Creative Ignorance: Nāgārjuna on the Ontological Significance of Consciousness." *Journal of the International Association of Buddhist Studies* 30.1–2: 139–73.

Siderits, Mark. 2007. *Buddhism as Philosophy: An Introduction*. Aldershot, England: Ashgate.

Silk, J. A., ed. 2000. *Wisdom, Compassion, and the Search for Understanding: The Buddhist Studies Legacy of Gadjin M. Nagao*. Honolulu: University of Hawai'i Press.

———. 2007. "Good and Evil in Indian Buddhism: The Five Sins of Immediate Retribution." *Journal of Indian Philosophy* 35.3: 253–86.

Skilling, Peter. 2004. "Mahāyāna and Bodhisattva: An Essay towards Historical Understanding." In *Phothisatawa Barami Kap Sangkhom Thai Nai Sahatsawat Mai* [Bodhisattvaparami and Thai Society in the New Millennium], edited by Pakorn Limpanusorn and Chalermpon Iampakdee, 139–56. Bangkok: Chinese Studies Center, Institute of East Asia, Thammasat University.

Smith, E. Gene. 2004. "Banned Books in the Tibetan-Speaking Lands." In *21st Century*

Tibet Issue: Symposium on Contemporary Tibetan Studies, Collected Papers, 364–81. Taipei: Mongolian and Tibetan Affairs Commission.

Smith, Jonathan Z. 2004. *Relating Religion: Essays in the Study of Religion*. Chicago: University of Chicago Press.

Sopa, Geshe Lhundup, Michael J. Sweet, Leonard Zwilling, and Dharmarakṣita. 2001. *Peacock in the Poison Grove: Two Buddhist Texts on Training the Mind: The Wheel Weapon (Mtshon Cha 'Khor Lo) and the Poison-Destroying Peacock (Rma Bya Dug 'Joms) Attributed to Dharmarakṣita*. Boston: Wisdom Publications.

Sørensen, Per K., ed. 1986. *Triśaraṇasaptati: The Septuagint on the Three Refuges*, by Candrakīrti. Vienna: Wiener Studien zur Tibetologie und Buddhismuskunde.

———. 1999. "The Prolific Ascetic lCe-sgom Śes-rab rdo-rje *alias* lCe-sgom źig-po: Allusive, but Elusive." *Journal of the Nepal Research Centre* 11: 175–200.

———. 2002. "A XIth Century Ascetic of Buddhist Electicism: Kha-rag sgom-chung." In *Tractata Tibetica et Mongolica: Festschrift für Klaus Sagaster zum 65* Geburtstag, edited by K. Kollmar-Paulenz and C. Peter, 241–54. Asiatische Forschungen 145. Wiesbaden: Harrassowitz.

Sørensen, Per K., Guntram Hazod, Ṅag dbaṅ bstan 'dzin 'phrin las, and Tshal pa Kun dga' rdo rje. 2007. *Rulers on the Celestial Plain: Ecclesiastic and Secular Hegemony in Medieval Tibet: A Study of Tshal Gung-thang*. Vienna: Verlag der Österreichischen Akademie der Wissenschaften.

Sparham, Gareth. 1987. "Background Material for the First of the Seventy Topics in Maitreyanātha's Abhisamayālaṃkāra." *Journal of the International Association of Buddhist Studies* 10.2: 139–58.

———, trans. 2006. Abhisamayālaṃkāra with Vṛtti and Ālokā, vol. 1, *First Abhisamaya*. Fremont, CA: Jain Publishing.

Staël-Holstein, Alexander von. 1977 [1926]. *Kāçyapaparivarta: A Mahāyanasūtra of the Ratnakūṭa Class*. Shanghai: Commercial Press, 1926. Reprint, Tokyo: Meicho-fukyūkai, 1977.

Stcherbatsky, Th., and E. Obermiller, eds. 1992 [1929]. *Abhisamayālaṃkāra*. Bibliotheca Buddhica 23. Leningrad: Academy of Sciences of the USSR, 1929. Delhi: Sri Satguru Publications, 1992.

Stein, Rolf Alfred, and Arthur P. McKeown. 2010. *Rolf Stein's Tibetica Antiqua: With Additional Materials*. Leiden: BRILL.

Steinkellner, Ernst. 1990. "Is Dharmakīrti a Mādhyamika?" In *Earliest Buddhism and Madhyamaka*, edited by David Seyfort Ruegg and Lambert Schmithausen, 72–90. Leiden: Brill.

Strong, John. 1992. *The Legend and Cult of Upagupta: Sanskrit Buddhism in North India and Southeast Asia*. Princeton, NJ: Princeton University Press.

Study Group on Buddhist Literature. 2004. *Jñānālokālaṃkāra: Transliterated Sanskrit Text Collated with Tibetan and Chinese Translations*. Tokyo: Institute for Comprehensive Studies of Buddhism, Taisho University.

———. 2004. *Vimalakīrtinirdeśa: Transliterated Sanskrit Text Collated with Tibetan and Chinese Translations*. Tokyo: Institute for Comprehensive Studies of Buddhism, Taisho University.

Suzuki, D. T. 1932. *The Laṅkāvatāra Sūtra*. London: Routledge and Kegan Paul.

Sweet, Michael J. 1996. "Mental Purification (*Blo Sbyong*): A Native Tibetan Genre of Religious Literature." In Cabezón and Jackson, *Tibetan Literature*, 244–60.

Takasaki, Jikidō. 1966a. *A Study on the Ratnagotravibhāga (Uttaratantra)*. Rome: Istituto Italiano il Medio ed Estremo Oriente.

———. 1966b. "Dharmatā, Dharmadhātu, Dharmakāya and Buddhadhātu: Structure of the Ultimate Value in Mahāyāna Buddhism." *Indogaku bukkyōgaku kenkyū* 14.2: 78–94.

Takchoe, Sonam. 2007. *The Two Truths Debate: Tsongkhapa and Gorampa on the Middle Way*. Boston: Wisdom Publications.

Tanji, Teruyoshi. 2000. "On Samāropa: Probing the Relationship of the Buddha's Silence and His Teaching." In Silk, *Wisdom, Compassion, and the Search for Understanding*, 347–68.

Tatz, Mark, trans. 1985. *Difficult Beginnings: Three Works on the Bodhisattva Path by Candragomin*. Boston: Shambhala Publications.

———. 1988. "Maitri-pa and Atiśa." In *Tibetan Studies: Proceedings of the 4th Seminar of the International Association for Tibetan Studies*, edited by Helga Uebach and Jampa L. Panglung, 473–81. Munich: Komission für Zentralasiatische Studien Bayerische Akademie der Wissenschaftern.

———. 1990. "Tattva-Ratnāvalī: The Precious Garland of Verses on Reality." In *Researches in Indian History, Archaeology, Art and Religion: Prof. Upendra Thakur Felicitation Volume*, vol. 2, edited by G. Kuppuram and K. Kumudamani, 491–513. Delhi: Sundeep Prakashan.

Tauscher, Helmut. 1988. "Paramārtha as an Object of Cognition: Paryāya and Aparyāyaparamārtha in Svātantrika-Madhyamaka." In *Tibetan Studies: Proceedings of the 4th Seminar of the International Association for Tibetan Studies, Schloss Hohenkammer, München 1985*, edited by H. Uebach and J. L. Panglung, 483–90. Munich: Kommission für Zentralasiatische Studies, Bayerische Akademie der Wissenschaften.

———. 1999. "Phya ba Chos kyi seng ge's Opinion on *prasaṅga*." In *Dharmakīrti's Thought and Its Impact on Indian and Tibetan Philosophy*, edited by Shōryū Katsura, 387–93. Proceedings of the Third International Dharmakīrti Conference, Hiroshima, November 4–6, 1997. Vienna: Verlag der Österreichischen Akademie der Wissenschaften.

———. 2003. "Phya Pa Chos Kyi Seng Ge as a Svātantrika." In Dreyfus and McClintock, *The Svātantrika-Prāsaṅgika Distinction*, 207–55.

———. 2009. "Remarks on Phya pa Chos kyi seng ge and His Madhyamaka Treatises." *Tibet Journal* 34.3: 1–35.

Thiện Châu, Thich. 1999. *The Literature of the Personalists of Early Buddhism*. Delhi: Motilal Banarsidass.

Thurman, Robert A. F. 1976. *The Holy Teaching of Vimalakīrti: A Mahāyāna Scripture*. University Park, PA: The Pennsylvania State University Press.

———. 1984. *Tsong Khapa's Speech of Gold in the Essence of True Eloquence: Reason and Enlightenment in the Central Philosophy of Tibet*. Princeton, NJ: Princeton University Press.

Thurman, Robert A. F., et al., eds. and trans. 2004. *The Universal Vehicle Discourse Literature: Mahāyānasūtrālaṃkāra*. New York: Center for Buddhist Studies, Columbia University, and Tibet House US.

Tillemans, Tom J. F. 1990. *Materials for the Study of Āryadeva, Dharmapāla, and Candrakīrti: The Catuḥśataka of Āryadeva, Chapters XII and XIII, with the Commentaries of Dharmapāla and Candrakīrti: Introduction, Translation, Sanskrit, Tibetan, and Chinese Texts, Notes*. Vienna: Arbeitskreis für Tibetische und Buddhistische Studien, Universität Wien.

———. 1999. *Scripture, Logic, Language: Essays on Dharmakīrti and His Tibetan Successors.* Boston: Wisdom Publications.

———. 1999a. "Dharmakīrti, Āryadeva and Dharmapāla on Scriptural Authority." In Tillemans, *Scripture, Logic, Language*, 27–36.

———. 1999b. "How Much of a Proof Is Scripturally Based Inference?" In Tillemans, *Scripture, Logic, Language*, 37–51.

———. 2007. "Trying to Be Fair to Mādhyamika Buddhism." In *Expanding and Merging Horizons: Contributions to South Asian and Cross-Cultural Studies*, edited by K. Preisendanz, 507–24. Vienna: Austrian Academy of Sciences.

———. 2011. "How Far Can a Madhyamaka Buddhist Reform Conventional Truth?" In Cowherds, *Moonshadows*, 151–65.

———. 2016. *How Do Mādhyamikas Think? And Other Essays on the Buddhist Philosophy of the Middle.* Somerville, MA: Wisdom Publications.

Tola, F., and C. Dragonetti. 1985. "Nāgārjuna's Catustava." *Journal of Indian Philosophy* 13: 1–54.

———. 1987. "Śūnyatāsaptati: The Seventy Kārikās on Voidness (according to the Svavṛtti) of Nāgārjuna." *Journal of Indian Philosophy* 15: 1–55.

———. 1995. *On Voidness: A Study on Buddhist Nihilism.* Delhi: Motilal Banarsidass.

Tomabechi, Toru. 2009. *The Adhyardhaśatikā Prajñāparamitā: Sanskrit and Tibetan Texts.* Vienna: Austrian Academy of Sciences Press.

Tribe, Anthony. 2016. *Tantric Buddhist Practice in India: Vilāsavajra's Commentary on the Mañjuśrī-Nāmasaṃgīti: A Critical Edition with Annotated Translation of Chapters 1–5 with Introductions.* New York : Routledge.

Tsuda, Shinichi. 1974. *The Saṁvarodaya-Tantra: Selected Chapters.* Tokyo: Hokuseido Press.

Tucci, Giuseppe. 1947. "Minor Sanskrit Texts on the Prajñā-pāramitā, 1: The Prajñā-pāramitā-piṇḍārtha of Diṅnāga." *Journal of the Royal Asiatic Society of Great Britain and Ireland*, no. 1: 53–75.

———. 1956. *Minor Buddhist Texts.* Rome: Istituto Italiano per il Medio ed Estremo Oriente. Reprint, Delhi: Motilal Banarsidass, 1986.

———. 1958. *Minor Buddhist Texts.* vol. 2. Rome: Istituto Italiano per il Medio ed Estremo Oriente. (Sanskrit and Tibetan editions of *Bhāvanākrama–1.*)

Uebach, H. 1990. "On Dharma-Colleges and Their Teachers in the Ninth-Century Tibetan Empire." In *Indo-Sino-Tibetica: Studi in Onore di Luciano Petech*, edited by P. Daffina, 393–417. Rome: Bardi.

Vaidya, P. L. 1958. *Lalita-Vistaṛa.* Buddhist Sanskrit Text Series 1. Darbhanga, India: Mithila Institute.

———, ed. 1960. *Bodhicaryāvatāra of Śāntideva witḥ the Commentary Pañjikā of Prajñākaramati.* Buddhist Sanskrit Texts 12. Darbhanga: Mithila Institute.

Van der Kuijp, Leonard W. J. 1983. *Contributions to the Development of Tibetan Buddhist Epistemology: From the Eleventh to the Thirteenth Century.* Wiesbaden: F. Steiner.

———. 1987. "The Monastery of Gsang-phu Ne'u-Thog and Its Abbatial Succession from ca. 1073 to 1250." *Berliner Indologische Studies* 3: 103–27.

———. 1991. "Review of Jñānagarbha's Commentary on the Distinction between the Two Truths: An Eighth-Century Handbook of Madhyamaka Philosophy by Malcolm D. Ecker." *Journal of the American Oriental Society* 111.2: 402–5.

———. 1992. "Notes Apropos of the Transmission of the *Sarvadurgatipariśodhana-tantra* in Tibet." *Studien zur Indologie und Iranistik* 16: 109–25.

———. 2014. "Some Text-Historical Issues with the *Bodhicittavivaraṇa* by *a* Nāgārjuna and the Tibetan Commentarial Literature." In *Himalayan Passages: Tibetan and Newar Studies in Honor of Hubert Decleer*, edited by Benjamin Bogin and Andrew Quintman, 117–41. Somerville, MA: Wisdom Publications.

Van der Kuijp, Leonard W. J., and Arthur P. McKeown. 2013. *Bcom ldan ral gri (1227–1305) on Indian Buddhist Logic and Epistemology: His Commentary on Dignāga's Pramāṇasamuccaya*. Vienna: Arbeitskreis für tibetische und buddhistische Studien, Universität Wien.

Varghese, Matthew. 2008. *Principles of Buddhist Tantra: A Discourse on Cittaviśuddhiprakaraṇa of Āryadeva*. New Delhi: Munshiram Manoharlal.

Vetturini, Gianpaolo. 2007. "The bKa' gdams pa School of Tibetan Buddhism." PhD diss., School of Oriental and African Studies, University of London.

———. 2013. "The bKa' gdams pa School of Tibetan Buddhism." PhD diss., revised, School of Oriental and African Studies, University of London.

Vitali, Roberto. 2004. "The Role of Clan Power in the Establishment of Religion (from the *Kheng log* of the 9th–10th Century to the Instances of the dByil of La stod and gNyos of Kha rag." In *The Relationship between Religion and State (Chos srid zung 'brel) in Traditional Tibet: Proceedings of a Seminar Held in Lumbini, Nepal, March 2000*, edited by Christoph Cüppers, 159–88. Lumbini, Nepal: Lumbini International Research Institute.

Vorobyova-Desyatovskaya, M. I., with Seishi Karashima and Noriyuki Kudo. 2002. *The Kāśyapaparivarta: Romanized Text and Facsimiles*. Bibliotheca Philogica et Philosophica Buddhica 5. Tokyo: International Research Institute for Advanced Buddhology, Soka University.

Vose, Kevin. 2009. *Resurrecting Candrakīrti: Disputes in the Tibetan Creation of Prāsaṅgika*. Boston: Wisdom Publications.

———. 2010a. "Authority in Early Prāsaṅgika Madhyamaka." *Journal of Indian Philosophy* 38: 553–82.

———. 2010b. "Making and Remaking the Ultimate in Early Tibetan Readings of Śāntideva." *Journal of the International Association of Buddhist Studies* 32.1–2: 285–318.

Wallis, Glenn. 2003. "Advayavajra's Instructions on the Ādikarma." *Pacific World*, no. 5: 203–30.

Wangchuk, Dorji. 2007. *The Resolve to Become a Buddha: A Study of the Bodhicitta Concept in Indo-Tibetan Buddhism*. Tokyo: International Institute for Buddhist Studies of the International College for Postgraduate Buddhist Studies.

———. 2009. "A Relativity Theory of the Purity and Validity of Perception in Indo-Tibetan Buddhism." In Franco and Eigner, *Yogic Perception, Meditation, and Altered States of Consciousness*, 215–37.

Wayman, Alex. 1977. *Yoga of the Guhyasamājatantra: The Arcane Lore of Forty Verses*. Delhi: Motilal Banarsidass.

Wedemeyer, Christian K, trans. 2007. *Āryadeva's Lamp That Integrates the Practices (Caryāmelāpakapradīpa): The Gradual Path of Vajrayāna Buddhism according to the Esoteric Community Noble Tradition*. New York: American Institute of Buddhist Studies, Columbia University.

———. 2010. "*Cette fraude littéraire ne peut tromper personne*: Jo nang Tāranātha and the History of the gSang 'dus 'phags lugs." In *Studies in the Philosophy and History of Tibet*, edited by M. Kark and H. Lasic, 145–74. Proceeding of the Eleventh Seminar of the International Association for Tibetan Studies, Königswinter, 2006. Andiast, Switzerland: International Institute for Tibetan and Buddhist Studies.

Westerhoff, Jan. 2010. *The Dispeller of Disputes: Nāgārjuna's Vigrahavyāvartanī*. Oxford: Oxford University Press.

Williams, Paul. 2009. "Is Buddhist Ethics Virtue Ethics? Toward a Dialogue with Śāntideva and a Footnote to Keown." In *Destroying Māra Forever: Buddhist Ethics Essays in Honor of Damien Keown*, edited by John Powers and Charles S. Prebish, 113–40. Ithaca, NY: Snow Lion Publications.

Wogihara, U., ed. 1932–35. *Abhisamayālaṃkārālokā Prajñāpāramitāvyākhyā by Haribhadra: The Work of Haribhadra*. Tokyo: Toyo Bunko.

———, ed. 1971. *Sphuṭārthā Abhidharmakośavyākhyā*. Tokyo: Sankibo Buddhist Book Store.

Yiannopoulos, Alexander. 2012. "Luminosity: Reflexive Awareness in Ratnākaraśānti's *Pith Instructions for the Ornament of the Middle Way*." MA thesis, Rangjung Yeshe Institute, Kathamandu, Nepal.

Yonezawa, Yoshiasu. 2008. "Vigrahavyāvartanī: Sanskrit Transliteration and Tibetan Translation." *Journal of the Naritasan Institute of Buddhist Studies* 31: 209–333.

Yoshimizu, Chizuko. 1993. "The Madhyamaka Theories Regarded as False by the Dge lugs pas." *Wiener Zeitschrift für Kunde Süd- und Ostasiens* 37: 201–27.

———. 1997. "Tsoṅ kha pa on don byed nus pa." In *Tibetan Studies, Proceedings of the 7th International Seminar of the International Association on Tibetan Studies, Graz, 1995*, vol. 2, edited by E. Steinkellner et al., 1103–20. Vienna: Verlag der Österreichischen Akademie der Wissenschaften.

———. 2005. "A Tibetan Buddhist Text from the Twelfth Century Unknown to Later Tibetans." *Cahiers d'Extrême-Asie* 15: 127–64.

———. 2010. "Źaṅ Thaṅ sag pa on theses (*dam bca', pratijñā*) in Madhyamaka Thought." *Journal of the International Association of Buddhist Studies* 32.1–2: 443–67.

———. 2013. "Reasoning-for-others in Candrakīrti's Madhyamaka Thought." *Journal of the International Association of Buddhist Studies* 35.1–2: 413–44.

———. 2014. "Indo-chibetto bukkyo niokeru chūganha niyoru ronrigaku hihan no kaimei" [Clarification of the critic of logic by the Madhyamaka school in Indian and Tibetan Buddhism]. *A Report of Grant-in-Aid for Scientific Research* (B) 16520044: 1–106. Mie, Japan: Faculty of Humanities, Mie University.

Zimmermann, Michael. 1999. "The Tathāgatagarbhasūtra: Its Basic Structure and Relation to the Lotus Sūtra." *Annual Report of The International Research Institute for Advanced Buddhology* (Soka University) 2: 143–68.

Index

O

P

T

About the Author

James B. Apple is professor of Buddhist studies at the University of Calgary. His research focuses on the critical analysis of Mahāyāna sūtras and topics within Indian and Tibetan Buddhist forms of Buddhism. His books include *A Stairway Taken by the Lucid: Tsong kha pa's Study of Noble Beings* (2013) and *Stairway to Nirvāṇa* (2008).

Studies in Indian and Tibetan Buddhism
Titles Previously Published

Among Tibetan Texts
History and Literature of the Himalayan Plateau
E. Gene Smith

Approaching the Great Perfection
Simultaneous and Gradual Methods of Dzogchen Practice in the Longchen Nyingtig
Sam van Schaik

Authorized Lives
Biography and the Early Formation of Geluk Identity
Elijah S. Ary

Buddhism Between Tibet and China
Edited by Matthew T. Kapstein

The Buddhist Philosophy of the Middle
Essays on Indian and Tibetan Madhyamaka
David Seyfort Ruegg

Buddhist Teaching in India
Johannes Bronkhorst

A Direct Path to the Buddha Within
Gö Lotsāwa's Mahāmudrā Interpretation of the Ratnagotravibhāga
Klaus-Dieter Mathes

The Essence of the Ocean of Attainments
The Creation Stage of the Guhyasamāja Tantra according to Panchen Losang Chökyi Gyaltsen
Yael Bentor and Penpa Dorjee

Foundations of Dharmakīrti's Philosophy
John D. Dunne

Freedom from Extremes
Gorampa's "Distinguishing the Views" and the Polemics of Emptiness
José Ignacio Cabezón and Geshe Lobsang Dargyay

Himalayan Passages
Tibetan and Newar Studies in Honor of Hubert Decleer
Benjamin Bogin and Andrew Quintman

How Do Mādhyamikas Think?
And Other Essays on the Buddhist Philosophy of the Middle
Tom J. F. Tillemans

Luminous Lives
The Story of the Early Masters of the Lam 'bras Tradition in Tibet
Cyrus Stearns

Mipham's Beacon of Certainty
Illuminating the View of Dzogchen, the Great Perfection
John Whitney Pettit

Omniscience and the Rhetoric of Reason
Śāntarakṣita and Kamalaśīla on Rationality, Argumentation, and Religious Authority
Sara L. McClintock

Reason's Traces
Identity and Interpretation in Indian and Tibetan Buddhist Thought
Matthew T. Kapstein

Remembering the Lotus-Born
Padmasambhava in the History of Tibet's Golden Age
Daniel A. Hirshberg

Resurrecting Candrakīrti
Disputes in the Tibetan Creation of Prāsaṅgika
Kevin A. Vose

Scripture, Logic, Language
Essays on Dharmakīrti and His Tibetan Successors
Tom J. F. Tillemans

Sexuality in Classical South Asian Buddhism
José I. Cabezón

The Svātantrika-Prāsaṅgika Distinction
What Difference Does a Difference Make?
Edited by Georges Dreyfus and Sara McClintock

Vajrayoginī
Her Visualizations, Rituals, and Forms
Elizabeth English

Wisdom

About Wisdom Publications

Wisdom Publications is the leading publisher of classic and contemporary Buddhist books and practical works on mindfulness. To learn more about us or to explore our other books, please visit our website at wisdompubs.org or contact us at the address below.

Wisdom Publications
199 Elm Street
Somerville, MA 02144 USA

We are a 501(c)(3) organization, and donations in support of our mission are tax deductible.

Wisdom Publications is affiliated with the Foundation for the Preservation of the Mahayana Tradition (FPMT).